P9-DMB-629

FROM
EVE
TO
DAWN

FROM
EVE
TO
DAWN

A HISTORY OF WOMEN

VOLUME 3:
INFERNOS AND PARADISES

MARILYN FRENCH

McArthur & Company
Toronto

First published in Canada in 2003 by
McArthur & Company
322 King Street West, Suite 402
Toronto, Ontario M5V 1J2

National Library of Canada Cataloguing in Publication Data

    French, Marilyn, 1929-
    From Eve to dawn : a history of women / Marilyn French.

    Maps on lining papers.
    Includes bibliographical references.
    Contents: v. 1. Origins — v. 2. The masculine mystique —
    v. 3. infernos and paradises.
    ISBN 1-55278-268-9 (v. 1).—ISBN 1-55278-323-5 (v. 2).—
    ISBN 1-55278-346-4 (v. 3)

    1. Women—History. I. Title.

    HQ1121.F74 2002   305.4'09   C2002-900455-1

Design & Composition: *Mad Dog Design Inc.*
Jacket Design & f/x: *Mad Dog Design Inc.*
Interior Map: *Jamie French*
Cover photo copyright: *Joanna McCarthy/Getty Images*
        10149643 Woman Rajasthan India
Endpapers (Peters Projection): *Akademische Verlagsanstalt FL-9490 Vaduz, Aeulestr. 56.*

Editors: *Rosemary Shipton and Jane McWhinney*
Proofreader: *Wendy Thomas*
Indexer: *Gillian Watts*
Printed in Canada by *Friesens*

10 9 8 7 6 5 4 3 2 1

"As if from Eve to Dawn
Your own name changes."
— Barbara Greenberg

To Barbara Greenberg and Margaret Atwood

CONTENTS

Volume 3

INFERNOS
AND
PARADISES

PART SIX

THE NINETEENTH CENTURY: CAPITALISM TRIUMPHANT

THE NINETEENTH CENTURY ROILED WITH CONTRADICTION. It was the lowest point in women's history: a male historian has pointed out that nineteenth-century British women had fewer rights than Babylonian women possessed when Hammurabi's Code was written.[1] Moreover, British women were no worse off than women in other Western countries, and perhaps better off than women in Eastern societies.

But the nineteenth century was also the period in which women as a caste for the first time stood up en masse and demanded an end to subjugation. Hard-earned victories gradually won them the right to acquire advanced education, to learn a profession and actually practise it, and to own their personal property. From the perspective of this book, it is the most cheering period in female history, the moment the tide began to turn.

It was just such a period for workers, too (many of whom were now women); they also began to stand up and protest wages that were inadequate to maintain life, as well as inhumane working conditions and hours. Middle-class people, including many women, sided with the workers, arguing also that tiny children should not be working in factories, tied to machines, and that all children should be decently fed, healed, and educated.

But of course, such arguments would not have been necessary if the actual conditions of life were not so hellish. Cities were overcrowded, filthy, and unhealthy; factories were unsanitary and unhygienic, and workers were treated worse than animals. Yet even so, agricultural workers often found factory work preferable to work on the farm, which was brutally hard and demeaning.

To complete the picture of this age of contrasts, it was also a period when socialists (and others) began to envision better ways of living, inventing utopian schemes for living and working in harmony with nature and the machine. Some of these schemes were realized, in towns that still stand (as ruins) in England and the United States. But none of them were successful, largely because men continued to exploit women.

The industrial hells wrought in northern cities were paralleled by imperialist expansion in the south and east, in Africa and Asia. The horrors described in Joseph Conrad's great novella "Heart of Darkness" occurred in this period. The nineteenth century's cruel expropriation of Africa and Asia reverberates today, having created problems that still persist.

CHAPTER 1

IMPERIALISM IN AFRICA

ETWEEN ABOUT 1830 AND THE SECOND WORLD WAR, two
developments changed the human condition itself. One was
the invention of power-driven machines that brought on the industrial revolution, changing not only the kind of work people did but
also where, with whom, and under what conditions they worked
and lived. The other was the emergence of a new vision of humanity, a new morality. Enlightenment ideas subverted the passive
acceptance that characterizes much religious thinking. People burning with new conceptions of human nature and human rights envisioned new possibilities for living.

Power-driven machines gave humans greater control over matter and in some ways offered an easier life than they had imagined
possible. But men's exploitation of this new power and of the people who worked the machines created infernos – working and living conditions more terrible than any large population had ever
endured. Reacting to such conditions and armed with the new
vision of humans as creatures with *rights*, people began to devise
social and political arrangements that would foster human well-

being and rebuild their societies. The resulting movements – abolitionism, socialism, feminism, utopian, social welfare, and labour movements – sometimes at odds with each other, sometimes overlapping, did create beneficial changes, but also some of the cruellest societies on earth.

For, everywhere, the new moral vision was ignored or co-opted by men with a newly intense and insatiable drive for power – domination through wealth or influence, and control through might or knowledge. These two tendencies, in opposition, intersection, and interconnection, gave the nineteenth century its character. Technology provided a means to ease the human lot, but it also created a dehumanizing hell on earth; at the same time, a new sense of power and right infused human images of alternative ways to live and attempts to realize heaven on earth. This chapter examines women's involvement in both sides of this dichotomy, their strategies for living and for changing their lives.

As the new ideas of freedom and equality that inspired revolutions in late eighteenth- and early nineteenth-century Europe affected Western attitudes toward Africa, humanitarian groups, especially in England and the United States, began to protest slavery. Slavery was finally abolished – if mainly for economic rather than humanitarian reasons. Individuals and groups may have been morally motivated but societies were not. Moralists' efforts to push through emancipatory legislation were supported by early capitalists because a free-wage labour system was cheaper than slavery. The capitalists' goal of exploiting the resources and markets of what we now call Third World countries militated against depleting those populations. Their own countries had plenty of workers who did not have to be kept.

Britain's economy did not depend on slave labour, so its abolition movement began earlier and was stronger than that in the United States, where in 1860 slave-produced cotton made up 60 percent of exports. Britain passed laws in 1807 barring British subjects from slave trading, and in 1833 abolished slavery and slave trade in Canada and its Caribbean, Indian Ocean, and South African colonies (but not in India or other Eastern possessions). Thereafter, taking a high moral tone, Britain used influence and sometimes force to prevent other nations and their colonies from trafficking in and earning profits from the cheap labour of slaves English colonies were by then denied – although some Britons continued to trade slaves.

Of the other major slave-holding powers, France and Portugal, France was the first to prohibit slavery in its colonies. But this 1794 prohibition was a response to massive slave revolts in Martinique and St. Domingue the previous year. Napoleon later reinstituted slavery. After the English defeated Napoleon in 1818, the French, yielding to British pressure, outlawed slave trading, but barely enforced the ban. The 1848 French Revolution brought to power humanitarian thinkers who abolished slavery on French soil, including French colonies and possessions. Still, colonists had ways of deceiving governments, which themselves were not always averse to being deceived. Some of the cruellest instances of European viciousness to Africans occurred after abolition.

In Portugal slavery was merely whispered against until 1836, when the export of slaves from Portuguese territories was outlawed. Slave trade continued quite openly just the same. Portugal outlawed slavery in its territories in 1878, but slaves were shipped to French and Portuguese islands in the guise of contract labour well into the twentieth century. The Portuguese government impressed Africans to work in Portuguese mines until Mozambique became independent in 1975. Then labour became more "voluntary."

In the nineteenth century, European states expanded their power base in Africa simply by calling a region a "colony," subject to their law and power. They made deals with individual Africans to provide slaves and other commodities, using the age-old techniques of patriarchy – male supremacy, co-optation, and divisiveness – to undermine and destroy local solidarity. Africans devised strategies to survive, accommodate, resist, or oppose European power. Women used all tacks: they maintained their people, subverted foreign impositions, and led resistance movements. This section begins the discussion of women's experience in the nineteenth century by looking at the way the treatment of women in Africa was affected by predations of slave trading in the imperialist period.

Slavery's Destruction of African Societies

Slavery had a profound effect on all Africans, but it affected men and women differently. It treated men individually, women as a caste. Africans of both sexes were enslaved and transported; but of Africans involved in trading, only men profited. After the British and French governments abandoned the slave trade, it was taken over by Angolans, Brazilians, Americans, Dutch, English, and French commercial firms that insinuated themselves along the coast. Backed with capital from their lineage, African men ran these new commercial centres as merchant lords over all-male households. They charged Europeans customs fees, regulated local business, provided auxiliary services, and sent goods to the interior on credit. A successful man called his household his "town" and demonstrated status in the old way – collecting wives, clients, and slaves. He educated his sons and nephews, trained them in the business, and gave them a patrimony in slaves.

Some slaves remained slaves even after the decline of the "peculiar institution": they were "slaves of the church," agricultural and household slaves attached to missions. Missionaries required agricultural slaves to marry and live in clusters near the mission. All household slaves were male – boys and young men; women could not enter mission houses. After the missionaries left, the "slaves of the church" went on living in all-male enclaves. Both sexes were impressed to serve an overlord to work on his or her behalf; but owners valued women as providers – of food, sex, and children – and men as worker-sons being trained to take over an all-male institution.

Kongo

In dealings between Africans and Europeans, only formal political power counted; Europeans were comfortable dealing man-to-man with Africans but would not accept female African leaders. In dealings with Europeans, African men gained power – and cash. No longer dependent on women, they could buy food and goods that wives had formerly provided. Exposed to new languages and customs, they gained education and experience as merchants and brokers. In time, matrilineal inheritance faded and women's elite status crumbled; they became wives, not sisters, sequestered at home and segregated at public events.[2] Some merchants reportedly offered visiting European men sexual use of their wives or daughters. Territories like Kongo may have remained sexually integrated even after class stratification, but they were now transformed into patriarchal societies in which only men functioned publicly and women were relegated to back rooms. As social mobility increased for men, it decreased for women.

People in the interior still followed the old ways, but the foreclosure of women from coastal commerce kept women out of the new commercial world. Women found new markets for their crops, supplying the *barracoons* (pens for slaves awaiting export) near the coast. When slave trade ended, they sold foods like groundnuts to Europeans for cash. As commerce expanded, women offered more variety at local markets and opened roadside food stands to cater to commercial caravans. But barter was still the rule: few women had cash, needed to purchase European goods.

Aside from commerce, the only way to get rich was by tribute. The old tribute system had died; men now controlled roads and markets, and granted titles. On the coast almost every man, even a low-level worker, could afford a slave; slaves were in such demand that they could negotiate their working conditions. But female slaves could rise in status only through marriage and motherhood, and all wives – royal, free, or slave – did field work. No woman had leisure; rich men's wives had only the help of co-wives. Some scholars believe that women may perhaps have preferred polygyny because it lessened their workload. Some co-wives developed close bonds. There were virtually no women in politics; Kongo was now an outpost in a Western commercial network in which women had lost most of their power.

East Africa: Zanzibar

The city-states of east Africa, which had grown rich by controlling trade routes, were invaded and conquered by Portugal in the sixteenth century. Over the next 200 years, various New World, Asian, and north African states contested to control the rising demand for slaves. In 1840, after conquering the Mazrui rulers of Mombasa, the Sultan of Oman, Seyyid Said, moved his headquarters to Zanzibar and consolidated his control over the east African coast, neighbouring islands, slave routes, and major trade centres and towns in the interior, creating the Zanzibar commercial empire. Zanzibari rulers set the conditions under which Asian and European merchants could reside and trade in the empire.[3]

As the Atlantic slave trade declined in the early nineteenth century, slave trading in East Africa expanded. After British, American, and Indian financiers wrested control of trade routes from Muslim Zanzibari rulers, the Arabs built huge coconut and clove plantations on Zanzibar. By 1850 they dominated the world clove market. African plantations were little worlds centred on a compound where owners lived with their family and servants. Until the mechanization of farming, plantation agriculture relied heavily on slave labour. Huge farms dedicated to few crops required enormous amounts of human labour and were most profitable when that labour was unpaid.

Basil Davidson writes that African slavery was not like that of the New World. In America, slaves could not marry, testify in court, or own slaves; they were overworked, often punished, whipped, tortured, separated from their families, and killed. African slaves were more like European serfs or peasants.[4] An observer of the Ashanti (Asante) of West Africa, quoted by Howard Zinn, attested that slaves could marry, own property or slaves themselves, and swear oaths as competent witnesses. "An Ashanti slave, nine cases out of ten . . . became an adopted member of the family, and in time his descendants so merged and intermarried with the owner's kinsmen that only a few [knew] their origin." Africans tended to absorb slaves into their families to increase their lineage, and even made them their heirs. In Sierra Leone, slaves were never overworked and never punished so as to draw blood. Zinn quotes John Newton, slave trader turned anti-slavery leader: "The state of slavery, among these wild barbarous people, as we esteem them, is much milder than in our colonies. For as, on the one hand, they have no land in high cultivation, like our West India plantations, and therefore no call for that excessive, unintermitted labour, which exhausts our slaves: so, on the other hand, no man is permitted to draw blood even from a slave."[5]

But if conditions there were less excruciating than in the New World, they were still very abusive: slaves died young and did not reproduce. Plantation work did not *use* slaves, it *consumed* them. Over half of Zanzibar's slaves were women. Work was divided by sex: men picked cloves, women separated the buds from the stems, spread them on mats to dry, and supervised the drying, which took about a week. When slaves threatened slowdowns, wanting piece-work wages and a five-day week, the Arabs gave them Thursday and Friday (the Muslim holy day). On these days, slaves could hire themselves out to carry loads, clean copra (coconut shells), do construction, tote water, or make products to sell, and keep their wages. Asians and Europeans, who were barred from owning slaves, hired slaves on their days off, directly or from their owners.

Owners established a hierarchy to keep slaves under control, writes Frederick Cooper.[6] Lowest in rank was the new unskilled plantation worker, *mtumwa mjinga* (stupid slave); then came those brought to the coast as children and socialized locally: *wakulia* ("people brought up here"). Above them were the locally born *wazalia*. The highest rank, except for concubines, were the skilled workers – carpenters, masons, metal workers, door carvers, and boat builders – solely male trades. Women could reach high rank only as seamstresses or concubines. Muslim law held that concubines could not be resold in an owner's lifetime and were to be freed at his death. Actually, they were freed at caprice by owners who were moved by a show of submissiveness. *Wazalia*, often freed with nothing after years of labour, ended up as serfs, *wahadimu*, still dependent on their former owners for land, shelter, and work. Some remained on the plantation as tenants or servants after their owner died, and, when the British took over East Africa, became their tenants, sharecroppers.

Women slaves worked in the fields, sold produce for the mistress in town markets, and carried goods outside the house in daylight. *Wazalia* were often house slaves; in the 1890s Mtoro bin Mwinyi Bakari outlined their work (*mzalia* is the singular of *wazalia*).

> The work of the [female] *mzalia* is to serve in the house, to wash vessels and plates or clothes or to be taught to cook, to plait mats, to sweep the house, to go to the well to draw water, to go to the shop to buy rice or meat; when food is ready, to dish it up for the master, to hold the basin for him to wash his hands . . . to wash his feet, and to oil him; but only if his wife approves. If the wife wants to go into the country or to a mourning or a wedding, she accompanies her, and if she has an umbrella, she carries it.[7]

In societies with huge disparities in wealth and power, the privileged, always fearful of rebellion, must justify their superiority. Their claims must contain enough seeming truth to be swallowed by the oppressed. Today, the rich justify their wealth on grounds of merit and hard work; they claim to be more talented or to work harder than others. Since some rich people do work hard and are talented, the claim seems real, and other grounds for privilege – inherited status, inherited wealth, willingness to exploit – melt into invisibility. For millennia, male superiority has been rationalized by the claim that it is based in nature. Legal and institutional leashes on women cast an aura of truth on the claim. Whites made precisely the same claims about blacks, claims that were "proven" true by similar leashes. Arab slaveholders, who at first did not hold the racist belief that dark skin denoted inferiority, justified black slavery by devising an ideology making Africans uncultured outsiders.[8]

Owners knew that to keep their slaves they had to control a huge class which might over generations become conscious of its solidarity and strength and rebel or resist. Slaves living within thinking distance of their homelands might flee. To reconcile them to subjection, the Arabs presented slavery as a reciprocal arrangement placing obligations on both slaves and owners. Although owners granted concessions under pressure, they presented them (like a five-day week) as generous benefits conferred by a superior people. Their major weapon was religion: the Arabs assimilated Africans to Islam, offering them religious instruction and encouraging them to spread it among themselves – to a degree. The problem was that Islam preaches equality. So owners concocted a two-tiered religion that accepted slaves as lower-level Muslims with fewer obligations. Muslims in the city of Lamu relegated slaves to one section of the mosque, barring them from certain rituals (as they did women). They invented a symbolism associating free Lamuans with light, heaven, and purity, and slaves with nature, beings too earthbound to understand more than the basic precepts of Islam. Close contact with slaves would contaminate free Lamuans; Arabs were better Muslims.

Arabs devised rituals to reinforce divisions among slaves, as well as between slaves and free people or owners. Each rank of slaves dressed differently: male plantation slaves could not wear caps, shoes, or *kanzus* (sophisticated coastal clothes). Female slaves, because they were forbidden to wear veils or headcloths, were probably harassed in street, field, and market. *Wazalia* were permitted to shake hands and eat with owners and free people. At special feasts, high-ranking male slaves could sit with free men (only concubines could sit with free women). The sexes were segregated. Slaves addressed their owners not by name but by "Mwinyi" or "Bwaba" (Master). In time, free Arab women were expected to call men of their own class "Master," reinforcing women's subordinate status.

Physical punishment was always the core of discipline on plantations, but Zanzibar lacked the armed force to back slave owners or intimidate the labour force, especially in remote agricultural districts. Harshly punished slaves often fled to establish Maroon villages or join maverick potentates who challenged the sultan's authority. Once Christian missions became secure havens (in the 1870s), slaves took refuge with missionaries opposed to slavery.

Africans adopted Arab culture; they spoke Swahili, wore coastal dress, and converted to Islam, often with ardour. Some owners rewarded acculturation by giving slaves (especially *wazalia* who had learned to follow coastal ways) a greater role and more responsible positions in household rituals and social activities. But the situation was delicate: by adopting Islamic culture slaves undermined the owners' myth of slave inferiority. Owners had to grant slaves some rights, but to acknowledge them as Muslims or human beings equal to their owners would subvert the entire premise of enslavement. And since Muslims may not enslave other Muslims, the conversion of slaves to Islam created a tricky problem. In particular, slave women were never expected to follow Islamic sex and marriage laws decreeing adultery a crime; many slave women were *required* to perform "adulterous" acts.

Indeed concubines and their offspring presented plantation owners with their worst problems. In Islamic law an owner cannot sell a concubine after she bears him a child, and he must free her in his will. Concubines' children were legitimate and free, the juridical equals of wives' children. In some regions Muslims ignored these laws. East African Muslims, wanting to augment their kin-groups, obeyed them to a degree, but did not value the children of concubines equally with those of wives. Some Arabs made concubines' sons lesser kin to free sons, but daughters were always slaves. In Mombasa concubines' children were part of both worlds; in Malindi, most respected families accepted concubines' sons but not their daughters. The royal dynasty of Zanzibar imported expensive prestigious Caucasian and Ethiopian concubines, and *their* sons became princes. Racism had become a factor in the ranking of people.

All over East Africa, people wanted slave women for plantation and domestic work. Since they fetched higher prices than men, no woman not bound to a man was safe in the interior. Slaves could be resold, and free women could be sold. Widows whose husbands' lineage agreed were sold. Some gave themselves as slaves to a known man to escape sale. Marcia Wright describes such a woman from central Africa. Narwimba, whose husband had died, was afraid for herself and her children. She went to her husband's nephew, and begged him, "Take me to wife; so that we might be protected."9 Some captured women committed suicide, leaping from dhows into the Indian Ocean. Fugitives were severely punished if they were caught. Missionary David Livingstone, for example, came upon a woman who had been tied by her neck to a tree to die slowly for this "crime." Slave raids into the interior multiplied, and rulers sold their own subjects to fight off the raiders for cash to buy guns and ammunition. Slave and ivory trade generated powerful chiefdoms and kingdoms as Arabs, Asians, and Swahili battled for control.

Shambala

After the 1830s, when the Kilindi had conquered the Shambala, they began trading with the Zanzibar commercial empire for slaves, ivory, imported cloth, and firearms. As the Zanzibar empire expanded and needed more slaves, slaves became the Kilindi's most important export "product." Over time, they had to travel farther and farther afield to find them, and they increasingly pulled men from farm work to go on slave raids or to defend villages and trade routes from raiders. Subject peoples disliked letting their homelands get run down, and resisted mainly by fleeing. The Kilindi's hold weakened. Chiefdom raided chiefdom, men sold children and wives or used them to pay fines for minor or invented crimes. Settlements unprotected by a state could not defend themselves.

It was a terrifying time, an old man remembered: "People simply seized and sold one another. If someone came across you and you weren't very strong he would just grab hold of you. Off to be sold you go." Women and children were most easily kidnapped, and women dared not leave their houses to work in the fields without armed guards: crops withered and people starved. Women killed their babies rather than see them starve or be enslaved. Traditionally, women whose husbands abused them, or whose kin failed to help them in need, had committed "cooking pot suicide": they would concoct an ancient poisonous herbal potion, and, cursing their kin – especially brothers and sons – would give it to their young children to drink and drink it themselves. Like desperate Chinese and Japanese women, they had no power but to die; and in Africa too, the act of cursing and suicide was seen as a pollution of the entire lineage. Since families wished to prevent this, the threat of suicide could sometimes work to women's advantage.

But in this period, suicide was not a strategy; enslaved women committed suicide and murdered their children in despair. Whole villages picked themselves up and moved to remote mountains to escape the raids. Subject peoples like the Bondei broke away from Kilindi rule, murdered as many Kilindi as possible, and re-established their old patrilineal groups. Late in the century, a Kilindi chief explained: "Every Kilindi needs to make war so he can capture slaves to sell for gun powder." Slavery created a vicious cycle: people needed guns to capture slaves to trade for guns to get more slaves. By the 1890s, East African agriculture declined to subsistence farming: the region was ruined.

The Cape

African societies that tried to maintain their traditional structure –
like the peoples of the misnamed Cape of Good Hope in present-
day South Africa – were cruelly pressured and often simply crushed.
Moreover, whites acted secretively, blaming Africans. Since only
whites kept written records, their false version of events was often
enshrined as truth. Recent research has revealed the truth about a
phenomenon called the *mfecane*, "the crushing," supposedly a progressive trampling of blacks by blacks in the period of the Zulu
leader Shaka (1810–30).

The term *mfecane*, coined by a white, has no African root,
writes Julian Cobbing; it describes a total fabrication.[10] In brief, two
Britons, Moffat and Melville, claimed that Zulu aggression against
other black societies had displaced a society, which then crushed the
next society, continuing in a domino effect. The massacres supposedly left (African) women and children homeless and starving, and
godly Christians took these refugees back to their settlements and
tried to find work for them.

Moffat, a missionary, and Melville, a government commissioner, wrote from their base in Natal that revolutions in northern
'Nguni societies southwest of Delagoa Bay had brought a fierce
insane Zulu chief, Shaka, to power in the early 1820s. (In fact, no
people called 'Nguni existed.) Moffat and Melville described an
1823–25 Zulu rampage led by Shaka, whom they credited with
inventing the *ibutho*, transforming battle tactics with short stabbing
spears and "horns and chest" battle formations. Although Shaka was
a real person, the weapons and formation had long predated him.
But the British public believed the claims. Whites wanted to usurp
African land and slave raids, but England had abolished slave trade,
and the public would not support aggressive war. To justify military
action, Moffat and Melville created a false history, writing that
Shaka had made a treaty ceding Britain considerable land but was
not fulfilling it (the Zulu knew nothing of this allegation until

1828) and was depopulating Natal. Histories still maintain that the expansionist Zulus overran other societies, precipitating a chain reaction as groups desperate for land fled inland, each overrunning the next society, with genocidal effect.

In fact, according to Cobbing, the Zulu were crushed between two white fronts. British relations with Shaka were utterly mendacious, and the British eventually arranged to have him murdered. British abolition of slave trade in 1807 meant that settlers in the Cape Colony could not *increase* their slaveholdings, although in 1823 they still owned slaves. (To abolish slave *trade* is not to abolish *slavery*.) British frontier policies were so cruel toward Africans that the English lived in fear of reprisal, and in terror banned all blacks but the Khoi (whom they called Hottentots) from working on Colony farms. From 1812 blacks could be shot if they were seen west of the Fish River; after 1819, if they stepped west of Keiskamma. Blacks who were dispossessed from their land could not travel for work.

Originally, the Khoi, Capetown herders, had welcomed and traded with the Dutch, the first whites to intrude on their land. But when British explorer Henry Stanley imported cattle with sleeping sickness, Khoi herds were decimated. In addition, smallpox brought by whites almost annihilated the Khoi, leaving so few that the British lost their fear of them and forced them into serfdom between 1809 and 1812. The San (Bushmen) might also have been pressed into serfdom if the British had not already genocidally exterminated them. When more settlers were sent out from Britain in 1820, a labour shortage threatened the colony's existence, so British traders and missionaries began raiding the Delagoa Bay region for slaves. The missionaries had co-opted the Griqua, a frontier people, and in 1827, 1832, and 1837 Boers joined British-led Griqua in attacks on the area.

Neither the British government nor the British public could be told that Britons were raiding for slaves, so Moffat and Melville concocted reports of battles at Dithakong and Mbolompo against a fictional tribe of Mantatees and an army 100,000 strong led by Mantatisi, mother of Sekonyela, the Tlokwa leader, whose name conveniently resembled "Mantatee." Calling Mantatisi (or Mmanthatisi) a fierce woman, they compiled an entire history of her leadership of her cannibalistic people in a sub-continental holocaust that wiped out nearly 2 million blacks. In reality, Mantatisi was a leader remembered by her people for saving them, not for leading them in a war that conveniently emptied the area so that Europeans could move in during the 1830s and 1840s.

Moffat and Melville's reports won support and sympathy in England by describing the actual refugees as marauding bands of semi-demonic *cannibalistic* women and children who ravaged the countryside like locusts. They saw "bones littering the veld" after savage wars among blacks (the bones, real enough, came from their own slave raids) which left hordes of refugees wandering the countryside. What could Christian men do but take in these homeless, hungry folk with no place to go, weeping mothers searching for their kidnapped children? To help the missions deal with this misery, whites in London, Glasgow, Paris, and Boston poured money into mission societies.

But the battles waged against "savage" Africans to save "innocent" women and children were actually slave and cattle raids. The Griqua took cattle as their cut; the missionaries got cattle, women, and children. The British force killed as many men as possible because the Cape slave market wanted only women and boys. By 1824 they had brought several thousand new slaves into the colony. Slaves were given a tiny wage, almost nothing, to disguise their real state, which was that they were sold and bought and could not leave. White farmers sometimes accompanied the raiders, seizing a slave so as not to have to pay for her. In 1822–23 Moffat and Melville invented a second "horde," the "Fetcani" (a Tembu word for bandits used by the Boers to describe any people whose cattle *they* raided). When the British governor sent armies across the Kei to capture people for slaves under the pretext of a

Zulu invasion, the story was that the "Fetcani" had driven the Tembu from their land. In reality, an army directed by whites surrounded Ngwane villages before dawn and attacked, killing 70 people and plundering 25,000 cattle. In a second attack hundreds of Ngwane were killed, their cattle and over a hundred captives taken, mainly women and children.

Given such events, the Zulus were essentially forced to become militaristic: their choice lay between that and annihilation. But militaristic states always oppress women, and to this day, the Zulu remain male-dominated and militaristic. The men own the cattle exchanged as bridewealth; women are required to be subservient to husbands, husband's "mothers," "fathers" (men in a paternal relationship), and senior brothers, especially during their early probationary and childbearing years. After the 1870s white South Africans also encouraged male domination and delegated judicial authority in both the home and community to elder indigenous males. Wright states that even today the people of this region – the Zulu, Swazi, and Basoto – are extremely sexually stratified and nationalistic in a way that is utterly congenial with the doctrines of apartheid. This partially explains the conflict between the African National Congress and the Kwazulu that raged throughout the struggle against apartheid, and reverberates still today.

Accommodations to Slavery

Women Traders in West Africa

After the European invasion, resourceful independent West African women, like other African women, tried to use Europeans for their own ends. They succeeded for a time, but were finally crushed. Some West African women were coastal traders with a long history of economic independence and initiative. According to legend, queens ruled coastal Senegal, Gambia, and Upper Guinea; rich women ruled West African villages when the Portuguese arrived. The first Portuguese traders worked from ships, later settling in coastal and riverine villages. For commercial advantage, they formed relationships with the most influential women who would have them; in return for trading privileges, the women tended the men and taught them African customs.

George Brooks has studied these women, called *senoras, signares, senhara,* or *senhoras.* Most lived on the tiny islands of St. Louis and Gore, in Senegal, and had high social rank, great beauty – Brooks sounds quite in love with them – and style, wearing splendid brilliantly coloured clothes and gold and silver jewellery.[11] These sharp businesswomen owned ships, houses, and large bands of slaves. They knew how to acquire wealth and also how to enjoy it: they built two-storey houses with large airy rooms opening onto verandahs, and lived in luxury and comfort, giving balls at which their slaves entertained. These women never sold their slaves, many of whom were artisans, and treated them indulgently. The *signares* nursed the Europeans during their frequent illnesses. (Between a sixth and a fifth of Europeans died each year in the unfamiliar Senegalese climate. In the rainy season, July to October on St. Louis island, three of every ten Europeans died.) In the eighteenth and nineteenth centuries, long after the Dutch had displaced the Portuguese, to be in turn displaced by the French, men viewed these women with great respect, and integrated themselves into the women's lives. Until the British came. When they got to Senegal, they built a fort, described by the man sent to manage it as a "dismal heap of ruins [inhabited by] the most mutinous, drunken, abandoned fellows I ever met with." Brooks writes that they were racist "rootless" bachelors, reckless gamblers, and alcoholics who would not associate openly with African women.

Sierra Leone, like Liberia, was a colony founded by former slaves who could not return to their homelands. In 1792 the Sierra Leone Company established the colony with a thousand Nova Scotian and American slaves who had supported the British during the Revolution, writes E. Frances White.[12] They were joined in 1800 by Jamaican Maroons who had fought the British to an impasse and accepted relocation in settlement. As the British tried to end slave trading, their ships intercepted slave ships and took the captives to a British naval base in Freetown, where 50,000 West African recaptives eventually settled. The British tried to meld these people into a tribe called Krios. ("Creole" means krio-speaking in Africa.) Other fugitive slaves joined them and the people traded African palm products and kola nuts for imported European goods. The overwhelming majority of Sierra Leoneans were Yoruba, Ibo, or Popo, from today's Nigeria and Benin.

Most female recaptives in Sierra Leone were Yoruba. Since they shared a similar background and were often from the same ethnic group, the culture they created had a Yoruba character. The Yoruba reversed the common African division of labour: men farmed and women marketed the produce. This arrangement gave Yoruba women independence – freedom to travel long distances while trading and the freedom to divorce. They divorced to advance themselves economically and could do so because they were financially independent of their husbands. Also, they grew up in fairly urban economically developed areas and were not intimidated by Freetown. But by tradition, West African women did not trade until they were past forty: young wives, who were held responsible for feeding the family, were pressed into domestic and farm work. As they usually worked alone, they produced little surplus. Men tried to keep wives from earning money, fearing they would repay their brideprice and divorce them. (Men realized they exploited women.) The British, trying to "civilize" the Africans, imposed monogamy, which would have undermined women traders if a large number of newly arrived recaptive women had not fallen into British hands. They "apprenticed" the newcomers to men who made them work in the fields or carry produce, so that older women could continue to trade.

By 1830 many Freetown women were prominent traders; some were famous, like the Hausa recaptive Betsy Carew, who married a Bambara butcher, Thomas, and supplied meat to the army.

Adorned in gold earrings and a coral necklace, she made formal calls on Europeans and sent one of her sons to London to school. The couple later expanded their business into retailing imported liquor. Another contractor for the British government, Elizabeth Coles, supplied the military with meat and vegetables from her large garden. Most traders worked on a small scale, but in 1838, thirty Sierra Leoneans ran factories; women, never as successful as men, ran factories on the rivers, reaching their peak of success in the 1870s.

Inland Africans resented traders, who tended to exploit or cheat them, and hated the English for offering their runaway slaves refuge in Freetown. Inland men didn't like their women to see Sierra Leonean women traders' freedom and autonomy. So they kidnapped, murdered, or enslaved women traders. Elizabeth Coles (not the woman above) was a twenty-five-year-old from a peninsula village who went inland to Senehu to trade in 1888, protected by her landlord, Madame Yoko, a pro-British chief. When Senehu was attacked, Coles and three other Sierra Leonean women were captured. The others, who made the mistake of speaking English, revealing their identity, were killed. Coles, enslaved, survived by acting ignorant of English. She was recognized by a Temne trader and rescued.

In 1895 England declared Sierra Leone a protectorate and imposed taxes. Interior groups – the Sus, Temne, Yoni Temne, and Masimerah – rebelled. But the British, perhaps strategically, blamed coastal peoples for the war and bypassed them to ally with hinterland chiefs and local elites, penetrating ever more deeply in order to appropriate inland territories. Unable to operate without British protection, the traders and their culture died out.

Resistance to Slavery: Male States, Female Leadership

Some Africans tried to resist European predation by building power bases of their own. Both women and men created such bases, but women generally made themselves powerful centres around which people gathered in loose organization, while men built highly centralized military states. Women never ruled in such states but acted in them on every level, as slaves (women were the first to be enslaved, last to be freed), administrators, and slave owners.

The Yoruba and the Oyo Empire

Slave traders reached present-day southern Nigeria about 1650, and seized 1.5 million people along its coast from the late seventeenth to the early nineteenth century, writes Babatunde Agiri.[13] This region was home to the Yoruba, some of whom used profit from the slave trade to build a state, the Oyo Empire. They hoped to protect their own people from being transported by providing the Europeans with foreign slaves they had bought, captured, or coerced as tribute from other Yoruba groups or their neighbours, the Bariba, the Hausa, and the Nupe. To protect its own people, the Oyo Empire became itself a slave-state.

In the 1790s European wars disrupted slave trade in West Africa, breaking Oyo's connection to the Atlantic trade. With its economy disintegrating, the army rebelled in 1817; Dahomey stopped paying tribute and intervened. When uprisings shook the Muslim Ilorin Emirate, some fortified cities withdrew and merged with Dahomey into a new Yoruba state, the Oyo Empire. Built for resistance, the empire was militaristic: army chiefs maintained standing armies and ruled its cities, which did large-scale slave trading. Neighbours scurried to protect their people, often in vain. Historians believe that a state became necessary to defend people against European aggression.

An *alaafin* ruled the Oyo Empire; nobles in the *oyo mesi* (council of state) headed lineages with huge numbers of wives, slaves, and other dependants. The army was made up of slaves, some of whom were specialists in the care and use of horses. Since the cavalry was the backbone of the Oyo army, slaves were essential to sustaining the empire. Slaves managed provincial towns, collected caravan tolls and taxes, and acted as messengers, farmers, and household servants. Slavery was intrinsic to Yoruba thinking: the Yoruba religion emphasized the importance of one's kin-group and of *ori* (destiny, one's inner, spiritual head). People's well-being depended on their *ori* and on ritual sacrifices to the gods at Yoruba shrines. Ambitious people were told to be patient and prudent in order to develop a good character. Inequality was a given. The Yoruba metaphor for the social entity was a hand: as fingers of unequal length are all useful, so people of unequal status were useful in the community – even slaves who had slave parents or those who had lost the higher status of their natural families through misbehaviour like theft or misfortune, capture in war, or kidnapping.

In a climate in which freedom was vulnerability, free men in need of protection attached themselves to lineage leaders as clients. Called "slaves" of the chief, they had to pay tribute at ceremonies and sometimes work on a chief's farm a number of days a week, but they were not bound and could switch allegiance easily. There were also "pawns," mainly females pledged as collateral for loans. Their bondage was often endless, as they had to pay off the loan *and* the interest on it. A child pawned by her father lived with and served his creditor, who fed her. Parents unable to feed their own children often pawned them to someone who could; if the parents could not redeem them, they remained in bondage their whole lives. If they ran away, debtors had to find or replace them. Adult pawns served a mutually agreed number of days a week.

Exposure to Western ideas led some Yoruba to abandon their traditions. Although transported Yoruba maintained their traditional religion in the New World, a new generation of African men adopted the Western value of individual achievement. Scorning the Yoruba idea that good behaviour propitiated *ori*, they became war captains, aggressive and skilled at fighting, farming, and trade. To have their importance recognized in Africa, they had to own many other human beings. Anna Hinderer, a nineteenth-century Western observer, wrote: "There are no riches in [Yoruba land]; slaves and wives make a man great in this country."[14]

Doubts about the efficacy of the Yoruba gods drew many Yoruba to Islam or Christianity, neither of which justified slave revolt. Islam condoned slavery, and Catholic missionaries in Oyo in the 1840s were divided about it; some deplored slavery, and some bought slaves or assisted the slave trade. But both groups challenged Yoruba religion and social structure. The British too were equivocal. A decade after landing at Lagos in 1851, they decreed it a colony and themselves its rulers. As they moved further into the interior, they rarely protected black Christian communities from slave traders, but did send military excursions to stop slave exports, and in the 1880s and 1890s tried to stop them inland.

Methodists and the Church Missionary Society (CMS) opposed slave trade and slavery, and the CMS helped make Sierra Leone a haven for fugitive African slaves. But after Britain had emancipated slaves in its territories in 1833, the CMS *supported* domestic slavery. Missionaries wanted to convert Africans to Christianity, but the religion did not appeal to them. Sierra Leonean Yoruba Christian converts returned to Yorubaland to proselytize after their emancipation. The most prominent of them, Bishop Samuel Crowther, a leader in the anti-slavery campaign, would not have been able to convert African slave owners if he had opposed domestic slavery. So he supported it, claiming African slavery was humane. His group also insisted on compensating owners for freed slaves.

In 1879 the CMS forbade Christians to own slaves. A minister who tried to enforce the rule was confronted by a group of Egba converts led by prominent women trader slave owners who declared that people would rather go into the interior with their slaves than remain without them. Local mission workers warned the CMS that preaching against slavery could cause the widespread murder of white missionaries and the extirpation of Christianity in Africa. Ironically, of all African slave owners, both white and black, Christians treated their slaves most harshly and worked them hardest, insisting on the "Protestant ethic" of hard work.

The gradual defeat of the entire continent of Africa was probably inevitable, given the Europeans' superior arms and their intense drive for acquisition. No African of the colonial period permanently overcame the Europeans. Men built militaristic, hierarchical states to keep their people under control and oppose the Europeans. Women created networks that enabled their people to maintain some integrity and dignity, as well as helping African cultures survive. Both failed: women were killed, and states collapsed. Africa fell under Europe's heel. But the women's legacy of courage and unity fed a continuing resistance.

Nehanda of Zimbabwe

African women retained their ancient aura of spiritual power into the modern era. Some, like Nehanda of Zimbabwe, used it in overtly political ways. Nehanda Nyaksikana, a Shona religious leader and prophet, lived between 1863 and 1898. The Shona believed she incarnated the spirit of the original Nehanda of the Shona, who had lived in the fifteenth century. According to legend, when her father, the chief, died, it was the practice that a son had to commit incest with his sister in order to rule (females must still have inherited the right to rule). Discovering that one of her brothers was willing to do so, Nehanda was so dismayed that she disappeared into a cleft in a rock. The rock was then named after her, and her spirit was said to return to guard her people whenever they needed to resist.

Centuries later, in the late 1880s, the British invaded Mashonaland to exploit the people and their land: the invading expedition was financed by the British South Africa Company, which had major mining interests in South Africa. The guiding spirit of the enterprise was Cecil Rhodes, who became enormously rich from those interests. The Shona believe Nehanda Nyaksikana had taken on the original Nehanda's spirit to lead them in resisting.

Nehanda led the Shona in the Chimurenga war of resistance, from 1896 to 1897. Other peoples joined them, including the Ndebele. Nehanda's headquarters lay in the Musakain Mazoew district, an impregnable mountain fortress pierced by a network of caves, inaccessible except through treacherous narrow passages. It had plentiful water, grain storage, and cattle kraals. From this retreat, Nehande chose targets: mines, trading posts, police stations, white settlers, and African collabourators. Her army won control of most rural areas and forced the British to ask for reinforcements to protect their settlers. A white settler wrote: "At the present moment Nianda [sic] is the most powerful wizard in Mashonaland and has the power of ordering all the people who rose lately and her orders would in every case be obeyed." (Nehanda was a general, but female, therefore a *wizard*.) The British made deals that divided the Ndebele and the Shona; they then made peace with the Ndebele and focused entirely on the Shona.

In December 1897 the British captured Nehanda and Kagubi, a male leader; contrary to all military protocol, they killed her – something they would not do to a white military opponent – hanging her on April 27, 1897. A white Catholic priest wrote:

> Everyone felt relieved after the execution as the very existence of the main actors in the horrors of the rebellion, though they were secured in prison, made one feel uncomfortable. With their deaths, it was universally felt the rebellion was finished, their bodies were buried in a secret place so no natives could take away their bodies and claim that their spirit had descended to any other prophetess or witchdoctor. The younger generation, it was hoped, now knew that the white Queen [Victoria] meant to reign.[15]

Yaa Asantewa and the Asante

After Ghana fell, its people went on living as they had for centuries. With its huge forests and plentiful water, Ghana was stable: homesteads and fields were occupied for generations by the same people, including the Akan clans, which grew into states. In the 1670s Osei Tutu tried to unite the Akan states, ostensibly to overthrow neighbouring Denkyira but really to dominate the confederacy himself, writes David Sweetman.[16] With a priest, Osei invented the myth of the Golden Stool, a wooden stool decorated with gold that floated down from heaven during a ceremony. The stool became the symbol of Asante unification, and reigning rulers were said to be "on the stool." But no one sat on it; it was considered more exalted even than the ruler, and during ceremonies, sat on its own throne higher than the ruler's.

The Akan states retained many matricentric customs: chiefs had to be descended from a certain female line and inherited their status from their mothers. The queen mother and her advisors might rule themselves or choose a ruler (*asantehene*) from among her grandsons or great-grandsons. Women often led troops into battle, and they filled high offices and supervised women's affairs. The *asantehema*, the king's wife and co-ruler, had symbolic status but also participated in state councils. Princesses were involved in political power struggles. These facts suggest that women retained considerable power in Asante lineages.

By 1750 the Asante Empire almost reached the sea, but the Asante never assimilated those they conquered or dispersed their armies. So, whenever they seemed vulnerable, their subjects rebelled. Asante disputes over British efforts to end the slave trade led to wars in 1811 and 1816. An uneasy truce lasted until 1874, when the Asante attacked the British, who retaliated by invading the country. Reaching the Asante capital, Kumase, they declared it a colony, deposing the *asantehene*. But neither superior British arms nor the civil war over succession that mired the Asante for a decade could break the people. They were almost wholly destroyed and their king exiled when, in a final drive to repel the British from their land, the Asante made a woman their leader.

In 1884 Nana Afrane Kuma ruled Edweso, an Asante state, with his mother, Queen Yaa Asantewa. In a civil war, he sided with Prempeh I, of Yaa Asantewa's Oyoko clan. The British signed treaties with and offered protection to states that rebelled against the Asante.

Prempeh was "enstooled" in 1894; in 1896, when the British set up a protectorate at Kumase, they ordered Prempeh to pay for the expedition. When he refused, they exiled him and his supporters, including Nana Afrane Kuma and Prempeh's mother, also a major political figure.[17] Thinking they had finally won the war, the British established a residency in Kumase and built a fort for their adminis-trators. When the new British governor paid a visit, he ignorantly and arrogantly demanded the golden stool to sit upon.

This electrified the people, and they silently left the ceremony. Three days later, war erupted – the Yaa Asantewa war, named for the woman who led it. In April, Yaa beseiged Kumase, trapping the British in their fort. Their major ally, the king of Bekwai, was too frightened of Yaa to send reinforcements to help them, and he could barely keep his men from joining her. By mid-June, with thirty Britons a day dying inside the fort, the remaining men tried to escape. Yaa Asantewa let them go. In July British reinforcements with Maxim guns arrived in Kumase; they retook the city and set out to capture Yaa Asantewa. She and her soldiers resisted until the end of September, when the British surrounded the forest she was hiding in. She spat in the face of the officer who arrested her, but the strength of the Asante resistance had forced the British to respect her and they treated all their captives as prisoners of war – there were few executions. They exiled Yaa Asantewa and her son to the Seychelle Islands, where she lived another twenty years. Yaa was defeated but she had forced the English to recognize the Asante people. The Asante still sing about "Yaa Asantewa, the warrior woman who carries a gun and a sword of state in battle."

Resistance to Male Domination

East African Spirit Mediums

Most African societies had some degree of male domination before Europeans arrived, but the invaders increased it by generating war and militarism. Many Europeans dealt only with men, thereby nullifying women's power; they turned entire regions into predatory jungles where women were safe only if they were "owned" by a man. In the next phase of domination, the European states completed the patriarchization of the continent by imposing Western notions of property rights and law. But women continued to resist male supremacy, some through religion.

Africa has a long tradition of female spiritual leadership. Women like Nzinga of Angola, Amina of Hausaland, Beatrice of Kongo, and Nehanda of Zimbabwe were spiritual leaders who had military or political skills. Some women used spiritual power and the beliefs of their societies to improve their lives and those of other women. Such women, known as spirit mediums, were active in local spirit-possession religions. Iris Berger has studied this tradition among nineteenth-century East African women in southern and western Uganda, Rwanda, Burundi, and northwestern Tanzania, where local religions were often devoted to a legendary hero who was apotheosized – seen as a god. Among the leaders and their large followings were both females and males.[18]

In East Africa patrilineal clans farmed and herded in scattered settlements with a centralized political structure stratified by class and occasionally by ethnicity. Men were superior to women, but upper-class women were superior to lower-class men and a few upper-class women had wealth and authority. But only men had political power, legal rights – the right to inherit cattle and land and to act independently outside the home. Women were not supposed to speak in public or even look a man in the eyes; if questioned, a woman was expected to avoid answering, claiming ignorance. Most women were totally subservient to their husbands and fathers, who retained authority over them throughout life, even after marriage. Women who rose above their sex-based status did so by gaining the favour of a male superior, mainly by manipulation, lying, or flattery. Women had authority only over children, younger sisters, and their husbands' subordinates. Burundian men claimed women were stronger than men, and so more suited to physical labour, but inferior to men because they were clumsy, lacked agility, were unable to control their emotions, and were prone to jealousy. Although women's part in childbearing was passive – men planted "seed" in their "earth" – it was said to age them more quickly than men.

Women could be rainmakers (it was a hereditary profession and the chief rainmaker was famous), and they could be spirit mediums, who entered trances during which they were "possessed," inhabited by the spirit of a departed god who spoke through them to the living. Spirit mediums, called Bandwa, were members of religions; they dressed strikingly in animal skin or bark cloth and enjoyed considerable respect. A potential medium was sent a sign, perhaps a long illness, after which she was ritually initiated. Indeed, the approved cure for women who went into trances, grew ill, and cried was to join a religion. They became part of a secret society higher than ordinary society. Only a few were professionals; most lived ordinary lives between ceremonies during which they danced, made rhythmic music, spoke in an esoteric language, adorned themselves, and acted out roles.

All observers noted that women, the mainstay of the religions, were predominant. Most were childless women who had to worship the ancestors of their husbands' lineage, and whose husbands would approve their devotion to a religion that might help them get pregnant. But Berger and others believe that women often used religion to gain the authority and status their society denied them and to assert themselves in the face of male domination. Some religions gave a "possessed" wife control over her husband during trances: she might order a man to drive his other wives away, terrify him into ceasing to beat her, demand control over household goods, or order her husband to carry or hire someone to carry the heavy burdens he had laid on her. The subtext of religion seems to have been to impel husbands to treat their wives more fairly.

Some rituals allowed women to share men's prerogatives and status. In Busoga only men were allowed to sit on stools, but female mediums sat on skin seats during trances; in some ceremonies, women wore male ceremonial dress, sat on stools, carried spears, and judged trials. In others, possessed women could act like men, speak inconsiderately, and abuse parents or superiors without paying compensation afterward. Religion could alter women's oppression, and also give temporary relief. There were rituals that reversed class distinctions (most members were lower-class); men could reverse gender, dressing as women and insulting others during trances. The assumed status was held only during possession: after it, people reverted to their usual status. High-status men could allow women or lower-class men this liberty without risking their positions in the social order.

Some African priestesses and mediums became powerful and prestigious figures.[19] Only "great witches" and royal princesses could own or inherit property, but some mediums became rich. In Nkore the female diviner Nyabuzana owned land and a palace and had such high prestige that in ceremonial dress she could claim any cow she wanted. The role of spiritual outlaw – priestess, medium, or soothsayer – fits the cultural image of women and empowers dispossessed women in many cultures.

Despite government declarations abolishing slave trade and slavery, and some efforts to enforce them, African slavery lasted into the twentieth century – and still exists, mainly for young women. Europeans impoverished Africa, killed or exported its people, expropriated their land, and eroded its culture. The number of Africans enslaved may be as high as 250 million – between 1500 and 1800, 11 million were transported, almost 8 million across the Atlantic to Brazil and the Caribbean, and 3 million across the Sahara, Red Sea, and Indian Ocean. A healing fact that does not mitigate their tragedy or that of the people they left behind is that their descendants now enrich societies across the world. Africa and its traditions endured, largely because of African women's powerful resilient behaviour in the face of patriarchy – in both its indigenous and imported forms.[20]

CHAPTER 2

INDUSTRIALIZATION

THE INDUSTRIAL REVOLUTION BEGAN AROUND 1780, when machines were invented to manufacture cloth faster than humans could. By 1800 water- and steam-driven machines were producing energy to make chemicals, iron, and pottery. By 1850 railroads were crossing continents.

The first country to industrialize was England, then the richest country in the world, with its many colonies and a navy huge enough to reach them, their resources, and their markets. For the British, as for all governments, national interest meant the interests of the ruling class, and Britain used its power over colonies to benefit British capitalists. By placing tariffs on foreign imports, it thwarted colonial industries and forced colonies to produce raw materials so that they had to buy British manufactures. A tariff on Indian cloth, for example, made India's major export prohibitively expensive in England, stimulated domestic cloth production, and left the Indian economy even more vulnerable to British demands. The capitalist system dictated the work of colonists, and industrial states thwarted the development of colonial industry. Capitalism revolutionized life globally.

Another reason the industrial revolution began in England was the availability of British workers. The overwhelming majority of Europeans lived on the land and grew their own food. In 1830, 60 percent of French and Italians, over 70 percent of Prussians, 90 percent of Spaniards, and 95 percent of Russians farmed. Most Britons worked on the land but few owned any: England had wiped out its peasant class. A few landlords with thousand-acre estates had appropriated *half* the country. Landowners leased land to tenant farmers, and hired the landless, or farmers with tiny plots, for day wages to grow crops mainly to sell. Some grazed sheep on their land, even enclosing village commons to prevent their pure-bred sheep from mixing with other varieties. In England, displaced peasants became a desperate labour force willing to work for a pittance, whereas France still had a sturdy lower middle class of very conservative peasant landowners, who rarely emigrated. Many Britons emigrated, and many Germans; in Germany, rich men freed their serfs in return for a third to half of their land.

Before British landowners ejected the peasantry from the land and industrialization began in Europe, most people had a place to live. They may have been bowed down by arduous work that did not always suffice to keep them from starving, but they were bound to that work and to their land. Industrial labour was actually *less* onerous than life on the land; industrial ills *seem* worse because they are more documented. Systematic studies of the conditions of workers' lives began in the nineteenth century. The impulse to make these studies arose from the new belief that conditions could be altered to make them more bearable, that life could be improved. It is important to bear in mind as we examine workers' conditions that peasants' lives may in some ways have been worse.

The industrial revolution transformed the nature of work by tapping new energy sources; and it also transformed the relations between classes. Peasants and nobles gradually became workers and

owners. A new elite arose: men with capital. Capitalism revolutionized society by putting a new concept of human relations into practice. The feudal system was based on a notion of bonds of rights and
obligations; the capitalist system is based in an ideology of freedom
which claims that instead of being contracted by bondage to others
or to land, a free person contracts with another free person to buy
(or sell) labour. This formula – men buy labour, not people – sepa-
rates production from reproduction; but its rhetoric of freedom
(people cannot be bought) and individualism is accompanied by a
profound indifference to the survival of masses of humans.
Capitalist ideology claims that labour can be freely bought and sold.
But in truth, unequal ownership of resources bars the majority from
such freedom. For a huge dispossessed class utterly vulnerable to
capital's demands, *freedom* means the freedom to starve or work for
any wage offered. The wage that connects capital and labour is a
constant cause of struggle; the workers' only sustenance, providing
maintenance, renewal, and reproduction, is the capitalist's major
item of budget savings.

Older traditions lingered after capitalism emerged: workers like
domestic servants, farm or textile workers, and seamstresses were
still housed and fed by their employers, families or mill owners who
provided dormitories. Such workers remained bound – under surveillance, forced to obey their employer's orders – but employers
also remained responsible for workers' safety, health, and diet. Increasingly, though, employer responsibility ended with the wage.
Profits were staggering, yet wages were so low that workers could
not live on them. Owners hired mainly women and children, paying them abominably. In 1833 a family of five needed at least 20
shillings a week to survive, but only 2000 of 12,000 Glasgow cotton mill workers averaged more than 11 shillings a week. Average
wages in 131 Manchester mills were under 12 shillings. Nor could
people avoid the factories; weavers, a large prosperous and skilled-
labour force, were decimated by competition from machines. From
1795 to about 1834 weavers' wages fell by 83 percent: 500,000

weavers and their families starved to death.

As manufacture moved to factories, "putting-out" work (piece-work done at home) declined, making it harder for artisan or peasant families with a little land to survive. Many became landless seekers of waged work: proletarians. Families swarmed to cities expecting to work together as they always had and at first were hired as families, including children over five or six. (Men soon separated themselves from women and children.)[1] At first, the factory system was the leading edge, not the dominant mode of production. Most work was still done traditionally, and most female workers were still domestic servants. Feeling they had to establish the upper hand over labour, factory owners created a highly regulated, heavily policed environment.

To force workers to show up, they held back their wages or tied them to contracts for twenty-one years. Discipline was harsh: the slightest infraction could mean instant dismissal, transfer to the worst job, or a fine. No one had any autonomy; discipline and work rhythms were imposed by others. People resisted factory discipline, not because they did not want to work but because they resented losing control of their labour. Factory work was regulated by bells or whistles: arriving ten minutes late could mean losing a whole morning's wages. Workers had to work fourteen to eighteen straight hours at the same task with only a short break – or none at all – to eat. Forbidden to talk or walk about or rest for a moment, they could only wait for the next bell or whistle. In some factories they had to gobble food down beside their machines. They were literally not given time or place to pee: toilets were scarce or non-existent. Owners buying only labour ignored workers' bodies or minds – giving no thought to their fatigue, health, safety, morale, personal refreshment and renewal, or ability to produce healthy children.

Factory foremen were most savage to women and children, considering them mere property. Managers tied tiny children to machines to keep them awake and upright; like husbands in home workshops, they beat children and women and used women sexually, threatening punishment or dismissal for resistance. Parliamentary and official inquiries from 1800 on regularly record male supervisors molesting female workers, cuffing and strapping children, dragging them from sleep and weighting them with iron as punishment.

Factory conditions were appalling. Open machines had dangerous moving parts that could injure the children who cleaned under or around them. Over 50,000 children worked in mines hauling laden underground trams, often for twelve hours at a stretch. Women too hauled coal trams. Tiny children put in charge of the doors that ventilated the mines sometimes fell asleep, imperiling everyone in the mine. Trapped gas frequently exploded. Textile mills were unventilated and workers breathed in fibres that later caused fatal lung disease; the lead used in making glazed pottery poisoned workers. Underfed workers suffered spinal curvature and bone deformations from standing still for long hours.

After fourteen or more hours of numbing work, and a walk to and from the factory that might add an hour at each end, women, men, and children stumbled through smoggy smoky cities to cramped basement rooms without windows or drains, or to cold dark hovels or corners of flats without water or toilets – the first slums. Crowded filthy cities lacked sewers or drains, garbage rotted in the streets, and gutters stank of excrement and urine. Factories, railways, and chimneys polluted the air. On the pittances they earned, people ate poorly; rickets was common. Epidemics swept the crowded slums, and thousands died of cholera, typhus, and tuberculosis. And during the frequent economic downturns, people lost their jobs and their small hold on life. In 1810 factory workers rioted, chanting "Bread or blood!" They stole to eat; from 1805 to 1833, larceny convictions in England rose 540 percent; over 25,000 people were hanged, most for petty theft. In 1842, one in eleven Britons was a pauper.

We have not yet seen the full consequences of the industrial revolution: we are still living them out. It made life less arduous for millions *and* it impoverished millions; it enriched life by introducing items once unavailable or non-existent *and* it created more stress, pollution, noise, and ugliness. It changed the air we breathe, our diets, the pace of life, and the way we look at life. Its most serious immediate consequences were social; the rich used their wealth mainly to amass huge fortunes by exploiting workers. People newly imbued with the Enlightenment idea of human rights were outraged at the wretched lot of the mass of humanity. Protesting their misery in riots and strikes, the poor learned class-consciousness, a revolutionary development. They became aware of themselves as a coherent group with a place in history, exploited by and struggling with another group. They learned to protest not as individuals or in informal groups but *collectively*. Their struggle triggered the political movements and revolutions that constitute the history of the modern age.

Working-Class Women

Industry operated initially on the same assumptions as the traditional family labour system. Eager to keep the price of labour low and the supply high, owners happily let men and women fight it out. The price of labour depended on organization; men organized in the precapitalist craft guild system used their solidarity to control wages and access to the labour supply. Men's insistence on patriarchal privilege infused the wage struggle, which was really a male war against women. Refusing to demand that women should earn the same as men, men battled to control the labour market *and* the family through wages. Very quickly, men's wages became the family wage. Owners were pleased to pay women less and keep them in low-level jobs.

Women who remained at home to maintain the family and raise children were still productive, but because capitalist thought excluded renewal and reproduction from productive labour (defined as production of surplus value, or profit), their work was considered valueless. (Recall that some simple societies define whatever women produce as worthless even when it sustains the group, and value only what men produce, or define women's work as non-work.) Without wages, women had no voice in a family. As production moved to factories where jobs were sex-segregated, the two sexes were less likely to work together. In an agricultural society, most people worked at home, together; in industrialized society, people's jobs distanced them from home and from each other. Work became "homosocial," a word coined by Carroll Smith-Rosenberg to describe same-sex social affiliations.[2] Sexual segregation had always existed in institutions like the Catholic Church, universities, the military; in this century it became near-universal and gender roles rigidified.

Texile Workers

Most factory women worked in textiles. In 1835 almost half of English cotton-textile workers were female, and this number increased over the century. British factory women saw work as a contribution to their families, not as a means to economic independence. Françoise Basch describes the atrocious conditions in most mills.[3] Temperatures averaged 30°–35°C or higher, the unventilated air in carding workshops was permeated with fluff that lodged in the lungs, and the noise was deafening. Girls of eleven assigned to wet-spin linen stood barefoot in water; water flowing from the spindles soaked their clothes and saturated the air with steam twelve to fourteen hours a day. Workers lost limbs to machines, suffered vitamin deficiencies, exhaustion, blindness, ulcers, asthma, and – most often in textile work – tuberculosis.

What may have been the first textile mill in the United States opened in 1822 in Lowell, Massachusetts, with all elements of production under one roof. The Lowell system was designed to maintain tight control over workers, mainly daughters of local Yankee farmers drawn to the mills by the promise of their own wages. Most of them planned to work only until marriage and sent all or part of their wages home. The Lowell Manufacturing Company put them in dormitories with strict rules: "The Company will not continue to employ any person who shall smoke within the Company's premises, or be guilty of inebriety, or other improper conduct. . . .The doors must be closed at ten o'clock in the evening, and no person admitted after that time without reasonable excuse." The girls did the same tasks as at home – weaving and spinning – but the work was mechanized and conditions were oppressive, as shown in a poem some of them composed: "Amidst the clashing noise and din/ Of the ever beating loom/ Stood a fair young girl with throbbing brow/ Working her way to the tomb."

Wherever industrialization occurred, the same pattern appears: all workers were overworked and underpaid, but women were given the most difficult, menial jobs, had no hope of advancing, and were paid less than men.[4] When Russia industrialized in the late nineteenth century, women filled the factories. By 1914, millions worked in industry, almost half a million in textiles alone, many under fourteen years old. In every trade, women were given the heaviest and hardest labour (this was still true in the Soviet Union). In wood depots and sawmills they lugged the heaviest loads. Any machines available were given to men, and women worked manually. Yet the minimum female wage was 17 rubles a month, the male, 21.

In the first textile mills in France and Italy, male owners, like the Lowell owners, acted *in loco parentis* for young female workers, decreeing rules of conduct to limit their mobility and freedom – they sometimes even tried to arrange marriages for them. Control over girls' lives served owners' interests: they guaranteed the workers' presence and reinforced control of their work. Families were content because daughters' wages were sent *directly to their parents*. In England, not until the 1890s could single working girls living at home keep some of their own wages; French and Italian servant girls went on sending money home even when they no longer expected to return to marry and live. Patriarchal controls over women were maintained in all circumstances.[5]

But industry offered young women opportunities they had not had since patriarchy began. Industrial capitalism had contradictory consequences for women. On the one hand, it exploited and damaged them by placing them in dangerous and unhealthy environments, forcing them to work inhumane hours at repetitive tasks for low wages. On the other, it offered single women the possibility of liberation from the oppressive patriarchal family. Work in the Lowell mill, for instance, gave young American women independence from their families. Family life was extremely oppressive for daughters, as other family members saw them as servants who were expected to do menial work, serve, nurse, and obey with little freedom. Working and living together away from home, young female American mill workers discovered sisterhood, solidarity, and class-consciousness. Lowell women formed a literary club, writing and reading their work to each other, and producing a magazine, *The Lowell Offering.*[6] They formed deep bonds, so when owners increased hours (without extra pay) or ordered speed-ups (more production on faster machines without extra pay), their solidarity made them the first Americans to strike.

Thus capitalism, which elevated patriarchy by turning its major value, power, into the *only* value, also destabilized it by enabling women for the first time in history to become economically independent. Despite the patriarchal solidarity inherent in the deal the mill owners made with New England farmers – "Send us your daughters and we will guard them as you do and they will earn money for you" – the Lowell mill girls used their situation to develop the solidarity to resist both owners and family.

But the power that solidarity had given the Lowell mill women did not last. Women moved back and forth between mill and farm to help their families seasonally, despite rules that mill owners made to prevent this. In the 1840s a huge influx of Irish emigrants arrived seeking work. Competition made Yankee women fear giving up a job, and employers came to prefer the Irishwomen: fleeing famine and poverty, they were desperate enough to work for low wages and terrified enough to fear being organized. The patriarchal strategy of divide and conquer worked: Yankee and Irish competed in enmity, unable to unify in a common cause.

When unions began organizing northern workers, mills moved south and appealed to white women from rural areas. Having analyzed the family labour system, and knowing that women and children did the essential work on farms, owners presented factories as a refuge for impoverished countrywomen tenant-farmers and their children. They lured families by offering mill-owned houses on condition that at least one person per room work in the mill.[7] Women especially were drawn: the first to apply for mill work were those who had worked hardest in commercial farming: female heads of household, widows, single women, and itinerant labourers. Once again, capitalism empowered women while exploiting them.

Home Workers

Some women worked at home, doing "piece-work" or "sweated labour." Later, they worked in sweatshops: indeed, the industry of New York, London, and European cities was built on sweated labour, the low-priced labour of women and children.[8] At first, shoe-making wives and daughters did binding for male household heads, who were paid for the finished shoes. Later, shop bosses in shoe manufacturing centres like Lynn, Massachusetts, dealt directly with pieceworkers, hiring women to stitch and bind the uppers at home, while men worked together in shops. When the sewing machine was invented in 1855, men pushed women out of shoe manufacture entirely (until the end of the century). Thus isolated, women could not organize to resist. Women pieceworkers were paid appalling wages: a woman trying to supplement a man's inadequate pay by sewing might work as long and hard as he, but earn under $2 a week compared to his $10–$15.

Moreover, married women felt they had to conceal their labour. Charlotte Woodward, a glove sewer, one of the few paid workers at the women's rights convention in Seneca Falls in 1848, explained:

We women work secretly in the seclusion of our bedcham-
bers because all society was built on the theory that men,
not women earned money and that men alone supported
the family. . . . But I do not believe that there was any community in which the souls of some women were not beating
their wings in rebellion. For my own obscure self I can say
that every fiber of my being rebelled, although silently, all
the hours that I sat and sewed gloves for a miserable pittance, which, as it was earned, could never be mine. I wanted to work, but I wanted to choose my task and I wanted to
collect my wages. That was my form of rebellion against the
life into which I was born.[9]

Piece-work was not just poorly paid but risky: women returning bundles of finished work might be told they had done poor
work and be paid less than the agreed price or nothing at all. If
demand for a product waned or the economy contracted, they were
given less work and they starved. But women with small children
had little alternative to piece-work. Factory owners, who always
limited married women's opportunities, did so increasingly over the
century, preferring young single women, believing them more malleable and reliable. Still, piece-work earnings of women from cultures which forbade women to go out without a male guard could
shift their families from starvation to survival.

Artisans' homes were also workshops. In weavers' households,
small children carded and combed, older daughters and wives spun,
and fathers wove. Without cooperation, weavers could earn little.
Whole families did laundry in Parisian households, but women
always did the soaping and ironing. Parents willed their shops to
daughters as often as sons. Craftsmen's wives often helped them
with tailoring, shoemaking, or baking, or kept the shop, selling
goods and keeping accounts. In households where men did putting-
out work at home for a manufacturer, wives often negotiated the
terms of workloads and wages. Wives of Lyon and Saint-Etienne

silk weavers transported raw materials and finished products back and forth. They were beasts of burden, carrying heavy loads over long distances, but as liaisons between their husbands and manufacturers, they got the pay for the finished work. Wives of English knife-makers performed similar functions. The practice was so common in some trades that when craftsmen started to work in factories, employers still gave their wages to their wives.[10]

Women in the Needle Trades

Sewing requires great skill, but seamstresses lived in great hardship. Four months of the year, they worked an average twelve- to thirteen-hour day; during the two London "seasons" – April to August, October to December – they often worked twenty hours straight. They averaged eighteen, sitting all day in tiny dark airless workshops either freezing or overheated. Fifty seamstresses worked in one large room sunlit by day, lamp-lit at night, rooms so hot and oppressive that young women sometimes fainted at their work. At night they slept crammed into cells, eighteen in a room with one window, or five in a single attic bed. They had ten minutes for breakfast, fifteen or twenty for tea or dinner after the working day. They sometimes simply lay down on the floor and curled up for a few hours without eating, then started work again.

Long sedentary hours severely impaired workers' health: while working, they drove themselves, and fainted when they finished. They had poor digestion, weak lungs, and pains in their sides, and the circulation in their hands and feet simply ceased from lack of exercise, "never seeing the outside of the door from Sunday to Sunday." All seamstresses' eyesight was damaged and all were ill by the end of the season. But since owners discharged sick women, they feared to complain and continued working, harming their health further. Most were "second hands" earning board, lodging, and £20 to £30 a year. Healthy youngsters from the country became so ill they had to leave the trade, most often to become ladies' maids.

Many seamstresses described their food as "insufficient and unwholesome." With poor food, and horrible work hours and working conditions, many had swollen ankles, spinal curvatures, tuberculosis, asthma, and blindness: many English needlewomen ended their lives in the North London Ophthalmic Institution. They were not paid enough to live. At a labour meeting, slopworkers, trousermakers and seamstresses compared notes: 151 had never slept in a bed; 508 had to borrow clothes to attend the meeting; four or five owned underwear; only five had earned over 5 shillings the week before.

Capitalism created this wretchedness but it also created the conditions to change it. People working together could organize: a rhetoric of freedom provided a basis for action. A group discussion in England at a labour meeting led women to form the Association for the Aid and Benefit of Milliners and Dressmakers in 1843. Asking employers to end Sunday work, respect the twelve-hour day, and pay a minimum weekly wage of 9 shillings, the association set up an employment office to find seamstresses jobs in shops that abided by these requests. It urged employers to add extra staff during peak periods instead of grossly overworking the regular staff, and offer medical supervision of workers (who often fainted or fell ill over their work). It encouraged owners to install some form of ventilation.

American needlewomen also founded unions. The United Tailoresses Society (UTS), a trade union, was founded in 1831; the Shirt Sewers' Cooperative Union formed between 1851 and 1853 to sell its products directly to the public; the Sewingwomen's Protective and Benevolent Union acted as a mutual aid society and trade union in 1864–65; and the Working Woman's Association (WWA) functioned in 1868–69 as trade union, debating society, and feminist pressure group.[11] The most militant, the UTS, was run by tailoresses themselves, who developed a coherent theory of economic exploitation – systematized class and sex oppression based in male dominance. With the solidarity conferred by pre-industrial organizations, men fought for a "family" wage. They demanded higher wages on the grounds that they supported women and children. But most women and children worked, many men were not married, and married men with families often abandoned or barely supported them. Louise Mitchell of the UTS argued: "When we complained to our employers and others of the inequality of our wages with that of men, the excuse is, they have families to support from which females are exempt. Now this is either a sad mistake or a willful oversight. How many females are there who have families to support and how many single men who have none."

The WWA was founded by feminists Susan B. Anthony and Elizabeth Cady Stanton, who also founded the newspaper *Revolution*. If their main goal was to recruit women workers into the suffrage movement, they also wished to help them. Feminist analyses of oppression focused on sex struggle, and male exploitation of women. This generated conflicts based on fear of male judgments, as suggested in an 1868 *New York Times* piece on the WWA:

> A meeting of ladies was held at the *Revolution* offices for the purpose of organizing an association of working women who might act for the interests of its members in the same manner as the association of working men, regulating the wages, etc. of [members]. . . .Mrs. Stanton thought the name [of the new association] should be Working Woman's Suffrage Association. Miss Augusta Lewis said that woman's wrongs should be redressed before her rights were proclaimed and that the word "suffrage would couple the association . . . with short hair and bloomers and other vagaries."

The focus on sex struggle alienated working women who were less exploited by their men – who were also exploited – than by their employers. They felt class struggle was essential: the WWA lasted less than a year.

Even organized workers were overmatched by employers and money interests, and no strategy guaranteed success. Strategies that avoided the confrontation created by class theory produced only short-term benefits for a few; strategies based in economic analysis were also short-lived, although seeing economic oppression as man-made helped women develop the thinking and confidence they needed to counter notions of natural female inferiority. Needlewomen's organizations did not achieve their stated goals, but they succeeded by developing a political analysis.

Women, who in general welcomed industrial production, soon saw that it could make them independent or leave them destitute, and felt it necessary to reiterate a fact that still needs reiteration: many women do not have men to support them. Some people blamed women for this fact, refusing to acknowledge the injustice of an economic system that allowed only men a living wage. Women explained they had lost husbands or fathers in the Civil War, and received no recompense. But they did not want pensions and especially did not want charity: charitable institutions were wretched and humiliating and jobs created by charities lowered everyone's wages. Women wanted work. Despite the enormous wealth around them, they did not attack the rich, nor did large numbers of them follow advice to migrate west, where they knew no one. They attacked the system, becoming the first American workers to analyze class structure.[12]

Boston entrepreneurs mechanized the garment industry early, mainly because of a labour shortage. The Irish influx in the 1840s made cheap unskilled labour available and in 1846, Elias Howe of Cambridge invented the sewing machine. When Britain allied with the south during the Civil War, the north stopped importing British cloth, placing a greater demand on domestic producers. By 1865 Boston factory owners had created the "Boston system" of dividing mechanized tasks, a sewing assembly line: one person did only facings, another only buttonholes, and so on. By eliminating the need for multiple skills, manufacturers could hire unskilled workers for low wages, and throw accomplished seamstresses and tailors out of work.[13]

Women in Trades

Women seem to have been hired as telephone operators as soon as phones became available to the public in 1879, and they made up the great majority of telephone operators. Male operators worked mainly at night. Late in the century, women went to work in offices: the first British government department to hire women as clerks was the Post Office. A busy subculture of women worked on their own, market women, servicers like carters, petty traders, street hawkers, laundresses, and boardinghouse keepers, who swelled cities over the century. They also learned trades they were later excluded from, like mailmaking, brickmaking, and mining.

Much of what we know about working women comes from a Victorian gentleman, Arthur Munby. Obsessed with working women, mainly their dress and manners, he observed and interviewed them, and wrote a book that tingles with his titillation. He is constantly wondering if their work made them less "ladylike" or "feminine"; he is thrilled by women in "male" guise – trousered, dirty, swaggering, roughly dressed.[14] The middle class saw women doing manual labour as "degraded" because, unlike ladies, who always had chaperones, they were alone, vulnerable to sexual approach (the men who accosted them were *not* seen as degraded). In fact, labouring women were as sexually free as men in their culture and ended up married with families, just like ladies.

Brickmakers worked barefoot, legs bare to above the knee, in stained ragged clothes, with mud-stained faces and hair. Their foul mouths shocked Munby. Most were young. Munby noted that a thirteen-year-old would have been "pretty in face and form" if she were clean and healthy, but the flush in her cheeks was from exhaustion, not health. He watched her move weakly, unsteadily, raising a twenty-five-pound mass of clay on her head, balancing it as she squatted to pick up another twenty-five-pound mass which she held against her stomach. Lumbering six or seven yards with her burden, she lay it on a moulding bench, repeating these actions for ten to twelve hours every working day.

Many women and children worked in mines doing very arduous and low-paid work. Deep in the mines everyone worked naked or half-naked. Women wore old trousers and a shirt – improper and undressed in a period when corsets and bustles and layers of petticoats were prescribed. Basch describes women bent double in water up to their knees lugging heavy loads of coal. Girls of six or seven went down first and came up last, working the doors for ventilation and to let corves (metal tubs or baskets used to haul coal) pass through. Women guided and pushed corves along the gallery rails, and in narrow seams, got down on hands and knees harnessed to a belt with a chain that passed between their legs to draw a sledge over considerable distances along sloping galleries. In unprofitable shafts, owners saved money by having women rather than rails or pit ponies convey heavy baskets of coal.[15]

Laws barring underground mine work by children and women were passed in the 1840s, impelled by Lord Ashley, who in 1842 published a report on child labour in mines, with illustrations and woodcuts for parliamentarians who did not care to read. He proposed new legislation in a two-hour speech that moved his audience to tears – and to the passage of an act forbidding female labour underground and the apprenticeship of children under eleven. These laws were modelled on an 1833 law barring the employment of young children in textile mills and establishing an eight-hour workday for children over nine – the first major industrial legislation enacted in England. In 1844 laws banned night work and fourteen to sixteen-hour days for women and children under eighteen, decreeing a maximum of twelve hours of labour and strengthening safety regulations and the powers of factory inspectors. In 1847 a ten-hour day was imposed on women and youths under eighteen; later laws decreed that their hours must fall between morning and 7 p.m., thereby ending night shifts.

Such laws seem humane, but real humanity would have included men under their terms. Lacking that, the laws injured those they were intended to help. Adherents of laissez-faire policy opposed such laws, warning that women in mining regions would be unemployed; mine owners argued that women had a right to choose their own work and that mothers' indefeasible rights over their children would be violated by state regulation of children's labour. The rhetoric of rights served the mine owners' desire for cheap labour; and they ignored mothers' rights when it came to child custody. Owners who used women in mines with seams too narrow for horses to haul coal would be ruined if they had to use men (who got higher wages) for this work, warned a millionaire colliery owner: they would shut the mines, forcing women and their families to starve.

But even people who perceived the needs of working-class families opposed laws barring child labour on the grounds that a child working in a textile mill could relieve a mother from work so she could tend younger children. In 1833 legislators opposed to child labour laws argued that limiting the working hours of infants would force "the mothers of families to work in mills; a consequence which is much deprecated as extremely mischievous." French inspectors supposed to enforce an 1841 child labour law frequently reported that families needed their children's wages.

In the 1830s and 1840s, England and France passed laws requiring manufacturers to educate child workers; this led to a marked decline in illiteracy, but not to universal education. An anguished schoolteacher in the industrial north wrote in 1861: "At ten, sometimes nine or eight, even the weakest children are stolen from us to be sent to ruin their bodies and lose their souls in the dust and disorder of workshops for a few sous a day."[16] In 1867 an inspector in Reims charged that children's education was sacrificed for "the material interest of the family"; in 1870 inspectors in Sommes reported that about six hundred children between seven and thirteen years received no schooling whatever. But some understood: "One of the principal causes of school non-attendance stems from poverty, from the need above all to satisfy those material interests which affect their very existence."

Even after law made school compulsory, mere thousands of

children attended English factory schools. Cities had inadequate facilities for public education, but there were even fewer in the countryside. Manchester children studied erratically between three and twelve years of age, but remained largely uneducated. They might go to school, but if the family was desperate, money was short, or jobs opened up, they were sent to work – selling matches, running errands, or working in tobacco shops.

Domestic Servants

Westerners derided the African style of exhibiting status – having a large entourage of dependants – but nineteenth-century middle-class Europeans used the same symbol. Social scientists studying status found its surest determinant to be the number of "deference givers," and accorded middle-class status only to families with at least one servant. Middle-class people surrounded themselves with "rituals of order," presenting themselves as public images, works of art freed from the realm of the necessary. Conventions that lower-ranked groups use back doors, deal only with servants, or use titles when addressing upper-ranked people enabled elites to appear free from realities like uncombed hair, unwashed faces or, as Edith Wharton's mother scornfully declared, untidy drawing-rooms. The drive to disassociate the self from necessity is unspoken and probably unconscious. Likely unaware of their own psychological dependence on servants, people did what they could to bind servants into economic and physical dependency on them.

Most waged workers were employed in agriculture or domestic service. In Milan, in 1881, 1901, and 1911 censuses, most waged women were domestic servants; the second largest group were needlewomen. In 1881 one out of every twenty-two Britishers was a servant; in London the proportion was one in fifteen. Until the end of the century, over a third of working Englishwomen were under twenty and a third of those between fifteen and twenty were servants: girls of nine or ten were in service. In 1911, 35 percent of working women were servants. People increasingly hired females, writes Leonore Davidoff, not just because men demanded higher wages but also because men were less amenable to control.[17] Girls, seen as property by their families, were used to supervision. A servant's life was determined by the household she worked in: in a big house with a staff of servants she might have some autonomy, a high standard of living, and considerable authority over others. But most were "slavies" in lower-middle-class suburban or artisan households or lodging houses. American James Fenimore Cooper wrote that the servant in his Southampton lodging house in the 1830s was "worse off than an Asiatic slave."

Yet many European women preferred domestic service to factory or shop work with their risky freedoms.[18] Families also preferred it and usually kept sons at home to work the farm, sending daughters out into service where they would be safe in a family environment, and guaranteed a room, food, and clothing. Wages were low, but they could save their wages for their marriages – domestic work gave them enough security to defer marriage until they found men who pleased them.

But not in the United States, where domestic service was the least desired work. American women wanted independence above all, and servants were on constant call and under constant surveillance. Before the Civil War, women considered domestic service "immigrant work" fit only for unskilled newcomers.[19] Black women, who made up a huge contingent of servants, preferred work in which they were not at the beck and call of a white family and had time to take care of their own families. Female domestic servants worked from before dawn until their employers went to bed, but were on call twenty-four hours a day. Employers closely supervised the morals (read "sex life") of female, not male, servants – yet male employers regularly sexually harrassed or raped girls who had virtually no redress. Working alone, servants could not organize collectively or protest, and they depended on references. Factory work involved long but discrete hours, and when they ended, workers were free.

Servants were in an uneasy position because most women were

actually servants in their own homes. Work by a woman without a contract stipulating her wages was considered voluntary: dependent sisters, aunts, or cousins were really unpaid servants. Like female kin and wives, paid servants were confined to the home, responsible for chores and subject to the caprice of the master. Unlike wives, servants were paid for their work and not legally bound to provide sexual service. But wages were tiny, sex was often coerced or demanded, and, if a woman became pregnant by a master or his son, she was cast off and dishonoured. Discussing the situation of servants and wives in nineteenth-century England, where law decreed "husband and wife are one and the husband is that one," Davidoff shows how arrangements bolstered male control.[20] For example, in European cities, maids from different households slept together on the top floor of blocks of flats. When London flats were built, this feature was deliberately omitted so that families would not lose control of their servants. Most English families lived in one-family houses with gardens that allowed easier surveillance and confinement of servants.

Domestic servants experienced domination intimately. Of the conflicts between masters and servants that reached the police courts, most concerned broken contracts (with servants charging masters four times more frequently than the reverse).[21] But many complained of physical or emotional abuse. It was no longer acceptable for employers to beat servants, but some pushed woman servants around or boxed their ears or scolded them humiliatingly, calling them "silly girl," "lazybones," or "blockhead." Young servants were most unhappy about being confined; some were daring enough to sneak out at night. Many employers felt they had the right to search servants' personal belongings or read their letters.

Male employers exposed themselves to servants, frightening some into bringing charges. But formal cases only hint at the rampancy of sexual harassment. Male employers regularly cuddled, kissed, or touched female servants' bodies. In the morality of the time, acts that caused no visible injury were harmless, and most servants suffered silently. But male employers and upper servants commonly raped or seduced young girls, making them pregnant. In such cases, not only was a servant girl alone dishonoured and disgraced, but she alone had to face the consequences of an act she may not have been able to control. Some were discharged; others gave their babies to charities. However men rationalized such acts, they symbolized the real employer/servant relation of domination and powerlessness, class exploitation in the domestic sphere, imposed on women not just socially but also personally.

Shop Clerks and Prostitutes

To be a salesclerk in a fine shop was a prestigious position, but clerks worked very hard and even the highest paid earned pittances. In nineteenth-century France, shop girls worked thirteen- or fourteen-hour days, from about eight in the morning. They had to walk up and down stairs to fetch merchandise and were sent on errands, often climbing forty flights of stairs a day. In 1876 and even in 1901, British clerks often worked eighty-five hours a week. The time allotted for meals – thirty minutes at midday and fifteen to twenty minutes for afternoon tea – included the time to reach and return from an eating place. They suffered from digestive troubles and anaemia and had to be on their feet constantly, even when not waiting on customers or tidying stock.[22] Shops were not affected by the newly passed laws covering factory workers, and were drafty and poorly ventilated, with glaring gaslight. Toilets were dank, small, and not sex-segregated; many small shops had none at all.

Reformers, especially Americans, deplored women working as shop clerks, considering department stores portals of prostitution: people were sure that poor young women exposed to luxuries they had never seen before and would never be able to afford would be turned to prostitution.[23] A 1915 study of department store saleswomen showing that the highest paid clerks most often turned to prostitution "proved" that rising expectations were the motivation. But perhaps the women were better paid *because* they were prostitutes, since the main prerequisite for working in a shop was dressing well and being attractive, and clothes were expensive. Women without proper dress were turned away; shop girls had to be stylish. French clerks might run up and down stairs all day, but they had to dress formally on wages of 1 franc a day, 3 to 12 in commissions.

Everything was stacked against them, and many women survived only by becoming prostitutes. Almost all prostitutes had another job, usually as servants or seamstresses. Needlewomen's wages were so low that many became whores to eke out a living. Female garment industry workers were paid starvation wages. Shop clerks had to dress well. Not only were women paid half as much as men for comparable work, but *in no occupation did women workers earn enough to support themselves independently.* Moreover, fair game for male employers – and often told to initiate the household sons sexually (some derived pride from the function) – servants gained sexual experience. A servant fired when *her* "crime" (sexual activity with the master class, seen as unfortunate but normal) became known often was driven to prostitution.

Prostitution could earn a living. Surveys of prostitutes show that most came from the working class and became whores to stay alive, and most had jobs that paid too little to live on. Many American prostitutes interviewed in the late nineteenth and early twentieth centuries were unskilled workers earning $4–$6 a week when they needed $9 a week to survive alone. In Italy most registered prostitutes were country-born peasants, single, and poor; they became prostitutes when they moved to the cities, in lieu of or along with other work: in 1875, 7 percent of them worked in the textile industry, 23 percent in garment making, and 28 percent as servants.[24]

By mid-century, prostitutes thronged every major city, military base, and even the countryside.[25] In England, every commission of inquiry into rural prostitution blamed starvation wages. W.R. Greg called them women "for whom there is no fall . . . for they stood already on the lowest level of existence."[26] Reports are filled with women like a young unemployed milliner who went on the streets to feed her father, a docker who was ill and could not work, and workers who sold their bodies to feed their children. Most working-class women did not set out to be prostitutes, but entered "the life" gradually, after a seduction and betrayal, or as a temporary measure when they or their families were in economic difficulties.

Almost every city in late nineteenth- and early twentieth-century America had a thriving "red-light" district.[27] Patronage of bars and brothels was open, amounting to *de facto* legalization of prostitution. Brothels covered an economic gamut, catering to different classes of men and specific tastes. A few luxurious houses offered "special" services to the rich and highly placed, politicians and gentlemen, for $5 to $10 a trick. Some houses charged a dollar or two, drawing a middle-class clientele. Older, less attractive prostitutes charged 50 cents for a quickie in shabby tenement brothels called "cribs." Some walked the streets, although fewer than today. Prostitutes too had a pecking order and class snobbery: each rank considered those below them economically "trash" who cheapened the status of the profession.

But some women gained independence and a supportive female subculture through prostitution. As whores, they could profit from a sexual war in which women were usually victims. Some earned enough to live alone, which was impossible in waged work, domestic service, or marriage. Some earned enough to spend money on fun and luxuries, things other women could not afford. In the past, prostitutes were the only class of women living outside male control (even nuns had to obey priests and the church hierarchy), and prostitution was often the only paid profession men allowed women. To have women sexually available to all, men had to enable them to live outside the control of other men. Later, it was the only profession in which they let them earn a decent living.

Although prostitution is created by male demand, patriarchy lays the onus of sexuality on women: women, not men, are responsible for the sexual morality of society. Prostitutes violate the morality that women are expected to uphold. Men keep women in a vise in patriarchies: demanding that women fulfil the function of sexual availability, they pay prostitutes enough to live but also label them criminal and place them beyond the protection of law; as wives, they were deprived of property or rights over themselves and their children.

Prostitutes have always been treated with contempt, and after the Protestant revolution, have been cast out from society as beneath consideration, undeserving of civil or political rights. During waves of reform, societies arrested, whipped, expelled, or transported prostitutes. Trying to check the spread of venereal disease in garrison towns and seaports, in 1864, 1866, and 1869, England passed the Contagious Diseases Acts, which transformed the prostitute into "a conduit of infection to respectable society."[28] The bearer of disease, the scapegoat carrying the sins of society in her genitals, she was an object of class guilt, "a powerful symbol of sexual and economic exploitation under industrial capitalism."[29]

Society's Attitudes Toward Working Women

Protective legislation ostensibly arises from compassion for women and children. Its adherents use a rhetoric of pity; those opposed to it use a rhetoric of freedom. In both cases, rhetoric masks real motivation. Those who opposed protective laws wanted a continued source of cheap labour; those in favour feared female independence. Neither cared about what the actual people wanted.

Protective laws often did not use the term *women*, including women in the category of "young persons" as if they were minors. Both Ashley's 1842 speech and Engels' *The Condition of the Working Class in England* in1844 stressed that women's labour led to the "dissolution of family ties," to social disintegration. Reports by factory inspectors, observers, and officials obsessed about the immorality of female factory workers, married or single, as demonstrated by increased illegitimacy, widespread promiscuity, prostitution, alcoholism, and delinquency. Whether women with families worked like their husbands, supported the family when a husband was unemployed, or had no man to support them (40 percent of Englishwomen were unmarried in 1841) was irrelevant: women's working for wages destroyed the fabric of the family.

There *was* a serious increase in illegitimate births in many European cities from 1750 to 1850, not because of female immorality but because of a new male freedom. Rural sex had always been relatively free; couples usually deferred marriage until pregnancy proved a woman's fertility. In 1850 the London *Morning Chronicle* declared "co-habitation before marriage . . . almost universal" in rural areas. Country women could rely on men's promises of marriage: few men dared break them in villages, where the moral force of the entire community pressured them to accept their responsibility. Men needed mates to survive; children repaid their cost within a few years by work in household and farm. Marriages might be unhappy, husbands might abuse wives, but illegitimacy was rare.

Such customs could not be enforced in cities lacking community, and where mates and children were not economic necessities. Statistics then and now show that many men evaded responsibility for children. Young rural women who went on believing promises of marriage learned that country rules did not apply in cities. The requirement that domestic servants be single meant that women either went without sex and affection or had affairs. Many men broke their promises because they earned too little to support a family or had a chance to work elsewhere, but those who simply chose to ignore responsibility could not be forced to accept it. In such cases, a woman could either abandon her baby or struggle to feed it on wages insufficient to support even one of them.

Illegitimacy rates increased in this period even in the English countryside, perhaps because most men were landless and immune to community pressure. European birth rates were high because people were living longer and producing more children. Birth rates began to fall in France after 1820 when French peasants began to use contraception, probably *coitus interruptus*. Infant and child mortality also declined somewhat in the nineteenth century, but mortality rates varied greatly by economic class (as they do today in the United States). The wealthy in England and France enjoyed better health and lived longer than the rural or urban poor. Life expectancies were appallingly low and infant mortality rates high in the urban slums of industrial cities. Of babies born in 1850, half reached fifteen with two living parents; less than 10 percent reached fifteen with both parents and all siblings alive. Working-class people's health and longevity were also affected by their work: some occupations shortened lives.

Illegitimacy, alcoholism, prostitution, and "promiscuity" were no more common in women factory workers than among servants or farmwomen. The upper classes, men especially, had always enjoyed sexual freedom. Only the middle class inhibited sex, preferring emotion repressed. Adherents of protective laws declared that female immorality threatened the social fabric, but what they really feared was female independence. Paid work outside the home, especially if it freed women from the restraints of Victorian dress and manners, might inspire them to defy other restraints. Legislators argued that factory work kept women from devoting themselves exclusively to their families but feared the challenge to male dominance of a breadwinner wife and a husband who stayed home to tend children, clean, and cook (which of course few men did). Legislators cried that women who supported the family "virtually turned [their husbands] into eunuchs."[30]

Lord Ashley was shocked that women workers formed clubs and associations to "meet together to drink, sing and smoke" and "gradually [acquire] all those privileges which are held to be the proper portion of the male sex." Indeed, the idea of "privilege" underlay the entire controversy.[31] "Protection of women" was code, like "protection of the family" today, for preserving patriarchal customs. In mid-century England, of 6 million women over twenty, half worked in industry, and over a third supported themselves. People who earned wages instead of depending on inheritances could ignore their parents' dictates about marriage. In regions where waged work was available, more couples married and younger than before, following *their* desires, unconcerned about property or money. In some regions, couples did not bother to marry, but simply lived together in what their contemporaries called "concubinage" (compromising only the woman). Such unions had always been common but seem to have increased in nineteenth-century England and France. They were known to last, often happily, especially between workers in the same trade. Parents in these liaisons did not abandon their children.

Once children were forbidden to work, mothers with babies had to find work to feed them; laws "protecting" women from night work or heavy lifting kept them in the lowest-paid jobs. Later laws required employers to pay women giving birth and caring for newborns; these laws functioned to keep employers from hiring women at all. Women and children were driven from hardship to starvation. Nevertheless, arguments over protective laws continued throughout the century and into this one. The issue divided even feminists, who had no economic agenda beyond their concern for women's safety and health or their freedom and economic status. Protective legislation that applies only to one sex divides the labour force, injuring all its members. A similar problem resulted from men's insistence on dominating unions.

Moreover, protective laws did not confront the real problem: an economic and political structure that consigned reproduction to an invisible domestic realm, and treated it as a *non-productive* activity requiring no support. By patronizing female reproduction as entirely women's concern, a trifle or luxury women chose for amusement, industry pushed women into a desperate situation.

Married Women

It is no exaggeration to call nineteenth-century working-class women's situation desperate: single women could not earn enough to live, married women could not get jobs, mothers with mates who could not or chose not to support their children watched them starve. A Frenchman of the period observed: "A single woman cannot earn a living in Paris. . . .A good half of young workers, if not the majority, find themselves with this alternative: to live in privation or to marry."[32] Patriarchies force women to marry, often through family pressure. Nineteenth-century Western women were forced into marriage by economic pressure. Women had to marry: single mothers married men who had not sired their children; servants married – usually men of higher status.

But married women could not get work, especially as industrialization increased. In agricultural France of the 1860s, 40 percent of married women worked family farms or ran family businesses; in 1896, 52 percent of single and 38 percent of married women worked outside the home. But in industrial England in 1851 only 25 percent of married women had paid work; by 1911, 69 percent of single women but only 9.6 percent of married women had jobs, most in their husbands' business, running small beer houses or provision shops. Women did what they could to help support their families, in cities, planting vegetable gardens or raising animals, usually pigs and hens, to supplement the family diet and sell the surplus. They opened cafés in their houses or set up outdoor stands to sell prepared food or drink. A knife-maker's wife in Sheffield, England, bottled a fermented drink she called "pop" to sell to city residents in summer.

In the United States the only large group of regularly employed married women besides blacks (valued as domestic servants) were immigrants in New England textile mills. Native-born educated women often looked down on them as ignorant, but immigrants resourcefully adapted their skills to local requirements. Southern Italian women used to picking fruit and vegetables found similar work in Buffalo, New York; those on New York's lower East Side sewed or made paper flowers with their daughters at home, while their husbands dug ditches or swept streets and sometimes kept house and cared for children when their wives found work in factories and sweatshops. Married Irishwomen who knew only farming quickly learned enough to become domestics and cleaned New York office buildings at night so they could tend their children in the days. European married women usually worked in the least industrialized enterprises; with less separation between home and workplace, they were more able to control their own work rhythms.[33] Married women, clustered in poorly paid, episodic, and temporary marginal work, nevertheless contributed 10 percent to 50 percent of family incomes. Recent studies demonstrate what past studies have suggested – that women spend most of their wages on the family, while men spend much of theirs on themselves.

All industrial societies up to the present have treated women as marginal workers for whom work is a secondary priority. Since women everywhere have also been expected to take responsibility for the unpaid maintenance of households and children, employers and governments have viewed them as dependants who wrap work around their primary concerns, wifehood and motherhood. Employers have paid women low wages when they were young, assuming that their fathers supported them and they needed only "pin" money; and they did not train or promote them, or expect them to advance. After marriage, they hired women at need, paying them little, on the assumption that they were merely supplementing their husbands' incomes. Working-class men won the wage war against women: men fought for and got a "family wage" whether or not they had a family, while women in industrial societies worked seasonally, irregularly, part time, at home, for pittances.

The home, which middle-class writers saw as a comfy nest for reproduction and renewal, protected from the brutal aggressive male public world, was for women a site of power struggle and labour. This was true for all classes, but worst for working-class women. Reproduction was a great burden; renewal was not possible. The conditions of work in industrial society made it difficult and sometimes impossible to raise a child and feed it at the same time. When mothers were absent for hours every day, children suffered, especially infants.

Babies whose mothers could not nurse them were bottle-fed animal milk or soup; in the nineteenth century people did not know about sterilization, so such feeding could give them fatal digestive diseases. Infant mortality rates were high in regions where mothers worked long hours away from home: mothers were blamed. Working mothers pressed daughters of seven or eight into tending younger children or left infants with aged women who were not always scrupulous, and might use contaminated milk or not feed nursing babies often enough. They often fed babies unnourishing bread soaked in sugared water. There were accidents – burns, falls, drownings. To make babies sleep, caretakers used alcohol, laudanum, morphine, or opium-based narcotics that could bring on convulsions.

The alternative to bottle-feeding was wet-nursing, widely practised in France. Louise Tilly and Joan Scott write that if a baby survived the trip to the wet nurse (often a long distance over rough roads), if the nurse had enough milk to nourish it with the other children she cared for, and if it survived the many hazards of infancy when tended by someone likely to be indifferent, then the child was returned to its parents at an age when it could care for itself. Most infants never returned.

For mothers, survival of a family was more important than any one life. French working couples prospered when both partners worked for wages, but with babies their situation deteriorated. Children needed supervision and cost money; pregnancy, nursing, and tending children reduced a wife's earnings. Wives had to maintain the household, husbands to support it, both almost alone. Things improved when children reached about eight and could contribute to the family earnings. But when children left to set up their own households, aging parents again on their own earned less; if illness, injury or "other crises overtook them, misery often ensued again."[34] The longer children lived at home, the better off the family: families whose children found waged work near home were better off; children could stay home longer if a family had enough to live on: it was a vicious cycle. Remaining home strengthened children's ties to their mother, the heart and soul of the family, whose concern and work kept it alive.

In the traditional division of labour, men ran farms or shops and women managed households. When people began to work outside the home, men still expected women to shoulder the entire domestic burden. They tried; they marketed, cooked, sewed, cleaned, and mended clothing and gave the children most of whatever education they received. Because poor women lacked *things* – furniture, dining or kitchen equipment, objects requiring dusting – housework was less onerous than it became, but work in tiny tenement rooms never ended. The poorer the family, the heavier women's work. Women's major task, finding food, fuel, and water, took hours every day, entailing "scores of errands out of the house."[35]

Women and children sacrificed for men. Contemporary autobiographies record Alice Linton's father, for example, eating butter while the rest of the family ate margarine; one father regularly ate bacon as his family watched hungrily.[36] George Acorn's father took "all the meals we had so anxiously provided without the slightest thought or consideration." Wives said nothing about their poor diets. A woman recalls her mother regularly dining on "kettle-bender" (crusts with hot water, pepper, salt, and a bit of margarine), careful to eat her meal "before father came in for his." A husband might help plan a meal and send the children out to buy haddock, say, then feed them the head and tail. Studies of working-class English budgets from 1860 to 1950 show that 7 to 8 pence a day was spent on men's food, while the rest of the family lived on threepence or less a day; wives' and children's lower nutrition and caloric intake are well documented.[37]

When a major expense like a childbirth approached, women saved by giving children less food and starving themselves. This practice was not rooted in female self-sacrifice; it was strategic: women gave men what they wanted *in order to keep them and their wages*. Denied their desires, men might abandon their families, as many did. A wife's failure to cater to her husband's wishes, even if he did not support her, was a major violation of men's marital rights. Ellen Ross writes that such failures were a primary factor in assault cases tried at Old Bailey, like that of Robert Plampton, who stabbed and killed his wife, Emily Maria, one afternoon for pawning his blankets when he wanted to take a nap. Women needed husbands, who brought potential pregnancies and beatings but also money, unobtainable elsewhere, into the household.

Men blamed pregnancies on women and considered children one of the irritations attendant on taking a wife. A popular song of the time, "Don't Have Any More, Missus Moore," implied that the mother was solely responsible for the Moores' twenty children. A woman wrote about hearing her father complain to her mother (who bore nineteen children), "I can't hang me trousers on the end of the bed . . . that you're not like that [pregnant]." Fertility rates were high among London's poor. The usual birth control methods of the period, abstinence and *coitus interruptus*, required male cooperation, but men took no responsibility for sex *or* for children, often raping or beating women who refused intercourse. Some did refuse: London mothers were known for assertive opinions. Others may surreptitiously have used sponges, douches, and, later, diaphragms.

Men often concealed the amount they earned from their wives, giving them only a small allowance, while keeping the rest for tobacco and drink.[38] And they had a legal right to their wives' wages, which many drank up, leaving the family to starve. Harriet Robinson often saw American men searching the Lowell mill for their wives.

> The laws relating to women were such that a husband could claim his wife wherever he found her, and also the children she was trying to shield from his influence; and I have seen more than one poor woman skulk behind her loom or her frame when visitors were approaching the end of the aisle where she worked. Some of these were known under assumed names, to prevent their husbands from trusteeing

their wages. It was a very common thing for a male . . . of a certain kind to do this. . . depriving his wife of all her wages, perhaps month after month.[39]

As a result, many children saw their fathers as enemies. Adult siblings robbed each other and stole from their fathers, but of hundreds of theft cases listed in newspaper and court records for the years 1869 to 1889, not one described a child stealing from a mother. Mothers held families together by caring and taking responsibility. This may be universal but is documented among working-class families in England, working-class and slave families in America, and in most of Africa. The mother-child relation created the loyalty and sense of family obligation that marked the working class. Many observers noted especially strong bonds of affection between working-class mothers and children, who knew that their mothers sacrificed for them and protected them from their fathers. Children gave mothers "affection and gratitude. . . .Should the mother die, her little ones weep. . . their only friend is gone." When education became compulsory, mothers had to maintain families without help from school-aged children – and the age was gradually raised. After the 1870s they had what their husbands gave them and their own pitiful earnings.

While women struggled to maintain families, men maintained solidarity in a strong pub culture. Many popular music-hall ballads about starving children in pubs begging fathers to come home with money for food reflected this situation, as did the popular temperance movement in the United States. Men's indifference to women and children is not a matter of boyish irresponsibility; an ethnographic study of male pub culture shows it arises from hatred of women, sexual objectification of and preoccupation with controlling them.[40] In this sex war, males expressed their contempt for women publicly, verbally and physically, while women, isolated from each other, lacking solidarity and perceiving the taboo on female anger against men, hid their hostility to men.

When men did come home after spending the "family" wage at

a pub, many beat their wives and/or children. Ross quotes one woman: "I should say seven out of ten of the wives down my way feel their husbands' fists at times, and lots of 'em are used shocking." It was generally believed that men had the right to beat wives, but women sometimes left men because of violence, or because men threatened to murder them or attacked their children (this is said to have been rare in the period), or refused to support them or insulted them sexually. One woman told a police court missionary, "I would forgive anything but the filthy names he calls me." She was indeed forgiving: at twenty-three, she was deaf in one ear and had a broken nose from her husband's fists. Wives feared debilitating injury and venereal infection transmitted when drunken husbands raped them. The "sympathetic" police court missionary declared wives living with husbands had to submit to rape. Women did not leave husbands from sexual jealousy; Ross notes that in contrast to contemporary French, German, and Spanish popular music, British music-hall lyrics lacked sexual passion. Male violence to women pervaded working-class society.

Husbands and wives had utterly different relations to children and money, the two major components of family life, and little tolerance of each other's needs.[41] Couples "lived together" only by being economically and sometimes sexually interdependent. They even had different neighbourhood friends. They shared goods, services, and sites – shops, pubs, streets, doorways – with people of their own sex. Most women valued children, kin, enough money, and intimacy, not with husbands but with their mothers, children, sisters, grandmothers, and neighbours. Men and boys moved further from home than women, and spent time with other males in talk or drinking, sports, politics, and gambling, often in pubs.

London women too hung out in pubs, but always in groups, not alone, often with their babies and children. (After a 1908 law barred children, pubs became male domains.) Every Monday women took their valuables to a pawnshop to get some cash to tide them over the week, redeeming the item on payday so as to have it over the weekend. Afterwards, they stopped at the pub to chat. Female neighbourhood networks created a community on which women depended; to a large degree, wives' social skills determined their families' well-being. Neighbourhood women shared linens, washtubs, clothing, or items to pawn in times of need. Even if they were not friends, woman neighbours helped each other in emergencies like serious illness or eviction, taking in a beaten wife for a night, an evicted family for a longer period. Women neighbours tended the sick, did their laundry, brought fuel and built fires for them, and prepared their meals. They collected money for big expenses like funerals, but rarely asked help from non-kin men.[42]

This behaviour was rooted in compassion and good-heartedness, but it was also insurance. No one knew when she might need similar help. Poor neighbourhoods had more female-headed households than wealthier neighbourhoods (then as now, in all ethnic groups). Middle-class observers were struck by poor women's compassion for needy children; poor as they were, they pitied children. A man with a criminal reputation visiting a very poor South London district met a woman who kept six children in her "wretched room." Two belonged to a widow who had lived above her but was jailed for assaulting a police officer. The woman had taken them in and intended to keep them until the mother was freed – if she could: "It was only neighbourly-like and my heart bled to see the poor young'uns a-cryin', and that wretched and neglected and dirty." Woman neighbours often acted as extra parents, feeding neighbours' hungry children, and sometimes even adopting them.

But this honourable taking of responsibility makes life harder for women, who are often blamed for things they cannot control. In the nineteenth century, a woman's dress and sexual, social, and drinking habits largely created a family's – even a street's – reputation for respectability, and mothers were blamed for children's plight. On a winter day in 1856, an agent of the Children's Aid Society of New York saw two barefoot, thinly dressed, but cheerful children gathering bits of wood and coal on the street. They explained they were finding fuel for their mother and agreed to take him to meet her. Their widowed mother earned what she could street-peddling, but had had to sell everything for food: their room was bare and unheated. As they spoke, she sat on a pallet with two children younger than the foragers, rubbing their hands. The agent remarked on the sweet tidy children, but blamed the mother in his report: "Though for her pure young children too much could hardly be done, in such a woman there is little confidence to be put. . . . It is probably some cursed vice has thus reduced her and . . . if her children be not separated from her, she will drag them down too."[43]

Urban Life

For centuries Europe's urban poor lived in the streets, working, playing, and resting in marketplaces and squares. Middle-class observers with notions of privacy were fascinated by the public domestic life of the London poor.[44] The same phenomenon occurred in nineteenth-century New York, where the streets teemed with children peddling, huckstering and scavenging, stealing, or selling sex.[45] Adults scavenged too: like today's bag-people, rag-pickers lived on cities' detritus. Street kids slept in groups in nooks and crannies, orphans, abandoned children, or runaways from destitute homes. Sexually abused or beaten children sought the streets, which offered a way to survive. Platoons of six- and seven-year-olds sought fuel for their mothers, ransacking docks, lumberyards, demolished buildings, and artisanal districts for chips, ashes, wood, or coal to take home or sell. New York children convicted of theft and jailed in the juvenile house of correction in the 1850s had been convicted of stealing a bar of soap, a copy of the *New York Herald*, lead or wood from demolished houses, and a board worth 3 cents. A New York journalist wrote that along with malefactors, the city jail held young boys and girls "caught asleep on cellar doors or [those] suspected of the horrible crime of stealing junk bottles and old iron!"[46]

Children rarely stole from people, but some were muggers or pickpockets – dangerous work, but easy enough to learn from men who hung around hotels or business districts, and a single theft could reap a month's wages for a domestic servant, a week's for a seamstress, several weeks' for a huckster. Juvenile prostitution was a permanent street feature; not yet a crime, it paid girls more than any other work. In the 1830s John R. McDowall, head of a reform society, complained that "females of thirteen and fourteen" walked on fashionable Broadway "without a protector, until some pretended gentleman gives them a nod and takes their arm and escorts them to houses of assignation." A journalist walked a mile up Broadway one night in 1854 and counted almost fifty girls soliciting.

In formal reports, reformers blamed women more than men for this situation. Women – widows, abandoned wives, orphaned working-class daughters – were poor: female self-support *meant* indigence. Middle-class reformers insisted that women's poverty was caused by negligence. Mothers of street children were bad parents but also sub-human, like prostitutes. Their inability to demonstrate true womanhood by creating a home placed them outside the pale of humanity. Over the century new ideals of domesticity and the proper role of women had created a new image of civilized society. Social arbiters merged gender and class ideologies to sanctify the home as a private (hidden) space presided over by women, inhabited by children, and frequented by men. Dangerous streets indicated a corrupt family life. Early in the century, philanthropists saw the poor as providence's creations; mid-Victorians thought poverty could be abolished by training the poor, mainly the young, to be better workers, citizens, and family members.

People who believed it was possible to change conditions increasingly emphasized control. New York created a police force in 1845, reformers broadened definitions of crime, and "experts" testified that family relations, not industrial capitalism, caused the visible, widespread, and seemingly permanent misery of city life. Promiscuous sociability, the "almost fabulous gregariousness" of the poor, offended the walled-in middle class; perceiving a crisis, they solved it by ending street life. Middle-class reformers forced the poor to stay indoors, to hide their poverty. They won their battle against street life without ameliorating poverty in any way. By destroying the street life of the working poor, reformers annihilated urban communities and a vital way of using urban space.[47] Streets emptied of life became the haunts of predators, especially dangerous for women.

In 1824 the Society for the Reformation of Juvenile Delinquents set up a House of Refuge to train offending children by corporal punishment and solitary confinement. The Children's Aid Society used a gentler strategy, putting poor children in foster homes to be cared for by "loving gentle women" thought to be so by nature. Poor city children were first sent to nearby farms where labour was scarce, but in 1854 the CAS began sending groups by rail to Illinois, Iowa, and Michigan. By 1860 it had "placed out" 5000 children. The CAS ignored the rights of working-class parents, seeing it as a positive good to separate their children from them. They took children without their parents' consent or, sometimes, even their knowledge. Moral reformer Lydia Maria Child wrote in 1843 that the greatest misfortune of "the squalid little wretches" in New York streets was that they were not orphans. The CAS remedied this: it manufactured orphans.[48]

Despite its declared intention to use the "innate" kindness of women to remould poor children, the CAS relocated mainly boys to be overseen by men, who also ran its Newsboys' Lodging House, where newsboys could sleep and eat for a few cents. The female staff of the CAS were not paid (men were), and ran programs for girls aimed at moulding them into wives and mothers dedicated to domesticity, who knew middle-class standards and would use them in their homes and families. Such re-education came to dominate reform programs for working-class females. The settlement houses of turn-of-the-century New York offered mothers housekeeping lessons, brainwashing vast numbers into assimilation into America.

CHAPTER 3

UTOPIANISM

AND SOCIALISM

A S THE EIGHTEENTH CENTURY ENDED, EUROPE WAS IN CRISIS. Old regimes were tottering because their economic systems were inadequate to industrial society. Huge inequities in income had created widespread misery. Political agitation flamed into riot as protestors demanded food, rights, autonomy, or secession in the United States, Ireland, Holland, Belgium, France, and Geneva. Since France dominated Europe and political thought, its ground-breaking revolution profoundly affected the whole continent. By killing their king, the French had flouted all claims of elite divinity. For a time Napoleon's wars occupied Europe, but after his defeat in 1815 waves of French-inspired revolution swept Europe.

The first wave of revolution (1820–24) was centred in the Med-iterranean region.[1] The second (1829–34) convulsed all of Europe west of Russia. In 1830 France overthrew its Bourbon kings, and Belgium won independence from Holland. Most other uprisings were put down, but Irish Catholic emancipation (1829) encouraged further agitation against Britain.[2] In 1847–48, a third wave of almost simultaneous revolutions occurred in France, Italy, the German states, most of the Habsburg Empire, and Switzerland.[3]

Revolution was a reaction to the bankruptcy of a traditional morality that considered some humans superior to others, granting great privilege to a divinely appointed elite and relegating most people to rightless misery. New ideas of human rights and equality opened minds to the possibility of creating political structures that would divide power differently and grant a political voice to a larger proportion of the population. Then as now, conflicts focused on how much participation to allow what people. Conservatives advocated constitutional government and an extension of the suffrage to more men (but not to the masses). Radicals advocated a government responsive to the people and universal manhood suffrage – extending the vote to all adult males. If this was radicalism, heaven knows what they would have called any movement that argued for women's suffrage. No problem: no one did. Yet some well-intentioned people did want to ease women's oppression. Their attempts are the subject of this section.

Building "A Heaven in Hell's Despair"

The philosophy called "socialism" (the word first appeared in 1831 in France) emerged in the early decades of the nineteenth century, and was based in a humanist vision of universal emancipation in an ideal communal society with no inequality, including sexual – a utopia. Utopian thinker Charles Fourier believed: "The degree of emancipation of women is the natural measure of general emancipation." An entire generation of socialist thinkers before Marx (followers of Fourier and Saint-Simon in France, Robert Owen in England, American Fourierites, and Transcendentalists) was committed to female freedom as part of their wider struggle for human liberation.[4]

Yet in the twentieth century many socialists scorned feminism in both its suffragist and second-wave manifestations, as a middle-class movement – as if sex struggle for freedom and status were less revolutionary than class struggle. Feminism is often portrayed as a movement of privileged women ambitious for male prerogatives, rather than as a philosophy that challenges prerogative itself, the very basis of patriarchal moral, economic, and political systems. Both socialists and capitalists reject feminism because it advocates the abolition of male privilege and structural changes more radical than either care to contemplate.

To portray feminism solely as a movement of leisured middle-class "ladies," men had to write early socialist feminism out of history – and this is exactly what they did. Histories that even mention women's rights usually begin with the "Rights of Women" debate of the 1790s and then leap to the Victorian period. Capitalist texts dismiss utopianism by associating it with socialism; Marxists scorn utopianism for not being based in "scientific" thinking.

Most utopias hold socialist ideals of cooperation and sharing, but utopianism is a separate trend with a long tradition in philosophical literature. Francis Bacon, Rabelais, Thomas More, and Daniel Defoe created fictional utopias before the nineteenth century; William Morris, Edward Bellamy, Charlotte Perkins Gilman, and Freda Hossain during it. Utopian works all stress equality, but they define the concept in different ways. All utopias are concerned with social justice, harmony, and individual and sexual freedom, but not all are feminist. William Morris, for example, envisioned a society of justice, equality, harmony, and sexual freedom for men, as if women did not require such things; Gilman and Hossain, on the other hand, were unable to envision a utopian world with men present in it.

Utopian socialists wanted to abolish class divisions, money, the state, and the separation between public and private. When feudalism died, the sense of kinship weakened for both sexes. Eighteenth-century ideas of freedom and rights infused political discourse, opening the possibility of new collectivities and classes; industry transformed conditions so that women's liberation became thinkable, and nineteenth-century utopian thinkers began to see the power differential between men and women (sexual politics) as fundamental to other inequities. The early industrial age was turbulent because industry revolutionized both the nature of work and relations between the elite and the workers; and it changed relations between women and men, women and work, and women and the family. Both capitalism and industrialism are patriarchal, but they are also (unlike feudalism) dynamic and offer the means for destabilizing patriarchy. They made collective action possible.

Nineteenth-century utopian socialists tried to devise social and economic structures to resist the separations imposed by capitalist industry. Envisaging workers as wholes – both ends *and* means – as people who could create wealth for themselves and not just be instruments for creating wealth for others, they wanted to integrate production and reproduction. They saw that women needed economic security *while* they were reproducing and maintaining society, recognizing the hardship women suffered when they were neither paid nor supported in their "natural" (as many still saw it) work. But women were not their primary concern and they did not examine their preconceptions; they did not ask if it was just to require one sex alone to be responsible for reproducing and maintaining all of society. Only a few, mainly women, used utopian ideas as the basis of feminist theories. All nineteenth-century utopian thinkers derived their ideas from Enlightenment thought in France, Scotland, and England.

France

The only important *philosophe* who unswervingly supported women's rights, the Marquis de Condorcet (1743–1794) argued that to deprive women of political rights on the pretext that their pregnancies and indispositions (menstruation) made them unfit was as absurd as to deprive man of the vote because of his attacks of gout. During the Revolution, women had given the King a list of their grievances *as a sex*, asking for equal rights in civil and political status, education, and work. Excluded from men's political clubs, women formed their own: chocolatière Pauline Léon and actress Claire Lacombe founded the Revolutionary Republican Women Citizens Club; Théroigne de Méricourt marched for women's right to bear arms and founded the Club des Amis de la Loi between 1789 and 1792. Olympe de Gouges' "Déclaration des Droits de la Femme et de la Citoyenne" urged women to create their own National Assembly as men's political and social equals and repudiate the privileges granted the "weaker" sex. Among her demands were an end to illegitimacy and more flexibility in marriage.

Frenchwomen's solidarity and awareness that their problems were tied to their sex were almost immediately suppressed: the Jacobins banned their clubs and barred them from public or political activity in 1793. In a final blow, Napoleon's retrogressive Civil Code of 1804 reaffirmed patriarchal values, private property, the absolute authority of men over wives and children, and the double standard. Depriving women of any legal or property rights, it placed them in legal subjection. Not until Napoleon fell did reformers again begin to address social problems.

Claude Henri, comte de Saint-Simon (1760–1825), a believer in Christianity and industry (he coined the word "industrialism"), believed that capital and technical "progress" could remake society. He and his disciples wanted to create a new elite of engineers and scientists who would use the laws of industry to end exploitation of the poor and the subjection of women. Saint-Simonians held the sexes complementary, accepted women in public roles, and valued sentiment over reason. When Saint-Simon died, his disciples built a school (later called a society), run by Barthélemy Prosper Enfantin, a banker with advanced engineering training.

Between 1829 and 1831, 200 women came to Saint-Simonian lectures on religion, finance, and social subjects. Some became missionaries in or near Paris; a hundred worked in Lyon. Most were kin or close friends of male members. One married couple donated their entire fortune to the community. But women did not throng to the sect, as they did to other religions that promised them equality, because the gap between rhetoric and practice was too obvious. With twelve women and sixty-seven men, the ruling clique was male-dominated; in Paris, no woman was ever allowed to act as a priest or preach the doctrine in public. Men had special uniforms to mark their solidarity, the sexes sang different songs, and the calendar commemorated important events related only to men.

Still, Saint-Simon's ideas deeply affected many women, who, for the first time, sought alternative lifestyles. Most Saint-Simonian women were urban working class: a group calling itself "femmes prolétaires" in 1832 founded the first feminist newspaper, *La femme libre* (*The Free Woman*), and published forty issues before running out of money.[5] Suzanne Voilquin (1801–1877), a laundress and embroiderer who co-edited the paper, complained: "At bottom, the male Saint-Simonians are more male than they are Saint-Simonian." Calling women an oppressed caste, the newspaper urged them to unify across class lines, arguing that "the emancipation of woman [would bring] the emancipation of the worker." The paper concentrated on women's rights in marriage and divorce, education, training, and shelter for poor, homeless or unmarried pregnant women and widows. When the Saint-Simonian church collapsed in 1834, some members remained feminist socialists, and resurfaced in 1848. Their sophisticated analysis of class and gender oppression foreshadowed the feminism of the 1848 revolution.

Of all early Utopian thinkers, Charles Fourier (1772–1837) placed the greatest emphasis on women's liberation. His complex theory traced human evolution through historical stages distinguished by the dominant mode of conjugal relations. In 1808 he traced the "progressive liberation" of women in marriage as "the fundamental cause of all social progress." "Social progress and changes from one era to the next are brought about by . . . the progress of women towards liberty, and social retrogression occurs as a result of a diminution in the liberty of women."[6] He considered women equal and similar to men, and the catalysts of change.

Their emancipation was indispensable to universal freedom.

Humans would progress by stages to Harmony, the ultimate goal, living in communities called *phalansteries*. Hating the family, Fourier envisioned couples united by love as long as it lasted. He proposed communal domestic work: communal kitchens, daycare centres, and sewing workshops. But he did not imagine men working in them. Like William Morris in his utopian novel, *News from Nowhere*, he conveniently believed that women enjoyed and wanted to cook, clean, raise children, and serve men. Fourier theorized radical reorganization ending the wage system and sexual inequality. Fourierist communities in France foundered when they were charged with moral turpitude for their unusual sexual practices.

Louis Blanc (1811–1882), a politician and journalist horrified by industrial society's competitiveness and exploitation of workers, campaigned for manhood suffrage. He thought the vote would enable working men to control the state, and fund "Associations of Production," a network of self-governing workshops guaranteeing everyone jobs and security. (Such workshops were established in Paris during the 1848 Revolution.) Before Karl Marx, Blanc predicted private enterprise would wither away with the state. Pierre Proudhon (1809–1865), an anarchist (advocate of self-government), wanted fair wages and prices based on the amount of labour needed to make goods, not whatever the market could bear.

Flora Tristan (1803–1844), influenced by many socialist-utopian thinkers, joined no group or party. The natural daughter of a rich Peruvian, she worked in a lithographic workshop and was forced to marry her boss, who beat her. When she left him, she lost her property and custody of her three children, regaining them only after he tried to kill her. Her famous assertion that all women were pariahs emerged from these experiences. Envisioning economic development liberating women morally, emotionally, and economically, she devoted herself after 1835 to feminist-socialist activities and writing *Nécessité de faire bon accueil aux femmes étrangères* (1835), *Pérégrinations d'un pariah* (1838), *Promenades dans Londres* (1839), and *L'Union ouvrière* (1843).[7]

Recognizing that a new class had emerged from a particular historical moment, a political/economic/social situation, Tristan urged workers to free themselves five years before Marx produced the *Communist Manifesto*. Workers, pariahs of the earth, had to liberate themselves as a class, but women, "the proletarian of the proletarian," suffered special problems as mothers, workers, and prostitutes. For Tristan as for Fourier, women's emancipation underlay that of workers. She urged workers to use collective action and form inclusive unions or committees.

Tristan's ideas for workers' unions and the "right to work" grew popular in 1840s France. She urged yearly dues of 2 francs a person to pay missionaries to convert more workers and a workers' representative to the National Assembly, and most important, to build workers' "palaces," homes for 2000–3000 children and old people, with farms and workshops. Children would be educated identically to develop intelligence, love of humanity, and skill with crafts. For Tristan socialism and feminism were one entity. She championed female education, marriage reform with the right to divorce, and women's right to do any work whatever. But seeing women mainly as mothers, she could not imagine them liberating themselves: men had to emancipate women. Harrassed by police and misunderstood by workers, she decided in 1844 to tour France and preached her gospel of cooperation and brotherhood directly to workers. While touring, she came to see herself not as a pariah but as a *femme guide* whose mission was to save the world. Exhaustion made her vulnerable to typhoid, and she died in Bordeaux in 1844.

England and Scotland

Edmund Burke supported the American Revolution but vilified the French in *Reflections on the Revolution in France* (1790). The French Revolution inspired Englishmen like scientist Joseph Priestley, minister Richard Price, and James Watt, inventor of the steam engine, to urge the overthrow of privilege and absolutism in England. Thomas Paine urged democracy in *The Rights of Man* (1791–92).

England's old tradition of Christian communitarianism had produced visions of harmonious egalitarian societies like Thomas More's *Utopia* (1516). The pre-nineteenth-century utopians concerned with women's status (seventeenth-century Diggers and eighteenth-century Shakers) had built communities based on sharing, cooperation, and equality and aimed at earthly felicity and spiritual regeneration. Socialist utopians believed that humans could achieve harmony by communal ownership and character transformation. Determined to end sex and class oppression, they focused on women's rights, believing, like the French utopians, that societal regeneration required female liberation.

The eighteenth-century *querelle des femmes* between haters and defenders of women did not produce a distinct consistent feminist political position. The first coherent feminist theoretical statement, Mary Wollstonecraft's *The Vindication of the Rights of Woman*, introduced the idea of "gender," manufactured sex roles. Wollstonecraft argued that womanhood was artificially created to serve male desire: society moulded girls into personal slaves for men. Men praised as "sensibility" a compound of slavish traits – servility, cunning, and "infantile imbecility." The social order consigns women to a stultifying, crippling way of life, she wrote, but "virtue can only flourish among equals." Wollstonecraft too believed that human political and social liberation depended on female emancipation, and her regenerative vision inspired both *Enquiry into Political Justice* (1793) by her future husband, philosopher William Godwin, and "Spensonia," a plan for an agrarian communist utopia by Thomas Spence, a working-class pamphleteer.

Godwin, determined to find ways to achieve and maintain both equality and individual liberty, concluded that the two could co-exist only if private property (which bred inequality) and government (which constrained individual freedom even when benevolent) were eliminated and replaced by a global system of small communities, economically maintained by small self-managed farms and workshops governed democratically by local councils. Both Spence and

Godwin advocated marriage reform: in Spensonia, women, married or single, would participate in a communal land economy on the same basis as men and have the same political rights, except that married women's domestic responsibilities kept them from sitting on government councils. Divorce was permitted and women's marital status was equal to their husbands' (if equality is possible when one sex alone is responsible for reproduction and maintenance, and the other for governance). Female suffrage, Wollstonecraft's ideas on female education, Godwin's and Spence's anti-marriage arguments, and the poet Shelley's eloquent depiction of a new era of sex equality aroused much discussion in British radical newspapers of the 1790s.

But events in France – the 1792 Terror, the 1793 overthrow and execution of Louis XVI, and the proclamation of a Republic – terrified the British ruling class and appalled the middle class. While preparing for war with France, the government feared British workers across the country who supported it. It suspended the law of habeas corpus, suppressed worker protest, banned radical societies, and arrested their leaders. Landlords, industrialists, magistrates, and churchmen hired vigilante squads to hit suspected reformers. After a "Church and King" mob burned down his house in 1793, a man wrote to a friend: "I cannot give you an idea of the violence with which every friend of liberty is persecuted in this country." The upper class became even more conservative, condemning any questioning of sex roles as revolutionary and reviling Wollstonecraft's *Vindication* (which had earlier been well received) for advocating promiscuity. Wollstonecraft became infamous: Horace Walpole called her a "hyena in petticoats." Feminism was vilified by respectable people: in 1798 a liberal women's journal declared itself "relieved to report" that the champions of female equality, who were as inimical to the happiness and interest of the sex as those who preached the doctrine of liberty and equality to men, were no longer regarded as sincere and politic friends.

By making feminism taboo and identifying women's rights with sexual libertarianism, free thought, and social revolution, conservatives forced feminists to become radical. (When there is no possibility of society absorbing a new doctrine, adherents focus on changing society.) Society hysterically feared that sexual equality would subvert all social institutions – church, marriage, and family. Feminists, responding to the hysteria, began to equate their goals with radical workers' "levelling" goals, linking sex-struggle with class-struggle. This connection and Wollstonecraft's ideas underlay the Owenite movement a quarter-century later.

Robert Owen (1771–1858), a Welsh visionary influenced by Godwin and Jeremy Bentham, believed character was moulded, not innate. He married a woman whose father owned a large cotton mill in New Lanark, Scotland, took over the mill, and tried to create a model environment, improving working conditions, building model houses and schools (free to his workers), and establishing social security. He was still a capitalist, if a benevolent one, when in 1820 he attacked capitalist enterprise and proposed creating communities without private property or salaried work, where people shared, living separately but raising children communally. Finding no support for his plan in England, he emigrated to the United States in 1825 with his son, Robert Dale Owen, and built New Harmony, Indiana. But in 1829 he went back to England to found the National Consolidated Trades Union. After it failed, he left the labour movement and became a spiritualist.

But Owen's ideas had extraordinary influence. His text on marriage, *Lectures on the Marriages of the Priesthood in the Old Immoral World*, damned the family, and advocated civil marriage and easy cheap divorce, which liberal Nonconformists also demanded in that period. Like many men, Owen was a feminist in his head, not heart, admiring Wollstonecraft, seeing the justice of women's protest, but still accustomed to female servitude. His major social statements, like *The Book of the New Moral World*, are visions of an egalitarian future. He tried to ease women's lot by having women share "their" work in community kitchens, cooperative nurseries and daycare, but that both parents should do caretaking and raise children never dawned on him. He was authoritarian, at best paternalist, which may be why his experiments in communal living failed. Obsessed with marriage, he blamed it for almost every social ill – prostitution, adultery, syphilitic degeneration of the species, and the destruction of pleasure and sensuality.

But the movement called Owenism derived less from Owen's ideas or activities than from a generation of conscious, organized radicals. Owenism was not a hierarchical movement dominated by one person, but rather, like today's feminism, a swell of autonomous individuals united by their beliefs. Most Owenites were upper working class, many lower middle class, a few wealthy. At first it attracted radical intellectuals, but in the 1830s and 1840s its appeal widened. From 1840 until its demise, hostile commentators wrote contemptuously of "crowds of women" regularly attending Owenite events around the country: hundreds heard Owenite lectures on women's rights, scores wrote to Owenite newspapers on women's issues, usually under pen names. Women, who rarely spoke in public and never for themselves, were speaking on their own behalf. The Owenites, unique among social movements because they wanted to abolish all relations of power and subordination, including sexual inequality, decided to form exemplary societies which would show the world that, as an Owenite woman wrote, "men and women may meet in equal communion, having equal rights and returns for industry . . . and equal attention given to the cultivation of their whole nature, physical, moral, and intellectual."[8]

Many Owenite feminists had middle-class backgrounds. A middle-class woman easily slipped into poverty, even starvation, if she did not marry, if her husband abandoned her, or if her father left her a house but no income. It was nearly impossible for a middle-class woman of the period to support herself. Those with education became socialists and wrote for working-class journals, trying to make a living as journalists, writers, or lecturers. But polemics against middle-class female idleness or marriage for property had no meaning to working women, for whom idleness meant starvation. Feminists urged "industrial emancipation" on women longing to be free of it. Yet feminists were vital to Owenism.

Whatever their background, Barbara Taylor writes, most Owenite women were like George Gissing's "odd women," daring to think and act in defiance of the social conventions that constricted women. Only their passionate discussions of serious issues marked them as deviant, and their repudiation of the deforming dress of nineteenth-century "ladies" made them outré in ladies' company. The first to assert Owenite feminist ideas publicly, Anna Wheeler and Frances Wright, came from rich families with prestigious male connections – which is why their careers were recorded.

Anna Doyle Wheeler (1785–1848), born in Ireland to a progressive family, married at fifteen and bore six children. She read constantly, especially Wollstonecraft and texts on the French Revolution, and finally fled her home for Guernsey, then France, where she met Tristan and Fourier. She was drawn to Saint-Simonian feminists, whose work she translated for the Owenite journal, *The Crisis*. By the 1820s she was a militant Owenite, organizing trade unions, speaking before radical Unitarians in London, and involved with William Thompson (1775–1833), an Irish landlord who had joined Owen's cooperative movement. Thompson felt that women deserved a better life and advocated they be given financial support during pregnancy, communal child care, and the chance to work for wages outside the home. Such changes would lead to female economic independence and a more perfect society.

In 1825 Thompson and Wheeler produced the *Appeal of One Half of the Human Race, Women, Against the Pretensions of the Other Half, Men, to Retain them in Political and thence in Civil and Domestic Slavery: in Reply to a Paragraph in Mr. Mill's Celebrated Article on Government*. Published in Thompson's name, it was partly Wheeler's work, and was written to refute James Mill's thesis that women were sufficiently represented by their male kin and did not need the vote. (His feminist son John shared this conviction.) The

Appeal was the first socialist analysis of women's condition in England: it argued that competitive pursuit of personal wealth was incompatible with democracy and sexual equality, condemned the double standard and hypocrisy of marriage, and urged birth control. Previously, only poets had questioned women's exclusive responsibility for social and biological reproduction, Taylor notes. Even Wollstonecraft accepted this "duty," merely urging that women be allowed other activities too. By questioning it, the *Appeal* offered a new morality.

Wheeler lectured at South Place Chapel in London, where radical Unitarians and women's rights advocates like W.J. Fox, Harriet Taylor, and John Stuart Mill met in the 1820s and 1830s. Fox's *The Monthly Repository* often published pieces on women's position; Harriet Taylor wrote *The Enfranchisement of Women* in 1851; her husband, Mill, a liberal philosopher who supported women's emancipation, wrote *The Subjection of Women* in 1867. The Owenite press published radical or liberal feminists like Mary Leman Grimstone, Harriet Martineau, and Anna Jameson. Margaret Chappell Smith and Eliza Macauley lectured on economic theory; Smith, one of the most popular Owenite lecturers in the 1840s, discussed currency reform and the history of English financial institutions. Other Owenite feminists wrote on mathematics, natural science, and the most advanced thinkers of the period, including Wollstonecraft, Godwin, Shelley (feminists' favourite poet), and Owen. Few other non-socialist radicals publicly supported women's cause in the first half of the nineteenth century.

Emma Martin (1812–1851) succeeded Wheeler as the movement's leading feminist publicist. Born and raised in a Bristol middle-class family, Martin had little education, yet in 1830 she became proprietor of a ladies' boarding school and editor of *The Bristol Literary Magazine*. An ardent Baptist, she attacked Owenites who denied divine inspiration to the Bible. Somehow, while raising a family, running the school, editing the magazine, and working for her church, Martin learned languages (including Hebrew and

Italian), basic medicine, physiology, and enough theology to dis-
comfit the clerics she debated later in her career. Miserable in her
marriage, she discovered feminism and in 1839 took her children
and left her husband (who took all her property) and joined the
Socialists. She began to lecture as a freethinking feminist, at first
receiving a small salary from the Owenite Centre.

Reversing her earlier religious conviction, she promoted socialism
as the only cure for sexual inequality, and wrote anti-religious tracts.
She was close and loving with her daughters, but had trouble supporting them: she had to pay for child care when on lecture tours or
take them with her and expose them to the risks of travel and local
animosity (she was sometimes stoned in the streets). The fact that she
took a lover and had another child did not make things any easier.
Class background was irrelevant to women supporting themselves;
any woman who gave up middle-class status was treated as "common." Barbara Taylor believes such experiences led Owenite feminists
to identify strongly with working-class people and to see women's
oppression as a cross-class phenomenon. Martin taught, kept a shop,
and did midwifery, but could not earn enough to support her family,
and had to ask for help publicly. She died young and penniless.

Utopian Communities

Owen argued that labour was the source of all society's wealth and
that workers' poverty was not natural or inevitable but a result of
the unjust appropriation of their work. He urged workers to work
for themselves by creating communities that collectively owned the
means of production and distribution. Owenites had founded four
cooperative societies by 1828; by 1830, there were three hundred.
By 1832 five hundred cooperative societies flourished, and Owen
set up a National Equitable Labour Exchange, a bazaar where workers could trade their products for "labour-notes" representing the
amount of work time invested in them. Receiving "a just reward"
for their work, they cut profiteering distributors out of the loop. A
London activist wrote: "The Labour Exchanges will make all mas-

ters, no servants or slaves."

Owenites drew up models for communities where like-minded people, not kin, could live in justice and felicity. In most models large connected residences had private bedrooms for adults and dormitories for children. A major concern was getting rid of *private* housework, the "unproductive and repulsive drudgery" that William Thompson calculated occupied nine-tenths of a woman's time. Thompson planned a mechanical laundry and scientifically arranged kitchens; the London Co-operative Society suggested that all adults rotate housework. Child care and education too were to be done collectively. Robert Cooper, a Manchester socialist, designed a model in which children under eleven did housework (which he must have imagined required no knowledge or skill); those aged twelve to twenty-one were responsible for "production of wealth," those twenty-two to twenty-five for its preservation and distribution. Between the ages of twenty-five and thirty-five, people would teach – in his words, direct the "formation of the character of the rising generation." At thirty-five, people governed, and at forty-five, freed for artistic or intellectual pursuits, they became community advisors. At each level, women and men would perform exactly the same tasks. This plan was never realized.

In 1821 twenty-one artisanal families formed a community at Spa Fields, Islington. Women shared domestic labour, freeing themselves to teach and sew, and they pooled their wages to pay for children's education which, like child care, was collective. In County Clare, Ireland, in 1831, twenty-four farming families formed the Ralahine Association on communally held land. They set up collective housekeeping, and an infant school to care for children during the twelve hours a day the women worked in the fields. But since women's wages on this commune were half of men's (as in the outside world) and women were still responsible for children after school hours, it hardly altered their hard lives.

Owen's community in Hampshire, Queenwood (or Harmony), was also agricultural. Each woman had to perform one domestic task for a month, and the heaviest work was done by hired labour. Everyone rose at six and worked in the fields. Women not on cooking duty also went to the fields, returned at eight for breakfast and went back to the fields until supper. At night, there was singing, dancing, or classes – a "female" class was held once a week. To lighten women's workload, Owen in 1842 began a controversial, expensive building program including a kitchen with elabourate machines. Despite their goal of easing women's burden, Owenites never questioned why women alone were responsible for all domestic maintenance. Women resisted or left many communities. Men's refusal to take care of themselves and their children was more powerful than any principles they adopted. It was male chauvinism, not theoretical inadequacy, that destroyed egalitarian communities.

Most Owenites disliked traditional religion and its conventions. Offended by the legal non-existence of married women, the double standard, and men's right to beat their wives, and wanting to end marriage based on money and private property, they tried to invent alternative forms of marriage. Disputing scripture, Martin, Fanny Wright, and others contended that mutual loving egalitarian unions could emerge only from free thought and love. Owenites sifted through anthropological data for alternatives to traditional marriage, writing on women and marriage in such exotic places as Turkey, in works like "Amazon Women of the Lost Islands," and "Primitive Peoples of the Geenkonki Delta." Some reworked scripture into socialist theology or Christian millenarianism (belief in the Second Coming of Christ), their communism permeated by female mystical and moral pre-eminence, the "Doctrine of the Woman" or "Woman-Power." Accepting nineteenth-century middle-class ideas of female moral superiority to men, they attributed to women the redemptive power to fulfil "Woman's Mission" to reform the world.

In his community, Owen ruled that a couple wanting to marry should announce their intention three months beforehand, then proclaim their bond before the assembled community. They could declare a wish to divorce any time after a year, but had to wait six months before the union was considered ended. Divorced people could remarry. Thompson felt that each person over a certain age should have a private bedroom, even after marriage. Acknowledging that sexual liaisons would occur, he drew the line only at parenthood: the right to sexual liaison did not mean the right to reproduce. To separate the two required what Thompson called "individual prudence" or "individual measures to limit population" (contraception). Owen was accused of importing condoms into New Lanark (with its largely female workforce) and never denied it.

However, neither sexual puritanism nor an ideology of free love with social and economic independence solved women's problem. What they wanted was a mutual relationship with men, a way to provide for their children, use their abilities and avoid enslavement by domestic maintenance. But no utopian scheme expected men to share responsibility for maintenance and support of children; thus, while women might enjoy sexual freedom, as long as they bore the responsibility for children, they needed husbands legally bound to support them. Therefore, most women did not want to see marriage abolished and pressured the Owenites not to urge it; they chose marriage as a civil contract that included the possibility of divorce. Female lecturers dwelt on the pleasures of faithful marriage and the miseries of sexual exploitation.

Owen was devoted to education and encouraged women to participate in group educational activities and classes in subjects like housewifery, while Owenite women wanted classes in subjects that might free them from the household and train them for other work – reading, writing, history, and arithmetic. But few such classes were given: men's resistance affected everything. It was not Owenism but a patriarchal system that created women's double bind: only women were denied a living wage and political rights, only women were held responsible for children, only women were socially outcast for being unmarried. Twenty years after Wheeler left her husband, she wrote: "I am a woman and without a master: two causes of disgrace in England." All "masterless" women were pariahs; Owenite women were shunned even by broad-minded liberals. Freethinking women were *witches, she-devils, whores.*

Some women chose not to marry, but some could not find husbands. In the 1830s the high ratio of women to men (who tended to marry late) left many women single. Middle-class women who would not become unpaid servants to male kin became destitute; working-class women could find jobs but not a living wage. The Owenite women discovered that in the real world it was hard to find a man and impossible to survive without one.[9] An editorial of the period argued: "A woman's wage is not reckoned at an average more than two-thirds of a male, and we believe in reality it seldom amounts to more than one-third (and wives have no wages at all). Yet, is not the produce of female labour as useful? . . . The industrious female is well entitled to the same amount of remuneration as the industrious male."

In 1844 Owen was expelled from the governorship of Queenwood, and Owenism collapsed as a united movement of radical thought. The Owenite movement matters to us now because it tried to integrate work and private life, men and women, capital and labour more commodiously than any other movement before or since. Its defeat was also the defeat of integrated thinking: no wide-scale movement since has had this goal. The Owenite analysis of class exploitation anticipated Marxism and was even wider, addressing oppression in the workplace, marketplace, school, and home. The utopian socialist movement was the first arena of massive struggle waged by a popular feminist movement and adherents of cooperative production. Both were defeated: nineteenth-century feminism was defeated by men's adamant refusal to take responsibility for maintaining themselves and their children; cooperative production was defeated by capitalism. But utopian socialist thinking helped shape the future and lived on in later feminism and the modern cooperative movement.

Other Political Struggles

Owenism was one strand in the social protest that disquieted England in the first half of the nineteenth century. During the Napoleonic war that began the century and the depression that followed it, rising prices and falling wages sent thousands of working-class men and women onto the streets in food riots, strikes, and protests. The government suppressed them, hiring spies to unearth evidence against them. The hardest-hit area (then as now) was the industrial north where "radicals" agitated for wider franchise. Workers called Luddites (for Ned Ludd, who supposedly led a demonstration in Nottingham with his wife and co-leader "Lady Ludd") smashed machines or attacked workers who refused to join unions. It took repeated clashes between demonstrators and the army or police – shopkeepers who withheld taxes and formed their own national guard, a cholera epidemic, the king (William IV) hearing rumours of "miners, manufacturers, colliers, and labourers" about to rebel – for the government to pass a Reform Bill (1832) extending franchise to men who paid £10 or more yearly in rent on land held on sixty-year leases: a mere 3 percent of the population.

Corn Laws and Poor Laws also aroused general ire. Corn Laws protected English landowners by placing duty on cheap imported grain so as to keep the price of bread high. This hurt the poor, who pressured manufacturers for wages high enough to buy bread, in turn irritating manufacturers. Poor Laws granted paupers help only in their natal parishes. People who moved regularly seeking work were stranded by this rule, but the number of paupers strained local resources. The Poor Law passed in 1832 reflected the self-righteous morality of a tight-mouthed middle class (vividly portrayed in George Crabbe's *The Borough*). Blindly sure that poverty was a moral flaw rooted in poor character, that jobs were available to anyone willing to work, the government ended the dole and ordered the indigent to be confined in workhouses under conditions so grim they would want to get out. But an early 1840s depression forced the government to re-institute the dole. In 1846 *manufacturers'* pressure led parliament to repeal the Corn Laws.

Female and male workers formed Friendly Societies offering mutual aid insurance, and set up cooperative stores. There were about five hundred such societies with over 20,000 members by 1831. After the 1832 Reform Act, women organized politically to fight oppression by the police, the church, and the privileged. Appealing to "natural rights" and the Bible, in 1837 they demonstrated against the Poor Law. Workers organized trade unions: textile workers and miners formed the National Association for the Protection of Labour; 30,000 joined the Operative Builders Union. The Women's Stocking Makers of Leicester joined Robert Owen's Grand National Consolidated Trades Union of Great Britain and Ireland in calling for a general strike in 1834. This led the government to decide to stamp out unions, prosecute Grand National leaders, and transport them to Australia. Thousands of women marched demanding bread in a general strike in Lancaster in 1843. Employers required workers to sign pledges that they would not join unions.

After 1835 socialists, despairing that the union movement would create a foundation for a workers' commonwealth, turned their energies to transforming traditional thinking. Economic cooperation had failed, but universal enlightenment and cultural reconstruction might succeed. Believing the only way to end the treatment of women as property was to end private property itself, Owenites decided that building a New Moral World required not just abolition of private capital but moral and psychological education to transform human competitiveness. Correct "Character Formation" was essential to social re-creation, therefore all institutions responsible for Incorrect Character Formation – authoritarian education, orthodox religion, patriarchal marriage, and familism – must be destroyed or altered. Socialists could not change institutions but could challenge the hold of one, religion, on common people. Declaring socialism the "Rational Religion" that would supersede orthodox Christianity, they decried scripture. The clergy retaliated. Violent debate between Christians and social scientists exploded in working-class meeting halls. In their offensive against socialist "immoralism," the clergy stressed women's sexual behaviour, provoking a new breed of propagandist – Owenite feminists struggling to free their minds from patriarchal Christianity. They lectured and wrote, and the work of a few voluble women swept England, Scotland, and Wales between 1838 and 1845, making everyone aware of the Woman Question.

Some Owenites joined a growing male labour reform movement called Chartism, which flourished from 1838 to 1848. Members wrote a "People's Charter" and circulated it across the country; millions signed it. This "Charter" demanded electoral reforms that had been proposed before 1832: universal male suffrage, secret ballots, annual parliamentary elections, the abolition of property qualifications for members of the House of Commons, salaried House members, and equal electoral districts. Chartism was looser and larger than socialism, with a huge militant female membership. It incorporated a wider range of attitudes. During its peak years, tens of thousands of women campaigned for the Six Points, led mass demonstrations, organized campaigns, prayed in Chartist churches, taught in Chartist Sunday schools, and sometimes attacked the military and the police. Chartism was a working-class movement; it rose from the ashes of defeat of socialist women, and its women were militant, but not feminist. William Lovett, a Chartist leader, idealized the home as a private retreat, extolling homemakers (and his own wife) as "Angels in the House," indicating that middle-class women's constriction within domesticity was filtering down to the working class.

A backlash against all this agitation (perhaps orchestrated) insisted on even greater confinement of women. Women who helped support their families felt the growing disapproval. New ideas of female respectability made it even harder for women to act politically than earlier, when political women like Emma Martin were publicly slandered. Women were now barred from pubs, where many political meetings were held, and a burgeoning moral reform movement held alcohol to be anathema to respectable womanhood. Near mid-century, Victorian sentimentalization of the home and the patriarchal family pervaded all classes; even tough working women shrank into "home-centredness and inferiority." Soon, the idea of separate spheres came to be seen as Natural and Right. The domestic, dependent, private female sphere was rigidly segregated from male work, politics, and public life.

Some socialist organizations endured. But the socialist utopian movement, united by one goal – a New Moral World – from 1820 to 1845, splintered into trade unionism, social science, practical cooperation, spiritualism, free thought (called Secularism after 1850) and feminism, with a small left wing. By the 1860s the Trade Union Congress stated that it intended to work for an economic structure in which wives could remain at home, their proper sphere. The British labour movement has strongly opposed women's employment ever since. Socialism, too, buried feminism, labelling it bourgeois and personal. But in Britain and France – and later Russia – the first socialism was feminist and feminism was socialist.

Early feminism, humanistic and revolutionary, challenged all hierarchies at all levels. Its radical ideas and experiments with social-ist communities horrified the articulate middle class, which quiv-ered at feminists' desire to transform society utterly, to turn the world "upside down." Public reaction radicalized upper- and mid-dle-class women, for whom feminism was a simple plea for justice. Moderate feminists arguing for extension of the vote to upper-class women had to spend considerable energy proving their loyalty to capitalism and elite privilege. The demise of Owenism eased their problem: once it was forgotten, middle-class women could agitate for feminist reform without being seen as socialist, sexually immor-al, or subversive. By 1860 "women's rights" had enough moderate adherents to be respectable. Working-class radical feminism was for-gotten entirely – by everyone.

The United States

Egalitarian enlightenment ideas did not take root in working-class nineteenth-century Americans: after a revolution in the name of equality, the state declared it achieved. Since the New Moral World already existed, there was no need to build one. America's ruling class still uses a rhetoric of achieved revolution, ignoring the nation's vast inequities, privilege, poverty, and conspicuous injustice. Because America lacked a tradition of utopian socialism, when feminism emerged, it lacked a socialist or utopian agenda. The women's rights movement grew instead from moral reform societies, temperance, and abolitionist movements.

But industrialization transformed American social and economic life too. People hoping for a higher standard of living went to work in industry: disrupted by urbanization, weakened kinship and community bonds, and alienated from their work, they sought comfort in religious movements like evangelical renewals. The Second Great Awakening began in the south in the late eighteenth century, moving east between 1810 and 1825. Intensely emotional thousands professed themselves reborn. Throwing off the burden of Calvinist predestination and obsession with sin, they tingled with optimism and godliness – a huge number of women among them.

Many formed alternative communities and millenarianist sects – from the Revolution to the Civil War nearly a hundred fledgling utopias sprang up across the country, like Economy, Pennsylvania; Fruitlands and Hopedale, Massachusetts; Pleasant Hill, Kentucky; and Nauvoo, Illinois. Religious communities prepared for the Second Coming or a Golden Age – Shakers in Massachusetts and New York, Amana in Iowa, Oneida in New York. Owen's and Fourier's ideas crossed the Atlantic, inspiring secular communities intended to be new societies – Owen's New Harmony, Indiana (1824), North American Phalanx, New Jersey (1843), and Brook Farm, Massachusetts (1841). Fourierist communities tried to alter conceptions of private property and sexual politics, but like their European counterparts, suffered from disparity between theory and practice, rhetoric and action. None realized sexual equality or economic justice.

Some communities tried to free women from the burden of childbearing by requiring celibacy. Rappites, Zoarites, and Shakers saw that conventional marriage kept women from sexual equality, and either wanted to free them from the pain and danger of childbirth, or believed that chastity made people spiritually pure. Women converted to such religions more than men. Celibate societies expected to increase their numbers by conversions and adoptions, not births. The Shakers were founded by Ann Lee, an illiterate young woman from Manchester. Hounded by the Church of England, she and eight followers came to the United States in 1774, settled in New Lebanon, New York, and built the first Shaker (named for a convulsive dance used in their ritual) church in 1787. Lee believed she was the Christ: the Shaker Manifesto reads: "Do we believe in Jesus, the Son of God? Most certainly, and we also believe in Ann, the Daughter of God." Unique among religions with goddesses, the United Society of Believers saw women as equal to men.

As more people joined, Shakers moved across the country, building villages organized by rules governing all areas of life. Each community had its own government and resources. New members had to abandon their biological families and renounce bonds of flesh and kinship in celibate abstinence devoted to "Our Father in Heaven and Mother Ann." Many converts had yearned for relief from bad marriages or financial problems; women especially longed to avoid marriage in a world of legal male dominance and no birth control. Lee passed strict rules of sexual segregation: members lived in segregated buildings or at opposite ends of buildings, shared rooms with those of their own sex, and entered common areas like dining rooms by different doors. Sisters and brothers could not shake hands, pass one another on staircases, or hang their garments together. Married couples were separated.

The sexes worked apart, men in the fields or at carpentry, women at domestic tasks – cleaning, cooking, laundry, and bread-baking on a rota system.[10] Shaker women were equal to men but the traditional division of labour remained. Sisters had to mend the brothers' clothes and clean their rooms when they were absent. The only concession to female "fragility" was that brothers had to help sisters with heavy tasks and do the milking in bad weather.

Stereotypic ideas pervaded the Shaker religion too: although their deity was bisexual, Shakers identified maleness with intellect and femaleness with emotion. But the Shakers seem to have *practised* the sexual equality and the appointment of women to posts of authority asserted in their Manifesto; witnesses noted two Elders and Eldresses, three Deacons and Deaconesses overseeing an equal number of women and men at meetings. Shakers still endure.

In 1826 Robert Owen and his son established America's most famous utopian socialist community at New Harmony, Indiana. It allowed a variety of living arrangements: one or two families lived in a small two-storey house, each family with its own chamber and alcove. Toddlers lived in a communal nursery, older children in a school. Single residents lived in communes, visitors in boardinghouses. Common spaces – dining rooms, kitchens, laundries, halls for dancing, music, and meetings – were open to all. Privacy and community existed at work, play, and household tasks.

For Owen, the main culprit in societal disease – private property – was marriage, which turned love into a power relation and fostered social ills by barring divorce. He wanted to eradicate or weaken the family, he announced in *The New Harmony Gazette*, to change "from the individual to the social system: from single families with separate interests to communities of many families with one interest."[11] Education was necessary for this, and he urged that year-old babies go to school. Parents balked and sent them at two: there were three to four hundred pupils in 1826. Geologist-pedagogue William Maclure believed the sexes had equal capacities and that female political power would improve society: education might even enable women someday to vote!

But New Harmony's leaders accepted inherent sexual differences that fostered traditional power relations. Girls and boys both learned mathematics and natural history (among other subjects) but different manual tasks – boys made shoes, did weaving and carpentry; girls washed clothes, cooked, and served. Everyone in New Harmony had to work; in theory, all were equal. But passbooks for use at a communal store were issued only to husbands. Women worked harder than men – for the community and for their own families. Since family work was not *real* work, it had to be done on weekends, when men could play sports or study. Women quarrelled about class: middle-class women objected to doing the same work or eating at the same table as lower-class women. Resentment led to defection, and turnover was swift; the community never cohered. The final blow was the failure of the textile mill, its economic mainstay, after Owen let the community manage it. New Harmony lasted only two years, from 1825 to 1827. Its economic failure was rooted in the moral failure of people who could not give up sex- and class superiority.

When Owen returned to England in 1829, his son, Robert Dale Owen, remained and edited *The New Harmony Gazette*. In 1830 he wrote the first birth-control tract printed in America, *Moral Physiology*. Insisting that women had the right to decide on birth control, he urged smaller, better-educated families. He represented Indiana in Congress in the 1840s and worked in the anti-slavery and spiritualist movements, but he is mainly remembered for his radical causes and his collabouration with Fanny Wright.

Frances (Fanny) Wright (1795–1852) was born to a prosperous family – her Scots father manufactured linen – but she had to educate herself. Fortunately, she had access to libraries and read Byron (and cut her hair like his), Epicurus, Wollstonecraft, Bentham, Hume, and other Enlightenment thinkers. She became an audacious anti-church intellectual, writing essays on Epicurean philosophy and three-act plays on political themes before she was twenty-one. Yet she doubted herself; impatient of convention, she was also extremely beautiful and anxious about her strangeness in a period that believed "young ladies ought only to have such a general tincture of knowledge as to make them agreeable companions to men of sense." By her mid-twenties, she had published several books and was known as a literary lady. In 1818 she visited the United States and recorded her impressions. Her strong democratic views pleased Americans but were virulently attacked in England. Deeply attached to General Lafayette, the aging hero of the American and French Revolutions, she proposed to him. He affectionately declined, but returned to America with her in 1824. She visited New Harmony and was immediately converted.

The next year Wright bought a plantation in Nashoba, Tennessee, spending most of her fortune to build a cooperative community. A staunch abolitionist, she bought black slaves and set them to work to earn back their purchase price while being educated for freedom. Her anti-church feminist principles led her to ban marriage in her community. This outraged the neighbours, who said that Nashoba men, far from honouring the "free and voluntary affection" Wright urged, intimidated or forced women into sex; but Gerda Lerner's interpretation is that it was the liaisons between people of different races that shocked even abolitionists.[12] Whether what occurred was rape or simply interracial sex, the resulting scandal demoralized the Nashobans. Wright was already notorious among her Tennessee neighbours for her positions on religion and feminism and her customary appearance: she cut her hair short and wore a loose tunic over bloomers – dress originally designed for New Harmony women. In 1828 Nashoba disintegrated: exhausted, Wright went to New Harmony to recuperate and met Robert Dale Owen.

The two moved to New York City, edited *The Free Enquirer*, and organized political groups (nicknamed "Fanny Wright Societies") to lobby state legislatures for universal free education. They founded the first labour party in the United States, the New York Workingmen's Party, which won a major victory in the 1829 election. Wright, who had become famous for a speech at an Indiana fourth-of-July celebration in 1828, was the first woman in

America to make lecturing a career. She urged free education in boarding schools for all children over the age of two, to inculcate egalitarianism – she did not mention the liberation it would offer women. Wherever she appeared, midwest or east, her ideas and appearance stimulated controversy. She crusaded for universal education, communitarian economic enterprises, and above all, rights for women, which included birth control, reform of the divorce laws, protection of women's property rights, and sexual mutuality – which was popularized as "free love."

Yet Wright, like most others who opposed conventional monogamous marriage, believed in monogamy and herself married in a traditional ceremony, only omitting vows of obedience. For arguing that sexual intercourse should involve the "unconstrained . . . unrestrained choice of both parties," Wright was attacked as a "decadent and immoral" promoter of "lewd and promiscuous behavior."[13] The popular press labelled her "the Whore of Babylon." The argument that women should have rights over their own bodies and should be able to make love when (and only when) they choose is interpreted by many men to mean they are sexually indiscriminate.

In 1830, feeling damaged by her notoriety, Wright gave up lecturing. The next year, pregnant, she married her lover, Owenite Phiquepal d'Arusmont, and moved to Paris to try conventional family life. In 1844 she divorced her husband and returned to America to resume writing and lecturing. He (Owenite only in name) took her inheritance and custody of their daughter, Sylvia, who became entirely estranged from her mother. Fanny Wright ended up a victim of the very abuses she had long attacked. The most famous of contemporary feminist radicals in America, she lived vividly ahead of her time, and her writing was nearly as popular as Owen's.

Also in a perfecting spirit, Unitarian minister George Ripley in 1841 founded Brook Farm in West Roxbury, Massachusetts. New England farmers, artisans, and intellectuals were attracted to the cooperative farm, inspired by Ralph Waldo Emerson's transcendentalism to believe they could rise above materialism and find felicity in a communal life providing work, play, and spiritual nourishment. Brook Farm had a hundred members at most, but its writers or teachers (like Nathaniel Hawthorne) and its famous quarterly, *The Dial*, attracted students from outside the community to its school. In 1845 the community organized Fourierist phalanxes, strictly regimented work-living units. As regimentation kills spirit, however, members left. After an 1846 fire, it died.

Massachusetts-born Margaret Fuller (1810–1850) visited Brook Farm with enthusiasm but did not join (Hawthorne disparagingly portrayed her there, in *The Blithedale Romance*). The Transcendentalist elite – Emerson, Bronson Alcott, Henry Thoreau, Orestes Brownson – had high regard for the erudite Fuller, who in 1840 co-edited *The Dial*. She left Boston in 1844 to become the first woman reporter on Horace Greeley's *New York Daily Tribune* and grew famous as a journalist and critic. In 1846 her job took her to Europe, where she met the most famous writers of the time, including George Sand, the Brownings, and Thomas Carlyle. While in Italy to support Italian independence, she fell in love with and married Italian marquis Giovanni Angelo Ossoli. When the Italian revolution collapsed, Fuller sailed back to America with her husband and baby; they all drowned in a shipwreck just offshore.

Fuller passionately believed in sexual equality and argued it persuasively and cogently in *Women in the Nineteenth Century* (1845). Examining women's inferior social status, she attacked the morality of laws that prevented wives from owning property or inheriting from their husbands. With brilliant originality she demonstrated that women's subordination (which she compares with that of slaves) was rooted in men's universal scorn. Laws institutionalized men's unfounded superiority over women by defining marriage as ownership of women rather than as a mutual relationship. Fuller enriched her arguments by allusions to myth, history, contemporary events, and figures like Sand, Germaine Necker (Mme de Staël), salonist Pauline Roland, Wollstonecraft, and abolitionist Angelina

Grimké, and she boldly analyzed the attitudes to women of "great" men like Swedenborg and Fourier.

But like her contemporaries – indeed, like many women today – Fuller was impeded by an essentialist view of the sexes. In a world devoted to power, the belief that women are *by nature* more humane and compassionate, less aggressive and acquisitive than men, justifies the status quo and its division of power. Essentialists, ascribing moral superiority to women, can only plead for equality on mystical or religious grounds (as Fuller did), which move the world of *Realpolitik* not at all. Fuller was a major figure ahead of her time and is important today, but she had little influence on the thought of her period.

Socialism and Revolution

The utopian socialist communal experiments were creative responses to the oppressiveness of the power differential between classes and sexes. All failed but, like the communal experiments of the 1960s, they were different enough from each other that it is hard to generalize about the causes of their failure beyond their members' inability to go beyond sex or class superiority. But the ideas behind the experiments inspired other movements. Class-conscious workers, acutely aware that they were exploited by the rich and the governments behind the rich, blamed *them*, not Nature or God, for the misery and destitution blighting every city.

The poor, writes Eric Hobsbawm, "found themselves in the path of bourgeois society" without traditional protections. They had three choices: they could strive to become middle class too, let themselves be ground down, or rebel; but becoming bourgeois was profoundly distasteful to workers, who despised the individualistic ethic of every man for himself.[14] Intellectuals horrified by industrialization used Enlightenment ideas of human rights and equality to build a new economic morality – socialism. As socialist utopians experimented with alternatives to capitalist industrialization, social

PART SIX: THE NINETEENTH CENTURY: CAPITALISM TRIUMPHANT

philosophers wrote, argued, and formed political groups and trade unions. Meantime, mounting human misery erupted in riots, uprisings, and finally, revolutions.

In the early nineteenth century, absolute monarchs ruled all European states except England (whose middle class had rebelled in the seventeenth century); kingless states like Poland were swallowed up. But kings had become absolute only in name; for centuries they had regularly had to compromise with ambitious nobles and reform economic structures to placate their people. Needing middle class money and support, some members of the nobility encouraged the progressives, intimating that the king might "modernize" society. But this was a lure: all kings were steeped in the values of traditional landed aristocracies and were blind to alternatives. Every rational thinker, even princes' advisors, knew serfdom had to end, but no king ended it: that took revolution.[15]

In 1848 most of Europe was still agricultural. Illiteracy, poor communication, and geographical isolation kept most people ignorant of events not conveyed by their priest or a traveller; few could read the handful of newspapers that existed. Eastern Germany, Russia, and the small Danube states were semi-feudal; their peasants were serfs. Prussia had freed its serfs, leaving them with little or no land, forced to work as labourers for landowners who controlled local government and police but paid almost no taxes. As industrialization spread, a new class emerged: the landless disfranchised unskilled workers living in permanent insecurity whom Marx called the *Lumpenproletariat*. They thronged to cities, which swiftly became crowded, squalid, unsanitary, and unsafe.

These people rose up everywhere, sometimes dangerously; some were violently suppressed. Radical thinkers discussed ways of curing society's ills. Friedrich Engels (1820–1895), whose German father was a partner in a Manchester cotton factory, went to England in the 1840s and spent two years working in the mill, observing workers' lives. He wrote vividly of slum life, the dehumanization of workers, and their alienation from their work, in *The Condition of the Working Class in England in 1844.* Noting "class-consciousness," he predicted that the workers' awareness of themselves as a group with common interests opposed to owners' interests would lead in time to revolution.

Engels' ideas impressed Karl Marx (1818–1883) and the two became friends and collabourators. Marx, born to a prosperous German family, studied at the University of Berlin and became editor of the *Rhineland Gazette.* From the start he criticized society and used his editorship to advance change, angering his publishers. Dismissed, he went to Paris, and met Engels in 1844. They decided to try to work out a coherent theory of revolutionary change. But Marx was expelled from Paris and went to Brussels, where he founded the German Working Men's Association and the Communist Correspondence Committee, later called the Communist League. These groups had few or no members and were dedicated to study, not revolution. But the Communist League grew. When it met in London in 1847, Marx transfixed the hundred or so members by denouncing their declarations of universal brotherhood and urging class war. They asked him to write a statement of principles for them in the next two months. Drawing on Engels' and his past work, Marx hastily wrote a text (generously sharing authorship with Engels, who repeatedly insisted that Marx alone had written it). As Europe exploded in 1848, *The Communist Manifesto* appeared. Although barely noticed in the turmoil, it changed the world.

Marx challenged Georg Hegel's idea that history was driven by ideas in conflict. Hegel claimed that when antithetical ideas synthesize (as red and blue synthesize into purple), progress occurs. For Marx, however, conflict and resolution (dialectic) were based in economics, not ideas; history was a record of class struggle, of conflict between owners (bourgeoisie) and workers (proletariat) over material goods (thus, dialectical materialism). Over time, the method by which material goods were distributed had changed from feudal manorialism to capitalism. Capitalism was a necessary stage in human progress, but would be overthrown. A proletarian dictatorship would take over the means of production *and* the distribution of material goods until capitalism and capitalist thought were eradicated. When the bourgeois state withered away, true communism would emerge as a utopia on earth.

Marx's first sentence, "A spectre is haunting Europe – the spectre of Communism," challenged the world.[16] He used the word "communism" rather than "socialism" because so many forms of socialism existed at the time. "Communism," an older, less loaded word, had a stricter meaning: communal ownership of goods. Asserting that "philosophers have only given different *interpretations* of the world; the important thing is to change it," Marx read history to that end. His analysis of the leading edge of capitalism remains pertinent and profound, even if capitalism had only just begun in 1848 and did not become revolutionary until railroads launched the iron and steel industries, producing the internal-combustion engine, Fordism (assembly lines), and our own burgeoning electronics industries.

Before 1848 most radical groups believed political power rested in franchise and focused on demanding universal male suffrage. Marx insisted that property, not the vote, conferred political power. He defined "value" as the labour-time required to produce goods; workers sell their labour-time for *full value* – the wages necessary to "reproduce" them – keep them alive for the next day. But owners price things above workers' wages, so workers produce "surplus value" which is appropriated by capitalists, who own the means of production – the factory, machines, and raw materials. The Communist goal was the abolition of private ownership of capital.

Marx saw that capitalism separated production from reproduction, the sphere in which labour-power is reproduced. He did not develop his thought about reproduction (biological or social); he granted it value, but did not incorporate it into his theory. This set a precedent; later socialist thinkers ignored the work of childbearing and family maintenance. Engels, however, was concerned with women's oppression and wrote a semi-historical account of its emergence, *The Origin of the Family, Private Property and the State*, which remains important to many socialists. In 1883 socialist theorist August Bebel argued that women were the first humans placed in bondage and should be counted as part of the workforce. But Marx, not Bebel, was the father of most modern socialisms. Marx envisioned capitalism as a dynamic system allowing social change so radical that the powerless could become the authors of history, but he did so *after* the defeat of women in socialism and the restoration of patriarchal priorities in organized labour. Patriarchy triumphed in later socialism as it did in later Christianity and later Islam. Once the formative stage of a movement has passed, men move to exclude women.

Nevertheless, socialism was a revolutionary new human discourse; by interpreting social structure in terms of class struggle – the exploitation of labour and collective action challenging it – socialist thinking provided a language and a set of values for a feminist agenda. But it was complicated by three facts: women participate in both sides of the class struggle (are members of the exploiters and the exploited); at the same time, all women are oppressed by men, including men of their own class. Women's loyalties are further fragmented by their primary responsibility for maintaining men and raising children (some male) to take a place in society dictated by their father's position.

Based on the principle of equality, socialism has treated women better than capitalism in some ways. Socialist states gave women access to education and jobs with decent wages long before "democratic" states did so. But women in socialist states suffer from the same discrimination found in the utopian communes and capitalist states: patriarchal bias. Women supported socialism ardently, and it affected millions of women. But it failed them. This failure is not unique: no system has yet been devised that acknowledges women's true centrality to reproduction and maintenance.

Revolutions broke out across Europe in 1848. In explanation, historians cite the greater population of Europe: people crowded into towns with no work. The potato crop failed in 1846 and subsequently, wheat in 1847. Poor harvests, aggravated by international financial and industrial crises, caused widespread unemployment, business failure, and starvation. Hungry people rioted, but even before these crises they had been politicized, affected by socialist ideas, ideas of democracy. After 1815 groups worked to wrest a share of political power. Secret brotherhoods called Carbonari, headed by army officers, emerged in Italy and spread through Europe in the 1820s, forcing the kings of Naples and Spain to promise constitutions based on the French revolutionary constitution of 1789–1791. A Belgian insurrection overthrew Dutch rule.

While all governments claim concern for the "national interest" and stress nationalism in times of crisis, the events of the mid-nineteenth century show that rulers are more concerned with protecting their own class and its privileges than with the well-being of their citizens.[17] Privileged classes sell out less-privileged citizens of their countries to preserve their privilege – as the Spanish did in this period.[18]

After Napoleon's defeat, Bourbon monarchs returned to rule France. When the reactionary Charles X tried to undo all that remained of the revolution – restoring aristocratic privilege to the detriment of the middle class – France rose in revolution. Workers, artisans, students, writers, and men and women demanding a republic (Republicans) erected barricades in the streets – more barricades in more places than ever before or since. (The 1830 revolution turned the barricade into a symbol of democratic insurrection.) From behind the barricades they fought soldiers and police, who were reluctant to fire on the people. Charles abdicated, raising the revolutionaries' hope for a republic. But Charles was not the only impediment to a wider sharing of power: a powerful group of bankers, merchants, and industrialists put the duc d'Orléans on the throne (calling him Louis Philippe of *the French* – not of *France*), and granted franchise to 100,000 more males. The heroism of the revolutionaries won nothing except a new consciousness, an awareness of common cause with workers which generated a proletarian-socialist revolutionary movement in Paris.

Workers, students, and writers formed secret societies to study socialist theory, publish attacks and satires, and mount riots. In 1834 the government outlawed political associations, and Paris and Lyon became war zones. The army massacred hundreds and arrested 2000 republican leaders. The elite's stubborn rejection of even moderate change drove moderates into the republican camp. Revolutionaries circumvented the law against political meetings by holding "banquets," and in 1847 mounted a nationwide protest that culminated in a mass banquet in Paris in February 1848. The government effort to squelch it ignited revolution.

Marshal Bugeaud, notorious for his brutality during an 1834 uprising, was ordered to crush this one. He sent four columns of troops to clear the streets. Untrained in street fighting, the troops were soon overwhelmed. Bugeaud's withdrawal demoralized Louis Philippe and his advisors: the king abdicated. A provisional government of ten male parliamentarians and journalists was appointed (seven republicans and three socialists, including Louis Blanc), with George Sand as unofficial minister of information. Paris bubbled with activity: republicans from abroad came to observe and enjoy the great event, newly legal political clubs sprang up everywhere, political journals proliferated.

Jeanne Deroin (1810?–1894), who had tried to organize a worker's union and was imprisoned in the 1840s, resurfaced during the 1848 revolutions. With the other Saint-Simonians (Eugénie Niboyet, Suzanne Voilquin, and Désirée Verret) who had co-edited the first feminist newspaper, *La femme libre,* in 1832, Deroin founded a political club and a new journal, *La voix des femmes.* It called for marriage reform, the right to divorce, and economic opportunities for women. The first issue argued that improving men's lot does not necessarily improve women's – a fact that has had to be rediscovered in every new feminist generation.

Blanc tried to set up a system of national workshops to train workers, distribute goods as a cooperative, and offer unemployment benefits, but apart from a midwifery training school for women, they became only a set of traditional charity workshops, offering minimal wages for hard, often pointless labour. In a France racked by unemployment, the project drew over 60,000 people to Paris in a few months, terrifying the middle class. Under pressure from radicals, the government decreed universal male suffrage; but at the next election men elected mainly conservatives. The government closed national workshops to new members, claiming they drained the budget.

Spontaneous mass uprisings at the Pantheon and Bastille cut Paris in two. Barricades went up in the poorer eastern *quartiers*; people seized weapons from gun shops or homes. Without an overall plan, and with only local leaders, 40,000–50,000 people took to the streets. The government later claimed the rebels were rootless vagabonds, but most were small-scale artisans, skilled workers established in their crafts and communities, men and women desperate enough to risk death to express their wishes.[19] They were crushed. This time the government imported rural soldiers willing to shoot city folk. The artist Meissonier, a captain in the National Guard, described a common scene: "When the barricade in the rue de la Mortellerie was taken, I . . . saw the defenders shot down, hurled out of windows, the ground strewn with corpses, the earth red with blood."

After three days of cruel street fighting and 12,000 arrests, the government hunted people down, sending most to Algerian labour camps, crippling the Parisian left for a decade. The defeat was so total and brutal that it annihilated radicalism not just in France, but throughout Europe. The government immediately held an election, hoping a strong president could silence dissidence. The reactionary favourite, Louis Napoleon Bonaparte, Napoleon's nephew, won overwhelmingly. Conservatives voted for him, hoping he would protect their property from the radicals; workers liked him because his book, *The Extinction of Pauperism*, offered surefire schemes for prosperity, and because he had a relationship with Blanc and anarchist Pierre Proudhon. Louis Napoleon wanted to be dictator. He won Catholic support by immediately returning control over schools to the Church and re-establishing French deference to the Pope. He won over the workers and the bourgeoisie by creating old-age insurance and laws favouring business. Three years later, he was elected dictator by a plebiscite.

News of the revolution flew across Europe, inspiring political actions in many cities; in nearly every European city with over 50,000 inhabitants in Western and Central Europe, the working poor rebelled.[20] They toppled the rulers of the Austrian Empire, rulers of German and Italian petty states, and temporarily discomfited aristocrats across Europe. But the revolutionaries were not united, and after all the killing and suffering new elites replaced the old: stratification did not vanish.

The 1848 revolutions did not produce democratic socialism or unify states. Nor did they much improve conditions for most people. But they changed the political system of Western Europe by replacing the aristocracy with a bourgeois elite. For the rest of the century the "grande bourgeoisie" – industrialists, bankers, and high-ranking civil servants – comprised a ruling class as adamantly opposed to democracy or socialism as any aristocracy. Authoritarian regimes stopped liberal reforms at the Rhine, and eastern European rulers were successful at suppressing their revolutions. Huge estates remained in Central and Eastern Europe, but the serfs were given their freedom, which somewhat eased their condition. In some states, reform governments were succeeded by repressive regimes more sophisticated in repression, although more aware of the potential danger of revolution and also of the necessity of integrating the working classes into larger society through education. French, Prussian, and Austrian governments began to offer primary education to the masses. Western governments permitted protest to be gradually institutionalized in trade unions and political clubs.

Parisians rose up again in March 1871, forming the Paris

Commune and declaring themselves autonomous. Thousands of women participated in this struggle with the Versailles government, literally interposing their bodies between the Versailles troops sent to suppress the revolt and the Paris National Guard defending the Commune on the Montmartre hills.[21] They drove ambulances, sewed uniforms, wrote for the Commune press, taught Commune children in newly reclaimed public schools, and defended the city of Paris on gunboats along the Seine. Women, newly claiming public space as "citoyennes" (women citizens), were creating the Commune as a structure in which women and workers could rule themselves. But to the government and the elite, women's presence in this transformed public space was a transgression and defamation of the sexual geography of public order that supported the French republic itself.[22] They saw women in the public sphere as whores, thieves, she-men with the audacity to carry guns and wear pants.

The Paris Commune fell, but revolutionary ideals continued to be transmitted over generations by artists and writers. Daumier was often imprisoned for his satirical cartoons on Louis Philippe; in 1849, Dostoievsky was condemned to die (and marched to a wall but not shot) for revolutionary activities; Pushkin was punished for involvement with the Decembrists. George Sand influenced the leaders of the 1848 uprising (as well as Marx and Bakunin), and wrote position papers for the provisional government. She went on writing sympathetically about women and the poor.

In 1848 the *revolutionary* government barred women from political activity and closed Jeanne Deroin's feminist journal. But she ran for the legislature in 1849, and then organized a federation of workers' unions with Pauline Roland, another ex-Saint-Simonian. Both were arrested by the republican government in 1850. Roland died in 1851 and Deroin went into exile in England, but their ideas influenced women like Flora Tristan who, with other feminists, placed female exploitation within a broad, coherent context, influencing people like the painter Rosa Bonheur and initiating a tradition of social protest that was resuscitated by the British women who invented the social protest novel.

These two decades of war, and the ideas and new sense of power engendered by revolutions of rights affected institutions in every major European state. However, changes in borders, laws, and institutions were minor compared to the profound transformation of the political atmosphere. Revolution raised consciousness everywhere. Nationalist and socialist agitation continued, workers formed unions, and feminism became broader-based. The tide of *thought* had turned. Hobsbawm interestingly suggests that autocratic governments tended to mistrust all intellectuals, even reactionaries, because once people accepted their right to think rather than the obligation to obey, the end of despotism was in sight. After 1850 all major European states were forced to grant more democracy. But the new elites ruled by more devious methods. What did not change was male domination of women – everywhere.[23]

CHAPTER 4

MIDDLE-CLASS WOMEN
IN ENGLAND

A NEW GENDER IDEOLOGY PERVADED the English-speaking world in the mid-nineteenth century. As ideas of rights and social justice spread more widely, ideas about women *narrowed*. In this period, women lost property rights; they also lost legal identity at marriage and were forced into domestic roles as tight as their corsets.

The Cult of Domesticity (or Cult of True Womanhood or Doctrine of Separate Spheres), which was central to nineteenth-century middle-class thinking about gender, slowly filtered down to the working class. It was an unattainable ideal for black Americans: an area of failure for black men who could not support women as the ideal required and for black women, who, even if supported, could never be "ladies." While many today scorn the image of a pious, sexually pure, submissive, domestic woman as false or constricting, it remains powerful in many media. The ideal was invested not just with moral superiority, but with *glamour*: the "lady," with her upswept hair, high-buttoned blouse, tiny waist, flowing skirt, bent neck, and sweet smile, sat on a velvet couch, protected from the harshness of life, an icon to be desired and emulated.

Revolutionary changes in printing made possible national distribution of magazines, the first mass medium. Magazines (often edited by women) and books like Catherine Beecher's *Domestic Economy* and *Godey's Ladies' Book* by Sarah Josepha Hale became the purveyors of woman's new image. It was still purveyed in the 1950s via *Good Housekeeping, Ladies' Home Journal, Woman's Day*, and romance novels. In this myth, a standard against which real women were measured, Woman was the pivotal figure in a morality upheld by religion, law, and science. Her function was to stand still yet do what was necessary for men to devote their energies to aggressive, acquisitive competition. Woman's moral excellence exemplified virtue; without it, men claimed, society would fall into viciousness. Western morality was split like Chinese yin and yang between a public sphere, ruled by men, and a separate, private domain, ruled by women. The marketplace was distinct from the home. All sexual divisions of experience are said to be complementary, to offer "separate but equal" powers, but all really maintain inequality. Men could enter the private realm – indeed, owned and controlled it – but women were excluded from the public.

The idea of True Womanhood grew partly out of Republican Motherhood, the sop men threw to women who had supported the American Revolution and wanted its promised rewards – liberty and equality. True Womanhood was defined by four virtues: piety, purity, submissiveness, and domesticity. Religion assigned Woman the role of guardian of the family against the moral corruption of the marketplace.[1] To fulfil this role, she had steadfastly to guard her "purity," the source of her power. Purity essentially meant asexuality. Woman's transcendence of sexuality gave her the moral force she was to use to cool or contain male sexual passion, which (presumably) was beyond male control. This concept is staggering. Most previous societies gave men control over women's bodies, but none considered women asexual or would have tolerated women's thwarting male desire. What was going on here?

Medieval Christian European men had seen Woman as a temptress threatening male godliness. But godliness took on a new character in nineteenth-century England and America. Divine traits were apportioned one to a sex. Especially after Darwin, theorists considered selfish aggressiveness a necessary trait in man's battle for survival of the fittest: virtuous men were killers in the struggle that was life. To complement this new definition of Man, Woman was redefined as an incarnation of love, the other divine aspect.

A new class was emerging. Lacking the semi-divine ancestry claimed by aristocrats, the middle class (or bourgeoisie) had to fight for the privileges formerly reserved to nobles – the right to make policy and law, to govern. Men who rose to this class had the energy and will for lonely struggle in the service of a new god, success. They became rich and powerful, but their success required putting power foremost and sacrificing most pleasures. The greatest threat to such dedication was thought to be sexual desire, which leads men to lose control and abandon the goal, or cede it to another who should properly be subordinate.

It was considered self-evident that the sexes were different species with different aptitudes. Man was active, Woman passive; Man was the "architect," Woman "the soul" of the house. Innate male intellectual capacity for creation, invention, and synthesis justified Man's role as doer, creator, and discoverer. Nature denied Woman such abilities: her judgment was fit only for detail and trivialities. Therefore the role best suited to her, the occupation that most satisfied her dependent nature was, as social historian W.R. Greg wrote, the role of servant. "They [female servants] are attached to others and are connected with other existences, which they embellish, facilitate and serve. In a word they fulfill both essentials of a woman's being: they are supported by, and minister to, men." In herself Woman was nothing: "[Women] are . . . from their own constitution, and from the station they occupy in the world . . . relative creatures." As real men dedicate themselves to domination, true women dedicate themselves to service.[2]

As objects of male desire, women in patriarchal societies are always held responsible for human sexuality, but now men were demanding that women thwart male sexuality. That women lack desire was an idea that had floated around in the West for centuries – you can find it in Shakespeare – but asexuality never *defined* the female until the nineteenth century. (Indeed, patriarchal societies often see women as sexually ravenous.) A new society needed a new Woman: "In men the sexual desire is inherent and spontaneous. In the other sex, the desire is dormant, if not non-existent," wrote Greg. Virtue transformed Woman from Eve to Mary, the "angel in the house." Motherhood, which had been one task among many, became women's central task, as the work that women had done for centuries was now performed outside the home. Society blinded women to diminishment by haloing them: Woman was "the natural and therefore divine, guide, purifier, inspirer of the man," wrote Charles Kingsley.[3] Her power derived from submission to Man, but she was the centre of the family, the source of all thought, feeling, and influence, with absolute power over the spirit of man, peace, war, and the fate of humanity: "The hand that rocks the cradle/ Is the hand that rules the world."

Of course, not every woman was a True Woman: working-class and black women were barely human. Class was of the essence, and even middle-class women had to prove themselves True by remaining virgins before marriage, faithful after it, and by creating a safe, spiritual domestic environment with every creature comfort. Home – the realm of Woman – existed, like her, as Man's reward, offering relief from a harsh cruel world. By serving as nurse, cook, child-tender, spiritual advisor, midwife, housekeeper, teacher, floral arranger, and producer of needlework, Woman tempered, soothed, and transformed the male, who was hardened by the necessity of acquisitive aggressiveness into a being capable of virtue.

The actual situation this myth masked was not pretty, and the condition of this paragon far from divine. According to law and the precepts of religion, a husband owned his wife, who might have "no will of her own, no opinions, nor any feelings but in accordance with the will of her lord and master." Both servants and wives were subject to a male master's extensive control, one that reached into all areas of the subordinate's life.[4] Wives and servants did the same work; all but the wealthiest women did manual labour in the household, and all wives were responsible for managing it and any children. Both were physically abused and threatened with beating, a major source of men's control, more often used on wives than servants. Despite much evidence of widespread male violence in the home, not until the twentieth century was it openly admitted that wife-beating is not limited to working-class men. Nevertheless, women, not men, were scrutinized for sin. Wives were supposed to satisfy husbands' desires miraculously on whatever money they were given. The worst sin a working-class wife could commit, Françoise Basch writes, was to envy the privileged classes, to harbour "that sense of injustice which is the seed of social revolt."

Nineteenth-century ladies' clothes (which few working-class women could afford, fortunately for them) emphasized maternity and constriction. At puberty, girls were put into corsets to minimize waistlines, laced in so tightly that their ribs became deformed. Some died from the constriction, but all corseted women had trouble breathing: the "fainting-couch" had a real function. Corsets pushed the breasts up, exaggerating their size; bustles exaggerated the size of buttocks, making women all "T and A." They also wore layers of long skirts, sometimes over hoops, which impeded mobility considerably. Dress reform was an issue in feminist campaigns that urged women to wear bloomers (long full pantaloons) or at least to eschew corsets.

Women and Institutions in England

Science on Women

Scientists based their assertions of women's inferiority in every dimension except the moral on solid "facts": women, for example, were weaker than men physically. And they were: working women had poor, often inadequate diets and were overworked at jobs that ruined their health; "ladies" never exercised and wore deforming clothes. All women lacked the self-esteem vital to good health. Man had so dominated Nature that he had transformed the longer-lived, more enduring sex into "the weaker sex." To be female was to be sick: doctors blamed this on the female procreative system. Women, a different species from men, grew not from a rib but a uterus, "a highly perilous possession" exerting "paramount power" over them. A professor wrote in 1870 that "the Almighty, in creating the female sex, had taken the uterus and built up a woman around it." Male doctors fixated on the uterus, finding it the source of every female disease and the reason women suffered twice as many ailments as men. Tuberculosis in men was caused by environmental factors; in women by reproductive malfunction.[5]

All exclusively female physical functions were considered inherently pathological. Menstruation and menopause endangered life. And if puberty developed all of the *male* body ("the principles of life superabound in his constitution, and he vigorously performs all the noble pursuits assigned him by nature"), it made girls moody, depressed, petulant, capricious, and sometimes sexually promiscuous ("women . . . always preserve some of the infantile constitution").[6] To survive puberty, young ladies (only ladies could afford to consult a physician for this "disease") were ordered to pursue a strict regimen of domestic tasks like cooking, bed-making, cleaning, and child-tending. The cure for menopause was exactly the same; doctors claimed it was aggravated by sex, socializing, gaiety, or any mental activity whatsoever. There is great hostility in the medical literature on menopausal women: male physicians loathed them, calling them physically repulsive, stupid, dull, and jealous of the young.[7]

Despite the powerful uterus, women were *by nature* asexual. William Acton, a doctor in the Royal Medical and Chirurgical Society, wrote on urinary and sexual diseases and prostitution. In 1857 he published *The Functions and Disorders of the Reproductive Organs*, a work that amazingly ignores completely the anatomy and physiology of *female* reproductive organs. Discussing female sexuality only in relation to male desire and attitudes toward marriage, and anxious to allay male fears of married sex, Acton offers a fascinating view of female sexuality. The mistresses and courtesans a young man frequents before his marriage are unbalanced, nymphomaniac; the lady he will marry, on the other hand, will certainly be ignorant of sex and without desire: "Love of home, children and domestic duties, are the only passions they feel." Marital consummation will cause her only suffering and distress, but the husband may rest assured that "the act of coition takes place but rarely in the life of the couple."

Indeed, most nineteenth-century ladies *were* ignorant of sex when they married, and perhaps many did lack desire. Doctors did not always invent their perceptions: their writings betray that they, the experts, had not the slightest idea of how to make love to – as opposed to have sex with – a woman. If doctors did not understand female bodies, ordinary men were unlikely to. If a woman had absorbed the fact that sex was sinful, and feared the mysterious act, she may have disliked being banged, especially since she was the one who could get pregnant. Freud was not the only doctor ignorant of the workings of the clitoris, the organ second only to the uterus in destructive power.

The first use of the emerging field of gynecology was the surgical removal of female sexual organs – clitoris, foreskin, or ovaries. Clitoridectomies were said to cure "mental disorders" like "sexual desire or sexual behaviour," pathological when they appeared in women. They were performed occasionally in England and often in America after the 1860s. The last known case occurred in the United States in 1948, to "cure" a five-year-old girl who masturbated. At the end of the nineteenth century "great surgical operations are performed on girls, veritable tortures: cauterization of the clitoris with red-hot irons was, if not habitual, at least fairly frequent."[8] And women who were too "masculine" – assertive, unruly, or aggressive – were by a strange twist of logic "cured" by losing their ovaries.

Ignorance is forgivable when it is helpless, but poetry shows that people have known about clitoral function for millennia: nineteenth-century physicians could have discovered it if they'd thought twice. That they did not, but high-handedly defined female sexuality without bothering to study female bodies or consult women, demonstrates the psychological ambience of the period. Men simply nullified female reality, refused to deal with it or with contraception. Bearing, feeding, and tending too many children killed women, and men who loved and tried to support families were sometimes swamped by ten or fifteen children. Few wanted so many, yet nineteenth-century society utterly forbade contraception.

Contraceptives existed; Owenites and the Oneidans knew of some. Between 1820 and 1826, clandestine propaganda for contraception was published but little else appeared over the century.[9] Medical literature shows that abortion, the most primitive form of birth control, was widely used after the 1860s, but contraception was taboo until Margaret Sanger: even feminists opposed it. Contraception gives women a degree of control over their lives and bodies, which was not allowed. Yet ironically, as motherhood was being touted as a spiritual and civic duty, white middle-class women's fertility rates steadily dropped. A woman's average number of children fell from 7.04 in 1800 to 6.14 in 1840, 4.24 in 1880, and 3.56 in 1900; presumably "moral superiority" had successfully restrained male sexuality.

Despite their supposed Natural Aptitude for motherhood, women were historically thought to contribute little to the conception of children. Pre-nineteenth-century scientific accounts of reproduction attribute the form or "active" element of embryos to males.[10] Aristotle held that women, "passive" reproducers, merely provided space and material sustenance for the fetus – the oven for the bun. Females were infertile males; menstrual fluid, "stunted semen," generated females when a surplus interfered with development. Aristotle thought both sexes the same species, but saw females as "mutilated males." Galen believed, with Hippocrates, that both sexes produce seed, weak and strong varieties: strong seed from both parents produced males, weak seed females. Both parents make a material contribution but only males provide the active element in forming an embryo. With the male as model, Galen saw ovaries as "testes," drawing them to resemble testicles and the uterus as an inverted penis. Seventeenth-century medical authorities urged couples who wanted male offspring to eat hot or dry meats, avoid intercourse until "the seed was well developed," or arrange their bodies during copulation so the seed fell to the right side of the womb.

There were a few scientists after 1500 who considered the reproductive function of both sexes perfect and distinct, and females not defective versions of males. For Hieronymus Fabricius (1537–1619), semen stimulated female organs to produce eggs; Anton Van Leeuwenhoek (1632–1723) believed female eggs existed only to nourish the sperm, the source of embryonic form. Swiss physiologist Albrecht von Haller (1708–1777) thought the embryo existed in miniature in a pre-fertilized ovum. Not until German scientist Karl Ernst von Baer (1792–1876) used a microscope were scientists sure that female ova even existed. Observing female dogs, von Baer concluded that embryos originate in ova formed in the ovary *before* fertilization. Males *did not* create female life.

Scientists, who believed in domination and were certain there was only one true parent, began to fear that the female was that one. The argument that the true parent was the one who carried the ova much disturbed the medical profession. Embryology was placed on a modern scientific basis when Oskar Hertwig (1849–1922), observing the actual fusion of male and female nuclei within the egg of a sea urchin, demonstrated in 1879 that only one spermatozoon entered the ovum of a starfish. It had taken nearly 2500 years to "prove" that mothers as well as fathers passed on traits.

Nineteenth-century medical research "proved" that women's reproductive organs controlled their brains and that males were more intelligent than females. Phrenologists studied bumps on the skull that "proved" women, Jews, and Africans intellectually inferior to white Christian men. Nineteenth-century scientists assumed that large brains took up more space than small ones, that size meant greater intellect and complexity, and that the skull bulged to accommodate a large brain. When they found more bulges on the skulls of white Christian males than others, their assumptions were confirmed. And when evidence did not support the theory (and some phrenological evidence even demonstrated the opposite), researchers simply suppressed the data and manufactured the desired evidence.

Law on Women

Married women were legally non-existent in nineteenth-century England; they could not enter into contracts, own property, or control children. A woman's husband was the absolute master of her body, property, and children; she was a chattel. *The law did not recognize mothers*, stipulating that children must obey only fathers: "During the father's life, the mother is entitled to no power . . . but only to respect." If a father died, his nearest male relative became his children's guardian. A husband could force a wife to stay with him against her will, even confining her. A woman who committed adultery lost all rights to maintenance and could be legally separated and abandoned, but men were not penalized for adultery. In fact, a man whose wife left because he was unfaithful could pursue her and sue anyone who took her in; she could not get support without a court order establishing need. Only those with £1000 to pay Parliament for a Private Member's Bill could divorce. Few women, but about two hundred men managed this before 1857.[11]

Separated wives had no rights to their children, not even to visitation. Fathers automatically got custody. Yet philosophers insisted that women did not need the vote because husbands adequately represented their interests, because, men claimed, women and men had identical interests, because, in law, man and wife were one flesh.

As laws "protecting" working women locked them into more complete dependence on men, other laws restricted their options. The Reform Act of 1832, which extended suffrage to more males, inserted the word "male" into voting qualifications for the first time in British history. Earlier, the few women who owned large pieces of property had been able to vote. But when in this period a female property owner petitioned Parliament to allow single females with the necessary pecuniary qualifications to vote, the reformed democratic, egalitarian House of Commons burst into laughter.[12]

European women were similarly disinherited, as men everywhere legally wrote them out of rights to property and control of their bodies. In terms of rights, the nineteenth century was women's nadir. From the late twelfth century, men had steadily eroded women's rights, succeeding in the nineteenth in extirpating them entirely – as working-class women's wretched degradation and middle-class women's silent misery attested. But some men were horrified by this situation, and women were down but not out. Their struggle for economic, legal, and social liberation was a major element in the ferment that characterizes this century.

Most British reformers shunned any suggestion of radical change in social structures. Both socialism and feminism were anathema. Reformers of both sexes took for granted that women had a "special" talent for mothering and that their vocation was the family. Few pointed to the contradiction between women's reality and their exalted image. In *Society in America* (1837), political reformer Harriet Martineau mocked the idea of women's influence, their power to sway "the judgment and will of man through the heart . . . .One might as well try to dissect the morning mist." Bessie Rayner Parkes questioned "this mysterious moral fluid"; Marion Reid compared women's "all-powerful so-much-talked-of influence" with their real lack of rights, remarking that instead of "With all my worldly goods I thee endow," a groom should say "What is yours is mine; and what is mine is *my own*."[13]

Most British feminists focused on a specific injustice like

divorce law or single women's difficulty supporting themselves. Caroline Norton tirelessly argued that courts – not fathers' whims – automatically grant wives and separated mothers custody of children under seven and the right to visit older ones. The day before John Stuart Mill married Harriet Taylor in 1851, he wrote a solemn denunciation of the "odious powers" conferred on husbands by marriage. In 1855 Barbara Leigh Smith convened some women to pressure Parliament for a bill allowing married women to keep their own property. Anna Jameson illustrated single women's problems by using 1851 census data – there were half a million more women than men in England; three-quarters of single women lived on their own earnings. In 1865 Harriet Martineau showed that a third of women over twenty-one supported themselves.

Their pressure bore some fruit. An 1839 law allowed mothers to petition courts for custody of children under seven and the right to visit older ones. The 1857 Matrimonial Causes Bill eased divorce for the poor by allowing it in cases of adultery, cruelty, or desertion – but only men could sue for divorce on grounds of adultery. Women had to show that a man's adultery had been aggravated by desertion, cruelty, rape, buggery, or bestiality. (This double standard lasted until *1929.*) The bill also allowed women whose husbands had deserted them to petition for protection of their assets, and legally separated women to ask for *feme sole* status in regard to property acquired by inheritance, gifts, or earnings (this status acknowledged a woman the owner of her goods and chattels, able to make and be bound by contracts, take responsibility for debts, sue, and be sued). A *feme sole* had the same legal rights as a man but not the same political rights – all women, of any status, were barred from professions, universities, political office, and the vote.

In 1857 Leigh Smith and other feminists founded the Association for the Promotion of the Employment of Women to ease "the unhappy condition of women who had to earn their bread." It ran training programs, urging employers to hire women in expanding areas like clerical work. In 1858 "the ladies of

Langham Place" – Barbara Leigh Smith Bodichon, Parkes, Adelaide Procter, and Jessie Boucherett – launched the first English feminist newspaper to be entirely written and published by women, *The English Women's Journal*,[14] which became the hub of British feminist agitation. As feminist networks expanded, the *Journal* described Emily Davies' campaign to open public exams to girls and found a women's college, suffragists lobbying Parliament, new women's clubs, model housing projects, and unusual jobs that were available.

Historians consider the decade 1867–77 to be a turning point in the Victorian era. The second Reform Act of 1867 extended the vote to men of the lower-middle and better-off working class, another step toward democracy. Mill tried to amend this bill to substitute the word "person" for "man" to open the door to votes for women. His amendment was defeated but seventy-three Parliamentarians voted for it. The same year, a commission inquiring into schools called feminists Emily Davies, Frances Buss, and Mill to testify. Its report led to swift improvements in secondary and higher education for women, enabling Davies two years later to found Girton College, the first English university to admit women.

In 1868 birth control was publicly discussed for the first time; in 1870 the important Married Woman's Property Act was passed under strong unified feminist pressure. This gave wives the right to their own earnings, revenues, inheritances, investments, rents, and cash gifts over £200. An 1873 law granted courts the power (it was not required) to give mothers custody of children up to sixteen, but in 1878 mothers got custody of children under ten only if the father had committed "aggravated assault."

Women's legal status intensified their inclination to live in homosocial worlds and to form strong bonds with female kin; they used female networks to counterbalance their lack of authority in the family.[15] By helping and supporting each other and leaving their property to each other, women exerted collective moral, social, and financial pressure on family men.[16] A disfranchised caste, women created a self-sustaining world: alimony was rare, so female relations helped divorced women; a woman about to give birth, knowing she faced death, relied on her sisters to protect her children from a future stepmothers' abuse. Young widows turned to female kin for emotional and economic support, and older ones depended on daughters to tend them in illness.

Religion on Women

Institutions have contradictory effects. Nineteenth-century religion bolstered the imprisoning image of the pure Victorian wife and mother, but it also offered women another identity, embracing them in a community in which they could use other talents and access an authority more powerful than that of their husbands. By the late eighteenth century, women dominated most religious congregations in numbers and activity. But after 1850 many feminists attacked religion as the main bulwark of sexual hierarchy, and the root of female oppression.

Nineteenth-century Christianity sentimentalized the home, with its religion of domesticity under women's moral influence. The clergy denounced women's efforts to expand their role beyond the home as threatening the balance of power in the family and the balance of moral forces in the state. That women had a unique moral mission was an idea popular with both feminists and anti-feminists. For male and female anti-feminists, it made confinement at home palatable by exalting Woman ruling the world from her home in purity and righteousness. For feminists, it was a basis for legitimacy: if women were morally superior, society should heed them. But many feminists denied there was an essential, innate femininity, a single, universal female character.

Anti-feminists were not unaware of the contradiction in the new female role. One woman wrote: "It might seem inconsistent to claim for woman a spiritual role at least equal to that of her husband and at the same time accede to her social subordination [but] the one quality on which woman's value and influence depends is the renunciation of self."[17] The anonymous author of *Domestic Tyranny*, *or Women in Chains* (1840) disagreed:

> Far be it from my intention to claim or uphold any privi-
> lege which would in the least degree militate against the
> Scriptural injunctions, "Wives submit yourselves to your
> husbands, as is fit in the Lord." I would at the same time
> draw attention to the particular terms of this command-
> ment, "as is fit in the Lord," which certainly imply not a
> degraded or inferior being in the scale of His creation, or
> one who was unworthy or incompetent to appreciate such
> an injunction, but on the contrary, it is particularly
> addressed to them as responsible and self-governing agents,
> who are also required to search the Scriptures to know the
> will of the Lord.

The author's scriptural search led her to conclude that wife-beating,
male appropriation of female property, and the denial of the vote
were not part of a Divine Plan; rather "it . . . seem[ed] implanted in
our nature by the Almighty to rebel against oppression."

The nineteenth-century English Christian revival (like that in
twentieth-century America) was overtly anti-democratic and systematically suppressed ideas tending to female liberation. Women,
the mainstay of virtually all nineteenth-century congregations, were
allowed only auxiliary roles in revivalist churches. They were cary-
atids, woman-shaped pillars supporting the roofs of temples owned
and controlled by men. Ministers who preached that women were
"God's own repositories" refused to let them direct philanthropic
activities; only splinter Methodist sects let women preach in the
1830s. British women of the period, feminists or not, shared an
evangelical frame of reference.

As the century advanced, the cult of domesticity generated
opposing tendencies. Middle-class women used their "moral superiority" to redefine and expand the private sphere; working-class
women, especially the better-off, adopted middle-class values.

Working-class men became increasingly opposed to their wives' working outside the home. The ideal working-class wife had been an essential, if secondary, provider who also maintained the household; now the ideal working-class wife was a housewife, an unpaid servant. The new ideal was not foisted on working-class women: they chose it. Of their few options, staying home to raise their children was the least onerous form of oppression open to them.

Single Women

It was crucial for women's well-being, integrity, and pride to find a way to feel and act independent. This was difficult for single women – and there were a great many in this period. Biology caused women to outnumber men in most nations; there were not enough men for all women even if all men married. But single women were supposed to devote themselves to serving their families. Women who stayed single in order not to be domestic servants, but to study or make art were thwarted by this demand. Even if their household had servants and they were not consumed by domestic work, propriety required behaviour that killed the spirit. Economically dependent, and suffering the servility that doing tedious, unchallenging, repetitive domestic work entails, single women were miserable. They were forbidden to engage in any physical or mental activity and, confined by dress, custom, and law, could do little more than sit at windows gazing out at life. Tennyson in 1852 wrote "The Lady of Shalott" about a young woman for whom life happens in a mirror on her wall.

Single women were guilt-ridden about undone domestic tasks, and most profoundly, their failure to use their abilities, talents, and initiative. Even more than the wife, the spinster, representing purity, goodness, and virginity, was supposed to sacrifice herself to all who needed her. Many succumbed to mysterious debilitating diseases. Brilliant American Alice James, sister of Henry and William, suffered most of her life from strange ailments. Some of her diary entries suggest she was not entirely unaware of the connection between her ill health and her repression of rage: "How sick one gets of being 'good,' how much I should respect myself if I could burst out and make everyone wretched for 24 hours." Trying to be as pliant and submissive as society required, she felt suffocated (like Edith Wharton, born fourteen years later) and died at forty-four in 1892.

Even if single middle-class women came from well-to-do families, many had to make a living. Inheriting a house or some money no more guaranteed survival than working for wages: single women were haunted by money worries. But the nineteenth century was the first period in history in which middle-class women could live on their own wages (however poorly) free from conjugal or clerical authority. The struggle to accomplish this independence transformed some of them into leaders in the battle for women's rights, heroic pioneers who laid a foundation on which later generations built institutions extending far beyond their plans.[18] Realizing the feminist vision – changing society while enjoying themselves – they were bored when not working in their vocations. They did not enter male arenas like politics, but expanded the domestic realm to include workhouse, hospital, and school.

In the eighteenth century, a year or two of "finishing" school became fashionable for middle-class daughters. Despite the poor education that these schools often provided, they broke the isolation that prevented female solidarity: girls of the same age and class formed close friendships with each other at a formative and anxious time of life. Nineteenth-century families still educated their daughters at such schools, and they too often developed lifelong friendships even though few lived near or saw each other much after marriage. Many of these friendships were "romantic," youthful lesbian attachments. Since women were supposed to be asexual, such relations were not considered threats to society but rather as preparation for marriage. Indeed, married women used them to release subversive longings: Charlotte Brontë confided her deepest fears to Ellen Nussey, Florence Nightingale to "Clarkey," her friend Mary Clarke in Paris, and Geraldine Jewsbury bolstered Jane Carlyle. What labelled a woman "deviant" was her refusal to marry; only when women's communities offered an alternative to marriage did their friendships come to be seen as a threat. Few working women could afford to live alone, and communal living was cheaper and more pleasant than lodging in a boardinghouse. Women's communities offered companionship and privacy, fostering self-development.

Education and Women

From the 1840s women struggled for female education, opening secondary schools and offering lecture series. In 1848 Queen's College London was founded to educate governesses so they could demand higher wages.[19] Open to girls over twelve, it taught secondary school subjects but, like advanced educational institutions, provided lectures and grades. In 1849 Elizabeth Reid, a firm feminist, founded Bedford College and insisted that women themselves govern it. Queen's and Bedford were non-residential; they emphasized remedial work to prepare girls for degree-level study. But girls living at home were drained by domestic drudgery.

Female colleges opened in Oxford (Royal Holloway) and Cambridge (Westfield) but, lacking sufficient financial backing, they had inadequate libraries and teachers and so failed to draw students. Many male journalists were outraged at the thought that women might study independently, free from domestic labour; families reluctantly bore the expense of educating daughters, whose education, unlike their brothers', would neither add lustre to the family name nor prepare them for a profession or high-level job in the civil service. For women, college was just a time away from home to live and learn together; the only profession open to them was teaching. Still, the major problem for promoters of female higher education was girls' inadequate early training.

In 1867–68, a Commission of Enquiry on Schools found educational institutions deficient and declared in favour of higher education for women – in principle. Women like Davies and Buss, who had been working for this end for some time, moved swiftly: in 1869, Davies (1830–1921) opened Hitchin (later Girton) College. She knew that without rigorous training, women could hardly pass Oxford or Cambridge honours exams, which were geared to boys' preparation, years of classical and mathematical training. Women's failure of such exams would be attributed to intellectual inferiority; if they passed an easier exam, their claim on "men's" jobs would be weakened. Davies determined that her students would study for the Cambridge "Tripos" exams, following exactly the same course as men. But boys' education began at seven, and girls were already behind when they began the compulsory program of Greek, mathematics, and classics; Davies was not even sure Cambridge examiners would grade women's papers.

The examiners did agree to do so, and in 1872 three females passed the Tripos exams with (unofficial) honours. The women felt they had won a major victory and had proven themselves men's intellectual equals despite their erratic training. In 1881, although women were still barred from university lectures, they were officially admitted to university exams by convincing sympathetic dons to repeat their lectures for female audiences. Struggling steadily against the tide, by 1894 women took the same exams as men in all fields except medicine; by 1897 they were accepted marginally in the English university system.

The privileged women who attended residential colleges were probably the only women in England not required to do household labour and account to someone for every moment of their day. They could set their own rhythms and follow their own inclinations, in the company of others who delighted in learning. All college founders stressed the importance of a room of one's own. When Davies was planning Girton, she spent no money on landscaping but made sure each woman had a bed-sitting room — a space completely in her control, often for the first and last time in her life. The luxury of privacy was enhanced by the pleasure of community; these women retained their college friends and the memory of a female community throughout their lives. Many joined sisterhoods for social work and nursing.[20]

Female educators disagreed over whether education provided personal enrichment or preparation for a career. They were troubled that only a tiny elite could enjoy university education and that men still scorned them as incapable of furthering knowledge. Female teachers and administrators were trapped in a triple bind: despite their erratic schooling, they had to appear intellectually superior to men simply to be accepted as equal. They had to comport themselves rigidly in a respectable and conformist manner, and had the added burden of responsibility for students in an era when doctors declared that learning "unsexed" women and drained their "maternal energy," causing the "decline of the species." Physicians repeatedly attributed infertility, brain damage, or mental breakdown in a female patient to mental work. And female educators had to forfeit politics: Davies stopped supporting women's suffrage for fear of jeopardizing Girton's reputation.

Nevertheless, teaching was single women's most important occupation throughout the nineteenth and into the twentieth century. As democratic movements demanded universal education, more elementary and secondary schools were established in Britain. Educating children was considered appropriate work for women, an extension of their domestic role; it offered them a respected low-paid career, and teachers in boarding schools rediscovered the harmony of work and community of their college years.

Near the end of the century, men began to question their assumptions about women. Scientist Nicholas Cooke's book *Satan in Society* revealed facts, shocking at the time, about young girls' sexual habits. Authorities began to doubt that women were sexless, leading male "experts" to question the warmth and intimacy of women's relations with each other. This distrust arose just as female solidarity was creating a powerful political women's movement: suddenly, student-teacher relations were suspect as homosexual; schoolgirl crushes on teachers were said to cause permanent disturbance; friendship between teachers was labelled abnormal. While writers like D.H. Lawrence in *The Rainbow* (1915) and Clemence Dane in *Regiment of Women* (1917) portrayed lesbians as malevolent, power-hungry, and manipulating, everyone ignored the pervasive male homosexuality in Oxbridge colleges. Now female educators were suspect for both hetero- and homosexuality.

The Foundations of Nursing and Social Work

The middle class of the 1800s could remain unaware of the plight of the poor only by blinding themselves to it. Middle- and upper-class men had the political power to change the situation, but the poor could only agitate, threatening collective action, or attract sympathy by dying visibly in great numbers. They did both, and if most prosperous people averted their gaze, some tried to alleviate the situation. Male legislators passed laws to ease problems; men organized agencies dedicated to social welfare. Women formed organizations to press for legal change and did social work with the poor, usually directly.

Charitable work was permeated with class distinctions. Men and women established Protestant religious orders for women in high church (Anglican) and low (Evangelicals and Dissenters). Most low-church women started simple institutes to train, coordinate, and pay small wages to devout single working-class women who became visiting nurses (who also propagandized for religion). Middle- and upper-class women joined sisterhoods founded and dominated by high- and low-church male clerics, who dominated the public aspect and expected religious women to obey them in all church matters. But deaconesses and sisters carved out areas of expertise and power in male-dominated churches.

Middle-class women, who had been raised by money to a status "above nature," might patronize, despise, or fear lower-class women as an inferior species. But some began to work with them, albeit condescendingly. They helped some poor women, but they were also helping themselves. Their activities constitute the first major example of female solidarity across classes; their interaction forced both to recognize that their problems were often similar. This recognition fuelled the first large-scale feminist movement in history. For the first time since the emergence of patriarchy, women broke class and colour lines to support each other.

In 1813 Elizabeth Fry (1780–1845), a Quaker minister, wife of a banker and mother of (eventually) ten children, visited Newgate Prison. Three hundred women and their children, confined in two squalid wards, cooked, washed, ate, excreted, and slept on bare floors. The wards and their nearly naked occupants stank with filth. Without guide or precedent, Fry determined to amend these women's conditions and help them earn a living upon their release. She organized middle-class female volunteers to donate supplies and visit the prison every day; with the donated materials, the prisoners made clothes that Fry arranged to sell in a prison shop run by the volunteers. Profits went to the prisoners – half when their work was sold, half at their release. Fry also set up a school to teach children and young women to read, knit, and sew, and had cleaning equipment brought in for prisoners to scrub the wards and do laundry every Saturday. Contemporaries watched Newgate women's wards transformed into a well-run family or workshop.

A known expert on prison reform, Fry was called to testify on the subject, and visited almost every European country as a prison consultant. But British lawmakers favoured strict discipline and a "silent system," and did not heed her. In 1833, Fry founded a refuge for women prisoners at Kaiserswerth, near Dusseldorf, with German pastor Theodor Fliedner and his wife. This developed into a medical centre with a lunatic asylum, orphanage, infirmary, and hospital to train nurses, teachers, and "poor visitors" (welfare workers). By 1870 forty-two havens modelled on Kaiserswerth had been built and womaned with "sisters." Florence Nightingale, heroine of her age, fought to train there.[21]

Nineteenth-century hospitals were filthy corrupt warehouses

full of the dying poor, tended by old or alcoholic women, often ex-prostitutes. Authorities believed women had innate abilities to teach and nurse, yet they did not want ladies trained or paid, and discouraged pioneers who wanted to reform hospitals and nursing, which required recruiting and training a different kind of nurse. Florence Nightingale (1820–1910) transformed nursing from the most menial to the most exalted female job.

Believing no one but a sister would willingly do such work, the educated public identified nursing with religious commitment. Sisterhoods worked the way the public most admired – without pay. English reformers thronged to Kaiserswerth; and French Roman Catholic nuns and German Lutheran deaconesses initiated wide-scale reform movements, setting new standards of sanitation and conscientiousness. During an 1848 cholera epidemic in Devonport, Lydia Sellon set up a sisterhood to help the poor, and St. John's nurse training school opened in London.

Nightingale, of a wealthy pious family, was deeply religious; she heard a "call from God" when she was seventeen, but could not then act on it. Endowed with the energy and intellect of a genius, she found the life of a middle-class woman stifling to the point of death. "The family is . . . too narrow a field for the development of an immortal spirit, be that spirit male or female," she wrote in *Cassandra*. She rejected marriage with young journalist Richard Monckton Milnes because she did not want to live "someone else's life."[22] But she could not break away from her family (and did not until her thirties) or yet know what she wanted to do.

After a despairing youth, at the age of thirty-one she wrote in anguish, "What am I that [other women's] life is not good enough for me? Oh God what am I? . . . Why, oh my God cannot I be satisfied with the life that satisfies so many people? I am told that the conversation of all these good clever men ought to be enough for me. Why am I starving, desperate, diseased on it?" A year later, she had moved from guilt and self-hatred to criticism of society: "Why have women passion, intellect, moral activity – these three – and a place in society where no one of the three can be exercised?"[23]

She found herself when she decided to train as a nurse. Overcoming many obstacles, she studied at Kaiserswerth and Paris. When England went to war with Russia in 1854, she hounded the government to let her nurse the wounded. She took thirty-eight nurses to the Crimea, where they tended 10,000 men. (Of these nurses, twenty-four were Anglican or Roman Catholic.) Although Britain won the war, 118,000 British and allied soldiers died of cholera and other illnesses. Nightingale knew many deaths had been caused by poor sanitary conditions, which she had tried to improve. In 1856, on her return to England, she was celebrated as a national hero. Her fame enabled her to raise money to establish the Nightingale School of Nursing at St. Thomas' Hospital in London. She dedicated the rest of her life to raising standards in nursing and hospital care in the British Army, London slums, and India. Publicly she was self-sacrificing, but it was her adventurousness that inspired young girls of her period to make her their role model.

Nightingale opened her school in 1860 with fifteen pupils. She believed the key to improved medical care was hospital organization and staff training, and she made innovations that are now standard practice (describing them in an 1869 book).[24] Nurses had no rooms at hospitals, but slept in the same wards as male or female patients, or in wooden cages on landings. Nightingale had a wing built in St. Thomas' Hospital as a nurse's residence, and required that night nurses be given rest time during the day. She also demanded hot and cold water throughout the hospital, elevators, and other conveniences. Modelling her staff on the army, she treated trainees like soldiers at war against disease, dirt, and sin.

Nightingale chose St. Thomas' for her school because she trusted its matron, Mrs. Wardroper, who had reformed the nursing staff as soon as she was appointed in 1854. As Nightingale's "general," she helped set up a program requiring each probationer to account minutely for her time and undergo monthly evaluations of progress *and moral character* which entailed harsh punishments for trespasses like "making eyes" or wearing untidy uniforms. Probationers worked a fifteen-hour day, seven days a week, rising at 6:00 a.m., breakfasting, and making fourteen beds and washing each patient between 7:00 and 8:00. The ward sister came on duty at 8:00 and read prayers, then the "pros" washed all ward utensils – dressing bowls, spittoons, bedpans, et al.; at 10:00 they gave out snacks and helped with dressings. At 12:45, as they gobbled dinner to have time for rest, the ward nurse and sister served the patients in the ward.

At 1:30 the doctor made rounds with students. This godly being was waited on by a sister carrying an inkpot and a pro with a basin of water in which the doctor washed his hands after touching patients. Dedicated pros listened carefully to him, hoping to learn something about medicine. After some free time at 3:30 and a tea hour, they returned to the ward to wash patients again and prepare them for the night, applying new dressings, poultices, and liniments. New patients were usually admitted then. At 8:30 a quick supper, at 9:00 prayers, and then they could relax, write letters, read, and study. They also had to attend lectures squeezed in haphazardly, sometimes at 8:30. Study too had to be crammed into the few free hours. Lights went out at 10:30. Pros were assigned to a ward for three months, and then shifted to night duty to learn to serve breakfast, roll bandages, and complete the day nurses' work. They had a rare free afternoon, but the regimen was designed to eliminate all but the most determined candidates.

Although nursing was promoted as sacred, hospitals retained their unsavoury aura and nursing its dubious status until the 1880s, when reform changed their reputations. But sheltered middle-class women were not drawn to nursing until Nightingale's model was widely adopted. Then, the profession grew so fast that by the end of the century nursing had become a major female occupation along with teaching, shop sales, and clerking, and the one respectable job open to women that did not offer competition to men. In the 1860s and 1870s nurses were paid more than any other women workers, and trained nurses advanced rapidly because they were in short supply. By the 1890s, however, they earned less than teachers or social workers. And by 1900 nurses everywhere were poorly fed and overworked, treated with utter indifference. Their complaints – execrable living conditions, long hours, and low pay – were dismissed as reflecting a lack of devotion.

Matrons, who made all decisions regarding nurses, tried to give the profession prestige *by eliminating working-class women!* When matrons in London's voluntary hospitals spoke of "raising standards," they meant having only single "ladies" in the field, a longer training period, and more rigorous rules and discipline. Nursing leaders exploited Victorian women's belief in their self-sacrificing nature: they probably shared it. Nurses' poor food, long hours, and low pay fit women's image of commitment, spirituality, and piety. Martha Vicinus argues that of all female occupations, only nursing broke the rule of separate spheres. Nurses worked daily with male professional or social equals, so nursing leaders had to create a place for women in a male world. Yet nursing is a pre-eminent example of separate and unequal spheres: in hospitals today female doctors are still regularly taken for nurses.

Religious Orders and Prostitution

Women were drawn to religious communities by a longing for spiritual fulfilment or because they had worked informally in philanthropy and wanted to work more effectively in an organization. Some wanted the safety of a uniform: women were not supposed to walk in the streets alone, but a uniformed sister or deaconess, instantly recognized as a nurse, home visitor, or missionary, was protected by her uniform in body and reputation. Thus armoured, a woman could venture into the world alone, walk slum streets – experience "life" raw.

In the 1840s William Gladstone (a member of Parliament, later prime minister), seeing sisterhoods as a way to enable women to do good works while controlling them, proposed, along with other laymen and clerics, the foundation of an Anglican sisterhood. The first

Anglican order, "Park Village Sisters," was founded in 1845; most women who joined came from rural parishes and market towns across England and had been reared in large, authoritarian families with patriarchal religions. Used to surveillance and obedience, they adapted easily to religious communities, even over family opposition.

Anglican sisterhoods imposed severe rules on their members: rigorous training for one to three years, separation from kin and friends, constant surveillance of their spiritual devotion, behaviour, and relations with others. Sisters were not trained in theology: choir sisters (wealthy women) learned a complex set of services; lay sisters (poor women) the correct way to clean and pray. They had little free time and rarely deviated from regulated prayer, work, eating, sleep, and recreation.

Some sisterhoods founded and ran institutions like hospitals, orphanages, schools, and penitentiaries. The Sisters of the People lived together and went to the slums every day to work with the poor. The largest, the Wesleyan Sisters of the People, was founded in 1887 for devout educated Methodist women who wanted to work as teachers, nurses, and missionaries. There were others: Roman Catholic sisters worked alongside sisters from the Salvation Army in the London streets. All female church workers except Anglican sisterhoods were controlled by local ministers; all wore uniforms and followed a regular worship schedule. By 1900 churches had full-time professional women.

But many criticized women who left home for being unwomanly and abandoning their domestic duties. Sisters and deaconesses worked so hard and lived so austerely that no one could say they left home for an easy life. On the contrary, it was apparent that such women *preferred* arduous labour and austerity to home life, which, as Nightingale wrote, was stultifying, boring, and unloving even for her, a favoured daughter. This was hard for people who idealized domesticity to swallow. Not recognizing that women have selves, they could not comprehend their accepting almost any hardship to freely choose their lives, live with some autonomy, and do meaningful work.

In this period syphilis ravaged the population; children were often born with the disease. In major cities 45 percent of men had syphilis and, according to one study, 120 percent had had gonorrhea; in another, one man in five had syphilis and many repeatedly caught gonorrhea. Of course they contaminated their wives.[25] Appalled doctors blamed prostitutes. Agreeing with W.R. Greg that prostitution was ineradicable, they tried to keep disease from spreading by regulating prostitutes' hygiene, as France did. During 1864 to 1869 Parliament passed the Contagious Diseases Acts, which required medical exams for prostitutes in garrison towns and ports. All known or suspected female prostitutes had to be examined periodically or risk up to three months in prison. A doctor wrote: "Prostitution is a transitory state, through which an untold number of British women are ever on their passage" – most later married.

Women in the orders were convinced that their innate moral superiority helped them to work with prostitutes. Low-church women worked with the poor, tended the sick and homeless, and reformed "fallen women." Society assumed that Evangelical women – educated, devout, "pure" Englishwomen – represented the highest form of Christianity, and simply by example could draw out the latent goodness in others. Actually, they were often ineffectual and self-righteously intrusive, although indefatigable, going out night after night to offer streetwalkers food, a place to stay, training, hoping for "rebirth" in Christ.

Sisterhoods set up slum missions and Homes of Refuge to *protect* "repentant" prostitutes. Prostitutes entered these penitentiaries voluntarily, but were prisoners once inside. They could never be "forgiven" and were not allowed to forget their "sin"; they were taught to define themselves by their history. Although the sisters were enacting maternal roles in a culture that glorified motherhood, their program was designed to crush the penitents' maternal feelings, ignoring their need to be mothered and placing their children in adoptive homes. Even if a penitent fully submitted to the discipline, she could never become a full member of the religious community. Penitents lived isolated from each other and from the sisters, who knew the poor were inferior to the upper classes. A measure of these women's privation is that some preferred the sisters' stern attentions to none at all and asked to stay permanently – especially older women who could no longer face the struggle of earning their living outside, or had no loved ones there. They were the sisters' "successes": a special "Magdalen" order was created for them to guard new arrivals.

After the 1870s attitudes toward prostitution began to change: people criticized the Houses' punitive approach and turned more attention to poor neighbourhoods and children. Like penitentiaries, orphanages offered moral indoctrination, instead of trying to create a welcoming environment. The sisters physically cared for and disciplined children, to teach them to avoid sin (sex). They maintained class and sex status, teaching girls domestic skills, not job skills, and exhorting slum women to accept their position, not change it. Churches wanted large memberships, not social change.

The Professionalization of Philanthropic Work

By mid-century, women were doing social work outside religious orders. Wealth had increased and women with more leisure time sought useful work. Philanthropy opened life to them, enabling them to cross class lines, meet women of other classes, and observe poor people's private lives. The poor welcomed them into their homes, blaming women less than men for their oppression. Pioneers like Mary Carpenter, Louisa Twining, and Octavia Hill devised new approaches to child welfare, workhouse arrangements, and model housing. By the 1890s a leisure-class woman without volunteer work was a rarity. Charity work gave women a sense of purpose and the profound satisfaction of helping others; it exposed them to "real life" (from which class protected them), and was their only opening to public life. As charity groups and government bureaux offered more services, they needed professionals to guide and train a virtual army of volunteers – by 1893 about 20,000 British women worked full time and half a million part time in philanthropic projects.

Most active female social workers served as poor-law guardians, on school boards, and in low-level government offices, representing the interests of poor women and children. When they began to struggle for suffrage, women cited their experience with working-class women and children, effective leadership at the local level, and public service as proof that they were worthy of the vote (something men did not have to prove).

Mary Carpenter devoted her life to creating separate penal institutions for children; Louisa Twining successfully reformed poorhouses. Perhaps the most respected female reformer was Octavia Hill (1838–1912), who invented an approach to philanthropy that helped the poor through personal contact. With money from John Ruskin, Hill purchased a block of houses and rented them to poor families in 1865. She trained a corps of female volunteers to collect the rent each week and intervene in tenants' lives to help them find jobs and child apprenticeships, or to teach women housewifery and home decorating. Tenants who did not pay rent promptly were evicted; Hill was proud of guaranteeing a 5 percent return on investment in model housing. But most slum landlords earned twice that and were not induced to imitate her.

In the 1860s Hill founded the Charity Organisation Society (COS), a key organization intended to umbrella overlapping London charities. Its approach accorded with Hill's notions of self-help. It investigated all appeals for help: a volunteer visited each applicant with a questionnaire and wrote a case report. A committee determined who deserved aid. Evidence that kin could help an applicant or that a family member drank meant automatic rejection, but the respectable few who were accepted were given full assistance, which was followed up by investigations and reports. The poor hated the attitude of superiority permeating the COS, and asked for aid only when desperate; the COS hated and attacked groups that simply gave money directly to the poor. Hill's approach was adopted by government welfare agencies of that period in the United States.

Other approaches existed. Socialist and pacifist women founded settlement houses on different lines or crusaded for reforms, working alone or with friends. They pioneered school health inspections, kindergartens, open-air schools for sickly children, and clinics for pre- and post-natal care. But all settlements attracted idealists willing to sacrifice their comfort in the belief that middle-class virtues would "improve" the poor. These "settlers" – as they were known – had no idea that the poor had something to offer their "betters." They wanted to do good, but were imbued with contemporary society's values. Their metaphors came from colonial wars: middle-class women "purified" the slums by their mere presence, "purging" evil under the banner of cleanliness. Like colonists, they "civilized" slum "natives" with sanitation and middle-class speech, deportment, and manners. While their brothers emigrated to colonize exotic places, sisters "emigrated" to the wilds of the East End.

But in fact the process *was* mutual: charity work gave women freedom. No other work – teaching, nursing, or mission work – gave them the mobility to move in forbidden districts. Seeing life up close, they touched reality and brushed danger, adventure, in a way not otherwise possible. Also, they could dress and eat simply and use simple manners without losing respectability. Not until after the First World War did "settler" Muriel Lester work up the courage to walk on Regent Street (in London's fashionable West End) without gloves; yet in the East End, settlers had gone without gloves and hats in the summer for decades. In the slums, middle-class women could walk the streets in safety because they were known as ladies: accent, posture, and demeanour marked them as settlers. Settler women got back as much as they gave.

In time, social workers had to acknowledge that their best efforts were inadequate to the problem. Whatever they did, they could not erase the fact that a third of the people in the world's richest city lived in destitution. By 1910 they were seeking other remedies, mainly suffrage, hoping that a voice in the laws of the state might enable women to deal with the hunger and ill health that were rife in slum neighbourhoods. Many organizations investigated working-class women's conditions. The Fabian Women's Group, founded in 1908, studied how wives spent the money their husbands gave them, and proved conclusively that they could not feed, clothe, and house their families on their paltry allowances. Other studies of women factory workers, shop clerks, and servants arrived at similar conclusions. Socialist thinkers argued for sweeping change in tax law and government services.

But as government took over philanthropy, it marginalized or drove out the women who had created it. Virtually all settlers were single women with a wish to help women and children; they had instituted child welfare, schools for the handicapped, and mothers' services. Women's settlement leaders tried to make philanthropy a paid profession, opening schools to train social workers. But payment of trained settlers was erratic and very low until after the First World War. Professionalization of work invariably transforms it. Just as professionalization of medicine narrowed its scope and excluded all but Christian males, professionalization of social work narrowed its scope and put men in charge.

Professional social workers saw themselves as experts on poverty, superior to both non-professionals and their clients; they were concerned primarily with methods and systems, ignoring community and friendship. Even women who felt that government institutionalization of the work was necessary were unhappy working for the state, doing more bureaucratic work and having less personal contact with clients. The state put women in subordinate positions, preparing cases, managing centres, or staffing offices; women were assigned mundane tasks and had no control over policy, which was entirely in men's hands. The British government's failure to consult settlers with their extensive knowledge about and connections with those it was trying to help transformed philanthropy from a personal expression of middle-class benevolence to an impersonally managed bureaucracy.

CHAPTER 5

MIDDLE-CLASS WOMEN IN THE UNITED STATES BEFORE THE CIVIL WAR

THE VALUES URGED ON AMERICANS were similar to those urged on British women. The cult of domesticity was powerful in America, and if class was less important than in England, slavery and racism were more so. In America as in England laws were passed to alleviate the woes of industrialization and women's legalized victimization. And in America too, women were among the first to point out similarities in the condition of poor people and women.

Women Writers in England and the United States

Writing, especially fiction, was a major means for middle-class women to urge social change. Writers can call attention to a situation, and arouse sympathy or propose solutions for it. Most men who wrote about poverty offered prescriptions – W.R. Greg, for instance, urged women to become servants. Women, on the other hand, wrote mainly to elicit sympathy for the poor; women pioneered the "social protest" novel. Most of the men who followed them are remembered; the women are not (although a few have recently been resuscitated). Yet women's social protest novels were well written, had great impact, and were primarily responsible for bringing the injustice and inhumanity of social and economic conditions to the attention of a wide audience.

Women invented social protest fiction and dominated the form throughout the nineteenth century.[1] Historians date protest from Thomas Carlyle's 1839 statement: "A feeling very generally exists that the condition and disposition of the Working Classes is a rather ominous matter at present; that something ought to be said, something ought to be done, in regard to it."[2] But long before that, Hannah More had written *The Lancashire Collier Girl* (1795), Maria Edgeworth *Castle Rackrent* (1800) and *The Absentee* (1812), Harriet Martineau *The Rioters* (1827) and *The Turn-out* (1829), and Charlotte Tonna *The System* (1827). As Carlyle's monograph was being printed, Frances Trollope's *Michael Armstrong, the Factory Boy* and Tonna's *Helen Fleetwood* were appearing in serial form in English journals.[3] Middle-class women began writing out of pity for the downtrodden, perhaps identifying with the disenfranchised. But they gradually recognized their shared oppression. Elaine Showalter dates this awareness to around 1880, when women began to depict men's domination of women along with economic oppression, and a new set of feminist writers appeared: Charlotte Brontë, Elizabeth Gaskell, and George Eliot.[4]

Like men, female authors varied in background, religion, and political leaning. Some, like Tonna, stressed female domesticity (she condemned preferential hiring of women over men for demeaning it). Eliot was agnostic, Tonna ardently Low Church Evangelical, Gaskell Unitarian. But all were deeply concerned with human well-being. Trollope and Tonna depicted women with large families, Elizabeth Stone and Geraldine Jewsbury, uneducated women;

Stone, Gaskell, and Fanny Mayne portrayed vulnerable working- and lower-middle-class orphans and motherless girls. All vividly portrayed the futility and tedium of middle-class women's lives, the misery of being confined to domestic labour, and the disaster of being seduced and abandoned. Forced by censorship (unofficial but more severe for women than men) to omit or skim over sex or brutality, they nevertheless presented life in more concrete detail than male novelists working with similar material (Benjamin Disraeli or Charles Kingsley, for example) and far more accurately presented women's friendships and interactions across class lines.

Americans were slower than the British to depict class or sex oppression, but, as in England, women did so before men and were consigned to oblivion. Rebecca Harding Davis (1831–1910) published *Life in the Iron Mills* in 1861. The daughter of a well-to-do mill manager in Wheeling (then in Virginia, a slave state), and bound by the constrictions placed on young middle-class women, she spent tedious hours gazing out the front window of the Harding house as "long trains of mules dragged their masses of pig iron and the slow stream of human life crept past, night and morning, year after year, to work their fourteen-hour days six days a week."[5] *Life in the Iron Mills* claustrophobically depicts the stifling of a working-class man with the potential to create art. Tillie Olsen believes that Davis wrote the novel in utter identification with "thwarted, wasted lives . . . mighty hungers [and] unawakened power."

Davis married for love and often supported her family by writing, yet her husband treated her as a subordinate. Her son, a writer too, was more famous but less accomplished. Davis wrote until she died at seventy-nine, but the only literary journal even to mention her passing was *The New York Times*, which noted that the mother of Richard Harding Davis had died. The *Times* obituary recalled that *Life in the Iron Mills* had "attracted attention from all over the country . . . many thought the author must be a man. The stern but artistic realism of the picture she put alive upon paper, suggested a man, and a man of power not unlike Zola's." Olsen's comment:

"They did not mention that she had preceded Zola by two decades."

However, women novelists were gradually excluded from the literary establishment. Before 1840 many women wrote good novels that were financially successful.[6] After their work won respect for fiction as a form, men became attracted to its lucrative rewards and edged women out of the field. A male elite of editors redefined the novel as "Art" and claimed it as men's territory, dismissing women's fiction as fit for "mass audiences, passive entertainment, and flutter." Fewer women were published, and even fewer were successful, after the 1840s; only a few were admitted into the sanctified precinct of art.

The Economic and Political Background

The United States was run by large landowners and capitalist merchants from the time of independence until 1801, when the Democratic-Republican party elected Thomas Jefferson president. Jefferson's party worked to abolish privileges of birth, wealth, and established religion. Wanting rights extended to all citizens, they successfully campaigned to add a Bill of Rights to the Constitution. As the country grew richer, divisions of class and urban and rural populations widened, but there was a safety valve – a new frontier. Jefferson's 1803 purchase of "Louisiana" doubled the size of the country; settlement of the Northwest Territory – western New York and Ohio (and later the southwest, taken from Mexico) – gave the poor and dispossessed a chance at independence in a largely classless society.

In 1829 anti-privilege Democrats made Andrew Jackson president. Declaring all men politically equal (except slaves, Native Americans, and women), they fought for universal white male suffrage and election (not appointment) of government officials. In the first half of the century, the thousands of immigrants thronging to America from Scotland and England assimilated easily. But after the

1840s Irish fleeing the famine, Germans, and other Europeans encountered bias against their religion or language. No law demanded it, but all institutions, schools, and courts used English. People who worked outside the home picked up enough to get by, but homebound women did not and suffered doubly, living in poverty in an alien land, cut off from communication.

American laws denied women any rights, and legal change was painfully slow, state by state. In 1855 Michigan revised its laws to let married women keep and manage their earnings and property; New York passed a similar law in 1860, other states later. These laws created a new class: women with property but not franchised. Qualified by property standards, they were prevented by their sex from voting, serving on juries, or holding public office. Not until 1911 did a Michigan law grant married women the right to choose to work for wages; before that, husbands determined whether or not their wives could do waged work. The first new laws granted married women control over inheritances and gifts, not over the wealth they helped accrue in a farm or business.

Nineteenth-century American women followed the same pattern as British women: accepting men's definition of them as morally superior domestic creatures, they used it as a lever to smash barriers by extending the meaning of "domestic." In America too, single women first opened new professions to women and here too, women's dominance of congregations and "Great Awakenings" gave them confidence in their right and ability to speak and act publicly. But American women had another tool. The men who denied them political rights gave them a sop, honouring them as "Republican Mothers" and granting them education. Now women used revolutionary rhetoric to justify reforms like abolition and the franchise.

Women in Protestant sects founded missionary and charitable societies, converting neighbours, kin, and friends and forming tight-knit circles determined to purify the world by ending prostitution, intemperance, or slavery. They challenged male appropriation of church leadership: as early as 1850, Antoinette Blackwell earned a divinity degree from Oberlin College, becoming America's first female minister (but Oberlin Divinity School did not accept another woman for nearly forty years). Still, by 1880, 165 women were accredited ministers – the Universalist Church alone had thirty-five.

Unlike British women, American women leaders rejected religious orthodoxy. Quakerism, the most egalitarian religion, supported liberal causes, raising women's confidence by encouraging them to speak at meetings. In the first half of the nineteenth century, agrarian Quakers strongly advocated Indian rights, communitarianism, abolition, and temperance.[7] Of fifty-one leading feminist abolitionist leaders, twenty-one were raised in Quaker, Universalist, or Unitarian families.[8] Most leaders raised in orthodox or evangelical sects left them for these churches or none. Quakerism had lost its egalitarian edge: men increasingly dominated meetings, relegating women to a separate, subordinate sphere. When these women organized to aid the sick, poor, orphans, homeless women, or slaves, they based their right to speak and act not on religion, but on female moral superiority. Still, when the feminist movement exploded in America in 1848, a large percentage of its members were Quakers.[9]

American Women Use Their Education

In Education

Protestants let women learn to read so they could teach children religion, not realizing that women turn any instrument they are given to their own purposes. Literate women wanted their daughters educated, but no institution of higher learning would take them until Emma Willard opened a seminary in Troy, New York, in 1821. She taught her students they were intellectually equal to men, and she travelled tirelessly, lecturing, giving workshops, promoting education.[10] Her graduates founded or taught in schools across the country; over 200 schools founded in this period were modelled on Willard's "Troy ideal."[11] In 1837 Mary Lyons founded Mount Holyoke, in Massachusetts, considered the oldest women's college in the United States, and Oberlin became the first co-educational college in the country (but female students had to clean rooms and do laundry for male students!). Massachusetts opened the first state normal school (teachers' college), Lexington Academy, in 1839.

In the struggle for higher education, women often used the argument of female moral superiority. Even the assertive Willard advocated "true womanhood" as the goal of female education (but more of her graduates had careers and they had fewer children than less-educated women). Sophia Smith founded Smith College in Massachusetts in the hope that "the higher and more thoroughly Christian education of women" would prepare them to purge "the evils of society," especially "the filth" in literature. But some women wanted knowledge, not True Womanhood. The first woman's literary club in the United States was formed in 1837 in Lowell, Massachusetts, that hotbed of female solidarity.

The career of educator Catherine Beecher was a paradox: she spent her life in the public realm *urging other women to stay home.* The sister of novelist Harriet Beecher Stowe, Beecher believed women could influence society by teaching, and she built schools across the country, concentrating on the educationally deprived frontier. She would persuade backwoods communities to fund schools, then staff them with her protegées. Her *Domestic Economy* was the most popular and important housewifery text of the ante-bellum period.

Women thronged to teaching, the one profession by which single middle-class women could live independently. By 1870 they made up over half the 200,000 primary and secondary school teachers in the country. Of course, they were paid half as much as men, at best 60 percent, and "feminization" had its usual effect (the more women, the lower the status and pay). Women were also kept at the lowest echelons: by 1850 they dominated grammar-school teaching, but were only slowly hired by secondary schools and colleges and almost totally excluded from administrative jobs. White Anglo-Saxon women began to be promoted (in negligible numbers until the mid-twentieth century) only after women from other ethnic backgrounds entered the field. In the 1880s female teachers were dismissed for marrying: working-class women, black and white, were allowed to do back-breaking labour whether married or single, but "ladies" with husbands were not permitted to work for pay.

There were some advantages to living in a country without traditions. The British used tradition to exclude women from schools, but the American educational system was just forming, and many new colleges followed Oberlin in accepting women – Antioch (1852), University of Iowa (1856), Swarthmore (1864), and others out west. By 1880 nearly half of America's colleges accepted both sexes. Still, most new land-grant colleges had a "gender-differentiated" curriculum. In 1865 forty-one male and no female students were enrolled in traditional college courses, and sixty-six women and no men in the normal school at the University of Wisconsin. Old prestigious men's colleges opened sister schools with second-class status. In 1874 Harvard opened Radcliffe; although its students were taught by Harvard faculty, they were barred from Harvard College libraries. In 1889 Barnard opened with its own faculty, but students used Columbia University's library and other facilities. In 1887 Tulane opened Sophie Newcomb College, which was emulated in 1891 by Pembroke/Brown.

The career of Graceanna Lewis of Media, Pennsylvania, illustrates the difficulties erudite women faced in this time. An ornithologist and scientific illustrator, Lewis applied for a job on the Swarthmore College science faculty in the early 1860s. When a male naturalist also applied, Lewis withdrew, feeling less competent than he. Maria Mitchell, professor of astronomy at Vassar, urged Lewis to apply for a similar position there. Lewis had to have an income – she supported herself by teaching in a high school – and the Vassar job would give her professional recognition and status. John Cassin, curator of birds at the Academy of Natural Science in Philadelphia, and Spencer Baird, secretary of the Smithsonian, wrote strong letters supporting her, but she was rejected in favour of a male geologist. She went on working and in 1868 published the first of a projected ten-volume *Natural History of Birds*, a catalogue and general scientific treatise on ornithological classification. Its critical and popular success led to invitations to present papers at the American Association for the Advancement of Science.[12]

This triumph would have assured a man a prosperous career, and in 1870 Lewis was nominated for the Philadelphia Academy of Natural Science, supported by George Tryon, ornithology curator, and by librarian Edward Nolan. She was rejected, but a week later the board reversed its decision, admitting Lewis and two other women. Important as this was to her status, she had to earn a living. Still unable to get a job in a college, she returned to teaching in a high school. But she was too old and learned for such work: intellectually, emotionally, and physically drained by living at a girls' boarding school, she fell ill in 1871 with "an affection of the brain." For two years she lay in bed, attended by her sister, Dr. Rebecca Fussell, sliding into invalidism.

In succumbing to the overwhelming social pressure against independent women, Lewis became a statistic in a campaign to prove that learning was injurious to females. While women tirelessly strove for learning, male debate raged around them, deprecating their capacities while ignoring what they actually achieved. Marshalling "facts" from biology and neurology, academics and scientists "proved" women to be physiologically and intellectually inferior to men. One authority reported that average male European brains weighed forty-nine grams and female brains only forty-four grams: ergo, women were intellectually inferior to men. The greatest threat was that Woman, formed around a uterus, would damage it with study. Massachusetts-based Edward Clarke argued that women, being creatures of their bodies, must limit other activities to realize their biological destiny, motherhood. His best-selling *Sex in Education* (1873) used Darwin and Spencer to give sexism and misogyny a scientific basis. He cited studies of college women to demonstrate that education had given them dysmenorrhea, acute and chronic ovaritis, *prolapsus uteri*, hysteria, and neuralgia *inter alia*.

In Writing

Yet women built successful careers in journalism and literature in this period. Wide female literacy led to a veritable explosion of periodical literature for women in this century, magazines dealing with motherhood, housekeeping, health, recreation, morality and religion, reform, fashion . . . everything but politics. Editors dictated the style and substance of such journals, and many of their editors and writers were women. Some "female" literature contained progressive ideas, and many female writers openly scorned males, but the progressives were not the scorners. Scorn for males is so pronounced in some pieces that today's critics call them feminist. But just as the women who express most scorn for men today are right-wing women who feel that abortion enables men to evade their responsibilities, the nineteenth-century women who most condemned men and their realm were those who most exalted domesticity and motherhood. Feminist journals were *in competition with* those that exalted mothers and homemakers.

It was in this period that people began to define feminism as a political movement that aimed at equality for women in the public realm and was hostile to traditional "feminine" values and culture. Simultaneously, advocates of domesticity developed value systems hostile to the male world, challenging male hegemony by stressing feminine values and female culture. The conceptual division of women's movements into a "feminist" struggle for political equality and a "feminine" struggle for a protected moral-domestic sphere remains a damaging fissure in female solidarity.

To the chagrin of authors like Nathaniel Hawthorne (who sneered at "scribbling women"), women dominated the literary market in nineteenth-century America, outselling Hawthorne and other men. Male critics horrified by women writers' "unfemininely bitter wrath" belittled their work and subject matter, ignoring it when they could. Scholars re-evaluating women's work today discover critical prejudice against both female authors and female form. Male-oriented critics accept only one pattern as fulfilling the conditions of art: a single figure is pitted against his environment, struggles, and wins or tragically loses. Life is a battle waged in lonely exile for a personal goal. This is the pattern adopted by most male writers. Women tend to see life as experience suffered, enjoyed, endured; their protagonists usually live amid a community that eases their struggle or pain.[13] Male novels, like male histories, tend to exemplify male power; female writing tends to describe the quality of experience. Critics decreed only one kind of legitimate, excellent, Art. Emily Dickinson (1830–1886), arguably America's greatest poet, remained virtually unpublished all her life.

It was women who wrote the first social protest novels in the United States as well as in England. While some women writers idealized domesticity and sentimentalized family relationships, others wrote harsh books about women locked in cruel marriages, their arduous manual labour and economic dependence. Their most common image was the villainous husband. Mary Virginia Terhune (Marion Harland), Catharine Maria Sedgwick, Lydia Sigourney, Caroline Gilman, and E.D.E.N. Southworth, as well as other ancestors of the great female writers of the end of the century – Willa Cather, Ellen Glasgow, Harriet Beecher Stowe, and Kate Chopin – produced novels of power and import.

It was hard for Victorian women to see themselves as serious writers. Catharine Sedgwick denied that she cared about her craft or was concerned with style, or that the reception of her work mattered to her emotionally or financially: "My *author* existence has always seemed something accidental, extraneous, independent of my inner self. My books have been a pleasant occupation and excitement in my life . . . but they constitute no portion of my happiness." Edith Wharton lived later, yet never lost a sense of shame about her work. She was famous and supported many people but concealed the act of writing much as Jane Austen concealed her texts with embroidery. Wharton worked in bed mornings, and appeared downstairs beautifully groomed and ready for the day, about eleven. In her autobiography (1934), she made light of her writing. Her disavowal of serious intention eased the way for male critics eager to belittle women writers to dismiss her work after she died. Although important in her time, she was barely remembered by 1950. Only recently has her greatness been recognized.

Critic Ann Douglas claims nineteenth-century American culture was "feminized" by a sentimentalism that diminished our really great (i.e., male) authors and produced modern consumerist culture – ads and sitcoms depicting happy families with happy problems.[14] She does not discuss how politics dictate literary standards (including her own), or consider men's exclusion of women from modern culture. Douglas blames the women who tried to uphold humane standards and a vision of felicity for the victory of the power-seeking makers of modern culture who exploit and degrade such standards in the marketplace.

In the Arts

Writers learn by reading widely and exercising their skill. Graphic artists and musicians, however, must learn technical skills. In the past, most female artists, composers, and musicians were related to men who were trained in an art. Eight American female artists, for example, were related to artists – the nieces, granddaughters, and a daughter-in-law of Charles Wilson Peale, daughters of Gilbert Stuart and Thomas Sully, and Thomas Cole's sister earned their livings as painters.[15] Women were not sent to art school or apprenticed to masters no matter how much talent they showed, so their only possible way of learning was from male kin. Few women were able to study abroad as men did, and in any case, art teachers so disregarded female pupils that they would undermine the confidence needed for a career in art. A woman who overcame all these obstacles still had hardship surviving: over half the women in the New York Historical Society's *Dictionary of American Artists: 1564–1860* were financially dependent on male kin because they were paid so little for their work.

Two art schools that took women opened in 1851–52: the Philadelphia School of Design and Cooper Union Institute School of Design for Women in New York. But women were still barred from life classes – the sex that gives birth was forbidden to look upon the naked human body! Such barriers continued into the twentieth century: Canadian painter Emily Carr, born in 1899, wrote about them in *Growing Pains*.[16] Women continued to challenge this taboo or tried to compensate for the handicap by attending anatomy lectures at medical schools to acquire the detailed anatomical knowledge that they needed. Most accepted what they could not change, and painted flowers, still lifes, portraits, and miniatures.

A few American woman sculptors were successful in the 1850s – an extraordinary accomplishment given the requirements of the field. Since sculptors *had* to study abroad, they needed money; and they needed commissions for work. In short, they needed people of means with confidence in them. Harriet Hosmer, Vinnie Ream, Emma Stebbins, and Edmonia Lewis all became successful sculptors. The government commissioned Ream to design memorials to Abraham Lincoln and Admiral Farragut; New York City commissioned Stebbins' "Angel of the Waters" for Central Park. Lewis, half-black, half-Indian, born on a Chippewa homeland in upstate New York, studied at Oberlin and in Rome, and was the first black artist to become nationally known, especially for a bust of H.W. Longfellow.

Hosmer, the most famous of the three, was supported by her physician father, a teacher and patron. Critics attributed Hosmer's "Zenobia" to a man; she sued, but rumours persisted that she had not created the work. She was charged with indecency for portraying a female naked: a critic wrote, "Her want of modesty is enough to disgust a dog. She has casts for the entire female model made and exhibited in a shockingly indecent manner."

American women expressed their creativity in traditional female arts, embroidery, lacemaking, and quilting, which they made a fine art. A quilter frequently plans her design, chooses her pattern and colours, and collects fabric scraps by herself, but nineteenth-century quilters met in female networks to sew. The quilting bee, popular in America, offered companionship to women who were isolated in households, and gave them a chance to use their skills to create useful objects. Quilts traditionally copied set designs but many nineteenth-century quilters illustrated narratives or events. Quilters sometimes signed their work (they were not naïve artists), which then became heirlooms handed down over generations. Not until the late twentieth century were they acknowledged to be works of art.

In Medicine

The profession that attracted American women in the greatest numbers was medicine. As in England, war provided the impetus for women to entering nursing. When the Civil War erupted in 1861, both northern and southern women mobilized. A Cooper Union rally drew more than 3000 New Yorkers, who founded the New York Central Association of Relief, governed by a board of twenty-five, of which twelve were women. They oversaw the collection and distribution of supplies and trained nurses to work in hospitals and on battlefields. This agency, one of 7000 in the Sanitary Commission, was the most important and effective institution created by women during the war. It ran fairs, bazaars, and large two-week fairs in major cities; with the millions it raised, it bought supplies for poor soldiers, widows, and orphans. Southern women made similar efforts, but were less successful.

Women were effective enough that both Confederate president Jefferson Davis and Union president Abraham Lincoln gave them official ranks. In June 1861 Lincoln named Dorothea Dix Superintendent of Nurses for the Union Army. Knowing the social pressure she was up against, Dix stipulated that applicants be at least thirty and "plain." Attractive women (and male patients) protested, but Dix wanted to avert potential attacks on moral grounds. Attacks were still made, but thousands of women (among them author Louisa May Alcott) volunteered. Some wanted to experience the adventure and danger of war, others wanted work that gave them dignity. Still others, their livelihoods destroyed by a war that took men from marriage and farm, needed the 40 cents a day, food, shelter, and transport that came with the job.

Nurses left their hospital wards to tend men on the battlefields, but had to *fight* to help; military regulations barred them, and doctors preferred to let men die rather than accept female help. Only the wounded welcomed nurses, and despite their great contributions, army nurses were eventually eliminated. Independently of the army, Clara Barton nursed and single-handedly raised thousands of dollars for food and medical help for Union soldiers. Barton, single, thrived on this work; after she was ousted in 1863, she became an invalid. In 1870, when the Franco-Prussian War broke out, Barton seized the chance to organize nursing aid. At its end in 1871, her health failed again, and she lost her eyesight. For ten years she languished – until she conceived the idea of a medical group that crossed national lines in emergencies. Founding the first American Red Cross chapter in Danville, Massachussetts, restored her energy and well-being.

Southerners were even more appalled than northerners at "ladies" tending "ruffians" (their own soldiers): most Confederate enlisted men (and wounded) were lower class. But southern women brushed off all objections, helping all soldiers: one said, "A woman's respectability must be at low ebb if it can be endangered by going into a hospital." Some brought slaves along to help and protect them. The single Sally Tompkins turned a friend's house in Richmond, Virginia, into a twenty-two-room infirmary. It flourished after Davis made her a Confederate Army captain. "Cap'n Sally" treated almost 1300 men over time, of whom only 75 died.

Nursing opened doors to white women only. In the 1890s white nursing leaders followed Britain in upgrading nursing by recruiting only middle-class women. The "professionalization" of nursing excluded blacks. Southern states barred black women from registering for examinations or gave them more difficult examinations. Racism justified whites' hiring black nurses but treating and paying them as servants. Black women could not even train as nurses until black hospitals and nurse training schools opened in the 1890s.[17] (Blacks were also barred from hospitals as patients – the great blues singer Bessie Smith died when no southern hospital would admit her.) When black health-care institutions opened, white professional groups refused their workers membership. White women were as responsible for such policies as men.

This situation continued until war again made men aware of women's skills. Mabel Keaton Staupers, a black nurses' advocate, was executive secretary of the National Association of Colored Graduate Nurses (NACGN) from 1934 to 1946. In 1945 the Surgeon-General of the Army threatened to draft nurses to fill the severe shortage. Staupers publicly confronted him, demanding that the army use black nurses. She generated huge public support for removing American health-care institutions' quotas for blacks (*that kind* of quota was acceptable). In time, once blacks were welcomed into the American Nurses' Association, they dissolved the NACGN. But recognizing that the American Nurses Association (ANA) marginalized and ignored them – very few black women held leadership jobs in the ANA – they founded the National Black Nurses' Association to solidify their voice and their lobby in 1971.

Conditions were worse for women who wanted to be doctors. Few women broke into the profession before the Civil War. The first American woman doctor, Elizabeth Blackwell, earned a medical degree from Geneva Medical College in 1849. She then studied in Europe, and returned in 1851 to New York, where she tried to start a medical practice. But male doctors shut hospital doors to her. With her sister Emily and Maria Zakrzewska (who later taught at New England Medical College for Women), who were also barred from practice, Blackwell founded the New York Infirmary for Women. Not even a desperate need for doctors during the Civil War could break men's prejudice against women, and no women were commissioned as physicians by either side until 1864, when

Dr. Mary Walker was sent to the front at Chattanooga, Tennessee. Captured, she was traded for a Confederate physician and made supervisor of the Female Military Prison in Louisville. President Andrew Johnson gave her a medal.

Insurgent feminism provided the impetus for women in medicine. In 1849 the first feminist convention in Seneca Falls, New York, persuaded men to found the Central Medical College, a coeducational medical school in Syracuse, New York. Feminist philanthropists founded medical schools for women. Quaker activist Ann Preston worked tirelessly to raise money for the American Woman's Medical College in Philadelphia, founded in 1850 as the first medical school to offer a medical course and the M.D. to women. For over a decade, the Philadelphia County Medical Society denied it accreditation. Preston raised money from women to send promising young Emmeline Cleveland to study advanced obstetrics at the Paris Maternité Hospital. Preston founded the Woman's Hospital of Philadelphia, and on Cleveland's return she headed obstetrics at the college and became the first female surgeon in the United States at the hospital.

Like many practising male doctors, Harriot K. Hunt was self-taught. After practising medicine for fifteen years, she applied to Harvard medical school in 1850. The faculty allowed her to attend lectures, but male students protested and the administration ousted her. Sexism is stronger even than money: in 1878, twenty-five years after Hunt's expulsion, when hundreds of women were already doctors, Marion Hovey offered Harvard $10,000 to admit women to its medical school. Harvard refused. The first elite institution to accept the carrot was Johns Hopkins, which accepted a large gift from Mary Garrett on condition that it train female physicians.

Medical school was a cruel and undermining harrassment for women, and after they completed the academic work they still could not build practices. By barring women from hospitals, men effectively kept them from seriously practising medicine: men *without* formal training prospered better than formally trained women.

Women fought state by state, lobbying legislatures and demanding that women's prisons and asylums (a new development) have woman doctors on staff. They finally prevailed by founding women's hospitals, the New York Infirmary for Women and Children (1854), and the New England Hospital for Women and Children (1862).

The first male-controlled hospital to hire a woman doctor was Mount Sinai, New York, which put Annie Angell, a graduate of the Women's College of New York Infirmary, on its staff in 1874. By the 1880s thousands of women were practising medicine, but even hospitals that admitted women doctors allowed only one or two. Fearing female encroachment, male doctors urged reforms to improve and standardize medicine. Both sexes practised medicine without licences, but the reforms worked only to the exclusion of women.

In 1850 women made up 2 percent of the physicians in Boston. This number soared after they founded their own medical schools and hospitals: by 1890, 18 percent of Boston's doctors were women; at 200, they outnumbered woman lawyers in the whole country. To *professionalize*, Tufts and Boston University medical schools, formerly coeducational, placed a quota on women students. This type of retrenchment spread across the country: Northwestern Medical School simply closed its women's division in 1902. In 1890 women made up *a quarter* of the students in Michigan Medical School; in 1910, about 3 percent. As women swarmed into the public world, men all but closed the entry doors to them. Colleges like Wesleyan, which had been coed for decades, suddenly barred women; others established quotas.

In Social Work

American women turned also to philanthropy. In the colonial period, charity was the obligation of city elites, mainly women. After the Revolution, elite groups created networks of secular organizations modelled on English humanitarian societies to help poor widows, the sick poor, and distressed slaves. Church-sponsored groups aided the poor or ran charity schools for poor children. In New York early philanthropists tried only to alleviate the sharpest pains of poverty: it did not occur to them that they could eliminate it.[18] They gave the poor firewood, food, or used clothing, without trying to alter their lifestyle or attitudes. But as wealth grew, so did destitution. Poverty overran the resources that patricians wished to devote to it, and charity groups buckled. Philanthropists began to seek ways to eliminate poverty.

The well-to-do resented the poor for simply integrating charity into their lifestyles after the Revolution, relying on relief agencies regularly instead of applying to them only in crises. In addition, the grim almshouse, built as a last resort for the elderly, impaired, sick, and mothers of small children, who could not help themselves, was used as a periodic haven by people who, the well-to-do presumed, could. The huge expansion of "outdoor relief" galled those who felt that need was sin and wanted the poor to live under punitive regulation. Contempt for relief recipients, coupled with admiration for English methods, led New Yorkers to found the Society for Prevention of Pauperism (SPP) in 1817.

The gentlemen of the SPP shifted the focus of charity from the *needs* to the *habits* of the poor. British-inspired categories and statistics demonstrated that the causes of poverty were the vices of the urban poor: imprudent hasty marriages, ignorance, intemperance, idleness, thriftlessness, gambling, and promiscuous sex. The SPP's first three reports did not even mention unemployment. They felt that charity to such people only bred indigence, even though New York mayor Cadwallader Colden's 1819 investigation of the almshouse found not one soul "unfit" for charity. Some elite women still held the old view of philanthropy, but SPP men were considered authorities by policy-makers and populace. Their cure was hard work and severity – lifting price controls on bread (a traditional way of preventing starvation), setting stricter licensing laws for taverns, founding savings banks to encourage prudence, and putting treadmills in insitutions to deter laziness. In 1823 they installed a treadmill in the penitentiary.

SPP views dominated American policy toward the poor until after the Civil War, when many women entered philanthropy. Like Englishwomen, American women imbued with belief in female moral superiority but lacking occupation affirmed their sense of worth by weaving the poor into sentimental embroideries of domesticity. Women wanted to improve the family lives of the poor, pointing their male colleagues toward domestic arrangements in tenements. They entered philanthropy through church work. The first large nineteenth-century female organizations had religious goals – they sought moral reform, sending preachers on missions to the frontier and ministers to "uncivilized areas." They entered public spaces to raise money, hand out Bibles, or sell religious tracts. But they had energy and time, and proposed projects to church auxiliaries – collecting food, clothing, and money, as well as visiting the needy or immoral in their neighbourhoods to give help or advice.

Women's groups sprang up everywhere. In small communities, women of different religions worked together harmoniously to combat increasingly visible poverty, disease, and social displacement. Over a thirty-year period, the Boston Fragment Society aided more than 10,000 families with gifts of 40,000 pieces of clothing and $20,000. The New York Charity School taught hundreds of students each year. The Female Hospital Society of Philadelphia, organized by the Quakers in 1808, gradually began offering needy women paid work instead of charity, helping many. As in England, women charity workers had closer contact with poor people than did men, and so saw the problems of the poor more clearly. It was middle-class women who first made society aware of poor women.

For the brunt of poverty fell on working-class women. The educational benefits that the Revolution had granted women aided middle-class not poor women. The dignity working-class men derived from a revolution that defined them as citizens and freemen was undermined by industrialization, which prevented their autonomy. Lacking importance in the political and social world, they built a world they could dominate, a fellowship of labourers centred in the workplace and tavern. This male solidarity was bolstered by their power over women in the family. Similar working-class male cultures arose in every industrialized country – France, Germany, and Russia, as well as England and America. In all of them, men tormented their families by spending much of their pay on tobacco and drink, and coming home drunk to abuse wives and children.

Many women were hit by drunken husbands, but poor women saw their starving children beaten when the money that the man drank up could have fed them. Temperance became their major priority. Men's consumption of alcohol in early nineteenth-century America was staggering. Adults averaged six to seven gallons a year of alcohol in 1810 – seven to ten in 1820 – and few women drank any. By comparison, in 1986, with women drinking, annual adult consumption was about .84 gallons. In 1826 women founded the American Society for the Promotion of Temperance, a "cold water army." By 1834 it had a million members in more than 5000 local affiliates.

Women's next priority was prostitution. Men too worked to eliminate prostitutes, blaming them for polluting society; most women reformers saw them as depraved, but also as victims. They were certainly the latter: in America, too, most prostitutes worked for wages that could not keep them. Of 2000 whores in New York City jails surveyed in 1858, almost half worked as servants, a quarter as seamstresses. Over 60 percent were immigrants, 75 percent under twenty-five years old, most teenagers; *half had children*, of which half were illegitimate; 75 percent were single or widowed; the others had alcoholic husbands or had been deserted. Half had syphilis.

Before the Civil War, in New York City there was one prostitute to every sixty-four adult males; by 1890 the number of prostitutes had multiplied six-fold. Nineteenth-century attitudes toward sex still exist: women are held responsible for all sex performed without a marriage licence.[19] A young Presbyterian minister, John

McDowall, in 1830 rationalized that women's moral depravity was more threatening than men's because "a few of these courtesans suffice to corrupt whole cities, and there can be no doubt that some insinuating prostitutes have initiated more young men into these destructive ways than the most abandoned rakes have debauched virgins during their whole lives."

Women advocates of moral reform, however, blamed both sexes. In 1834, upon organizing the New York Female Moral Reform Society, they declared: "The licentious man is no less guilty than his victim and ought, therefore, to be excluded from all virtuous female society." They were amazing: bands of ladies stood outside brothels, jotting down the names of men who entered, or went in themselves to get information about runaway daughters or offer help to any woman held hostage. They invaded brothels en masse, praying and singing to discourage business and to try to win over sinners. They printed men's names in their journal, *The Advocate,* and hired the Reverend McDowall and two assistants to visit whores in jails, hospitals, almshouses, and brothels. They sponsored reformatory homes to turn prostitutes into virtuous domestic servants (this regularly failed). They had little effect, but continued angrily to attack "the lascivious and predatory nature of the American male."

In Abolition

In 1830 slavery was a political, not a moral issue: women were its greatest enemies. Men controlled anti-slavery organizations, but women made up the numbers and did the endless work. They prayed in groups, "memorialized" (petitioned) legislators to abolish slavery, raised funds to support abolitionist journals and agents, and gave "ladies' fairs" to sell handmade articles bearing anti-slavery messages or emblems. Society considered commerce a male domain, but did not criticize such fundraising activities, which proved extremely lucrative even as they raised consciousness. Yet they also reinforced women's auxiliary role in the movement, for the proceeds supported men's abolitionist work. Women also boycotted produce, cotton, or manufactured goods produced by slave labour. Only gradually did they overcome their fear of male hostility to expand into male terrain – public speaking, writing, editing, and serving as delegates to conventions.

The first women to speak publicly against slavery, the Grimké sisters, Angelina and Sarah, had the daring, courage, and moral commitment to leave their South Carolina slaveholding family to go north, join the abolitionists, and speak before "promiscuous" (mixed sex) audiences. Women who spoke in public were notorious (as Fanny Wright had discovered) and the young Grimkés were savagely attacked more for usurping the male prerogative on public speech than for their position on slavery. This provoked them to address women's rights in their anti-slavery talks.

At first, women worked state by state to make the nation aware of the evils of slavery by speaking, drafting petitions, and arguing with people they asked to sign. When congressman (and ex-president) John Quincy Adams submitted a petition urging abolition signed by 148 Massachusetts women to the House of Representatives, Virginians "raved incoherently . . . pounded the table with their fists . . . cursed Massachusetts and . . . wished that the women of the state might swing from a lamp-post." As anti-slavery petitions flooded Congress, hysterical Southern members passed a "gag rule," enabling them to table petitions for abolition without acting on them. This added free speech to anti-slavery demands, especially for women – as Angelina Grimké said: "The right of petition is the only political right . . . women have." Women intensified their effort, staged prayer vigils, mounted fairs, and converted men (among them the later leaders Wendell Phillips and William H. Seward) to "the Cause." The campaign gave women a taste for militant activity, and opposition radicalized them: anti-slavery adherents (who had urged patience and peaceful ways to combat the evil) became impatient abolitionists.[20]

The first American women's anti-slavery society was founded by black women in Salem, Massachusetts, in 1832.[21] That year too

Maria Weston Chapman and others tried to organize white women in a Boston Female Anti-Slavery Society. Chapman spent her life on the Cause: she edited *The Liberty Bell*, which advocated abolition, and ran fairs to raise money for the movement. She persuaded writers like Margaret Fuller, Harriet Martineau, Henry Wadsworth Longfellow, and James Russell Lowell to join the Cause, and took over editorship of the *National Anti-Slavery Standard* from Lydia Maria Child from 1844 to 1848. (Child had been an extremely popular novelist until she published an anti-slavery pamphlet, *An Appeal in Favor of that Class of Americans Called Africans*, in 1833.) Chapman, called the "Lady Macbeth" of the movement, was the confidante of black leader Frederick Douglass, who complained of being patronized by white male abolitionists.

Philadelphia female abolitionists gathered around Lucretia and Joseph Mott, active Quakers. Lucretia Mott (1793–1880), who was licensed as a Quaker preacher in 1821, became the best-known woman abolitionist. In 1833, when Philadelphia was hosting the American Anti-Slavery Society (AASS) convention, the convention president in an afterthought invited Quaker women, including Mott. When she rose to speak, however, the men protested: women could attend meetings but not speak. Mott was not one to bow to pressure: she had six children, yet made her home a station on the Underground Railroad and had hidden a fugitive black woman in her carriage under the noses of armed guards. As a minister, she was used to public speaking and was unintimidated by men's presence. She prevailed, making several suggestions that were adopted as resolutions. But none of the women present was allowed to vote on the resolutions or sign the final document. Mott went home and founded the Philadelphia Female Anti-Slavery Society, and acted as its president for the next quarter-century.

But American abolitionism was always a minority movement. Unlike temperance, it never won popular support. Abolitionists annoyed, provoked, and incensed audiences, and were considered dangerous radicals or even lunatics. They were regularly heckled on platforms, and often tarred and feathered. Women's image of pious purity did not exempt them from violence: they may even have been men's main target. On the first day of the second Anti-Slavery Convention of American Women in Philadelphia in 1838, men stoned the delegates; on the second, a mob burned the new Pennsylvania Hall (planned as an abolitionist centre), to the ground. Authorities watched, doing nothing.

The major male abolitionist, William Lloyd Garrison, was a radical disciple of "Perfectionist" John Humphrey Noyes; an advocate of immediate emancipation of slaves without compensation, he refused to work with people who urged gradual solutions. He opposed hierarchy, denouncing clerical and political authority, church and state, as bulwarks of slavery. His radicalism made him women reformers' comrade: he repudiated the institutions that barred them from the public realm. This extraordinary man welcomed women as equal partners.

Clergymen who cited scripture to defend slavery now quoted it to silence women, sparking a growing feminist consciousness and reinforcing women's bond to Garrison, whose anticlerical arguments had given the Grimkés ammunition against clerical censure. When clergymen tried to silence them, they and other female pioneers questioned the clergy's role in oppressing blacks and women. Women's rights were problematic for many men in the anti-slavery movement: Theodore Weld feared that "undue" attention to the "woman question" might distract people from the more "immediate" problem of slavery. Succumbing to unrelenting male pressure, the Grimkés dropped women's rights from their speeches. Sarah published a feminist manifesto, *Letters on the Equality of the Sexes, and the Condition of Women*, in 1838, and then retired with her sister from public life. Angelina married Weld that year.

It is dismaying that a progressive liberal egalitarian movement denied women equality, but it is an even more bitter irony that a movement to eliminate racial oppression was racist. White women called African women the "reason" that drove them to face reality –

the arguments and heroism of African women inspired white women to "strike out on their own."[22] Yet when the Grimkés first came to Philadelphia and attended Quaker meetings, Africans were segregated from the congregation. Noticing two black women sitting apart, the Grimkés joined them – Sarah Douglass, a schoolteacher, and her mother Grace. When they became friends, Douglass told the sisters about the discrimination they had endured from Quakers. They wrote a pamphlet about it, but no one in the United States would publish it.

The Philadelphia Society was remarkable for integrating black and white women when even the most liberal Protestant societies were segregated. Among the city's free black women working alongside whites were Charlotte, Sarah, and Marguerite Forten (daughters of prominent black shipbuilder James Forten), Harriet Purvis, and Sarah and Grace Douglass.[23] Enslaved black women fought as they could.

One of these was a woman called Isabella, enslaved to a white man in Kingston, New York. Her owner, who inherited her family, did not want to feed her old father, and freed him with no means of support. He also forbade her to marry a man she loved, flogging her in front of him. She later married a man her owner approved of and had thirteen children, most of whom he sold. In 1817 New York State emancipated slaves over forty, but doomed younger ones to ten more years of bondage. To cut their losses, owners illegally sold their slaves out of state (African-Americans were at risk as long as even one state supported slavery). In 1826, believing she would be sold south, Isabella fled to a local abolitionist couple who helped her sue to free her son Peter, who had been sold in Alabama. She won and went to New York City to work as a servant. Illiterate, she worked in the abolition movement under the name Sojourner Truth.

In 1851, at a women's rights convention in Akron, Ohio, a clergyman ridiculed weak helpless women for wanting rights. The audience scornfully heckled the women activists, who sank, defeated. An old black woman stood up in the audience, then came forward to sit on the steps of the pulpit. Some white feminists feared that alliance with abolitionists might injure their cause, and hoped the presider, Frances Dana Gage, would not give the podium to this known abolitionist, Sojourner Truth. As Gage described it, the woman "moved slowly and solemnly to the front, laid her old bonnet at her feet and turned her great speaking eyes to me. There was a hissing sound of disapprobation above and below. I rose and announced 'Sojourner Truth' and begged the audience to keep silent for a few moments." Sojourner faced the clergyman:

> The man over there says women need to be helped into carriages and lifted over ditches, and to have the best place everywhere. Nobody helps me into carriages or over puddles, or gives me the best place – and ain't I a woman?

She raised her strong old bare arm.

> Look at my arm! I have ploughed and planted and gathered into barns and no man could head me – and ain't I a woman? I could work as much and eat as much as a man – when I could get it – and bear the lash as well! And ain't I a woman? I have borne thirteen children and seen most of 'em sold into slavery, and when I cried out with my mother's grief, none but Jesus heard me – and ain't I a woman?

Sojourner Truth seized the occasion and turned it around, electrifying the audience. She never stopped working against racism. A decade after the Akron convention, she protested black segregation in "Jim Crow" streetcars, pressuring Congress to ban segregated cars in the district of Columbia. After the ban was imposed, she repeatedly confronted streetcar conductors who refused to pick up blacks, bellowing, "I want to ride!" as they passed her. One day, the conductor of a streetcar she entered tried to shove her off: she pushed back, and he dislocated her shoulder. She took him to court and won: he was dismissed. Before the trial ended, she said, "the inside of the cars looked like pepper and salt."[24]

The clergy's treatment of the Grimké sisters stirred abolitionists like Lucy Stone to shift their efforts to women's rights, and they lectured on the subject throughout the 1840s. The election to AASS office of Abby Kelley, a young Quaker, opened a major rift in the male-dominated group. Male abolitionists who patronized Frederick Douglass and other black male abolitionists, scorned white female support. Calling women's issues an unnecessary distraction from the "real" problem of slavery, they opposed Kelley's election, and seceded to form a separate group (Garrison dubbed them "New Organization Men"). After the split, AASS men mobilized to end the struggle for equality once and for all. The problem came to a head at the 1840 World Anti-Slavery Convention in London.

Garrison's group, endorsing equal standing for women, sent female delegates to the World Anti-Slavery Convention in London that year. The convention refused to seat them. Delegates Mary Grew, Lucretia Mott, and all other women were relegated to a gallery behind a curtain where they could see but not participate in the events. Black abolition leader Charles Redmond, Garrison, and Nathaniel Rogers joined them there, but the women were humiliated and outraged by the cold hostility of the men who blamed them for the split. Elizabeth Cady Stanton (1815–1902) a newlywed there as her husband's guest, was propelled by the experience (and Mott's tutelage) into political feminism. On the sidelines of this convention the two made plans for a women's convention.

In Feminism

Ferment about women's rights had bubbled since early in the century, heated by women like Fanny Wright, the Grimkés, Lydia Maria Child (the self-supporting writer was furious to learn her husband had to sign her will to make it legal), and others. When legal reforms to merge common and equity law began in the United States in the 1830s, feminists lobbied for the inclusion of the women's rights that had been recognized by some courts – to own property, make contracts, sue, and testify in court.

After London, Mott returned to Philadelphia and Stanton to Boston. Stanton's husband moved the family to Waterloo, New York, where, isolated from friends and worn down by the drudgery of tending the six children she bore in eight years, she became depressed and determined to work for women's rights. When the Motts vacationed in upstate New York in summer 1848, Stanton met with Mott, her sister Martha Wright, Mary Ann McClintock, and Jane Hunt (four Quakers) to plan a women's convention. Within a week, they had put a notice in the newspaper, chosen a chapel for the meeting, written a "Womanifesto" based on the Declaration of Independence and an agenda. Stanton insisted on woman suffrage – her husband was so put out that he left town during the meeting.

Despite scant publicity, 200 women turned up at Seneca Falls, New York, on July 19–20, 1848, as well as forty men – which convinced the convenors not to bar males as they had intended. Besides, the organizers, afraid to chair the meeting, asked Joseph Mott to do it. But women did speak. Although nervous in her first public appearance, Stanton announced their purpose: to right woman's wrongs. Frederick Douglass not only attended but was the only man to speak in favour of woman suffrage. Many activist Hicksite Quakers came and a hundred signed the Declaration of Sentiments passed by the convention, which included equality in education, employment, at law, on public platforms, and the vote.

The personal revolt of a small group of women began a revolution that has not ended. Women as a group were protesting the treatment of women as a caste. Women willing to confront overwhelming institutionalized discrimination and men willing to admit its injustice joined to change it. The first feminist revolution explicitly to challenge patriarchy had begun.

The Seneca Falls meeting was followed by a Woman's Rights Convention in Rochester the same year, mainly to discuss suffrage, the most disputed of the eleven Seneca Falls proposals. The women's declaration did not claim a higher moral nature or special talents for women, but asserted it was the "duty of woman, whatever her complexion, to assume, as soon as possible, her true position of equality in the social circle, the Church, and the State." Urging women "no longer to promise obedience in the marriage covenant" but to let "the strongest will or the superior intellect . . . govern the household," they urged women to claim equal authority "on all subjects that interest the human family," especially their economic status. Pointing to the women who "plied the needle by day and by night, to procure a scanty pittance for [their] dependent famil[ies]," they condemned a man's "legal right to hire out his wife for service" and take her wages as a "hideous custom" reducing women "almost to the condition of a slave."

Immediately afterwards, Amy Post and Sarah Owen organized the Working Woman's Protective Union, which in the next years found jobs, temporary shelter, and child care for fugitives – female slaves and battered wives. Union women helped each other recast their marriages in egalitarian ways, act independently of their husbands, demand equality in decision-making, travel, speech, and the education of daughters and sons. Two months after Rochester, the Congregational Friends proclaimed: "When we speak of the Rights of Woman, we speak of Human Rights." With "common natures, common rights, and a common destiny . . . [e]very member of the human family, without regard to color or sex, possess[es] potentially the same faculties and powers, capable of like cultivation and development and consequently has the same rights, interests, and destiny." For the next sixty years, Congregational Friends worked in various causes to foster equality for all women.[25] Women of all backgrounds welcomed the movement so warmly that within three years a national convention was possible. The 1851 convention repudiated the doctrine of separate spheres: "We deny the right of any portion of the species to decide for another portion . . . what is and what is not their 'proper sphere': . . . the proper sphere for all human beings is the largest and highest to which they are able to attain."

Then as now, feminism had no central control: women chose to concentrate on grassroots organizing. Women acted as they chose – withholding taxes to protest their lack of representation, challenging institutions that excluded them, protecting women's wages from husbands, publishing journals and tracts urging divorce reform, child custody, temperance, anti-slavery, and moral reform, or urging women to give up corsets and stays for tunics and loose-fitting pants like Fanny Wright's (called Bloomers because Amelia Bloomer adopted the style). State by state, they pressed for legal change: fourteen states had reformed married women's property laws by 1860, when New York allowed women their own wages. Others followed.

The New York law resulted from a fierce campaign. Feminists targeted certain regions for attention; in 1853–54, under Susan B. Anthony (1820–1906), the greatest feminist leader of this generation, they campaigned to reform New York laws. Anthony, born to an abolitionist family, began her political career working for temperance. When male delegates to a temperance convention in 1852 refused to let her speak, she resigned from the society and with Stanton founded the New York State Women's Temperance Society. She was one of the few women who shared Stanton's priority of suffrage in that period: the two became lasting friends and made a formidable team. In 1854 they devised the strategy of inundating the New York legislature with petitions from women for three demands: control of earnings, suffrage, and child custody after divorce. The reform laws that New York passed in 1860 were the most advanced in the nation – and perhaps the world.[26] They granted women the right to sue in court, keep their own wages, and exercise more control over a husband's property at his death.

The outcry was huge. Some of the new laws were in fact intended not to redress women's wrongs but to assist bankrupt men to keep their property by putting it in their wives' names. Ignoring this, journalists reacted to women's gains by lampooning feminists, harping on superficial issues like dress (as in the 1970s they harped on "bra-burning"). Politicians deplored the "emasculation" of men who "gave in" to women's demands, calling them "husbands in petticoats." Mobs of men with guns and knives menaced women public speakers while police stood by idly. But not all women supported feminism. Women who accepted a "separate sphere" feared male anger or the consequences of independence and disliked feminism, fearing its militance. And feminism seemed a luxury to lower-class women pre-occupied with survival – nor did feminists fully understand working-class needs. Only Anthony even tried to ally with them.

The nineteenth-century feminist movement has been faulted for its narrowness. Few feminist groups welcomed black women; only the temperance campaign and those for women's right to keep their wages cut across class lines. Feminism was a white middle-class movement whose successes benefited mainly that class – at the time. Women without any political voice managed to change sexual politics through sheer unremitting effort and dedication, and their achievement benefited *all* women later. What is hardest for late-twentieth-century feminists to accept is the racism so evident in certain feminists – yet our record is only a little better. Without ignoring flaws in the movement, we must acknowledge the difficulty of building female solidarity across the divisions carefully created and stoked by patriarchy over eons.

Despite their revolutionary ideas on one subject, middle-class women, like any people anywhere, had absorbed the beliefs, not to say prejudices, of their period. These not only belittled other classes and colours but also themselves. They were often hobbled by a sense of inadequacy and wrongness when they defied their social role. Single women in public arenas in this period were afraid of public scrutiny of their "femininity," because they lacked the usual "accoutrements of womanhood," husbands and children.[27] The inspired speaker Mary Grew, editor of an abolitionist journal *Pennsylvania Freeman*, declined an invitation to address the American Anti-Slavery Association because she had not "sufficient voice to fill the Tabernacle." Married women like Stanton were too frightened to speak at Seneca Falls.

In Black and White Women's Networks

Carroll Smith-Rosenberg has written about a "female world of love and ritual" that flourished unnoticed by indifferent nineteenth-century men.[28] Networks of female friends sustained women emotionally and gave them a voice. Some of these networks grew into larger groups dedicated to a chosen form of social amelioration, or exclusive clubs with literary leanings (which men mocked). Chicago's Fortnightly Club invited guest lecturers to discuss recent books like George Eliot's *Middlemarch*. Ladies' Clubs sprang up in major cities and in Rockland, Maine; Selma, Alabama; Quincy, Illinois; Cripple Creek, Colorado; and Walla Walla, Washington.

After the Civil War women's clubs grew more thoughtful and feminist. The most famous was founded in protest. Professional women had expected to face barriers when they entered the public sphere, but as more women entered professions, men became more antagonistic and erected new obstacles. When the New York Press Association barred well-known journalist Jane Croly from a banquet for Charles Dickens in 1868, she and her friends founded a club called the Blue Stockings, which attracted many prominent New York women: poets, editors, writers, musicians, professors, artists, teachers, physicians, lecturers, philanthropists, and a historian. The club (later called Sorosis) supported suffrage and other feminist demands, but also focused on working-class women.

The Chicago Women's Club, founded in 1876, contained departments dealing with reform, philanthropy, education, the home, art and literature, philosophy, and science. Within a decade, it had over 200 members; five years later, 400. The majority of women chose to work in the most activist sections – education, philanthropy, and reform. They pressured the Cook County Insane Asylum to hire women physicians and during a severe depression in 1893 provided poor women with money and cheap lodgings. They co-founded useful organizations in Chicago – the Legal Aid Society, the Public Art Association, the Protective Agency for Women and

Children – and raised money for an industrial school for boys. The club improved the condition of the poor in Chicago. Its members were activist and often feminists, but it never officially endorsed women's suffrage. Still growing in 1900, it set a limit of 1000 members.

In 1873 The Ladies' Social Science Association based mainly in the Northeast and Chicago, tried to create a national women's network. This popular club fostered early consciousness-raising – open discussion of marriage and sex. In 1889 Sorosis called a national convention, drawing delegates from over sixty organizations nationwide, to form the General Federation of Women's Clubs (GFWC). GFWC founders planned a network of clubs focused on literature, art, or science, but the federation soon moved into civic reform activism. By the 1890s nearly 100,000 American women were club members; by 1910, 800,000 women were part of a "municipal housecleaning" movement to improve neighbourhoods and cities, as well as create kindergartens and libraries across the country.

The YWCA (Young Women's Christian Association), founded in New York in 1858, had at least thirty-six branches by 1873. To help women help themselves, it offered single women newly arrived in cities from abroad or rural areas inexpensive lodging, training in domestic service and other "female" occupations, and a job placement service. The conservative YWCA helped women adapt to, not break barriers. Even so, it was torn by conflict: some members wanted to exclude blacks or accept only Protestants in good standing with their home congregations; some sided with black leaders who saw it as a rich resource for black girls and women. It chartered segregated affiliates in the north but not the south until it became national in 1906. After the First World War, northern branches accepted all classes, creeds, and colours, but southern branches kept blacks in separate branches. Since it did not bar black women, like most national groups (including the GFWC), it was considered liberal and enlightened.

Women's "moral superiority" did not keep them from oppressing others. Knowing how it feels to be excluded for a quality one cannot change, they still excluded black women. As men justified excluding women on grounds of stupidity or emotionality, white women justified barring black women for "moral impurity." Middle-class black women dealt with such insinuations directly. Josephine St. Pierre Ruffin wrote: "Year after year southern women have protested against the admission of colored women into any national organization on the grounds of immorality of these women. . . . The charge has never been crushed, as it could and should have been at first." Fannie Barrier Williams eloquently told a white audience at the 1893 World Columbian Exposition: "I regret the necessity of speaking to the question of the moral progress of our women because the morality of our home life has been commented on so disparagingly and meanly that we are placed in the unfortunate position of being defenders of our name." She shocked them by asserting that white men caused black female "immorality." But nothing changed.

Since the 1790s black middle-class women had formed their own clubs, mutual aid societies based on traditional African female networks to assist mutual survival.[29] Members of the Daughters of Africa, the African Female Band Benevolent Society of Bethel, the African Female Benevolent Society of Newport, Rhode Island, and the Colored Female Religious and Moral Reform Society of Salem paid dues, pooling them to pay women benefits in times of sickness or death, give widows and fatherless children money and visits, and clothe children in African Free Schools. In the 1830s they changed their focus to "mutual improvement." Wives and daughters of ministers, teachers, and businessmen – the African-American elite – founded self-educational groups. Members of the Afric-American Female Intelligence Society of Boston, the Minerva Literary Society, and the Colored Ladies' Literary Society met at each other's homes to read their essays and poems.

Abandoning hope for integration, black clubwomen created their own national network through *The Woman's Era*, a paper published in Boston. In 1896 the National Federation of Afro-

American Women, with branches in sixteen states, merged with the Colored Women's League of Washington (the largest black female organization in the United States) to become the National Association of Colored Women (NACW). Uniting over a hundred women's clubs, it set up a communications network and sponsored publications and conventions to bring women together. A major step for black women, the NACW was neither an auxiliary to a male group nor a minority in a white female group but a group directed by and oriented to black woman. Its first president, Mary Church Terrell, born to slaves during the Civil War, earned a degree from Oberlin College in 1884. A teacher and the first black woman named to the D.C. Board of Education, she expanded the NACW to almost 50,000 members and over a thousand clubs.

Deeply concerned about the health of black women and children, the NACW established social programs. Educator Olivia Davidson wrote: "Three fourths of the colored women are overworked and underfed, and are suffering to a greater or lesser degree from sheer physical exhaustion." White middle-class female social workers addressed themselves to white working-class women in similar conditions but NACW women had a different perspective from whites. They knew that almost all black women bore the burden of raising children yet worked for wages all their lives, and that most black girls could find work only as servants in homes where white men sexually exploited them. Williams wrote in pain about the constant stream of letters she received from southern women "begging [her] to find employment for their daughters . . . to save them from going into the homes of the South as servants as there is nothing to save them from dishonor and degradation."[30]

Leaders felt it urgent to educate girls to help them escape from whites' power and to disprove white myths about black women by personal example and through their works. Their near-religious reverence for their mothers (who deserved it) inspired deep belief in the moral strength of true womanhood. As sexually pure, pious, and domestic as their white counterparts, middle-class black women came to feel their monopoly on virtue obliged them to "better the race," "uplift" the poor. Educated, prosperous, leisured, they saw poor black females as "The Black Woman's Burden."

Despite their class bias, they did much good. Northerners helped southern migrants by creating residences for young working-class women, kindergartens for their children, and mothers' groups with seminars in child care and home economics. In 1896 the Illinois Federation of Colored Women's Clubs opened Phyllis Wheatley Home for Girls, a residence, social club, and employment bureau for young women. Faculty wives and their friends living near Spelman and Moorehouse colleges in Atlanta formed the Atlanta Neighborhood Union, which built a park and health centre for black children and sponsored homemaking and woodworking classes, mothers' clubs, and scouting troops. Northern urban women founded organizations to help southerners who migrated in answer to ads placed by northern employment agencies. In 1897 Victoria Earle Matthews founded the White Rose Industrial Association and Working Girls' Home in New York City to protect black female servants from exploitation. Black women opened branches of the National League for the Protection of Colored Women in New York, Philadelphia, Memphis, Baltimore, Washington, and Norfolk to give migrants rooms, education, and jobs. Black men supported these groups, even joining them.

White middle-class American women were more willing to work with different classes than with different colours, perhaps because lower-class women did not expect equality. Earlier, we noted the 1848 founding of a Working Woman's Protective Union to help poor women, fugitive women slaves, and beaten wives. In 1863 New York women started a Working Woman's Protective Union to coordinate city relief programs for women, find them jobs, and provide money. Women in Travelers Aid Societies met incoming ships to offer immigrant girls lodging at a YWCA home and protect them from "white" slave traders. They could live in YWCA boardinghouses for $3–$4 a week and once they found work, female-staffed agencies helped them in other ways. Female immigrants' main problem was that employers often capriciously refused to pay them. The Chicago Women's Club set up a protective agency; in its first year, over 156 women filed complaints, a third of whom made charges that their wages were unjustifiably withheld.

Women's clubs in many cities formed Women's Exchanges to help poor women who could not work outside the home. For $5, a woman could join an exchange that sold items she made at home, giving her 90 percent of the purchase price. The New England Women's Club gave subsidized lunches to middle- and working-class women and offered evening classes to train them in marketable skills. One dedicated woman could make a great difference in a city. Lucretia Longshore Blankenburg, daughter of the first woman doctor in Philadelphia (who named her for Lucretia Mott), made a difference in that city. She co-founded the New Century Club, which ran a night school for working-class women; she taught bookkeeping, started the New Century Guild, a working-women's club, lobbied the police to hire matrons, and persuaded the Philadelphia school board to appoint women. As president of the Philadelphia Women's Suffrage Association, Blankenburg fought for years to get the major white women's club federation to support it, succeeding in 1914.

CHAPTER 6

THE CIVIL WAR
AND ITS AFTERMATH

I N 1860 THE SITUATION OF AFRICAN-AMERICANS was worse than
ever. In 1820, 13 percent of the 2 million blacks in the United
States were free; by 1860, the African population had nearly doubled but only 11 percent were free. After independence, free
Africans bought land in New York and Pennsylvania, and in the
early nineteenth century they moved into southern Ohio and
Maryland. Most bought small farms, but a few acquired urban
properties in New Orleans and Philadelphia, as well as New York,
Cincinnati, Washington, D C, and Baltimore. When slave trade
ended in 1807, owners could only replenish their slave holdings
through natural increase so they began to coerce women slaves to
produce children. Two women owned by a Virginia planter named
Cohoon had seventy-three descendants.[1] Before the Civil War, free
black men were artisans and mechanics, and 4000 blacks, most in
cities, owned slaves. White men's lust gave black women some
mobility: once slave trade ended, more black women than men were

freed. More free black women lived in the south, and lived better than men. Most black heirs got property from their mothers.

Abraham Lincoln lightly charged Harriet Beecher Stowe with starting the Civil War by writing *Uncle Tom's Cabin.* But while abolitionism contributed to it, the Civil War was not fought primarily over slavery. Northern businessmen who manufactured goods in competition with English imports wanted protective tariffs; southern planters wanted free trade. This conflict, heated by abolitionist pressure, drove the south to secede from the Union in 1861. For the country at large, the Civil War was a struggle for supremacy between national and state law. But it would determine the future of white southerners and African-Americans. Many blacks fought for the Union, proving themselves among the most skilled, courageous soldiers despite prejudicial treatment.[2]

Woman Spies, Soldiers, and Workers

Women took many roles in the war. Army nurses acted as scouts and spies; Dr. Mary Walker (see chapter 5) was sent on an intelligence mission.[3] Belle Boyd, a Confederate Army nurse, joined the army in her teens and became famous for courage and expert horsewomanship. Riding thirty miles one night to tell a Confederate officer about a plan for a secret attack, she was betrayed and captured in July 1862. The northern press smeared her as a "village courtesan" who got information by sexual means. Jeanne d'Arc (found a virgin when she was captured) was similarly accused: such smears keep women from acting in the world.

Rose O'Neal Greenhow, a widowed society woman, lived in Washington, DC, with her eight-year-old daughter. In 1861 the north suspected her of spying and placed her under house arrest, forcing her to sleep with her bedroom door open, censoring her mail, and denying her newspapers and contact with friends. They used her house to imprison other suspected spies – it became known as Fort Greenhow. Freed in 1863, she immediately ran the northern blockade to sail to France, placed her daughter in a convent, and embarked on diplomatic work for the Confederacy. She sailed home in 1864, carrying gold and documents in a diplomatic pouch. Outside Wilmington, Greenhow sighted Union patrols who might seize the ship and tried to elude them by rowing to the harbour. She drowned when her boat capsized, a martyr to the Confederacy.

Another southerner, actress Pauline Cushman, sympathized with the North and declared her principles publicly, yet she remained extremely popular in her native New Orleans. Cushman was able to glean information about Confederate plans and transmit it to Union officers when she toured border states with her theatre company. In 1864 the south caught her with plans she had stolen from a Confederate engineer. She managed to escape but was recaptured and sentenced to death. Union soldiers rescued her and she resumed her acting career in the north.

Many women disguised themselves as men to join the armies as soldiers – more than four hundred were found out. Sarah Edmonds became Franklin Thompson, a male nurse with the 2nd Michigan Cavalry. In 1865 she published an account of her adventures as nurse, spy, mail courier, and soldier. The government granted her a pension of $12 a month in recognition of her service to her country (but not until 1884). Ellen Goodridge went to the front with her Union fiancé; Franny Wilson of New Jersey fought with Union troops for a year and a half before being wounded – and exposed – at Vicksburg. Most female soldiers were discovered wounded, in hospitals. Southern women were far less likely to adopt this disguise, and those who did had usually accompanied their husbands. But southerner Amy Clark remained a soldier after her husband was killed at Shiloh, and was exposed only after capture by the north.

Southern women were less likely than northerners to abandon traditional roles, but not because they were weaker or less spirited. They had the harder lot, since most of the war was fought on southern territory. They suffered terribly from shortages. After a long seige, when the only food in Vicksburg was rats, women instigated food riots and looted government warehouses. When Union soldiers occupied the south, they took over southern houses, forcing the women in them to cook, clean, serve, and do laundry. As Union troops moved on, they stripped farms bare of food and valuables, and often burned the houses down. Toward the end of the war, they adopted a "scorched earth" policy, burning crops in the fields. When Confederate soldiers arrived, southern women welcomed and fed them, but they consumed whatever the Union men left. Yet southern women were infamous in the north for their spirited hostility toward Union soldiers, so much so that one officer ordered that any woman showing disrespect for Union soldiers was to be treated like "a woman of the town." Neither victory nor defeat eased the lot of women in occupied areas.

A new job area opened to women during the Civil War – white-collar work. Lack of men led storeowners to hire women; female shop clerks were paid as little as $5 a week for long hours – sometimes over a hundred hours a week. Yet it was probably because of the pay that women kept these jobs when the war ended. Before the Civil War, a few women were hired as clerks in the patent office. War opened jobs for women in the civil service. Frances Spinner, appointed Treasurer of the United States in 1861, hired about a hundred women for government service; other government offices did the same: nearly 500 women worked in Washington by 1865. Spinner paid women $600 a year in 1861, and $720 by 1865, which allowed them to live decently. Other government departments, especially the Post Office (an all-male preserve until it hired women to work in the Dead Letter Office), paid women half or a third of what men earned for doing the same work. Still, women earned more than they could elsewhere, doing relatively clean safe work, and they eagerly sought government jobs. They earned excellent work records.

But good work did not prevent them from being fired when the war ended. Officials insisted that "government girls" give way to returning veterans, in some cases arguing the impropriety of men and women working in the same office – even though they had done so harmoniously for several years. The men got rid of women, who made up only 3.3 percent of office workers in 1870. But the precedent for white-collar women workers had been set, and by 1880 the percentage of women working in offices doubled; by 1890, it tripled. By 1900 women filled over 75 percent of the jobs in private and government offices; two-thirds of all typists and stenographers were females aged fifteen to twenty-five. As white-collar work was feminized, however, wages fell and, despite their numbers, women were not promoted but continued in low-level jobs. Most were single and lived with their parents, and they took what they could get.

Once the war was over, men everywhere expected women to return to their pre-war status. This was impossible. An estimated 620,000 men had been killed in the conflict, nearly a generation of young men. Women who had struggled to keep the children alive and the farm productive during the war had to pick up the broken pieces of their lives. The situation was worst in the south, where they were left with houses in ashes, scorched fields, and a devastated countryside. Alabama alone had 80,000 destitute widows. Sexual imbalance persisted in the south until the 1880s.

Transcontinental Shift

Men who survived the war sought a better future by heading west or north or south to Spanish America. Entire families moved west for a clean start; over 350,000 people made the long trek overland to Oregon, California, and points along the way. In 1879 7000 blacks moved to Kansas, fleeing persecution by southern whites; many fled elsewhere – men to escape violence and find work, women to protect their children. In the spring, homesteaders loaded supplies and valuables into Conestoga wagons for the five- to seven-month journey, covering fifteen to twenty miles a day along the Platte River valley on the north central plains, across the Rocky Mountains into Wyoming.

The journey was easier for men; women were still expected to do all the work of maintaining the family – cooking, mending, laundering, healing, and tending children. They had to gather dry buffalo dung for fuel and cook over an open fire: "From the time we get up in the morning until we are on the road, it is hurry scurry to get breakfast and put away the things . . . pulled out last night," one woman recalled. Every night they had to reverse the process, unpacking utensils, gathering fuel, and cooking – often burning themselves. Afterwards, the men relaxed around the fire while the women cleaned utensils, clothes, and children before they could sleep. But the most unpleasant experience was to be pregnant while travelling over rough terrain and to give birth in a Conestoga wagon. Many died.

These women developed great hardiness and learned to drive wagons and handle weapons. And once the journey was over, homesteaders built one-room sod or log houses miles from the nearest neighbour. Sod houses were always covered with a layer of dust; some had grass floors. Log houses had chinks and were drafty; women stuffed the chinks with rags and mud. Furniture that had not been brought in the wagon was rudely crafted. Roofs leaked so badly that women kept their skillets covered so that mud, rain, and muck would not drip into dinner. The mark of a seasoned pioneer was that she no longer bothered to wear gloves when she collected buffalo dung. One man remembered his mother making biscuits: "Stoke the stove, get out the flour sack, stoke the stove, wash your hands, mix the dough, stoke the stove, wash your hands, cut out the biscuits, stoke the stove, wash your hands, put the pan of biscuits in the oven, keep on stoking the stove until the biscuits are done. Mother had to go through this tedious routine three times a day." And it was only one step in producing meals.

As usual on farms, women worked in barnyard, dairy, and vegetable garden, earning money from butter and eggs, and providing food for the family. Homesteaders spent surplus money on machinery to lighten men's work, or on new barns, rather than on conveniences to ease the drudgery of women. As always, women's huge contributions to their households were simply expected and gave them little voice in financial decisions. Many died of hardship – one walked five miles to find a tree tall enough to hang herself on.[4] One Nebraska homesteader went through four wives: he left a bride behind when he went west, and then married a woman who went mad on his isolated farm. His third wife, a mail-order bride, deserted him after two weeks, so he ordered a wife from Europe. She became pregnant almost immediately and had to remain, but was miserable, her daughter wrote.

The Homestead Act, passed by Congress in 1862, allowed anyone twenty-one or over, or the head of household, to stake a claim to 160 acres for $14 and receive final title if they showed they had lived continually on the land for five years and improved it. The wording of the law enabled women to stake claims and a fair number did. Mary O'Kieffe's husband regularly disappeared; she finally packed up her belongings and her nine children and left the family farm on the Missouri River. With her children, she "hitched the horses, loaded the cultivator, strapped a cage of poultry to the wagon-top and made a fifty-one-day, 500-mile trek," to claim land in Nebraska, build a sod house, and prosper.[5]

Even before the Homestead Act was passed, women went west alone, some when gold was discovered at Sutter's Mill, California, in 1849. When a man named Guerin died in 1857, his destitute widow cut her hair, put on pants, named herself "Mountain Charley," and embarked on a career as a male wagon-train driver to California for thirteen successful years. In towns that were nearly all-male, adventurous single women worked as cowgirls and sharp-shooters, or in dance halls, saloons, and brothels. All single women in the west were considered whores; whatever their sexual activities, most eventually married. Some became models of respectability; some grew rich in marginal occupations. Irish-born Mary Josephine Welch migrated to the United States in her teens. In 1867, single and twenty-three, she left Chicago for the mining frontier, settling in Helena, Montana, near Last Chance Gulch. Calling herself

"Chicago Joe," she ran the Red Light Saloon, importing women from Chicago to work as dollar-a-dance "hurdy-gurdy girls." She took part of their earnings – as much as $50 a night. When newspaper accounts celebrated Chicago Joe's Valentine's Day ball, moral reformers were outraged. In 1873 they succeeded in making dance halls illegal.

The south had more women than men, the west the opposite – Wyoming had six men to one woman. To lure women west, the Wyoming legislature granted them citizenship – the right to vote and hold office. Feminist activists gained the vote in Washington Territory, Idaho, and Utah – where female suffrage backfired.

Joseph Smith's Church of Jesus Christ of Latter-day Saints was often persecuted. The sect was driven from upstate New York to Illinois and, after Smith was killed in 1844, it followed Brigham Young to the barren salt flats of Utah. Smith, eager to attract women to his sect, supported women's societies, but in the 1830s established polygyny. Some think he hoped to draw older single women and widows unlikely to marry, but it is more likely he wanted to attract men to a sect whose moral code forbade both men and women from extra-marital sex. Young had twenty-seven wives. Suffragists, arguing that Utah women needed to outlaw polygyny, won the right to vote in 1870. But female Mormons obeyed their church fathers, and barred women from public office. They used the franchise to give men political control of the state.

Native American Women

In their advance westward, whites trespassed on and appropriated Native American land. In the Northwest Ordinance of 1787 the government pledged: "Utmost good faith shall always be observed toward the Indians; their land and property shall never be taken from them without their consent." But from Washington on, presidents violated the treaty. As Justice John Marshall was defining Native Americans as a "dependent nation" within the United States (1832), President Andrew Jackson was fomenting war on Indian societies that blocked frontier settlement. The army forced Indians off their land in cruel massacres; they retaliated with raids. By the 1840s, war on the frontier was constant.

Some of our knowledge of Native American customs in this period comes from people kidnapped by Indians. Texan Rachel Plummer, who was held by Comanches for almost two years, was appalled by women's status in Comanche society: "The women do all the work, except killing the meat. They herd the horses, saddle and pack them, build the houses, dress the skins, meat, etc. The men dance every night, during which, the women wait on them with water." She did not note that white women too did most of the work, or that whites also excluded women from their councils.

Like European Americans, Native Americans divided labour by sex, but did not regulate sex the same way. A Moravian minister who spent years with Native Americans, mainly Delawares, wrote: "Marriages among the Indians are not, as with us, contracted for life; it is understood on both sides that the parties are not to live together longer than they shall be pleased with each other. The husband may [leave] his wife whenever he pleases, and the woman may in like manner abandon her husband." A male observer of the Cherokee resented their view of adultery – perhaps seeing it as female usurpation of a male right. The Cherokee, he wrote, "have been a considerable while under a petticoat government, and allow their women full liberty to plant their brows with horns as oft as they please, without fear of punishment."

A woman of the Fox tribe recalled a strict division of labour and training – girls and boys were raised separately and trained differently, but the sexes had complementary status and responsibility. When she left her lazy, abusive first husband, no law stopped her; she alone made the decision to marry a man she loved, who waited until the time she set to approach her. Choosing not to interrupt her active sex life by having children, she drank a potion given her by a wise woman to prevent pregnancy. But when her husband died, she decided to marry a last time to have children and found the wise woman again. "Is there perhaps a medicine whereby one might be able to have a child if one drank it?" There was; she drank it, became pregnant, and later had several children.

After the Civil War, Native Americans were confined to reservations, their numbers severely reduced by war and the disease and famine it brought. Their children were taken away and placed in schools to "Americanize" them, "to kill the Indian and save the man." The Dawes Act (1887) forced white notions of private property on Native Americans, destroying with a stroke of a pen an age-old tradition of communal ownership. When Oklahoma entered the Union in 1906, Indian Territory ceased to exist.

The Situation of African-Americans[6]

Emancipation did not make freed slaves citizens. The government passed three amendments to the constitution: the Thirteenth abolished slavery; the Fourteenth made blacks citizens; the Fifteenth forbade discrimination on grounds of race or prior status and granted males suffrage. After passing Congress, however, the amendments had to be ratified by two-thirds of the states. Intense lobbying ensued. Women were in conflict about the Fifteenth Amendment. Some, like abolitionist Sarah Parker Redmond, worked for black male suffrage despite the exclusion of women; others, like Sojourner Truth, predicted that exclusion would lead to the domination of black women by black men. It is noteworthy that she used the future tense.

Slaves lacked all rights – civil, political, economic, or social – so any sexual domination among blacks was situational, not legal. It lacked an institutional base. Any male dominance drew from American culture or African tradition, compounded by women's tendency to bolster pride and confidence in those they love, especially those continually beaten down. African-Americans lived in the same overall society as whites, but their position within it required different strategies for survival.

Like whites, African-American men wanted dominance, felt that manhood needed continual proof, and associated freedom with manhood. In 1773, when revolutionary fervour swept the colonies, black male slaves petitioned the Massachusetts legislature for freedom on the grounds that as slaves they *lacked authority over their families*. They asked: "How can a husband leave master and work and cleave to his wife? How can the [wives] submit themselves to . . . husbands in all things?"[7] At abolitionist meetings in the 1850s black male leaders complained: "As a people, we have been denied the ownership of our bodies, our wives, home, children and the products of our own labour." They urged black "mothers and sisters" to "use every honorable means to secure employment for their *sons and brothers*." In William Wells Brown's early African-American novel, *Clotel* (1861), black women are accused of wanting to become their white masters' lovers.[8]

Knowing that male slaves scorned cooking, sewing, laundry, cleaning, bathing children, or picking lice out of their hair, owners punished them by forcing them to do such tasks. A Louisiana cotton planter made male offenders wash clothes and forced chronic offenders to wear women's dresses. A historian reported that men treated this way were more tormented by what they considered public humiliation than by harsher punishments: "So great was their shame before their fellows that many ran off and suffered the lash on their backs rather than submit to the discipline."[9]

As oppressed women sacrifice solidarity if they accept traditional patriarchal class divisions, oppressed groups lose solidarity if they accept patriarchal sexual divisions. Men who feel they must prove they are men invariably choose to prove it by dominating women rather than by refusing domination by other men. No group or class of men seems immune and African-American women's extraordinary resourcefulness and endurance seems only to have intensified African-American men's need for superiority.

The burden shouldered by slave women was an extreme form of that borne by other women.[10] Until the nineteenth century most women were responsible both for reproduction (and the enormous tasks associated with it) *and* for production. Slave women were not uniquely but extremely oppressed. To cement their control, white owners denied slaves any power over their lives, including the right to marry (yet scorned them as sexually unbridled). Family had great meaning for slaves, so keeping a family together was an act of defiance. Since owners regarded slave children as *their* property, an intact family was a triumph and gave people a place of their own in the midst of dispossession and alienation. African mothers had always been the centre of the family, struggling to maintain its integrity and welfare.[11]

Owners who gave skilled jobs only to males and never gave slave women authority over men in work, rarely made sexual distinctions on grounds of strength. Owners made women carry very heavy loads and work long hours, barely lightening their burden when they were pregnant or nursing. (Yet they wanted strong healthy babies who fetched high prices.) But slaves helped each other. Jacqueline Jones wrote about the Bell family on a Virginia wheat farm. During the harvest, Frank Bell and his four brothers followed their parents down the long rows of grain so that "one could help the other when dey got behind. All of us would pitch in and help Momma who warn't very strong." The overseer forbade families to work together, believing "dey ain't gonna work as fast as when dey all mixed up," but the driver was Bell's uncle, who "always looked out for his kinfolk, especially my mother."

James Taliaferro recalled that his aunt Rebecca ("a short-talking woman that ole Marsa didn't like") was usually assigned more work than other women. His father one day counted the corn rows she was allotted, and told her she had twice as many as anyone else. Indignant, Rebecca confronted the owner. Only after threatening to sell James' father for meddling did he grudgingly reduce her workload. On another plantation, fieldworkers surreptitiously added handfuls of cotton to the basket of a young woman who "was small and just couldn't get her proper amount." (Slaves had to pick a certain amount each day. Failure meant a whipping.) Even the work of house slaves was hard and endless: only about 5 percent of all adult slaves worked as house servants, and during the harvest season, all slaves, even those in the house, had to go to the fields to pick cotton.[12]

Children too were treated without sexual distinction. All were dressed in a "splittail shirt," a knee-length smock slit up the sides: "They call it a shirt iffen a boy wear it and call it a dress iffen the gal wear it." Children between six and twelve lugged kindling for woodboxes, built fires in bedrooms on chilly mornings and evenings, made beds, polished shoes, washed and ironed clothes, and stoked fires while whites slept at night. They fetched water and milk from the spring-house and meat from the smoke-house, set the table three times a day, helped the cook, served meals, "minded flies" with peacock-feather brushes, "passed the salt and pepper on command," and washed dishes. In the house, they swept, dusted, served drinks, and fanned visitors. White mistresses gave their babies to slave children barely beyond babyhood themselves to bathe, diaper, dress, groom, and entertain. Children on farms "gathered eggs, plucked chickens, drove cows to and from the stable, and 'tended the gaps' (opened and closed gates)." In fields they acted as human scarecrows, toted water to workers, and hauled corn shocks. As an old woman, ex-slave Mary Ella Grandberry said she "disremember[ed] ever playin' lack chilluns do today."[13]

The central irony in slave women's history is that *because* owners ignored physical differences in fieldwork, slaves maintained a strict sexual division of labour in their households and communities. The home, such as it was, was the place where slave men's pride could be rebuilt by women following sex rules traditionally African or copied from whites. For black women, the family was the centre of resistance to oppression; for white women, the family was the centre of oppression.

Free African-Americans lacked property, education, or white acceptance, and faced a terrible struggle for survival in which it must have seemed essential to pull together, not separately. And they felt strongly that black women's refusal to work in white homes annulled white power over blacks. Women supported by men could pay full attention to their own families. Most stopped working in the fields or worked only at harvest time. Outraged southern men noted that "negro women are now almost wholly withdrawn from field labour"; statistics show that not only did many wives stay home, but those who still did field-labour worked like humans, not slaves – shorter hours and fewer days a year.

Production fell drastically in many regions. Aware that "women were as efficient as men in working and picking cotton," landowners enraged at losing their unpaid workforce blamed "female loaferism" and forced black women to work for them. Lucretia Adams of Yorkville, South Carolina, told the Freedmen's Bureau, which negotiated labour contracts between planters and blacks, that eight drunk white men seized and assaulted her, saying, "We heard you wouldn't work. We were sent for . . . to come here and whip you, to make the damned niggers work."[14] Intimidated workers remained silent, fearing complaint might lead to reprisals. Whites seized black children to "apprentice" them, supported by southern courts. In Maryland alone an estimated 10,000 children were bound to labour over their parents' objections.

Discrimination against African-Americans continued on every level and the government ignored its promises to give them land. Still, blacks succeeded for a time. After a post-war tour of the south, Frances Harper reported that African-Americans "were beginning to get homes for themselves . . . and depositing money in the bank . . . . They have hundreds of homes in Kentucky."[15]

Whites determined to put a stop to this: they paid blacks so little that a man could not earn enough to support a wife and children. In 1867 they resuscitated a sharecropping system used on feudal manors in Europe as feudalism was collapsing. Landowners offered landless men cabins on their plantations, providing tools, seed, and use of the land. In return, sharecroppers paid landlords a share – usually half – of the crop they raised, usually cotton. This form of labour departed radically from the "gang" farming characteristic of plantation slavery and from the wage economy that characterized northern industry. It involved private individuals working land not theirs for a return on their labour – an incentive to hard work. Landlords won a good return on land they could not afford to pay workers to farm. Black sharecropper husbands assumed the main responsibility for agricultural work; their wives assumed the responsibility for maintaining the family and helped the men on the land, especially during planting and harvest. Children too worked in the fields at those times, so the whole family worked in relative safety from intrusion by whites.

Although this arrangement helped landless families, it imposed the traditional division of labour and power; this division was also reinforced by the black church, which, like white churches, exhorted wives to submit to husbands. Female herb doctors and "grannies" were revered in the black community, but men dominated black political and religious organizations, holding all positions of authority. Like white men, they felt they had a right to dominate and to beat their wives, an abuse that greatly increased in this period; what black men needed to bolster egos damaged by white persecution or exploitation was *domination*.

Few African-American women could afford the luxury of refusing to work for whites. Women without men or whose men lacked land had to work for wages, often as domestic servants; many were the economic mainstay of their families. Yet black male writers blamed such women, insisting that their husbands were actually able and willing to support them, and that they worked for whites merely to obtain finery and luxuries. African-American men chose to emulate the white patriarchal model whenever possible. Some black women welcomed dependency, some were forced to accept it, and some resisted it.[16] The pressures on black women to accept the white middle-class model were great: all women are taught that male pride and ego depend on female dependency, but black male pride had suffered incalculably. But both sexes suffered for their allegiance to a patriarchal family structure.[17]

A small class of middle-class African-Americans had thrived in the United States for over a century before the Civil War. They went north: free African-descended Barbadians and other islanders, escaped or freed slaves. They were cautious because they were always in danger. Yet they educated their children and many became teachers. The first known African-American teacher, Catherine Ferguson, an ex-slave, in 1793 opened Katy Ferguson's Schools for the Poor in New York City. In 1851 white Myrtilla Miner opened the Miner School for Colored Girls in Washington, DC; in 1852 the Institute for Colored Youth was founded in Philadelphia. After the war, young northern-born middle-class black women ran schools for freed people funded by the American Missionary Society and other philanthropic groups. No schools opened in the south until Josephine Griffin pressured Lincoln to let her collect volunteers to help freed blacks find food, homes, and establish schools.

With Lincoln's sanction, Griffin founded the Freedmen's Bureau, under whose aegis people moved south to teach former slaves: by 1869 it had 9000 teachers, of which half were women. Susie King Taylor, laundress for the first black Union regiment, nursed the wounded, then became a teacher. Charlotte Forten, an educated middle-class black, gave up a comfortable life up north to teach African-Americans on the Union-occupied Sea Islands off South Carolina. For the two years that Forten lived and taught in Port Royal, she kept a diary – the first black female diary published in the United States, one that remains inspiring reading today. Black and white northerners who moved south encountered hostility, ridicule, and even violence, yet many remained even after Union troops withdrew in 1877. They prepared the way for the civil rights movement of the future: W.E.B. Du Bois called them the "tenth crusade."

Educated or not, black women could find few jobs after the war. Although the number of female field workers in the south dropped sharply in the 1870s, only women supported by men could afford to reject fieldwork. Most freedwomen did the same work as slaves – stuck in it by their skin colour, years after most white women had gone to factories and offices.[18] As late as the 1930s, over a quarter of black working women in the United States did agricultural work; most others were domestic servants or washerwomen. The situation was identical in the north. Between the Civil War and the First World War, black women flocked to northern cities but most could find work only as servants. Women with small children could not live in a white household and could only wash white men's shirts at the going rate of 13 cents a dozen. In 1900, 84 percent of black working women were servants or laundresses; in 1960, almost a third of African-American female workers were domestic servants and over half the country's 2 million domestic workers were black women.[19] Until recent decades, black women constituted a permanent service class in America.

Since white churches barred or discriminated against African-Americans, black congregations built their own churches. But the black clergy who defied Paul's dicta on slaves accepted his position on women and systematically denied them leadership within the church.[20] Like white women in support positions in their churches, black women essentially held the church together, teaching Sunday school, counselling and sponsoring youth groups, singing in the choir and establishing their own missionary societies. Some nineteenth-century black women Baptists created a feminist theology, using Bible stories to justify a more aggressive public role for women within the Church without breaking with orthodoxy. Over male objections, women in the African Methodist Episcopal Church preached, claiming that their call arose from extraordinary visionary and spiritual experiences. Fannie Jackson Coppin and a committee of women at the Mother Bethel African Methodist Episcopal Church opened a home for destitute young black women.[21]

When reconstruction ended in 1877, northern troops were withdrawn and the Freedman's Bureau became, wrote Du Bois, a "dead-letter." White southerners amplified their campaign to re-establish white supremacy and destroy black political power and prosperity, which had been gradually increasing. By 1889 black men were disenfranchised in the south. Each locality had a subterfuge for accomplishing this, like poll taxes, or literacy tests not given to whites. White school administrators diverted funds allocated to black schools to white ones, state governments legalized segregation, and whites began to use terror, subjecting blacks to mob violence and lynchings. Between 1890 and 1915, the white campaign of intimidation was so extreme that few blacks challenged it, and many moved north, preferring its racial discrimination and *de facto* segregation to the south's Jim Crow laws, a rigid system of apartheid enforced by terrorism.[22]

Once African-Americans were free, racism intensified. Racism, the claim that one race is superior or inferior *humanly* to another or others, is a strategy like sexism (the assertion that one sex is superior or inferior humanly to the other), devised to justify legal, social, economic, and political subjugation of a group.[23] African-American slavery was *always* racist; white indentured servants were all eventually freed. Africans differed from Europeans not only in colour but also in culture, and people tend to rank differences. Slavery came to an end in the United States but racism did not. The extremism of southern terrorist organizations was not anomalous; racist hatred of blacks in the United States was and is almost as profound and pervasive as woman-hatred (*almost* because woman-hatred is more pervasive – men of colour are also misogynist – and is worldwide). Gradations in skin colour are probably the first thing we notice about people after their sex.

In both north and south, whites cooperated in actively or passively impeding blacks, denying them decently paid jobs, residence in their communities, jobs in their workplaces, and places in schools and other institutions. Under persecution, thriving black communities dwindled into dirt-poor ghettos full of neglected children: both parents had to work just to survive, no child-care facilities existed or money to pay for them if they had.

After the industrial revolution, the middle class in England, the United States, and Europe treated the working class similarly and caused them similar suffering. But some middle-class people pitied and worked to ameliorate workers' situation; more important, workers themselves achieved a rough solidarity, a class-consciousness that enabled them to fight for decent lives. Their numbers and solidarity frightened governments and industry into making concessions to them. Whites had far less empathy for blacks; the racist myth assumes that blacks hate whites and are a mortal threat to all whites – although as we have seen, the oppressor always hates the oppressed far more than the opposite. Every black-consciousness movement that has arisen in the United States has been swiftly and brutally suppressed, and black leaders imprisoned or killed. Blacks remain about 15 percent of the population of the United States; they lack the numbers to threaten to shut down society. Under J. Edgar Hoover, the FBI pursued a policy of intimidation even against the non-violent campaign of Martin Luther King Jr. When blacks frighten industry or government, those bodies do not hesitate to use force. Public outcry is limited to blacks and a few whites because whites, who far outnumber blacks, have been convinced by racist propaganda.

Racism was fostered by intellectuals who taught that blacks were subhuman, morally degenerate, and incapable of education. Their ideas were based in the work of scientists (who "scientifically" defended the enslavement of Africans) like Dr. Cesare Lombroso (who also cast contempt on women and Jews: see chapter 8), whose book, *Criminal Man* (1876), asserted that men with non-Anglo-Saxon features tend to love "idleness and orgies," pursue evil for its own sake, lust to murder, mutilate corpses, and "tear . . . flesh and drink . . . blood." A similar campaign was waged against immigrants who came to America in the late nineteenth century. Theodore Roosevelt and Henry Cabot Lodge upheld "eugenic" ideas foreshadowing those of Hitler. Xenophobia spread as the "science" of eugenics taught that certain groups – mainly Latins, Slavs, and Jews – tended to be feeble-minded and must be sterilized so as not to pass on the trait. "Manliness," the great good, required white racial solidarity and a warrior ethic; European anarchists and socialists were "effeminate" and decadent. By 1900 reformers fully believed in hereditary criminal tendencies and "irredeemable deviance." Massive propaganda campaigns in the 1950s and 1960s quieted such views, but they still thrive.

People concerned with True Womanhood were oblivious to black or working-class women. Only "ladies" were human – other women were outside the realm of discourse. The elevation of "ladies" (the word automatically excluded blacks or workers) led to the onus of sexual sin and evil in the world being placed on female "non-ladies," especially blacks. Society at large assumed that black women were *inherently* immoral, sexually licentious. The irony that this judgment was the result of their victimization by white men is too cruel to bear.

Southerners justified violence against blacks by claiming they were protecting the virtue of "white womanhood." They were also implicitly warning white women who were asserting themselves in the new climate. The "pursuit of the black rapist represented a trade-off . . . the right of the southern lady to protection presupposed her obligation to obey."[24] White men had always abused white women, belittling them, taking black slave lovers, battering them when they were drunk. Suddenly these same women were "unsullied alabaster icons," so delicate that a black man's glance could pollute them.[25] But a myth of "knights" protecting chastity gave violence a Christian religious basis.

The south's persecution of black men of course harmed black women. A nineteenth-century historian wrote that blacks were so degenerate they could not survive without slavery and white supervision, and that black men raped white women in disgust at the "wantonness" of black women.[26] His view was not extremist; it was mainstream thinking. From the post-Civil War until the civil rights movement, black women in America were perceived – and treated – as sexually available to any man.

Vigilante groups – the White Citizens' Council, The Knights of the White Camelia, The Knights of the White Magnolia, and the Ku Klux Klan – used terror as a weapon. All lynched blacks; the Klan soon became a terrorist gang. Sheets concealed their faces, transforming men considered pillars of the community into outlaws whose trademark was lynching, often in a brazenly public carnival atmosphere. They castrated blacks and fought over body parts as trophies.[27] Black executions increased in time: an average of fifty-seven black men a year were lynched in the 1880s; in the 1890s, 116 blacks every year except 1892, when 162 souls were lynched – four outside the south. The murders were invariably presented as retribution for black men's approaching white women but in the climate of the south at that time, black men did not even dare to look at white women – and five people hanged in 1892 were women.

A woman led the fight against lynching. Ida B. Wells (1862–1931), born six months before the Emancipation Proclamation to slaves in Holly Springs, Mississippi, went to a local Freedman's Aid Bureau school. But when she was fourteen, her parents and three siblings died in a yellow fever epidemic. Claiming she was eighteen, she applied for a teaching job to support her remaining four siblings and taught in Holly Springs until she was twenty-two, when she moved to Memphis. There, she refused to leave the all-white "ladies" car of a train (she had all the attributes of a lady but blacks could not be "ladies"), and was thrown off. Wells' account of this experience for a black-owned newspaper opened a new career for her. When she wrote about Memphis schools providing inferior education for black children, she was fired from her teaching job. She then earned her living by her pen: travelling throughout the south, she wrote about black people. In 1889 she bought into the *Memphis Free Speech*, and became editor.

The peak year of lynchings, 1892, changed Wells' life. Three young black men were lynched for raping a white woman. Wells knew their real crime was running a successful grocery store in competition with a white one. She wrote a powerful condemnation of the lynching, urging blacks to move to Oklahoma Territory. Thousands did. She remained in Memphis to boycott the city trolley system until a mob of whites invaded her newspaper office, destroyed the press, and threatened her life. She took them seriously, moved north, and embarked on a campaign of lecturing and writing about white terrorism against blacks. Her pamphlet, "Southern Horrors," itemizes the extent and acceptance of lynching in the south, stressing that such murders had nothing to do with white women or sex, but were racially motivated executions.

The indefatigable Wells founded women's clubs and anti-lynching committees in the north; she toured England, lecturing and gaining considerable support for her anti-lynching movement. In 1895 she married, settled in Chicago with her husband, Ferdinand Barnett, and published *A Red Record* (with an introduction by Frederick Douglass), which recorded the lynchings of the three previous years in brutal detail. Wells was part of an 1898 delegation which demanded that President McKinley act on the lynching of a black South Carolina postmaster. Huge public anger rose against her, but she never stopped. Around 1900 she joined other crusades like the Niagara movement, a campaign for racial equality led by Du Bois, and helped found the National Association for the Advancement of Colored People (NAACP).

A feminist, Wells joined the woman suffrage movement despite southern white suffragist protest; she criticized Susan Anthony for allowing segregation in the movement. In the course of her career, she argued with everyone. She rightly accused WCTU head Frances Willard of racism; she defied the United States Secret Service when it threatened to arrest her for treason if she would not stop publicizing the government's hanging of nineteen black soldiers who defended themselves against an attack by white soldiers. She fought with important black leaders like Booker Washington, who did not support equal rights for blacks and was for much of his career an apologist for white supremacy, and with Du Bois and the NAACP, for the weakness of their anti-lynching program. Wells was one of a handful of women who, unlike male leaders, refused ever to compromise for the sake of profit, advancement, or obedience to a party. Like Emma Goldman and Rosa Luxemburg, she ended her life in political isolation. Like them, she remained steadfast to the truth as she saw it, and looking backward, we must acknowledge her vision as indeed true.

The Black Middle Class

Black women educated their daughters: an African-American woman passed the bar exam in the 1880s. The first female physicians to practise in the south were black. Around 1900 Booker T. Washington's National Business League listed thousands of accomplished black women: journalists, writers, artists, 164 ministers, 160 physicians, 10 lawyers, 7 dentists, 1185 musicians and music teachers, and 13,525 educators.[28] Blacks developed class-consciousness and a new militancy; some joined Marcus Garvey's Universal Negro Improvement Association (UNIA), the only serious African nationalist movement to emerge in the United States.

Marcus Garvey, a charismatic West Indian, declared that European imperialism was dying. Insisting that blacks would never be treated as equal in the United States, he urged they return to Africa to create a new united society. Calling himself Provisional President of Africa, he planned to buy a steamship to transport people to Liberia. Drawing poorer blacks (who had reason to agree with his negative estimate of their future in America) partly by disparaging light-skinned blacks, he held huge UNIA rallies with pomp and pageantry – complete with plumed hats, medals, titles, and parades – established an African Orthodox Church with a black Virgin and a white Satan, and supported women's rights.

As soon as the First World War ended, the United States government began a campaign to root out "subversives" – people who dissented on any ground from the capitalist status quo – by creating a division of the Justice Department under J. Edgar Hoover. One of its targets was Garvey. In 1920 Garvey held the first UNIA convention in Madison Square Garden, and the following year sent the first UNIA mission to Liberia. In 1923, Hoover arrested Garvey for mail fraud, imprisoning him for three months until President Harding ordered him released. Two years later he was convicted and imprisoned, and in 1927 President Coolidge commuted Garvey's sentence and deported him as an undesirable alien.

Many middle-class blacks and black intellectuals opposed Garvey. The intellectuals were creating a brilliant new culture in northern cities, centred in Harlem and called the Harlem Renaissance. It began just after the First World War, and was perhaps rooted in black music, the first characteristically American music and, worldwide, the most influential music of the twentieth century.

Blacks had distinguished themselves in the arts before the twentieth century: we have previously noted New England poet Phillis Wheatley and sculptor Edmonia Lewis (1843–1900?).[29] The first novel by an African-American was by a woman. When Harriet E. Wilson published *Our Nig* (1859), whites ignored it because the novel dealt with northern racism in a period when northerners felt self-righteous because they were fighting for abolition. When the novel was rediscovered, it was deemed so good that it was said to have been written by *a white man posing as a black woman*.[30] Many black women wrote in the late nineteenth century: the best known are Frances Ellen Watkins Harper, Alice Dunbar-Nelson, and Anne Perry.[31]

But in the 1920s African-American music, art, and literature suddenly flowered magnificently. Harlem was a centre of excitement: while exhilarating Garveyite rallies drew huge crowds at Liberty Hall, the 135th Street YMCA presented speakers like Du Bois and plays by Du Bois, Angelina Grimké, or Georgia Douglas Johnson, and a new generation of black poets read at the 135th Street branch of the New York Public Library (now Schomburg Center). Paul Robeson appeared on stage; offered a theatrical career, he turned it down for law school. Artists like Bessie Smith, Josephine Baker, Louis Armstrong, and Duke Ellington performed in Harlem nightclubs, which were in the height of fashion. (Yet clubs like Connie's Inn and the famous Cotton Club accepted blacks as performers only, not as patrons. They were also too expensive for most blacks. Some clubs were mixed and some all-black.) Downtown, all-black musicals and revues were staged for the first time, with huge success; Edna Guy did classical dance; and Marian Anderson sang at Town Hall.

In Europe, where jazz and black music were adored, black singers like coloratura Marie Selika and soprano Caterina Jarboro built operatic careers, and sculptor Meta Vaux Warrick (1877–1968) and portraitist Laura Wheeler Waring studied and exhibited. Warrick studied at the Pennsylvania School of Industrial Arts and the Colarossi Academy in Paris, where she met Saint-Gaudens and Rodin. Returning to the United States, she married Solomon Fuller, a physician, in Framingham, Massachusetts, and over his opposition built a studio with her own hands. Although insufficiently appreciated in its own time, her powerful work inspired later generations. Augusta Savage (1900–62), another inadequately appreciated black woman artist, was born in Florida and was one of the first women to study sculpture at Cooper Union. Sculptor Selma Burke (1900–95) is remembered for the Franklin Delano Roosevelt profile on the dime. The greatest artists of the movement were Warrick and Aaron Douglas (1898–1979) one of the Harlem movement who broke with academicism to create a brilliant African-American style.[32]

In the 1920s Douglas met Du Bois, the Harvard-educated editor of the NAACP magazine *The Crisis*, and did designs and illustrations for *The New Negro* (1925), the literary anthology edited by Alain Locke that first brought widespread attention to Harlem Renaissance male writers like James Weldon Johnson, Countee Cullen, Langston Hughes, and Sterling Brown. Locke, a philosopher, devoted a 1925 issue of *Survey Graphic Magazine* exclusively to Harlem artists; it became the manifesto of the movement. Some intellectuals wanted African-American artists to withdraw from American culture entirely. Locke wanted them to express their

Americanism with pride in their history and culture – African heritage, black traditions, and community life.[33]

Jessie Fauset (1885–1961), who published *There Is Confusion* in 1920, was the first woman identified with the Harlem Renaissance to publish a novel. Described as the "most prolific novelist of the Harlem Renaissance," she published four novels between 1924 and 1933 and edited *The Crisis*. An advocate of black pride, she tried to reach all of America.[34] Claude McKay, a Jamaican living in Harlem, issued *Harlem Shadows* (1922), the first book of poetry published by a Harlem Renaissance poet, celebrating black beauty. Other black literary figures like poet James Weldon Johnson, who edited an anthology of Black American verse, Jean Toomer, author of *Cane* and other novels, poets Countee Cullen and Langston Hughes, as well as Carl Van Vechten, whose novel *Nigger Heaven* deals with Harlem life, all helped bring a new consciousness, a new language into American culture. Nella Larsen, who had a Danish mother and a black father from the Virgin Islands, published *Quicksand* (1928) and *Passing* (1929). But the most important woman connected with the Harlem movement was Zora Neale Hurston (1901–60).

Black colleges and universities lacked the trust funds that supported white institutions, with portfolios built up over decades by prosperous alumni. Howard University, the largest black college in the United States, depended on Congress for funding, and government funding means government control. In the repressive 1920s it was discovered that the Howard library contained a book promoting socialism. A Congressional reprimand forced the president of Howard to apologize, vowing that the school neither taught nor advocated socialism. Zora Neale Hurston protested in *The Messenger*, the most militant black journal of the period, that the president "should have informed the body that we could teach what we liked and if the money was withheld, we would have the satisfaction of being untrammeled."[35] After Howard, she went to New York to study anthropology at Columbia with Franz Boas and in 1925, became editor of a black journal, *The Spokesman*, stressing literature based on black folklore. She published her first book of poems in 1926, but did not attain her full stature until after the Harlem Renaissance, publishing three novels between 1934 and 1948. The most famous is now a classic: *Their Eyes Were Watching God.*

The Harlem movement spread to Washington, DC, Cleveland, and Chicago, strengthening African-American confidence and identity. Then the Depression hit and the movement was over. Langston Hughes later wrote: "Between 1919 and 1929, Harlem was in vogue." Economic recessions always wipe out the poor first, and the Depression gradually ravaged Harlem. It was never the same again. During the 1930s many blacks turned to Communism as their only hope. The great majority of blacks were thrust back into poverty and marginality, but the monuments of the Harlem Renaissance remain to inspire future generations of blacks and whites.

White terrorism made normal life impossible for blacks in the south. When the urgencies of the First World War forced northern industry to open jobs to blacks, a mass migration occurred: 2 million blacks moved to northern cities between the two world wars. Whenever possible, black families tried to educate their children, and in periods of prosperity many entered the middle economic class. But black middle-class people were not treated as part of "the middle class"; they were shut out of middle-class and even poor white neighbourhoods clear across the United States.

Wealthy, middle class, or poor, blacks lived in segregated communities, attended black churches, and joined black social organizations. Their lives were circumscribed by the black community and they were either ill at ease or outright terrified in the white one. Whites remained ignorant of blacks, if not downright hostile. At first blacks could express themselves or take the lead only in church: the church was their shelter.[36] Black class structure was modelled on that of the master race – the elite were light-skinned – but it accorded people status for education and correct behaviour rather than for income.

During the First World War, some African-Americans who

moved north to take jobs in industry earned decent wages for the first time in their lives; they sent their children to standard integrated schools, voted, held office, and gained confidence in themselves as part of the larger world. As male doctors, teachers, educated ministers, and small businessmen carried their families into the middle class, their wives formed social clubs and reform societies, becoming leaders in anti-lynching and suffrage campaigns.

The Temperance Movement

The most important nineteenth-century female society was the Women's Christian Temperance Union (WCTU). A temperance society had been formed by men and women earlier in the century, but it was sidetracked by the Civil War. In the depression years of 1873–74, women in the midwest protested male drinking. Imitating itinerant preachers, they invaded town bars singing hymns and reciting scripture, praying and urging temperance. Nearly 25,000 women took to Philadelphia streets in an 1874 "Women's Crusade": they protested at 406 bars, pressured 38 church members to evict saloons from their property, persuaded 80 bartenders to resign, and extracted pledges of temperance from 280.[37] They formally organized as the WCTU.

National officers sent Plans of Work to WCTU locals detailing suggested strategies. In 1874 they recommended holding Gospel Temperance meetings "in the streets, billiard-halls, and churches . . . offering the Gospel cure for intemperance," with women moving among the audience playing the tune of "Jesus, Lover of My Soul" to invest the act with the solemnity of a religious service, urging people to come forward and sign a pledge. When Frances Willard (1839–98) became president of the WCTU, it became a political force. She ran it from 1879 until her death.

Born to educated parents in Wisconsin, Willard was a genius: with only a mediocre education at a female seminary, and after only a few years of teaching, she became president of Evanston College for Ladies. When Northwestern University absorbed Evanston, she became dean. Dealing with an all-male board of trustees and a president who was her ex-fiancé may have radicalized her, because after three years she sought another vocation. Rising equally swiftly in temperance work, she became head of the Illinois chapter, then the national union, in months. Temperance was not a passion but a vehicle for Willard; her goal was always to attract apolitical women into a militant women's rights movement.

Temperance drew women like no other cause. Most WCTU members were middle class, not poor women visibly victimized by husbands who drank their wages and abused their families. We may surmise what went on in middle-class homes. The women of the WCTU were convinced that banning alcohol would purify the world of evil. Soon after her election as president, Willard (called "St. Frances" by her followers) launched a campaign, collecting 180,000 signatures on a petition to prohibit the sale of alcohol. Within a few years, the crusade had spread to every state in the union. Willard then extended her "Home Protection" campaign, arguing that only the vote would enable women to fulfil their True Womanhood and protect their homes from the "demon rum."

By 1880 the WCTU had become the largest female organization ever seen in the United States, international in scope and organization, and the largest reform movement of the century. Over 200,000 dues-paying members and thousands more sympathizers embraced the notion of woman's "separate sphere." They founded their reform philosophy on it, seeing temperance agitation as a natural extension of their roles as wives and mothers protecting the home. Accepting a narrow role at first, they expanded it, storming streets, taverns, and legislatures to "purify" them in the name of the home. More than any other female society in nineteenth-century America, WCTU members were conservative, domestic, pious, respectable middle-class married white women who never touched alcohol or tobacco, went to church regularly, and were sexually irreproachable – precisely what society demanded they be. They were pressuring men with the very morality that men insisted they uphold, and temperance literature contains a certain retaliatory aspect. Noting that "in the popular division of responsibility . . . the father may be a moderate drinker [but] the failure of the boy to grow up good and pure is adjudged to be his mother's fault," it stressed mothers' importance and responsibility.

Injustices suffered by other groups mattered less to Willard than her constituency and its aim, "to make the whole world *homelike*." She said this was her goal: maybe it was or maybe this was the only discourse available to her. For it is true that many women who crusaded in the name of domesticity and the Home never married, had children, or managed homes. Willard was single and worked with an exclusively female support network that included single women like Catherine Beecher and Sarah Josepha Hale, who supported themselves by advising women on domestic matters but never ran their own homes. Other female agitators had marriages unconventional by nineteenth-century standards: Elizabeth Cady Stanton discarded her husband; Lucy Stone found a supportive one.

In 1881 Willard succeeded in obtaining WCTU endorsement of woman suffrage. Although some suffragists were uncomfortable with WCTU support, they welcomed the hundreds of thousands of women it added to the movement. When Willard died – before Prohibition became law – her organization reverted to its old form, becoming a single-issue lobby. Her great accomplishment was not banning alcohol, but raising the consciousness of thousands of middle-class women about their importance to society and their right to a voice.

Settlement and Prisons in America

Idealistic young college graduates in America were inspired by the British settlement movement, and in 1886 Stanton Coit founded the first settlement house in the United States, the Neighborhood Guild in New York City. Settlement swiftly became a female cause as young educated middle-class women seized this outlet for their abilities. In 1889 seven Smith College alumnae rented a tenement on New York's Lower East Side for a settlement house. Other women founded settlements in Boston, Philadelphia, and Pittsburgh; Jane Addams and Ellen Gates Starr founded Hull House in Chicago; and Lillian Wald founded the Nurses' Settlement in New York. In 1894 Susan Chester, a Vassar graduate, built the Log Cabin settlement near Ashville, North Carolina, to adapt urban reforms to a rural area. She started clubs for girls and women, revived the weaving industry, and created a library. Local people regularly walked eleven miles to her cabin to use the cherished library.

Jane Addams, one of those sickly middle-class single women who "proved" men's claim that women were weak, was educated by her wealthy family and then was expected to spend her life at home caring for aging relatives. She understandably collapsed with "nervous prostration" and was treated by Dr. S. Weir Mitchell (who also treated Edith Wharton). His Hospital of Orthopedic and Nervous Diseases specialized in female "nervous complaints." A spinal problem kept her bedridden for six months and in a leather, whalebone, and steel corset for two years. But when she founded Hull House (and, perhaps, acknowledged her sexuality) she recuperated. Her dream was to transform the poor community by helping poor women find work: she later said that helping others helped her even more. Their same-sex relationships sustained Addams and Lillian Wald throughout their lives.[38]

Most settlement workers focused on practical programs like child-care centres, kindergartens, manual training, and industrial education. Hull House collected money to feed striking Chicago textile workers in 1896. In 1910 Addams derided the idea that "the sheltered, educated girl has nothing to do with the bitter poverty and . . . social maladjustment which is all about her, and which, after all, cannot be concealed, for it breaks through poetry and literature in a burning tide which overwhelms her; it peers at her in the form of heavy-laden market women and underpaid street labourers, gibing her with a sense of her uselessness."[39] When she wrote this, over four hundred settlements thrived in America.

Most American settlements were non-sectarian; workers lived in the settlement houses, their relations with their poor neighbours uneasily progressing from suspicion to affection. The overwhelming majority of settlers (three-quarters) were women, young, single, and college-educated. A tiny group in the poor masses, they were extremely effective, keeping their organizations flexible and personal. Female "settlers" had special clarity about the connection between poverty, prostitution, and other female crimes.

In 1857 reformers sympathetic to women accused of crimes, especially young ones ("juvenile delinquents") established the first reform school for girls, in Massachusetts. Like sisters in British penitentiaries, women superintendents in reform schools had an exalted notion of their task. One wrote: "It is sublime work to save a woman, for in her bosom generations are embodied, and in her hands, if perverted, the fate of innumerable men is held."[40] Reformers tried to train women in domestic skills; most American reform organizations were not tied to a church, but reform was pervaded with moralistic thinking based in religious notions of purity and taint, especially when it concerned women.

Sex determined what was a crime. Men were jailed for (alleged) violence to property or persons, but women could be confined in reformatories or lunatic asylums for masturbating or sex before marriage – or "wantonness." Some girls were incarcerated for life for such acts. Early reformers kept them from "temptation" by locking them in reformatories and teaching them domestic skills to "redeem" them. Once reformers accepted eugenic theories that viewed criminal tendencies as hereditary and deviance irredeemable, they confined women with no effort at reform.

Many institutions were extremely punitive, using solitary meals, permanent handcuffing, and imprisonment in dungeons to control inmates. In a rare case of organized resistance, women in the New York Hudson House of Refuge rioted to protest the dungeon and extreme corporal punishment in 1899. Late in the century, prison reformers worked for separate prisons for women. Women in mixed prisons were treated very harshly – at Sing-Sing Prison, they had their hair cut off, were gagged, locked in straitjackets, and kept in solitary confinement cells without windows or light. Such abuses roused feminists to work for prisoners' rights as "their sisters' keepers." In female prisons, female superintendents used gentler means to keep order.[41]

Utopian Visions after the Civil War

The early socialist agricultural cooperative communities had been forgotten, but some people devised cooperative techniques geared to industrial society. In 1868–69, Melusina Fay Peirce, the wife of a Harvard professor, published a series of articles in *Atlantic Monthly*. She argued that women should do two things "as the conditions not only of the future happiness, progress and elevation of their sex, but of its bare respectability and morality. First: They must earn their own living; Second: They must be organized among themselves." She urged cooperative stores, kitchens, laundries, and bakeries; she suggested that groups of women do housework cooperatively, billing husbands for the service on the same scale as skilled male workers. Men did not want their wives working to "make other men comfortable," but public kitchens and cooperative dining halls became popular late in the century, some supported by the settlements. Single women ran an impressive array of cooked-food delivery services, cooperative dining clubs, and communal bakeries and laundries, and they delivered prepared food by horse-drawn carriage or automobile in towns from Evanston, Illinois, to Palo Alto, California, from 1869 to 1920.

Edward Bellamy's *Looking Backward*, published in 1888, became one of the century's best sellers. The hero of Bellamy's utopian novel awakes in 2000 to a world in which women have full political and economic equality. The state supports pregnant women and pays for domestic work in public kitchens and dining rooms, day schools and nurseries, freeing women from economic dependence on men. The novel inspired the political Nationalist movement.

Charlotte Perkins Gilman (1860–1935) became spokesperson for the movement. Gilman, grandniece of Harriet Beecher Stowe, was a complex and important figure.[42] Her father deserted the family when she was seven, and her childhood and adolescence were very unhappy. Her brother was sent to MIT and earned a degree, but Charlotte was allowed only a short stay at the Rhode Island School of Design. She married at twenty-four but, after giving birth to a daughter the next year, had an acute breakdown. Despite severe depression, she began to write. When she recovered, she divorced her husband. When he remarried, she gave him custody of her daughter, Katherine, and went off to write and lecture in Europe and America. In 1892 she published the powerful "The Yellow Wallpaper," a claustrophobic account of a woman driven mad by the seemingly loving ministrations of her doctor husband.

Gilman went on to publish *Women and Economics* in 1898, a brilliant analysis of modern industrial economy and women's position within it. Society confuses women's sexual and economic functions, in a holdover from the past that is anachronistic in modern industrial society. Gilman urged economic reorganization to give women equal participation in public life and enable them to develop fully into independent human beings who contribute to society, "rather than creatures of sex": men sell labour for survival but women, denied wage-earning jobs, were forced to sell sex to survive. Her next book, *The Home: Its Work and Influence* (1903), accused the single-family home of wasting resources and isolating women. She proposed "French flats" (apartments), in which wives, not domestic servants, would be paid for household maintenance. Mechanized household gadgets only chain women to the house: professional services should launder, wash diapers, prepare food, and do other household tasks. Gilman also wrote utopian novels: *Herland* (1915), the most famous, was serialized in her magazine *The Forerunner*, which for fifteen years published feminist analyses of law, education, fashion, and sports. Gilman was another expert on domesticity who had repudiated it in her life.

CHAPTER 7

WOMAN SUFFRAGE
IN AMERICA AND
GREAT BRITAIN

In America

THE AMERICAN SUFFRAGE MOVEMENT was an uneasy alliance of
women whose main bond beyond their sex and inferior status
was work in some area of reform. Few were militant feminists. Some
were active abolitionists; most were evangelicals working in moral
reform, political conservatives who claimed a right to political
action on grounds of moral superiority. Their vision of women as
superior collided with the feminist vision of women as like men.
Conflicting interpretations of Woman's Nature produced a tension
that characterized the suffrage movement (and women's movements
into the present) in debates over education, protective legislation,
maternity leave, and other issues.

In the early republic, some women had the franchise: in 1783
New Jersey granted the vote to all residents of age worth £50. Only
two women voted in 1787, because of confusion about eligibility,

but few women had £50. Women's participation in local elections (in large numbers in 1797), aroused male resentment: newspaper articles ridiculed "petticoat politics," warning of a legislature "filled with petticoats." Men opposed to women's voting often claimed that slaves did too; an 1806 election was voided after reports that women, blacks, and white men voted more than once. After John Condict, a Republican representative from Essex County, New Jersey, was nearly defeated by women's vote, he led a campaign to limit eligibility. In 1807 New Jersey limited the franchise to white male adults with property.

In the nineteenth century, women made giant steps toward full citizenship, but won not one victory for woman suffrage. Men feared suffrage more than any other reform as a threat to "the family," that is, to male supremacy. Too cowardly to admit this explicitly, they argued that women who wanted the vote were insulting their husbands, who always voted in the best interests of the entire family. Woman suffrage would generate domestic chaos (two voices instead of one), unsex women, and emasculate men, as women abandoned housekeeping and child-rearing, leaving them to men.[1]

Suffragist-abolitionists were disturbed by the Fifteenth Amendment because, in granting suffrage to freed slaves, it added a word never before used in the constitution – *male*. Introducing sex discrimination into the constitution affronted all women, especially abolitionists. In essence, the drafters of the amendment were rubbing female abolitionists' noses in their victory: women were being made to pay for abolition. Suffragists, outraged that men whose slavery they had fought to end had been granted a right denied them, became racist: patriarchy had triumphed again.

Citizens could work to pass the amendment extending suffrage at least to black men, or work against it. Most male and some female abolitionists lobbied for the amendment, dissociating themselves from the women's movement. In 1865 the charismatic antislavery orator Wendell Phillips told suffragists he was setting aside female suffrage to ensure franchise to newly emancipated black males: "I hope in time to be as bold as Stuart Mill and add to that last clause 'sex.' But this hour belongs to the negro." The *negro* was apparently male. Devastated by the amendment's wording, bitterly disappointed by the desertion of black and white abolitionists whose cause they had championed, women in the suffrage movement split. Elizabeth Stanton, Susan Anthony, and others in the National Woman Suffrage Association (NWSA) rejected the Fifteenth Amendment. Lucy Stone, her husband Henry Blackwell, and Julia Ward Howe accepted it and left the NWSA to found the American Woman Suffrage Association (AWSA).

The adamant opposition to the women's movement, which had originally called for a total makeover of society, had forced it to narrow to a single issue: suffrage. Some contemporary feminists fault the single-minded pursuit of suffrage, a strategy that ignored other needs and relinquished hope for larger change. But men obstructed every proposal that might relax legal and social constrictions on women – even those that would benefit men, like contraception. Given the fierce opposition, it may have been necessary to concentrate on one issue.

In addition, a footnote: the December 1999–January 2000 issue of *Ms. Magazine* featured interviews with a dozen women a hundred years old or older. One of the questions asked them was what event was most important for women during the preceding century. Nine of them said "the vote"; two said feminism (or women's lib); and one, a Chinese woman whose feet had been bound as a child, cited the end of footbinding. People now disenchanted with the political scene dismiss the importance of the vote, but the women who lived through not having it, then having it, know better.[2]

Over the century, middle-class women's birth rate dropped by half. The decrease from an average of 7.04 children for each married woman in 1800, to 3.56 in 1900, suggests that women took control of reproduction somehow. They were given very little information about contraception or their sexual and reproductive organs; doctors authoritatively offered false advice, designating as safe a time of month when we know now conception is most likely, or insisting that women could not get pregnant if they did not reach orgasm. Women often refused sex or made men withdraw before orgasm – which should have made men welcome birth-control devices. Ignorance of birth control was wilful. Rubber condoms were advertised and available in the east in the 1850s. A diaphragm-like "womb veil" invented before 1864 was banned in the United States until the 1920s.

A small group of feminists, including the redoubtable Victoria Woodhull, argued for contraception to limit family size. (They did not claim to want to free sex from conception or ease women's burden: such ideas were too radical for the times.) But men opposed "planned parenthood." In the front line against contraception were religious leaders, backed by a male establishment that feared giving women such freedom. Theodore Roosevelt's denunciation of contraception as "race suicide" (white women must reproduce or the nation would be overrun by "hunger-bitten hordes") was popular with elite southern whites. In 1872 New York's YMCA, to enforce the ban on immoral material (anything mentioning sex), hired investigator Anthony Comstock "to prosecute, in all legal forms, the traffic in bad books, prints and instruments." He later worked in the same job for the United States Post Office so zealously that the ban was called the "Comstock law." His first victim was Victoria Woodhull.

Born in 1838 in Ohio, one of ten children, Woodhull was neglected and uneducated, a vagabond. In her teens, she turned to spiritualism. She married at fifteen but continued to travel, earning her living as a clairvoyant for a decade. Beautiful, intelligent, and enterprising, she divorced, remarried, then met Cornelius Vanderbilt. She persuaded him to back a New York brokerage company that she founded with her sister, Tennessee Claflin. Woodhull, Claflin, & Co., the "Lady Brokers of Wall Street," made a fortune and in 1870 persuaded socialist Stephen Pearl Andrews to publish a weekly paper, *Woodhull and Claflin's Weekly*, which offered radical feminist ideas even about sex: equal rights for women, "free love," ending the double sexual standard and sexual hypocrisy. Woodhull became famous (or infamous); the popular press called her "Mrs. Satan," "Queen of Prostitutes." Yet she appeared in the Congress speaking in favour of woman suffrage.

This extraordinary woman argued that the Fourteenth and Fifteenth Amendments granted citizenship to everyone born or naturalized in the United States; women were citizens, and suffrage was a right of citizens which could be endorsed by a mere Congressional Act. Her 1871 speech won the support of Stanton and Anthony (and of the NWSA), who had been ambivalent about Woodhull. Hundreds of women went to polls in 1871 and 1872. Anthony went to one in Rochester, expecting to be turned away and planning to sue, but was allowed to vote. Two weeks later, federal marshals banged on her door and arrested her for voting illegally. She lost her court case but used it to publicize woman suffrage. Woodhull tried to take over the NWSA; when Anthony thwarted her, she started her own Equal Rights party, which nominated her for president and Frederick Douglass for vice president (without his knowledge). Douglass disclaimed the nomination, and no campaign was launched.

But Woodhull's most scandalous act was her revelation in 1871 of an adulterous love affair between Henry Ward Beecher, a famous reform minister, and Elizabeth Tilton, wife of his best friend, reformer Theodore Tilton, both his parishioners. The affair had long been rumoured; Woodhull may have published it to expose sexual hypocrisy in the middle class, but people were less shocked by the affair than by her defying propriety in revealing such behaviour in moral leaders. Tilton sued Beecher for misconduct. The sensational trial dragged on for weeks and ended in a hung jury: Elizabeth Tilton could not testify in her own defence. It harmed the women's movement: Beecher had been president of the AWSA; Stanton and Anthony, who defended Elizabeth Tilton, were tainted.

People associated the Beecher-Tilton affair and Woodhull's "free love" with the women's rights movement.

By the 1890s publicly approved laws muzzled contraception advocates and banned birth-control devices and information. The only means to limit family size were abstinence or abortion. From 1800 to 1830 there was (estimated) one abortion for thirty live births; by 1850 the figure was one in six. Since it was illegal, women without sympathetic doctors (fortunately, many doctors were sympathetic) had to resort to riskier practitioners. Two-thirds of the women who sought abortions were married, 60 percent had one child or more. Those too poor to pay for an expensive illegal procedure aborted themselves. Many died rather than bear another child: in the 1920s, one of two pregnancies was aborted.

Sojourner Truth and Stanton predicted that the constitutional amendments would deepen sexual antagonism: "Woman will then know with what power she has to contend. It will be male vs. female, the land over." Both Stanton and Anthony seemed most offended by the right of lower-class men – ex-slaves, indigents, immigrants – to vote, when middle-class women could not. Stanton was outraged at "refined" white women being ruled by men from "the lower orders of Chinese, Africans, Germans and Irish, with their low ideas of womanhood." Anthony fumed: "While the dominant party have with one hand lifted up *two million black men* and crowned them with the honor and dignity of citizenship, with the other they have dethroned *fifteen million white women* – their own mothers and sisters, their own wives and daughters – and cast them under the heel of the lowest orders of manhood." Like the European feminists who tried to offset class fear by urging that only propertied women be granted suffrage, Stanton suggested giving middle-class white women the vote to outweigh "the Freedmen of the South and the millions of foreigners now crowding our shores." Giving black men the vote, she said, was giving them a virtual licence to rape. As usual, rage was directed *below* rather than above.

Still, blacks worked for woman suffrage. Sojourner Truth, Frances Harper, Sarah Redmond, Mattie Griffith, and Hattie Purvis – all well-known abolitionists – crisscrossed the country by stagecoach, train, and steamboat, sometimes trudging on foot to carry the crusade to towns in Ohio and upper New York State, Wisconsin and down the Missouri River to Kansas City. Frederick Douglass, the six black men in the Massachusetts House of Representatives, and seven of eight black congressmen from South Carolina supported woman suffrage. Inspired by Victoria Woodhull, Mary Ann Shadd Cary registered to vote in the District of Columbia in 1871.

Their huge effort did not succeed during their lives, but Stanton and Anthony have an importance beyond the movement they founded, despite their racist and classist attitudes. They were first to realize that women would not succeed as long as they linked their demands for themselves to demands for others. Imbued with the female ethic of self-sacrifice, women had always tied their needs, like ribbons, to abolition, temperance, or industrial reform packages. Stanton and Anthony saw that women had to work by themselves for themselves in an independent women's movement. They also saw that organization was vital to success.

In 1887 Alice Stone Blackwell, daughter of Lucy Stone and Henry Blackwell, initiated a merger of the AWSA and NWSA into a National American Woman Suffrage Association (NAWSA) with Stanton as president. Perhaps exhausted by the failure of their forty-year effort, Stanton and Anthony adopted a strategy of "expediency." A movement that had begun by demanding justice in human rights was reduced to arguing that votes for women would offset the "foreign influence" (immigrants and black men) in politics. A new generation of suffragists, led by Carrie Chapman Catt and Alice Blackwell, found Stanton rigid and old-fashioned; they could deal with her only through beloved "Aunt Susan" Anthony, who took over as NAWSA president in 1892. But Catt too argued that the nation was threatened by foreign men's votes and wanted them revoked in favour of middle-class women.

Anthony asked Frederick Douglass to absent himself from the next NAWSA convention – *Douglass*, who had spoken at Seneca Falls! The 1895 convention, the first in the south, was to be held in Atlanta, and she feared he would be an embarrassment. Stanton pleased the southern audience by warning against enfranchising "illiterate" women, but Anthony and Stanton's daughter, Harriet Stanton Blatch, voted against her proposals. Stanton, a prolific writer and the intellectual force of the movement, was dejected by the mean narrow thing her cause had become and turned her attention to religion as a major antagonist to women's rights. From 1895 to 1898, she issued the *Woman's Bible*, a commentary on biblical passages on women. Her brilliant work gained her a host of new enemies; even NAWSA voted 53 to 41 to repudiate it officially.

But Stanton was right about the church: Christian churches worked fiercely, if covertly, against suffrage. The most visible lobby opposing woman suffrage, the liquor industry, feared women would vote for prohibition. (The Eighteenth Amendment prohibiting the sale of alcoholic beverages was passed in 1919 *before* women won the vote, and was later repealed. The industry did not foresee that women would someday drink.) Businessmen fought woman suffrage on economic grounds but, like clergymen, camouflaged their views by declaring that God had not intended women to vote.

The 1899 NAWSA convention refused to back a resolution that black women need not ride, according to the Jim Crow laws, in railway smoking cars: claiming NAWSA could not control railroad company policy, Anthony rejected black women's cause. Fearing defection by white southern women if it supported black women, NAWSA let white men dictate its policy. Blacks outnumbered whites in many of the southern states that barred black men from voting. Southerners feared they could not thwart women too: as W.E.B. Du Bois explained, "You can bribe some pauperized Negro labourer with a few dollars at election time, but you cannot bribe a Negro woman."

Yet white women's rejection did not deter black women from working for suffrage – it spurred them on. Fannie Barrier Williams pointed out: "The exclusion of colored women and girls from nearly all places of respectable employment is due mostly to the meanness of American women, and every way that we can check this unkindness by the force of the franchise should be religiously done." By the 1900s the NAACP had a female-staffed suffrage department, and black women's suffrage clubs thrived in tens of American cities. The indomitable Harriet Tubman, Frances Harper, and Mary Church Terrell addressed suffrage meetings.

NAWSA remained divided over the best way to win the franchise. Anthony wanted to concentrate on a constitutional amendment; others urged working state by state. But local campaigns proved disappointing: of four hundred mounted between 1870 and 1910, only seventeen led to referenda and only two approved suffrage. In 1900, worn out by *fifty years* of meetings, speaking, writing, trudging from door to door begging for signatures on petitions, enduring ridicule and hostility, travelling across the country (shocking for a woman alone), sleeping in carriages, suffering frostbite: exhausted and defeated, Susan Anthony resigned – although she remained the vital force and head of the movement until her death in 1906. Her friend Elizabeth Stanton died in 1902. The Seneca Falls generation died feeling they had failed.

In 1907 suffragists, including Stanton's daughter, Harriet Stanton Blatch, met in New York City to discuss ways to revive the crusade. They founded the Equality League of Self-Supporting Women (later the Women's Political Union – WPU), which by 1909 had 19,000 members including Rose Schneiderman and Charlotte Perkins Gilman. In 1910 the WPU launched a new campaign – large-scale demonstrations and parades showing the movement's broad base. A newpaper account of a 1912 march read: "Women who usually see Fifth Avenue through polished windows of their limousines and touring cars strode steadily side by side with pale-faced thin-bodied girls from the sweltering shops of the East

Side. . . . All marched with an intensity and purpose that astonished the crowds that lined the streets.[3]

Younger suffragists Alice Paul, Blatch, and Lucy Burns had worked with British suffragists and urged more militant action. They wanted to adopt the British strategy of holding current administrations accountable and protesting against the party in power. The day before Woodrow Wilson's inauguration as president in 1913, they marched in Washington. Ida Wells tried to join the contingent but whites, insisting that southerners would not accept her, urged her to march with a "colored delegation." She disappeared into the crowd but when the parade was underway, suddenly stepped among the Chicagoans and finished with them.

By June 1916 women had won suffrage in presidential elections in twelve states. Hoping women might bloc-vote in the next election, Paul formed the National Woman's Party (NWP) to campaign for pro-suffrage candidates, but its spirited anti-Democratic campaign did not defeat Wilson. In 1917, with the First World War raging in Europe, the NWP picketed the White House with demands for suffrage. For months, the police remained passive and Wilson courteous, but after the Russian Revolution the Russian Kerensky, whose revolutionary government had granted woman suffrage and other rights, visited the White House. Suffragists held up banners announcing that the United States was not a democracy but the fief of Kaiser Wilson. Male onlookers, some uniformed military men, attacked them violently. Only women were arrested – over five hundred picketers – and nearly a hundred were imprisoned.

Imitating British women, they went on hunger strikes in jail, and American prison officials, like the British, retaliated with forced feeding, martyring the women. Wide publicity roused so much sympathy for them that the government was forced to back down and in March 1918 the District of Columbia Court of Appeals invalidated all prison sentences and illegal arrests of peaceful protesters. Wilson, not personally opposed to woman suffrage, shifted his stance to support it, joining with NAWSA and the NWP to back a federal statute, the Susan B. Anthony Amendment, which passed the House and went to the southern-dominated Senate.

Black women and the NAACP feared an alliance of white suffragists and southern racists, so the NACW's Northeast Federation, representing 6000 black women, applied en masse for membership in NAWSA. NAWSA leaders were appalled: terrified of the south, they were willing to sacrifice black women to gain the vote for whites. They asked black women to defer their aims for the time being for the sake of the *larger cause* – white franchise! While this conflict was hanging, the Senate passed the Anthony Amendment. It still had to be ratified: women faced another fourteen months of lobbying, speechmaking, petitioning, travelling, before the Nineteenth Amendment was finally passed in 1920. The fight for woman suffrage took seventy-two years.

Carrie Chapman Catt wrote that simply to remove the word "male" from the constitution, American women had to conduct "56 campaigns of referenda to male voters; 480 campaigns to get Legislatures to submit suffrage amendments to voters; 47 campaigns to get State constitutional conventions to write women suffrage into State constitutions; 277 campaigns to get State party conventions to include woman suffrage planks; 30 campaigns to get presidential party conventions to adopt woman suffrage planks in party platforms and 19 campaigns with 19 successive Congresses."

Then the official women's movement collapsed, lost cohesion.[4] The strategy of Alice Paul's NWP was concentration on single issues. Believing franchise alone would not change women's status, she urged a constitutional amendment guaranteeing women economic and legal equality. When the Equal Rights Amendment was submitted to Congress in 1923, Crystal Eastman remarked it was worth fighting for even if it took ten years! But focusing on the ERA meant ignoring other matters of vital importance to women – birth control, *de facto* disfranchisement of black women, peace, and protective legislation. The NWP dismissed these as "diversionary and divisive," the same grounds on which abolitionists sixty years before had renounced the cause of woman suffrage.

But at the moment feminism was falling into disrepute, a host of women's organizations sprang up, many formed by former suffragists.[5] The New League of Women Voters, the National Consumer's Leagues, Business and Professional Women's Clubs, the National Congress of Parents and Teachers, and the American Association of University Women: each had its own specific agenda. They sometimes allied, but solidarity was a thing of the past: the movement had won the only cause that united it.

Analysis of the conflicts between women's organizations in this period shows they defined womanhood differently.[6] They might argue about protective legislation versus equal rights, disarmament versus military preparedness, prohibition versus repeal, but the core of their conflicts concerned the Nature of Woman. Protectionists urged laws forbidding employers to order women seen as "overburdened and vulnerable" to carry heavy weights, do hard labour during pregnancy, work excessive hours, or at night. Stressing woman's difference from man, especially as reproducer, they discussed her *need* to work. The NWP and career women saw women as eager, robust and similar to men. Stressing the social construction of gender, they talked of women's *preference* to work.

Maybe people were so indoctrinated by the age-old division of women into madonnas and whores that they could not see beyond it. No one condemned defining women by one trait – sexuality seen as sinful – which allowed women only asexuality or licentiousness. No one argued that all beings are both vulnerable and strong, or that women's "special" needs were in fact their responsibility for maintaining the human race and supporting their families at the same time. One cannot challenge stereotypes of women without challenging stereotypes of men, received ideas about the nature of nature. The same issues split British women after suffrage.

In Great Britain

For a decade after William Thompson and Anna Wheeler's *Appeal of One Half of the Human Race* in 1825, not one systematic radical analysis of women's status appeared in England.[7] In 1843 Mrs. Hugo Reid's *A Plea For Women* argued that suffrage was women's only recourse from injustice, the only tool that could end the oppression of half of humanity by the other. After the 1857 Divorce Act, some sensational, widely publicized cases of divorce and separation shocked the public into awareness of infidelity and violence in respectable upper-class families. Frances Power Cobbe warned that marriage was a lottery in which any woman could pick "an unfaithful or cruel husband," but no one protested the plight of wives until 1868; even then feminists barely mentioned the areas of greatest suffering: men's rights to women's property, earnings, children, and divorce. They did not address birth control at all.

Because the idea that women were human beings intellectually – or even potentially – equal to men was too radical for Englishmen before the twentieth century, British feminists could not fight for women on that ground. Owenite socialism was long forgotten in society's obsessive pursuit of respectability, and the women in feminist causes were eminently respectable. Many had worked in campaigns to abolish slavery or repeal Corn Laws. They had learned through such campaigns that sustained pressure by organized groups had an effect despite women's lack of political voice, and they brought this knowledge to the emergent women's movement. The anti-slavery crusade had made them aware of the similarities between slaves and women and that female abolitionists were in the vanguard of feminism in America after 1840. British abolitionist Anne Knight wrote the Grimkés after the 1840 London Anti-Slavery Conference refused to seat female delegates: "Yes, dear Angelina dear Sarah, your noble spirits lighted a flame which has warmed [us who] thought not of our bondage."[8]

By 1850 the position of upper middle-class women had

improved enough, especially in education, that they could contemplate achieving political equality with men of their class. Harriet Taylor and John Stuart Mill bolstered this hope. Taylor's "The Enfranchisement of Women," in the *Westminster Review* (1851), asserted that women were equal to men and so were entitled to political equality; Mill's *The Subjection of Women* (1869, written with Taylor), asserted that women were human beings equal to men and should have a political life and realize their natural abilities.

The impetus for the first British women's suffrage society came in 1866 from the great Barbara Leigh Smith (Bodichon) and from prominent woman pioneers in education, medicine, and legislative reform. When the first eminent feminist, John Stuart Mill, was elected to Parliament in 1865, the group was galvanized to collect 1500 signatures on a petition for female householders to vote. In 1867 Mill made the first major public statement on woman suffrage in the House of Commons, generating new suffrage groups and persuading more people to sign petitions, especially in Manchester, where 13,500 signatures were gathered. The first public meeting of Smith's suffrage society was held in London in 1869. After Mill presented a bill for woman suffrage, feminist leaders pursued a policy of regularly presenting private members' bills to the House of Commons. In 1884 Liberal prime minister William Gladstone promised that if women joined a group *he* had set up, they might "earn" the right to vote. He betrayed them, and women abandoned the strategy of pleasing male leaders.

From 1893 to 1906 Manchester textile workers – the best organized female industrial workers in England – joined the suffrage movement by the thousands. A coalition of female trade unionists, socialists, and Women's Cooperative Guild organizers with socialist principles strategized winning the franchise by organizing working-class wives who were more radical than middle-class suffragists.

The lives of working-class wives were hard even if they did not work for wages: "No cause can be won between dinner and tea, and most of us who were married had to work with one hand tied behind us," wrote one. They cooperated: when a woman spoke or went to London on business, another tended her children or prepared her complaining husband's dinner. As political activists in socialist or labour groups or women's trade unions, they well understood the degree of male opposition they faced. No trade union or the Labour Party – or even the radical Independent Labour party – *ever* supported woman suffrage. Most men wanted women home washing clothes and cooking meals. One man slapped his wife's face publicly on her return from a meeting; others did worse in private. During women's speeches, men heckled them, crying, "Go home and wash the pots!" or "What about the ole man's kippers?" One woman lamented: "Public disapproval can be faced and borne, but domestic unhappiness, the price many of us paid for our opinions and activities, was a very bitter thing."[9]

For two decades, suffragists concentrated on raising the consciousness of educated women, but women of all classes flocked to the movement despite almost universal press hostility. The National Union of Women's Suffrage Societies pressured members of Parliament and the Liberal party, constantly marched, and held fund-raising bazaars, membership drives, and educational meetings. Emmeline Pethick-Lawrence exhorted audiences to work for suffrage not for "the Vote only, but what the Vote means – the moral, the mental, economic, the spiritual enfranchisement of Womanhood; the release of women, the repairing, the rebuilding of that great temple of womanhood, which has been so ruined and defaced." British feminists knew to fight for themselves from the first.

Emmeline Pankhurst, convinced by her experience as a Poor Law guardian that profound change was necessary, joined the suffrage movement in the 1880s, and in 1903, with her daughters Sylvia and Christabel, formed the Women's Social and Political Union (WSPU). In the early 1900s thousands of formerly apolitical middle-class women contributed their time, energy, and money. Fiery, young, impatient women of all classes joined the WSPU, the most militant suffrage group. With the motto "Deeds, Not Words," WSPU members were willing to disrupt or break laws to call attention to the cause.

In 1906 the Pankhursts moved the WSPU to London to be near Parliament and government offices. Emmeline and Frederick Pethick-Lawrence joined Christabel and Emmeline Pankhurst in leading the WSPU. They ruled autocratically, fearing their swiftly growing organization would lose force if it bogged down in democratic decision-making. They sold their journal on street corners, organized thousands of meetings, rallies, and colourful marches throughout the country, and heckled Liberal speakers at by-elections, demanding party support. In under three years, they had seventy-five organizers (they started with one) and an £18,000 income. But in June 1909 Emmeline Pankhurst and eight well-known women were rudely turned away from Parliament. Outraged suffragists smashed government office windows; 108 were arrested. One went on a hunger strike to protest the refusal of the Home Office to grant women political prisoner status – the first use of the device. She was freed, but other women who followed her example were forcibly fed on the orders of King Edward VII.

Midge MacKenzie's *Shoulder to Shoulder*, a great film on the British suffrage movement, portrays the force-feeding. Three or four female guards open the cell door for a doctor carrying a long rubber tube; the prisoner sits up on her cot, protests; is pushed down; two hold her down forcibly, the other gags her. The doctor inserts the tube (often used repeatedly without cleaning) into a nostril or the mouth, pouring a mixture of milk, bread, brandy, and often an anti-vomiting agent down it. The procedure left its victims nauseous, cramped, with headaches and sores in mouth, nasal passages, and stomach. Most also suffered severe indigestion and constipation. But the worst part was the anticipation, waiting in agony, hearing their comrades screaming in pain. Some women broke down under the strain, expecting to die.

Lady Constance Lytton nearly did. Gently reared, she lived with her mother, as a dutiful daughter of the nobility until her late thirties. Sylvia Pankhurst claimed that years of dependency had left her extremely anxious about hurting others or asserting herself. Yet when this "childlike" woman decided to join the suffragists, she chose the militant wing – although her decision deeply distressed her family. Her health was poor, but in 1908 she led a delegation to the House of Commons and in 1909 threw a stone at Lloyd George's car in Newcastle. On both occasions she was arrested and sent to jail, where her rank procured her gentle treatment. So in 1910 she dressed like a worker and gave a false name when she was arrested. Sent to Walton prison, Liverpool, she was forcibly fed eight times despite her weak heart. When the authorities discovered her name, they released her, but she was "more dead than alive," irreparably damaged.

Constance's sacrifice galvanized her brother, Lord Lytton, to back a bill enfranchising a million Englishwomen heads of household. In July 1910, the "Conciliation Bill" passed the House by 139 votes, but contention between Commons and Lords led Parliament to dissolve and Prime Minister Asquith procrastinated. Constance Lytton was jailed again, and suffered minor heart seizures throughout 1910–11, culminating in a stroke in 1912. She survived until 1923, an ardent supporter of suffrage no longer able to act politically. She never stopped hating prison doctors.

The WSPU women continued to destroy property; they chained themselves to the fence around the meeting house of the British cabinet and broke windows in Parliament Square – unthinkable acts for British *ladies*. They were attacked, however, simply for occupying public space. Men pawed, pushed, pinched, or punched them in the breasts, groped under their skirts, spat at them, threw stones, whispered obscenities in their ears, hurled rotten fruit. The police arrested and imprisoned the *women*. On November 18, 1910 ("Black Friday"), a large delegation of suffragists set out for the House of Commons, but they were violently attacked by police and male bystanders. They fought back for six hours, while *four men and*

115 women were arrested. Police officials had called in East End police rather than the usual "A" Division police, who knew and liked the suffragist delegations. East End police regularly dealt with the poor and did not scruple to treat women brutally. The revelation of how far men were willing to go to hold women down shocked middle- and upper-class feminists.

In 1911 the WSPU began systematically to smash windows. Convicted women were sentenced to prison with hard labour. They continued. After they attacked expensive West End shops, the police raided WSPU headquarters. Christabel Pankhurst fled to Paris, broke with the Pethick-Lawrences, and led the WSPU from abroad. Now semi-legal, it operated underground, changing headquarters and local leaders regularly to evade raids. For two years, members bombed letter boxes and fuse boxes, smashed street lamps, cut up golf courses, and burned empty houses. The public grew hostile. Memories of violations – forced feeding, blows, violence – in their bodies, memories of betrayals and male contempt in their minds, left the women angry and desperate, martyred. But none died until 1913, when, as the king rode to the Derby, Emily Wilding Davison hurled herself in front of his horse crying "Votes for women!" The WSPU was in disarray, its leaders in jail or being hunted down; Davison's funeral was its last major demonstration.

That year, the home secretary pushed through Parliament a bill allowing the government to free hunger strikers until they recovered their health, then re-arrest them. Called the "Cat and Mouse Act," it gained huge publicity for the WSPU, which was delighted also by its "mice," who adeptly eluded re-arrest, then appeared with stunning drama at meetings. The cycle of arson, imprisonment, hunger strikes, release, and re-arrest continued until the First World War broke out in August 1914. Although Sylvia urged WSPU members not to support the war effort, most of them did. Emmeline Pankhurst worked tirelessly, travelling throughout England rallying women to work in munitions factories and essential services. Although she was acting as a patriot, she had an eye on the war's end, when women would be rewarded by the franchise. Sylvia, more radical, broke with her mother and sister, seeing the war as a patriarchal device to submerge class differences in nationalism. She denounced the government for the war and for exploiting female labour, and worked with some success to gain equal pay for women, and safeguards and decent working conditions in hazardous munitions and airplane factories. Her mother repudiated her. Sylvia continued to work for the rights of East End working-class women. Emmeline Pethick-Lawrence joined Jane Addams' international peace movement. The glory years were over.

After the war, Parliament granted suffrage to all men who had fought in the war, without property or residency restrictions, but did not mention women. When suffragists protested, it granted the vote to single women and wives over thirty of men listed on the Local Government Register. This age limit prevented women from becoming the majority of British voters: 8 million British women were enfranchised in January 1918. Moderate women's suffrage groups redirected their energies to electing women to Parliament and lobbying for bills on "women's issues." Women could not yet claim *all* issues were their issues, as all are men's. For years, feminists pressured Parliament to remove the age limit on women voters, but did not succeed until 1928.

At the end of the campaign, militants looked back at their eight years of battle as an exalted period: women had been central in British political life, making upper-class men shudder under female assault for the first time in their lives. American women used the Cult of True Womanhood to expand the notion and in the process destroy it; Victorian Englishwomen's militancy radically defied their socializing, but was also its epitome. Inculcated with the belief they must spend their lives serving others and sacrificing the self, they used their training in hard work, service to the community, religious faith, discipline, extraordinary idealism, and self-sacrifice to serve *their own* ends. From 1906 to 1914 over a thousand women went to prison and thousands more were arrested. The WSPU's legacy to later generations was a new image of woman as rebels, articulate, visible, and organized.

Women's most striking advances resulted from the war, when they took jobs formerly reserved for men. They worked as skilled engineers (mechanics in America) in munitions plants, on farms, as chauffeurs and ambulance drivers. As in the United States, educated women found administrative jobs in the civil service, managing new wartime bureaucracies. That their filling "male" jobs made the men at the front feel emasculated suggests the weak base of the male psyche. When the men returned, male solidarity forced women out of their jobs, but during the recession that followed the war many men could not find work. Men never fully reasserted their former dominance over women, who, once they could support themselves, could reappraise just what men gave and what they cost.

After winning the vote, women did not maintain the strong sisterhood achieved by suffragists. They did not vote as a bloc, but allowed class (in the United States, colour) divisions to fragment their voice. Both egalitarians and protectionists concentrated on legislative reform, but in trying to assimilate into the male political world, they cut themselves off from other women. Feminists usually lost political contests, and political parties shunned them as liabilities (it is unclear which caused which). Women made only minor changes in the organization or regulation of industry, the church, military, or the government – to this day they have not been able to influence the policies of such institutions. Male solidarity and prejudice and women's continuing acceptance of responsibility for children combined to perpetuate female inequality in the marketplace. Working-class women were still paid least, and were the least skilled in the least pleasant jobs – they remained marginal, easily dismissed or replaced.

These unwon fights do not diminish what women did accomplish. Middle-class women utterly transformed their position in the nineteenth century. However, the contradictions that pervaded their actions also characterized the results – and contradictions were rife. In a period that idealized motherhood, women halved their family size. Confined within the domestic realm, they embraced the confinement and simply proclaimed their sphere to be the world. Required to be angels devoted only to family, and presiding in isolation at home, they organized. Organization was a necessary condition for their success. For the first time in history, women achieved large-scale solidarity.

Women's reform networks succeeded because their power base – home and church – was considered their legitimate sphere. Adopting a rhetoric of domesticity and purity, they circumvented established male authority structures and institutions, which did not at first perceive them as a threat. Men saw women's networks as auxiliary and separate; women considered them central. Their dynamic conception of their appropriate sphere allowed them continually to expand it. Perhaps some used the rhetoric of True Womanhood cynically, but most believed it. Although powerful when they acted in concert, individual women remained hobbled by belief in female asexuality, moral superiority, and the appropriateness of certain arenas for their sex, not to mention their sense of sex as tainted. Such beliefs, along with biases of class and race, led women to disavow other women. They milked the Cult of Domesticity, which united and fragmented them at the same time.

In a little over a century, women in England, the United States, and other European states altered the course of patriarchy. Every ancient patriarchal state made the confinement of women in the domestic sphere – their exclusion from a voice and civil rights – a primary rule of society. And suppression of the female, once achieved in states like China, India, and Japan, remained immovable for millennia. Capitalism, with its emphasis on rights and individuals and its division of people and experience into rigid spheres, made feminism possible. Nineteenth-century feminism did not overturn patriarchy but damaged it enough to make further gains possible in the twentieth century.

Women fought for suffrage around the world. First to win it

were New Zealanders, in 1893 – but no New Zealand woman held a high-level political position until 1947. Women in South Australia won the vote in 1894, and it was the first state to allow them to stand for parliament, but other Australian women had to wait until 1947. Finnish women voted in 1904 after only twenty years of agitation; Russian women in 1917, after the revolution. Sometimes women won suffrage but remained barred from high-level political life. In Norway, women won the vote in 1913, but did not begin to stand for high political office until 1945; Sweden, 1919 and 1947; the Netherlands, 1919 and 1956; Germany, 1919 and 1956; Brazil, 1932 and 1982; and Turkey, 1934 and 1971. In Egypt, men adamantly opposed woman suffrage until 1956.[10] Other countries surrendered even later. But women won. And they won with only themselves – without weapons, political rights, or much wealth, they had only their minds, bodies, spirits, voices, influence, charm, rage, tenderness, and strength to turn the world around. And they did.

CHAPTER 8

LABOUR MOVEMENTS

M IDDLE-CLASS WOMEN HAD THE LEISURE TO FIGHT for political
and economic rights; working-class women struggled to survive. Reformers tried to ameliorate poverty, not eradicate it, which
would require economic and political changes they were unable or
unwilling to contemplate. But segregated people develop a group
consciousness and come to see that their problems are not individual but collective. Once they realize that not personal failure but the
structure of society itself causes their difficulties, that they are the
sacrificed in a system designed to benefit another group, they feel
empowered to fight to change that structure or win a voice in it.

In America

Before the Civil War

Five million immigrants flooded the United States between 1815
and 1865; 80 percent settled in northern industrial cities. Many
took low-paying factory jobs. The overwhelming majority of textile
workers in America were single white women. Working conditions

were atrocious. In the 1820s to 1830s, women in Lowell, Massachusetts, factories worked twelve to sixteen hours a day in huge hot noisy rooms, with no fresh air, running water, or toilets. Meals were provided but the women had to run to a boardinghouse, eat, and return in only a half-hour: many became ill. In 1845 they took a major step and created the Lowell Female Labour Reform Association; the company punished them by ending support for their literary journal. The women went on strike, demanding a reduction in the workday from fourteen to ten hours. They lost, but Sarah Bagley, an association leader, had them sign a petition for a ten-hour day and sent it to the Massachusetts legislature, which opened an inquiry into factory conditions – the first in the United States.

Profits were high but owners wanted more. They bought larger, faster, noisier machines, and had workers tend more machines for less pay. They cut hourly wages, adding hours to make up the difference. In 1825 woman tailors in New York City organized and tried to shame employers by publicly naming those who paid women 10 to 18 cents a day. When this had no effect, they struck. Women struck in Dover, New Hampshire, in 1828; they too failed, but after further pay cuts in 1834, 800 women unionized and struck. The company hired scabs (non-union workers), forcing them to sign agreements not to join any union, and broke the union. The national press, widely reporting female labour agitation, warned mockingly that government might "have to call out the militia to prevent a gynecocracy."

In 1844 Allegheny and Pittsburgh cotton workers agitated for a ten-hour day; in 1845, with Manchester mill women, they threatened to "declare their independence," to "make war" on the Fourth of July if their demands were not met. Owners blackballed the leaders, locked out any who would not work twelve hours and hired scabs. Workers protested this and in October, a riot erupted in a Pittsburgh mill. The government was completely behind the owners and sent strong-arm men to put it down, but workers outnumbered the thugs, beat them off, and took over the plant. They won a ten-hour day, but their wages were reduced. Although many women wanted to strike again, most settled for reduced hours.

Whatever method they used – strikes, walkouts, or shutdowns – workers did not win permanent improvements. Without coordin-ated campaigns or sophisticated strategies, they were no match for wealthy owners with government support and an endless supply of scab workers. Owners resourcefully countered workers' efforts – if forced to pay higher wages, they raised rents at company boarding-houses; if forced to grant shorter days, they lowered wages and ordered increased production (speed-ups) that undermined work-ers' morale and health; and they hired scabs, abundant in an era of massive immigration and poverty. They set worker against worker. Dropping any pretense of common purpose with the farm commu-nity, mill owners fired native-born women, hiring easily intimidated destitute illiterate immigrants often unfamiliar with English. But labour protest continued as tailors, shoemakers, and laundresses unionized in cities across the country.

But the greatest obstacle that working women faced was men. Women averaged a quarter of men's wages, yet most male unions refused to support women's strikes (women supported men's – for example, cotton workers at Pawtucket, Rhode Island, joined male co-workers in a strike protesting wage cuts and longer hours in 1824). Husbands or fathers used violence to keep women from attending union meetings or joining strike lines. Men prowled around women's meetings and promised women easier lives, then lured them into prostitution. Men defended *their* turf: the small percentage of men in cotton manufacture were better paid than women, and all supervisors were men. Some argue that women were not promoted because they did not remain long at their jobs – in 1836, only 18 of 233 female employees at one mill had worked there over six years. But women left because they knew they would not be promoted. In the 1860s about 300,000 north-ern women and 12,000 southerners worked in textile, shoe, and clothing factories, and in printing, keeping their jobs twice as long as the earlier generation – yet men still held all managerial positions.

When it came to women, hostility between male owners and male workers melted. Whatever their struggles with each other, men united in opposing any step that would allow women independence. Both wanted to exploit women – owners to pay them low wages, husbands and fathers to keep them in servitude. Even men whose lives would be easier if their wives earned higher wages fought women's attempts to improve their lot. The interests of men of different classes coincide when the issue is maintaining patriarchal control and dominance over women.[1] Discussion of the sexual division of labour and "woman's place" in production pervaded American journals and newspapers from 1850 to 1880.[2] Writers on the sexual division of labour identified different occupations as "female" or "male," but all believed their ideas were Natural Law.

The American Labour Movement after the Civil War

Still, there are moving examples of men cooperating with women. Collar laundresses in Troy, New York, worked twelve- to fourteen-hour days in 100° temperatures from furnaces heating water for their tubs; they washed, blued, dyed, and rinsed, and lifted heavy hot irons to press the detachable collars and cuffs of men's shirts. For this arduous labour they were paid $2–$3 a week. In 1864 they unionized. Troy unions of male puddlers and boilers in the iron industry supported them, and the Troy Collar Union thrived. Its 400 members donated $500 to striking bricklayers in New York City and $1000 to Troy iron moulders striking in 1866. When the laundresses struck in 1869, the male unions sent them $500 a week and promised "to continue the same for weeks to come rather than see such a brave set of wenches crushed under the iron heel of these laundry nabobs." But the company starved the women, who had to swear to renounce the union to get their jobs back. The invention of paper collars broke the union in 1870.

Shoe binders formed the first national women's union; it had over forty lodges from Lynn to San Francisco but did not last long.

After the Civil War, a few male unions accepted women – in 1867 the National Union of Cigar Makers embraced women and blacks. When the Women's Typographical Union disbanded after nine years, men accepted them in the national union on equal terms with men (but never chartered another women's local). Women supported men, though: during an 1877 railroad strike, 100,000 men and women faced police, militia, and federal troops. The press was horrified not by armed forces being used against citizens in a bitter fight but by an "Amazonian army" of "enraged female rioters," an "unsexed mob of female incendiaries."

However hard life was for white workers, it was worse for blacks. They still had no choice of work and were paid too little to live. They could still resist inhumane employers only by feigning illness or incompetence or failing to show up for work. Until the First World War, 10 percent of African-Americans lived in northern cities where men had trouble finding work and women supported the family by domestic and personal service work. Three-fourths of southern African-Americans lived on farms or plantations as share-croppers, unskilled labourers, laundresses, or domestic help. Most unions rejected all women, emphatically black women, who worked only as domestics and laundresses. So black women started their own union in Mississippi, the Washerwomen of Jackson, in 1866. Washerwomen unionized in Galveston, Texas (1877), Atlanta (1881), Greenville, Pennsylvania (1886), and Bibb City, Arkansas (1889). Some struck for higher wages. Few won.

Between 1880 and 1930, when the United States restricted immigration, over 27 million people, most from southern and eastern Europe, emigrated in desperate need. Three million Italians migrated from 1880 to 1910, as well as millions of Poles, Czechs, Slovaks, and other Baltic peoples. Pogroms in the 1880s to 1890s propelled 2 million East European Jews from their ghettos, about three-quarters from Russia. Over 90 percent settled in the United States. Greeks, Portuguese, Armenians, and Syrians risked the journey hoping for a better economic life. Hard as life was in America, it was worse elsewhere. Farmhands in Sweden earned $30 a year with room and board in the 1870s; in America they earned $200 a year. Pennsylvania mineworkers earned $40 a month, railroad workers $1–$2 a day. Passage to New York cost $12–$15 from England, $30 from Copenhagen: emigrés could save enough to bring their families to America.

It was hard to get to America and terrible afterwards. Millions of immigrants packed slum rooms or flats without running water, toilets, or even heat in teeming neighbourhoods infested with fleas, bedbugs, and lice. Single men rented sleeping space in a family's kitchen. Arriving with little or nothing, many spoke no English and were grateful for the meanest jobs. They ate poorly, contracted tuberculosis or pneumonia. Women, as always burdened doubly, tried to earn money to help the family while raising the fruit of their repeated pregnancies. They aged quickly, and their poor diet contributed to a staggering rate of infant mortality.

America responded to foreigners, with their odd languages and poverty, with virulent xenophobia. In the 1840s–1850s, to guard "white natives'" prerogatives, "nativists" formed the Know-Nothing Party. An anti-Catholic movement began in the 1880s. The two-and-a-half-million-member American Protective Association tried to limit immigration with stricter naturalization laws. Anti-Semitism grew, and clubs and resorts adopted a "Gentiles only" policy. German Jews who had been assimilated for decades suddenly found themselves *persona non grata*. Discrimination in housing and jobs followed. In 1891 the government enforced anti-pauper laws at Ellis Island and other ports of entry. Jews who had been stripped of property by Eastern European governments had to prove they had money or relatives in the United States.

Perhaps the most vicious xenophobia was directed toward the Chinese. Thousands of single men imported to build the Central Pacific railroad during the Civil War stayed on afterward to work in western mines, farms, and canneries, and faced what Florynce Kennedy called "horizontal hostility" – antagonism directed at equals rather than oppressors. White male workers blamed their low wages not on exploitative employers but on the Chinese, who lived on almost nothing. Such hostility reproduces itself: abused exploited men exploited and abused their women in turn.

Most Chinese women who entered the United States between 1840 and 1880 were slave prostitutes. Chinese families often sold girl children into servitude. By 1850 the business of certain Chinese societies was importing girls for west-coast brothels – the secret society Hip-Yee Tong alone imported 6000 females from 1852 to 1873, many just children. Their lives were awful; they aged fast, and died young. Some were promised release from their contract after a fixed term, which never came; many were forcibly addicted to opium. When their plight became known, public outrage prodded the California legislature to investigate prostitution in 1876. A San Francisco pastor explained:

> The women [generally] are held as slaves. They are bought or stolen in China and brought here. They have a sort of agreement to cover up the slavery business, but it is all a sham. . . . After the term of prostitution service is up, the owners so manage as to have the women in debt more than ever, so that their slavery becomes life-long. There is no release from it. . . . Sometimes women take opium to kill themselves. They do not know they have any rights, but think they must keep their contracts and believe themselves under obligations to serve in prostitution. . . . They have come to the asylum all bruises. They are beaten and punished cruelly if they fail to make any money. When they become worn out and unable to make any more money, they are turned out to die.

Tension over hiring and wages between white and Chinese workers culminated in the Sandlot Riot of 1871. America's solution was "Keep orientals out." Legislators hysterical about "the yellow peril" in 1882 passed the Chinese Exclusion Act, the first law barring immigrants in the United States. It banned all females from China (barely affecting brothel keepers, who kidnapped girls within California). Whites hoped that without women, Chinese men would return to China. Some did, but more stayed. In the west, anti-Chinese fury erupted in major riots in Tacoma, Seattle, and Wyoming in 1885. In the 1920s, hysterical waves of paranoia led to the deportation of masses of Chinese.[3]

On the east coast, mill owners hired new immigrants at low wages (lowering wages throughout the industry) and let working conditions deteriorate. During the Civil War, the south stopped sending raw cotton north, closing northern mills. Desperate mill women swarmed to cities seeking work in the needle trades. The invention of the sewing machine revolutionized the garment industry – a man's shirt that took fourteen hours to sew by hand was made in an hour on a machine – and the number of sewing machines doubled during the war. After the war, owners moved their factories south; Irish immigrants began to leave New England textile towns, and impoverished French-Canadians moved in. There was always another wave of poor people to exploit, and conditions in the garment trades grew worse as sweatshops sprang up in most cities.

Garment workers put in fifteen- to sixteen-hour days in stifling, crowded, dimly lit workshops; some slept on fabric piled on the floor to save rent. Most were women: in 1900, 65 percent of New York City seamstresses were single Jewish girls paid so little that many became prostitutes to survive. The top men in a shop earned $10, women $3 to $6 a week. Work was ranked: only native-born white women could work as shop girls for $5 a week or librarians for $3 – badly paid, but less injurious occupations. Daughters of immigrants were barred from "genteel trades." Until the Civil War, except for 2 million unpaid slave women, the vast majority of women worked only at home; only about 10 percent earned any money. By 1880, mainly because of immigration, 2 million women worked for wages (the figure doubled in the next decade).

In 1881 the Noble Order of the Knights of Labor chartered the Working Women's Union. The Knights, a combination of secret fraternal society and reform organization, admitted workers and middle-class men, excluding "parasites" – lawyers, saloon keepers, bankers, stockbrokers, and professional gamblers. It supported equal pay for equal work and equal treatment for women and blacks. When it became open, it admitted women: at its peak its 700,000 members included 50,000 women. Female Knights struck in Yonkers, New York, in 1885: 2500 women picketed the mill. The company called the police, who were so violent to the women that the public pitied and helped them, enabling them to hold out for six months and win their demand: *rescinding a pay cut.*

As strikes grew more frequent and damaging, employers used heavier hands. When steelworkers struck at Andrew Carnegie's steel mill, he hired immigrants, had them shepherded off the boats that brought them from Europe right into sealed locked boxcars, and transported them right *inside* the mills, to live and work at gunpoint. Speaking no English, the men had no idea what was happening. Such repressiveness climaxed in the Chicago Haymarket riot.

On May 1 (May Day), 1886, 80,000 mostly male workers marched down Michigan Avenue, then met with women tailors to plan a general strike for an eight-hour day. On May 2, Lizzie Swank, a brilliant labour organizer, marched with hundreds of women from the garment district, stopping at each shop along the way to urge women workers to join them.[4] Even the *Chicago Tribune*, a hostile newspaper, was moved: "The ranks were composed of women whose exterior denoted incessant toil, their in many instances worn faces and threadbare clothing bearing evidence of a struggle for an uncomfortable existence. As the procession moved along the girls shouted and sang and laughed in a whirlwind of exuberance that did not lessen with the distance traveled."

On May 3, as workers rallied peacefully in Haymarket Square, the police advanced, ordering them to disperse. A bomb exploded, the police fired on the crowd. No one knows how many were killed

– 200 were injured. On May 4 a police dragnet arrested almost every activist in the Chicago labour movement, charging eight with murdering policemen in the riot (which was probably staged by police killed by their own crossfire). Only one of the accused was even in the square during the riot and he was on stage in public view. Nevertheless, the government executed five men.

As industrial capitalism became more firmly rooted, the Knights' rank and file lost hope for a cooperative commonwealth and focused on practical working problems. The Order's leaders did not respond to this shift, and could not overcome employers' strong attacks after the Haymarket affair. The organization lost two-thirds of its members in two years, from 1886 to 1888.

In the 1890s, 1 percent of Americans had more income than the bottom 50 percent: the top 1 percent earned 25 percent of the national income, the bottom half less than 20 percent. People starved: women abandoned babies on doorsteps; children, at least ten thousand, lived on the streets and slept in areaways. (Jacob Riis photographed them in his 1890 study of the tenements of New York, *How the Other Half Lives.*) The Chicago Women's Alliance launched a campaign for compulsory education for children in 1889, eventually forcing passage of a bill establishing a twelve- to twenty-four week school year for children aged seven to fourteen, with half-days off to work.

The gains won by female organizers' efforts seemed imperman- ent in these years, but they lasted: in 1878 few women had the courage even to attend a union meeting, but in 1886 hundreds of women marched for an eight-hour day and in 1903, 35,000 marched in Chicago on Labour Day.[5] Early organizers raised work- ing women's class-consciousness and taught them that they had the right to a decent wage and decent working conditions, and the right to fight when they were denied – which was news to these uneducated women.

The women's local that marched before the Haymarket mas- sacre disintegrated after it, but organizer Elizabeth Morgan persuaded Samuel Gompers of the American Federation of Labor (AFL) to charter women in a union of mixed occupations – a "federal" union – a catch-all to unionize men in different trades when there were not enough to found a trade union, or to organize women or blacks separately. Male locals rejected women and blacks but Gompers himself chartered federal unions to bypass locals. Federal unions brought together large numbers of working women from different trades, as well as housewives. A women's union meeting could be a social function (men met in saloons). The disadvantage of having separate unions was that male and female locals in the same shop bargained separately, sometimes against each other, and women usually lost; or men bargained for both, trading women's raises for their own.

The AFL claimed to be egalitarian, to support women and equal pay. But it really tried to keep women disorganized, slotting them into the Union Label League, whose only function was to propagandize for goods with union labels. Leaders claimed the AFL could not organize women because they were unskilled and the AFL charter was for skilled workers – but they would not let women apprentice to learn skills. Groups of women workers who applied for admission to the international in a craft were rejected. If they appealed this, AFL leaders said they had no control over the decisions of an international; if they asked for a charter as an independent local, they were refused because that would violate the jurisdiction of the international in that craft. Thwarted at every juncture, women were demoralized. The AFL stand harmed not just women but the entire labour movement.

WTUL and Triangle

There were only four women delegates at the 1903 AFL convention at which William English Walling and Mary Kenney first set up a national Women's Trade Union League (WTUL) modelled on the English WTUL. In an effort to organize *all* workers in trade unions and gain equal pay for equal work, an eight-hour day, a minimum wage scale, and woman suffrage, the founders set up locals in Chicago, Boston, and New York. Lacking male union support, the New York local turned to middle-class women – professionals and wealthy women drawn to the WTUL by sex solidarity. But few understood labour problems, and class and ethnic divisions generated argument in the League, for example, debate over whether the New York WTUL should focus on organizing downtown Jewish or uptown "American" girls. Constant debate about whether to concentrate on organizing or legislation split along class lines, with workers supporting the former. The AFL was now conservative (it voted to exclude Chinese from the United States); the WTUL was split between conservative and socialist policies.

In November 1909 a small waistmakers' local in the International Ladies' Garment Workers Union called for a general strike against New York shirtwaist manufacturers. Thirty thousand workers spontaneously answered the call – the strike was called the Uprising of the Thirty Thousand, or "the women's movement strike," because the WTUL led the entire women's movement from the Fifth Avenue elite to Lower East Side socialists to support the strikers, mainly teenaged girls. It rented Cooper Union for the meeting. Workers from three shops (Leiserson's, Rosen Brothers, and the Triangle Waist Company) had already struck; the meeting was to exhort others to join. The hall overflowed; union leaders frantically searched for others. Beethoven Hall, the Manhattan Lyceum, and Astoria Hall also filled and overflowed. At Cooper Union, the stage was full – of *men*. Gompers, other union officials, a woman from the WTUL – none of whom worked in a shirtwaist shop – spoke.

Suddenly a young woman from the audience stood up and asked for the floor. Despite rumblings of disapproval, the chairman held that as a striker she had as much right to speak as he did, and she walked to the platform. Clara Lemlich had helped found the shirtwaist local, had led the walkout at Leiserson's, which sent thugs to beat her up on the picket line. She knew precisely what the women were up against and how profound their anger and anguish were. She spoke rousingly in Yiddish, then put the motion for a general strike. The entire hall rose to endorse it.

The women, many only girls, starved as they picketed through a cold winter. Leiserson's thugs regularly beat them up, especially Lemlich, who had six ribs broken. Police arrested the women and sent them to the workhouse. Leiserson hired scabs; they themselves were so disgusted by the owners' tactics that they joined the strikers! The heroic women held out for thirteen weeks, up to a thousand women joining them every day. Three hundred and thirty-nine shops settled, but each separately, consequently without major gains. One of the two biggest makers, Triangle, refused to recognize the union and settled partially, rejecting (among other demands) open doors and adequate fire escapes (foremen locked the doors to keep the women from sneaking out for air): all garment factories were firetraps. The next year, Triangle went up in flames. When the alarm went off, one exit was aflame, the other locked: workers had no way out. The shop went up in minutes: piles of fabric lay everywhere and so much lint hovered that the very air burned. Women leaped from the fire escape in burning clothes to be impaled on a spiked iron fence below it. A hundred and forty-six died, hundreds were injured.

Triangle's two owners were tried for negligence, but were acquitted. One was later fined $20. The press claimed the fire was started by a smoking worker. Rose Schneiderman of the WTUL spoke at a memorial meeting after the fire: "This is not the first time girls have been burned alive in this city. Every week I must learn of the untimely death of one of my sister workers. Every year thousands of us are maimed. The life of men and women is so cheap and property is sacred. There are so many of us for one job it matters little if 143 of us are burned to death." Public outrage eventually forced the passage of fire safety laws in factories.

A depression from 1907 to 1909 devastated the labour movement; marginal workers (women) lost their jobs or accepted lower-paid ones and dropped out of unions. In Chicago, women's union membership fell from 37,000 to 10,000; not one female local remained in 1910. About 8 million women worked for wages, most in factories where they earned $2 to $6 a week, a third as much as men doing comparable work. Associations of working and middle-class women fell apart too when groups like San Francisco women concerned primarily with suffrage refused to support a strike of streetcar conductors; the workers felt betrayed and abandoned the group.

The IWW

In 1905, revolutionaries from the Western Federation of Miners and the Socialist Party founded a new union, Industrial Workers of the World (IWW) – the "Wobblies." Mother Jones was one of the founders. The IWW wanted to destroy capitalism through class solidarity and uncompromising class war, and to create a base for working-class production after capitalism disappeared. Their goal was visionary but their practices were geared to achieve realistic working-class solidarity. Trying to avoid the exclusionary practices of the AFL, they organized by industry, not craft, welcoming everyone in an industry – migrant and unskilled workers, immigrants, Asians, women, men, whites, and blacks in a south still dominated by the Klan and its lynch mobs. The IWW analyzed oppression in socialist terms, dividing the world into workers and capitalists. It mobilized blacks and women as workers who would be liberated when wage slavery and the class system ended, but it ignored their special experience.

Socialist groups arose in America late in the century, usually at times of economic hardship. The collectivist aspect of socialism drew great numbers of women; women helped shape it, but its narrow analysis always bothered them. At the first socialist International in The Hague in 1872, an American delegate defied the party to announce: "The labour question is also a woman's question, and the emancipation of woman must precede that of the workers." The party held that "universal suffrage cannot free humanity from

slavery. . . . The gaining of the vote by women is not in the best interests of the workers." Marx had implied that women's condition was
a gauge of society's progress, but American socialism was created
mainly by German immigrants imbued with patriarchism. Annoyed
by suffragists and bourgeois reformers, they demanded that women
reject suffrage for socialism, and then relegated them to ladies' auxiliaries. When the Socialist Party of America was founded in 1901,
only 8 of its 128 delegates were women.

The IWW also opposed woman suffrage, but was the only
labour organization to discuss birth control; it also made good use
of women during strikes. While the AFL slotted women into
"union label leagues," and the socialists kept them in auxiliaries,
IWW organizers enrolled workers' wives in locals, especially in the
west (wives too were oppressed by employers). For example, bosses
in the Mesabi iron mine traded men safe jobs in the mines for sexual use of their wives or daughters. The families of workers who
lived in company-owned houses were evicted during strikes. As
workers or wives, women proved more militant than men; they
stood in the front ranks wielding rolling pins, brooms, and pokers
to battle scabs; they were beaten, fire-hosed, and arrested – everywhere. When fish dealers reneged on an agreement with striking
fishermen, their wives hurled rocks at them. An IWW organizer
ordered them to go home quietly. "Who are you?" they roared. It
was their fight.[6]

But because it never saw women's problems as distinct, the
IWW could not address them. Since it considered women's locals
and support for women's rights disruptive of class solidarity, despite
repeated suggestions by feminists like Sophie Beldner, Elizabeth
Gurley Flynn, Joe Hill, and Frank Little (the latter two killed for
their politics), it never recruited large numbers of women, and hired
only three female organizers in its history.

IWW men were reluctant to treat women as equals and scorned
them, saying they resisted organization, and would probably marry
soon. Men did not see that unions did not guarantee women

equality in marriage or help them produce and raise children. *Nothing did.* Women's only hope for decent lives lay in finding decent men who would support them. A fertile woman's well-being depended on her personal relation with one man; joining a union would impede, not help that.

The 1912 Lawrence Strike

The IWW tried to organize workers in Lawrence, Massachusetts, in 1905, with little success until 1911, when the Atlantic Cotton Mill, wanting to lay off 40 percent of its weavers, ordered workers to tend twelve looms at a piece rate of 49 cents rather than seven at 79 cents. The weavers mounted a small strike: strong IWW support brought it public notice. The IWW issued frequent bulletins and imported major speakers like the young socialist "rebel" Elizabeth Gurley Flynn and IWW agitator James P. Thompson. After Thompson spoke, the IWW intensified its campaign with mass meetings indoors and outdoors, leaflets, and stickers.

On January 1, 1912, a law reforming labour practices in Massachusetts went into effect, barring women and children from working over fifty-four hours a week. Not foreseeing this would lead to a pay cut, reformers did not lobby against it. The Italian IWW local held a meeting and voted to strike if pay were cut. Other groups agreed. On January 12, they anxiously opened their envelopes: the company had deducted two hours' pay. Two hours' pay was 30 cents; this bought five loaves of bread. Five loaves a week meant the difference between surviving and starving.

Deciding "Better to starve fighting than to starve working," 20,000 people struck that day. Owners and journalists were dumbstruck: Lawrence was barely unionized – only a few hundred men were in the AFL, a few hundred in the IWW. Half the mill workers were women and children too worn down to protest: women could not even take time off for childbirth, squatting between looms to give birth. In an age when the average lawyer or clergyman lived to sixty-five, spinners died at thirty-six; 172 of 1000 of their children

were born dead, *all* children were malnourished. IWW leader Bill
Haywood explained: "It was a chronic condition. These children
had been starving from birth. They had been starved in their mothers' wombs. And their mothers had been starving before the
children were born."

They struck in sub-zero weather in falling snow, swarming out
of the mills to throng the streets; groups went into factories to pull
workers out. Owners placed men on the bridge leading to some factories to turn hoses on workers who approached. Enraged strikers
entered a mill and broke machinery and windows and tore fabric
from the looms. Owners demanded the mayor call in troops; the
mayor called the governor, who called the National Guard, including Harvard students freed from class to "have their fling at
these people"; they roamed the town, itchy. IWW knew what the
strikers were up against. An organizer warned: "You can hope for no
success on any policy of violence. . . . Remember the property of the
bosses is protected first by the police, then by the militia. If these
are not sufficient, by an entire army. Remember, you are also armed
. . . with your labour power which you can withhold and stop production." They encouraged strikers to restrain rage and preserve
organization. They brought in outside contacts who publicized the
strike and raised money for the strikers. But the spirit of struggle
really rose from the strikers' desperation: it "existed before the IWW
came and after it left."[7]

When the company called in scabs, thousands of women spontaneously picketed. An army of women surrounded the mill district
and took control of the streets. Firing into the crowd, police killed
a young striker, Anna Lopezza, but charged two IWW leaders with
her murder. Police harrassed strikers, arrested them, and jailed some
for a year for obstructing the sidewalk! (At least they ate in jail.)
Major IWW leaders like Haywood and Flynn stayed on, helping,
working, and later testifying to the courage and resourcefulness of
the workers, who maintained soup kitchens and commissaries,
investigated cases needing special relief, and kept their own books.

The strikers carried banners announcing what they wanted – "Bread and Roses" – which gave the strike its name. Women, half the strikers, were violent too. Some met a policeman on the bridge, grabbed his gun, club, and star and were removing his pants when he was rescued. Arrested, they were sentenced to jail terms by a judge who informed them "in awful tones that the body of a policeman was sacred." As the strike wore on, women grew more active, making street confrontations, dismaying owners, the police and the press, who whined, "One policeman can handle ten men, while it takes ten policemen to handle one woman." Husbands and priests tried to keep women out of it; Haywood and Flynn held meetings to heighten the women's confidence.[8]

Strikers began to send their children to sympathizers in other cities, where they would be fed and kept safe from the soldiers (who were assaulting them). But once the children were photographed in the press, their visible emaciation and illness drew national attention to the Lawrence workers' plight. Angrily, the owners sent police to assault the next batch of women and children who went to the railroad station. News reports of "cossacks" beating women and children got even more coverage, but the act outraged women. Announcing that even soldiers with bayonets had mothers and would not attack a pregnant woman, a tiny Italian woman and another woman, both pregnant, led women picketers. The soldiers beat and arrested all of them; the pregnant ones miscarried. This was reported in a Congressional committee.

Public opinion and Congress pressured the owners to settle, and they began negotiations in March. They accepted a 25 percent raise for the lowest-paid workers (earning 9 cents an hour), lesser raises along a sliding scale, time and a half for overtime, and no retribution against strikers. The success of the Lawrence strike led to other strikes across New England, which were all quickly settled. Twenty-five thousand textile workers gained by the Lawrence strike.

American Socialism

At its founding in 1901, the American Socialist Party endorsed equal political and civil rights for women, including suffrage. A large party with a broad political base before the First World War, it won some mayoral and congressional seats and almost 700,000 votes for socialist presidential candidate Eugene Debs in 1912. Party members were active in the AFL and the WTUL. But its most important role was providing political discourse. No other political body did this: the two major political parties disagreed on some points, but no one – not they or suffragists or trade unionists – wanted or dared to challenge capitalism itself. Only socialism offered an alternative to a capitalist organization of society; only socialism had a different political perspective. It drew women who could not accept the limitations of other movements.

Socialist women's groups arose in many American cities to discuss issues the major parties ignored and to give women a forum where they would not be overshadowed by men. Female membership grew tenfold in a year, and the party published a huge body of literature aimed at working-class women. But once a substantial percentage (10 percent) of the party was female, there were rifts over suffrage strategy. At this time, some European suffragists were demanding the vote as property owners on the same terms as men. Many middle-class women's organizations opposed protective legislation for female factory workers, which socialists favoured. At a convention of women socialists, Clara Zetkin and other German socialists decided to work for suffrage independently of suffragist groups because of such differences.

But in the United States, the main opponent of protective legislation was the AFL, and no suffragist group supported limited franchise. Socialist women were already working with suffragists to support the shirtwaist-makers' strike. American socialist women bowed to the party decision because they felt they needed to seed the ground for class struggle by urging socialism along with suffrage.

Moreover, suffragists had never acknowledged the socialists' huge contribution to the shirtwaist-makers' protest, and barred them from certain public platforms, fearing public identification with them. *Everyone* assumed the vote would make women fully equal to men in society and end female oppression and male hostility overnight. Socialist *men's* opposition to woman suffrage subverted American socialism. In 1912 radicals sympathetic to the IWW left and conservatives (who gave nothing to the WNC) abolished the Women's National Committee as too expensive and ended publication of the newspaper. Many women left the party or lapsed into inactivity.

When the First World War erupted, nationalist "patriots" fervently supported it. The Socialist Party (SP) opposed it as an imperialist struggle forcing working-class men to kill each other, deflecting their attention from their real enemies, capitalists. No one foresaw that a pointless war would eradicate an entire generation of young European men (and many women and children), and mark the end of the leisure class along with the old European social/economic structure. NAWSA suffragists and WTUL members supported the war, hoping for a post-war reward of franchise; many took government jobs. Alice Paul's NWP protested despite the war, picketing the White House asking how Woodrow Wilson could make the world safe for democracy he did not have at home. The AFL pledged not to strike for the duration. Some feminists (like Jane Addams) were pacifists; the IWW and most socialists opposed the war.

Then as now, people who opposed wars were called traitors and persecuted: NWP picketers were mauled by soldiers, arrested, sent to the workhouse, and went on hunger strikes. They were forcibly fed. Socialists were hounded, jailed, and murdered. At the end of the war, the government used it to justify suppression of dissent (a similar "Red Scare" followed the Second World War and the attack on the World Trade Center in New York in 2001). It targeted labour groups for elimination despite their support for the war, showing that capitalism, not war, was the issue. Unions that were inactive during the war were vulnerable to a massive government union-busting campaign that destroyed steel, meatpacking, dock-worker, and lumber unions and shook many others: the AFL lost over a million members. Organized labour suffered a serious decline, losing about half its members between 1920 and 1933.[9] Socialist groups were fragmented by raids, persecution, deportations, and quarrels over strategy after the Russian Revolution. Dissent from capitalism had become a crime, a heresy.

In this climate arose a heroine.[10] Rose Pastor, born in Poland in 1879, immigrated with her family to Cleveland to work making cigars. At twenty-four, she became a journalist on a Yiddish newspaper in New York City and in 1905 married J.G. Phelps Stokes, a millionaire reformer of one of America's oldest richest families. Labelled "Cinderella of the Sweatshops" by the press, Rose led her prince into the Socialist Party to organize hotel and garment workers, mounting a legal defence of strikers in Paterson in 1913. With her husband, she left the Socialist Party because most members opposed American entry into the First World War; a year later, she left him to return to the party. Speaking against the government for war profiteering got her indicted for anti-war activity in 1918 and sentenced to ten years in prison under the Espionage Act. Eugene Debs, head of the Socialist Party, spoke in her defence at her trial. Her sentence was overturned on appeal, but Debs' speech was used to convict him for "espionage." Her experience with the United States government persuaded her that only revolution would alter it. Scorning feminism as "bourgeois and elitist," accepting separate women's committees only to aid the spread of socialism, she left the Socialist Party in 1919 to help found the American Communist Party.

Prosecuted for founding the Communist Party (and other "crimes"), she did not go to jail, probably because of Stokes' wealth. Her marriage faltered on its political and class differences. Divorce thrust her into poverty; she lived by writing and speaking. In 1927, she married V.J. Jerome, a Communist eighteen years younger than she, with whom she lived happily, if in poverty. In 1929, demonstrating at a rally demanding withdrawal of United States troops from Haiti, she was clubbed by the police, after which her health declined. Rose Pastor Stokes died of breast cancer in 1933, true to her principles unto death.

African-Americans in the Early Twentieth Century

The First World War was a turning point for African-Americans. Before it, northern mills did not hire black women, although a larger percentage of black women than white did waged work. Few unions accepted women, even fewer blacks until the Committee for Industrial Organization (CIO) was formed in 1935. (Yet in 1920 the AFL Hotel and Restaurant Employees' Union had ten black locals in the south; the CIO-affiliated United Domestic Workers' Local Industrial Union in Baltimore had one in 1942.) After black women could join, the white male leaders of industrial unions bartered the interests of blacks and women to protect or consolidate their own gains; their strategies often led to the complete exclusion of blacks from workplaces. Scarce in industry, unwelcome in unions, isolated in white households, black women could only protest individually, informally.

In 1900 less than 3 percent of wage-earning black women worked in manufacture. In 1910 more than 700,000 black women in the south worked for pay, most in tobacco plants as stemmers, the lowest job in the industry hierarchy. They did the "dirty" jobs – sorting, cleaning, stemming tobacco – working apart from white women (who did "cleaner" jobs, inspecting and packing tobacco). White men presided over the entire workforce, supervising black and white women and black men who hauled hogsheads of tobacco from "dirty" prefabrication departments of the factory to "clean" manufacturing and packaging departments. Chicago meatpackers, too, relegated black women to "dirty" sectors, the most disagreeable jobs – hog-killing and beef-casing – "under repulsive conditions."[11]

Amalgamated Meat Cutters and Butcher Workmen locals never organized black women and wanted them eliminated from the labour force.

Linked by the physical and verbal abuse they endured from white foremen, by shared racial, sexual, and class oppression, black female tobacco workers became race, class, and sex conscious. Aware of black female power, if not feminism, they formed factory networks that extended into communities, overlapping with church groups and women's clubs. Network support gave individual women courage to protest their working conditions and treatment.[12]

Black club-women founded a Women Wage-Earners Association in Washington, DC, to teach black working-class women how to organize to demand better wages, housing, and working conditions. In 1917 a branch in Norfolk, Virginia – 600 domestics, waitresses, nurses, and tobacco-stemmers – protested. They were ignored and the stemmers (about half the organization) struck. Domestic servants followed (hitting whites at home), then stemmers' husbands and most oyster-shuckers. Since the country was at war, the government had extreme powers and threatened to arrest as subversive those who refused to work. But 3000 white male navy-yard workers who had recently struck for higher wages were not arrested. Black workers were, breaking the strike and the Norfolk branch.

Persecution in the south drove black workers north when jobs opened up to them during the First World War. Northern domestic servants earned $8 a week, twice or more what a black woman earned in Mississippi. But the south that persecuted them did not want them to leave: police seized blacks from northbound trains and arrested labour recruiters. For a time, southern employers raised wages and improved conditions. But 500,000 blacks went north in this period, a million and a half more before the next world war.

By 1920, *100 percent* more black women worked in manufacturing and mechanical industries than a decade earlier. For the

first time they could use machines in laundries and garment factories and were hired as clerks, stenographers, and bookkeepers, as
social workers, counsellors in schools and courts, public health
workers, pharmacists, bacteriologists, and chiropodists. For the first
time, they were accepted in the same jobs as white women, but only
because whites left them. As white immigrants left factories for
higher-paid work in munitions plants, blacks took their places.

But the situation in the north was not much better. Black
women remained the most oppressed group in the country: of the
2 million who worked for wages in 1920, almost half were servants,
almost half were in agriculture. They made up only 6.7 percent of
industrial workers. Yet this tiny gain incited the worst anti-black
violence ever seen in America: after the First World War, they were
attacked by mobs, lynched, and caught in sudden outbursts. In
1917 blacks marched silently down Fifth Avenue in protest. So
many blacks were lynched in 1918–19 that the NAACP held a
conference on the subject and published *Thirty Years of Lynching in
the United States*. The government tried but failed to suppress it. In
1919, as the black 369th Infantry Regiment returned from France
and marched up Fifth Avenue to huge cheering crowds, Attorney
General Palmer launched the "Red Scare" by creating a special division of the Justice Department headed by J. Edgar Hoover to spy
on, raid, and eliminate radicals and blacks, including Marcus
Garvey. That year, twenty-five race riots exploded in cities across the
country. A nationwide steel strike in 1920 caused a major defeat for
organized labour. The United States was growing increasingly
repressive.

The white backlash succeeded: industry cut back black hiring
and fired black women as 4 million soldiers returned to the workforce. Industry slowed down, immigration resumed, and the KKK
reorganized, spreading from Maine to California. In 1921 Missouri
Representative L.C. Dyer sponsored a bill supported by Garvey's
UNIA, the NAACP, and the YMCA, making lynching a federal
crime, but the KKK and Nativism had the political clout to force

passage of the National Origins (or Immigration Restriction) Act in 1924. It excluded all Asian immigrants and limited Europeans by nationality to 2 percent of those who had immigrated in 1890.

Thousands of black women were out of work and those with jobs had their wages reduced. Tradeswomen could work only in black-owned businesses (even in Harlem, only a fifth of businesses were owned by blacks). Unions, always hostile to blacks, again excluded them, virtually shutting them out of industries they had been working in, like garments and furs. The civil service had begun hiring black women, but President Wilson blocked this practice, and discrimination spread to municipal civil services. The telephone company, department stores, insurance companies, and restaurants refused to hire blacks or gave them only the most menial jobs.

Oddly, black women could work in the professions, where competition was lighter. By 1920 two of ten black university graduates were female; in 1921 three black women earned PhDs from prestigious schools. But in fields requiring college or post-graduate degrees, black female legal, medical, educational, and social workers earned paltry incomes compared to their white counterparts. Huge numbers of black women were forced back into the jobs reserved for women – domestic service and prostitution.

Heroines

Despite the Red Scare, some feminists with strong socialist views, like Jane Addams and Lillian Wald, opposed America's entering the First World War and were able to continue their work. Crystal Eastman, Margaret Sanger, and Emma Goldman, reformists dedicated to female sexual freedom, were a generation younger than Wald and Addams. Eastman, a journalist and attorney specializing in labour conditions and injuries, drafted the first New York worker-compensation law, the model for such laws across the country. An early supporter of female athletics, she toured the United States with champion swimmer Annette Kellerman, promoting "women's right to physical equality with men."

Eastman founded the New York branch of the American Union Against Militarism, the "mother" of the American Civil Liberties Union, and served as executive director with Wald as president.[13] In 1914 Eastman, Addams, and Emmeline Pethick-Lawrence created the Woman's Peace Party to try to keep the United States neutral in the First World War and stop it from invading Mexico in 1916. Eastman, Wald, and Addams dined with Wilson and his advisors at the White House and lobbied Congress, trying to influence events. After the United States entered the war in 1917, Eastman and Roger Baldwin worked in the Civil Liberties Bureau (renamed ACLU) to protect the rights of conscientious objectors and dissenters. The government used the war to justify domination and technology and to stifle dissent.

The Espionage Act and Sedition Acts of May 1918 made certain wartime acts retroactively illegal, and legalized removing radical publications from the post (in line with Comstock's focus on mail in an earlier wave of enforced conformity). Dissenters were imprisoned (including Eastman's brother Max) as well as thousands of anarchists, socialists, labour leaders, and conscientious objectors. Some were deported in the Red Scare following the war. These acts radicalized Eastman, who came to believe that capitalism had to be (peacefully) destroyed if liberty was to be possible. With Max, she started a protest magazine, *The Liberator*. Believing socialism stood for democracy, equality, and liberty but not for women's rights, she created a women's rights program around sex and reproduction, accepting birth control and "free love." Addams disavowed her. Blacklisted in the United States, she moved to England but failed to find work and died at forty-seven in 1928.

Margaret Sanger, a visiting nurse on Manhattan's Lower East Side and socialist IWW supporter, had helped strikers in Lawrence and Paterson. Daily exposure to poor women convinced her that birth control was necessary. In 1913, in France to study birth-control methods, she found that despite the Catholic Church and government allowances to mothers of large families, the French working-class birth rate was declining. Returning to the United States, she started a magazine, *The Woman Rebel*, devoted to female sexual freedom, and was indicted by the U.S. Post Office for "a philosophical defense of assassination" for writing:

A woman's body belongs to herself alone. It is her body. It does not belong to the Church. It does not belong to the United States of America. . . . The first step toward getting life, liberty and the pursuit of happiness for any woman is her decision whether or not she shall become a mother. Enforced motherhood is the most complete denial of a woman's right to life and liberty. . . . Once the women of the United States are awakened to the value of birth control, these institutions – Church, State, Big Business – will be struck such a blow that they will be able only to beg for mercy from the workers.

Sanger thought birth control would ease poor women's lot and free them sexually but also strengthen the working class. She fled the country until her trial (which she wanted to turn into a public forum), but before leaving she published a pamphlet, "Family Limitation," a digest of her knowledge of contraceptive techniques (douches, condoms, sponges, diaphragms, and suppositories) that contested claims that *coitus interruptus* harmed women's health. She urged that sex be mutually fulfilling, not an imposition of men's conjugal rights. The pamphlet was printed clandestinely but 10 million copies were issued and many more mimeographed, handcopied, or typed over the years. Thousands of grateful readers of both sexes sent small sums for Sanger's trial.

Throughout Sanger's career, the IWW had been her strongest ally, despite its reluctance to espouse birth control. But the government had destroyed the IWW. The IWW did not seem to understand the repressive potential of class rule: it never acted secretly, keeping open membership lists and a loose organization with no mode of communication but the mail.[14] When the government decided to eradicate the IWW during the First World War, it was able to seize all its publications and members in a few raids, and then prosecute and jail people on flimsy charges. Sanger had to look elsewhere for help. She found it in Emma Goldman.

Emma Goldman (1869–1940), arguably the greatest American political figure of her era, disappointed her Russian Jewish family by being a girl. With three female children by a first husband who died, Emma's mother felt it urgent to remedy her failure and have a son. Both parents cared only for sons. Emma's father suffered from repeated business failures and brutal Russian anti-Semitism, and took out his rage on Emma and her sister Helena, beating them continually, especially after their brother died. He sent Emma to live with an uncle who took her out of school and used her as a servant, treating her as cruelly as her father (kicking her down a flight of stairs). Two kindly woman neighbours rescued Emma from him and restored her to her family. She went to work as a seamstress and was raped: her angry father tried to force her to marry. After threatening to jump into the Neva River, she and Helena decided to go to America and live with their sister Lena.

They settled with Lena in Rochester, where Goldman worked as a seamstress, less happily than in Russia: the American factory was modern but regimented. St. Petersburg seamstresses talked and sang while they worked; in Rochester, conversation was utterly forbidden – foremen stood over the women working at their machines. Not only were workers isolated but Goldman's ideal of Jewish solidarity crumbled – the factory was owned by a wealthy German Jew who exploited Russian Jewish immigrants. With little formal education, Goldman educated herself with political novels like Chernyshevsky's great *What Is to Be Done?* whose heroine Vera Pavlovna escapes from an exploitative family, starts a flourishing communal female workshop, and lives in sexual freedom.

She moved to New Haven, Connecticut, to work in a unionized corset factory with decent working conditions. She also found comrades, Russian immigrants who gathered after work to discuss socialist and anarchist theory. She was fascinated by the level of discussion and by anarchy. Through her friends she met German anarchist Johann Most, an eloquent speaker despite an apparent facial deformity. Once a member of the Reichstag and German Social Democratic Party (SDP), he edited the *Berliner Freie Presse* and wrote a popular summary of *Das Kapital*. Expelled from Germany, he went to London where he published *Die Freiheit*, an anarchist journal. Most, impressed with Goldman's eloquence, trained her in public speaking. But she noticed he lost interest whenever she expressed her own ideas. Another ideal collapsed as she saw that even a man committed to individual freedom, opposed to all inequities and hierarchies, expected to dominate women.

Goldman became politically and sexually involved with Alexander (Sasha) Berkman, an anarchist. In 1892, workers at the Carnegie Steel plant in Homestead, Pennsylvania, struck for higher wages. Henry Clay Frick, chairman of Carnegie, replaced them with scabs, and locked them out of their company-owned houses. The strikers stood firm; he sent 300 Pinkerton men to attack them, and three Pinkertons and ten workers were killed. Outraged, the twenty-two-year-old Berkman decided to kill Frick with Emma's help. She planned and financed the assassination attempt: Berkman managed to get into Frick's office and fire three shots, seriously wounding Frick, but he was captured. The act that Emma expected to trigger workers nationwide to take over factories instead sent Sasha to prison and Emma underground, and provoked a new wave of repression. Workers' organizations were fractured by arguments over tactics. Emma began privately to question the wisdom of violent acts like Berkman's.[15]

Goldman later defined anarchy as liberation of the human mind from the dominion of religion, liberation of the human body from the dominion of property, and liberation from the shackles and restraints of government. For her, anarchy meant a "release and freedom from conventions and prejudice" without denying life and joy: "I want freedom, the right to self-expression, everybody's right to beautiful, radiant things," she wrote. All her acts bespoke an unwavering commitment to all people's right to live free from oppression. Anarchy offered no political program but a morality no political group was prepared to realize.

Goldman surfaced at an 1893 rally in Union Square, New York, to speak and march with a red banner alongside unemployed women and girls. The next day she was arrested, charged with "inciting a riot and . . . disbelief in God and government," and sentenced to a year at Blackwell's Prison. Her brilliance in court won her wide press coverage and on her release she found herself a national celebrity. In the next years, she visited Vienna (learning about Freud) and London, meeting major European radicals like Louise Michel, heroine of the Paris Commune, and anarchist Peter Kropotkin, who believed modern technology could maintain a cooperative communist society and that revolution was a natural process, not a violent overthrow. In 1900, Goldman returned to the United States, worked as a midwife-nurse (having trained in jail), and lectured on contraception, which she felt integrated her life. She thought that contraception abetted sexual revolution, helped free women, and subverted government efforts to leash personal freedom.

In 1906 Goldman founded an anarchist journal, *Mother Earth*, as an alternative to *Masses*, the socialist journal. Aimed at a less intellectual but more radical readership, it presented political messages from literary figures and Goldman's mix of politics and art. She found the suffrage movement hostile to labour and never worked for women's suffrage. But she spoke on an even more provocative subject, female sexual freedom, as well as birth control. At every talk she gave in every city, she sold Margaret Sanger's magazine, *The Woman Rebel*, which had been banned from the mail for "obscenity" – birth-control information. When Sanger's husband William was arrested for giving a visitor to his home a copy of her pamphlet "Family Limitation" in 1915, Goldman wrote an editorial in *Mother Earth* condemning legal censorship. Her eye was always on principle – not advantage, influence or power, or the power, influence, or status of a party. This was true of no male leader.

As the possibility quickened that America would enter the war, Goldman's speeches linked war and birth control, warning that America's increasingly repressive atmosphere was related to war preparations: a country at war subordinates all needs and dissent to the State's desire for unity. After the United States declared war on Germany, she continued to speak against conscription. Attendance at her speeches was huge: once, 5000 filled the hall and 30,000 massed outside as she urged workers to copy the revolutionaries who overthrew the Czar in February. After one speech the government arrested hundreds of draft resisters. Since the government was using her talks to entrap prospective war resisters, she chose not to speak again but only write. But she was arrested the next day, along with Berkman, who was now out of jail. The arresting officer carried not a warrant but the June issue of *Mother Earth*, which, he said, held enough treasonable matter to send them to jail for years. They were found guilty of "conspiracy against the draft," and after declaring Goldman "probably the greatest woman of her time," the judge imposed the maximum penalty for conspiracy against the draft – two years in prison and a $10,000 fine.

Under the Espionage Act, the government arrested thousands, especially foreign anti-war agitators and radicals, giving the longest sentences to Bill Haywood of the IWW, Eugene Debs, Socialist Party head, and Kate Richards O'Hare, major socialist activist and reformer. Mail censorship increased. The Postmaster banned a book of essays by Voltairine de Cleyre for pieces on Goldman and sexual slavery; her linking of sexual freedom and anti-militarism threw him into virtual hysterics.[16] Most dangerous, the government felt, was "Justice for the Negro," a Wobbly leaflet pointing out that while black soldiers were asked to fight for democracy abroad, ninety-one blacks had been lynched at home.

The Alien Immigration Act of 1917 gave the government power

to deport foreign-born anarchists. Arrests became arbitrary when the war ended in 1919: paranoia generated "Palmer raids" on groups connected in any way with foreign, anti-war, or radical activity. When Joseph Kershner, whom Goldman had married and left years before, died in January 1919, she was no longer a citizen by marriage and the government sought a way to deport "Red Emma" as it had long wanted to do. It hired a woman to infiltrate the anarchist network as Goldman's secretary and report on the activities of "those damned kikes." Early on December 21, 1919, a bitterly cold day, Emma Goldman, Sasha Berkman, and 247 others guarded by 250 soldiers each with a rifle and two pistols, were marched onto a dilapidated military ship, and expelled from American soil. America had cast out its greatest moralist.

With Berkman, Goldman went first to Russia to observe the revolution. She spoke Russian, knew many radicals visiting there, and was a figure of considerable stature, so she could observe widely. And what she saw was misery. Goldman complained to Lenin, who received her graciously, persuading her and Berkman to help build the revolution. For a year they toured the country, seeing poverty everywhere, hearing about people's disillusion, and their terror of the Party and of the secret police, the Cheka. She learned of the ghastly conditions in prisons, discrimination against intellectuals, and pervasive anti-Semitism. With Berkman, she decided to tell the world what she had seen.

Her criticism of the revolution lost her what friends she had left; in the next months, Goldman and Berkman were imprisoned in Latvia on Bolshevik orders, while American officials hysterically mounted defences against her possible return. Two years after their deportation, the pair left Soviet space, sailing into a void, friendless, without destination. Because her loyalty lay with humanity, not any cause, Goldman was abandoned. In the next years, she wrote her autobiography and lectured in England, Holland, Denmark, and Germany, continuing to warn the human race of threats to its freedom, arguing that Hitler's fascism showed the same disregard for the individual as Lenin's Soviet Union and American capitalism. Hope gone, Goldman died in May 1940.

Women in American Labour after 1930

Millions of American working women who strategized, organized, and protested were also defeated. During the first phase of labour struggle, they were beaten mainly by capital, as employers succeeded in "hungering" them out. Men and male unions helped some women's unions during this period, but in most cases, men impeded or cut women out entirely. White men used trade unions, which could have united all workers to stand fast against employers, as a weapon to defend relative privilege against other workers.

When the Committee for Industrial Organization (CIO: later called the Congress of Industrial Organizations) was formed in 1935, women were more accepted by organized labour, and by the end of the Second World War, neither AFL nor CIO unions barred women from membership; only the International Brotherhood of Bookbinders had separate women's locals (common in pre-war years). More women had staff positions too, if mainly on the local level, but only one, the United Federal Workers, had a woman president. Few women sat on national executive boards. The most impressive (but atypical) was the United Electrical Workers, whose organizing staff was over a third female in 1944 – almost matching its 40 percent female UEW membership.[17]

Some women union leaders developed and promoted special programs to meet the needs of women, despite male leaders' opposition to their advanced ideas. Their efforts led many unions to provide child care and other community services for women workers and to negotiate contracts providing maternity leave without loss of seniority. By the war's end most unions had endorsed the idea of "the rate for the job," or equal pay for equal work. Unions rarely confronted the real inequalities by trying to eliminate differential wages for "men's" and "women's" jobs, but in 1942, the UEW negotiated a contract with Westinghouse that raised only women's wages. The system of job classification by sex was almost never challenged. A 1944 study of twenty-five industries found that men's hourly earnings were 50 percent higher than women's, and 20 percent higher on unskilled jobs.[18]

According to a United States Women's Bureau survey of 13,000 women workers in war industries in 1944–45, 75 percent wanted to keep their jobs when the war ended. While they expected to be laid off disproportionately because of lower seniority, and neither demanded nor expected preferential treatment, they felt they deserved the same protection as men. They thought that returning veterans should displace workers of either sex only if they had more seniority. Their effort to establish nondiscriminatory seniority systems was quite successful – four-fifths of the union contracts covering 75,000 women workers in a Midwestern war industry area in 1945 demanded plant-wide rather than departmental seniority; only a fifth stipulated separate seniority lists for women.[19]

Thus, while women expected to bear the brunt of initial layoffs, if they were recalled according to seniority, post-war industrial expansion should have reincorporated them into the labour force of the industries where they had done "war work." But often they were not recalled. The UAW affirmed unequivocal support for "Protection of Women's Rights in the Auto Industry," laying out a detailed model policy on equal pay, seniority, and other rights, but did not specify penalties for violating them. Many locals continued to negotiate contracts that openly discriminated against women, and locals had to enforce contracts with formal protections against discrimination. Many shop stewards simply ignored inequities or failed to pursue women's grievances.

The single most important change in the make-up of the labour force after the Second World War was the dramatic rise in female participation; the recent stagnation of the labour movement resulted from its failure to deal with that. Indeed the extent to which industries are unionized is strongly inversely related to the representation of women workers in their labour forces. AFL unions' successful exclusion of women (and people of colour) from craft occupations helped to rigidify the sexual division of paid work.

No matter how large their female membership, mixed unions remain male-dominated. When the WTUL merged with the Amalgamated Clothing Workers of America it became 75 percent female, but it has never had a woman director or high officer at the international level and has a tiny female presence on its executive board. No woman held high office in the IWW, despite the importance of women members like Elizabeth Gurley Flynn. Rose Pesotta complained in 1944 that despite its 85 percent female membership the International Ladies Garment Workers Union (ILGWU) reserved only one seat on its executive board for a woman; in the 1980s, the ILGWU sometimes had two women on its board of twenty to twenty-three members. A few small AFL unions had women presidents, but no woman ever sat on the AFL-CIO Executive Council. No woman had ever been president of the AFL-CIO and, as of 1986, none had been regional director. After John Sweeney, a reformer, was elected head of the AFL-CIO in 1995, however, things changed. Sweeney doubled the representation of women and people of colour in high-level posts; women, once 6 percent of department heads, now comprise 50 percent. Women head the two largest departments, international affairs and field mobilization. He also created a working-women's department, and a program open to any working woman, unionized or not. Now, 13 percent of the Executive Council, and 15 percent of the Central Labour Council are women.

A female onslaught in the 1970s and 1980s forced skilled trade unions such as electricians and plumbers to accept female members. But the men harassed women; they ganged up against those hired singly or by twos verbally abusing them or refusing to speak to them at all, hung obscene pictures in the workplace, endangered them or used physical violence. However they could, they drove women out. Yet reluctance to make common cause with women and minority workers still undermines organized labour as a whole.

Governments, still elitist, continue to want to destroy organized labour. Three miners' strikes occurred in 1989 – in the (then) Soviet Union and Poland (socialist states that prohibited strikes), and in the United States, where miners in three states struck against the Pittston Coal Group. Only in the United States were strike leaders imprisoned. The American press, which gave wide coverage to the strikes in socialist countries barely noted the American one. Since Ronald Reagan successfully broke the air controllers' union in 1981, companies have been hiring "replacement workers" (euphemism for scabs), and firing strikers. Since unions excluded so many people, "replacement workers" are easy to find. Unions' failure to organize workers worldwide has contributed to allowing multinational corporations to arrange to have goods produced where production is cheapest. Clothing manufacturers avoid paying union scale by transferring production to Korea or China or southeast Asia, where they can pay workers too little to survive.

Owners are power-hungry and greedy, but so was labour: the history of white men in the American labour movement is ignoble. They called themselves *the workers* as if only they laboured to survive. Cutting out all women and men of colour, they seized their piece of the pie. Men who once guarded their privileges in massive steel and automobile industries now pound the sidewalks of Houston and Dallas seeking work or live homeless in New York. The American labour movement turned its back on its own early standards – to create a just and felicitous society – and made its own destruction possible. All workers lost as a result.

At present, union leaders are trying to reform the movement and revive the organizations' past unity and moral force. They have opened their ranks to women and people of colour. But labour unions, which in the 1950s boasted a membership of 38 percent of the workforce, now have only 9 percent. This defeat was caused not by labour, but by owners, who moved their factories to other countries in the world – to nations that do not have laws demanding healthful safe environments or wages sufficient to maintain life – to avoid having to abide by labour laws in the United States. Other owners have shifted to staffs largely made up of part-time or contract workers, to avoid having to pay for medical care, pensions, and other benefits. Few workers nowadays earn enough to support families, which must have two working members to survive. The labour organizations that sixty or seventy years ago urged the unionization of the world's workers were on the right track. But that has not occurred yet.

In England

It was the class-ridden English who devised a strategy with the potential to create an industrial society with a democratic, non-exploitative shape. Nineteenth- and twentieth-century labour history is a series of attempts by owners to wrest control from workers' organizations to restructure labour to suit their ends, and workers' attempts to resist this usurpation. Labour lost.

Laws passed in England in 1824–25 gave male organizations (descended from guilds) the right to bargain collectively, allowing them to become full-fledged trade unions and preserve the guild hierarchy of apprentice, journeyman, and master. From the start, male trade-unionists wanted women – "wives and daughters" – to be "in their proper sphere at home, instead of being dragged into competition for livelihood against the great and strong men of the world," as a labour leader said in 1875.[20] Men who felt their jobs threatened by women earning half their rate challenged not the wage rate but women's right to the jobs. Textile unions adamantly excluded women, striking when owners hired them, yet they could not prevent the hiring of skilled women at half wages. Cotton spinners urged women to form their own unions, and many did in the 1830s and 1840s: female and male Glasgow spinners and power-loom weavers joined to raise money to fight for equal pay.

Spinners' unions accepted only men who could afford high entry fees and dues. High dues enabled unions to pay their members during strikes, but strikes also affected workers without an organization or strike fund – like women. Without wages, they starved, so were available as strikebreakers, "knobsticks," scabs. To prevent this, spinners finally accepted a separate organization of piecers and cardroom workers. The Bolton Association of Cotton Spinners admitted women to its piecers' section in 1837. Other unions or union sections were soon organizing piecers and cardroom workers. It was ludicrous to exclude women from unions in an industry in which they predominated, but spinners and cotton weavers admitted them only slowly over years.[21]

In the winter of 1833, the Derby silk industry locked out all workers, initiating a struggle that generated such anger and solidarity among workers nationwide that they created the Consolidated Union. During this strike, women founded union lodges, networking with neighbouring women in other industries, who supported them. They joined cooperative workshops and led large demonstrations, fighting with – even stoning – the police. A union man wrote: "From the determined heroism [of these women] I could scarcely believe but that I was surrounded by the descendants of the 'Maid of Orleans,' and are these, I ask . . . to be subdued by the fancied power of the monied capitalists? No, gentlemen of Derby . . . retire from the contest with these Amazonian females; defeat will be yours."

Seeing radical action as an extension of their family duties encouraged women's militancy, but limited its forms. Workers' groups adopted the traditional family sexual division of labour and power. Before 1830 no woman led a sexually mixed union; the Consolidated Union had members in mixed trades, yet women were usually organized in separate lodges, and men's lodges took the initiative in all ventures. Women seem not to have protested or suggested other ways: the old ways were just transferred to the new system. In virtually all industries women worked on different elements or phases of production from men and were paid less. They often organized alongside men, but many mixed organizations collapsed and were replaced by segregated ones. Tension between the sexes grew as owners retooled and debased or eliminated the need for craft skills, hiring unskilled workers – usually women – for less pay. Female labour threatened skilled male workers, who formed sex-segregated unions with men who wanted women out of their industries and unions entirely.

Nineteenth-century industry exploited women almost as cruelly as it did children, but male colleagues did not step in: government did. Government, however, did not regulate industry but its victims, forbidding women and children to work underground in mines. This gratified male miners, whose organizations had been trying to bar women from underground work because they kept "lads and men from getting their proper wages." Many male trade unionists lobbied Parliament to limit the hours women could work, hoping further restrictions on women would limit men's hours "behind the women's petticoats." One union lobbied for hour limitations and proportional quotas on women, and a ban on married women.

After women textile workers unionized, no drive to organize women workers occurred until 1874, when Emma Paterson founded the Women's Protective and Provident League. Paterson intended the league to be a central body that helped set up individual unions, hoping that once women knew how to run a self-reliant, self-supporting organization, the league could withdraw but stand ready to help a union in trouble. At first, it helped unionize women bookbinders, milliners, mantle-makers, and other needlewomen in London, all very small groups in areas traditionally regarded as skilled or semi-skilled "women's work." It soon became controversial for its opposition to protective legislation. Its middle-class leaders felt that women had the right to any job and hours they wanted, and that if hours were to be limited, collective bargaining, not legislation should negotiate them.

A few years after Paterson died in 1886, the league responded to changes in trade unionism by changing its policies, financial base, and name; it became the Women's Trade Union League (WTUL). Lady Dilke, who led the league after Paterson's death, wanted to shift from middle-class donations and subscriptions to a firm financial base in the trade union movement and devised a plan allowing any bona fide trade union admitting women to affiliate with the WTUL for a halfpenny a year per female member, for which WTUL would help organize women and raise strike funds. By the 1890s sixty unions, including thirty local cotton worker groups, had done so.

Changing its policy on protective laws, the WTUL now championed them. Female factory inspectors, the first women in responsible government jobs, were few in number but enormously important to women in factories and trade unions. They travelled extensively around Great Britain to factories, back-street workshops, even to wild Donegal; they had detailed knowledge of the laws governing factories and the ability to argue a case in court – thirty years before British women were admitted to the bar. Courageous outspoken women devoted to their work, they went far beyond their assignments to investigate areas where improvement was needed, suggesting new laws or extensions of existing acts. Their annual reports provided an authoritative foundation for campaigns for further laws to protect women workers.

Unlike cotton unions, heavy woollens workers' unions, most in Yorkshire, were often started or virtually run by women. The industry was not organized until 1875, when owners in the Dewsbury area (over fifty manufacturers, two or three finishers, and twelve dyers) colluded in cutting wages. Hannah Wood, Ann Ellis, and Kate Conran founded a Heavy Woollen Weavers' Strike and Lockout Committee and struck, raising a strike fund of £1200 in six weeks. These women had no inhibitions against speaking in public and at one meeting spoke to 9000 people. Throughout the strike, they pleaded for unity of male and female workers. The strike was settled and their union became the first branch of a General Union of Textile Workers.

A government report on strikes and lockouts in the textile industry listed ninety-nine labour disputes in 1898 (fewer than in the five
previous years) involving 24,978 workers, directly or indirectly. Of a
labour force 42 percent women, 32 percent men, and 26 percent
youths, proportionately more women than men were involved in
lockouts and strikes. Non-unionized women relied on local trades
councils to help organize, support, and negotiate for them after they
struck. Unions were reluctant to organize women otherwise.

Trade unions closed to skilled women did not even consider
organizing the most gravely exploited workers – unskilled factory
women. When radical WTUL women urged such organizing, they
were criticized by people like journalist Annie Besant for advocating
unworkable schemes. If workers (like the match workers she had
mentioned in a recent column) went on strike, hundreds of others
would beg for their jobs, she wrote. The column, headed "White
Slavery in London," described conditions at Bryant and May, whose
female employees worked ten to eleven and a half hours a day, earning from 4 to 9 shillings a week, burdened by innumerable fines: "If
the feet are dirty, or the ground under the bench is left untidy, a fine
of 3 pence is inflicted; for putting 'burnts' – matches that have caught
fire during work – on the bench" they were fined 1 shilling (a quarter of the wages of some). If they were late for work, they were shut
out all morning and docked 5 pence from their day's pay of 8 pence.

When Bryant and May told the press that they were suing
Besant for libel, she announced she would stand by the statements
in her article. The company dismissed three women known to have
talked to Besant and asked workers to sign a statement swearing
Besant's claims were false. They refused, and the company fired a
woman they believed to be a ringleader. All the women in her
department left with her; soon, all 1400 women at Bryant and May
walked out. They held public meetings, demonstrated, and sent a
deputation to ask the home secretary to prosecute Bryant and May
for imposing illegal fines and deductions. Still calling Besant's
article a "tissue of lies," the company dropped its libel suit. A

delegation of "match girls" went to the London Trades Council (LTC) for help; they received £20 for the strike fund and an offer to mediate. The LTC helped them draw up a grievance list and arrange a meeting among the strike committee, trades council members, and Bryant and May directors. The company acceded to almost all the women's demands. All fines and most deductions were abolished, the "pennies" restored, and no retribution was exacted. Most important, the company acknowledged the union. The Match Girls' strike inspired other unskilled workers' unions.

During this period, women began to infiltrate white-collar work, entering civil service by a circuitous route. In 1870 the government took over the telegraph system, placing it under control of the Post Office, which was obliged to retain female telegraph operators who had worked for the private companies. A postal official saw advantages to hiring women, and his brief became the basis for female employment in civil service. He preferred women to men in clerical work because they were quick, accurate, and happier at sedentary occupations. The wages offered would draw a better class of women than men, with the added benefit of superior education – they wrote and spelled better and "where the staff is mixed, the female clerks will raise the tone of the staff." In addition, he wrote:

> Women are less disposed than men to combine for the purpose of extorting higher wages. . . . Permanently established civil servants invariably expect their remuneration to increase with their years of service. . . . Women, however, will solve these difficulties for the Department by retiring for the purpose of getting married as soon as they get the chance. On the whole, it may be stated without fear of contradiction that, if we place an equal number of females and males on the same ascending scale of pay, the aggregate pay to the females will always be less than the aggregate pay to the males; . . . and further, that there will always be fewer females than males on the pension list.

The government hired forty women in the savings bank in 1875. Appalled, the men in the office threatened an "indignation meeting" to protest employment of women as causing "grievous dangers, moral and official." Beyond that, they said, women would not be strong enough to write cross-entry acknowledgments, which required "heavy pressure by means of very hard pens and carbonic paper"[!] But the advantage of cheap labour outweighed male prejudice: women became a significant presence in government offices.

In 1906 Mary Macarthur founded the National Federation of Women Workers (NFWW), which lasted only until 1920 but organized more women, mounted more strikes, and did more to establish women's unions than any other group, largely because of her leadership. A freelance journalist, she kept books for her father, a successful Ayr draper. Covering a shop assistants' union meeting for a conservative Scottish newspaper changed her life: "I went to a meeting in Ayr to write a skit on the proceedings; going to scoff, I remained to pray." Impressed with the "truth and meaning of the Labour movement," she joined the union. In 1902 she was elected branch president (the only female president in Scotland), and president of the Scottish National District Council. Involved with the Independent Labour Party, at a 1902 conference, she met Margaret Bondfield, an organizer of shop assistants in the south, who gave Macarthur the confidence to move to London. At twenty-three she was secretary of the WTUL and threw her considerable energy into organizing it and its finances properly. Macarthur stayed connected to WTUL; she created the NFWW as a militant union for women in unorganized trades or trades with unions that rejected women. Workers' only weapon in this period was the strike and between 1906 and 1914 the federation mainly led strikes. The first league leader with experience in trade unionism and the labour movement, Macarthur died in 1921, only forty-one years old.

Tailoring

In the eighteenth century, tailoring was men's work. With the strongest union in England, tailors controlled prices, hours, and labour recruitment through apprenticeship. They strictly limited female employment to dressmaking and millinery, which were lower paid and unorganized. Tailors' wives, unlike those of weavers, did not help them, so only masters could support a wife and family. Tailors' wives earned money by embroidering, making necklaces and mantuas, and selling milk. A journeyman with a working wife could live decently: the family could afford a servant, a few amenities (some books or a piano) and he could enjoy local cultural and political life. Men needed wives to work but felt disgraced if their wives worked away from home, so wives kept shops, did homework and laundry, or took in lodgers. Whatever a wife did, she earned little.

Capitalists reorganized industry in the early nineteenth century and hired "puffers and sweaters" who subcontracted jobs to home workers. Aiming for maximum profit, they sought workers who would take low wages. They found women. The tailors' union, trying to prevent production outside workshops, which they controlled, struck and won. Francis Place, a master tailor in 1824, wrote: "It will be found universally . . . where men have opposed the employment of women and children . . . their own wages are kept up to a point equal to the maintenance of a family. . . . Tailors of London have not only kept up, but forced up their wages in this way."

During the Napoleonic Wars, the government needed cheap military uniforms, and developed a system in which wholesale fabric producers contracted with small masters or unemployed journeymen. They in turn hired cheap labour, often women, to make ready-to-wear – "slop" clothing – in their homes or sweatshops. Slop clothing, cheaper than "bespoke" (made to order), became very popular. New quality clothiers opened "show-shops" of clothes made to standard measurements, driving master tailors out of business. The union protested: "Have not women been unfairly driven from their proper sphere in the social scale, unfeelingly torn from the maternal duties of a parent, and unjustly encouraged to compete with men in ruining the money value of labour?"

In 1834, 9000 London tailors struck for higher wages, a reduction in hours, and the abolition of piece- and home-work. All concerned knew they wanted to put an end once and for all to female tailoring; they threatened women's outwork and show-shop employment, declaring, an editor wrote, a "war against the female tailors." Owners used editorials in their mouthpiece, *The Times*, to lament "dictatorial" union treatment of "honest and industrious females" and hired women scabs. Union men assaulted women and seized their materials. But the men were divided: some supported women's right to work but condemned the shops that hired them. The union accused owners of lying to "turn our mothers and sisters against us"; some wanted to set up a (separate) women's union. Socialists, favouring equality, opened a cooperative workshop during the strike. John Doherty, head of the Lancashire cotton spinners union, said the problem of women was serious, but its solution obvious: men, he exhorted, should "acknowledge the natural equality of women . . . include them in all [their] schemes of improvement." An editorial in *The Pioneer*, an Owenite newspaper, urged equal pay and women's inclusion in unions. In the end, however, the tailors lost.[22]

The Pioneer editorial laid out the options for male unionists who wanted to move beyond defensive sectional militancy toward egalitarian class organization: "Women have always been worse paid for their labour than men and thus, they have been taught to regard this inequality as justice." Since they were "content with merely a portion of man's wage, even when their work is equally valuable," they could be used to undercut men's wages. To prevent lower wages, tailors organized against female employment.

It is not right, the editorial continued, for male workers to undercut the wages of other men; it would not be right for female workers to do this either, if women were equal to men, with the same rights and privileges. "But since man has doomed her to inferiority, and stamped an inferior value upon all the productions of her industry, the low wages of woman are not so much the voluntary price she sets upon her labour, as the price which is fixed by the tyrannical influence of male supremacy. To make the two sexes equal, and to reward them equally, would settle the matter amicably; but any attempt to settle it otherwise will prove an act of gross tyranny."[23]

Women wrote of their male antagonists, "It is clear enough from this whispering spirit of jealousy . . . that the men are as bad as their masters." If the idea of women meeting and organizing outside the home, beyond the direct control of husbands or fathers terrified some men, the idea of women organizing, earning the same wages, and cooperating in work, appalled them. But by refusing to recognize women, excluding them from their unions, and retreating from a demand for equal pay and decent working conditions, the craft unions injured women and destroyed themselves.

Men's loss of domination of crafts led to a breakdown in their sexual authority. They equated losing the power that seemed inherent in their craft, and losing the feeling of strength they derived from status in all-male industries and unions, with a loss of manhood. Losing the powers of purse and status weakened their sense of superiority over women, which had been constructed by customary and legal prerogatives. But men's loss did not liberate women, who were forced into deeper poverty. A study of wife-beating in London in the 1840s found that when women replaced men as the major breadwinners in artisan households, men responded violently, asserting physically an authority that had lost its material foundation. Men's already strong opposition to married women's employment was heightened: a wage-earning wife symbolized male degradation. They believed that a "real man" kept a dependent wife at home.

Women too supported the family wage and bought the ideology of domesticity; it was oppressive and imposed from the outside, but it was the best choice then open to working-class women, given the hideous working conditions and low wages of the time. In the end, though, men's loss of dominance in the family liberated women as they challenged other forms of male dominance.

Printing

Male printers staved women off for a little longer. Printers' organizations were rooted in medieval guilds; the many female printers of the fifteenth and sixteenth centuries probably took over their dead husbands' shops – girls were never allowed into the hierarchy of apprentice, journeyman, master.[24]   Printers derived great self-importance from an exclusive craft that barred all women and most men and which required literacy, a mark of status. Few applicants were accepted as apprentices, and printers' sons got precedence. On finishing their training, they were ritually initiated; journeymen became part of an elite group of artisans – citizens, Freemen of the City. Union shops were called "chapels," suggesting printers' awed sense of themselves.

Manufacturers, who constantly seek new production methods requiring less skill, developed Linotype, a mechanized typesetter that needed only one semi-skilled operator. The Typographical Association (TA) informed owners that its members would run the machines and share the profits; shorter hours and training it made possible. The TA and the London Society of Compositors (LSC) were strong enough to enforce this (a commentator called the TA "an army of guerilla bands," the LSC "a panzer division"). British compositors even did unskilled jobs in the trade to retain exclusive control of the composing room. Publishing grew wildly over the century and employers' profits were high enough to satisfy them. As hand-compositors retired or died, younger printers found work in the growing market. By 1900 socialist ideas had penetrated the TA, which allied with what became the Labour Party to unionize the unskilled, and helped form a national Federation of Printing and Kindred Trades to unite all male printers' unions in Britain.

In the world of printing, women were complete outsiders. Few women did printing – 300 in 1851, 700 in 1871, and 4500 in 1891 – and almost none were compositors. Neither the TA, the Scottish Typographical Association (STA), nor the LSC needed explicitly to bar women, because unions controlled apprenticeship. The unions showed their true colours in an unusual conference held in London in 1886 to deal with the "threat" of women compositors in Edinburgh.

When male compositors in Edinburgh went on strike in 1872, owners hired women and trained them to fill the men's jobs. By 1900 Edinburgh had 750 female compositors. Owners in other Scottish cities began to hire them, and during a depression men bitterly blamed women for male unemployment. Paying women less than men, Scottish firms could undercut London firms, and they began taking their business. The three typographical societies met to deal with this. Wanting to keep women out of the craft altogether, but also to ensure that if women got in, they could not undercut men's wages, they passed a seemingly illogical resolution: "That while strongly of the opinion that women are not physically capable of performing the duties of a compositor, this Conference recommends their admission to membership of the various typographical unions, upon the same conditions as journeymen, provided always the females are paid strictly in accordance with the scale." They knew no employer would hire women at the same wage rate as men, given men's hostility and the limitations of the Factory Act (the protective law that curtailed women's work hours at night).

Men claimed women could not physically do work they were already doing because it involved too much standing and lifting heavy weights. They simply ignored women's work in mines, laundries, and similar industries. They warned that handling type could "destroy the powers of maternity in women." British union histories still dismiss men's antagonism toward women as incidental fall-out from the class struggle, given employers' exploitation of cheap female labour. "Had nothing but class interest been at stake, the men would have found women acceptable as apprentices, would have fought whole-heartedly for equal pay for women and the right of women to keep their jobs at equal pay."[25] Instead, they tried to eliminate women from their trade.

What was at stake for men was, as one man wrote, the male need for women to be men's servants, "housekeeper, cook, and several other single domestics rolled into one."[26] This ideal, presented as fact, won union men a "family wage" and kept women out of work. Yet many union men did not marry, many of those who did were negligent toward their families: many women and children were destitute. Men received a "family wage" whether they had families or not; and women did not receive decent wages whether they had families or not. In the period of the First World War, a family wage was paid on behalf of 3 million fictitious wives and 16 million fictitious children – the supposed dependants of bachelors – while real women and children starved.[27] Men claimed that status was an emotional necessity, ignoring women's physical needs: "I felt degraded following the footsteps of generations of compositor-forefathers before me, at having to descend to such vile practices" as working alongside women; if women did the work, "some of the shine would go out of the job for me. Prestige might not be exactly the right word, but it carries what is known as a macho bit, composing. It's man's work." Composing was men's work; "it has always been regarded as men's work . . . a large number of men are attracted to the trade because it is a man's employment." The presence of even one woman transforms it into "women's work."

Unthinkable as it was that women should join the all-male trade society that gave men self-respect as artisans and as men, it was equally unthinkable that employers would hire women at the same wages as men. The printers' societies tactic succeeded. A few bold employers went on using women at low rates, but no women were admitted to the English TA; Jane Payne, accepted by the LSC, resigned in 1898. Feminists tried to organize women compositors in Edinburgh, but the STA was unwilling to accept them.[28]

Male hostility toward women became hatred in 1904 when Glasgow printers asked owners for a wage raise. When the arbitrator denied the request on the grounds that by excluding women, compositors hobbled Glasgow firms in competing with Edinburgh firms, union branches in other Scottish cities rose up against women. Solidarity brought victory; after a fifteen-week strike, Aberdeen printers won a promise that no more women would be hired at case (hand-typesetting) or on machines. The Dundee branch had all women compositors fired but two; Perth got all its females fired.

Edinburgh compositors delayed until 1909 the crusade against women that the trade had been anticipating. In the interim, the monotype machine was introduced. It separated the two parts of printing, setting type and casting. Typesetting could now be done like typewriting, on a keyboard like other female jobs. Now the Edinburgh men were threatened by women in both hand and machine composing. Late in 1909, the Edinburgh branch of the STA sent a "memorial" to printing masters: get rid of women. As printers agitated, employers vaguely agreed to reduce the number of "girls" at case. This was a ploy – female keyboard workers threatened compositors at case. The men asked for backing by the local Federation of Printing and Kindred Trades, unskilled men in the Warehousemen and Cutters' Union, and the National Society of Operative Printers' Assistants. In return, they promised to help their drive for recognition by employers.

Three hundred women compositors signed a petition and sent it to the masters and their association. Temperate and reasonable, they argued the unfairness of firing them: they were competent, they had been doing the job for forty years, and they too were part of the labour movement. They begged the men at least to listen to them before acting further. The STA exploded, saying their petition had been produced by a small coterie of outside feminists "engaged in political warfare. . . . The vast majority of girls knew absolutely nothing either of the memorial or its authors." Any women com-

positors involved were surely the better paid. "The bitterest opponents to this funny little game . . . are . . . the ranks of the girls
themselves," who did not want "the sympathetic help of a class
political body, or My Lady's tea parties." The men, strong in "conscious righteousness," knew they had "the moral backing and financial support of the entire trade in the UK. . . . We are going into
battle. Let us stand together like comrades and brothers."

Brothers indeed. The largest group of men ever to attend a
union meeting in Edinburgh turned out to hear the employers'
response to "The Woman Question," breaking all records "for size
and solidarity of feeling." Employers promised not to hire any new
women compositors for seven years. That was not enough: the men
held out until employers agreed not to hire any new women at any
job for six years (until June 1916) and to have men run all future
keyboards of composing machines. As older women compositors
eventually died off, the agreement became a ban on women in the
industry that was still in force in 1953.

In no industry did sexual segregation change from 1901 to
1971. Women workers remained clustered horizontally in certain
types of work, and vertically in the lower ranks of seniority and pay.
They predominated in clerical and secretarial work (80 percent),
occupying a few low-level managerial jobs, usually supervising
women's work. They were 11 percent of workers on national newspapers, 28 percent on local and provincial newspapers, and 5 percent of newspaper managers. On newspapers, women held mainly
clerical, canteen, and cleaning jobs. In 1977 not one woman compositor worked on a national newspaper, and only 300 (with over
11,000 men) worked on regional papers. Then came the computer.

In the second half of the nineteenth century, British working-
class men organized against women. To keep women economically,
socially, and politically dependent, working-class men denied them
jobs and a living wage; to accomplish this goal, labour historically
colluded with its class enemy, and British labour politics became
centred on the single issue of the male wage, and male economic

power: no egalitarian wage politics existed. This struggle also reinforced men's belief that they had no responsibility for – were exempt from – concern about "women's" realm: reproduction and renewal. Finally, working men's economic struggle affected theories of social change in Britain: the main impetus to Owenism, and its most profound challenge to capitalism – to ward off the division of experience into categories of production versus reproduction and renewal – was sacrificed to the male ego.

The suffrage movement was dominated by middle-class women with (often) little comprehension of the plight of their working-class sisters, but some middle-class women were sympathetic and many working-class women worked in the suffrage movement. Indeed, feminists struggled to be heard within every socialist organization. But feminist ideals were disregarded by Marxist groups like the Social Democratic Federation and by larger, non-Marxist bodies like the Independent Labour Party. Labour politics became a mirror image of capitalist politics, obsessed with power, profit, and male ego at the cost of all other concerns. In the late nineteenth century, British socialism revived within labour and reflected its values. Politics became a nightmare like a Russian doll: each constituency replicated the others on a different scale. There were no alternatives: the nature of socialism was transformed. Capitalism had the potential to challenge patriarchy by creating a free labour market; people freed from the old bonds of blood and feudal kinship could have transformed the patriarchal family into an egalitarian relation. But labour politics thwarted that challenge as socialists ignored the brilliant socialist insight that the worst evil of capitalism was its sundering of integrated life.

By the time Marx's work was translated into English, British socialism was already firmly patriarchal. Marx's perspective and terminology, his couching of problem and solution, stressed strategy more than ideals. It gave socialists a more acute awareness of the obstacles impeding a revolutionary movement, and as they systematically adopted a Marxist approach, as communism acquired clearer direction and focus, it was masculinized (in the sense in which the word is used in this study), filed to a sharper but narrower point. At the same time, it was transformed from a possible alternative to patriarchy into a variation of it.[29]

CHAPTER 9

THE WAR AGAINST WOMEN

B Y THE NINETEENTH CENTURY, women in much of the world seemed subdued by the combined forces of religion, law, and male will, which did not shrink from physical coercion. Some women were destroyed by subjugation; others found ways to survive within it; some grew stronger because of it. But however effectively it inhibited women's bodies and acts, it never tamed their powers of thought. Women can behave within the boundaries allotted them and yet not be defeated. However constricted and oppressed, women have always fought for power over their own lives using psychological, emotional, and sexual strategies. Men deeply resent this. Having defined women as submissive and obedient, having appropriated women's sexuality and taught them that virtue – even the right to life – lay in accepting male ownership; having denied women any political and most economic rights and, to differing degrees, education, they still had to *think* about them, guard against them, deal with opposition often of the subtlest variety. Men who believed male definitions and saw women as inferior, slavish, stupid, and incompetent *by nature* were outraged when women protested or demanded rights.

This contradiction between orthodox definitions of femaleness and women's actual wilful behaviour leads men to divide women into categories of madonna or whore, a division that has always reflected not actual women but men's sense of the hostility and personal will that lie beneath women's compliant surfaces. The propaganda campaigns waged by dominators always convince *them* that their rule is necessary, deserved, good. But dominators are shocked and outraged when the dominated suggest, however subtly, that they have minds and purposes of their own. Since the orthodox definition of Woman does not grant her the selfhood to possess a purpose, men interpreted female wilfulness to be aimed at undermining *them*, as malign, evil.

In the industrial west, as women rose up to demand rights, they had to argue that they were part of the human species, with the same needs and desires and therefore the same rights as other (that is, male) humans. Barriers of law and custom cannot be blown down with a huff and a puff: even the moderate reforms described in this book took decades, lifetimes to effect. But during the struggle, both sexes continued to live in traditional relationships; even women who tried to change traditional expectations, however, remained subject to them. Working-class women who had freed their minds of received ideas enough to walk a picket line were married to men unwilling to cook their own dinners. Leisure-class women might have felt free as they hurled a rock at a window but could not for more than that moment forget that they were dependent on a father or husband for their very food. However active women might have been in unions or demonstrations, whatever their class, *all* women were subordinate to men, whom they had to pacify, placate, or disarm. Men who believed in the rightness of their rule quite correctly felt manipulated.

There have been many revolutions in history, uprisings of classes, ethnic groups, races, and struggles by discrete groups to throw off the domination of other discrete groups. But before such groups can revolt, they must forge self-consciousness. Slaves cannot rebel when they live isolated in separate households; they require community, consciousness of themselves as an oppressed group. Women are oppressed *as a caste:* that is, *all* women are oppressed because they are women, regardless of class, colour, or religion. But women live in isolated units *with* their oppressors, and – except for the women's communities found among the aboriginal Australians – have nowhere on earth to flee (with their children) where they can be free. Female oppression was legitimated by abstract external forces – law, religion, and custom – but those who enforced that oppression were women's most intimate kin – fathers, husbands, brothers, and sons. Civil war is the cruellest kind because it sets members of the same nation against each other, sometimes even brothers. But women's rebellion invariably sets women against their families, the very men on whom they must depend.

Painful as this is for women, it is not without pain for men, some of whom are aware of the justice of women's cause. Some nineteenth-century men tried to redress injustices in the world or their own families, but most were convinced of male superiority. When they saw women acting in the world, they presumably felt, like Dr. Johnson, that they were seeing a dog walking on its hind legs. They blustered in Parliament, pubs, and at home; wrote scurrilous articles, beat their wives, and did scientific or philosophic work that bolstered their stance.

Since most cultures define the sexes as opposites (at best, complementary opposites) rather than as members of the same race, change in the definition of one necessarily alters the definition of the other. If women changed role, men would have to as well (the change men feared above all in the late nineteenth century was the subject of innumerable cartoons showing men pushing baby carriages). Whether women accepted the role of domestic angel, stretching it to cover the world, or rejected the role to demand fulfilment, men dealt with their fear, discomfort, and rage not by examining themselves or their institutions, but by blaming women. These attitudes inform the scientific disquisitions, novels, poetry, and art of the period – the most remarkable fact about which is their obsession with Woman.[1]

While artists obsessively focused on the naked female, continually redefining Woman, they rarely depicted active healthy forward-looking working-class women. A.J. Munby was one artist who did sketch some working-class women. In comparing his sketch of himself and a colliery woman with a photograph of them, we see that in the sketch Munby is drawn far thinner and more bodiless than he is, and much taller than the woman; her sex is indeterminable, her bearing somewhat menacing, and she is filthy. The photograph, on the other hand, shows Munby under his hat only a fraction taller than a strapping young girl, who is more erect and vigorous and less menacing than in the sketch.

This chapter focuses on male attitudes toward women as shown in cultural artifacts. I have drawn largely on two analyses: Bram Dijkstra's *Idols of Perversity: Fantasies of Feminine Evil in Fin-de-Siècle Culture*, and Klaus Theweleit's *Male Fantasies: Women, Floods, Bodies, History*,[2] both of which acknowledge considerable interpretive help from feminists. Dijkstra concentrates on the years 1880 to 1920 and Theweleit on Germany from 1918 to 1923, from the end of the First World War to the emergence of Hitler.

After 1850 Western painters suddenly produced hundreds of images of Woman as Dying Swan, reflecting a reality of the era: idle, repressed middle-class women like Clara Barton, Jane Addams, Charlotte Perkins Gilman, Florence Nightingale, and hosts of others who did not recover from their malaise, who, like Alice James, languished because they were forced into inactivity and purposelessness. No one painted active, starved, exhausted sick working-class women. Science in this period defined Woman as sick by nature, but art romanticized, eroticized, this condition. Artists' depictions of spiritually luminous beautiful women, white, dying, or dead, ignored totally women's misery and rage, transforming pain into glamour. Languid beauties expire orgasmically and seem to cry out for a firm clasp by strong male arms. Such paintings often bore the names of literary figures – the most popular were Shakespeare's Ophelia (who had the advantage of going mad), George du Maurier's Trilby (a passive creature controlled by an evil Jew, Svengali), Zola's Albine (who needs a male for completion), and Tennyson's virgins, Elaine and the Lady of Shalott, doomed to die without having lived. That Tennyson may have been projecting his own sense of life does not alter the fact that he projected it onto females.

Anthony Ludovici wrote popular advice books on the "woman question" in this period. He criticized men who exalt women, writing that a man who remains faithful to a wife who fails "to stimulate him adequately" places himself disastrously "under the empire of women."[3] Dying erotic women seem to need men but make no demands on them, giving them the pleasure of feeling desired without having to fulfil "virile" responsibilities.[4] It is unthinkable that these beautiful weak females in need of "saviours" would ever stand up to demand rights or decide to get jobs.

By the 1860s and 1870s, feminism terrified men, who portrayed it as a kind of madness, female delusion, regression to a primitive stage of human existence. Men had a more intellectual moral sense; women, with intuition and a *natural* need to be absorbed by men, required male guidance. In 1869 one male writer warned that if women won the vote, they would destroy American society, wreck public virtue, and end "our new-born, more beneficent civilization."[5] Another cautioned that the idea of rights could profoundly injure the fragile feminine mind, exciting it to "feelings of indignation and dissatisfaction with [her] present condition," and leading her to "cease to be the gentle mother, and become the Amazonian brawler."[6] Certain that the absence of sexual desire in women was the foundation of a healthy society, he warned that newfangled notions of education were leading Woman to abandon purity. This man had earlier written a book praising female friendship, but now he cited research by French scientists showing that female masturbation was widespread, fostered mainly by female boarding schools where masturbation "is . . . acquired and practiced." Female friendship can even lead to the depths of degradation, for "the same bed often receives the two friends."[7]

The hostility to femaleness implicit in the desire to control them (because only what constitutes a threat needs to be controlled) became evident as the virtuous domesticity of earlier portrayals of groups of women gave way to portrayals of ugly and voluptuously sexual females. In 1886, in *Psychopathia Sexualis*, Richard von Krafft-Ebing described a condition he named "masochism" after Leopold von Sacher-Masoch, a popular author of soft porn whose heroes are sexually aroused by humiliation and pain. Krafft-Ebing thought masochism, "the wish to suffer pain and be subjected to force," was a perversion when it *appeared* in men, but was *built into* women. *Nature* gave Woman "an instinctive inclination to subordination to man," an "instinct" for "servitude." This was not a new idea. In 1858, P.-J. Proudhon wrote: "Woman does not at all dislike to be treated a bit violently, or even to be raped."[8] Male authors usually plant masochism in female, not male, figures, but it is men who are obsessed with it and have written most of the sado-masochistic literature. (Emotionally honest James Joyce alludes to Sacher-Masoch's *Venus in Furs* in *Ulysses* to suggest the masochism of his *male* hero, Leopold Bloom.) The French, who first discussed arousal by punishment, called it "the English disease," believing it infected British boys from frequent beatings in public school.

Female masochism intoxicated artists. The end of the century is crowded with characters like Zola's *Nana* (1880), Trina in *McTeague* (1899) by Frank Norris (whose theory of women was drawn from Schopenhauer), Concha in Pierre Louis' *Woman and Puppet* (1898), and Franz Wedekind's Lulu, who inspired an opera and a movie with Louise Brooks.[9] Oscar Wilde and Mark Twain testify to women's love of abuse;[10] Thomas Hardy makes a *female* character (Sue Bridehead in *Jude the Obscure*) say: "No average man – no man short of a sensual savage – will molest a woman by day or night, at home or abroad, unless she invites him." Coventry Patmore, who invented the phrase "angel in the house," had his finger on the pulse of his time, for he also wrote a stanza that inspired generations of painters and cartoonists:

Lo, how the woman once was woo'd;
Forth leapt the savage from his lair,
And fell'd her, and to nuptials rude
He dragged her, bleeding, by the hair.

Eugene Delacroix and a host of lesser-known artists painted harems thronged with naked women, bodies posed like "pin-up" girls in the grasp of or awaiting male ravagers. Masochistic, women were shown to *crave* rape and suppression, literally.

Experts sanctioned rape. Theories popular in the 1890s assert-ed that evolutionary progress in women was accompanied by diminished sexual drive: Harry Campbell, a London pathologist, believed the sexual instinct of civilized women was atrophying. This, they said, made rape *necessary*: men must take responsibility for reproduction if the human race is to continue. The newest thinking countered the theory that women did not become preg-nant without orgasm.[11] "The female must lend herself to the sexu-al act" but the example of "primitive" men, who regularly took women by force shows that female sexual drive is not essential to successful coitus: "woman need not be a willing agent" in sex.[12]

Indeed, rape was *better* than mutual sex. Cesare Lombroso and Guglielmo Ferrero, in *The Female Offender* (1899), warned against unleashing female sexuality because the sexual impulse was male. When awakened in women, it roused the inherent "criminal in-stinct" and made them "excessively erotic, weak in maternal feeling, inclined to dissipation, astute and audacious." They start to domi-nate, subtly or by force, and take up violent exercise. Such behav-iour, "vices," and dress make them resemble the "sterner sex" – a cardinal offence. "Normal" women are monotonous, look alike, and are impervious to suggestion. They are intuitive and *imitative* – their best efforts can produce only copies of men's. Charles Darwin said so, and a host of authors followed him, creating female characters who reflected the world without "ever really understanding it."[13] That women were inherently imitators, not originators, was a cliché in the 1870s.

Woman-hating attitudes became pervasive around 1900, as late nineteenth-century biologists, sociologists, and anthropologists wrote on sexual differences. Charles Darwin's *The Origin of Species* (1859) and *The Descent of Man* (1871) are important because they help us understand the evolution of the cosmos and humanity; but they also contain elements that were used politically. Many men used Darwin's notion of the survival of the fittest to justify predatory *male* (not female) behaviour. An 1866 essay, "The Darwinian Theory," claimed that the largest, strongest males get the best food and are most attractive to females, and transmit their powers to their offspring.[14] Differences in aggressiveness explain inequities among classes and races, why "the Negro, the Malay, the Mongolian, are almost precisely what they were five thousand years ago." Auguste Comte used Darwin's theory of natural selection to build a *System of Positive Polity* (1851–54), a "science of society" later used to justify domination as necessary for the survival of the fittest.

After Darwin's *Origin*, Herbert Spencer put huge amounts of energy into trying to prove that predatory individualism was an evolutionary force. Using complex, seemingly logical arguments, he showed that the widest inequalities existed in the most advanced societies and that the *natural* rulers of a society were its most "individual," intellectually advanced, financially successful men. Defining evil as "non-adaptation of constitution to conditions" (whatever conditions might be), Spencer traced a human "progress" from "barbarous lower" races to white Europeans, the acme of evolution, proving it by citing craniological evidence according Europeans larger brains than "the savage."[15] Carl Vogt "proved" in 1864 that non-Germanic peoples belonged "to the lowest races of man," citing craniologists who had shown that "the female skull is smaller" than the male's: "the skulls of man and woman are to be separated as if they belonged to two different species." The conclusions these men extracted from their false data are remarkable: not only did smaller skulls mean lower intelligence, but the skulls of European men were larger, compared to European women's, than African men's skulls were to African women's.[16]

Vogt called the German male the pinnacle of evolution and the African woman the nadir. But all women were said to be frozen at an early evolutionary phase: "We may be sure that, whenever we perceive an approach to the animal type, the female is nearer to it than the male." To find the "missing link" between humans and apes, science should focus on the female. Quoting Vogt, Darwin agreed in *The Descent of Man* that "the female somewhat resembles her young offspring throughout life." Spencer saw women and men as utterly different mentally and bodily, especially in powers of abstract reasoning and "the sentiment of justice – the sentiment which regulates conduct irrespective of personal attachments."[17]

The "brainless" woman (the dumb blonde) was a scientific fact. Since Woman did not need intelligence to be a mother, nature had not given her any, proving that maternity should be her only activity, and intelligent men should marry "healthy women, not brainladies." Education was not only wasted on women but made them "nervous and weak," said Paul Möbius, brilliant pathologist and inventor of the Möbius strip. Reflecting these ideas, Degas, Renoir, and a host of others painted zombie-like women, expressionless, sleepy, passive, empty, stuporous. One male critic noted a "fixed stupor of expression" on Degas' women; another gushed over Renoir's female "playthings," with their "beautiful, deep, azure, enameled eyes of dolls, of adorable dolls, with flesh molded of roseate porcelain. . . . [In an] original and perhaps very wise conception of the famous 'eternal' feminine . . . the artist has suppressed virtually completely any elements of intellect his models might have possessed [and] compensated for this by including in his work a lavish display of his own."[18]

These ideas influenced men's view of women and women's self-image, and contributed to cruel predation by contemporary Europeans in Africa and Asia; they also inspired twentieth-century experiments with social control like eugenics, lobotomy, mass imprisonments, and murder, culminating (but not ending, for this way of thinking is not dead) in genocide, the holocaust. The immediate effect on Europeans was less dramatic but calamitous – an obsession with children, girls and boys, who were erotic but ignorant and could demand nothing, and a fierce terrified loathing of mature females who were not passive lumps of flesh.

Erotic portrayals of children begin to appear just as Freud was suggesting (to Europe's shock) that children had sexual feelings. But if Freud's observations triggered such art, they did not supply its content. Whatever children's sexuality, only molested children see themselves as sexual commodities. Painters of this period did not depict childhood sexuality, but projected their sense of commoditized sex (the body as goods for sale) onto children. Emile Zola and the Reverend Charles Dodgson (Lewis Carroll), among many who were obsessed with young girls, eroticized their "innocence."[19] Paul Chabas, a hugely popular painter of the era, produced endless images of adolescent girls in sexually suggestive poses, like the girl in "September Morn." Males and females portrayed little girls as miniature courtesans appraising their wares. Even Carl Larsson, the great idealizer and sentimentalizer of domestic life who inspired a generation of chidren's book illustrators, was not immune. The appeal of the girl child lay in her paradoxical combining of malleability, sexual innocence, and knowingness, her precocious sense of herself as an object for men's gaze.

Even babies and little girls were tainted with depravity.[20] For some reason, young men were free of it. The true aesthetic and moral ideal was the sensitive adolescent, the grown boyish male, who could be heroic (girls could not) and as provocative as a girl without overtones of wily calculation.[21] He might be James Barrie's Peter Pan (Barrie was enamoured of young boys as Dodgson was of little girls), or a "blond God." Artists and thinkers used the young god-figure to personify the aggressive, evolving mind of man.[22] An emblem in philosophies like Oscar Wilde's, a familiar intellectual world view at the time – Platonic idealism with Darwinian overtones – the androgynous boy-god linked virulent hostility for the petty bourgeoisie with adoration of a Nietzschean ideal of power and transcendence. Transcendence of the material world means transcendence of nature; thus women (nature incarnate) cannot attain it. The ideal body suggested physical power without flesh, aspiration without materialism; his "rippling muscles and steel blue eyes" symbolized aspirations toward transcendence for many intellectuals then – and forty years later.[23]

Fin-de-siècle male intellectuals hated the bourgeoisie mainly for its materialism, its obsession with money, and its lumpish entrenchment in domestic comfort. And no one was more associated with domestic comfort than Woman, who maintained it, whose duty was to devote her life to it. Although women were not responsible for bourgeois enterprises or aggression, as upholders of its standards they incarnated the class for many men. Symbolic association occurs on a deeper level of sentience than logic; by association, all women were tainted. The rising chorus of speculation that Woman was sexual after all compounded her menace. Many sensitive men in this time had a horror of Woman, terrified by her encompassing body as if it would swallow them up, her mindless offering of domestic comfort as if it answered all need, and her clamour as she entered public space with other women to raise her voice and even her arm to overthrow the rule of Man. Artists from Edvard Münch to James Thurber and the later Willem de Kooning portrayed women as vampires, demons, and enveloping monsters.

Fin-de-siècle artists' view of Woman is extraordinary: passive, asleep, a zombie with inert flesh, an absinthe-dulled or syphilitic woman of the town, a "clinging vine" draining the life out of men, or a seductress practised in bestiality. Walter Pater called daughters in families "serpents" tempting the men in the household; other writers call Woman feline, "catlike," sinuous, serpentine, snake-like.[24] Women were connected with snakes: a Baudelaire poem describes a prostitute "coiling like a snake/ across hot embers." Her "fluid lips" promise unheard-of pleasures but "once she'd sucked the very marrow from my bones," she becomes "a slime-flanked mol-lusc full of pus," then a "cadaver taut with force/ Having gorged itself on blood," and finally, "scattered pieces of skeletal remains."[25]

Animals that Darwin thought were wildly promiscuous appear with women in many paintings – an antelope ("the most inordinate polygamist in the world") has nude women riding it; gorgeous naked women entwine with or fondle lions, wild boars, elephants, seals, huge dogs, and extremely long-beaked fowl.[26] Sometimes the connection between Man and Woman-animal is explicit. Sirens cavort in water, luring men to their death. Physically powerful, bes-tial Woman, driven by lust, threatens the male Knight of the faith.

Literature showing women as man-killers was immensely popu-lar. Sacher-Masoch and his cruel heroines were highly regarded by intellectuals, especially the French, who translated his complete works and made him a member of the Legion of Honour in 1883. Among his admirers were Zola, Victor Hugo, and Camille Saint-Saëns, whose opera *Samson and Delilah* portrays a woman who sub-verts a hero. Richard Strauss used Wilde's *Salome* as a libretto, and made his *Elektra* a madwoman, and his *Die Frau ohne Schatten* (with Hugo von Hofmannsthal) was barren. Alban Berg's *Lulu*, Antonin Dvorak's *Rusalka*, Paul Hindemith's *Mörder, Hoffnung der Frauen*, and Massenet's *Thaïs*, on similar themes, all date from this period. Ferrucci Busoni and Giacomo Puccini wrote operas based on Carlo Gozzi's *Turandot*, a man-killer.

Judith, the Jewish heroine who saves her town from Assyria by cutting off the head of the Assyrian captain, Holofernes, while he sleeps, was extremely attractive to male thinkers in this period. An extremely popular figure for woman painters in earlier eras, Judith had suggested their anger and desire for vengeance against men. As men became aware of women's anger, she became representative of all women. Salome was the "true centerpiece of male masochistic fantasies": a "virginal adolescent," a gorgeous exotic dancer with a virago mother and "a hunger for man's holy head," she epitomized the period's "libidinous fetishes."[27] As war approached, men painted Woman as its spirit.

Definitions of the sexes are interdetermined, and these convulsive redefinitions of Woman affected men's self-image. The same authorities who defined Woman defined Man. Women, stuck in an early phase of evolution, were virtually a different species from men; people of colour, too, exemplified a primitive stage of evolution. Cultures that find so much that is human repugnant, basically hate humanness itself. They are suicidal. Having declared most of the human race subhuman, men scoured the male sex for traces of contamination: any taint of effeminacy was damning (as a drop of Jewish blood would be forty years later). An 1895 article anatomizing "The Psychology of the Weakling" declared that men who were cautious, tolerant, respectful of others, and scorned violence were "unmanly."[28]

In 1903 Otto Weininger's *Sex and Character* electrified European intellectuals. Weininger was a twenty-three-year-old Viennese; his ideas were neither logical nor new, being derived from Plato, Schopenhauer, Kant, Darwin, Spencer, the social Darwinists, the woman-haters of *Mercure de France*, and Freud, who liked the manuscript. Weininger organized a "scientific" system, conflating ideas related at a deep psychological level. He produced his theory at a moment when Europe's intellectual climate was open to such things, and it became very popular. Ford Madox Ford lamented that the book "had spread through the serious male society of England as if it had been an epidemic." Wilhelm Fliess angrily accused Freud of leaking his ideas to Weininger, letting him steal Fliess's intellectual "property."

Weininger holds that the human race was originally bisexual; sex differentiation was its first step toward a higher form. The further the race evolved, the closer people came to pure maleness and femaleness. But since sex differentiation is never complete, human advance is retarded. Woman's body, the site of physical reproduction, is a negative pole; man's brain, spiritual understanding, is a positive pole. The more completely male Man becomes, the more spiritual; the more completely female Woman becomes, the more materialistic and brainless. Intellectual women are sexually intermediate: absolute females lack logic, morality, and souls. Association with such benighted beings hinders male progress to spirituality, so "homosexuality is a higher form than heterosexuality." Intermediate states notwithstanding, human beings are always either male or female. Men still have a sex drive, a vestige of femaleness, but if "man possesses sexual organs, her sexual organs possess woman. . . . Sexual excitement is the supreme moment of a woman's life." Women are parasites and cannot live without men or each other; man needs only himself.

Here Weininger touched a major strand in Western thought, one that runs like a barely visible deep stream feeding surface soil all the way from Aristotle: Man is defined by volition. Weininger projects Kant: "I am responsible only to myself; I must follow none other; I must not forget myself even in my work; I am alone; I am free; I am lord of myself." So pervasive, universal, and ancient is the definition of manhood as isolated heroism that we do not perceive its insanity. Men live – and writers create male characters who live – as if isolation led to triumph, utter transcendence. In fact, it leads only to death: isolation is desolation; all humans are responsible to each other, no one is free of the human condition, and no one totally controls even himself. Weininger accurately perceived the ultimate end to which his principles led. Since the major impediment to human progress is effeminacy, defined as men allowing themselves to be enticed by and come under the power of women, the only way to achieve transcendence was for men to free themselves of sex, forcing women to do the same: "The rejection of sexuality is merely the death of the physical life, to put in its place the full development of the spiritual life. . . . That the human race should persist is of no interest whatever to reason."

Like Vogt, Weininger linked women and "degenerate races" – Jews, blacks, "orientals." By inbreeding or failure to evolve, these groups had become effeminate and degenerate. Judaism in particular "is saturated with femininity." Jews, like Woman, did not see that property is indissolubly connected with the self, "thus they were "readily disposed to communism. . . . Greatness is absent from the nature of the woman and the Jew, the greatness of morality, or the greatness of evil." Opposed to the Jew and woman is the Aryan man, in whom good and evil are "ever in strife." True to his principles, the Jewish Weininger committed suicide a few months after his book was published. But his ideas lived on: his book was important to Hitler, who echoes the ideas in *Mein Kampf*.

Some writers linked transcendence with homosexuality, as distinguished from effeminacy, traditionally ascribed to homosexual men. André Gide's *Corydon*, which advocates male homosexuality, links "masculine idealism" and male aggression: "Periods of martial exaltation are essentially homosexual periods, in the same way that belligerent peoples are particularly inclined to homosexuality" (as both D. H. Lawrence and Yukio Mishima suggested). Stylistic innovation in the arts in this period had to be macho to stifle accusations of effeminacy: "to be original was to be masculine," tough.[29] Critics' most vicious attacks were reserved for women artists, all "imitative" of men. Writers, marginal to the world's power centres, were verbally belligerent, ruthlessly belittling the imbecile masses, "the infantile inferiority of nonwhite races, and the brainless inanity of women." The "gratuitous act" became their badge of power.

The ideological roots of Nazism and other horrors of our century are evident in this material. Moreover, men who failed in True Manhood were lower-class: the intelligentsia had contempt for the masses. One thinker wrote that a proletarian might gain enough intellectual dignity through self-denial and hard work to be included in the lower ranks of evolved manhood, but:

pauperism, prostitution and crime [are] the attendants of a state of society in which science, art and literature reach their highest developments. . . . If we should try, by any measure of arbitrary interference and assistance to relieve the victims of social pressure from the calamity of their position, we should only offer premiums to folly and vice and extend them further. . . . The sociologist is often asked if he wants to kill off certain classes of troublesome and burdensome persons. No such inference follows from any sound sociological doctrine, but it is allowed to infer, as to a great many persons and classes, that it would have been better for society, and would have involved no pain to them, if they had never been born.[30]

Even Karl Marx, whose work represents the point of view of the intelligentsia to what they would consider "lower" beings, workers, also regularly referred to lower-class men as "beasts" and "asses."

Marx expected the socialist revolution to occur in Germany, with its strong popular socialist party. After Germany lost the First World War, Chancellor Ebert, over socialist protest, tried to build a government with strong ties to the old ruling class. He created the Freikorps, a volunteer secret army. Ebert, a socialist, did not trust working-class soldiers from the regular army, which was in any case limited by peace treaty to 100,000 men. So he recruited demobilized officers, mainly from semi-commando units trained to penetrate enemy lines in sudden daring attacks. These men did not return their weapons as required but took them home, buried them in oilskin, and dug them up afterwards.[31]

Most Freikorps leaders came from a rural petty bourgeoisie with semi-feudal traditions – a class usually considered conservative, honest, and decent, the backbone of a country. Their fathers owned small estates, were ministers, military officers, civil servants, tradesmen, small farmers. From 1918 to 1923, the Freikorps, a set of "largely autonomous armies each commanded by its own charismatic leader," roamed Europe attacking "enemies" – Polish communists and nationalists, Latvians, Estonians, the Russian Red Army, and the *German* working class. A free-ranging gang of marauders, government-appointed but not government-controlled, it killed those it *chose* to kill. Some members were imprisoned or exiled, but most survived the relatively quiet years from 1923 to 1933 to follow a man who spoke for their values and attitudes. Becoming the nucleus of Hitler's SA, they reached high positions in the Third Reich; one was kommandant of Auschwitz.

The Freikorps was most active between 1918 and 1923, but literature about it does not appear until after 1933, when a spate of novels depicts politically aware soldier-heroes trying to build a national socialist (Nazi) movement. These works contain striking, strongly held, shared attitudes. The Freikorps was strongly anti-communist, but *communism* was code for nature, the body, and women. They loathed the same elements that intellectuals and artists scorned but with a major and devastating difference: the art of these men was killing. They *loved* killing.[32]

Freikorps writing is a literature of sons: its perspective is always that of a son trying to deal with mothers and sisters. Fathers do not have a voice in Freikorps books. Even authority figures write as sons, rebels who survived their father's disgrace (Wilhelm II's abdication) and intend to correct his errors. Even Hitler writes as a son: "The kaiser should have died at the head of his capitulating army." The father's surrender was an abdication of legitimacy; now it was the turn of sons.[33]

They are also brothers to each other and to women. The only positive relation men can have with women is as son or brother. A number of the Freikorps soldiers married each other's sisters or sister surrogates, women they considered pure, pious, domestic, and above all, virgins: "white" as opposed to "red" women. In letters to comrades, the men note their marriage but do not mention their bride's name, or mention it once and not again for the rest of their lives. They emphatically did not marry for love, but to avert lust;

they marry nurses (Germans call trained nurses *sister*) who nourish and comfort men, but are asexual – pale, cold as marble, unapproachable, the idealized cool white nurses on war posters, comforting wounded soldiers; the dead or dying women in paintings of heroes.

There were other nurses, "Red" nurses. Whenever the Freikorps attacked a working-class enclave, women were on or near the front lines, fighting alone or alongside men. The departure of men to war meant that working-class women had to support their families by working in factories. Food shortages during the war forced them to stand in long queues, and they had confrontations with the police in every German city. For the first time, German women demonstrated for higher wages and decent food rations; they even looted display windows. They learned how to operate in the world, to deal with male officials about wages or the rent on factory-owned housing, becoming in the process confident and authoritative. They changed, and their men were dismayed when they returned. These women supported their men in the socialist conflict after the war but, even when men seem to be praising their efforts, they have a "peculiar note of irritation," as in this report on miners' wives (emphasis mine):

> The spatial confinement in mining districts promotes a solidarity among women and men who are on strike or locked out. The same thing is difficult to muster in occupational groups living in a more scattered community. It isn't rare for women to take an active role in men's battles, where they often accomplish more than the men through picketing and related assignments. Once a woman has gotten fired up about the legitimacy of her demands, she almost amasses such enormous energy that *it puts most men to shame*. In the process she may often give free rein to her *temperament*, but at the same time she *calmly* takes the consequences into account. During the general lockout of the Ruhr miners in

May 1924, whole companies of female pickets assembled. Armed with sticks and moving along *secret paths,* they intercepted those men prepared to give in and go back to work, and drove them back to their homes. When the night shift changed, *it was a strange thing to see* the women marching out of their villages with burning lanterns, ready to surround every mine within a large radius.[34]

These fighting women called themselves "nurses." To the Freikorps, they were all prostitutes. Their leaders believed the women carried arms, and offered false evidence to prove it. One claimed that communist bands were entrenched in the hills: "In any camp . . . wild scenes could be witnessed of Red bandits strutting back and forth . . . surrounded by those most repulsive of characters, the Red 'nurses.' These women indulged even unwounded warriors with prophylactic attentions; and as for the men, the spring season was in their blood. They did it right there in the fields and forests." The Freikorps lusted to deal with Red nurses. A soldier who spied a couple making love later boasted that "a grenade had caught her off guard in the practice of her true profession." The terror these women inspired in Freikorps men is incomprehensible, even considering the woman-hatred and fear pervading men's associations with female sexuality in this period.

Indeed, it pervaded the opposition culture too. Socalists did not elect women to their executive councils, and paid women less than men even when workers' organizations themselves set wage scales. So did the Red Army in 1920: "Remuneration . . . is in accordance with the terms of the March 22nd bulletin: 165 marks for front-line troops; 40 marks for local service; 30 marks for female personnel." Demobilized men demanded that women be ousted from any job with status. Marx's values were similar: in a letter to Engels, he announced: "Yesterday morning, between six and seven, my wife [Jenny von Westphalen] was delivered of a bona fide traveler — unfortunately of the 'sex' par excellence." (That "the sex" was a common term for females in this period implies maleness was asexual.)[35] So-called proletarian literature of the 1920s never describes women acting politically or in the public sphere. In it too, men marry sisters or sister-surrogates who are spotless maidens, come from their own homeland, and belong to a category for whom they previously had "no time at all" – non-prostitutes. Hardworking, with clean houses, dutiful, pious, and devoted to the workers' movement, Red women too are "white."

Both sides blame women for failures. Fascist men blame women for communism; socialist men hold them responsible for communist defeats. Women were responsible for the failure of a putsch, a Freikorps officer explained, because they had the task of typing out appeals to the people. Men of all classes had similar attitudes. Educated writers, artists, and thinkers, and those who wrote German "proletarian" novels in the 1920s, all depicted the women of the opposite class as sexually depraved.[36]

Women are killed off in novels from both camps; the only important difference is that women in "proletarian" novels die for the good of the party, and not as gruesomely as in fascist works. The threat women embodied for fascist men was so great that it was not enough to divide women into good (asexual and nurturing) and evil (erotic and threatening): they annihilated both, beating or killing "evil" women and rendering the nutritive, "good" women lifeless. Attack on any woman not categorized as mother/sister is "essentially self-defence," so any act is acceptable. It is hard to say which was more brutal, Freikorps men's *acts* or the *language* in which they are described.

A recurring image in right-wing fiction and reportage is of women hiding weapons under skirts or aprons, grenades between their legs; women often attack men astride horses (which actual women did not have) and kill by cutting bits off them – ears, noses, heads, anything protruding, sometimes the genitals proper. The hidden weapons symbolize concealed penises; removal of body parts symbolizes castration – Freikorps soldiers "experience communism as a direct assault on their genitals."[37] Red women look ordinary, so men cannot wait to be attacked but must take the offensive, as a general urged in a pep-talk before a putsch:

> "It's a well-known fact that women are always at the head of these kinds of riots. And if one of our leaders gives the order to shoot and a few old girls get blown up, the whole world starts screaming about bloodthirsty soldiers shooting down innocent women and children. As if women were always innocent."

> We all laugh.

> "Gentlemen, there's only one thing to do in cases like that. Shoot off a few flares under the women's skirts, then watch how they start running. It won't really do much. The magnesium in the flares will singe their calves or behinds, and the blast flame may burn a few of their skirts. It's the most harmless device you can think of! So, gentlemen, no more warning shots! Flares between the legs will do the job best."

In reality Freikorps men bend women over, strip their buttocks naked, and whip them with riding crops; hurl grenades at their field kitchen trucks, shoot them as they weep over their children's bodies, club or beat them to death with whips if possible, rather than shoot them. Shooting showed respect; beating did not. The Freikorps planned to beat Rosa Luxemburg to death with a rifle butt; they shot Karl Liebknecht, German and male, and beat Jewish Leo Jogiches to death (see chapter 10). The actions are hideous, but the glee, the exaltation of their descriptions is worse: a contemporary novel urges: "With their screams and filthy giggling, vulgar women excite men's urges. Let our revulsion flow into a single river of destruction. A destruction which will be incomplete if it does not also trample their hearts and souls." Whether women block soldiers' paths, call out derisively, or offer to inform, they are the ultimate enemy. A living woman is a "stinking carcass"; the body of the woman whipped to death is "a bloody mass, a lump of flesh that appears to have been completely lacerated with whips." Prurient loathing pervades descriptions of specific parts of female bodies; mouth, buttocks, and genitals – beneath their skirts.

"Mouth" symbolizes vagina, "spittle," its secretions. A female mouth is nauseatingly evil, a "venomous hole" spouting "a rain of spittle." Soldiers punch a woman in the mouth, club one in the teeth with a rifle butt, shoot one's open mouth. Punishment on the buttocks humiliates; soldiers kick women in the rear, lash them with riding crops. They make a working-class woman "snort" from her "bare cheeks" and a redhead "with a loud screech, show . . . her behind." Freikorps men attack women from horseback, with whips, bullets, rifle butts, and boots – all phallic surrogates. They rarely touch them with their bare hands – only one slap is recorded in the texts.

When the sexual woman dies, order is restored to the world. Descriptions of murders of women often end with a sigh of relief, a "peculiar note of satisfaction ('and there was peace again in the land')" that distances the narrator from the horror and shame he must also somewhere feel.[38] Men's major emotion – "passionate rage" – cannot end until its object lies silent. But it can in fact never end, rooted as it is in loathing for the flux and substance of nature and body, the uncontrollability of *emotion*.

A new man emerged in the eighteenth and nineteenth centuries. His major activity was expansion. At home, he fought kin for territory, enclosed land, expanded cities. He extended his hold on the globe. The European assault on non-Western civilizations was symbolically a penetration of the female body; male domination of female in the patriarchal family and white male conquest of people of colour were two forms of the same drive. In all of this, women's bodies provided the "raw material" for the new man's images: they symbolize what he was trying to vanquish: desire, need, vulnerability, and his subjection to uncontrollable nature and emotion. Western art suggests men are obsessed with women after the eighteenth century. Even abstract sculpture focuses obsessively on female body forms, breast, and buttocks.

In the eighteenth century, having appropriated women's sexuality and reproductive powers, and limited their mobility and activity, men had tried to transform women's bodies to make them more sexually attractive to men: ideal women should alter their shape with corsets, learn "correct" posture, grace, elocution, and change their hair and eyebrows to achieve "beauty."[39] Manuals offered what gentlemen preferred: a 1715 *Frauenzimmerlexikon* (Ladies' Lexicon) listed thirty "required" components of complete beauty: women should be "in correct proportion" – not too fat or thin, with small, reddish ears which did not protrude much from the head. They should wear a gracious smile. Besides "lovely, agreeable speech" uttered with "pure and gentle breath," they needed "delicate skin, underlaid with tiny blue veins," a "long alabaster neck," and "tiny, narrow feet, well-proportioned and facing outward." Another manual prescribed the desired shape, size, and colouring of calves, knees, thighs, buttocks, and especially breasts. Women, who needed a man to survive, complied.

Eighteenth-century women were urged to feel (or show) passion but only if it was centred on men. The first books asserting that masturbation led to insanity appeared in 1716; it was later labelled deviant and punished by clitoridectomy.[40] Nursing one's baby was considered disgraceful and some marriage contracts stipulated the wife was to be relieved of the task (powders dried up breast milk in forty-eight hours). The breast was reserved for sexual use only. Women were also expected to be cultivated, to dance, sing, or play instruments, not for their own pleasure but as an adornment appealing to men. Literature praised specific female body parts, mainly breasts and vagina; poems were written to *die Schoss* (the womb or lap). Johann Besser's enormously popular *Die Schoss* (1700) pleased even the electoress Sophie and her court ladies. In such poems, the vagina of a high-born beauty is a sea of delights, a utopia. Geographies and ethnologies of this time contained physical portraits of women from the countries discussed.

A century later, however, society required women to renounce both the appearance and reality of sexuality. The middle-class revolution repudiated aristocratic eighteenth-century norms. In the nineteenth century, German industrial society, like the American and English variety, made "a contract for dominance that bases male production on the division of the sexes ('separate spheres') and the subjugation of woman-nature."[41]

The values of the Freikorps are not unique to it or to the Nazis. If they were, we would not only know who our enemies are, but they would be – blessedly – outside us and defeated. But even the well-meaning progressive German physicians and psychiatrists who tried to understand and deal with the war by writing a *Moral History of the World War* discuss "dark, vengeful feelings of degenerate femininity" and rape being "lustfully received by the woman who is defeated in love." Good liberal authors who distance themselves from gung-ho soldiers share the woman-hatred that is the foundation for machismo, fascism, and inhumanity. The Freikorps' values are not unique to any class, or unfamiliar to any of us. They are the values of men *and women* throughout the world.

My purpose in including this segment is not to analyze fascism, although it shows that fascism, rooted in fear and hatred of women, is an extreme, overt, and recent example of the bases of patriarchal systems. Fascism differs from other systems in its degree of hatred for humanness (seen as vulnerability and need); it locates transcendence in individual male power in the world, not beyond it, as religions do, or in a community, as socialists do. Nor is my point to demonstrate that ideas we call "fascist" derive from a foundation of "humane" arts and letters created by the most eminent men of their age – although this is also true. My purpose is to give texture to women's environment, to show what they were up against, and to contrast their actuality with men's images of them. The contrast is shocking.

PART SEVEN

THE TWENTIETH CENTURY: REVOLUTION

IN THE TWENTIETH CENTURY, EVERYTHING EXPLODED. The workers' struggle reached proportions that frightened the elite into severe repression and, finally, world war. The subtext of two world wars and a host of smaller ones was conflict over rights between the privileged and the underprivileged. Although this study is written in sympathy with the underprivileged (women as a caste were the first humans to be denied rights, regardless of the women of the elite, who might have some privileges but no rights), the fight was also a struggle between fascists and communists in which neither side was blameless or pure. But the entire century was ripped by this struggle, whether as war or conflict, in one part of the globe or another. The underprivileged won some battles, but the privileged have won the war—so far. The "new" global economy is a triumph of the elite, in the form of corporations, which now surpass nation-states in wealth and power.

The twenty-first-century elite may not be descended in blood from the nineteenth-century elite (although surely some members are), but it is just as privileged, despite the existence of many "democracies." The communist dream of the withering away of the state was really a dream of a vanishing elite, and the first act of communist leaders was always to fortify themselves as an elite. The dream of African revolutionaries focused on African leaders who would not exploit the people, but, with few exceptions, the new leaders not only exploited the people but robbed them blind. Democracy is supposed to be a guard against elitism, but it grew in elitist soil. It must constantly fight against its own foundation — patriarchy — which is an assertion of the most basic elitism, men over women.

The aggressive expansion of European states after the sixteenth century succeeded at a huge cost to life and well-being for humans and animals alike. It enriched and empowered a white male elite. Exploiting its colonies, the West (Western Europe and the United States) spread its culture across the globe and drained formerly self-sufficient societies. By the late nineteenth century, ancient "Third World" societies were prostrate before Western ships, guns, and ideas. Britain dominated most of the globe. The men who controlled technology and the wealth it reaped ruled not only their own countries but distant colonies as well-literally, the world. This new class, descendants of men who seized power in earlier insurgencies, joined by men who got rich in industry, exploited their subjects impartially. Most humans lacked rights.

Imperialist powers, aware of their colonies' resentment, relied on force to maintain a supremacy that was often the main reward for their effort-the costs of colonization could exceed its profits. Domination always destroys the dominator. Revolt begins at the moment of victory: however helpless and inferior dominated people may feel, they hate and wait (like Catherine de Medici), simmering with resentment and rebelliousness until they can expel the dominator. In the late nineteenth and twentieth centuries, Third

World colonized peoples and First World working classes rose up en masse. Most wars of this period were uprisings by nations or groups demanding rights or independence.

The twentieth century was convulsed by revolutions, genocides, and civil wars unparalleled in ferocity and scale. Technological developments — airplanes, submarines, rockets, tanks, and nuclear weapons — made the wars of this century more murderous than earlier conflicts, wider and more indiscriminate. Its two major wars, the First and Second World Wars, were not revolutions. No one has satisfactorily explained the first, and the second is seen as a war to halt German expansion, yet both were desperate attempts to divert and refocus the class and sex struggle.[1] Most uprisings of the century were won by the rebels, through war, passive resistance, or negotiation, yet change proved elusive.

No war succeeded in ending oppression. Former colonizers retain their power under new guises, and most indigenous governments have become oppressive kleptocratic cliques or were forced by external pressure into attenuated war (as in Mozambique, Tanzania, and Nicaragua). The stirring rhetoric of revolution disguises the fact that war is always a struggle for power and that the moral change always expected to follow victory cannot occur in a culture concerned primarily with power. Moral revolution, which changes values, cannot be violent, yet it is hard to achieve peacefully. The enduring changes won in the past century resulted mostly from peaceful movements by unions, black civil rights workers, and feminists. These changes modified the status quo and did not revolutionize society. Third World revolutions won independence for some states, but the economic hardship and power struggles among classes, peoples, and sexes still continue.

Women, at the bottom of every class, oppressed and discriminated against under the old system, remain so in the new. No revolutionary struggle, no matter how vocal its commitment to sexual equality, actually achieved it; no matter how strongly revolutionary leaders advocated women's rights before or during armed conflict, none accepted women as equals once it was won. Women's experience in struggle had local particularities, but men's treatment of women as a caste after the struggle is over is strikingly similar from nation to nation. Part Seven examines women's experience in three kinds of revolution-socialist, fascist, and nationalist.

CHAPTER 10

SOCIALISM IN EUROPE

THE FIRST ENDURING SOCIALIST GROUPS were formed in the 1860s and 1870s by the International Workingman's Association or the First International (1864–76). They were initially dominated by conservative artisans hostile to women's independence through paid work or political rights, men who wanted to return to the traditional households or guilds they controlled. More regressive than progressive, their socialism was less a vision of exploitation and community than an awareness that industrialization was making them obsolete. They wanted to stop factory owners from simplifying and dividing tasks so they could be performed by unskilled workers paid minimal wages. But industrialization could not be stopped and, as it spread, unskilled workers and landless farmers were drawn to Marx's vision of collective struggle. Abandoning nostalgia for the past, most of them took Marxist positions and accepted the idea of female equality promoted by Marxist intellectuals. Soon they and Marx dominated the movement.

The triumph of Marxist thinking in socialist parties in the latter nineteenth century gave women's rights issues theoretical legitimacy, but by the time conservative socialists were defeated, the socialist project had already been defined. Marx envisioned capitalism as a dynamic system allowing social change so radical that the powerless could become the authors of history. But his ideas triumphed after women had been defeated in the socialist movement, after organized labour had re-established patriarchal priorities. Despite some strong efforts to emancipate women, socialism failed women in the end.

Karl Marx and Friedrich Engels saw women as human and as oppressed, and they advocated their political rights and economic independence. But while Marx was aware of the importance of re-production, he never thought about how women were to go on taking sole responsibility for it and still be productive citizens. Neither Marx nor Engels seemed aware of the work and time required to rear children and maintain families, the crushing difficulty of combining these tasks with paid work; neither seemed to notice what wives, daughters, and other servants actually did all day. Their failure to address the hardship of reproduction and family maintenance set a precedent for later socialists to dismiss them as non-work.

Marx concentrated on the "masculine"-capitalist power and strategies for overthrowing capitalism. His focus validated that of later socialists, who were already drenched in disdain for "feminine" aspects of life. Their contempt extended beyond women to all human life, because scorn for women means scorn for the essential, the "necessary." From its inception, socialism was penetrated by disdain for the areas of life associated with the feminine.[1]

The socialist dream failed partly because of male indifference to the necessary, the realm to which women are consigned. Socialist men avowed principles of equality, yet denigrated feminism and treated sexual equality as secondary. To attract men, they were willing to sacrifice women. Yet socialist parties that ignored women failed, and separate women's groups were not formed until the Second International, from 1889 to 1914.[2] Repressive laws forced the German party to create a separate women's organization. The men had no premonition that this group would help it become the largest and most radical socialist party in the world.

Nationalism, not democracy, spurred the 1848 revolutions. Foreigners ruled middle-European and Italian states; Germany was a set of small confederated states with a common language until 1871, when Bismarck unified it under Prussian rule. Most German states, especially Prussia, had authoritarian political and moral systems lacking any conception of rights. In such a climate, women faced even greater obstacles than in England and the United States. When the German Social Democratic Party (Sozialdemokratische Partei Deutschlands, or SPD) was founded in 1875, it advocated the vote for *all* citizens. Some thought this phrase included women, but when August Bebel proposed adding "citizens of both sexes" (women were not citizens in all German states), the party voted it down. In 1878 Germany passed anti-socialist laws, forcing the party underground until 1890.

In 1889 Clara Zetkin (1857–1933) addressed the founding congress of the Second International in Paris. Her speech set the standard for socialists' attitudes toward women. Building on Engels' and Bebel's analyses, Zetkin assumed that socialists must support feminist struggles. Since working-class women were slaves to both capitalists and working-class men, she rejected collabourating with bourgeois feminists, who shared capitalist men's class interests. Rather, she insisted that work which permitted economic independence was the necessary basis of full emancipation for socialist women. When the party was legalized in 1890, its make-up changed. Industrial growth had created a larger proletariat open to socialist ideas. Unions grew, and by 1911 over a quarter of a million German women bakers, butchers, glaziers, woodworkers, leather workers, lithographers, metalworkers, and saddlers, among others, had joined unions. Bebel and Engels were widely read; Bebel, Wilhelm Liebknecht, and Karl Kautsky (followers of Marx and Engels) were its new leaders, and Zetkin was prominent. The 1891 SPD Congress at Erfurt voted for universal adult suffrage and for the abolition of sexually discriminatory laws. The "Erfurt Program" became a key text for socialists everywhere.

Zetkin demanded separate groups as necessary for women; the SPD wanted women in its ranks, mainly to keep them from undermining men. Since the law in many German provinces barred women from political activity, limiting them to "non-political" groups, the party ruled in 1890 that women could elect their own delegates to party conferences at special women's meetings. Circumvention of the law, rather than commitment to women or brilliant strategic insight, led the SPD to create a separate women's organization – the key to success for the German socialist women's movement. In their own group, women could speak and act publicly, without fearing male disapproval or mockery. Ottilie Baader (1847–1925), the "central Spokesperson" for "women comrades," headed 407 spokeswomen in the party hierarchy in 1908. By 1914 the SPD had 174,751 female members (twice the total membership of the French Socialist Party); 112,000 subscribed to the party women's paper, *Die Gleichheit* (Equality), edited by Zetkin. The German socialist women's movement was the largest political women's group in Europe between 1890 and 1914, and the standard for others.

By 1896 Zetkin had changed her mind about "bourgeois" feminism. Deciding it was "completely justified," she stopped criticizing it, but still insisted that suffrage was only a first step in the emancipation of working-class women. When Germany repealed laws barring women from joining political parties in 1908, the SPD dissolved its separate women's hierarchy. Zetkin objected so strenuously that the male leaders compromised, keeping the women's bureau but making it subordinate to the national party executive. Bypassing Zetkin and Baader, they appointed the younger, less-known Luise Zietz as the women's representative on the executive, perhaps imagining she would be more deferential to their authority on women's issues.

Legalization legitimated women's participation: within a year, women's party membership doubled to over 62,000, nearly 10 percent of the SPD. Among themselves, women were able to develop political skills, and they formed a nucleus to embrace the hosts of new recruits who were now joining legally. At Zetkin's suggestion, the 1910 International Socialist Congress designated March 8 as International Women's Day; after 1911, German and Austrian women mounted major demonstrations on that day, giving visibility to the socialist women's movement. When the First World War erupted in 1914, 16.1 percent of registered party members were women. Zetkin opposed the war as a capitalist struggle pitting working-class men against each other and wrote an essay exhorting socialist women to fight for peace: "When the men kill, it is up to us women to fight for the preservation of life. When the men are silent, it is our duty to raise our voices on behalf of our ideals." Early in 1915 Louise Saumoneau of France and socialist women in other countries clandestinely distributed Zetkin's essay. But the main opponent of war, the figure who towers over all others in this period of German history, was neither German nor a feminist: Rosa Luxemburg.

Poland and Rosa Luxemburg

She was born Rozalia Luksenburg in 1870 in Zamosc, Poland.[3] At five, Rosa was diagnosed as having a tubercular hip, put into a cast, and kept in bed for a year. Afterward, one leg was shorter than the other; years of painful treatments left her with a severe limp, unable to run or jump, and scorned by other children. She started school at ten, an ungainly Jew craving assimilation in a school system that took Jews by quota and persecuted them in countless ways. She protected herself by adopting an arrogant, assured facade. When she was twelve, a pogrom erupted in Warsaw. A mob marched from the Church of the Holy Cross to Jewish neighbourhoods, including the Luksenburgs', smashing windows, hurling stones, breaking into houses, and looting. Terror of mobs never left her, and she retreated into literature, mainly the poetry of Adam Mickiewicz, a Polish idealist who urged the destruction of a decayed world and the creation of one that would ease human suffering.

Most Polish girls were not educated: the daughters of aristocrats, rich landowners, and the intelligentsia went to expensive private girls' schools that were closed to Jews. Only boys attending Russian state gymnasia were exempted from the draft and eligible for university. In 1879, teaching in Polish was outlawed and it was declared a foreign language. Poles taught their literature and history underground, and repression backfired as young students receptive to patriotic fervour became rebels with their teachers' and their families' blessing.

Luxemburg did well academically and learned to control her limp and facial expressions; her mother designed her clothes to conceal her physical disproportion (her upper body was larger than her lower). By sixteen, she had found others in underground circles who were inspired by Mickiewicz and by social and economic works smuggled into Poland, often from Russia. She experienced the joy of political argument about the Catholic Church, Darwin, materialism and idealism, revolution and socialism. After graduating from the gymnasium at seventeen, she joined an illegal socialist group dedicated to building a workers' party and became a governess. No institutions of higher learning in Poland accepted women, so she applied for a passport and headed for further schooling in Switzerland – a country that swarmed with radical Polish students and offered political freedom.[4]

Luxemburg was raised on a diet of revolution. She was eleven in 1881 when Sofia Perovskaia and Alexander Zheljabov were hanged for assassinating the tsar, and thirteen when Aleksandra Jentys was imprisoned with Ludwik Warynski, who had founded the first Polish workers' party, the Proletariat. This pair inspired all young rebels: the beautiful, intelligent, elegant, cultivated Jentys had taught by day in the exclusive Institute for Girls of Noble Birth and plotted at night with her married lover, Warynski. From 1883 to

1885 they were held in the notorious Tenth Pavilion in the Warsaw Citadel, then exiled to Russia. When Luxemburg was fifteen, Maria Bohuszewicz and Rosalia Felsenhard were jailed in the same place. A Polish aristocrat, Bohuszewicz was head of the Proletariat's Central Committee at nineteen. Felsenhard, the daughter of a Jewish doctor and Bohuszewicz's friend and collaborator, courage-ously saved thirty pupils from a fanatical mob invading her class-room during an 1881 pogrom. Luxemburg was seventeen when both died en route to Siberian exile, still in their early twenties.

With many of their men in prison or Siberian exile or killed in insurrections, elite Polish women often managed landed estates as well as their children's education. Women's equality with men was a fact of daily life, in conspiracies, on the battlefield, and at home. Polish Jewish women had been liberated even earlier, ironically by their marginality. Polish culture exalted Christian women; Jewish culture ignored women, who escaped the constrictions of patri-archal families because no one paid attention to them. After the sev-enteenth century, they owned businesses and taverns, traded in liquor and fabrics, and acted as match-makers and go-betweens. In the 1830s they worked as bankers and merchants in Warsaw. They lacked prestige, regarded merely as rich Jews.

Luxemburg recoiled from identification with unassimilated Jews, scorning their dress, language (Yiddish), and ignorance, and associating them with Jewishness itself. Like a gentile anti-Semite, she slurred practising Jews. She had deep connections with women, but shrank from identification with women like her mother-agree-able housewives. She wanted to escape being stereotyped; she want-ed love, a home, a child, respect, acceptance as a Pole, and work for a cause. But no woman escapes her sex: Luxemburg was sexually slandered and belittled, like all women in the public eye. Her world saw her as a Jew with no roots, no tradition, no country.

Luxemburg joined a large Polish contingent in Zurich in early 1889. Polish men could not attend Russian universities unless they were politically acquiescent, and women were not accepted at all, so the entire Polish intelligentsia flocked to Zurich, where they formed a Union of Polish Students and a Polish National Museum. German and Austrian socialists also developed their theories in this safe haven – Liebknecht, Eduard Bernstein, Bebel, and Kautsky planned the SDP in Zurich. The German socialist club Eintracht had a good library, reading room, and lecture hall.

Rosa knew she was starting a new life: when she registered with the authorities, she spelled her name Luxemburg for the first time (and ever after). Through her German exile landlord, she met members of the German Social Democratic press and learned about political journalism. Enrolled in zoology courses, still unsure of her future career, she met Leo Jogiches in the fall of 1890. Jogiches had been born in 1867 in Lithuania, a land isolated from Europe by thick forests, moors, and swamps.[5] When Poland was partitioned in the 1790s, Lithuania became part of Russia, which suppressed its language and culture. An underground movement arose, centred in the university at Wilno (where Mickiewicz had founded a secret student society). In 1847 Lithuanian Jews opened a rabbinical seminary in Wilno, and the city became the most important seat of Jewish learning in the world (it was annihilated by the Nazis). Russia focused Russification on Jews, because of their vulnerability, leading Christian Lithuanians to condemn them as double traitors- to Christ and also to Poland.

Despite pogroms, at the end of the nineteenth century Jews made up over 40 percent of Wilno's population. Jogiches, the youngest son in a rich, cultivated, assimilated Wilno Jewish family, was sullen and withdrawn, deeply connected to his musician mother. Considering money-making exploitation, he left school, apprenticed himself to a locksmith, and agitated among Jewish workers. Like Luxemburg, he did not consider himself Jewish and scorned unassimilated Jews and their Yiddish. He dealt almost entirely with Jewish workers not because of any feeling of kinship but because most workers were Jewish. Despite his contempt for Yiddish, he learned it so he could communicate with workers who spoke nothing else.

When Luxemburg met him, Jogiches was famous for his dedication and organizational skill, and infamous for his tyrannical behaviour. He impressed her with his knowledge of political reality – she had been exposed only to theory and discussion – and she changed her field of study to economics, law, and philosophy. He began to study evolutionary theory, for Darwin's ideas were transforming European thought. They became secret lovers and remained connected, living together or in contact by mail, for the rest of her life. They planned a political platform: Luxemburg had long wanted to form an anti-nationalist Polish socialist party (she never comprehended the force of Polish nationalism) and, in 1893, they founded the Social Democracy of the Kingdom of Poland (SDKP) and a journal, *Sprawa Robotnicza* (The Workers' Cause). In her first public speech at the Congress of the Second International, Luxemburg asked recognition for the SDKP, impressing members with her brilliance and vitality – a noteworthy socialist at twenty-three.

She also had the humanity that makes her a heroine today. Luxemburg and Jogiches were always enmeshed in power struggles with each other. Both were utterly dedicated to socialism, but to him, life was less important than his image as the exiled stranger of all hero myths, Mikhail Bakunin's and Sergej Nechaev's revolutionary, the lost man with "no interests of his own, no cause of his own, no feelings, no habits, no belongings, not even a name. Everything in him is absorbed by a single, exclusive interest, a single thought, a single passion – the revolution."[6] Luxemburg hated this vision; she told Jogiches that life was not about *The Workers' Cause*, or the workers or the cause, but about living. To limit it to issues, pamphlets, and articles was to kill the soul. Like Emma Goldman, who wanted a revolution she could dance at, Luxemburg never lost sight of the whole in pursuit of a part, and never preached a deformed, deforming politics.

In 1897 Luxemburg was awarded a doctoral degree in law and political science *magna cum lauda*; a respectable publisher accepted

her dissertation, and her articles were published regularly.[7]
Luxemburg wanted to live in Germany, then the centre of socialist
agitation, but, as a Russian citizen, she was open to extradition on
political grounds. So Jogiches suggested she marry Gustav Lübeck,
the son of her beloved landlady. He agreed and, in May 1898,
Luxemburg left Zurich as a Frau, settled in Berlin, introduced herself to the SPD, and was sent to organize Polish workers in Upper
Silesia, which was controlled by Prussia. She had great success and,
despite strong German anti-Semitism and contempt for Poles, she
was accepted by German socialist leaders.

Eduard Bernstein, an important socialist theorist, questioned
Marx's dictum that intensified class struggle and pauperization of
workers would lead to capitalist collapse and world revolution. He
argued that neither was inevitable and that some of Marx's theories
were outdated. Knowing that a rigorous reasoned rebuttal would
make her reputation, Luxemburg wrote "Social Reform or
Revolution." Its publication led the SPD press commission to elect
her unanimously as editor-in-chief of their journal, a position no
woman had held before (or would hold again). Four months after
arriving in Germany, she was an internationally famous socialist.
She still called members of "the new Russian 'party'" – which
became the Communist Party of Russia in 1918 – rascals. She disliked the party's coteries and its smug, self-serving, self-congratula-
tory, conservative attitude, closed to new ideas. Yet she worked hard
to support it, writing, "Poor is the party in which a botcher, an
ignoramus like me plays an important role." She wrote on a wide
range of topics, including women's liberation, condemning middle-
class women's movements as individualistic and near-sighted, pursuing rights and freedom for themselves alone. Luxemburg was not
a feminist.

Yet she unfailingly upheld feminist values, even against the par-
ty. In her 1904 "Organizational Questions of Russian Social
Democrats," she criticized Lenin's political thinking in *One Step
Forward*. With great erudition, she attacked him on two contradic-

tory fronts, arguing that his "glorification of the inherent genius of the proletariat" about socialism and his distrust of the Social Democratic "intelligentsia" were not intrinsic to revolutionary Marxism, and denouncing his "ultracentralism" or autocracy:

> The "discipline" Lenin has in mind is by no means implanted in the proletariat only by the factory, but equally by the *barracks*, by the modern bureaucracy, by the entire mechanism of the centralized bourgeois state apparatus . . . The ultra-centralism advocated by Lenin is permeated in its very essence by the sterile spirit of a night watchman rather than by a positive and creative spirit. He concentrates mostly on *controlling* the party, not on *fertilizing* it, on *narrowing* it down, not *developing* it, on *regimenting* and not on *unifying* it.

As a socialist, not a feminist, Luxemburg attacked Lenin for his divisiveness in setting one group over others, his antidemocratic bent, and his love of centralized power – in cells, the party, and the Soviet state. Lenin's structures silenced the rank and file, who were expected only to obey; he cast the mould that strangled Eastern Europe until 1989–90 and transformed a liberating concept – socialism – into a synonym for tyranny. Divisiveness is a patriarchal means toward domination. Like Emma Goldman, Luxemburg opposed all tyrannies; her socialism was democratic. She never stopped attacking Lenin, but her opposition was not personal: they had great respect for each other, and she saw him and Jogiches as the most outstanding revolutionaries of the time. But she believed, with Marx, that a people's revolution must be accomplished by raising workers' consciousness, not by armed force. Her opposition to Lenin had an added motive: his centralist ideas would eradicate the Polish party, "turning it into one of the territorial organizations of the Russian party."

The "Bloody Sunday" massacre of January 1905 kindled strikes across Russia and Poland. Luxemburg's party, the SDKP(iL), which for years had only a few hundred members, grew to 2000 in late 1904 and 30,000 in 1906. The far more popular PPS was only slightly larger; the Bund, a Jewish workers' organization, had about 35,000. The three competed for worker support, mainly by the written word. Luxemburg published almost ninety articles in 1905 alone. Strikes were so widespread that they amounted to an insurrection, especially in Poland, where twice as many workers struck as in St. Petersburg, and three times as many as in Moscow.

Students and the intelligentsia joined the workers, who were rebelling not just for higher wages and better working conditions but against Russian domination. In Warsaw, a general strike protested a government-instigated pogrom of Bialystok Jews. In Russia, sailors from the battleship *Potemkin* mutinied to join the rebel cause. The Russians responded by imposing martial law on Poland, which Poles defied: in October, after a general strike in Russia, Polish railroad workers struck; industrial workers followed, swelling it into a "common fight against the tsardom," a strike so massive it paralyzed the country. The Russians defused it by promising Poles a constitution and civil liberties, political amnesty, and the abolition of preventive censorship. But once they had blunted the edge of revolution, they reneged.

Jogiches went to Warsaw in February 1905 to organize strikes. Luxemburg joined him in December, hectically writing articles to foment rebellion. Gratified by busy excitement, both ignored the fact that they were political outlaws in Russian Poland. In March 1906 the police arrested them and the government sought evidence of their political activity. The Polish party devised schemes for escape, but they were held in the dreaded Citadel. Investigators seemed as concerned with proving Luxemburg immoral as treasonous. Lurid articles in conservative German journals accused "bloody" Rosa of using sex to get German citizenship.

Luxemburg had been imprisoned before for insulting Emperor Wilhelm II in a public speech in 1904. She was efficiency itself in prison, meeting almost daily with a party official to manage party business and handling personal affairs – rent, Jogiches' tailor's bill – through letters to friends. Her spirits remained high, but her health suffered. When bribes freed her, she went to Kuokkala, in Finland, where Lenin was based. She would never return to Warsaw and never again live with Jogiches, who, tried and found guilty of attempting to overthrow the Russian Empire by armed insurrection, was sentenced to eight years of penal servitude. But he converted a guard and escaped after two months, went underground, and returned to Berlin in April 1907.

As Luxemburg came to know Lenin well, she admired him even more, yet spent most of her time writing "Massenstreik, Partei und Gewerkschaften" (The Mass Strike, the Political Party, and the Trade Unions), an argument for a socialism different from his. She asserted that a mass strike "cannot be artificially 'produced,' 'decided' at random, or 'propagated'"; rather, it is "a historical phenomenon that at the right time results from social conditions with historical inevitability." Spontaneity was better than organized action, the healthy instinct of the proletariat more effective than party leadership. Her assertion that prepared plans cannot keep pace with the spontaneous movement of the masses was validated in 1990, when the USSR fell after months of uprisings by masses in socialist states. Above all, she argued, mass political struggle cannot be directed from above by a central party organization: "The overestimation . . . of the role of organizations in the class struggle of the proletariat usually goes hand in hand with . . . disregard of the unorganized proletarian mass and of their political maturity."

Fundamentally, Luxemburg's socialism was the freedom to "think differently"; revolution meant fighting for a more humane social system. Human progress was moving towards moral virtue. *Realpolitik*, whether conceived by Marx or Lenin, was immoral and so unusable. Marx was concerned with inexorable laws of history, and Lenin with the dictatorship of the proletariat: they were both hard matters, to be taken seriously. But Luxemburg was concerned with the ethics of socialism and with workers' idealism – "soft," "feminine" matters – and she wrote no comprehensive work on social change. She has been discounted as a political theorist, yet events have proven her more astute than Marx or Lenin: Marx's laws of history have proven not "inexorable" at all, and Lenin's dictatorship was not of the proletariat. She underestimated the power of nationalism, but rightly saw it as a divisive force. Indeed, as nationalist movements have again flamed into life in middle Europe and Africa, they still feature intolerance and fascism.

Luxemburg believed that nationalism was fading in Europe.[8] She imagined that an international proletariat could fill the need to belong to a group, since working-class people have more in common with each other, in lifestyle and consciousness, than with the elites of their own nation. Accepting Marx's vision of proletarians – people with no national allegiance – she envisioned them united by common interests, not nation, race, or heredity.

In 1913 Luxemburg published her major work, *The Accumulation of Capital*. Rigorously, logically, she argues that capitalists can accumulate surplus value (profit) only by expanding into foreign markets or less-developed parts of their country. Capitalism needs non-capitalist markets to function and ultimately to survive, yet when it enters such places, it destroys them as independent entities, thereby destroying the demand necessary for it to realize surplus value – a condition for continued accumulation of capital. Capitalism must collapse because of the contradiction inherent in laws governing accumulation. (This theory, accepted by socialists and capitalists for decades, has not yet proven itself: capitalists are very resourceful.)

As ruling elites threatened by growing socialism and feminism inflamed their populations with nationalistic fervour, war became likely. In 1913 Lenin urged national self-determination, and German socialists supported Prussian militaristic self-aggrandisement. Luxemburg, back in Germany, urged German workers not to fight against workers of other states. In February 1914 she was tried for inciting public disobedience, and she put the Prussian government on trial by Social Democrat standards:

> Wars can be conducted only if the working people see them as just and necessary, or at least accept them passively. But once the majority of the working people concludes – and it is precisely the task of Social Democracy to arouse that consciousness and lead them to this conclusion . . . that wars are barbaric, deeply immoral, reactionary, and against the interests of the people, then wars will become impossible . . . According to the . . . prosecution, the party at war is the *army*, according to us it is *the entire people*. It is the people on whom the decision must rest whether or not to make a war . . . working men and women, old and young, and not the small section of the people wearing the so-called King's uniform.

But Luxemburg could not stop the war and she spent it in prison, muzzled.

In the post-war chaos, Prince Max, trying to prop up the monarchy, appointed a Social Democrat chancellor; a Social Democratic Republic emerged, created not by a desire for democracy but by panic, hunger, and disastrous military losses. Its survival depended on the very men who loathed it, Junker officers. The end of war exposed the divisions within Germany. For generations, people had thought German armies invincible. Theories of racial superiority pervaded European and American thought and made it inconceivable that heroic Teuton males could be vanquished. People who never saw the battlefields had no sense of the dimensions of the military catastrophe. Certain of victory, they were stunned by defeat and readily swallowed the propaganda campaign the army launched after the armistice, the "stab-in-the-back" theory: the superb German army and navy were destroyed by degenerates – socialists, communists, liberals, pacifists, and, above all, Jews. They had wrecked Germany by undermining the morale of non-combatants, the military, and honest patriotic Germans. In 1930 Joseph Goebbels declared that "the Jew is the real cause of our losing the Great War." And now the Jews were plotting to turn Germany over to the Bolsheviks.

Luxemburg was freed from prison without notice on November 8, 1918, at ten o'clock at night. She was forty-eight years old, frail, worn, and alone, yet she immediately plunged back into political work. Government propaganda did not distinguish between Spartacists (Luxemburg's party) and Bolsheviks, lumping them together in a red scare campaign. And, indeed, the (Soviet-led) Bolsheviks were trying to insinuate themselves into the German struggle. Luxemburg thus had to fight on several fronts at once. She never publicly criticized the Soviet regime, but never praised it either. To stress the Spartacists' similarity to Western socialists' goals and values and their difference from the Bolsheviks, she and Jogiches proposed calling their party "socialist" rather than "communist," but they were outvoted. (This difference remains important in leftist thinking today: communism refers to state ownership and decrees pronounced from above; socialism is real democracy, a form that has never been tried.) She tried to hold the international workers' congress in Germany to keep the Bolsheviks from dominating the future International. Failing, she instructed German delegates to Moscow to oppose a Third International.

Her strongest arguments were comparisons of Lenin's concept of revolution and her own. She condemned Lenin's means, especially terror, as the ultimate perversion of socialism, worse than the disease his regime was supposed to cure: "The proletarian revolution requires no terror to achieve its aims; it hates and despises mass murder." Liebknecht and Paul Levi (her lawyer and former lover) loyally supported the Bolsheviks. Except for Jogiches, she was isolated from her comrades: as the victorious Lenin was realizing a program she had criticized for fourteen years, the victorious German Social Democrats were, in her opinion, betraying socialism.

Everywhere she went, billboard posters, scrawls on buildings, newspapers, and leaflets denounced the Jewess devil trying to destroy good God-fearing Christian Germans: "Judah is reaching out for the crown. We are ruled by Levi and Rosa Luxemburg." Predicting pogroms against Jews in Germany, she went on with her task: to promote socialism while separating her league from Lenin's party and trying to counter government propaganda exploiting German fears of the Bolsheviks. The German government strategy was clever and successful; but in winning, it not only prepared the way for Hitler but eliminated an alternative that might have established a more humane and just socio-political system in Germany.

The Treaty of Versailles limited Germany to a 100,000-man army; the government evaded this restriction by establishing a "free" corps (Freikorps), a volunteer outfit of demobilized soldiers, officers, unemployed workers, fanatical nationalists, and adventurers (see chapter 9). It became a set of separate armies, each with its own captain and its own agenda. Rumours that the Bolsheviks were about to invade Germany justified their leaping into action. In city after city, they tore down and burned red flags. On December 7, 1918, the Spartacists demonstrated, with armed workers as guards; the next day they mounted a huge demonstration. On Christmas Day government troops fought revolutionary sailors occupying the royal stables: eleven sailors and fifty-six soldiers died. Paralyzing strikes and armed fights between workers and troops erupted all over the country. Social Democratic socialists and Spartacists attacked each other for betraying the revolution. On New Year's Eve, Luxemburg addressed the founding Congress of the Communist Party of Germany. She castigated the Social Democrats for supporting the war, allying with the Kaiser's army, and now using it against German (and with British help, Russian) workers. Only heightened economic struggle and the creation of a national assembly with worker representation would help revolution.

On January 4, 1919, the minister of the interior deposed the president of the Berlin police, Emil Eichhorn, an Independent

Socialist, the one man in government sympathetic to radical workers, the only one they trusted. Refusing to give up his post, he passed out arms to workers. Thousands took to the streets on January 5, occupying *Vorwärts*, the Social Democratic newspaper, and other buildings. That night, Germany's Communist Party and the Independent Social Democrats formed a Revolutionary Committee; next day they announced a "temporary" takeover of the government, asking workers to gather next morning at the Siegesallee to organize a general strike. Liebknecht endorsed the takeover without consulting his comrades. Luxemburg saw the insurrection as the realization of her vision of spontaneous uprising of the proletariat, but she feared it was turning into violence. On January 11, after five days of blasting grenades and sniper artillery fire between the government and the Spartacists, she wrote, "Ultimately one should accept history as it develops." Her dream of a reasonable struggle evolving into a just order had shattered amid the violent contest for power.

The Spartacist uprising was spontaneous but also disorganized. The army, however, was not. The Freikorps killed with relish, summarily executing anyone bearing a white flag, savagely beating workers, and mutilating their bodies.[9] As they killed, they jeered "Where is your Rosa?" By January 12 it was over. Some Spartacist snipers fought from rooftops at heavy artillery and machine guns, but troops occupied Berlin. On January 14 Luxemburg wrote in *The Red Flag*, "Order reigns in Berlin," adding that an order whose survival depends on ever more bloodshed "inexorably proceeds toward its historical fate – annihilation." The official war went on until the Weimar Republic was established; the unofficial, until Hitler took over.

Refusing to leave Berlin or abandon her comrades, Luxemburg went into hiding. She lay in bed all day. When the doorbell rang after nine that night, she got up fully dressed, took Goethe's *Faust* from the bedtable, put it in her handbag, and shut her small suitcase. Nailed boots clumped on the floor, her name was barked out, someone protested, and her door opened. A man with a gun on his shoulder stood in the doorway, staring at her legs. He ordered her to get her coat. She did not look at him or ask for a warrant of arrest: she knew there was none. She drew on her gloves. Soldiers surrounded her, marched her out, and pushed her into a car. She tried not to limp. They took her to the Eden Hotel, an army head-quarters. As she walked through the lobby crammed with soldiers, one shouted, "Röschen! There goes the old whore!"

Upstairs, officers asked her identity: "That's for you to deter-mine," she said. They marched her downstairs. News had spread that Red Rosa was there and a crowd had gathered. Impassive, Luxemburg walked past. A soldier dashed forward and cracked her on the head with a rifle butt. She fell. He smashed her again in the temple and raised his rifle a third time, but another soldier stopped him. The soldiers lifted her from the floor and carried her to the car and drove away. Those in the hotel heard the shot that penetrated her left temple. The car halted near the river; soldiers dragged her out of the car and threw her in a canal. "The old slut is swimming now," one said.

Liebknecht was killed the same night; Jogiches was beaten to death. In May 1919 Luxemburg's body was found in a canal lock and furtively borne outside Berlin for secret burial. Her body was decomposed, but the cause of death was murky: she may have been thrown into the water alive.

German Socialism after 1920

When the war ended, the socialist women's movement lay in ruins. The war had accomplished its real, unspoken purpose – to destroy the solidarity of workers necessary for a successful class struggle and the solidarity of women necessary for a sex struggle. The force behind the German women's movement, Clara Zetkin, was dis-lodged in 1908 after fighting the SPD leadership over retaining a separate women's organization. When she stood with Luxemburg and against the SPD to oppose Germany's entrance into the First World War, it expelled her and removed her as editor of *Die Gleichheit*. Appalled that a German government made up of leaders of the pre-war SPD could repress the Spartacist revolt against the Weimar Republic and connive at the murder of Luxemburg and Liebknecht, Zetkin joined Lenin's Third International to promote communism. But she was excluded from a real position of power within the Communist Women's International because her conception of communism was closer to Luxemburg's than to Lenin's.[10]

Euphoric at the Kaiser's overthrow and the founding of the Weimar Republic by SPD leaders, large numbers of women joined the SPD despite Zetkin's defection: in 1919 they constituted over 20 percent of SPD membership. But many soon left, dismayed by the conservatism of the SPD government: in 1923 women constituted only about 10 percent of the membership. As Hitler began his climb to power, however, women again joined the party most opposed to him and, in 1931, the SPD had 230,351 women members, 22.8 percent of the membership. The Second International was revived after the war, with Adelheid Popp in Zetkin's position, but the split between socialism and communism weakened the socialist women's movement and transformed it from a powerful independent radical force in the party into the women's auxiliary of a male party – except in Austria.

The platforms of most European socialist parties were dictated by the Second Socialist International, founded in 1889. The SPD, which dominated the International, required workers "to admit women into their ranks on an equal footing." This demand may seem innocuous – it merely gave women the right to join the socialist party – but no other European political party accepted women until after the First World War (a few parties had female auxiliaries). The International, faced with the same problem as feminist groups – the contradiction between equality and special protections for women – in 1893 passed a resolution proposed by Anna Kuliscioff of Italy requiring equal pay for equal work and stipulating that protective measures not be used to deny women jobs. It also passed a resolution proposed by Louise Kautsky of Germany naming the protections women should receive: an eight-hour day and prohibitions against night work, jobs harmful to women's health, and pregnant women working two weeks before and four weeks after childbirth. Not until 1900 did it advocate woman suffrage.

Many national organizations remained ambivalent about the issue: Belgian men opposed woman suffrage because, like Frenchmen, they thought women would obey the Catholic Church, a reactionary force. When the Belgian Socialist Party was on the brink of passing a bill substituting universal manhood suffrage for suffrage with property restrictions, a right-wing member of parliament tried to derail it with an amendment for universal suffrage. Belgian socialist women sacrificed themselves, ceasing to press for woman suffrage, so as not to jeopardize the bill's passage.

France

As France industrialized, a proletariat emerged with new ideas. After Germany defeated France in the Franco-Prussian War in 1871, a new conservative government tried to disarm the volunteer Paris National Guard. Fearing the government's conservatism and rural base, the guard refused to give up its weapons, decreed itself independent, and proclaimed the Paris Commune – a revolutionary committee – the true government of France. The uprising turned into civil war: Marx and the First International supported the Communards, while the middle classes recoiled from a "socialist massacre." True, the Communards had killed about sixty hostages, including the archbishop of Paris, but the government had killed 25,000 rebels in battle, executed twenty-six, and imprisoned or exiled thousands. The Paris Commune was defeated and the labour movement, devastated by war losses, re-formed only slowly. Marxists urged workers to accept industrialization as irreversible, to organize in order to reform or collectivize it, and to support women's rights.

French socialists had trouble uniting – there were five parties in the 1890s – but the Workers' Party eventually became the French Socialist Party. Socialist women formed groups, but none lasted until Elisabeth Renaud (1846–1932), Louise Saumoneau (1875–1950), and others founded the Feminist Socialist Group in 1899. A watch-factory worker's daughter, Renaud educated herself to be a governess in St. Petersburg. Returning to France, she married a printer who died after five years, leaving her two children and a mountain of debt. She opened a boardinghouse, taught French to foreigners, and attended socialist meetings. In 1879, as head of the French socialist women's movement, she led her following from a hardline Marxist party to Jean Jaurès' new Independent Socialist Party in 1898.

Saumoneau, a seamstress of independent mind, came to Paris from the provinces in 1897. Primed for political action, she left work one afternoon to attend a feminist meeting, which spent hours debating the morality of dowry. Resentful at losing half a day's wages for an irrelevant debate – families like hers did not give dowries – she determined to start a feminist group for working-class women. In time she met Renaud and others and founded the Feminist Socialist Group. Its manifesto protested the "double oppression of women, exploited on a large scale by capitalism, subjected to men by laws and especially by prejudice" and called for a socialist women's movement modelled on Zetkin's. They tried to work with feminists and socialists, but hit the class barrier at a 1900 feminist congress by proposing that domestic servants be given a full day off every week. The ladies were not amused.

In 1900, having organized a seamstresses' union and sister groups in three Paris working-class neighbourhoods, the group became part of Jaurès' party. The following year it began publishing a monthly journal modelled on *Die Gleichheit*. By 1902 it had a hundred members – a respectable number considering there were still three rival socialist parties, and even in 1905 only about two hundred socialist women in the Paris region. In 1902 Renaud and

Saumoneau argued; Renaud left, and Saumoneau led those who remained. Saumoneau hated feminism with a strange violence: she refused to help a woman printer barred from her job by male trade unionists because feminists might approve it; she advised against establishing separate women's groups in the socialist party because feminists might infiltrate them. Her stance was so uncompromising that she drove moderate women from her group. Yet the women (mainly seamstresses) in Saumoneau's group agreed with her, suggesting intense resentment about class among French women.[11]

The male-dominated Section Française de l'Internationale Ouvrière (SFIO), the socialist party that united in 1905, rejected the group's application to join, accepting women only as individuals. Consequently, the SFIO attracted the least number of women of all Second International parties, and it never became a significant force. In 1913 Marianne Rauze (1875–c.1950) gathered the leaders of the old Feminist Socialist Group, including Saumoneau, into a Socialist Women's Group. But it was an auxiliary organization for women already in the SPD, not a separate hierarchy. A year before the First World War erupted, it had only 300 members.

Italy

Italy united under a constitutional monarchy in 1861, but many Italians continued to identify themselves primarily by region or city, as Romans or Milanese or Tuscans. People from different regions often spoke different dialects; there was a wide gap between rich and poor and a sharp difference between the north and the south. The south, still agricultural and technologically undeveloped, was burdened by absentee landlords who lived on income from grain grown on land they owned but did not work. The system bred inefficiency; without subsidies, domestic grain cost more than imported grain. To keep southern landowners from rebellion that might topple Italy's fragile unity, the government subsidized domestic grain, annulling any motivation landowners had to increase efficiency or oversee their lands. The victims of this policy were the poor: subsidies guaranteed that the cost of bread, the staple of poor people's diet, remained high.[12]

In such a climate, class agitation was constant, and a united Socialist Party emerged in 1892. Italian socialism was unique: it lacked a separate women's structure, but two of its most important leaders were women, both, oddly, Russian-born: Angelica Balabanoff (1878–1965) and Anna Kulis`cioff (1854–1925). Balabanoff, a leader of the party's left wing, was not primarily concerned with women's issues. Kuliscioff helped to found the party and was the driving force in all its attempts to organize women. Exiled from Russia in 1877, Kuliscioff settled in Italy, took an Italian socialist lover, and had a daughter in 1881. When he proved incapable of accepting her as an equal, she left him to study medicine. As a gynecologist, she practised in a working-class neighbourhood in Milan, read Marx and Engels, became a socialist, and grew active in the Italian feminist movement. In 1884 she met Filippo Turati, with whom she spent the rest of her life. Both worked in the Italian Socialist Party from its inception until it moved further left in 1912. But she did not use her party rank to press it towards feminist positions until much later.

After Zetkin lashed out at the 1907 International Socialist Congress, Kuliscioff urged the Italian party at a 1910 party congress to support woman suffrage. Noting that the Italian party had proportionately fewer women than the German or the Austrian party, she proposed that it support woman suffrage "as an altogether indispensable, utilitarian and idealist necessity" to its life and development. Her resolution passed, and Kuliscioff began organizing women. In 1911 the party voted to fund a women's newspaper she edited; the next year, socialist women delegates attended the national party congress, which voted to establish a National Socialist Women's Union with Kuliscioff on its executive committee.

Balabanoff triumphed at the same congress, routing the moderates and taking control of the party from the Kuliscioff clique. She was supported by Benito Mussolini, whom she had made editor of the party newspaper – an action she rued the rest of her life. After Balabanoff's victory, Kuliscioff resigned her posts. Balabanoff took her place on the women's executive, although she had little sympathy for its purposes. In 1904 she had opposed "a feminist socialism since, for us, the so – called feminist problem does not exist." Once she realized the importance of organizing women, however, she took a major part in a 1904–5 campaign to organize Italian women working in Switzerland. Women participated in significant numbers in uprisings in this period: huge numbers had turned out in Milan on May Day 1898 to protest the cost of food, and in 1900 they joined Genoese dockworkers who put down their tools to mass in public squares to confront the police. In strikes in Turin and Florence in 1902, and in Rome in 1903, women stood in the front lines hoping the police and the army would respect their right to fight for bread and not shoot.

Balabanoff vainly opposed Italy's entrance into the First World War, an act that only intensified hostility between the government and the workers, especially in the northern industrial cities of Milan and Turin. The war made it convenient for governments to bar labour organizing and to treat strikes as insurrection, punishable by death. Protest was outlawed, but women rose up as workers and as housewives and transformed neighbourhood streets into sites of struggle. The war brought many Italian women into industry and, when inflation and food shortages aroused discontent, the socialists exploited the situation.

In August 1917 crowds of women demonstrated at Turin town hall, demanding an end to the war and more food.[13] On August 21, after more than eighty bakeries closed, declaring themselves out of bread, desperate women took their children and marched from their neighbourhoods to the plaza before city hall. Outraged that bakers had flour for expensive rolls for the rich, they demanded bread for their children. The next day, local officials hastily ordered bread from nearby provinces, but furious women led crowds that were vandalizing trolleys. Declaring "No food, no work," they inspired 2000 male railroad workers to strike. Once they had generated a communal strike, the women protested in their neighbourhoods. By August 27, 1500 had been arrested. Most men returned to work that day, but the women did not. The impetus for the women's uprising was the scarcity of bread, but they also demanded an end to the war and the return of their men. Married women resented the dual load of waged labour and household work.

The women's energy arose from their fury at a government that rarely heeded working-class men, never mind women. They turned a bread riot into a coordinated workers' effort to end the war, and many who were arrested were charged with spreading discord and pacifism. The war continued, but the communal strike planted an enduring spirit of resistance in Turin, the centre of Italy's metallurgical industry.[14] Metal workers and Fiat automobile workers struck again in 1919 and 1920, seizing factories and organizing workers' councils that were modelled on revolutionary Russian factory soviets.

The war left socialist parties in disarray, and the Italian party, like other European socialist parties after the war, split in 1921. Some, dismayed by the German socialists, moved to communism; Balabanoff, heartened by the 1917 Russian Revolution, helped found the Italian Communist Party. Kuliscioff remained in the Socialist Party, but in 1922 it split again and expelled Kuliscioff and her faction as reactionary. Mussolini and fascism ended Italian socialism completely.

Spain

Spain had declined since its famous conquests, "consumed with that which it was nourished by" – gold. From the sixteenth to the eighteenth centuries it was torn by wars and revolutions. Prime ministers ruled the constitutional monarchy, yet, despite universal male suffrage, poor men had no voice in elections. Their misery caused constant unrest among the urban working class and, from the mid-nineteenth century on, there were frequent communal strikes in the south, in Andalusia. People regularly overthrew local governments, set up democratic governments in their place, and ran them until the slow-moving inefficient government managed to move the army in to repress the insurrection. Many Spaniards were anarchists: they viewed anarchy as a movement that could give people direct democratic control of their cities and regions. Indeed, the Spanish revolutionary tradition of popular democracy was anarchistic until the Spanish Civil War of 1936–39.[15] Women were an important part of the long struggle for industrial and agricultural workers' rights from 1868 to 1923.

Spain did not really participate in the First World War, but it endured shortages because armies took precedence over ordinary people. Bread grew scarce and costly, and even the cheap anchovy that put protein in Spanish working-class diets soared out of reach. In 1918 rumours sprang up in working-class neighbourhoods near Malaga harbour that more fish was being exported. On the evening of January 14, Malaga women, determined to stop it, marched through the streets chanting denunciations of speculators and hoarders. They yelled to maids and laundresses at rich houses and expensive hotels, exhorting them to join their cause of regulating food supplies. At the railroad station, they seized food produced in Spain but destined for richer foreign markets; they auctioned huge boxes of fresh anchovies to each other at 30 cents a kilo and confiscated sacks of potatoes. Then they marched to the regional governor's office to demand that he lower the price of potatoes, fish, and olive oil. Doubting his promise to do so, they rushed to fish warehouses to make sure that fish merchants did not surreptitiously ship the fish out that night.

On January 15 hundreds of women gathered on the Alameda, Malaga's main street. They drove away men and children who tried to join them, shouting "Only the women!" They did not want to endanger others and hoped their sex would protect them.[16] They advanced on the city's administrative offices, which were shut. But they stayed, gradually joined by hundreds more women. The Civil Guard dispersed those in central administrative districts, but even greater numbers later marched to the governor's house to remind him of his promise. Then the Guard shot, killing Josefa Caparros and transforming a food riot into a feminist protest.

The Spanish government took pains to assign soldiers to unfamiliar regions, where they would not know the people or their dialect. When the women cried to the soldiers, "We are your wives! We are your sisters! We are your daughters!" the men did not understand them and fired as ordered. Forming a cortege for Caparros, the women treated her death as a murderous attack on all women. They asserted women's right to a voice in government when it failed in its duty to help them feed their families.

The women's actions precipitated other insurrections, but labour unions never tied male economic protests to the broader social concerns galvanizing working-class women. No anarchist or socialist group seized on the issues that drove women to mount communal strikes or used women's great energy and informal organization. Women's gallant struggles in Malaga, Barcelona, Valladolid, and Valencia remain largely invisible to this day.[17]

Conditions continued to deteriorate, but not until 1931 was the Spanish monarchy overthrown and a republic established by popular vote. The new leaders, mainly socialists, made some progressive changes, including granting autonomy to Catalonia, an anarchist stronghold. But Catholics and right-wing moderates overthrew the republican-socialist coalition and gained control of the republic in 1933. The new government was still too liberal for some and, in July 1936, General Francisco Franco led a revolution of reactionary nationalist military men who wanted to set up a fascist government headed by Franco's Falangist Party. Spain instantly split into warring republican and fascist zones. Anarchists, opposed to central government on principle, joined unionists, socialists, communists, and liberals to form a Popular Front. It won a plurality (by 1 percent) in the February 1936 elections; in July the organized anarchist movement seized factories, communalized farms, and tried to make self-government a reality – especially in Barcelona.[18]

Hitler and Mussolini sent Franco troops and arms, but Britain, France, and the United States adopted a "nonintervention policy" that made them appear neutral in a struggle that echoed their own domestic struggles. In all three countries, capitalists and class supremacists favoured fascism over support for workers. The Soviet Union sent aid to communist groups; Emma Goldman went to Barcelona, bringing moral support. Progressive people all over the world formed brigades to fight for the Popular Front against Franco and fascism. Young European and American intellectuals saw the war as a stand against totalitarianism, and Ernest Hemingway glamourized it. But it was hideous: for the first time in history, undefended villages and towns were battered into rubble and ordinary people massacred by aerial bombardment. W.H. Auden called it "the second crucifixion," and Picasso mourned it by immortalizing the tiny market at Guernica, the first victim of fascist bombing.

Early in 1937 Goldman – a Cassandra who had already warned the world against fascism – went to London to get help for the anarchistic Spanish Popular Front. Unfortunately, the communists – in the process of creating a totalitarian government in Russia – feared anarchism more than fascism. In May 1937 the Catalan government sent assault guards (a national urban police force created by the first republican government) led by communists to seize the Barcelona Telephone Exchange Building, which the anarchists had taken from the fascists the previous July. The attack became a sub-civil war: outnumbered, the anarchists surrendered.

The anarchists were abruptly expelled from the Popular Front government, but that was not enough for the communists, who were on a witch hunt. The communists withdrew from the Cabinet when the prime minister refused to prosecute Trotskyites for their part in the crisis, and a socialist prime minister formed a centrist republican government to accommodate them. Anarchists, betrayed

by the arrangement, ruefully recalled the slaughter and imprisonment of the anarchists who had helped win the Russian Revolution.
The Popular Front split, and the many arms and troops Germany
and Italy sent Franco enabled him to win the war after three years.
Spain became a rigid dictatorship ruled by Franco with the support
of the Catholic Church. The days of uprisings were over.

Under Franco, the country froze into stasis, like a village in a
glass ball. The church supported him because he gagged women
and sexual expression. Spanish women did not challenge gender
myths: told by church and state propaganda that they were submissive, secluded, frugal, and industrious, they contented themselves
with their central role in domestic life. Feeling the power that
comes from maintaining households and influencing children, convinced they were using the male mystique for their own profit, they
remained strangled in rigid lives.[19]

Conclusion

In principle, socialism is radical democracy, a philosophy holding
that all humans are fundamentally equal, not in ability but in
desert: all babies are born to grow, suffer, and die; all deserve an
equal chance to develop, learn, and be; and no individual has a natural right to superiority over any other. In principle, socialism is
directly opposed to patriarchy, an ideology of superiority that justifies hierarchical control by sex and by class, claiming that god or
nature has endowed a sex and a class with innate superiority.

No elite wants to lose the privileges with which it has rewarded
itself: all elites oppose equality. But the make-up of elites periodically
changes; new classes are generated by war or wealth or decadence.
Class is not static: it can change for an individual or a family. Dis-
lodging an elite that has held power for a few hundred years is
daunting but regularly done. What is overthrown is a given elite,
not the idea of elitism. Socialist revolutions were waged in the belief
that elitism itself could be eradicated: none succeeded. They failed

because the men who led them were themselves profoundly infected with elitism, especially the sexual variety.

Unlike class, sex is static: people are born as one sex or the other;
until the development of transsexual surgery, they could not change
their sex. And since the emergence of patriarchy, one sex has been
considered superior to the other. After several thousand years of
patriarchy, the idea of male dominance pervades culture and all
political, economic, and psychological structures. No new philosophy can simply offer equality as a principle. Special efforts must be
made to counter ingrained sexism, yet male socialists everywhere,
on grounds of practicality, gave equality of classes priority over
equality of sexes.

But it is foolish to imagine that an egalitarian society can be created omitting women. To ignore women's special contributions and
needs is, tacitly, to treat women as less than human beings – the
fully or semi-conscious belief on which the idea of elitism itself
rests. It is as difficult to end class dominance as sex dominance,
because what must be changed is not who will rule but acceptance
of dominance itself. The heartbreaking fact about socialist revolutions is that, despite the high principles behind them, they managed only to substitute one elite for another and to change the standards that determine class. Socialist societies only pretended to
eradicate class differences; as with earlier revolutions, they drew
from a new pool, but replicated the societies they replaced.

Patriarchy triumphed in socialism as it did in Christianity and
Islam. Once the formative stage of a movement has passed, men cast
women out. Discarding utopian visions for future society as "soft,"
socialists dismissed women's independent aspirations and concentrated on strategies for defeating capitalism. They derided feminism
as bourgeois deviationism, or conceded its justice but relegated it to
secondary status as a minor issue to be dealt with after the primary
struggle had been won. Dissident politics became a reflection of
mainstream politics.

Nevertheless, socialism was a revolutionary new human discourse that changed life for millions of humans across the globe. It incorporates a human ideal of equality, justice, and humaneness. That men tried to realize it through power unmitigated by humane values, and so created oppressive societies, does not alter the ideal – although it has damaged the name of socialism. It is important to see that whatever workers won in capitalist states – a living wage, improved working conditions, job security – was grudgingly given by governments and employers who feared that workers would otherwise turn to socialism. At the same time, rulers in capitalist states were fostering nationalism in order to mount a war that destroyed socialist movements and international associations of workers and women. After the Great War, socialist states remained isolated and embattled. The recent collapse of European socialist governments places the future of workers worldwide in jeopardy.

By interpreting social structure in terms of class struggle – exploitation of labour and collective action to challenge it – socialist thinkers provided the language and values for a feminist project. The feminist agenda is complicated by three facts: women participate in both sides of the class struggle; they are members of both the exploiters and the exploited; yet they are all in some way exploited by men. Women's loyalties are further fragmented by their sole responsibility for maintaining men and raising children (half of whom are males) to take a place in society dictated by the father's status.

Socialism, based on the principle of equality, treated women better than capitalism did – in several categories. Socialist states granted women the vote, among other rights, long before "democratic" states. Women supported socialism as ardently as religions that promised equality, and some continue to have faith in its principles. Its failure of women is not, after all, unique. Yet capitalism may be worse, for as European socialist governments collapsed, women lost many former freedoms and opportunities. In several countries, women lost the right to abortion. The Catholic Church succeeded in outlawing most abortions in Poland in 1993 and, despite considerable seesawing with more liberal laws governing abortion, it remains illegal there in most situations, making Poland and Ireland the only two Western states where women's ownership of their own bodies is not admitted.[20]

In all former socialist states, constitutions still guarantee fundamental rights and freedoms to everyone, regardless of sex, race, religion, or ethnic background, but in none did real equality exist. Women had high employment, but only in segregated areas, earning 20–30 percent less than men; they also had to do all the housework, shopping, and child care. Women in these states now face greater unemployment, making up about 60 percent of the unemployed in Poland, Bulgaria, and the ex-GDR, and perhaps even more in the former USSR. They also have lower unemployment benefits than men.[21]

Most former socialist states had quota systems designed to keep women's participation in Parliaments numerically high – but silent. Women made up about 30 percent of Parliament members in Poland, Hungary, and the Czech Republic, but those chosen for the job were usually young, inexperienced nonprofessionals without political backing. Thus, women were largely fillers: a minority, with even less influence than their numbers suggested.[22] Since 1989, when quotas were abandoned, far fewer women have been elected – an average of 8–14 percent of Parliament members. But those now participating are much more visible in the public life of the country, partly because their average level of education is higher than men's and they have considerable legislative and political experience.[23] Yet few of them see women as a distinct group with special problems. They dislike what they imagine is Western feminism and shun anything resembling it. Partly, they do not like our emphasis on individualism, seeing themselves more as part of families and communities; and partly they identify Western feminism with Soviet "feminism," a top-down organization that imposed central planning on localities to which it sometimes had little relevance.[24] "None of the existing groups is willing to join or submit itself to a larger structure," says Slawka Walczewska, co-founder of the Foundation of Women in Kraków. She adds that less centralized activities are more successful and "more difficult for the police to disrupt."[25] But Ann Snitow, of the Network of East-West Women, says that women's movements are cropping up everywhere in the former Soviet bloc. Clearly, these women will make their own way to their own brand of feminism – in time.

CHAPTER 11

REVOLUTION IN RUSSIA

T HE SLAVS WERE MATRILINEAL; their powerful autonomous women once controlled both the household and production. Mother right (to hold land, pass it to daughters, and confer blessings) persisted longer among the Slavs than other Europeans. Women ruled, made law, judged, testified in court, and fought in battles: a male historian in the nineteenth century said that women created Slavic civilization.[1] Religion centred on avatars of the Great Mother, self-inseminating deities who controlled natural processes. Russia converted to Byzantine Christianity (later, Slavic Orthodox Christianity) around 1000 CE, but goddesses and associations between femaleness and earth (called Mother Moist Earth) endured well into the Christian era. Wherever men tried to establish the male-supremacist religion, they had to suppress matrifocal traditions – a challenge that, in Russia, required extraordinary efforts.

Using traditional Christian tactics, men defined women as impure by nature, tainted, sinful, walking temptations to sin, and inferior to men in all respects. Priests taught that coitus was unclean, ordering people to cover domestic icons when they made love and to wash ritually afterwards. Since female, not male, sexual organs generated the uncleanness, priests soon forbade women to enter churches during or just after their menstrual periods or giving birth. Only menopausal women could bake communion wafers. Women were segregated in churches; around the twelfth century they were also segregated in the home.[2]

The degradation of women intensified under Tatar domination from the thirteenth to the fifteenth centuries, especially among the boyars – an urban elite. The Tatars, who were Mongol Muslims, believed that women's only reasons for being were to satisfy male desire and bear children, and that they should be kept in isolated subservience to men. Tatar women were veiled and confined to the house, where wealthy households had a female quarter or a tower (*terem*).[3] Men were raised to treat women brutally: the Tatar marriage symbol was a whip hung over the conjugal bed. The Russians eventually expelled the Mongols, but their attitudes towards women lingered: in the sixteenth century, Sylvester, a Christian monk, published a domestic guide, the *Domostroi*, with the imprimatur of the Russian Orthodox Church and the strong support of Tsar Ivan IV (the Terrible). It prescribes, in lip-licking detail, methods of punishing wives, who were ordered to remain silent about all domestic problems, including abuse.

To expel the Tatars, Muscovite society became militaristic and authoritarian at every level. Matricentry was still alive in the eighteenth century when Peter I (the Great) suppressed the use of the term "motherland," decreeing that it was now a "fatherland" (*otechestvo*) and that Batyushka Tsar (Little Father Tsar) would no longer marry Matushka Rus (Little Mother Russia) in the coronation ceremony. Yet peasants still considered Holy Russia a goddess, explaining, "Your fatherland is your mother." Peter adopted French manners and culture, which somewhat improved the treatment of upper-class women, who were now expected to go out with their husbands and were addressed politely in public. A 1702 law required prospective brides to be given six weeks to get to know their future husbands; a 1714 law prohibited parents from forcing girls into marriage. Such laws probably had little effect, but the custom of importing foreign governesses to educate wealthy girls enriched their lives somewhat.

Peter also made all slaves into serfs. Previously, about 10 percent of the population were slaves. Poor people sold themselves into slavery to survive, and the rich bought them more for prestige than for labour. Serfs were free in principle, but as the Russian state expanded and centralized, it encroached on their freedom. Workers on the land are immobile; landowners restricted their movements even further by forbidding them to move, legally, except during two weeks of the year or by imposing "exit fees" on those who wanted to leave their land. Bondage to land made them virtual slaves, and by the mid-eighteenth century, owners' formal power over serfs was absolute, short of deliberate murder.[4] Unlike African slaves in America, serfs shared the owners' ethnic background, language, and religion, but they became as different from them as African-Americans were from European-Americans. Serfs, who made up half the Russian population, were owned by a tiny group of noblemen with huge estates: in 1860 only one American owned over 1000 slaves, but 3358 Russian nobles owned over 1000 serfs, almost half the total. Most serfs belonged to men with over 200 acres, but some owned over half a million acres of land, with 10,000 serfs on estates in different provinces.

Serfs rarely saw their owners, who visited their estates infrequently. Stewards or administrative staffs managed the estates, extracting profit and controlling the workers. Serfs bound to land and to their owners were given little or no maintenance; rather, they were expected to provide for themselves and their owner. The harsh climate and poor soil produced low yields; serfs ate miserably and had an appalling death rate (over a third higher than slaves in the United States). Guarded on patrolled estates, serfs needed passes to leave and were punished for breaking rules or failing to produce what was required. They seem to have resented their arduous labour and long hours less than their lack of freedom – compulsion and interference in their personal lives. They could marry within the church, but owners could compel or forbid marriage to a person from outside the estate. There was far less forced sex than in America because the owners were absent, and there were fewer broken families because imperial decrees (though often violated) forbade splitting families or selling unmarried children. Serfs were also cruelly punished by the dreaded knout (whip).

Like African-Americans, serfs gained whatever sense of autonomy they had from their domestic lives. They lived entirely in a self-governing peasant commune (*mir*) that controlled village affairs. Free peasants lived in the same *mir*, sharing culture, language, religion, and work. But the Russian tradition of male dominance contrasted with female-centred African-American life: adult male serfs brutally oppressed their wives and children, treating them with the same cruelty that managers used on them. Since tyranny makes tyrants as unhappy as their victims, everyone was wretched. Nominal Christians, serfs were wary of and sometimes overtly hostile to priests – who supported serfdom and the nobles – and preferred folk superstitions about sorcery and spirits.

In the late eighteenth century, the German-born Catherine (the Great, one of two tsars to earn that title) wanted to ease serfs' lives. St. Petersburg nobles fought her, centralizing their power to lead peasants, serfs, miners, and Cossacks in a revolt that lasted over a year. It was eventually defeated, but Catherine was forced to back off. Strong, intelligent, and sympathetic to reform, Catherine fostered the work of other women, including Catherine Dashkova (Catherine the Little). Like the empress, self-educated and fond of the same authors, she became her friend. When Catherine became tsar, she made Dashkova director of the Academy of Sciences. She became its president, then president of the Academy of Arts – posts she held with distinction. As Tsar Catherine grew increasingly autocratic, a distance arose between them; when Catherine died, Dashkova was internally exiled, but returned to favour late in life.

Tsar Catherine refused male sexual regulation, scandalizing men, but she gave Russian women a new model. She also influenced Russian culture: she had French literature translated into Russian. Works by Saint-Simon, the Utopians, and especially George Sand sent Russian intellectuals into a ferment (Dostoievsky was deeply influenced by Sand's *Oscoque*) and introduced the idea of equality (male equality, not human) to Russian soil.

Serf resistance weakened the manorial system, and even aristocrats began to criticize serfdom. In 1825 Tsar Alexander died and was succeeded by his son Nicholas, the most rigid reactionary in Europe. The autocratic Nicholas created a secret police to secure his power; the Poles, expecting aid from Western Europe, rose up against him. No aid came, and Nicholas crushed the revolt and absorbed Poland into the Russian Empire. Despite his reactionary tendencies, Nicholas streamlined the bureaucracy and set Russia on the path of industrialization. Railroads, telegraph lines, and factories rose across the country. Peasants now worked in factories seasonally, but they lost their farms if they left permanently. Women did the farm work when men went to the factories. Marched daily from and to huge barracks where they lived, these men did unskilled work for twelve to fourteen hours a day for measly wages. Here, too, the factories were unsafe and unpleasant.

Towards Revolution

Socialist ideas were generating political agitation in Europe, and Alexander II, who succeeded Nicholas in 1855, tried to modify his autocracy. In 1861 he conceded some local control, reformed the judicial system, and emancipated 22 million serfs, granting them legal title to some of the land they worked. Men were given more educational opportunities, and councils and schools became forums for political discussion. But as middle-class Russians came to believe that reform was possible, the government swiftly banned political discussion in schools, councils, and the press. As moderate avenues to change were curbed, liberal Russians became radical nihilists, utopian socialists, anarchists, and terrorists.

Male revolutionaries courted women, who eagerly joined their cells but were shut out of leadership and decision-making and expected to provide casual sex: one group asked its women to support them as prostitutes. Political ferment in the 1850s and 1860s inflamed young women who were longing for education, jobs, and the right to leave their fathers' houses. Seeking ways to escape the oppression of middle-class families, they formed consciousness-raising groups to cleanse their minds of gender stereotypes.

Higher education was not available to women anywhere in the Russian Empire. Until the late 1850s, only daughters of wealthy men received secondary education in convent-like institutions, where they were virtually imprisoned and taught obedience, manners, and French. Punished for intelligence, enthusiasm, curiosity, or doing their hair, they were indoctrinated with a morality of absolute obedience and uncoiffed hair.[5] Middle-class girls were tutored at home in religion, arithmetic, domestic skills, French, and manners: how to dress, dance, and behave according to their class. Such schooling prepared them for their lives. The law forbade fathers to force them to marry, but few girls knew this restriction; all they knew was that the law decreed their absolute obedience to husbands. The only disobedience allowed was refusal to accompany a man sent to Siberia.

Like other European women, Russian women could not work, study, trade, or travel without a husband's express permission, and divorce was virtually impossible for them. Still, they had rights European women lacked: they did not cease to exist legally at marriage, and they could own and inherit property. Daughters inherited from fathers (though less than sons), and wives from husbands (a seventh of their real estate and a fourth of their movable goods). Consequently, Russian men boasted that Russian women were emancipated and needed no further liberation. As in the West, single middle-class women had the grimmest fate. Few inherited enough to live and, barred from work, they had to live with their families.

Russian women had few options. After emancipation, serf and poor gentry families could barely support their daughters. These young women went to cities seeking work, but few resources were open to them. In 1862 the first Russian organization created by women for women was formed by three educated, well-to-do women. The Society for Cheap Lodgings offered poor, single, genteel women not only rooms but writing, reading, and dressmaking classes and a publishing cooperative. Its deference to sexual conventions and elitism alienated politically aware young women, but it published some good books and gave women work experience while protecting them from city life.

Another successful project, the Sunday School movement, gave adults free reading lessons. Secondary schools were established in cities for girls of all classes between 1858 and 1860, but, since poor girls worked, most students came from urban families of moderate means. By 1875, 27,000 girls studied religion, Russian language and history, arithmetic, geometry, natural history, sewing, and some of the arts. Their training, intended mainly to prepare girls for motherhood, was far inferior to boys' education. In 1863 male bureaucrats and journalists opposed to female education seized on the discovery of some nihilists in these schools to urge the state, over the objection of several universities, to close women's schools and bar women from auditing lectures. Thereafter, girls had to seek university and medical training abroad.

Nihilism, a Russian movement rather like America's counterculture of the 1960s, became extremely popular in the 1850s. It had no program, but a consciousness exhibited mainly in unconventional behaviour, dress, and appearance. The movement fostered residential communes in which both sexes lived together, sometimes in sexual pairs. Many political groups advocated equality among all people, but only nihilists counted women as people.[6] Nihilist consciousness was moulded by novels like *What Is to Be Done?* written in prison by Nicolai Chernyshevsky. Published in 1863, it inspired generations of Russian women. Its heroine, Vera Pavlovna, escapes from a predatory family, trying to sell her in marriage, by eloping with a young idealist who promises to respect her bodily integrity. She builds a successful collective workshop for women and eventually creates a sex life based on her desire. Its male characters, as noble and strong as its heroine, create equally satisfying lives. The novel envisions a utopian future based on a collective economy in which female liberation is central; it implies that this future depends on individual transformation. Vera must overcome fear and deference to patriarchal superiors; the heroes must overcome those traits too, as well as sexual jealousy, possessiveness, and male rivalry if they are to become rational, socially aware rebels. This vision was radically opposed to that espoused by Dostoievsky, who attacked nihilist individualism in *The Possessed*. Nihilists wanted to change the world by being – not doing – good and were not always political. Female nihilists avoided organized movements, seeking liberation from all oppressions – family, marriage, and sexism.

Nihilist women wore plain dark dresses falling straight and loose from the waist, with white cuffs and collars, short straight hair, and often dark glasses. They smoked, some adopted rude manners, some did not bother to wash. Single or married, they ran away from home to study abroad or to join communes, form workshops, and live in communal residences, none of which lasted long. Yet their influence on the culture was enormous, and they were a popular literary subject. The word for nihilist woman (*migilistka*) was eventually used for any educated, progressive woman.

Organized radicals called Populists wanted to establish democracy and agrarian socialism. After 1860, most advocated a federated network of artels (work communes). Earlier radicals like the Decembrists had excluded women; the Populists welcomed them as equals, encouraging them to use their skills, though they rejected feminism and nihilism as too individualistic. They supported a social platform granting women freedom within the family and requiring them to work for wages. They drew a huge following of educated, idealistic young people willing to live underground and die in order to liberate "the people." Women joined individually, and the various workshops and artels functioned as cells to spread the new gospel. Many such groups were destroyed by the police. After an assassination attempt on the tsar in 1866, the police moved on all radical cells, attacking them in the streets and banishing or jailing them.

Russian women seeking an education often went to Zurich, a hub for Russian exiles. The city was a hotbed of political discussion centred on the theorists Michael Bakunin and Paul Lavrov, who debated the proper role of intellectuals in freeing the peasants. Lavrov believed that intellectuals should educate themselves thoroughly and use their learning to benefit the peasants; Bakunin felt that education increased the distance between classes and urged students to abandon it, work with the peasants, learn from them, and persuade them to join the revolution. Russian women students in Zurich founded the first Russian female radical organization.

Most women agreed with Bakunin and returned to Russia to join radical men in the Pan-Russian Social Revolutionary Organization to spread across the countryside and convert peasants to the revolution. But the men merely talked: the women actually lived locked in factories except on holidays, at hard labour for thirteen to fourteen hours a day, lying on narrow boards in filthy infested dormitories, and whispering to exhausted workers at night about revolution. The process was slow and, as they began to win converts, they were arrested and held in solitary confinement for three years before being tried.[7] But the "Moscow Amazons," as they were called at their trial, got to tell their stories.[8]

Zurich radicals absorbed by issues of "The People" and "The Revolution" gave perfunctory attention to the "woman question." They planned the abolition of the family, but postponed planning other reforms. Yet women dominated the Zurich political cells, so it was women whom the tsar attacked: in May 1873, charging female immorality, he ordered all women studying abroad to return home by January 1874. Most gave up study for revolutionary activism; in the spring of 1874, thousands of young people poured into the countryside to reach peasants in a movement of selfless dedication unparalleled in the nineteenth century. But they were young and amateur, and the police were right behind them: by fall, 1600 had been seized. Of these, 770 were arraigned (20 percent of them women) and about 40 tried, but hundreds died in exile, prison, and on the scaffold.

In 1878 the governor-general of St. Petersburg had a political prisoner whipped for not doffing his cap in his presence. The withdrawn, introverted Vera Zasulich hated corporal punishment and was outraged enough to become the first woman in Russia's revolutionary struggle to use a weapon: she shot the governor. He almost died, yet she was acquitted. Her act split Land and Liberty (Narodniks), the main Populist party. One group went on doing education/propaganda; the other became a terrorist group – The People's Will (Narodnaya Volya). Women, a substantial presence among Narodniks, made up a third of Narodnaya Volya.

The attraction of terrorism for Russian women suggests a powerful rage or, possibly, such narrow alternatives that death was not unthinkable. Of more than 2500 Russians charged with political crimes between 1873 and 1879, about 15 percent were women; of 43 sentenced to hard labour between 1880 and 1890, probably for terrorist acts, half were women. An eighth of the 5664 revolutionaries listed in the 1870s are female, but their proportion rises in extremist groups.

Narodnaya Volya imagined that Tsar Alexander's death would end oppression – a naïve hope at best. After six failed attempts, during which Vera Figner held the group together, it succeeded in assassinating Alexander II in 1881. The act was directed by Sofia Perovskaia, who was hanged – the first Russian woman executed for a political crime. Figner repudiated violence the moment the tsar was dead, but was arrested in 1883 and held in solitary confinement

for twenty-two years. The tsar's successor, Alexander III, then instituted greater repression. Insisting that Russians, unlike Western
Europeans, were sustained by despotism and mystic piety and
would collapse without them, he curtailed local councils' powers,
put rich nobles in charge of villages, expanded secret police powers,
and initiated a policy of "Russification" that was continued by his
son, Nicholas II. This policy involved imposing Russian culture,
language, and religion on groups that the tsar felt to be menacing.
The tsars forbade Poles to speak or read their own language,
suspended the Finnish constitution, and abetted pogroms – the
terrorist raids on Jewish hamlets in Russian-controlled territories.

Literate Russian women, inspired by John Stuart Mill's essay
"On the Subjection of Women," campaigned for higher education
in 1868. Aware that Russian women who studied in Switzerland
came home politicized, the government decided to educate them at
home and, in the 1870s, opened institutions of higher learning for
women in Moscow, St. Petersburg, and Kiev. But in the 1880s the
vacillating tsar closed all but the Petersburg school, which was highly successful despite the fact that the state gave it only 3000 rubles
a year. Fearing female politicization, the government let Mme
Rodstvennaya donate 50,000 rubles to found a women's medical
school in St. Petersburg. When war broke out in 1877, opening
opportunities to women, they comported themselves so heroically
and professionally as doctors in the Turkish phase of the war that
they became national heroines. Before the war, women with medical degrees were "learned midwives"; afterward, they were "women
doctors."

Historian Richard Stites thinks nihilist women were rebelling
against their families or social groups, aiming for personal, not
political, change. But personal change is political: personal liberation frees women to act in the public arena. Feminists worked not
to overthrow but to alter the system, and between 1860 and 1900
they won rights for women to do philanthropic work, found legal
societies, and attend universities. Impressive numbers of women

were graduated as lawyers, teachers, physicians, and engineers. At the turn of the century, feminists began to lobby for suffrage, property rights, divorce, and freedom of movement. They based their suffrage campaign on that of Finnish women, who won the vote in 1904 after only twenty years of agitation. Most suffragists were middle-class, but without the bias American and European suffragists harboured against working-class or black women. Despite the size and energy of the movement, despite the existence of four feminist parties, on the eve of revolution in 1917 no woman could vote. But then, neither could most men.

In 1894 only 3.9 percent of Russian boys and 1 percent of girls were in school. When numbers increased, proportions remained the same. Some day schools prepared girls for university, though the government periodically threatened to close these schools, charging that "children of cooks" had too much freedom. About 1905 female universities opened again. In 1914, 25,000 women enrolled in women's courses, and universities put women on a quota system. Jewish women's quota was 3 percent, and they were required to remain within the pale of the Jewish Settlement. Young Jewish women bribed janitors, made fictitious marriages, or listed themselves as prostitutes with the police to get the yellow ticket allowing them to live inside the pale. Whatever they had to do, they did, thronging to universities, more politically radical than males.

Once girls had degrees, they struggled to find work commensurate with their education. Most became lower-grade teachers or taught in girls' schools, where they were paid less than skilled female labourers (8–20 rubles a month). Some towns regulated female teachers, dictating their dress, behaviour, and residence (they had to live at least two blocks from any male teacher). Some became journalists, architects, or designers, and fifty engineers graduated from St. Petersburg Women's Technical Institute between 1906 and 1916. Women physicians, theoretically equal to men, were in fact confined to pediatrics and gynecology; in towns they could work only in maternity hospitals, girls' schools, and examining prostitutes in a police-supervised system. Still, by 1910, 1500 Russian women were doctors, two-thirds more than any Western nation in 1930.

A third of the girls in secondary education attended elite institutes or Russian Orthodox parish schools that trained priests' daughters to become priests' wives. These girls were poorly fed, strictly disciplined, forced to wear uniforms, and taught religion, liturgical singing, and embroidery. Entrance requirements at schools for elite girls were Russian, French, some prayers, counting to a thousand, and the absence of communicable disease.

Peasant women, a majority of the Russian population in 1897, were not educated. Hardworking, deprived, illiterate, and ignorant of their rights, they bore the brunt of men's scorn for all women. In some regions, brides had to give their grooms bedding and a whip. Wives in extended families had to have sex with their fathers-in-law when their husbands were away for long periods. But women were most oppressed by their mothers-in-law. Despite frequent pregnancy, they did heavy field work. A 1908 report showed that one-quarter of women forty-five years old had been pregnant more than ten times; one fifty-five-year-old, married for thirty-five years, had been pregnant twenty-four times and had two living children. As industrialization spread and men went to work in factories, most peasant women remained in village households. Laws passed in the 1880s and 1890s gave them the right to keep dowries, earnings, and a share of household property. "Women without a lord" attended *mir* meetings and ran them if the men were absent. Some left the *mir* to set up independent farms with husbands, or to work as hired hands or in cities.

Most women who went to cities became domestic servants, "the most rightless people in the Russian Empire" – 32 percent of the population of St. Petersburg and over 25 percent of Moscow's in the late 1800s. The few women who worked in factories were abused on every front: poorly paid, they worked for long hours in miserable conditions, were beaten by husbands, sexually exploited and humiliated by foremen, and harassed by male co-workers. Factory work was unregulated by law until 1885, and some owners imposed eighteen-hour workdays, with a two- and four-hour break. With few safety measures, leather tannery workers got damaged lungs and kidneys, while tobacco processors suffered from heart ailments, asthma, and eye damage. In Moscow, men used a woman's body to sweep chimneys.

During the Russo-Japanese War (1904–5), factory jobs opened to women. In the 1880s, women made up 25 percent of the labour force; in 1914, 40 percent. In towns, they slept at their machines, in a corner of another's room, or in tiny rooms of their own. Workers lived in a space that was, on average, the size of a telephone booth; too exhausted even to undress, people slept wall to wall on the floors of various rooms. Rural workers usually lived in factory-owned barracks. An industrial centre in Central Russia, located on a stinking polluted river, housed 44 percent of its district workers in a barracks with no washing facilities. Three or four families shared a room rank with unwashed flesh, where people shared beds in shifts. Both sexes endured such conditions, but women also suffered from frequent male drunkenness, the seigneurial code of foremen and managers (some factories were used as recruitment pools by white slavers and pimps), and reproduction. They aborted themselves, or they sold, abandoned, or killed their babies. The only baby tenders available were incompetent, negligent old women or children.

The government tried to limit night work for women: owners protested, but women themselves were resigned. Resistant to organizing, women only slowly developed the confidence to express their resentment towards owners and male workers who froze them out of extra work; then they complained about limits on their hours. Middle-class women aware of their situation tried to organize them in feminist or socialist groups. For the first time alliances sprang up between different classes of Russian women. Workers were easier to organize than farmers, and organized men and women demonstrated, struck, and mounted insurrections with increasing frequency and intensity.

The bloodiest event occurred during a peaceful demonstration. On January 6, 1905, 200,000 members of the Union of Russian Factory Hands, founded by an Orthodox priest, Father Gapon, marched to the tsar's winter palace in St. Petersburg to beg relief from starvation. Although the priest favoured lower wages for women, 200 to 500 women joined his march. Singing hymns, they carried icons and portraits of the tsar. Peaceable as they were, they refused to halt at order, and Russian troops opened fire on them. The marchers fled, but mounted Cossacks pursued them, littering Palace Square with a thousand dead and thousands more injured – including many women and children. The massacre added another "Bloody Sunday" to a long list of such dates, eliciting a wave of support that shut the city down by the autumn of 1905: owners closed shops and factories; lawyers refused to go to court; and valets and cooks deserted their jobs. Factories named women to investigating commissions, but the government would not seat them. Cooks convened a political meeting on the street. The police broke it up and chased them, but they headed for a women's bathhouse, stripped, and held the meeting. In Ivano-Voznesensk, 11,000 woman textile workers mounted one of the largest strikes ever held.

The tsar was pushed by this spontaneous, unorganized uprising (called the Revolution of 1905), as well as pressure from the Constitutional Democratic Party (formed by middle-class businessmen and professionals to push for a Parliament and for Western-style liberalization of Russia), to grant a constitution and a Parliament, the Duma, elected by limited male suffrage. But over the next two years, Tsar Nicholas rescinded almost all his promises. As a result, a host of political parties arose. Only the socialists (like the earlier Populists) favoured maternity protection and equal political and economic rights for women. The Social Democrats – Marxists advocating an international working-class movement – had quarrelled over strategy in 1903 and split into Bolsheviks ("majority") and Mensheviks ("minority"). Bolsheviks wanted a strong central party to foment revolution and set up a socialist state immediately. Mensheviks, in contrast, believing that socialism must be achieved gradually, urged a transition government like those in the West.

The Uprising

Marxist feminism was deeply influenced by August Bebel. A German Social Democrat, Bebel introduced labour legislation covering women to the Reichstag and addressed the first Social Democratic women's meeting. He published *Woman and Socialism* in 1879, five years before Engels' *Origin of the Family*, and revised it to include Engels' points. His book was enormously popular, issued in fifty editions in fifteen languages. He supported feminist demands for education, suffrage, acceptance in professions, right to divorce, and property ownership. He dismissed women's "natural calling" for motherhood as "twaddle," arguing that women should be able to dress as they pleased and be sexually satisfied. Few women were daring enough to make such demands. He asserted that men, not just capitalism, oppressed women. He felt that feminism alone could not redress a problem that was rooted in history, not biology, but that it could be altered in history. Bebel's attention to working-class, as distinct from middle-class, women was unusual, if not unique, and he deeply affected them.

In 1900 Nadezhda Krupskaya (1869–1939) published *The Woman Worker*, a Russian Marxist interpretation of women's oppression based on her study of women factory workers. Printed abroad and smuggled into Russia, it circulated illegally underground, in an adumbration of the *samizdats* (illegal underground publications in the Soviet Union), and led her husband, Lenin, to approve some protective measures for women and include an equal-rights plank in the party program after 1903. Lenin uncompromisingly advocated female political equality, but he repudiated feminist means to achieve it. Marxists hated feminism. Marx knew that the family replicated external economic relations, that wives were proletarians to their husbands' bourgeoisie, and that women were paid half as much as men. He asserted political equality as a prerequisite for human emancipation, but he never developed these perceptions and, in life, he was crudely sexist. A subterranean drive to dominate women informed all male Marxist political groups.

Alexandra Kollontai (1872–1952) was alone in this generation in combining feminism and socialism. A general's daughter, torn between work and family, she joined first the Mensheviks, then the Bolsheviks. Like other socialists, she denigrated feminism as bourgeois, urging women to join the proletarian movement. But she soon saw that women had to fight for themselves, and in 1905 she founded the Proletarian Women's Movement. To persuade working women to join her group rather than the feminists, who were organizing an "all-women's" movement, she and a few supporters propagandized among factory workers, taught them Marxism, and tried to deflect their resentment from men to the bourgeoisie until 1908, when police harassment drove her out of Russia.

By 1912, educational opportunities had produced thousands of professional women, many of them in prison, exiled to Siberia, or abroad for political activities. As workers protested ever more militantly, both Mensheviks and Bolsheviks intensified their efforts to organize working women: both groups celebrated International Women's Day (an important holiday in much of Europe) in 1913.[9] The Bolsheviks created the Zhenotdel, a women's affairs bureau led by Inessa Armand (1879–1920). With editors including Lenin's sister, Anna Elizarova, Armand planned to publish a journal, *Rabotnitsa* (Woman Worker) on International Women's Day in 1914. The police, who had given the editors permission to meet, charged into the editorial meeting on the eve of publication and arrested everyone except Elizarova, who was late. Thirty of the women were exiled. Working underground, Elizarova managed to get the magazine out and, before long, daily newspapers were taking up its concerns. *Rabotnitsa* was published until the war began in the summer of 1914, and it was revived in 1917. It still exists.

Many women saw the First World War as a chance to change the system. Well-to-do women went to work in hospitals; others took over utilities and transport as telegraphers, trolley drivers, conductors, and carters. Women were military drivers, one became a pilot (another woman pilot was turned away), and many became soldiers. A miner's daughter rejected by the army disguised herself as a man, fought in nineteen battles, and won the St. George Cross. While European feminists and socialists like Rosa Luxemburg spoke against the war, most ended by supporting it, hoping for a reward – suffrage.

Seemingly purposeless to start with, the First World War became a war of attrition – battles were fought until everyone was dead. But considering the class and sex protest current in the era, we may find, like analyst Walter Karp, that the underlying drive to war was to bury socialist and feminist agitation under a "larger" cause that would reinforce the old power structure and its rulers.[10] For this, the elite was willing to sacrifice an entire generation of young men and many women and children.

By February 1917, after three years of war, food and fuel were short and people in many European cities rose in revolt. Russia alone lost over 2 million soldiers, and the government made no effort to feed its civilians. Remembering their hunger in 1905, people had little confidence in government. In Petrograd, on International Women's Day, a "Bread and Peace" meeting exploded into a communal strike, triggered by the most militant women – textile mill workers in the Vyborg District – who walked off their jobs in outrage and influenced non-strikers to follow them. Marching to the Putilov factory, they called out the male metal workers, who joined them after ascertaining that the police would not shoot them.[11] Heading for the bakeries, the women called to those standing on the breadlines to join them, shouting: "Down with war and high prices! Down with starvation! Bread for Workers! Bread!" Singing revolutionary songs, they ransacked bakeries and grocery shops while the men marched to other factories, urging workers to leave their jobs and join them. The horde marched down Bolshoi Prospekt, a grand avenue lined with houses of the rich, nobles, and government officials, as well as a high school, university buildings, and a women's adult education centre. The women counted on help from the students, who were experienced agitators. They went to the army barracks and asked the soldiers to join them.[12] They grabbed the bayonets of soldiers in the streets, ordering them to "Put down your bayonets! Join us!"

Women in working-class neighbourhoods on Vasilevsky Island and in the Petrograd District took similar actions that day and in those following: thousands marched to the Duma, the symbolic centre of national political life. They stormed the jails, freeing male relatives, many of them imprisoned for joining unions or socialist cells. Women networked, sharing information about which retailers were speculators, and they looted food shops, attacking those speculators.

The political parties in the cities had decided against striking on International Women's Day because they knew working-class men were not prepared to revolt and they feared that huge numbers would be massacred or arrested. But few women belonged to these parties, which were male-dominated. The women's revolt included no demand for suffrage or equality; they merely asked the government to take responsibility, to help them nourish and raise the children.[13] Officials estimated that 87,000 workers struck on International Women's Day in 1917, drawing a crowd of 200,000, and swelling to 300,000 on February 24 and 25. Both sexes demanded an eight-hour day, an assembly, and a republic. When the crowd surged into Nevsky Prospekt in the centre of the capital, the tsar ordered General Khabalov to shoot if necessary, including women. On February 26 men took over the strike. The police fired into the crowd, which retaliated by burning police stations. Almost the entire working class of the city was on the street when the army arrived on Monday, February 27. Soldiers too were unhappy with the tsar, whose poor management of the war had been responsible for the deaths of masses of their colleagues. Women beseeched them to think of the good of society and to join the people in protest. The confrontation that followed was described by a tsarist officer:

> The only sound that could be heard was the resonant ring of . . . approaching hoofs. Then a girl walked out from the crowd. She wore a dark padded jacket and huge shoes with galoshes. A simple knitted shawl of the same color as the Cossack's coat . . . bound tightly over her head . . . she crossed over toward the Cossacks, walking swiftly and lightly. . . . A thousand eyes followed her and a thousand hearts were numb. Suddenly, she threw away some wrapping paper – and held out a bouquet of fresh red roses to the officer. [He] was young . . . his epaulettes flashed . . . his saber, polished like a mirror, was firmly held in a strong hand – but suddenly the blade wavered . . . and dangled . . . from the . . . white-gloved wrist. The officer leaned over and took the nosegay. A mad riotous shout went up – such a shout as I had never heard and never expect to hear again . . . a wild bellow of uproarious joy.[14]

This "eyewitness" account is a myth: in February 1917 there was no bread in Petrograd, much less roses.[15] But it tells the emotional truth of a revolution rooted in female values, led by women courageous enough to risk being shot. Across the city soldiers refused to shoot women; they put down their guns and mutinied, becoming revolutionaries. The tsar abdicated. Liberal Duma leaders and representatives of Petrograd workers (a governing council, or soviet) established a provisional government to plan the election of an assembly. Under feminist pressure, it granted women the vote, making Russia the first major power to do so. It granted women equal opportunity, pay, benefits, and civil service titles, and licensed them to serve as jurors and attorneys. It set up women's universities on an equal footing with men's. But it also supported continuing the war, and deferred workers' and soldiers' needs until its conclusion.

In April 1917 Vladimir Ilyich Lenin, the Bolshevik leader exiled in Switzerland, was smuggled into Russia by the Germans, who knew he opposed Russian participation in the First World War and hoped his presence would weaken it. Lenin brilliantly united soldiers, workers, and peasants and tried to connect with the female masses. Other revolutionary parties made similar efforts, but the Bolsheviks were most effective because of vigorous work by female organizers like Kollontai. Promising not to act independently of the party, they got permission to form a Bureau of Women Workers to spread information, lobby clubs and unions, and revive *Rabotnitsa*. Amid the chaos of revolt and squabbling leaders, they created a powerful network of female agitators to organize factory women. They also established a school for female factory workers which forged them into a force to win new recruits and demonstrate for Bolshevik positions.

The soviets wanted to end the war and redistribute land. They elevated Alexander Kerensky, from the Petrograd soviet, to prime minister. Rightists of different stripes, fearing radicalism, united in a military coup that the Kerensky government defeated. Lenin resolved to mount a coup from the left, but Leon Trotsky triggered the October Revolution by mounting a coup in Petrograd. The American journalist Louise Bryant saw the ragged women of Petrograd, who were physically deformed from overwork, malnutrition, and abuse, some carrying shovels, swarm into the streets to attack the Cossacks, running "straight into the fire without any weapons at all." "It was terrifying to see them. . . . The Cossacks seemed superstitious about it. They began to retreat."[16]

On October 25, 1917 (November 7 in the Western calendar), the Bolsheviks took power, initiating the grand experiment, the creation of a socialist state. At that time, women held high positions in soviet and party organizations and in the Military Revolutionary Committee. After the Bolsheviks urged women to vote for Bolshevik instead of feminist candidates in the First Conference of Working Women of the Petrograd Region held in Moscow weeks

PART SEVEN: THE TWENTIETH CENTURY: REVOLUTION

after the coup, Russian feminism essentially died. In 1918 the Bolsheviks moved the capital to Moscow, drafted a constitution, and made peace with Germany. But civil war raged through the country, supported by those who opposed the First World War. Everyone suffered, but women most of all. Whatever their adherence or combatant status, they were treated as prey by Bolsheviks (Reds) and anti-Bolsheviks (Whites) alike. One city declared it a crime for any woman to "refuse a Communist"; another decreed all women state property, along with the children born from this appropriation. Whites savaged Red nurses: in 1919 near Petrograd they hanged three nurses in bandages from the beams of a field hospital with Komsomol pins stuck through their tongues.

Women fought, some disguised as men, on every front with every weapon. They were riflewomen, armoured train commanders, saboteurs, spies: the female machine gunner became a stock character in Soviet literature. Zhenotdel organized Bolshevik women scouts, cavalry, commanders, and reconnaissance, as well as communications, food, and medical workers. They built fortifications, dug trenches, policed, waged psychological warfare and propagandized, and ran food and sanitary operations. Many fought in all-female units of roughly three hundred. During the Polish campaign, when a male regiment faltered, a female company charged and saved the situation, losing all but one member. Conditioned by fifty years of revolutionary activity to indifference to dress or social codes, women adapted easily to the rough comradeship of camp life.

Women were most important in political work. Kollontai, especially good at training women, organized them into departments, managing groups of about twenty to travel with a wagon of literature and their leaders ("commissars"). Women held responsible posts during and after the civil war: Bolsheviks (renamed Communists), committed to female equality, instituted the most sweeping program for female equality ever produced. By separating church and state, they removed religious restrictions on Orthodox Christian and Muslim women in one stroke. Lenin loathed the domestic enslavement of women to "barbarously unproductive, petty, nerve-wracking, stultifying and crushing [household] drudgery."[17] His government passed laws protecting pregnant and nursing women and those in heavy or hazardous work. The Family Code of 1918 abolished bastardy; gave women control of their own earnings, inheritance, and ownership rights; and granted married women the right to keep their own names, live where they chose, have their own passports, and obtain divorces. The government made prostitution illegal, abolished alimony (expecting everyone to work outside the home), and opened all educational institutions to females. Most important, it set up a women's organization to oversee these laws and programs.

But the country was in a shambles. Almost 10 percent of its population had been killed in the civil war; 7 million homeless children roamed the countryside in gangs, hunting for food with weapons found in deserted fields. Facing massive poverty and ignorance at home and frightening hostility from abroad, the Bolsheviks concentrated on strengthening the state by industrialization and collectivization. In such an environment, women's rights seemed inconsequential. Once the war was over, the government passed the laws women demanded and let it go at that: the army got rid of women; so did the government. Before the October Revolution, three women sat in the highest party echelons; after 1923, no woman held high rank. A few held middle-level administrative positions, and many participated in the political process at the lowest level, but men at all levels scorned women and their concerns, begrudging them time or money. The programs established for women were well-intended, but sexism was as endemic among Soviet as European men. After granting women the vote, these men made not the slightest effort to liberate them further.

Kollontai and Armand ran Zhenotdel, the women's organization, on a tiny budget with a small staff, sending organizers to villages, factories, and working-class neighbourhoods to start literacy classes and explain the new laws. They crossed the steppe to central Asia, stopping at camps and oases along the way to show films. They talked to the oppressed Muslim, Jewish, and Christian women of the Caucasus, Volga, and central Asia. Organizers asked the women to elect a delegate to Zhenotdel, who would spend three to six months observing public activities, then report to Zhenotdel and her village. Shy women aware of their ignorance bloomed. A Muslim woman described life in the 1920s: "We were silent slaves. We had to hide in our rooms and cringe before our husbands, who were our lords . . . . Our fathers sold us at the age of ten, even younger. Our husbands would beat us with a stick and whip us when he felt like it. If he wanted to freeze us, we froze. Our daughters, a joy to us and a help around the house, he sold just as we had been sold."

Men ferociously tried to prevent organizers from speaking to women, so they met in bathhouses, sewing circles, and women's clubs. When women newly aware of their oppression removed their veils, men began to kill them. In Baku, as a group of women left a women's club, men assaulted them with wild dogs and boiling water; the father and brothers of a Muslim woman of twenty who dared to appear in a bathing suit sliced her in pieces; an eighteen-year-old Uzbek activist was mutilated and thrown in a well. In three months in 1929, three hundred central Asian women were murdered for political reasons by their own families.

Despite male violence, the Zhenotdel women created programs for child care, orphan care, schools, food distribution, housing supervision, preventive medicine, public health, and anti-prostitution campaigns, among others. They informed enormous numbers of women who had never imagined they had human rights. People of both sexes were drawn to the communist vision – to eliminate poverty, offer equal opportunity to everyone, and create a just, humane society. Architects and town planners designed communities with communal child care, cooking, and dining, carefully providing private rooms for singles or couples and easy room changes for divorcing couples. They tried to plan communities so that space itself fostered male-female cooperation in tasks. Some communes were built; others formed in cities and in the countryside.

Men often ignored decrees of equality; the government lacked money for the compulsory education, child-care centres, nurseries, and communal laundries it had promised. Protective laws worked against women, making employers reluctant to hire them. Of jobs lost in the 1920s, women lost 70 percent; by 1928, women (mainly widows, divorcees, and single women) made up under one-quarter of the labour force. Last hired, first fired, lowest paid, and consigned to the most menial, heaviest work, they left jobs for the home if they could: but few men supported their families.

Sexual freedom meant liberty for men and maternity for women.[18] Wanting sex without responsibility, men charged women who rejected them sexually with "bourgeois prudery." Many couples lived apart; a few men did housework, but the overwhelming majority drank heavily, were unfaithful, and expected to be waited on at home. Wives asked the party to deduct a portion of their husbands' wages so not all would be drunk up. Annoyed at a dinner not ready or socks not washed, men beat their wives or forced them to give up their jobs. Women were abused by men at work too: the complaint most often brought to Zhenotdel was that factory bosses treated women workers like a harem. Easy divorce meant that men walked away from a marriage, leaving women with children to support: in 70 percent of the divorces in this period, men abandoned their wives and paid no alimony or child support. The divorce rate was very high – in 1927, four out of every five marriages ended in divorce. In the country, peasants married women, used their labour in the fields for a season, and divorced them after harvest, having gotten free labour. In the early 1920s, armies of destitute women swept into Soviet towns seeking food or work. Despite its illegality, many – including children – became prostitutes. In 1921 there were 17,000 prostitutes in Petrograd; a year later, there were 32,000.

Most commentators blame the failure of the grand communist

vision of sexual equality on the ancient sexism of the culture (and certainly it permeated society, women as well as men). But beyond that, laws and programs ignored the basis of women's status – their reproductive powers. To treat women as men's equals without reference to women's reproduction, and men's refusal to take responsibility for children, is to place women in the impossible situation of being expected to do everything men do, and to reproduce society and maintain it, all at the same time and alone.

Only Kollontai addressed herself to sexual relations and family life, advocating communal facilities for child-rearing to be maintained by collective labour. Lenin supported her: when Russian women thronged to a meeting and defiantly opposed giving up their children to collective care, Lenin took the time to address them supportively. Kollontai wanted voluntary public child care, not forced removal of children from parents, and successfully fought for maternity leave at full pay, nursing breaks at specific sites in factories, free pre- and post-natal care, and cash allowances. Seeing marriage as a mutual union of two independent people, she wanted sex to please women as well as men, scandalizing everyone. She hated sexual regulation – rules dictating virginity and monogamy, or decreeing illegitimacy.

Kollontai, concerned about society as a whole, argued that workers produced less when they were under surveillance. She believed, like Luxemburg and Goldman, that society must be remade from the bottom, by collective action of workers. This infuriated Lenin, who was authoritarian and believed in centralized bureaucratic authoritarianism, but she would not shut her mouth. He stripped her of her posts, sent her to Norway on a diplomatic mission, and made her ambassador to Sweden. Her career in the party was over, and so was the effectiveness of Zhenotdel: in 1930 it was dissolved. The party still held women's congresses and demonstrations, but they were mere echo chambers for male decisions, bearing no relevance to women's needs. After Kollontai's dismissal, the only woman with influence was Krupskaya, who handled propaganda and education. She continued in her posts after Lenin died in 1924, but clashed with Stalin when he took power and he ousted her from politics in 1925.

From the start, the Bolsheviks favoured authoritarian central control and hierarchy, and these characteristics marked the society they built. Like the tsars, who created elaborate bureaucracies, the communists ruled through committees, commissions, congresses, and an even more complex bureaucracy. Given a huge sprawling country whose population spoke different languages and followed different religions and customs, this may have seemed the only way possible to create a new kind of state; certainly it was easier than winning consensus from people at the grassroots level, as Kollontai, Luxemburg, and Goldman advocated. The communist state made huge inroads against disease, starvation, and illiteracy (illiteracy among women fell from 90–95 percent in 1919 to 60 percent in 1929) and improved opportunities for young people across the country. But the revolution was exceedingly costly for women: under the tsars they suffered oppression and discrimination; during the revolution they were arrested, interrogated, tormented physically and mentally, torn from their children, sent to camps, subjected to hideous conditions, beaten, raped, and executed. And then they got Stalin.

Stalin's Revolution

Stalin essentially waged a second revolution in the Soviet Union. Using a rhetoric drawn from old myths, he collectivized farms, launched giant industrialization projects mainly for arms, and transformed the USSR into a militaristic society. Acutely aware of capitalists' fear of socialism and the US government's itch to destroy the Soviet Union, Stalin closed the country. For the first time in history, a state built walls not to keep strangers out but to keep citizens in, turning home into prison. His paranoia, inevitable in dominators, had a factual basis, but he went amok. He murdered millions of citizens, many supporters of the revolution, and war heroes. Eliminating the revolutionary elite, he raised a new one – rural men who had become managers. Cities swelled with upwardly mobile peasant immigrants who worshipped a new god – Stalin. More patriarchal than the revolutionary generation, more imbued with middle-class values, Stalin ended egalitarian experiments, political discourse, and sexual freedom. In 1936 he re-established sexual regulations: "We need men," he pronounced, making divorce more difficult and costly, and outlawing abortion except under certain circumstances. Lesbianism was not officially banned, but he had male homosexuals jailed for eight years simply for their inclinations.

Stalin created campaigns to encourage women to attend technical and medical schools, partly by setting quotas. He propelled an underprivileged group of women into education. They began to invade previously exclusive male worlds – laboratories, construction projects, and technical colleges. By 1939, 81.6 percent of Soviet women were literate, and 58 percent of people in advanced education were female. Unlike Western women in this period, they studied agronomy, technology, sanitation, engineering, and animal husbandry. These careers did not save them from a double-bind, for Stalin also pressured them to have children. Propaganda featuring hale women adorned with maternity medals and embracing large healthy families – sons for the state – reinforced the idea that women were responsible for maintaining families. High-ranking men's wives, exempted from working for wages, were photographed decorating their husbands' offices or factory grounds; ordinary women, sunk in the endless labour that remains the lot of Soviet women, worked one shift away and a second at home. As the world tottered on the brink of the Second World War, Stalin initiated the "great terror," killing or imprisoning millions of loyal Soviet citizens. Only 10 percent were women, but that included almost all women who had reached any position of authority.

After Germany invaded the Soviet Union in 1941, government policy towards women changed again. The whole country mobilized: a million women joined the army; another 800,000 became anti-aircraft and machine gunners, snipers, tankers, pilots and bombardiers (some air regiments were entirely female), in signal or medical corps, as partisans, guerrillas, and saboteurs. Thousands of women were killed, wounded, tortured, and executed by the Nazis. Women made up the majority of miners and industrial workers producing weapons and a third of Baku oil-field workers. They also worked in civil defence.

But as usual, when the war was over, women were forced back into subservience. The government was obsessed with replacing the lost population. It put men in women's jobs and bribed them to marry with a grant of de facto head-of-household status and preference in inheritance. Abortion was made illegal; unmarried and childless people were taxed; the legal and economic rights of women in de facto marriages were abolished; and divorce was made difficult and costly. As a result, people simply separated, but women no longer had rights as common-law wives. They lost the right to file paternity suits, and children born outside marriage were again stigmatized as illegitimate and denied inheritance. Women who had been rewarded for having large families now had trouble supporting them: 20 million Soviet men had been killed in the war and there were 150 women to every 100 men in the USSR. Fortunately, women did get child allowances – and larger ones if they were single.

When Stalin died in 1953, the terror waned but did not disappear from the Soviet Union. His successor, Nikita Khrushchev, released millions from prison camps and reformed laws governing women. He made divorce simpler and easier to get, legalized abortion, instituted maternity leave, and restored co-education, which Stalin had largely abolished in 1943. Couples were neither encouraged nor forbidden to live separately, and separate personal and property rights remained the norm. By 1967 the divorce rate was 2.7 (per 1000 inhabitants), higher than the divorce rate in the United States at the time. Most divorces were initiated by women, and some dialogue about women's position was permitted.

Women in the Late Soviet Period

Since I began this book, much has changed. There is no longer a Soviet Union, and the political situation changes daily. Before the Gorbachev revolution, life was hard in the Soviet Union, though, by any scale, people were better off than under the tsars. Like the tsars, the communists created intricate bureaucracies and forbade dissent by imprisoning, exiling, or executing dissenters. Still, no one starved under the communists, despite a scanty and monotonous diet. Medical care and education were free, and illiteracy was eradicated among people under sixty. Girls, encouraged to study for the competitive examinations for advanced education, made up 52.2 percent of university students in 1982. The Soviet Union had the highest percentage of women in the labour force of any modern industrial society (almost 90 percent), and more women in medicine, law, and engineering than any Western state. In 1970, over 50 percent of technicians and specialists, and 40 percent of veterinary surgeons, agronomists, and livestock experts, were women.

Soviet women were more likely than Western women to reach top positions – one was a space pilot, the highest scientific rank, and many were permafrost experts, the second-highest. Women were among the top mathematicians, and they made up about 12 percent of the managers in industry, agriculture, transportation, lumbering, and communications. Over 90 percent of Soviet women worked outside the home, making up 51 percent of the workforce. The law decreed equal pay for equal work, equality before the law and in the professions, free or low-cost child care, and free birth-control devices, information, and abortion.

Yet, like Western women, most women were ghettoized in low-paid jobs – in cleaning (women are 90 percent of the janitors in St. Petersburg), building, and railroad construction. Women were 49 percent of factory workers and 46 percent of manual workers, though less than a third of them used mechanical lifting equipment. Men, who justify male supremacy by men's superior physical strength, gave women the heaviest lifting and carrying jobs. If there was a machine to do a job, a man ran it, thereby earning more money and higher status. Rural men were twice as likely as women to have some higher education, and they monopolized the administrative positions on collective farms. In 1961 women made up about half of the farm workers but represented less than 2 percent of farm directors.

Educated women did not escape discrimination. After university, women were slotted into lower-paid professions and, at every level, earned less than men – about three-quarters as much (a higher percentage, however, than women earn in the United States). Medicine was numerically dominated by women but poorly paid – a good mechanic earned more. Only surgeons were well-paid, and most of them were men. The majority of clinic physicians were women, who often saw thirty patients a day; the heads of the polyclinics were men, who earned much more. Law also paid poorly, except for judges and prosecutors – and here, again, most were men. Female teachers taught the lower grades, and most of the higher-paid administrative jobs were given to men. Professions dominated by women – medicine and teaching – paid less than engineering, which was dominated by men. An anonymous writer in a feminist *samizdat* asserted that middle managers were concerned only with preserving their privileges. Although there were some really good men in science, most "just drink vodka." The worker on whom everything depended was a woman – who was paid less, commanded less prestige, and also had a home to care for.[19]

Women have a home to tend because women must marry, wrote Ekaterina Alexandrova.[20] In the Soviet Union, every citizen was under surveillance, had a file, and knew that private lives were discussed at political meetings. To change jobs, enter an educational program, or go abroad, people had to present reference cards from their place of work or study, with an evaluation by superiors according to standard criteria. A normal card read "politically mature, morally stable." If this phrase did not appear, the person became a third-class citizen with drastically curtailed opportunities. Someone who married and divorced five times or had many lovers was in no danger: such behaviour was not considered morally unstable. Someone interested only in drinking, sex, or sports was normal. But one who did not abide by regulations, who read books, or prayed outside of work was not normal. And for women, normality meant marriage – not to be married was shameful and degrading. To be divorced was better.

This situation was hardly unique to the Soviet Union: everywhere, discrimination prevents women from using their talents and keeps them poorer and lower in status than men. But Soviet women carried a unique burden: they were expected to maintain the family and to bear and raise children without help in a society in which domestic maintenance was a nightmare. Tatyana Mamonova, editor of the first feminist *samizdat*, described the elements of daily life in the Soviet Union.[21] Soviet refrigerators were tiny and few families owned one, so someone had to shop every day. That someone was almost always a woman. To shop, she had to visit many small stores containing little or nothing, queuing three times in each – to order her purchase, pay for it, and receive it. Wherever they were, whatever they were doing, women were always ready to drop everything and rush to a store rumoured to have, temporarily, scarce items like toilet paper, oranges, soap, or tub stoppers and to stand an hour or two in a queue with the net bag they always carried. Men usually lined up for alcohol; women were the food foragers. Some cities had no fresh food. Arkhangelsk, a busy port, frequently had no butter, meat, milk, sausage, cheese, or fish. The only available food was dried soup and cheap canned goods. Irkutsk, on Lake Baikal, the biggest freshwater lake in the world, had no fresh fish when I was there in 1983.

Many studies show that, in all industrial countries, women work much longer hours and get less sleep and leisure than men, but the situation was extreme in the USSR. Men tended to put in a desultory day's work, went home, and drank, or sat in front of the television while women rushed from queue to queue, then cooked, cleaned, washed, and cared for their children. Many women, feeling they had no more time or energy to give, stopped striving for better jobs (yet, according to national polls, only 20 percent of Soviet women would quit their jobs if they could afford to). A survey of housework in the USSR revealed that marketing, child care, and housework took 275 billion hours a year – 90 percent of the time spent on paid work in the entire national economy – and most of it was done by women.[22]

Men's salaries were so much higher than women's that women gained materially through marriage, and many said it was impossible for women to live singly: they had to be married. But some husbands drank up their wives' paycheques and contributed nothing to maintenance, expecting to be waited on by wife-servants. Soviet laws against wife-beating were stronger than in the West, but Soviet men had an extremely high rate of alcoholism and battering was rampant. No shelters existed for battered wives or rape victims, and most women simply did not report such abuse. Social pressure militated against it – domestic problems were women's fault.

Contraceptives were hard to find, crude, and ineffective. Diaphragms came in two sizes; condoms, called *galoshi*, resembled their name. Lack of contraceptives made abortion the major form of birth control – there were four to eight abortions for every live birth in the Soviet Union – and the procedure was savage. Doctors in abortion clinics did not use anaesthetics – some tied women to chairs. When Yekaterina Nikolayeva had an abortion, the male doctor shouted at her for staring at his bloodstained gloves and sneered at a woman in pain: "You should have had second thoughts before. You're all fond of sweets, but you're not willing to pay the price."[23] The Soviet Union's backwardness in gynecology was startling, since two Soviet physicians, Drs. Platonov and Velvovski, orginated the technique of prepared childbirth in the early 1950s and taught it to Lamaze, who introduced it to the West. Yet it was virtually unknown in the USSR, where women's needs were disregarded during childbirth.[24]

Some feminist Soviet women tried to start a women's movement with a *samizdat, Woman and Russia: An Almanac to Women*.[25] The journal grew out of informal meetings of feminist women in Leningrad in the fall of 1979. (It was difficult to network in the Soviet Union, where even telephone books were banned.) The editors asked for and wrote articles, typed them on a manual typewriter (mimeograph machines were illegal in the USSR), using carbons to get every ten copies. Binding them in heavy paper (hard to get in the USSR), adding exquisite handpainted illustrations, they sent them out into the world. Mamonova, one of the editors, wrote that they tried to represent the mass of women, not an elite group. They were essentialists, assuming that women have a distinct nature and that givers of life are "naturally" opposed to war and violence. Considering the differences between women and men to be profound, they did not advocate equality, but tried to describe the realities of women's lives and women's unhappiness with systemic discrimination. The only political position they took was to favour peace. The first issue was passed from hand to hand by women in Russia, Estonia, and the Ukraine.

The KGB interrogated and intimidated the editors, threatening arrest if they produced a second issue. The courageous Mamonova nevertheless produced one, entitled *Rossianka* (Russian Women). In 1980 she issued a third, which travelled as far as the Caucasus, the Urals, and Central Asia. The four leaders of the women's movement were exiled; the rest remained at home, where they continued to write under pseudonyms. Feminism was illegal in the USSR. Another group of women produced a *samizdat, Marija* (Mary), which advocated a religious feminism that offended Soviet authorities on two counts.

Many female Soviet dissenters were religious women. Soviet culture in general was essentialist, and the only discourse available to most people to describe the importance of affection, nutritiveness, and refreshment was that of religion. Soviet women who wanted to assert different values fell back on the language and values of a religion that made them subordinate. Dissident women had no place to turn: the government accused them of treason and counter-revolution, while dissident men belittled issues affecting women as frivolous and divisive. The dissident press, Mamonova held, was dominated by "sexist language of the coarsest sort." Only Andrei Sakharov supported women at all.

The defeat of communism and the break-up of the Soviet Union has led to a chaotic situation in what is, once again, Russia. In a mad rush to emulate capitalist economies, men nakedly seek money and power. In such conditions, social ideals vanish and hoodlums flourish. In 1989, in the freest multi-candidate elections since 1917, less than 15 percent of the Congress of People's Deputies were women; earlier, 33 percent of the Congress were women. When quotas were dropped for the 1990 election to the Parliament of the Russian Republic, the proportion of women dropped from 35.3 percent to 5.4 percent. In a pre-election poll by *Argumenti i Fakti*, voters felt one of the most important qualities in a candidate was "being a man." Reforms in the direction of Western-style capitalism make those who cannot work on the "fast track" obsolete – the disabled, older workers, and women. Women fear they will become dependent on their husbands and lose all benefits. In Soviet society, housing, health care, and pensions all devolved on one's job.

The Russian Revolution and its aftermath are paradigmatic of every revolution waged in the twentieth century. Women fight, struggle, sacrifice, take responsibility, follow orders, lead, suffer torture, and die along with men. They work, nurture their children, and hope for a new society. Both men and women have been disappointed by every revolution, but a fair percentage of men earned new status, became the new elite, and offered the state broad-based support. Women's status remained unchanged: women who gained were usually married to men who rose. In waged work, women gained more in socialist revolutions than others, but socialist revolutionaries, conceiving of humans mainly as producers, ignored the reproduction and maintenance (refreshment, re-creation) necessary for human life.

Since the fall of socialism in 1989, Russian women have become invisible in the Western press, which covered women mainly as markers in the contest between socialism and capitalism. At present, a small, embattled feminist movement exists in Russia, but there are problems. Women shun feminism, imagining that the Western version resembles the Soviet version – a hierarchy headed by an authority figure who determines the required dogma. A huge problem in today's Russia is surviving in a free-for-all economy devoted to greed. Slightly more women hold political office in Russia than in the United States, but only a few have taken advantage of the new money-grabbing economy. There is a very high male mortality rate (probably due to alcoholism compounded by poverty), and men scapegoat women for the present situation. Imagining that the USSR made good on its promises to women, they say, "This is what helping women got us!"[26]

In 1992 a law was proposed in the Parliament on the Protection of Family, Maternity, Paternity and Childhood, decreeing that women with children under fourteen would work part-time, thirty-five hours a week instead of forty, and that women with three or more children should be paid a minimum wage. It also mentioned the rights of unborn children. Feminists, fearing that abortion rights were being undermined, approached the deputies. These representatives told them the bill expressed a reaffirmation of the state's commitment to care for pregnant women and urged them to wait for public debate before criticizing it. When they asked Deputy Gleb Yakunin (a well-known democrat) if the bill did not discriminate against women, he dismissed them, shrugging, "Why do women matter?"

No public debate on the bill occurred, and the women were told that nothing they could do would amend or stop it. But they persisted, using all their organizational resources: they contacted the mass media, lobbied the democratic deputies in Parliament, published critiques in academic journals, and kept the buzz going. Their organization issued a critique of the draft. Finally, the controversial items were modified or deleted. After a barrage of negative letters, faxes, and telegrams, the draft was killed. Still, the Parliament removed abortion from the basic medical insurance coverage provided by the Ministry of Health, passed laws covering medical insurance and family planning, and set up a government program on safe motherhood without consulting any women's groups or allowing public debate.[27]

As has happened in other former socialist states in which women were guaranteed seats in governing bodies, the proportion of women in the central government body dropped from roughly 33 percent in the late 1970s to 5.6 percent after the democratic elections of 1991 (roughly the proportion in Western nations). Russians voting in December 1993 faced a list of parties ranging from nationalist and hard-line communist to pro-reform and social democratic, and a women's movement acting as a party concerned with health care and other social issues. Surprisingly, the women's movement managed to receive 8 percent of the votes, breaking the 5 percent barrier. Elizabeth Waters and Anastasia Posadskay comment that, a decade earlier, neither democratic elections nor the existence of a party dedicated to defending the interests of women was even conceivable.[28]

In the years since, the women's movement has grown more open and has split into segments devoted to special concerns. In major cities, groups have been founded to offer shelter to battered women, give rape counselling, and fight violence against women. Discussion of men's predations on women is more open than it has been in the past. The foundations of a strong movement are being laid.[29]

CHAPTER 12

REVOLUTION IN CHINA

THE WESTERN APPROPRIATION OF THE WORLD described in volume 2 of this series, *The Masculine Mystique*, extended to Asia as well, and, in different ways, the West took over China, Japan, India, and Southeast Asia. In 1800 China was ruled by an incompetent Manchu dynasty and a scholar-official bureaucracy, adamant about retaining the status quo. A comfortable cultivated elite scorned trade, which had once made the Chinese Empire powerful, but taxed and charged commissions on all foreign trade. Canton was the only legal port of exchange for exports and imports, which had to be conveyed overland five hundred miles to the capital, Beijing. China exported silk, tea, and cotton cloth; it severely limited imports, demanding payment in silver. Western traders seeking greater profit began to bring in opium.

The Chinese had long used opium as a medicine and, in the seventeenth century, began smoking it as a drug. The emperor forbade the practice, but by 1829 China consumed millions of pounds of domestic opium plus over 4 million pounds imported from abroad. This trade was illegal, and therefore not taxed by the state.

China tried to stop opium imports, claiming they drained the country of hard currency. The Canton viceroy closed his door to representatives of the British East India Company, which brought in most of the foreign opium. Outraged and determined to force China to abide by their rules of trade and diplomacy, the British started the "Opium War" in 1839. When it ended three years later, China was forced to cede Hong Kong to Britain, open four other ports to foreign trade, and grant rights of residence in Chinese cities to foreigners who had been given diplomatic privileges – mainly immunity against prosecution for importing opium. During the nineteenth century, foreigners demanded expanded privileges, which they abused by extortion, recruiting Chinese for near slave labour in America and giving light punishments to foreign offenders out of reach of Chinese law.

The Chinese did all they could to circumvent the treaties. Conflict inevitably arose, but the superior arms of the West always won. In 1858–60 a British-French alliance invaded China, drove the emperor to Manchuria, and burned the beautiful Manchu summer palace. They demanded entry to eleven ports, the right to travel throughout the country, Chinese protection for Christian missionaries, and a legalized opium traffic. The humiliated Chinese rulers, acting haughty and superior, took no action, but individual Chinese began agitating to reform the government and regain control of their country. In Korea and Japan, too, in this period, people agitated for reform, rebelling against greedy rulers. But only in China did men's demands for reform include women, especially for an end to footbinding. Some Chinese women had earlier resisted their society's constrictions, but their acts were remembered only in oral history. One such challenge had been a widespread movement early in the nineteenth century of women in a region of the Canton delta who refused to marry. They were not trying to reform marriage law, but simply refused to marry or cohabit with men.[1]

Women's situation had changed little since the seventeenth century. Still bought and sold, living as virtual slaves within their husbands' family compounds, women were excluded from the lineage until they bore a son; they had no voice except to bully their daughters-in-law. A woman's life was dictated by her economic class. As always, women of the gentry were most constricted, under constant surveillance, locked in parts of large houses and rambling court-yards. Servants shopped and marketed for them. The movements of peasant women were restricted and guarded too, but they could not be segregated in small peasant houses. When indoor light was poor, they sat on their doorsteps to work. Village women fetched water from wells, did laundry in rivers, spoke to shopkeepers and ped-dlers, and in some areas traditionally did field work with the men during busy seasons. The poorest women were most free – non-Han ethnic minorities, servants, boat-women, water-carriers, fuel gath-erers, and scavengers moved about freely.

For the first three years of her marriage, a woman was forbid-den to leave her courtyard: a traveller in nineteenth-century China found that tens of thousands of women had never been over two miles from their villages, and then only to marry. Chinese women said they lived like a "frog in a well": in the early twentieth century, one told an Englishman that, in her next life, she hoped to be a dog, for then she could come and go at will. One worker recalled that, after she and her sister reached the age of thirteen, they were for-bidden to walk on city streets and, if a stranger came to the door of their house, they had to vanish into an inner room. In the district where she lived, even visits by women were regulated: they were for-bidden to visit on the first or thirteenth day of a month; when they visited, they could not lean against the doorframe, stand or sit on the doorstep, or touch it in crossing. Any of these acts might give them power over the family and might ruin it because women were unclean. Such drastic prohibitions suggest that men had endowed women with enormous power.

Obsessed with female chastity, the Chinese deemed it desirable that men should never relate socially to women in public or at home: at seven years of age, boys and girls were segregated in the household, forbidden to sit or eat together. When inquiries were made about prospective daughters-in-law, the highest praise possible was to say, "We do not know, we have never seen her." A custom in a southeastern village illustrates the status of Chinese women: if a male visitor called out "Is anybody home?" when the man of the house was away, the woman was to reply: "No, nobody's at home."[2]

The feet of women who worked in the fields were not bound (they were called "Big Feet"), but the gentry bound their daughters' feet. A few wealthy fathers educated their daughters and gave them considerable latitude. Taoist cultists called "Boxers" taught their daughters martial arts. Minority (non-Han) generals trained their children as soldiers: the daughters often became rebels or bandits. Lower-class women in priestly or medical families became nuns, shamans, herbalists, or midwives. Hakka women (a non-Han minority) had freer, less subordinated lives.

Western incursions affected all Chinese. Western industries established in Chinese cities changed the nature of women's productive work and immeasurably worsened their working conditions. But Westerners also used the Asian treatment of women as a metaphor for backward barbarity. They were able to shame some Chinese men, who began to urge reform of laws governing women: an end to footbinding and concubinage, and a call for women to be educated and granted respect and a measure of power in families, especially elite families. These reformers discredited the Ming saying: "Only the virtuous man is talented; only the untalented woman is virtuous." They coined the term "women's liberation," exalting the "good wife, wise mother."

No matter how Westerners treated their own women, no matter how arrogant and patronizing their treatment of the Chinese, they did advance women's cause and later took credit for creating feminist traditions in China. They accepted girls in mission schools and offered urban girls intellectually challenging curricula. Mission schools, run by teachers independent, curious, and unconventional enough to work and live in a foreign place, sometimes demanded devotion to a particular brand of Christianity as the price of admission. But once women had been educated to see themselves as humans with rights, they soon conflicted with the men who had originally supported their education, men whose goals for them were limited.[3]

As the West tightened control over Chinese commerce, domestic upheavals threatened the Manchu dynasty. The most serious, the T'ai p'ing Rebellion, erupted in southern provinces with high unemployment, inflation, and poor harvests. In 1851 a scholar who had failed the civil service examination three times and who correctly believed that the Manchus discriminated against southern Chinese, created a political-religious movement to overthrow them. Merging elements of ancient Chinese religious beliefs, Christianity, and utopianism, the T'ai p'ing rebels advocated land redistribution, communal ownership of property, and sexual equality. Hakka women co-founded the revolutionary force, and the T'ai p'ing platform urged a ban on footbinding, opening the T'ai p'ing examinations (a kind of civil service exam) and official positions to women, abolishing concubinage and prostitution, and establishing monogamous marriage based on mutual love.

T'ai p'ing women organized a fighting corps whose mere presence was said to undermine the morale of the imperial armies facing them. The T'ai p'ing captured Nanking in 1853 and used it as their capital for the next eleven years. They were eventually defeated in 1864 with the help of Western powers, who preferred to deal with a weak, corrupt government than the socialist T'ai p'ings. But T'ai p'ing women had already been defeated by their own men, who, despite Hakka women's loud disapproval, had reverted to a double standard, taking concubines, yet requiring chastity in women. The T'ai p'ing movement is important for its ideals, which were forerunners of those of the Chinese communists.

As the nineteenth century drew to a close, China lost outlying possessions to Russia, France, Britain, Japan, and Portugal. In 1900,

Boxers (a Chinese political society) attacked Christians and foreigners in Shantung and other northeastern provinces. Britain, France, Germany, the United States, and Japan avenged attacks on their embassies by sending armies to occupy and loot Beijing. But they continued to prop up the Manchu government, extracting concessions from it. The partition of China by Russia, Germany, France, Italy, and America seemed inevitable.[4]

The Boxer Rebellion was as much a protest against Manchu rule as against foreign domination. Continued disruption forced the government to modernize the army and public education, abolish the civil service examination, and plan to institute a constitutional system. China escaped Africa's fate of partition because it was not fragmented into different political units. In addition, the Chinese had supreme confidence in the virtues of their own civilization. Suspicious and contemptuous of foreigners, few Chinese collaborated – and collaboration is basic to colonial rule. In 1904 Sun Yat-sen founded the revolutionary Nationalist Party, the Kuomintang (KMT), which accepted both women and men. (I use the initials KMT here because they are standard in older works on China. Kuomintang is now transliterated as Guomindang.)

The Republican Revolution, 1911

As the West increasingly penetrated China, its wealth, power, and stability and its principles of individualism, freedom, and self-fulfilment inspired the Chinese reform movement of 1898, the Republican Revolution of 1911, and, later, the May Fourth Movement of 1919. All attempted to redefine Chinese social and political institutions and to eject foreign dominators. Women and men were both influenced by the West. Women working in urban capitalist factories, no longer isolated, discussed foreign encroachment and Western ideas of rights. Women's movements began to try to win the right to a public role. Educated women opposed Confucian reformism, feeling that the entire Confucian system should go.

Ardently patriotic, wanting to redeem China from all foreigners, they refused to join the Japanese Patriotic Women's Society and turned their rage at their families into fervour for the anti-Manchu republican revolutionary movement. Feminism and nationalism were intrinsically connected because a new society, with women participating, was inconceivable in a Manchu and imperialist China. Many young women joined revolutionary parties.

Women had limited but conspicuous roles in the 1911 Revolution. When fighting erupted in the north, Canton boat-women went there to nurse revolutionary troops. Nurses were desperately needed at the front, so one of the few Chinese woman doctors called a meeting in Shanghai to exhort women to volunteer as Red Cross nurses. On only one day's notice, almost a hundred women showed up and, next day, thirty or forty left for the front – but not with the Red Cross. The doctor recalled: "We were so angry, because the Red Cross in Shanghai said these men you call rebels are only thieves and robbers, bad men, they will not be grateful! But we knew they were brothers, our patriots, our homes. We *must* go help!" She founded the White Heart Society to do similar work, and her nurses remained at the front despite its horrors.

Women like Sophia Chang (who took her first name from the Russian revolutionary Sophia Perovskaia) carried messages, arms, and ammunition; she was the heiress of a rich merchant and gave her life and her father's wealth to the cause. Jin Jilan, a famous actress, was beheaded for spreading rebellion among the people after many years of using her income and contacts in the United States to purchase arms for the revolution. A Japanese journalist called the women arrested during the Canton uprising in 1911 "veritable walking arsenals," compared to whom "the militant London suffragette is nothing." (Obviously, the militance of the British suffragists had impressed much of the world.) The "modern Chinese woman daily . . . supplies arms and ammunition to her brother revolutionaries and is occasionally arrested with her tunic lined with dynamite." Soumay Cheng joined a KMT auxiliary, the

Beijing "Dare to Die" corps, formed to kill people considered obstacles to the creation of a new democratic government. They transported explosives in suitcases and in coat linings. Cheng volunteered to carry dynamite or bombs, thinking a girl would draw little notice. For months, she travelled twice a week back and forth from Tiensin to Beijing, lugging suitcases of explosives.

The most celebrated woman revolutionary, Qiu Jin (1875–1907), was born to gentry, classically educated, and became a poet. Her nutritive mother trained her to be independent but could not prevent her being married against her will to a wealthy landlord's son. He bought an official position in Beijing. As literature spread ideas of democracy and nationalist revolution, Qiu Jin became interested in politics. Having resented women's restrictions from her youth, she identified women's oppression by men with China's oppression by a Manchu dynasty servile to foreign interests. Offended by the corrupt luxury of official life in Beijing and by her husband's attitudes, she left him and her two children in 1904. She sold her jewellery to raise money to join Chinese students studying in Japan, where Chinese revolutionary organizations flourished. There Qiu Jin wore a man's long gown and black leather shoes, combing her hair back in a man's queue.

Returning to China, she became the first woman to join the KMT – with her mother's moral and economic support. She accepted a position as a schoolteacher in Shanghai and politicized her pupils and scandalized society by riding horseback astride and having female students do military drill. She founded China's first feminist newspaper, *The Chinese Women's Journal*, and wrote poems filled with outrage at male domination. Assuming the name "Qinxiong" ("compete with men"), she sometimes dressed in Western male gear with a jaunty cloth cap. She engineered a number of uprisings, which exploded prematurely and were put down, but her feminism and revolutionary enthusiasm aroused such animosity that she was arrested within a year. Under torture, she agreed to confess and said: "Autumn rain and autumn wind sadden us."

Beheaded at thirty-three in 1907, she became a Chinese martyr.[5]

The Nanking assembly voted to abolish the monarchy and establish a republic, and it elected Sun as president. He ceded the office to General Yüan Shi-k'ai, a pivotal figure who eased the Manchus out of power. Sun's party, renamed the Kuomintang, controlled Parliament; as it drafted a constitution, women revolutionaries pressured it for suffrage and full participation in politics.

In 1912 Tang Junying, a student who had returned from Japan, founded the Chinese Suffragette Society, which attracted mainly educated urban women who had participated in the republican revolution. Their program, aimed at easing the lot of all Chinese women, included suffrage and an end to footbinding, concubinage, child marriage, and prostitution. It called for female education, the creation of social services for women in industry, and raising the position of women within the family. To further these aims, the society set up schools, staffing them with its own members, and published a paper with poems, reports on foreign feminist movements, and articles on women's issues. It put out two versions – one in the language of the educated; the other in the popular vernacular.

Most activists were privileged – wives or daughters of male reformers and revolutionaries – or were teachers or students in the new schools. Only these women had the education needed for the confidence to protest, and the personal property (jewellery) to support it. They operated mainly in schools in Beijing, Shanghai, Canton, or Tientsin. Like the American Revolution, the Chinese republican revolution was a middle-class uprising, lacking a program to improve conditions for peasants. Sun was no democrat, and he believed that military rule was necessary to establish order in China. Only after the elite prepared the people could representative government evolve. Sun Yat-sen went down in history as the Father of the Revolution, but woman revolutionaries were later accused of "feminist reformism" for ignoring the needs of rural peasant women.

The new constitution made women citizens for the first time in Chinese history. It ordered education for girls, but granted them no political or social rights. Suffragists protested and forced their way into the House to get the president's attention, smashing windows and attacking military guards. The next day the Beijing Women's Suffrage Association marched to the Assembly House to demand women's rights: the men were so frightened that they called troops to protect them. The Suffragette movement was the first organized collective expression of feminism in China.[6] It was too small to affect the Assembly, but its example inspired provincial women to petition their own legislatures.

In 1913 General Yüan Shi-k'ai, who had never been a republican, asserted dictatorial powers, harshly suppressing reformist and revolutionary groups and banning all political activity. He dissolved suffragist unions and routinely executed women who kept their revolutionary weapons. Wanting a "strong man" who would keep the country weak, Western powers supported Yüan Shi-k'ai until he died in 1916. Then women again took military action and joined the National Army or the Assassination Corps, dressing and equipping themselves as men. China was still riven by oppressive warlords who contested for power when the Allies pressured China to declare war on Germany in 1917. But the Allies humiliated China at the Paris Peace Conference, treating it like a vanquished nation. Women students, outraged by this treatment as well as by their own, led a historic demonstration in Beijing on May 4, 1919 – the first massive manifestation of a moral revolution to uproot Confucianism and its three bonds of obedience. Students organized to eliminate Confucianism and imperialism, and to fight for nationalism and feminism in a movement named for its starting date.

The May Fourth Movement

In 1919 Chao Wu-chieh of Nanyang Street, Changsha, was prepared for a marriage against her will. Introduced to the husband her parents had chosen, she loathed him and refused. They forced her to don the elaborate Chinese wedding costume and sit in the ceremonial chair that would carry her to her husband's family home, where she would spend the rest of her life. As the chair was lifted, Chao Wu-chieh slid a dagger she had hidden from under its cushion and slit her throat.

It was not a remarkable event – in fact, such protests occurred regularly. But Chao's suicide happened during an emotional period in the life of a remarkable young man, Mao Zedong, who was not yet a Marxist. During the May Fourth movement, Mao wrote nine impassioned articles about Chao Wu-chieh, protesting the system that martyred her. Perhaps like Homer's maidens, he was weeping for himself. Mao had a loving nutritive mother but a despotic father, who bought an older girl as Mao's bride when he was a boy. This too was common: men bought girls to get work out of them until a son came of age and married her – slave and wife at once. When the time came for marriage, Mao ran away. When he was forcibly returned, he fought his father and did not marry the woman. Chao's suicide led Mao to connect the personal and the political.

The May Fourth Movement was a rebellion of youth against age and authority. Love and sex (called "the woman question") lay at its heart and were raised in almost every issue of a huge number of new periodicals, social critiques, and popular fiction that were now written in the vernacular. Profoundly critical of the traditional Chinese family structure, anarchist intellectuals of the May Fourth generation – feminist men like Li Ta-chao, Ch'en Tu-hsiu, and Mao Tse-min (Mao Zedong's younger brother) – advocated free choice in marriage, free love instead of chastity (for themselves), and divorce. Seeing only wretchedness in married life, Cai Zhang (Tsai Chang, who later led a national women's movement), her brother, and Mao Zedong vowed to remain single: some experimented with communal living. Mao optimistically wrote:

If we launch a campaign for the reform of the marriage system we must first destroy all superstitions, of which the

most important is destruction of the belief in "predestined
marriage." Once this belief is abolished, all support for the
policy of parental arrangement will be undermined . . . the
army of the family revolution will arise *en masse*, and a great
wave of freedom of marriage and freedom of love will break
over China.[7]

Male domestic tyranny was increasingly scorned by literate
urbanites. Ding Ling, one of China's most famous writers, attended
the Girls' Normal School in Changsha, a traditional school whose
"energetic, enthusiastic and unrestrained" students were eager to try
out every new idea they encountered. Society in this period, both
west and east, strongly disapproved of bobbed hair, for women's
long hair was symbolic. But as soon as they heard of it, the students
held a secret cutting session: eighty girls cut their hair and stood in
the street weeping over China's humiliation by foreign powers (they
were later killed because of this incident). The May Fourth
Movement resulted in women gaining access to education, the professions, and public office.

But some women opposed it. Hsiang Ching-yu had attended
Changsha's most progessive girls' school and had organized a co-
educational primary school aimed at inculcating missionary zeal for
sexual egalitarianism and anti-hierarchical thinking. She went to
France on a work-study program, where she supported herself by
factory work in a rubber plant and textile mill. Learning about proletarian life by living it and by studying anarchist, Marxist, and
social-democratic thought, she pronounced the May Fourth
Movement a "bourgeois fight of women against men" and argued
that women could be emancipated only by a socialist revolution.
Others, reaching the same conclusion, organized the Chinese
Communist Party (CCP) in Shanghai in 1921.

Civil War

Hsiang, her husband, and others in their work-study group joined the CCP from France. Its leaders were overwhelmingly male, except for a few intellectuals like Hsiang and Teng Ying-ch'ao, who married Chou En-lai in 1925. Unlike May Fourth anarchists, Chinese communist men were dyed in their society's age-old contempt for women and scorned women's rights groups, even those organizing women workers. After Hsiang returned from France in 1922, the CCP named her the first female Central Committee member and the head of a newly founded Women's Department modelled on the Soviet Zhenotdel. Hsiang was the kind of woman they could accept: always critical of feminism in China, she was exclusively concerned with organizing women workers. She was said to have organized over 100,000 women in Shanghai, Canton, and Hong Kong between 1922 and 1925. The party ignored female Shanghai cotton mill workers: in 1927 women made up 52 percent of Shanghai workers and 15 percent of party members, but no woman leader in the labour movement was a worker.

Loyalties were ambivalent in 1920s China. The non-communist Sun Yat-sen accepted the CCP into the KMT because he needed it: foreign domination was growing and the central government was challenged by regional warlords who had to be subdued one by one. As Western capitalism created new economic relations in growing cities, new classes emerged and the rural economy declined. Communist organizers from the USSR mobilized a revolutionary force of those who were angry with the corrupt warlords, with China's subservience to foreigners, and with the rigid hierarchical society. The CCP was controlled by Moscow, where Hsiang went to study Marxist-Leninist thought. Returning in 1927, she organized labour contingents in the Shanghai area. In 1923 the CCP joined a united front with the KMT.

The United Front wanted to maintain China's integrity and reform social, political, and economic structures, but it deferred reform until after it had defeated regional warlords and established a strong central government. It integrated the women's movement into the nationalist revolutionary movement by setting up a Central Women's Department. This linking of feminism to politics marked a turning point in the history of Chinese feminism. Trying to draw women to the revolutionary movement and pressure the government to legislate basic rights for females, the Women's Department successfully extracted resolutions from the KMT in 1924 and 1926 to enact laws decreeing free marriage, divorce, equal pay for equal work, and equality between the sexes; other laws granted women inheritance rights, prohibited trade in persons, and protected women who fled marital oppression. Its strategy was to train women to organize other women in the cities and the countryside.

Chinese industry was controlled mainly by Western capitalists, who worked women in silk and cotton mills of Shanghai, Tientsin, and Canton for twelve hours a day, seven days a week, for 12 to 15 cents a day. Most workers were indentured. Poor families rented their daughters to factory owners for part of their wages; owners provided their fare to the factory along with room and board. Many Shanghai women were involved in the labour movement at the grassroots level, some as organizers. Of all the unskilled workers in Shanghai, only female textile workers, male miners, and dockers dared to strike for better working conditions.

After Sun Yat-sen died in 1925, the young Chiang Kai-shek took over command of the United Front armies. Charging north from his base in Guandong (Canton) province in the "Northern Expedition," he conquered half of China's provinces and eventually become the political as well as the military head of the KMT. The United Front planned the Northern Expedition to politicize women as it traversed the countryside in a nation where four-fifths of the population were peasants. The Women's Department sent female organizer teams – women's unions three hundred or four hundred strong – after the armies of the Northern Expedition to instruct women on the revolution and their rights. They investigated women's complaints and helped girls who had been sold into prostitution by their parents, widowed daughters-in-law whose inlaws intended to sell them, girls about to be married against their will, and abused women and slaves. They provided refuge to oppressed women, and sometimes held kangaroo courts to try husbands for abuse. They marched convicted men through town in dunce caps, while the women followed shouting feminist slogans.

Male peasants, outraged by unstunted women – "big feet" – moving freely through the world and their villages, hated the women's unions for supporting women's rights, curbing their prerogatives, and helping women to divorce. Women, after all, were property. Older women who had developed ways to cope with oppression were also alarmed by the unions, which offended their sense of propriety and seemed to threaten their survival.[8] CCP men too grew wary of the women's unions: they considered men more important than women, feared men's default, and declined to risk it.[9] Mao Zedong supported the male CCP members and deplored acts that eroded "peasant" support (that is, male support), arguing that women would be liberated automatically once communists altered the political and economic structures. The separate struggle for women was unnecessary. However limited the CCP's liberation of women, it was enough to fuel KMT hostility for the party. When Chiang Kai-shek campaigned during the White Terror to wipe out the CCP in 1927, he focused mainly on women – leftists, CCP or KMT members, or those who had adopted "modern" ways. He terminated the KMT Women's Department. His soldiers stripped women who were wearing men's clothes to the waist and paraded them publicly, so "every man in town may see she is in reality a woman," before they killed them. They hunted down women with bobbed hair and shot them. In Canton they wrapped women considered CCP members in gasoline-soaked blankets and burned them alive. Everywhere, KMT agents or troops physically mutilated women, hacking off their noses or breasts and raping them before they murdered them.

In 1930 a KMT Civil Code granted women the right to choose their own husbands, apply for divorce, and inherit property. Adultery was made a crime for both men and women. Protective legislation for factory women would, it was claimed, lead in time to equal pay for equal work. Once this was done, male educators and officials declared that women were emancipated and announced there was no further need for them to engage in politics. Unlike American and European women, they claimed, Chinese women no longer had to fight male opposition. "Politics" became a code for communist doctrine.

The KMT attack on the CCP split China into two zones, one ruled by Chiang Kai-shek and the KMT; the other by Mao Zedong and the CCP. In 1928 the CCP made development of women's unions secondary to that of peasant (male) associations. The next year it retreated to rural Kiangsi, where it founded a soviet that the KMT tried to encircle. The party mobilized for war. Aware of rural men's hard-core opposition to women's liberation, it exhorted women not to join the army. Rather, they should urge men to join the CCP forces and take over the men's field work. Trade unions organized women into rear-guard defence units and encouraged them to sew for the army at the end of their day's work. A few women joined the army, but the CCP did not recruit them.

Still, the Kiangsi soviet passed radical marriage laws beneficial to women, banning infanticide, footbinding, prostitution, and tyrannical mothers-in-law. It granted free instant divorce to women and men, and it allowed divorced women property rights, land allotment, half of any property accrued during marriage, and custody of young children. Since poor women were entitled to their former husbands' farm work as economic support, divorce became economically feasible for them. And, because the laws required marriage and divorce to be registered, these events came under state control for the first time in China. Gradually, even accidentally, bureaucratization and centralization replaced tradition. Kiangsi women were politically active, making up 30 percent of the representatives to district congresses in 1930, and 64 percent in 1932.

The new laws and Kiangsi women's politicization provoked enormous male resistance. CCP cadres (official units) not only refused to enforce the new laws but punished women who asked for divorce. As the KMT campaign intensified, the CCP tried to boost men's morale by curtailing soldiers' wives' right to divorce (most young women were married to soldiers) and requiring a man's consent to a wife's application for divorce (a requirement that remained law even after the situation changed). Though CCP marriage laws were radical for their time, and special consideration for soldiers in wartime is understandable, this action was part of a longterm CCP tendency to sacrifice women to the "revolution."[10] A revolution that sacrifices women is a male fight – and should be so regarded.

In 1931 Japan invaded China's northeastern provinces (Manchuria), without formally declaring war until 1936. War with Japan exposed Chiang Kai-shek's (and his KMT government's) ambivalence about women and the women's movement. The moment war broke out, women were exhorted to pressure sons, husbands, and fathers to take up arms, and they were mobilized to take an active part themselves. Madame Chiang broadcast the first of many appeals:

> We women are citizens just as much as are our men. Our positions, our capabilities, and our lines of usefulness may be different, but we can contribute our share. . . . Today in Spain, women are standing in the fighting lines with their men; and during the Great War in every country they gave their best to aid in the realisation of victory. We Chinese women are not one bit less patriotic or less courageous or less capable of physical endurance than our sisters of other lands, and that we shall now show the world.

Women responded, forming their own fighting battalions and a War Service Corps that provided back-up services and fighters. The

Japanese were occasionally astonished to find their opponents female.

In the chaotic climate of 1934, the KMT tried to create some stability by a nationwide campaign – the New Life Movement. It re-canonized Confucius and traditional family virtues. It upheld unquestioned (unquestionable) rules defining correct relationships between rulers and ruled, generations, and the sexes. Chiang's program ignored the country's profound crisis and offered a familiar nostrum for social ills – return to the traditional family. Since the family is the primary locus of societal power struggles, and the "traditional family" is patriarchal, this method attempted to restore order by propping up absolute male power.[11]

Ignoring Japanese encroachment, Chiang directed his energies and resources to a fierce drive to eradicate Chinese communism. In October 1934 the KMT encirclement forced the CCP out of Kiangsi. It began a northward march to link up with other communist units. The Long March, which ended in October 1935, involved 100,000 men and 30–50 women: women with stunted feet could not march and stayed behind to till the land. They were killed by the KMT. In 1937 Japan launched a massive invasion of China, forcing the KMT and the CCP into a union that lasted uneasily until Japan's defeat in 1945. During this period, the CCP pattern of sacrificing women's goals to men's became entrenched: when Ding Ling exhorted the party to attack sexist attitudes in cadres and comrades, she was relieved of all official duties for two years. In 1943 the CCP formally foreclosed discussion of female social and political inequality.

During the war years, many Chinese women began working in textiles. Japanese occupation and a KMT blockade cut off cloth imports, and Mao urged women to spin, weave, and sew. By 1947, areas in CCP control were self-sufficient in cloth. Women cloth producers usually worked together, breaking the age-old prohibition against women leaving the domestic compound. Talking to each other politicized women, who eventually organized Women's

Associations and began to speak publicly. The CCP reformed land ownership when it expelled the Japanese from a territory. The party took land from landlords and gave it not to "families" (men) but to people – women and men. For the first time in over a thousand years, Chinese women had something of their own. Those who had never done field work began to do it, using their new self-sufficiency to escape abuse: 64 percent of all civil cases in CCP-controlled areas of northern China between January and June 1948 were divorce petitions, most of them made by women. Statistics suggest a turbulent reality in this territory in this period: of the 464 women who died violently, 40 percent, wanting divorces, were unable to get them and were either murdered or committed suicide.

The Chinese drove the Japanese out in 1945, but the Chinese people had no respite: like Soviet people, caught in the First World War, then revolution and civil war, the Chinese were caught in revolution, the Sino-Japanese War (the Second World War), then civil war. The War of Liberation took four years: when the People's Republic of China was established in 1949, women were among those on the presidium and they helped to write the new constitution. They made up 14 percent of the delegates elected by popular vote of the People's Congress in 1954 and up to 40 percent of elected officials in some districts; some headed town governments. The All-China Women's Federation formed in the spring of 1949 was perhaps the largest and most active single mass organization ever formed.[12] With 76 million members (the CCP had 11 million), it worked to support, unify, and direct thousands of Women's Associations across the country to teach women economic self-reliance and solidarity. In time, however, the Women's Federation became defensive about male opposition and stopped intervening to protect women's interests, especially if they conflicted with economic priorities.

The People's Republic of China

Under Mao Zedong, the Chinese Communist government made a serious effort to end the subordination of some men to others, and of women to men. With slogans like "Women hold up half of heaven" and "Anything a man can do a woman can do also," programs were established to redefine female roles and to give women equal status with men in both public and domestic spheres. The government used a three-prong strategy – passing equal rights laws, introducing women into production, and organizing them in their own interests.[13]

Among the Communist government's first acts was passing the Marriage Law and various labour and land laws. The first forbade extreme forms of abuse and reduced men's and kin-groups' power to control women in marriage and divorce; the latter gave women access to land and the right to work for wages and in political institutions. Entire communities opposed widow remarriage, but it was mainly men who opposed divorce. Land reform laws gave women the right to a share of family land when they left their husbands, so men often killed wives who planned to leave them. In regions where land reforms were not yet legalized, divorced women could not support themselves: either way, women suffered. Chinese women faced a long tradition upheld by men who did not consider them *jen* (human): Mao often reiterated that women were *jen* in his pamphlets on Chao Wu-chieh. The government made massive efforts to persuade people to obey the new Marriage Law, publishing and broadcasting propaganda condemning the old patriarchal system and advocating equal sexual relationships, and sending thousands of acting troupes to villages to dramatize the issues and offer literacy classes. Peasant women were shy of speaking in public and peasant men opposed change, so in every village cadres held meetings urging women to "speak bitterness" against men and mothers-in-law. They also singled out model couples for praise.

Believing that the expansion of women's economic opportunities was the most effective instrument of liberation, Communist officials adopted a number of strategies. First, they extended and reorganized production, separating it from the household in state-run industries and city workers' cooperatives. These enterprises employed almost the entire urban labour force, much of it female and full-time. Women adopted occupations previously held for men. A small group of carefully chosen women was trained for high-profile jobs, and successful women were publicized through awards at huge meetings and recognition in newspaper articles and documentary films. Among the acclaimed were steel workers in Anshan, train crews that drove, stoked, fired, and guarded trains, as well as pilots, lumberjacks, and crane drivers. Their example heartened countless women to seek jobs they might otherwise have shied from. Today women are highly visible in medicine, engineering, light industry, and service occupations.

Second, land reform gave peasant women at least putative independence. The knowledge that they owned land and could divorce or survive widowhood gave them an unprecedented sense of power. Sayings like "Marry a man, clothes to wear, food to eat" or "If you come, I shall feed you. If you go, you can take nothing with you" no longer described women's status. But in 1955 the Chinese government, imitating Stalin, imposed collectivism, set up communes, and encouraged women to engage in production equally with men. This standard is, of course, impossible for a sex that bears and rears children; moreover, neither sex had confidence in women workers. Most peasant women entered the collective in some capacity, but their involvement gave them a voice primarily in family decisions – on what crop to plant in their private plots, how to spend their money, or ways to solve domestic problems.

The third strategy for redefining women was creating separate women's organizations. Groups were established in cities, towns, villages, and the countryside to guard women's well-being, represent them in local community and larger political bodies, and help them acquire new skills. But no policy could dislodge women's oppression in the family – the seat of their first, crucial, formative experience. The Chinese government under Mao Zedong was unique in making serious efforts to empower women. In 1957 it launched a "Hundred Flowers" campaign to re-educate people about the responsibility for maintaining households, to pressure men to do half the work, and to allow women to register formal complaints with the government. But without day nurseries and jobs in newly established industries, women had few options. The next year Mao announced the Great Leap Forward, an ambitious program that urged women to work in construction, heavy industries like iron smelting, agriculture, and experimental agriculture, and tool research and development. It also founded rural People's Communes, which paid people according to their labour, and government-subsidized community facilities to help women with "their" responsibilities for raising children, supplying and preparing food, doing laundry, sewing, and other maintenance.

During this campaign, nearly a hundred million women joined the industrial labour force; others were forced to work in small-scale handicraft enterprises. Local service facilities appeared at a breathtaking rate: nurseries, collective dining rooms, laundries, and sewing and other service centres were hastily set up throughout the country.[14] But most were short-lived, closing as abruptly as they opened, without explanation. Some services survived, mainly in cities, but by the late 1970s they were spotty, not nearly fulfilling demand. The Great Leap Forward tried to substitute labour for capital, and the collective for the family, in a massive effort to transform China into an industrial society overnight. It was the most intense concerted effort ever made by any government to mobilize women in the labour force and, simultaneously, to reduce their double burden. It ended in economic disaster and a famine in which, China now admits, millions died. In this period, too, the government ignored male domination in homes and workplaces.

The Cultural Revolution of 1966, a complex, multifaceted political movement, was not concerned with women. Rather, Mao wanted to shake up oppressive power structures. He directed women to unite to oppose authoritarian bureaucracies and men's rule in the home; he urged them to study, organize, and criticize their families. As one critic expressed it: "It should no longer be a matter of who is supposed to speak and who is supposed to obey in a family, but a matter of whose words are in line with Mao Zedong's thoughts."[15] But authoritarianism cannot be ended by authoritarianism. Mao undermined his goal by replacing husbands' or fathers' authority with his own. He still expected women to obey. His egalitarian intentions were reduced to slogans as the government increased the personal pressures on women: it demanded that women play a man's role, yet gave them only rhetorical support. The Cultural Revolution's anti-authoritarian and anti-bureaucratic thrust propelled some women into high-profile, but short-lived, positions of power, while victimizing female intellectuals and leaders, who were criticized, demoted, physically assaulted, and imprisoned. Surveys from the mid-1970s showed women still doing most of the domestic labour. Nothing budged men's demand that women, whether working for wages or not, bear responsibility for maintenance and reproduction.

Women in Contemporary China

Communism vastly improved life for most Chinese. The Chinese government paid more attention to social needs like housing, medical care, and education than did the rulers of the Soviet Union. It subsidizes all housing in cities and provides social services free; peasants build their own houses and pay for medical care, but it is low-cost and generally good. Just over 76 percent of Chinese are literate. Women benefited from such improvements and from policies specifically directed at them: they hold jobs barred to them twenty years ago and have a voice in politics, if mainly at the local level. The Women's Federation keeps women visible nationally. The Communist government is repressive, but less so than the family control women lived under in the past.

But 70 percent of China's illiterate are female, and few women are in decision-making posts. Most prominent women are leaders' wives or women who deal with cultural affairs. Few women do even middle-level administration. The traditional division of labour remains unchanged, and women are paid less than men who do the same work. Only in conspicuous, usually male-held, jobs or in "female" professions are they paid equally with men, but they are not promoted at the same rate. Most female peasants and factory workers are confined to less-skilled jobs in lighter (not physically less demanding) industries, doing the most repetitive, unspecialized, unmechanized work. Urban women predominate in service, textile, food processing, and cooperative factories, while men dominate in the more skilled, mechanized, and higher-paid sectors. The same pattern occurs in the countryside, but where many men have been given jobs with more prestige and higher pay, women have been allowed a wider variety of agricultural tasks. A new division of labour has arisen in rural areas: men hold almost all the administrative and political jobs except the urban neighbourhood committees, which are made up largely of older retired community women.

Since marriage remains patrilocal in rural China, families and communities continue to prefer sons to daughters. Young men are welcomed into training programs and leadership positions: they have always lived in the village, worked on production teams, and are often related. Daughters leave the household and natal community at marriage, so parents and communities see no economic advantage in educating or training them. Single women, considered temporary residents, are discouraged from learning unusual skills when they leave school and are assigned jobs. Newly arrived wives need time to build up support networks. For all these reasons, women face great barriers in joining the political decision-making process. Sons remain to farm the land and care for aging parents: the only way labour can be recruited for the household is by a son getting married. Parents continue to try to control their children's marriages, and the sedan chair – the symbol of appropriation of a woman by a man's family – is still used in the countryside.[16]

Programs encouraging women to work in political or collective decision-making, which is often unpaid, failed because, in China, as in other states, the sexual division of labour in the household is unbalanced. No one can manage a household, hold a job, and do unpaid political work too. The work of rural women, who fetch water and fuel, produce and process food, is so overwhelming that many cannot work for wages, much less do unpaid political work.

China, a communist state subject to capitalist hostility, has, like the Soviet Union, felt compelled to spend its resources mainly on industrial and weapons development and to defer welfare programs, which most help women. Moreover, concentration on production lessens attention to reproduction and basic human needs. Pressing women to work in production, the Chinese government gave little thought to how they could work long hours and still care for children and maintain families. Socialist states exploit women's unpaid labour to subsidize their growth.

Since 1978, ideology has been eclipsed by "modernization," as China's leaders try to establish a market and increase productivity. The policy changes of most moment for women have been a new land policy and stringent limits on family size. The government now allocates farmland to peasant households rather than collectives. Since peasant families are still patriarchal and consider land the men's property, this policy has injured some women.

China's family limitation law is draconian. With a population of nearly a billion in a country with only 15 percent arable land, the government's anxiety is understandable, but people resent being allowed only one child. Resentment is so intense that the state modified the law in rural areas to allow two children. But the burden of birth control is usually placed on women, and preference for sons leads to violence against women who give birth to daughters and a resurgence in infanticide. That such events still occur after decades of campaigns for sexual equality is deeply disturbing, and the

Women's Federation has intensified discussion of women's issues. It is now more able to intervene actively in government policy on behalf of women.

Oppressive traditions persist. In 1989 women were still being sold as wives in China: tens of thousands in over twenty of China's thirty provinces and autonomous regions, 30,000 in Shandong province, and over 48,000 in Xuzhou in the years just preceding 1989. Wife-purchase was rampant in rural areas of Shandong, Hebei, Sichuan, and Henan, but local officials are loath to discuss it, insisting it is rare in their areas. The practice of wife-selling increased when social controls were eased in the countryside and people sought new ways to make money. Wife-selling involves a chain of abductors passing women through the country. After selling human beings was outlawed and peasants no longer had to buy wives at high prices, the cost of rural weddings rose. A wedding can cost $25,000, whereas a black-market wife costs only $500 to $800. It is unclear whether these wives have legal rights and, if so, whether local authorities would honour them.[17]

Despite women's significant presence, press coverage of the 1989 uprising in China focused on men, except for a nameless middle-aged woman caught by a television camera walking bravely into the path of a tank entering Tiananmen Square and standing still. But many women were imprisoned for daring to speak out for democracy, like Long Xianping, a professor at Xiangtan University, and Dai Qing, a prominent intellectual, reporter, and columnist for the *Guangming Daily*, a national intellectual newspaper based in Beijing.[18] Dai co-drafted a petition for more press independence and for direct talks between government propaganda officials and journalists to discuss the matter. She wrote a long study of Chu Anping, a free-press advocate damaged in Mao's 1957–58 intellectual purge, and articles arguing for the release of political prisoners. The first citizen to protest the ruining of China's environment, she launched a campaign against the Three Gorges project – a dam that, depending on its final size, will inundate between 11,000 and

114,000 acres of farmland along the Yangtze River, forcing nearly a million people to resettle.

Dai is not a Western-style liberal. She advocates what is called the "New Authoritarianism," the dictatorship of an ideal Confucian (strong, enlightened) ruler. Dictators in Taiwan, Singapore, and South Korea believe this description fits them; CCP leaders also like this image. But their attitude towards Dai changed when she publicly expressed sympathy for the students in Tiananmen Square – the first important intellectual to do so. Then on May 14, 1989, just before the first Chinese-Soviet summit in a generation, she begged the students to leave and seemed to withdraw from the movement. (We do not know if she was being pressured.) The students felt she had betrayed them, but so did the government. She resigned from the CP when the government suppressed the uprising on June 4. Seized by the police in mid-July and held incommunicado for months, she became a political prisoner in the infamous Qincheng Prison. The government claimed that her urging the students to leave was a pretext, that she was actually inciting them to make trouble. She was released in May 1990 and was offered prestigious posts abroad. Eventually she returned to China to agitate against the Three Gorges dam. The future of China, which has imposed repressive controls on speech, while allowing some forms of capitalism, is unpredictable.

The growth of a market economy in China enables some women to earn more and have more autonomy. But it also intensifies old problems, like prostitution, pornography, traffic in women, pressure on women to kill their female babies, and abuse of rural women who bear girls. Discrimination against women has also increased in state jobs and political life.

The All-China Women's Federation (ACWF), established in 1949, has continued its work, along with a coordinating committee on women and children set up in 1990 in the State Council. Twenty state agencies are represented on it, and the committee has power and authority to mobilize resources to work for women's benefit.

One of its projects, since 1989, has been a literacy and technical training campaign among rural women; by 1993 it had trained 120 million rural women, and 410,000 had earned the title of agronomist. In cities, non-governmental organizations address issues that are pressing for women. In Beijing, for example, women can find marriage and family counselling, a women's hotline, a singles' club (most members are educated women), and classes for teenage girls in understanding the changes they are undergoing. Also, the women's press has greatly expanded, and it is vital in documenting gender inequality and giving women a forum. More than forty magazines and newspapers focusing on women's issues are in open circulation, and the press has become increasingly vocal in exposing sex discrimination and supporting women's interests.[19]

CHAPTER 13

FASCIST REVOLUTION
IN GERMANY AND ITALY

A FTER THE FIRST WORLD WAR, men granted women suffrage in
Britain, the United States, Germany, Sweden, Latvia,
Lithuania, Estonia, and the states carved out of the old Austro-
Hungarian empire (Hungary, Austria, Czechoslovakia, Yugoslavia,
Romania, and Poland). Italy and France continued to deny women
rights: Catholics and socialists each feared that women would sup-
port the other. French women did not win the vote until 1944;
Italian women, until 1946.

Women gained political rights, but they were economically
marginal.[1] In Germany, improved working conditions in industry
drew labourers from the countryside; in France, oppressive landlord
traditions and inefficient farming methods drove workers to cities.
Farm workers, who were still virtual serfs, and war veterans
thronged to the cities, seeking better lives. In regions where agriculture was modernized, only men attended schools teaching new
agricultural technology; where it became big business, men claimed
that males would not accept female supervision and gave even

experienced skilled women lower-ranking jobs. Women left the farms even more quickly than men.

Competition between the sexes for jobs triggered conflicts in workers' organizations across Europe. Most unions rejected women. Only in Germany, where a social democratic government and Marxist tradition had created a powerful class-consciousness, were women unionized. Christian unions, which had been formed by anti-socialists to keep industry from usurping artisan labour, drew many women. In France, "free" (non-Christian), especially Marxist, unions upheld egalitarianism, but only in principle; Christian unions held fast to traditional dicta that women's place was in the home.

In 1919 the first International Congress of Working Women, held in Washington, DC drew female trade unionists from Asia, Europe, and America. It urged the International Labor Conference to require female representatives and proposed new labour stand-ards for all workers: an age of at least sixteen, an eight-hour day or forty-four-hour week, weekly rest of at least one and a half days, and daily rest of at least a half-hour. Women should receive free medical care and an allowance sufficient to support them for six weeks before and after childbirth. The congress argued that all workers should be protected against night work and work with toxic mater-ials like lead, and asked for international conventions to distribute raw materials equally throughout the world – goals still not met. By 1931, twenty-two nations had legislated six-weeks' leave for women after childbirth; fifteen more provided three to five weeks. But most maternity allowances were only 50–60 percent of a woman's basic wage, too little to sustain life. Many categories of workers were not covered, and those who were could not always regain their jobs after childbirth. These benefits were not extended to women in European colonies.

After the Depression of 1929, industry dug in its heels against the congress proposals, and the economic downturn propelled many women out of waged work. Large companies increasingly took business from small ones, and industry or services offered women who lost their businesses only low-paid dead-end jobs. The Depression justified governments that forced married women out of waged work, urging them to have babies to make up the population lost in the war. The female workforce grew younger as employers favoured shop girls and office workers under the age of thirty. In France, 408,000 female small proprietors lost their businesses between 1921 and 1936, and female waged workers increased by 179,000 as 156,000 men opened new businesses. Over 100,000 women became salaried workers. A similar shift occurred in Germany: from 1925 to 1933, independent women dealers in clothing, food, beverages, industry, crafts, inns, and taverns fell by 300,000 and white-collar female workers grew by about 250,000. In Italy, agriculture contracted, throwing women out of work. They were not hired by slow-growing Italian industry, which preferred men.

In this period, European governments began to be alarmed at the dropping birth rate. Prosperous families had limited birth for several centuries; after the First World War, so did working-class families. On farms, children were economically useful: they started to work at four or five; by ten or twelve they were experienced. But children were costly to raise in cities. By 1920, laws barred children from factory work and forced those held responsible for them – mothers – either to find child-tenders or stay at home earning nothing. Moreover, most children now survived infancy – it was no longer necessary to have several so that a few would live to adulthood. Men who wanted better lives agreed to limits on family size.

Demographers warned, however, that Europe was failing to produce enough of the "right breed," while "wrong" breeds multiplied madly in Asia, Africa, and India. For moralists, greater use of contraception and illegal abortion indicated a decline in female chastity, which they predicted would lead to the downfall of the West and the rise of Bolshevist "free love." Birth-control advocates, some of them feminists, played on people's fear of socialism to win support for eugenic measures, arguing that, with fewer children, poor people could live on their wages and stop agitating for wages that fit their needs. In the 1870s they created neo–Malthusian Leagues in Britain, France, Holland, and Germany, and, after 1900, held international conferences.

Freud's challenging ideas about sexuality, sensationalized, led to a rediscovery of female eroticism and bred new female images – the sexually free flapper, bachelor girl, and lesbian – that appalled moralists. But few women changed their lives as a result: most women who adopted freer sexuality did so for economic, not moral, reasons.[2] Many middle-class families lost their property when capital centralized during the post-war inflation or the Depression. Their daughters were freed from the restraints imposed on propertied girls; they had nothing to lose by adopting the sexual freedom customary to propertyless people. Since most middle-class women's behaviour did not change, moralists' anxiety was directed not against changing customs (as in the 1960s and afterward) but against female independence, sexual and economic. Indeed, they conflated the "working girl" and the "loose" woman into a figure whose mere existence threatened the fundamental values of middle-class life.

Fascism advanced in Europe by claiming it could deal with these problems. Conservatives believed that dictatorship was necessary to reverse the gains made by liberal politicians and labour unions. All Western cultures admired the strong man, the hero. Prominent men in England, France, and the United States supported fascism, but only Italy and Germany installed openly fascist governments.[3] Benito Mussolini and Adolf Hitler were passionate, eloquent speakers who roused audiences by exploiting their fear of socialism and their hatred of the rich. Historians who point out that Hitler and Mussolini were offered rule because the chief of state considered them the only alternative to socialist revolution rarely mention the importance to fascism of male fears of growing female power and the struggle for human rights. But fascist dictators immediately took steps to resubjugate women to the state, claiming they were healing society by reviving a "healthy" relationship between the sexes. Hitler, especially, was obsessed with harnessing women's reproductive power. Fascism was an attempt to repress both class and sex struggle and to revive patriarchal power in the guise of a concerned state.

Women supported fascism because it appealed to a past romanticized by time: Hitler invoked a mythic "Aryan" pagan past in which men were men (heroes) and women were women (subordinate and admiring), and they all lived in same-sex groups.[4] Mussolini invoked a similar mythic ancient Rome, in which fathers held absolute power and women were serene and satisfied. What makes these visions myths (like most modern depictions of nineteenth-century farm or small-town life in the United States or England) is their tacit message that life then was happy, free from conflict about money or between the sexes. *In ille tempore*, everyone knew their place and accepted it. Every appeal to the past shares this same characteristic.

Most European nations experimented with eugenics in the 1930s. The United States began to apply eugenic theories under Theodore Roosevelt. Many countries persecuted socialists and used the fact that many socialists were Jewish to justify anti-Semitism – which was already pervasive and openly expressed everywhere in the West. But only Hitler and Mussolini built national ideologies on prejudice, rooted in lies about socialism, race, and sex.

Fascism has been defined as a mix of extreme nationalism, statism (the belief that the state is supreme, has power over every facet of life, and owns the complete loyalty of all citizens), and militarism rooted in the conservative doctrine that life is a contest one wins or loses. These attitudes permeated twentieth-century fascism, which was also rooted in a belief in biological superiority. Fascists adapted socialist ideas of community to annul individual autonomy instead of increasing it.

In an ideal fascist state, parents' social and economic roles are taken over by the state: fathers need only inseminate; mothers, become pregnant and give birth. State-sponsored child care and educational institutions staffed by women assume responsibility for teaching racially acceptable children collectivist values. All have to sacrifice for the welfare of the state and are judged by their contribution to it, but the sacrifice varies by sex. Men are expected (symbolically) to be warrior-heroes ready to die; women are expected (literally) to smile, obey, support men, and give birth: old ideas in new packages.

Hitler and Mussolini, both of whom tried to realize the fascist ideal, had some similarities. They were raised in lower-middle-class Catholic homes by devout mothers and abusive, atheist fathers. Both drifted rootlessly until the First World War. Hitler openly scorned Catholicism and mocked priests as "skirts," while Mussolini wrote a novel of church scandal, *Claudia Particella, The Cardinal's Mistress*. Both avoided the draft until their countries entered the war, then enlisted as regular soldiers. And both were transformed by it.[5] They had the fire to inspire men – through Mussolini's Fasci di Combattimento, or Black Shirts, and Hitler's Sturmabteilung, or Brown Shirts – to join their paramilitary groups, swearing total devotion to Il Duce or Der Führer. Italy entered the Second World War siding with Hitler, but ended on the Allies' side, being, Mussolini felt, cheated of the rewards of victory. Like other Germans, Hitler blamed the German defeat less on the Allies than on German corruption caused by a Jewish conspiracy.

Nazi Germany

Germany's defeat in the First World War was intolerable to many Germans, who blamed it on a vague category of subversives inside Germany – marginal people like Jews and communists. Paramilitary units, the Freikorps, were formed to combat them. Hitler, a recruiter for such units, used communism as the great threat, but he also blamed a "Jewish conspiracy." In attacking labour unions for their socialism and capitalists for their wealth, he drew lower-middle-class support and, in 1923, tried to overthrow the government in "the Beer Hall Putsch." The president called out troops and had him imprisoned. For the next ten years he designed his ideal society and plotted strategy to take power, always building grassroots support for his National Socialist (Nazi) Party.

When he shifted from a strategy of armed revolution to legal political action, women, who had by then won the vote, supported fascism at the polls. Hitler made no particular effort to attract women, but neither did he publicly insult them, as some of his male deputies did. He claimed to honour mothers, yet did not live a "family" life – his incestuous affair with a niece ended with her suicide. After he became dictator, he took a subservient lover, Eva Braun, but did not marry her until just before they committed suicide together.

The six major political parties in the Weimar Republic welcomed women, ran them as candidates, and appointed them to lobby on "women's" issues. Even the most conservative politicians officially favoured equality. Only Hitler systematically excluded women from any responsibility in his movement. Yet in the early 1920s, women made up 20 percent of Nazi Party members, believing Hitler to be "a genuine German hero – honest, God-fearing and righteous."[6] Seduced by his racist vision of a new Germany based on traditional values, they believed Nazi propaganda that declared women equal and complementary to men: women of "inferior races" (Mediterraneans, for instance) might be inferior to men, but German women had always been equal to theirs. In time, they would breed a superior race (Aryans) who would rule society. Women believed that their Aryanism outweighed their femaleness.

But women joined the Nazi Party for another reason. Unlike political parties that welcomed women but anxiously scrutinized them for possible feminist activity, the Nazis had absolutely no interest in what they did. Just as more women joined socialist parties that allowed them to build separate hierarchies than those that did not, so Nazi women joined a party that allowed them to create their own organization, free from party surveillance, believing that this independence gave them greater access to power. Male Nazi storm troopers and leaders worked under constant surveillance to beat up "enemies" and stage mass rallies; Nazi women, meanwhile, planned their own activities and created their own ideology and structure in the Munich "Brown House." Taking the party's indifference as a mark of trust and respect, they started political clubs like Elsbet Zander's Red Swastika (later, the Order of German Women), which had 200,000 members by the late 1920s. Proclaiming herself Hitler's right-hand woman, Zander published a newspaper, collected large sums of money, and organized help for Nazi men and their families. The sixtyish Zander, single, childless, and dowdy, was a vibrant speaker who attacked feminists for "masculinizing" women and urged motherhood as woman's true vocation.

Another Nazi woman leader, Guida Diehl, had founded a movement, New Land, during the First World War to bolster civilian morale. After defeat, she mobilized it to fight communism. She did not officially join the Nazi Party until it was about to take over the government, but she worked independently to support it. She drew educated, civic-minded Protestant women, the most conservative members of the BDF (Federation of German Women's Organizations), by creating a substantial plan for women within a Nazi society. She disapproved of women working outside the household, but, recognizing that not all mothers had husbands to support them, proposed state subsidies for those who stayed at home with children. Women would no longer act in the public sphere but would build a separate women's legislature elected by them alone to balance the male legislature and defend women's interests.

With near-religious faith in the Führer, Nazi women worked to exhaustion, setting up soup kitchens, collecting food and clothing for poor party members, and sewing clothes for unemployed SA men (party storm troopers). They propagandized for Nazism door to door, passed out leaflets, nursed fugitive or wounded SA men, and risked arrest, or worse, smuggling campaign literature into German states where the party was illegal. They rejected the image of the "lady" – woman as decorative toy – yet violated their own definition of womanhood when they daringly faced down hecklers, harangued passersby on streets, marched behind the swastika, and smuggled weapons or messages past police check-points. Wearing Nazi uniforms, they were harassed in the streets, heckled by cries of "brown goose" or "Hitler whore!" They took pride in their solidarity, endurance, and, ironically, their "unfeminine" activities. One woman wrote that harassment "forged a unity among us that no power on earth could have rent asunder."

Apart from male Nazis, women interpreted Nazism as they chose. Hitler often used the term *lebensraum* ("room to live") to justify the German appropriation of Central European farmlands for a growing German population. But to middle-class Nazi women, the term meant "living room" – space that harmonized society, annulling class, sex, and political divisions. Nazi women's image of "loving womanhood" offset and softened the image of "powerful manhood" earned by brutal Nazi men hysterically predicting doom. It misled Germans about the nature of Nazism and an ideal Nazi society. But the women also misled themselves.[7]

The Depression hit Germany with special force because it depended on the United States for loans and trade. Its economic situation was desperate, with rampant inflation and nearly 30 percent unemployment among men (10 percent among women who customarily worked outside the home). Two million German men had been killed and thousands wounded in the First World War, so many women had unemployed husbands or none at all. Unable to earn much on their own, women longed for a "natural" order of "more masculine men and more feminine women." As incessant debate between socialists and conservatives paralyzed the Reichstag, Hitler decided to get the women's vote. In 1932, claiming Bolshevism had wrecked the family, he promised, if elected, to find jobs for all husbands – and husbands for all single women. Women's vote for the Nazis soared; the party moved from ninth to first place in the Depression years.

In 1933, seeing him as the only alternative to socialist revolution, President Paul von Hindenburg appointed Hitler as chancellor. The Reichstag granted him dictatorial powers and, when Hindenburg died, Hitler was supreme in Germany. During his decade of waiting to take national power, he had built a party with over a million members and 400,000 storm troopers, and he received the vote of a third of the German electorate (14 million people). Now about 5 percent of party members, women built support networks to mobilize women voters, garnering nearly half the votes that put the Nazis in power. Yet one of Hitler's first acts on becoming chancellor was to take over Nazi women's organizations and dismiss women from high-level state jobs. Gertrud Bäumer, a major figure in the women's rights movement for thirty years, worked in the Education Ministry and received one of the first termination letters. She protested, claiming she had long been of the "national socialist persuasion." Her feminist colleagues defended her, but she was expelled.

Middle-class working women rose to defend their right to work in such numbers and with such fury that, in the fall of 1933, the interior minister apologized for curtailing their participation and, at the next party rally in Nuremberg, the new head of the Women's Bureau (Frauenwerk), Gertrud Scholtz-Klink, endorsed this position. Women discovered that, if they showed enough zeal for the Nazis, they could get jobs in state agencies. The Nazis pretended that women had no function beyond reproduction and serving men, but they needed them as administrators, teachers, and social workers. Rigid quotas placed on women in universities were eased in time, but women never worked in Nazi institutes to train men for the elite.

Within a year, Hitler had expelled virtually every woman leader who had helped bring him to power. He wanted to handpick a different kind of woman leader, and his ministers experimented with various chiefs and organizational structures, even to making a man head of the Nazi Women's League. They sought the "perfect wo-man," who could lead women while obeying men and who fit Nazi values for womanhood, yet could give herself completely to the organization. She could be neither married nor unmarried. They found Gertrud Scholtz-Klink, a mother of four whose ardent Nazi husband had died of a heart attack during a party rally two years before. "Racially correct," opportunistic, and deferential, she ful-filled the requirements. She was to bring all non-socialist and non-communist women's groups under Nazi control.

Leaders of non-Nazi groups had to join Frauenwerk, expel all members with Jewish blood, and submit annual plans and financial and membership records to Nazi officials. In 1933 Protestant women leaders directed their 2 million followers to accept the Nazi state without reservation; the Vatican gave the same order to a mil-lion organized Catholic women. Even feminists bowed to Nazi hatred: the BDF decided to disband, but its member organizations purged Jewish women, who left "with great sadness" after decades of cooperative work with women they considered friends. Bäumer wrote in 1933 that since women rarely control the political struc-ture of the nations they live in, they must fight for rights within the context that exists.

When Nazi men finally noticed Nazi women, they ended their autonomy. They announced the new policy as soon as they took power: "There is no place for the political woman in the ideologi-cal world of National Socialism. . . . The intellectual attitude of the movement on this score is opposed to the political woman. . . . The German resurrection is a male event." Scholtz-Klink did her job admirably – in a few years, Frauenwerk had 8 million members free of Jewish blood or Marxist ties – yet after four years in office she complained that "she had marched with Hitler and often appeared on the same speakers' platform," yet never once had been "allowed to discuss any aspect of his policy on women." In 1942 Hitler wrote, "In no local section of the Party has a woman ever had the right to hold even the smallest post."

The Nazi revolution began as a protest movement, drawing people alienated by industrialization, threatened by socialism, or hurt by the Depression, people who yearned for the stability, community, and clarity of an imagined past. But very soon Hitler revealed his totalitarian vision, his intention to control everyone in society totally. He did not tamper with the Weimar Constitution, but for a time operated through it and existing agencies and bureaus. Finding this structure an encumbrance, he silently created Nazi Party agencies that duplicated the functions of the powerless Weimar bureaus remaining in place. Power centred in Hitler; SS power was disseminated by party bureaus. Without due process, the party simply took the right to imprison and murder, to control education, the press, the arts, and all political life, and, finally, to abolish the private realm.

The Nazis called their program of exterminating the Jews the "final solution," as if a problem existed. But Jews were scapegoats: those who blamed them for the German defeat in the First World War gradually blamed them for all the ills plaguing Germany. Once Hitler rid Europe of all the Jews, he intended to wipe out gypsies, Poles, the physically or mentally impaired, and the "inferior races," including many Germans. Hitler's genocidal program amounted to a campaign against humanness itself; only those who fit a narrow standard (so-called Aryanism) could produce a master race. It aimed at the heart of life – breeding, and therefore women. The Nazis outlawed birth control, amplified the harsh punishments already placed on abortion, denied permanent jobs to women under thirty-five, imposed quotas on those seeking higher education, and forbade women physicians to practise, except jointly with their husbands.

While forcing the "fit" to bear more children, the Nazis "pruned the unfit." They mounted a nationwide boycott against Jewish businesses, expelled Jewish children from public schools, and fired Jewish professionals from their jobs. They drafted laws forcing "racially unfit . . . Aryans" to be sterilized and ordering German social workers to send the deaf and dumb, mentally retarded, schizophrenics, alcoholics, and epileptics to eugenics courts, which assessed the damage their procreation would do to the "race." Estimates claim that over 375,000 people were sterilized, including prostitutes. The old, impaired, and feeble were killed, 150,000 of them in the "euthanasia" program after 1940.

The Nazis initiated programs aimed at women as soon as they took office. In 1933 the Education Ministry set up a program to teach girls new values – anti-Semitic "racial" science, physical fitness, home economics, and the equal importance of sexual and "racial" identity. It segregated most co-educational schools and, claiming that all children belonged to the state, pressured them to join youth groups. The Nazis wanted women indoctrinated with Nazi values, but gave their leaders inadequate funds or authority for the task. Nazi men treated women in the hierarchy contemptuously, allocated no money to "Nazify" girls' textbooks, and let "blacks" (Catholics) teach them.

Any state needs national unity and popular support most during war, yet, as the Nazis geared up for war in 1936, Hitler announced new programs that split what unity existed and dampened morale. He now urged women to work outside the home, created a new breeding policy, and attacked Catholic and Protestant organizations. His campaign against Jews had even more deleterious effects on the nation (not to speak of its victims). Like all large-scale efforts at control, the Nazi system was full of contradictions.

Frauenwerk had 9 to 12 million members, because every woman with a job or membership in a civic organization had to join, but few attended meetings or subscribed to Nazi journals. The primary affiliation for many women was religious clubs, until, under the new dispensation, Scholtz-Klink ordered members of Nazi organizations to resign from non-Nazi groups. Christians who had given their allegiance to the Nazi state because their churches assured them that Nazi and Christian goals were in harmony suddenly had to quit their church groups. They looked to church authorities for protection, but the clergy supported Hitler. Several women fought so hard to retain their autonomy, they were accused of treason. Catholic women were especially uneasy with Nazi policies of sterilization or abortion of the "unfit," but women of all religions were distressed by Hitler's new reproductive policy.

"Racial revolution" had been the heart of Hitler's plan from the start. After a massive pogrom in November 1938, Himmler unveiled Hitler's plan for breeding a "superior" race. Setting up special camps, the Nazis stocked them with "racially fit" single women and ordered SS soldiers about to be sent to the front to inseminate sons before they left. Pregnant women were then sent to maternity homes (with an allowance), and Germans were ordered to accord them more, or as much, respect as married mothers. This scheme had little effect on the birthrate but it shocked loyal citizens, especially religious women. Guida Diehl was appalled. And when rumours circulated that Jews were being deported, the anti-Semitic Diehl was horrified enough to write to Heinrich and Margarethe Grüber (who ran a clandestine mission to help Protestants with Jewish ancestors escape from Germany), deploring violence against the Jews. For this she was found guilty of treason, but, unlike other women, was not jailed because of her advanced age.

Women were urged to fill new Nazi needs – to take jobs and quit their roles as homemakers. Silently dropping restrictions and quotas, the Nazis paid women 75 percent of male wages. When women complained, the minister of labour declared: "There can be no basic equality with the man." Propaganda presented a new image: woman as both the eternal mother and the fighting comrade of man, while, simultaneously, Nazis wrote private memos calling them "geese" or "dumb prattlers" who lowered morale by cluttering up the streets as they stood in line to buy food. Women with big families resisted pressure to take low-paid jobs; middle-class women refused to sacrifice domestic servants to war work; and brides and young mothers preferred to stay at home. The Nazis gave soldiers' wives and widows high benefits, which were reduced if they took jobs. To please soldiers, the Nazis undercut their efforts to force women back into waged work.

In 1943, as the war began to threaten Germany, the Nazis forced women to register with the employment bureau. Many evaded this order, but others were given formerly male jobs in construction, munitions factories, shipyards, and foundries. Some were made "social workers" (prostitutes) with the troops in defeated countries. Whatever the circumstances, women were expected to bear and indoctrinate children with Nazism. Children, in turn, were supposed to report parents who failed in this duty. While scorning women as fit only for sex and reproduction, Hitler was obsessed with them. Even as Allied planes bombed Berlin, he was hiding out in a bunker, planning a post-war breeding program, a polygamous society in which every decorated soldier was allowed more than one wife. As Germany collapsed, Hitler announced that women were now equal, and he pushed them into the military as scouts, saboteurs, medics, communications aides, and messengers. But gave them no uniforms or weapons.

Jewish Women in Nazi Germany

Jewish Germans were aware of the anti-Semitism of Nazi speakers in the 1920s, but Germany was a liberal nation with a sophisticated culture. Many Jews considered themselves German, not primarily Jewish, and lived in liberal milieux, isolated from those who spewed such hatred. Racial, religious, and sexual hatred rumbles ominously underground in all societies – no Jew outside Israel, no black outside some African states, no woman anywhere in the world has not experienced belittlement, contempt, and hatred on such grounds. No one can predict if or when such emotions will erupt in action, and no one on earth could have imagined the horrors the Nazis would inflict on the Jews.

Hitler's planned "racial revolution" involved terrorism and probably genocide of Jewish Germans. Anti-Semitism pervaded

Nazi rhetoric in the 1920s, but the party platform never used the word "Jew": rather, it held that "only a racial comrade can be a citizen," and "noncitizens shall be able to live in Germany as guests only, and must be placed under alien legislation" – statements that intimate discrimination but not Shoah. Only once before he became chancellor did Hitler discuss anti-Semitic policy with his deputies: at a 1932 meeting, Nazi leaders agreed that if they took power violently, they would immediately and violently deprive Jews of citizenship, but if they took power legally, they would erode Jewish rights gradually by administrative means. SA men sporadically attacked Jewish lawyers, judges, businessmen, and community leaders; in several cities, SA men forced prostitutes to march through the streets carrying signs reading, "I have committed racial treason" or "I fornicate with Jews." In Nuremberg, Julius Streicher led an attack on Jewish community leaders, arresting fifty men and taking them to Dachau, where he beat them, forced them to eat their feces and drink their urine, and killed nine. But these were local actions, performed without official sanction.

Only in hindsight was Hitler's plan inevitable. After taking power in January 1933, he attacked socialists, religious objectors, prostitutes, homosexuals, and the "genetically damaged," shrouding his intentions for Jews in euphemisms. While many Christian Germans hated Jews, Protestants and Catholics also hated each other: religious hatred was pervasive but not violent. When violence erupted against German Jews in March 1933, Hitler worried about international repercussions – the Berlin stockmarket fell drastically and the Woolworth chain threatened to leave Germany. There were domestic repercussions too: the middle class, which did not protest mass arrests of communists or socialists, was appalled at attacks on middle-class Jews.

In 1933 Germany was not a nation of fanatic Jew-haters: it took six years of steady anti-Semitic propaganda and legislation to alienate non-Jewish Germans.[8] In the meantime, for each blow they received, Jewish Germans could cite a kind act, a piece of good luck, or hopeful counter-sign. Each new discriminatory law or anti-Semitic outburst sent Jews, with a history of persecution, reeling for ways to circumvent, adapt, or protest. But the memory of no pogrom could prepare them for Hitler's plan.

Hitler moved gradually: a boycott of Jewish businesses had failed miserably. Many decrees affected others besides Jews: quotas placed on Jewish university students included non-Jewish women; rules expelling Jewish doctors from the national health program and lawyers from the civil service exempted First World War veterans – exceptions which left half the "non-Aryan" doctors and 30 percent of lawyers in their jobs. Those harmed by such laws left the country. Some Jews welcomed an authoritarian state and even marched in Nazi parades. When Hindenburg ordered Hitler to ease anti-Semitic violence, many Jews were reassured.

Laws made it difficult for Jewish Germans to earn a living, but violence did not begin until 1938, when Goebbels began seizing Jewish property and deporting eastern Jews to Poland. After his parents were deported, a seventeen-year-old student in Paris shot a German diplomat: Nazis used his act to justify a national pogrom, *Crystalnacht*, on November 9, 1938. They arrested 30,000 Jewish men. Women scurried to save them, calling influential friends, offering bribes, writing appeals, and using clever ruses to fend off SS search and seizure. Women whose husbands remained free sought escape routes. Thousands of families left Germany, penniless except for what they concealed in their clothes. Some went "underground," adopting the names and manners of non-Jewish Germans with forged papers.

But many did not escape: 300,000 Jewish Germans went to the camps, and all but 5000 perished. In the face of such horror, women's talents sometimes saved them: some victims thought women survived the camps better than men because they shared and cooperated. Hannah Levy-Haas, a Jewish member of the Yugoslavian resistance imprisoned in Ravensbruck, wrote in her diary in 1944:

One thing here upsets me terribly, and that is to see that the men are far weaker and far less able to stand up to hardship than the women – physically and often morally as well. Unable to control themselves, they display such a lack of moral fibre that one cannot but be sorry for them. . . . To be sure, however, their behavior here is merely a continuation of their past.[9]

A few German women helped Jews and many Jewish women behaved with amazing nobility. The Nazis massacred between 5 and 6 million European Jews. Women helped to save some of those who survived.

Women Who Resisted

When the war was over and the Nazis were utterly discredited, their horrors unveiled to the world, many Germans dissociated themselves from the regime. Some were lying, but obedient patriots must have demurred privately and many people tried to circumvent unpleasant repercussions. Some historians now claim that most Germans were not fanatic anti-Semites. Why they participated in genocide remains debatable. Germans alone did not perpetrate the horror: huge numbers of Jews from other countries were slaughtered, and, proportionately, more Jews were killed in anti-Nazi countries reputed democratic (Holland or Norway) and the egalitarian Soviet Union than in Germany's allies – Italy, Hungary, or Romania.

Some Germans opposed fascism and offered passing kindnesses to persecuted Jews (as many women did); others resisted fascism and took actions that put them at risk.[10] Most accounts of resistance focus on men, but when survivors cite those who risked their lives to help them, they name women as often as, or more than, men. Socialist, communist, and religious women resisted Nazism, including Jehovah's Witnesses, a few Catholics, and Protestants. Many resisters were executed, as were several male and female socialist and communist Reichstag delegates from the Weimar Republic. The public outcry was enormous when a young mother, twenty-three-year-old Liselotte Hermann, was executed for treason. Fearing the damage to morale, the Gestapo did not execute another German woman until 1937, though they killed dozens in jail. But many women went undetected. Arrogant Nazi men shrugged off women as a threat, and women represented only 20 percent of those arrested for crimes against the state. Yet they actively rescued victims, maintained underground communications networks, distributed anti-Nazi propaganda, and gathered information. When men were caught, women ran the resistance groups.

As an inferior caste, women are profoundly aware of men's attitudes and how to play into them. They flirted with Nazi guards or acted maternal as they transported forged documents or harboured Jews. Gertrud Staewen recalled Protestant women collecting Motherhood medals from "Aryan" mothers to disguise Jewish women and children who were trying to cross the Swiss border. Carola Karg carried pounds of illegal pamphlets under a maternity dress as she did farm work on the French border. Maria von Maltzan arrived late at the train station, acting drunk, when she wanted to smuggle a news dispatch to Paris. Far fewer people resisted than bowed to or cooperated with the Nazis, and most of them are nameless heroes. But women were a significant presence among them.

Fascist Italy

Throughout the West, capitalist industry and education had enabled women to rise powerfully in middle-class or socialist movements and so win the suffrage and greater rights in most countries. Terrified conservatives cried for restrictions that would lock women into the home and family and reassert the authority of breadwinner fathers. Seeing life as a struggle among men (only), they justified greed for resources by pretending that all men started out equal.

The word "fascism" derives from the Latin *fasces*, a logo of a bundle of sticks surrounding an axe, representing the authority of the Roman state. Fascists believed in state authority and patriarchal gender roles. No longer able credibly to assert the will of god or nature's purpose, they made patriarchy impersonal and inevitable by substituting the power of the state for that of men (father, king). Thus, they spoke not of women's duty to husband and children, but of women's responsibility to serve their communities in special "feminine" areas of expertise. They urged state support of mothers whose husbands defaulted on their obligations.

Like the Nazis, Italian fascists touched profound yearnings by invoking a mythic past in which Rome flaunted its superiority over all other "races." In both countries, the fascist appeal to women was pervaded with paradox. Nazi and Italian fascist men derived much of their *élan* from the sexual exclusivity of their movement. They did not welcome women in their ranks, and they wanted their wives to obey them, not the state. Men's ambivalence about the place of women even informed fascist debate on women's dress. Uniforms meant women, like men, were citizens serving the state, but an ideal wife should dress to please her husband above all. Women in the party wore uniforms or distinctive clothing with an insignia denoting rank, advertising the victory of the fascist insistence that all citizens owed primary loyalty to the state.

Hitler and Mussolini asked men and women, all classes and both sexes, to stop struggling for rights and to sacrifice for the common good. But both men recognized that women, who bear the burden of reproduction, have special needs. Fascists pleased conservatives by promising to return women to exclusively domestic roles; they pleased women by offering them recognition and status for their special contribution. Using a traditional rhetoric, Mussolini and Hitler set out to forge a "modern" woman who would feel important in society without being independent. Propaganda encouraged women to engage in athletics; the New Mother (an alternative to the New Woman) was honoured with official awards in public ceremonies and the media. The Italian government funded institutes of home economics, backed radio programs aimed at "modern" homemakers, and tried to present motherhood as more desirable than wage labour. A cult of motherhood re-emerged in Europe in the 1930s, but only Mussolini and Hitler founded social programs on pro-natal policies and indoctrination of the young – the cornerstone of the fascist moral revolution. Whatever their attitudes, Hitler and Mussolini knew that women's support was vital. Both established separate women's organizations, but such organizations needed leaders – the very career woman they decried.

After Benito Mussolini, a schoolteacher with a mélange of socialist and conservative ideas, adopted socialism, Angelica Balabanoff, the head of the Italian Socialist party, made him editor of *Avanti*, the Italian socialist newspaper. Mussolini supported her in opposing the First World War, but soon reversed himself. Fired from *Avanti*, he founded a newspaper to rouse fervour for war and the Entente. When Italy joined the Entente in the spring of 1915, he felt personally victorious. Fascism had no platform until 1919, when Mussolini composed one advocating, among other items, universal suffrage, abolition of the conservative Senate, confiscation of most war profits, an eight-hour day, League of Nations membership, and "opposition to all imperialisms." Its support of equal rights for women led some women to join *fasci* (bands of units) in 1919, but Mussolini reversed himself in a more conservative platform in 1920. A Fascist Women's Congress in 1921 had only fourteen women delegates.

While Hitler bided his time, Mussolini threatened revolution in September 1922 with only 20,000 paramilitary followers. But his blackshirts compensated for their numbers by rigid discipline and extreme aggressiveness, and, in October, they marched on Rome. When the Fascisti occupied the capital, the old elite simply collapsed. The premier resigned, and King Victor Emmanuel III asked Mussolini to form a cabinet. Somewhat curbed by a king who could dismiss him at will and a Catholic Church with influence over the Italian populace that no German church wielded, he managed to create a fascist state based in nationalism, statism, and militarism. He abolished the cabinet, sapped parliamentary power by presenting voters with prepared lists of candidates, and eventually eradicated all other political parties. As prime minister and party leader, Il Duce, like Der Führer, used party police to purge the opposition.

As dictator, Mussolini repressed the socialists he once supported, but, for some years, non-socialist opposition parties ran candidates and even took posts in his government. Some non-fascists retained military or administrative jobs. Non-fascist newspapers kept some freedom and continued to be more widely read than government papers. Left-wing women felt the growing repression, but conservative and religious associations barely noticed it. Most middle-class women's organizations accepted his invitation to support the new state, and feminist groups refrained from criticizing fascism in theory or practice. Most Italian women were Catholic, and Mussolini had promised to wipe out atheism and communism. A pragmatist ruling an extremely conservative country, he bolstered male authority in the church. He also boosted the role of fathers by compensating them for loss of their political rights with more control over their families. After 1929, the church blessed the fascist state.

Mussolini devised a strategy to end class conflict. He placated workers by instituting huge public works projects; he quashed labour unions and put workers under the direct control of the government, which favoured employers. Female agricultural, textile, and tobacco workers struck to protest state-sponsored labour organizations, but in vain. He did not at first define women's status in the fascist state, but his leanings were suggested by the tone of the government newspaper. When a woman was named director of Milan's La Scala, it remarked: "Is our revolution so poor in men, that a woman should be appointed to the premier theatre of Italy?" He seemed to favour woman suffrage for a time, but was vague with the international press. Women were unsure of his policies until 1923, when he banned them from politics and urged them to do volunteer charity work: "Naturally, I do not wish to turn women into slaves. But it would be a personal affront to me if they voted. In our state women will count for nothing. . . . Women must obey. . . . Do you know how the Anglo-Saxons will end? In the Matriarchate!"

The fascists deputized women to organize female auxiliaries, but mistrusted women too much to make them independent. The state-founded Fasci Femminili, never given funds to be effective, had only 40,000 members in 1924. Its leader, Elisa Majer Rizzioli, who supported women's rights, had no effect on official policy. Most women featured in fascist propaganda were famous men's wives with glamour as writers or athletes. Fascist groups drew main-ly bourgeois urban women who were uninterested in careers and who did volunteer work. But the contradictions of fascism lured some young, educated, progressive women who scorned both tradi-tional female roles and feminism, woman looking to find in fascism a new image – a sexually free, vigorous intellectual wife striding into the future alongside her husband. Fascism offered them an escape from constriction within the family and an entry to public life, albeit without political rights. No Italian government had ever favoured female equality; whatever fascism offered was a plus.[11]

Despite his early contempt for the church, Mussolini allied with it. Sexually and emotionally, he was very different from Hitler. Mussolini lived with a woman and had two children with her. In 1925 he married her in the church and had the children baptized. His long-time "official mistress," Clara Petacci, and his many brief affairs did not conform to Catholic doctrine, but they did fit Italian custom, and he appeared to be a devoted family man. Mussolini could not afford to alienate the 98 percent of Italians who were bap-tized Catholics, and the quarter of the population who regularly attended Mass – almost all of them women. In 1929 he made the Vatican independent and gave it control of huge areas of public life – education and Catholic women's organizations with over a million members. The numbers of nuns almost doubled in a decade, and they began to do community work. In the nineteenth century the pope had denounced women's emancipation and communism as the two great threats to patriarchy and property. Strengthened by allying with the fascists, in 1930 Pope Pius XI issued a papal encyclical, *Casti Connubi*, defending men's absolute rights over their wives, which was handed out to couples at their weddings. The next year he issued *Quadrigesimo Anno*, ordering women to devote themselves to motherhood as their major function.

Mussolini reinforced the power of the church over society and the power of fathers over families. In 1929 "physical correction and discipline" was declared a husband's right; runaway wives were hunted by the police and imprisoned for two years. Adultery (an exclusively female "crime") was punished by two years in prison; rape was allowed if the rapist could show that the victim, whatever her age, had a bad reputation or was seductive. In 1932 Mussolini decreed that the murder of wives, sisters, or mothers for purported adultery was a crime of "honour," exempt from punishment. After this law, the homicide rate dropped by 50 percent: men stopped murdering women for fear of implying they had been cuckolded.[12] The drive to establish absolute male supremacy occasionally collided with the drive to increase the population. Dissemination of birth-control information was punished by two years in jail, and abortion even more severely. But if abortion was performed, with or without a woman's consent, in the interest of family honour as defined by a man, it was a minor crime. There was virtually no penalty for abandoning a child for "family honour," but abduction earned fourteen years of hard labour. As in ancient Rome, women and children were men's property.

The Italian economy improved a little in the late 1920s, like other European economies, but Italy suffered like them all during the Depression. Despite Mussolini's claim to have revolutionized Italian life, industrial progress proceeded at the same rate during, before, and after his rule. When economic crisis occurred, Mussolini blamed women and machines for taking jobs from skilled workers and ordered employers to hire no more women. Since such bans were issued frequently, they were probably not obeyed. The industrial north needed women for low-paid factory work, health care, and white-collar jobs. Despite rigid quotas, more and more women entered universities, particularly after men began to be drafted in 1935. A few even managed to become professionals. More women entered the service sector, working in transport, offices, and public administration. Poorly paid and rarely promoted, women continued to need work and employers to hire them.

Hitler demanded that Mussolini participate in the "final solution," but Mussolini was not obsessed with Jews. Large numbers of Jewish Italians were deported and killed, but Italy's – or Mussolini's – identity was not entwined with their eradication, so the Italian climate was less pervaded with horror, less terrifying than Germany's.[13] Mussolini's drive to harness reproduction had more impact on Italian women, who were secluded, than war and genocide. In 1925 he established a program to improve infant health; in 1929 he gave wage-earning mothers maternity leave; in 1933 the government granted small allowances to poor families with many children; and in 1934 it granted factory and office workers broad maternity benefits and let employers replace women by men even in jobs traditionally reserved for women.

As he prepared for war, Mussolini pressed women harder to reproduce, announcing a "battle for births" and promising state subsidies for child support, maternal relief programs, and a double income tax on bachelors. The popular press echoed his propaganda exhorting women to bear many children: "After the revolution, there will be bread and glory for all!" "Marry young . . . Marriage at 20 is a splendid thing," chirped the official newspaper. Ceremonies honoured extremely fruitful women; propaganda urged mothers to inculcate fascist values in their children.

But Italians refused to let the state dictate their lives. Despite severe penalties, they used birth control and abortion; infanticide, too, was high. Births increased somewhat during the 1930s pronatalist campaign, mainly because those born during the post-war "baby boom" reached childbearing age in those years. Whatever the law allowed, Italians married later – urban couples around twenty-five for women and twenty-nine for men.

Mussolini did not introduce a morality of "race" until the late 1930s. When deportations began and the government ordered all Italian Jews arrested, Jewish women went outdoors carrying forged Christian identity cards to get provisions for their families or to carry messages. In contrast, the police routinely strip-searched men and arrested all circumcised men with questionable papers. But over half the population still lived in traditional Catholic rural villages barely touched by government decrees. Few women in the south dared to walk in a public place without a male escort; such women barely knew what "nation" meant, living as they did in a bleak servitude approaching slavery.[14] Some women, exposed to ideas, had the confidence to fight and to join partisan units: the dedicated communist Lucia Canova, for instance, evaded arrest and joined a rural brigade, one of many partisans who attacked fascist military installations. Armed resistance existed in Italy, but not in Germany.

When the Second World War ended, fascism vanished, leaving no respectable intellectual heritage behind. The separate components of fascism are not automatically lethal, but they rarely occur separately. Nationalism (belief that a country or a people is superior to all others) is almost always accompanied by militarism (belief that a superior group must dominate all others or lose its superiority). Nationalism is inherently racist: superiority cannot exist without inferiority. When these fairly common beliefs include a quasi-religious faith in the great man, a hero-saviour who uses them to build a statist system, dictatorship is born.

People vary widely in their degree of sophistication about propaganda, image-making, and myth. Even the sorry history of the last century does not suffice to enlighten all of us. Both sexes are subject to appeals to a vague "law and order"; both yearn for a "healthy society" where everyone "knows her place" and does his duty. Most people are law-abiding and do not foresee what can happen when they allow police any sort of dictatorial powers. Fascism will endure as long as people are willing to sacrifice basic human freedom for the myths of a happy, ordered past.

CHAPTER 14

ANTI-IMPERIAL
REVOLUTION IN
LATIN AMERICA

WESTERN HISTORIANS CALL COLONIAL LIBERATION "decoloniza-tion," suggesting that divestment of colonies was voluntary. This terminology maintains the West's reputation for armed superi-ority and liberal political-social systems. But colonized people in Latin America, Asia, and Africa fought for their independence, often against harsh suppression. European imperial powers gave up at some point because either the wars or the colonies had become too expensive and troublesome. Colonies required huge infrastructures and military and bureaucratic superstructures; even with the loot the rulers extracted, most colonies were only marginally profitable. European states collected colonies for the same reason that Africans collected entourages and Londoners bought slaves: empire was a status symbol. In 1776 the Scottish economist Adam Smith noted the paradox that colonies had to be a liability, yet no imperial state would voluntarily give them up. Imperialism flourished mainly because it inflated the national ego.[1]

When European powers finally relinquished their colonies, they substituted economic for political domination and reaped even greater profits. Economic hegemony created what are now called Third World countries. Britain had the largest empire and, since the Seven Years' War in the mid-1700s, had controlled Canada, Australia, some Caribbean islands, and India; it had seized Egypt from Napoleon at the turn of the nineteenth century; and it controlled much of Africa. France had lost most of its Canadian and Indian empire to the British in the eighteenth century, retaining only a few West Indian islands, but it acquired a second empire, in Southeast Asia and Africa, mainly after 1871. Spain, Portugal, and Germany also held colonies, and the United States became tacitly imperialistic in the nineteenth century. Most Asian and African struggles for independence occurred after the Second World War, from 1947 to 1965; Spain and Portugal, however, began to lose control of their empires in the Americas in the early nineteenth century, after their wars with Napoleon.

Latin American Revolutions

The same stirring principles that inspired revolution in North America and France – the human right to liberty and equality – inspired revolution in Spanish and Portuguese America. But only in France were the most exploited people the nucleus of rebellion. To rise against oppression, people must have energy left over after their labour, exposure to ideas through reading or conversation, and, above all, a sense of legitimacy, a belief that they have the right to decide their own course in life. Oppressors try to ensure that their subjects experience none of these qualities. Exploited groups in North and Latin America lacked them all.

No Native Americans, Africans (free or enslaved), poor white men, or women instigated the American Revolution, although some supported it; none benefited from it. Latin America's population, made up of similar elements – Indians, Europeans, free and enslaved Africans – had far more mixed-blood people in greatly different proportions: Spanish colonies averaged 45 percent Indian, 30 percent mestizo, 20 percent European, and 5 percent African; Portuguese Brazil, in contrast, was 50 percent African, 25 percent European, and 25 percent Indian and mameluco. But only white males benefited from the various Latin American revolutions – and whites remained a minority in these countries, divided from each other by exclusionary practices. Rich Creoles resented European-born aristocrats and reserved the highest, most lucrative positions in church and state to themselves. Whites, bolstered by appropriational colonial policies, controlled all the wealth, so everyone else was wretched. Indigenous peoples resisted the encroachment on their culture of Europeans, whose policy was to convert them to Christianity and assimilate them. Beyond these visions, Latin America was split into small states that struggled separately from about 1810 to 1826.

The literate 10 percent of the Latin American population and Iberian aristocrats read Voltaire, Rousseau, and Jefferson, under whose influence they tried to reform the colonies. Most reforms were fiscal and administrative, but they did affect elite white women. After the Spanish Enlightenment, writers began to urge female education: Father Benito Jerónimo Feijóo, for instance, published his *Essay on Woman, or Physiological and Historical Defence of the Fair Sex* (1739).[2] He claimed that a female brain was "too soft for her to comprehend as much as a male," but "exceptional" women like Queen Isabella and Sor Juana de la Cruz showed that, with education, women could be valuable members of society.[3] Reformers stressed women's role as mothers to justify educating them, and began to treat motherhood as a civic function. Their delight in instructing women on character, health care, extravagance, and domestic affairs was muted by women's inability to read what they wrote, however, so, increasingly, they demanded female education. In the later eighteenth century, teaching orders for girls were founded in Buenos Aires and Bogotá.[4]

These schools treated girls mainly as future wives and mothers, teaching them reading, embroidery, religion, sewing, and music, but also Latin, arithmetic, and science. By 1802, 3100 girls attended seventy convent, municipal, parish, and private schools. Still, the overwhelming majority of Latin American girls were not educated. Upper-class girls were secluded: if they did go to school, they were taken out at ten and, thereafter, studied only music or drawing at home. Yet, as widows, they successfully managed property and ran plantations in Brazil.

Robert Walsh, the chaplain to the British ambassador to Brazil in the 1820s, wrote that "a common sight" in the Minas Gerais mountains was a woman riding with an attendant. She "dismounted like a man before us, without the smallest embarrassment," at a roadside store, drank a glass of sugar-cane brandy to "fortify her against the mountain air – remounted – examined her pistols" for readiness, and "again set off, her own protector."[5] Wives of *fazendeiros* (plantation owners), often widowed, managed their farms, slaves, "and in all respects assume[d] the port and bearing of their husbands." But once conditions grew easier, female independence was crushed. Richard Burton, the British consul in Santos, travelled extensively in Minas Gerais in the 1860s and reported that "the Mineira lives in . . . semi-seclusion. . . . In none but the most civilized families do the mistress and daughters of the house sit down to the table with the stranger."

The Spanish government tried to bring poor women into the labour force by abolishing guild rules banning women from crafts and ordering public schools to include vocational training in the curricula. Lower-class women did have a voice in their families' economic and social affairs. Indigenous women were important as mothers, producers of food, and traders, but not in governance, religion, or inheritance. Indians experienced tremendous social dislocation from *mit'a* (corvée), work in factories and mines, and *encomienda*, and women suffered more than men from these brutal customs that disrupted their households.[6] Inca, Aztec, and Maya women worked both inside and outside the home, but only aristocrats had influence. Noblewomen retained some legal rights, and in Aztec society, a few held high administrative, religious, or social positions.

Some Latin American countries fought for independence; others achieved it peacefully. Fighting occurred as often between rival leaders as between royal troops and rebels. Most rebels were unconcerned with the unequal division of resources in Latin America and revolutionary ideals soon faded. As it was, a tiny minority owned almost everything, and the huge majority were destitute.

Gradually, nationalism replaced religion as the main organizing principle of society.[7] The new elite, an intelligentsia aware of contemporary European ideas, gained power through the periodical press. Wanting to create a new industrial society based on liberal ideas about progress, they opposed the church. Uruguay and Argentina secularized education and promoted immigration to modernize the country. Since the Hispanic conquest, the church had defined women's roles. New elites regarded women as pivotal to the new society and reconsidered their nature and their function. Women had shown great courage in the independence movements, but, ignoring that model of female behaviour, men chose the cult of domesticity: women were mothers. They made single life impossible for women by abolishing convents, refuges, and cultural centres and dispersing the communities. This redefinition of women provided the foundation of the new societies.

Spanish South America

Enlightenment ideas and successful revolutions in both North America and France inspired Spanish colonists throughout South America to rebel. Spain's restrictions on colonists' rights to determine their own economic and political structure provided the goad; Napoleon's occupation of Spain in 1808 provided the occasion. American *criollos* (Creoles) used the French usurpation of the Spanish crown to justify forming juntas to take over the government.

The ruling *peninsulares* (Spanish-born) charged them with rebellion and sedition. When a conservative monarchy was restored to the Spanish throne in 1814, independence struggles surged in many regions of Latin America. Simón Bolívar led the revolt in northern South America, José de San Martin in the southern cone, and Miguel Hidalgo and José Maria Morelos in Mexico. The Mexican insurrection, begun in 1810, was a true revolution, based in a program of social reform to benefit the Indian and mestizo masses.

A Creole, Francisco de Miranda, tried to liberate Venezuela with British and American help, and he won. Five years later, provincial representatives declared Venezuela independent, and de Miranda returned from England as commander of the rebel armies. But he failed to take the country from Spain and, when an earthquake shook rebel-held territory, killing 20,000 people, Spanish priests cried that the earthquake was god's retribution for their sin. The armies collapsed, and Miranda was jailed with Bolívar's help.

Simón Bolívar, a rich, egotistical Creole rancher and fanatic patriot, fought with such fury that revolution splintered into civil war. He betrayed his friend Miranda for deserting the revolution and joined rebel forces in Colombia. He took Caracas in 1813 and was named head of the Second Venezuelan Republic in 1814. But Spain quickly regained control of the state, and Bolívar fled to Jamaica. Returning in 1817, he mustered an army, invaded Colombia, and decisively defeated Spain. He drew up a constitution for a United States of Colombia, including Spanish-held Venezuela, and kept trying to seize it, until he succeeded in 1821. Bolívar's lieutenant, Antonio José de Sucre, initiated a revolution in Ecuador and, in 1822, won a battle that assured its independence. Bolívar went to Quito and persuaded Ecuadorean revolutionaries to unite with Colombia and Venezuela to create a republic, Gran Colombia. When Peru was conquered in 1824, Bolívar, adored by the populace, created a constitution making Peru a republic, but giving all power to a president-for-life. Part of southeastern Peru then seceded, calling itself Bolivia in his honour. He gave it a constitution as autocratic as Peru's and made de Sucre its first president.

In the south, revolution arose from economic discontent. Buenos Aires merchants had built up a lucrative trade with Spain and Britain before Spain imposed monopolistic laws on them. They wanted freedom from these laws, so, in 1810, after Napoleon had replaced the Spanish crown with his puppet, Creoles in the city overthrew the viceroy and appointed a council to rule in the name of the deposed Ferdinand VII. But delegates from outlying provinces assembled at Tucumán in 1816 and declared themselves independent of Spain. Contention between the capital and the provinces, however, impeded the revolt.

José de San Martin, a Spanish soldier, fought the French in Spain and then returned to Argentina. Ignoring local quarrels, he had himself named governor of Cuyo province on the eastern Andes, then organized and equipped an army to invade Chile. From there he attacked Peru, the royalist stronghold in South America. With Bernardo O'Higgins, a Chilean with an Irish father, he conquered Santiago in 1817. The Chileans offered him a dictatorship but, intent on Peru, San Martin gave the post to O'Higgins. In less than a year he entered Lima and, in 1821, declared Peru independent and took the title of "protector" of the new government. San Martin thought that monarchy was necessary for stability, but he felt inadequate to the role. A poor politician and orator, and a reluctant ruler, he alienated his supporters and died in bitter obscurity.

Women of all classes participated in these struggles at every level – helping male kin, organizing and hosting political meetings, donating money, food, and supplies, and working as spies, couriers, camp followers, or combatants. They lost money, property, people they loved, and their lives.[8] Propaganda aimed at women, particularly in cities, urged them to act usefully in society and to stop living in seclusion. Convents and retirement houses, which were no longer regarded as proper places for women, became involved in social services. Women's groups also sponsored secondary schools for girls.

The bloodiest fighting occurred in Venezuela and Colombia. Women were not expected to fight in such battles, but some did: Evangelista Tamayo fought under Bolívar in the battle of Boyac; Teresa Corneja and Manuela Tinoco disguised themselves as men in the struggle. Bolívar's acknowledgment suggests the prejudice they met:

> Even the fair sex, the delights of humankind, our amazons have fought against the tyrants of San Carlos with a valor divine, although without success. The monsters and tigers of Spain have shown the full extent of [their] cowardice. . . . They have used their infamous arms against the innocent feminine breasts of our beauties; they have shed their blood. They have killed many of them and they loaded them with chains, because they conceived the sublime plan of liberating their beloved country![9]

Women worked as nurses in field hospitals. Upper- or middle-class Argentinian Creole women donated their jewellery and silver, money, horses, cattle, and property to finance independence movements. They organized *tertulias* and *veladas*, social gatherings in which women discussed politics with men. Mariquita Sanchez de Thompson, who, in 1805, had successfully petitioned the justice department for permission to marry the man she loved over her stepfather's objection, used her famous *tertulias* to form the Patriotic Society. In Caracas, Josefa Palacios and her husband, Jose Felix Rivas, gave *tertulias* to bring together Venezuelan liberals and intellectuals to articulate political grievances and find solutions. In Quito, Manuela Canizares launched the August 10 Ecuadorian insurrection at a *tertulia*, and in San Juan, Maria de las Mercedes Barbudo, the local agent of the Puerto Rican separatist movement, held group meetings in her house until she was exiled in 1823.

Latin American women were cconsidered innocents, incapable of deceit or seduction. This reputation simplified their working as spies and couriers, gathering or transmitting information on troop movements or military conditions in Spain. The most famous, the young Colombian Policarpa Salavarrieta, but known as "La Pola," was a seamstress raised in a separatist family. She worked in Creole homes and was able to scent out loyalties and learn about troop movements and manoeuvres. Captured in 1817, she gave a fiery speech before she was executed in Bogotá plaza.

During the wars, men became aware of women's leadership ability and stopped assuming that females were harmless, gentle, and weak. This recognition did not lead them to give women more power, however, but only to punish women insurgents more harshly. Many beside La Pola were executed, imprisoned, or exiled. Royalist women emigrated to Cuba or Puerto Rico, both of which were royalist centres.

Castas (women with mixed blood) were not welcome in such places. They survived by following men to war and maintaining them – by cooking, sewing, doing laundry, and providing sex. They tended the wounded, buried the dead, and bore the babies. The *Rabonas* of Peru created a semblance of normalcy during the entire period of chaos by providing for soldiers' needs – they "wash and mend their clothes, receive no pay and have as their only salary the right to steal with impunity."[10] Single, these women lived with the soldiers, ate and slept with them, and underwent the same dangers.

Portuguese America: Brazil

The Portuguese who colonized Brazil came from a culture much like Spain's, one highly stratified by both class and sex. Two-thirds of Brazil's population were African slaves, however, and there was only a small middle class, with no cities and few schools: 10 percent of the population was literate. When Napoleon invaded Portugal in 1807, the Portuguese king, Dom Joao VI, and his court, protected by the British navy, fled to Brazil. Upset by Brazil's backwardness, Dom Joao built hospitals, schools, colleges, and a bank, reorganized the administration, and sponsored new agricultural methods. Taking the colonists' part, he ended Portugal's monopoly over trade; he opened

Brazilian ports, abolished restrictions on colonial manufacture, and encouraged foreign immigration. Dom Joao patronized the arts and built a national library, museums, and a botanical garden.

When the Portuguese monarchy was restored in 1816, Brazil annexed Uruguay. In 1821 Dom Joao sailed back to Lisbon, leaving his eldest son, Dom Pedro I, as regent. Once in Lisbon, however, Dom Joao found himself beset by domestic conflict. He tried to curtail Brazilian autonomy and ordered his son home. But the minerologist José Bonifacio had converted the young man to the cause of independence and he defied the order, remaining in Rio de Janeiro. In 1822 Dom Pedro convened a Constitutent Assembly, proclaimed Brazil independent, and was named emperor. Brazil became the only Latin American state to win independence as a monarchy, not a republic.

Brazil's independence was achieved without war, but not without struggle. As in other Spanish colonies, women participated in this change. They agitated, provided forums for debate, and even joined the military. One ardent young nationalist, Maria de Jesús, was discovered when her father asked the army to seek her out. Illiterate, clever, quick, "with education she might have been a remarkable person," wrote one contemporary observer, Maria Graham.[11]

By 1826, all of South America was independent. Uruguay remained a province of Brazil until 1828; Argentina did not unify Buenos Aires and the provinces until 1853. But the vice-royalty of New Spain – Mexico, Central America, some West Indies islands, and Spanish territories in the United States – were all still colonies.

The Caribbean

Haiti, France's most prosperous colony in the eighteenth century, seethed with discontent. A few hundred whites, mainly French planters and officials, dominated half a million brutally exploited African slaves. Between them, hated by both groups, was a class of mulattoes, who were divided among themselves. In 1791 Toussaint L'Ouverture, the slave grandson of an African king, became the

African leader. When the French Revolution ended slavery in French colonies, he led a massive revolt against the slave owners. Like Nzinga of Angola, he used guerrilla tactics – his straggling force of fighters, barely trained and poorly armed, would hit and quickly run. It took ten years, but Toussaint gained control of the entire island: he issued a constitution and assumed dictatorial powers. Outraged, Napoleon vowed not to "leave an epaulette on the shoulder of a Negro" and sent a huge expedition to Haiti, led by his brother-in-law, General LeClerc. After two years of unsuccessful fighting, LeClerc offered to negotiate and invited Toussaint to his quarters. He had him seized and shipped in chains to a French prison. Africans rose en masse and forced the French out: in 1804 Haiti declared itself independent.

Santo Domingo shared an island with Haiti. It claimed independence in 1822, but Haiti invaded and occupied it until 1844. Santo Domingo was devastated by the revolution and the loss of its functions as a slave entrepot and sugar producer, functions that were taken over by Cuba. Immigrants from Florida, Louisiana, and Santo Domingo expanded and diversified Cuba's trade, introducing large-scale sugar production. The prosperous *criollo* Cuban elite feared slave rebellions and remained loyal to Spain. Puerto Rican Creoles had the same complaints about Spain as South Americans did, but the islands were key to Spain's colonial defence network: Spanish troops disembarked there for assignments on the mainland. Latin American rebels, mainly Venezuelans, tried to free the Antilles, but the strong Spanish military presence made it impossible. Cuba and Puerto Rico remained part of the Spanish Empire until 1898, when the United States took them in war. In the intervening period, Spain tried to make a profit by intensifying colonization and production on both islands.

There is little information about women in revolutions in the Caribbean until the 1860s, when bands of women collaborated with men in agitating for Antillean independence. Cuban women in the United States formed clubs to aid the rebels during the Ten

Year War, which began in 1868 when insurgents in both Cuba and Puerto Rico demanded abolition of slavery and independence. The Pact of Zanjón, which ended hostilities in 1878, granted neither, and the movement went underground until 1892, when exiles formed Cuban and Puerto Rican revolutionary parties. From 1878 to 1898 the clubs met on and off the islands and became very important in 1892, when the Mercedes Varona (a female hero of the Ten Year War) Club was formed for political agitation. By 1897, forty-nine clubs existed.

Elite women agitated within their own class. The Puerto Rican Lola Rodriguez de Tió is credited with writing the revolutionary anthem, while Mariana Bracetti sewed the banner of Lares. Others took more dangerous roles in secret societies. The Cuban Mariana Grajales, mother of the insurgent Antonio Macéo, was over sixty when the war began, but, with her daughters and Macéo's wife, Maria Cabrales, she gave rebel soldiers safe shelter and provisions. Women performed supportive acts that were fraught with danger: the government imprisoned, exiled, or executed people for their own acts or those of their kin. José Martí celebrated Grajales in the newspaper *Patria*, describing her egging on her compatriots while tending her dying husband on the battlefield and following, on bleeding feet, the stretcher bearing her wounded son. She nursed wounded Cubans or Spaniards. Martí, the poet-patriot of the revolution, central to the movement, called her the true mother of the Cuban nation. Despite women's work in revolution in Cuba and in Puerto Rico, female status improved only slightly. Today, however, it is normal for Caribbean families to be headed by women.

British-owned islands did not become independent until much later, but, throughout the British Empire, slaves were freed in the 1830s.[12] Jamaica and Trinidad (and Tobago) did not become independent until 1962. The British seemed unsure how to free the smaller islands: they tried various forms of limited federation and then abandoned them. Barbados gained independence in 1966, and, in 1967, Antigua, Dominica, Grenada, St. Kitts, Nevis,

Anguilla, and St. Lucia (and later St. Vincent) joined Britain as "associated states": they ran their own internal affairs, but Britain controlled their defence and external affairs. The islands found this arrangement unsatisfactory and, despite their small size, all but one chose independence: Grenada in 1974, Dominica in 1978, St. Lucia and St. Vincent in 1979, Antigua in 1981, and St. Kitts-Nevis in 1983. But independence in small states is somewhat meaning-less,[13] as the United States' invasion of Grenada proved in 1983.

Mexico

Creoles in Mexico were less powerful than in the rest of Latin America. They hesitated to rebel against Spain, fearing that ideas of liberty and equality might arouse Indians and poor mestizos to revolt. The first uprising occurred in the countryside, among Indians and the poor, led by the son of a poor Creole farmer, Miguel Hidalgo y Costilla. Defeated and captured, he was condemned by the Inquisition and shot. The rebellion continued, led by José Morelos, a mestizo who tried to set up an independent government. After four years, royalist troops captured and executed him. Augustín de Iturbide, the son of a prosperous mestizo landowner, fought for the royalists as a mercenary, then turned on them to demand independence and racial equality. He drew massive support, although his motivation was questionable. In 1821 he marched triumphantly into Mexico City without a fight and persuaded the Mexican Congress to name him Augustín I, emperor of a Mexican empire. But he ruled so harshly that he lost the army's support and was forced into exile in 1823. The next year, Mexico adopted a republican constitution like that of the United States, except for making Roman Catholicism the state religion.

Women were involved in these uprisings. They formed political organizations like the Patriotas Marianas, one of the first secular associations in Mexico to support the royalists. During the Cristero War, mounted by Catholics to keep Mexico from becoming a secular state, women mobilized to support the conservative church.

They also supported the rebels: Josefa Ortiz de Dominguez, La Corregidora, an early agitator for Mexican independence, warned the rebel forces of impending danger; Leona Vicario left her comfortable home to give embattled Mexican insurgents in the countryside some material assistance and she joined them in the fight.

Latin American revolutions were aimed at freeing propertied men from European control. But the proportion of propertied men was much smaller and they were much richer than their counterparts in the revolution in North America. The new states were economically and socially unbalanced. It is common, whenever masses of people are exploited, for the elite to place a despot in power. They hope a strong, repressive leader will keep the poor in line. For decades, the struggle continued in Latin America between proponents of dictatorship and anarchy, federalists and centralists, conservative Catholics and liberal anti-clericals, farmers-herders and urbanites. But the basic fight was, and still is, between a small minority of propertied men and everyone else. Land continues to be the source of most wealth, and insurgents regularly demand its redistribution. The plantation system remained almost universal well past its time, but, with slaves or semi-servile labour plentiful, landlords had little incentive to improve their methods of cultivation. In this environment, foreigners with money and ideas began to gain economic control.

Latin American Women after Independence

When the revolutions ended, men expected women to return to their traditional roles with their old social and legal status: they could not vote, hold public office, advocate, witness a will, or testify in court; nor could they be judges, lawyers, or priests, adopt a child, or act as guardian of a minor. Hispanic law considered the governance of children a "public ministry" suitable only for men. The law forbade women to dress like men, and granted men authority over women at home and in society, and over sons and daughters during the father's lifetime. Theoretically, children became personally and legally independent around the age of twenty-five, but most single women remained at home under the "protection" of male kin. Widows and emancipated single women could manage their own affairs, but married women had the right only to custody of children in most separations; to bequeath, own, and inherit property; and to keep their family surnames. Few women sued for divorce: unless a marriage contract stipulated otherwise, husbands controlled the wife's property. Wives could not enter legal contracts, work, or keep their wages without his permission.

Some scholars argue that Latin American women were confined to a separate sphere, but had equal power, because Marianismo, belief in the sacredness of the Virgin Mary, confers sacredness on motherhood and gives women moral force. But nineteenth-century Latin American Marianismo was a variant of Victorianism.[14] Women were rhetorically exalted in the family and in principle, but in reality, men dominated at home just as they did outside. Moreover, the religious model perpetuated sexual myths: "decent" (upper-class) women were believed not to feel sexual desire, while lower-class women, most domestic servants, and prostitutes bore the moral burden of the sexuality of the entire society.

Race and class divided women as always, but all classes of women took the elite as a model. Indian, African, and mestiza women populated the countryside, doing productive work, while rich landowners' wives set standards of behaviour. Some prosperous women headed households and found ways to own mines, haciendas, or businesses or to patronize religious and charitable institutions. Lower-class women worked as always in the fields, in shops, and as artisans and market vendors. Some theorists believe that patriarchy began with land ownership, and, interestingly, most Indians or mestizos who owned land lived in patriarchal patterns – until the number of people in the household outgrew its capacity to feed them. When land grew scarce, market economies arose, or land and labour became commercialized, female-headed or extended households emerged. Many such households existed at all levels of society. However, in all homes, women were central. Upper-class women, considered the pillars of society, derived power and pleasure from directing their children's socialization and education and overseeing a household, servants, and domiciled kin. Non-elite white women, Indians, Africans, and *castas*, with greater freedom in marriage and separation, were more likely to live in consensual companionship than in legal marriage.

Blood remained a key factor, and by the 1850s a handful of elite families dominated national and regional affairs. "Old" colonial families intermarried with "new" ones created by earlier intermarriage with Creoles, as some men grew rich in the financial and administrative chaos that followed revolution and married "up." They took government jobs that protected the interests of their class. These networks expanded and eventually dominated all aspects of Latin American society. Interest-based political and bureaucratic structures superseded the old family networks in the twentieth century, but non-elite families continue to use marriage, kinship, business association, and political influence in exactly the same way as the old elites. As we have seen, it is in family-based political systems that women often possess a role of major importance and considerable informal authority.

Women's Education

After the revolutions, "woman" was redefined as a dependent being. Having eliminated the one asylum women had, the convent, men defined women as mothers only, and they tried to harness them into service to the nation, rather than the church. To replace religious fervour with national fervour, men claimed the home to be an arena of stability and purity from which all "low" elements had been excised: "private life" sheltered men from turmoil, and women were the guardians of this realm. Again, women legislated powerless were made responsible for national "purity" and the patriotism, work ethic, and belief in progress of their children, whose "lazy habits" women were urged to wipe out. Rich women who had formerly sent their babies out to wet nurses were told to take a greater role in raising and educating them. To fill this role, women had to be educated.

The major propaganda medium was the periodical press, which was dominated by men who met in informal reading groups to circulate and discuss the latest European journals and books. They saw themselves as "apostles" and "redeemers" of their countries, chosen to speak for the voiceless and defining the parameters of national literature. To do that, it helps to listen to the voiceless, but these men saw women as only recipients of their knowledge.

Some efforts were made to provide women with a voice, as liberal men urged the expansion of secondary education on the familiar ground that educated women educated children, thereby benefiting the nation. In 1823 the Argentine government founded the Society of Beneficence of Buenos Aires to manage a public school system and appointed a group of elite women to run it. The society became a model for other charitable institutions and gave educated women a use for their talents, but had little effect on mass education.

As Argentina grew more prosperous, industry, agriculture, and commerce needed better-trained workers. Secondary vocational schools were set up to teach girls typing, accounting, telegraphy, and stenography. In 1907 the National Girls' High School No. 1 opened in Buenos Aires to educate girls in chemistry, natural history, anatomy, psychology, and geography, as well as the usual domestic science, music, and physical education. Most girls who attended such schools came from middle-class or immigrant families. There was no place for an educated elite in society: laws forced married Argentine women to get their husbands' permission to work, and they were forbidden from signing contracts.

Before independence, the Mexican government supported female education, claiming it would benefit men, and in 1842 Mexico City made education mandatory for all children seven to fifteen years old. The first girls' schools opened in Mexico City in 1869; other cities soon followed suit. But Mexican society undermined female education even as it fostered it: José Joaquín Fernández de Lizardi wrote a popular exemplary tract for girls, *Little Miss Quixote and Her Cousin,* in which he compared a "good girl," brought up virtuously to marry, with Little Miss Quixote, who was too smart for her own good. Lizardi believed that women merely parroted knowledge. He recognized the problems facing widows, but the only gainful occupation he could imagine a woman filling was watch repairing.

By the 1880s most Mexican legislators supported compulsory education and a standard curriculum. Late nineteenth- and early twentieth-century reformers like President Benito Juárez, educator José Maria Vigil, and legislator Justo Sierra urged secular education for women to weaken Catholic control over women (and thus over the family). Sierra wrote: "The educated woman will be truly one for the home."[15] But as soon as women had a basic education, they wanted more. This additional training, not so clearly "for the home," was strenuously opposed, and women were not accepted in professional schools until 1888, when Matilda Montoya entered the National School of Medicine. But many girls received vocational training for low-paid jobs as clerks and as telephone and telegraph workers.

Colombia's first public schools opened in 1821, but few accepted girls. In 1832 the Colegio de la Merced was founded to teach girls a traditional curriculum as well as Spanish, French, drawing, and music. To unify Colombian public education and create normal schools in each state, the first of many teacher-education colleges opened in Bogotá with eighty students in 1872.

In the slave-holding Brazilian empire, more class-ridden than any other Latin American state, only elite families willing to pay private tutors educated their children. In 1827 girls were admitted to primary schools to study domestic science; in 1837 normal schools, the only higher education available to them, opened to women. By 1873 there were about 5000 public and private primary schools with over 100,000 boy students and more than 40,000 girl students. In the late nineteenth century, some schoolteachers, like Francisca S. da Mota in Brazil, published feminist newspapers. But co-education was banned, and few men wanted to spend money schooling girls, so rich women studied abroad – Maria Augusta Generosa Estrella and Josefa Agueda Felisbella Mercedes de Oliveira, for instance, trained as physicians in the United States. Not until the end of the century was medicine (including nursing and midwifery) accepted as a career for women.

The Spanish colonies of Cuba and Puerto Rico were even more retrograde. Slavery was not abolished in Puerto Rico until 1873 and in Cuba, 1886. The emancipation of women took longer, partly because Latin American women themselves did not organize, and men were the main backers of female education. Celestina Cordero, a Puerto Rican educator of the 1820s, provided a model for later generations of women who founded organizations to promote female education. Men also urged women to demand rights. But the vision held out to women – that their education would serve others' causes (while they lived in the same confinement) – was hardly inspiring. Not until the last third of the century was educator Eugenio Maria de Hostos able to establish a public school system in Puerto Rico and to export his educational philosophy to Chile, Cuba, the Dominican Republic, and elsewhere in the hemisphere.

An exception to the general indifference about female education was the West Indies, where the majority of people were African, many of West African descent. West African women traditionally had freedom and autonomy as local traders and managed their own households within polygynous marriages, relatively free from surveillance or domination by husbands. When enslavement broke up their families, Africans set up matrifocal structures: Maroon communities were matrifocal. In both Maroon and slave communities, women, although subordinate to men, were the stable centre: they produced the food, controlled the Sunday markets, and maintained families, thereby linking elements of their African heritage with forms of resistance and solidarity. Their different view of women led people in Barbados and Jamaica to support education for both sexes, and women became teachers and nurses.

Everywhere in Latin America, attitudes were the same. Men feared educating women lest they rebel against their confinement; for the same reason, the upper classes feared educating the lower classes. When girls were given training, they were taught only the skills needed in the home. Normal school was women's only road out. As they took it, the school system, especially at the primary level, became dominated by women. Teachers were a driving force in all major movements for change in the twentieth century – and such changes in society expanded women's possibilities.

Women's Work, 1880-1930

Latin American economies were primarily based in mining (mainly of copper) and agriculture (mainly sugar and coffee) well into the twentieth century. Europe's and North America's hunger for raw materials enriched plantation owners, who expanded their holdings and devoured the land of small farmers. Once they were landless, these formerly self-sufficient people trooped to cities to work for wages or dwindled into peons on others' land. In some regions, individual Indians or entire communities were drafted for labour on haciendas; ironically, Indians were often resettled as peons on land they had once owned – in coastal areas of Guatemala and Peru, for example. Women were essential in peasant families: they worked for the hacienda family as cooks, seamstresses, weavers, and herders; helped grow the food that fed their own families; and reproduced and maintained them.

Indians kept aloof from Latin society, maintaining their own traditions. Women were largely responsible for preserving the ancient customs and work ethics: they enabled their communities to resist the dominant culture and religion, and also helped support them, running markets in villages and towns, and selling woollens, farm produce, and crafts.

Slavery dominated the culture of Brazil and the Caribbean

through most of the nineteenth century. Status determined one's life, and status was determined by race, colour, and ethnic background. The small white elite legislated itself all the political privileges and the economic and cultural opportunities. Most people were slaves. After the legal slave trade ended in 1807, slaves were American-born, many with mixed blood. There was no middle class, only free people of colour with none of the rights of the elite.

Pedro II, emperor of Brazil from 1840 to 1889, tried to emancipate its slaves. But extreme opposition from the rich, most of whom were plantation owners, slowed the process, which took almost twenty years. Finally, a rebellion overthrew the monarchy and established a republic dominated by the rich and the military.

Cuba and Puerto Rico had slave minorities: the population was largely Creole; *castas*, free and enslaved, made up the rest. Plantation owners, wanting a forced labour force, legislated one and required all peasants over sixteen to carry passbooks – work papers that limited mobility (just as Russians had immobilized the serfs, or South African whites had regulated the blacks). Instituted in 1849, this system remained in effect until 1873. Poor free women were forced to do agricultural labour – picking or thrashing berries in the coffee fields, or stripping, sorting, and bundling tobacco. In towns, little girls were pressed into domestic service, while the older women did laundry. Called *criadas*, they worked very long days doing whatever their employers ordered.

Early Latin American Feminism

After the mid-nineteenth century, feminists began to found their own newspapers and journals, but they still wrote articles exalting motherhood and the "sanctity" of the home. The Virgin Mary was their model for their claim that women were morally and emotionally superior to men. Women's books and essays, like men's, recommended education to make women better mothers. Latin American men who favoured female emancipation had different goals from women: they wanted free love, contraception, and easier divorce.

Women, worried about raising and supporting children, were more cautious about sexual freedom and concentrated on economic issues. Several women wrote political essays from a feminist perspective in the 1870s; María Eugenia Echenique in Buenos Aires, María Abella y Ramirez in Uruguay, Adelia de Carlo in Argentina, and Isabel Andréu de Aguilar in Puerto Rico. They all urged reform to make women better wives and mothers. Agitators not calling themselves feminists worked for woman suffrage and improved education, wages, and work conditions. They wanted the right to make decisions for themselves – to exist legally, eliminate the double standard, and improve working conditions for children and women.

Feminists, most of whom were educated abroad, became visible at the turn of the century. In 1901 Elvira López wrote that feminists in Argentina, Chile, and Uruguay wanted only economic and educational opportunities like men's; the Argentinian socialist Dr. Alicia Moreau de Justo insisted that women had to struggle alongside men, not against them, to combat capitalism. Cecilia Grierson, the first woman physician in Argentina, studied techniques for treating blindness and deafness in Europe and wrote medical treatises. On her return home, she founded one of the first institutes for studying and teaching retarded children.[16] Brazilian feminist Bertha Lutz was educated in Europe. She dared to suggest that the emancipation of women would benefit society, but urged woman suffrage in order to end female "parasitism" and make women responsible. Amanda Labarca, who studied in the United States, started feminist reading circles in Chile.

Feminists talked about emancipation and annulling laws preventing sexual equality, but were opposed not only by men but by women, who feared a "breakdown of the family." Many Latin American women were deeply religious and bowed to the conservative dictates of the church regarding sex roles. When religious war erupted later, they supported the church.

In 1887, women were 39 percent of the Buenos Aires labour force; in 1914, women in professions, industry, and commerce made up 22 percent of the country's workforce; by 1947, it was 31.2 percent. Yet they remained subject to male authority: men had the right to women's wages, and women could not vote or hold public office.

In 1910 Cecelia Grierson and Petrona Eyle organized the First International Feminist Congress in Buenos Aires. It drew women from Brazil, Paraguay, Uruguay, and Chile, and operated in several languages – Spanish, English, Russian, French, Italian, and German. The organizers invited major feminists and professionals like Dr. Julieta Lanteri Renshaw, founder of the suffragist National Feminist Party; Genia Chertkoff, who agitated for children's rights and against the social and sexual exploitation of women; Dr. de Justo, the socialist who founded the Committee for Women's Suffrage and National Feminist Union; Marie Curie; and Italian educator Maria Montessori. They sought common ground on civil rights, education, divorce, health, and domestic economics and passed a platform advocating equality for married women, equal pay, a divorce law, improved conditions for working women and children, and an end to the system where schools pressed women into traditional studies.

The Argentinian National Feminist Party and the Women's Rights Association did not begin to lobby for political rights until the 1920s, but they had swift success, pushing through protective legislation (though it affected only a minority of workers) and a Civil Code in 1926. This code changed the civil status of married women, giving them limited control over their earnings and the right to work without their husbands' permission, to sign contracts, and to separate from their husbands and retain authority over their children and household goods.

Revolution in Mexico

From 1833 until 1855, Mexico was ruled by Antonio López de Santa Anna, a Creole dictator supported by the church and the military. After bungling a war with the United States (1846–48) which lost Mexico its North American territory, he was overthrown by an

Indian reformist democrat, Benito Juárez. Juárez tried to end military and clerical privilege, separate church and state, and give church lands to the people. The elite mounted a war against him; they lost and, in the process, bankrupted the state. It had to sell church land to secular landowners, transferring the peasants from one exploiter to another. When Mexico defaulted on its foreign loans, Napoleon III sent troops to instal the Archduke Maximilian of Austria as a French puppet ruler. When France entered the Austro-Prussian War of 1866, Napoleon had to withdraw his troops from Mexico, and Maximilian's government collapsed. Juárez was elected president, but he accomplished little before he died in 1872. His successor was overthrown by Porfirio Díaz.

Díaz sought foreign investment, increased industry and trade, and built railroads. He balanced the budget by mortgaging Mexico to foreigners. Prosperity opened jobs for middle-class women in the professions, and for working-class women in textile factories, railroads, and other enterprises known for exploiting workers. The inevitable problems of industrialization followed – migration to cities, overcrowded expensive housing, poor sanitation, as well as low pay, unsafe and unhealthy work conditions, and lack of child care. Most rural women who came to the cities worked as servants. In Cuba in 1903, for instance, 70 percent of working women were servants; in 1919, domestic servants made up 50 percent of the labour force.[17] They suffered the usual fate of female servants: underpaid, overworked, sexually used, and cast out if they became pregnant. Many became prostitutes, whose numbers swelled; in 1907 Mexico City had 20 percent of the population of Paris, but twice as many prostitutes. Díaz required them to register and receive regular medical examinations. He repressed workers, sending troops to crush protests or strikes, and giving the rich the lands that Juárez had intended for the poor. At the end of the Porfiriato (1876–1910), half the population were peons on haciendas, communally owned villages had almost disappeared, 95 percent of rural families were landless, and 30 percent of Mexican mothers were single.

Mexican feminists were organizing before the 1910 Revolution. In 1870 Rita Cetina Gutierrez, a schoolteacher-poet, founded a feminist journal, *La Siempreviva.* Its editors created a secondary school that evolved into a state normal school. Women with knowledge and training demanded education for all women, decent wages, and reform of the Civil Code to eliminate the double standard and other inequities, thereby laying the groundwork for later reforms.

By 1910 the country was in revolution. Amid revolutionary rhetoric advocating social and economic reform, Díaz was overthrown and succeeded by a series of leaders played against each other by the United States. About a million people died in political uprisings between 1910 and 1917. Women fought on both sides – those devoted to the church fought with the elite; the others fought with the rebels. They were so fierce that several generals declared that, for the revolution to succeed, women would have to be "defanaticized." Some became famous, like the Zapatista La Coronela. Women were journalists, propagandists, and political activists, but, as *soldaderas,* they also had to grind corn and make tortillas for the armies. John Reed wrote that the Mexican *soldadera* follows her man into the army and becomes another soldier's woman when he dies. An American diplomat's wife offered a somewhat different account:

> A thick and Heartbreaking book could be written upon the *soldadera* – the heroic woman who accompanies the army, carrying in addition to her baby, any other mortal possession, such as a kettle, basket, goat, blanket, parrot, fruit and the like. These women are the only visible commissariat for the soldiers: they accompany them in their marches, they forage for them and they cook for them; they nurse them, bury them; they receive their money when it is paid. All this they do and keep up with the march of the army, besides rendering any other service the male may require.[18]

Several revolutionary generals and the first president of post-revolutionary Mexico, Venustiano Carranza, advocated female emancipation. A socialist general, Salvador Alvarado (later governor of the Yucatán), made the province a feminist centre from 1915 to 1924. Alvarado called the first two feminist congresses in Mexican history in 1916 to discuss political rights, secondary schools, and work, as well as divorce and birth control. The congresses drew mainly teachers, who approved resolutions favouring increased (and progressive) education and political participation for women. Alvarado's successor, the socialist Felipe Carillo Puerto, extended his programs, advocating woman suffrage and right to hold public office at the municipal level. Yet when a new constitution was signed in 1917 granting suffrage to all men over twenty-one and freedom of religion, it specifically denied women suffrage and excluded peasant women from the land reform program and land ownership.

At the First Feminist Congress of the Pan American League, held in Mexico City in 1923, feminist delegates from twenty Mexican states and North American women's groups overwhelmingly endorsed woman suffrage. Middle-class women, who gained most from feminism, tried to deal with the needs of poor and working-class women. But like middle-class women in England and the United States, they imposed their own standards, rather than learning what was needed at the local level. But sometimes the desires of the two coincided. Everywhere, huge numbers of women were entering the labour force, mainly in domestic service and textile manufacture. Throughout the continent, working conditions were brutal: women worked long hours for low wages without any provision for child care, health, or sanitation. A woman's suffrage movement emerged in Mexico, but women did not win the vote until 1958.

Activists: Labourites

Latin American working women linked political emancipation to improved working conditions from the first. They began to form unions in the late nineteenth century: in 1880 women in Mexican tobacco and textile industries unionized and struck for higher wages and better working conditions. In 1905 textile unions like the Hijas de Anahuac (Daughters of Anahuac) demanded a minimum wage and an eight-hour day. Puerto Rican women, also organized before 1900, had unionized coffee pickers, domestic workers, and women of Puerta de Tierra by 1910. Women in the Puerto Rican tobacco industry were elected as delegates to the Second Assembly of the Union of Tobacco Workers. Female unionists agitated for political and economic rights and the recognition of collective bargaining, usually under the banner of the Puerto Rican Socialist Party. In Argentina, working-class journals and the women's journal of the Argentine Socialist Party stressed the need for protective legislation for women.

In Mexico, unions fought the Díaz government, thereby aiding the revolution (which continued in various phases from 1910 to 1927). In Veracruz, severe inflation and unemployment caused widespread misery.[19] In January 1922, 3000 people at an open-air meeting asked a group of women and Heron Proal, a utopian socialist tailor with anarchist leanings, to lead a Revolutionary Tenants' Union. By March 3 it had drawn 80 percent of the population, many of them widows, sailors' wives, and working women. They held mass meetings, putting on plays to dramatize the political situation for illiterate people and fuel their sense of solidarity. The union called a rent strike to demand immediate rent rollbacks and recognition of the Tenants Union as the bargaining agent in determining fair rents and leases.

When the government threatened to use force, the strikers called an illegal public meeting at a park on July 5, 1922. At 8 p.m. Proal, the only male leader of the union, appeared, surrounded by forty women wearing red. The police and the army struck everyone they could reach. When the forty women shouted "Viva la Revolucion Social!" a crowd of 2000 echoed their cry. They tried to win over the soldiers by yelling "Viva el hermano soldado!" (Long live our soldier brother!). But these soldiers raised their rifles and fired into the crowd, killing some, wounding more, and arresting every union leader they recognized.

For months afterwards, women led periodical community demonstrations. Everyone involved agreed that women were the lifeblood of the Veracruz strike. In 1923 the Veracruz Union won a rent ceiling limiting increases to 6 percent a year, the right to a year's lease at a fixed rent, and the establishment of boards of tenants and landlords to rule on health standards. Such victories gave men a chance to participate in government, but women were still excluded. Many of the men who led the Mexican Revolution of 1910–17 advocated free love and easy divorce, but not the vote. After the revolution, the men formed a virtual one-party state dominated by a single institutionalized revolutionary party run on corporatist lines. Even now people can join it only as members of interest groups – workers or peasants, say – which hinders women who lack an extradomestic affiliation from political participation. Only recently have women been elected to the national legislature, and few hold positions in the judiciary. No woman has ever held a top position in the executive branch of the Mexican government.

Women were especially active in anarchist groups supporting female education and emancipation. In many Latin American countries, socialist and anarchist groups agitated for legal rights and protection for the growing numbers of women and children factory workers. First to do so was the Argentine Socialist Party, led by pioneers Alicia Moreau de Justo, Cecilia Grierson, Julieta Renshaw, and Elvira Rawson de Dellepiane. But they lacked a large following; Argentinian women could not vote until Juan Perón's regime. Even socialists were ambivalent about women's independence – newspapers like *El Socialista*, *La Comuna*, and *La Internacional* denounced exploitation of women and defended their right to work, but they also printed articles blaming women's oppression on their "nature." Of all the independence movements, only anarchism had a consistent ideology of equality. Other groups in which women were involved – the Peruvian Aprista Movement of the 1920s and various Communist parties – were not concerned about women's needs.[20]

Political Action after the First World War

When women in the United States and much of Europe won the vote after the First World War, they encouraged Latin American women to intensify their effort. But these women faced formidable opposition, and no campaign succeeded until the 1930s. Male dominance in Latin America had a special intensity, an adolescent cock-of-the-walk manner called "machismo" that has become the universal name for such behaviour. The double standard that pervaded Latin America after the First World War existed elsewhere as well, but was more openly and shamelessly acknowledged there.

Women, especially of the upper and middle class, were expected to be "pure" and faithful, patiently accepting men's sexual freedom. Argentinian men ran a white slave traffic, importing women from Eastern Europe for brothels in the capital. The *casa chica*, the "little house" where men had a second household with a lover and her children, is a venerated tradition in Mexico and Central America. Well-to-do men may make several such arrangements in a lifetime, but even poor men have them.[21] This system bolsters male pride by undermining women's independence: a woman who is totally or largely dependent on a man for survival will cling to and flatter him whenever he deigns to appear. In such a society, fighting for suffrage inevitably involved daily humiliation.

The United States dominated Cuba. In keeping with US foreign policy, it supported a series of corrupt, repressive leaders there. Women of all political persuasions joined the Cuban Committee for the Defense of Women's Suffrage, led by Pilar Jorge de Tella and Ofelia Dominguez Navarro, and helped oust President Gerardo Machado; they won the vote in 1934.

The United States governed Puerto Rico directly as a colony, but the island had a strong woman suffrage movement that won the vote in 1932. The movement diffused after its victory, but did elect 113 women to municipal councils. Maria Luisa Arcelay-Rosa, owner of a needlework factory in Mayaguez, was the first woman elected to the Puerto Rican House of Representatives. Owner though she was, she advocated progressive management practices, improved working conditions, and a daycare system. In 1936 María Martinez de Pérez Almiroty was elected to the Puerto Rican Senate, in a line of female representatives that continues today. Many women held municipal offices – Felisa Rincón de Guatier, mayor of San Juan from 1948 to 1968, was the best known. Many Puerto Rican towns or *municipios* have elected women mayors.

Brazilian women also won the vote in 1932, but, unlike its feminist pioneers, the suffrage movement there was concerned only with middle-class women. This male-dominated, repressive society impeded women's entrance into public life: while some women voted, most did not, and none was elected to a position of leadership.

Argentina is special because of the Peróns. Here, too, a few people had enormous wealth, but the majority were impoverished. When General Juan Perón, a member of the military clique ruling the country, became secretary of the Department of Labor and Welfare, he spoke out for women. He established a new political discourse welcoming women as equal partners in constructing the "new Argentina." Extolling the dignity of workers along with women's contribution to the nation, he created the first special Women's Division of Labor and Assistance to propose laws benefiting women. Perón banned piecework, established the principle of equal pay for equal work, encouraged female employment, and supported woman suffrage. A 1943 army coup brought him to power in 1946. For thirty-five years, bills extending the franchise to women had been submitted to and defeated by the conservative Argentine Senate; now Perón pushed one through a year after his election. He also created a new Peronist Constitution in 1949, modelled on the constitutions of the Weimar Republic and the USSR, affirming the rights of women, children, workers, and the elderly: it was one of the most progressive constitutions in the world. After a coup by the army in 1955, however, it was abolished and the old Argentine Constitution, copied from that of the United States, was restored.

In 1954 the Perón government passed a divorce law. (This law was also abolished by the army coup of 1955, which again made divorce illegal until 1986.) The party created social security programs and passed laws redressing inequality in pay and working conditions for women. By 1949 women made up 45 percent of industrial workers and 28 percent of the salaried employees in Buenos Aires; in 1950 they were nearly 22 percent of Argentine workers and half of those in textiles, garments, and chemicals. Between 1931 and 1940, female students in universities increased by 68.52 percent; from 1941 to 1950, by 139.51 percent; and from 1951 to 1960, by 153.62 percent.

Many historians – and Peronists – believe the charismatic Eva Perón was the architect of her husband's policies. She held no elected post and was not formally part of the government, but she influenced her husband with regard to poor workers. She headed the Eva Perón Foundation and sponsored the creation of women's centres in poor and working-class districts. These centres offered daycare and halls where women could meet and find free legal and medical care; lessons in language, painting, sewing, and other subjects; and attend lectures, conferences, and exhibitions on women's work. They raised women's consciousness of their rights and imbued them with Peronist ideals; they were later assimilated into the Peronist Women's Party, which Eva Perón also headed. As we know, a separate women's party tends to strengthen any movement, while it also allows women to learn political skills and become politically involved.

Eva Perón wanted to draw women away from Socialist and Marxist feminism and to elicit the blind devotion and loyalty of the members. She succeeded: by 1952 the Peronist Women's Party had 500,000 members in 3600 centres, and in the next election Juan Perón won 63 percent of the vote of the women to whom he had granted it. Upper-class women rejected Eva Perón because of her humble origins and sexual mores; older people criticized her politics and morals – she had openly lived with Perón before his election (he took her everywhere with him, treating her respecfully as his wife). But she offered an amazing role model to adolescents of the 1940s and 1950s, recalls historian Maria Gimenez, who grew up in Argentina in that period.[22] Working-class women appreciated her fiery anti-oligarchic, anti-capitalist rhetoric and the recognition, status, and real benefits she brought them. In 1951, for the first time in Argentina, more women than men voted (90.32 percent v. 86.08 percent), most for the Peronist ticket.[23] In another first in Argentine history, a large number of women were elected to national and provincial congresses, seven as senators and twenty-four as deputies to the National Congress.

Perón respected women, but had a traditional sense of their capacities. He considered women more loving and peaceable than men, and urged their participation in government on that ground. He favoured gradual reforms and cooperation between capital and labour. Eva Perón was more radical. She developed a unique combination of feminism and working-class consciousness which radicalized the working masses and made her the inspiration of the left wing of the Peronist party. When scholars discuss Peronism today, they divide it into an orthodox collaborationist wing, headed by Juan Perón, and a left wing, headed by Eva Perón.

When Eva Perón died at the age of thirty-two in 1952, she had touched the lives of millions of people, particularly women. The standard of living of working-class women and the status of all women were greatly improved by her policies and by her commitment to a wearying schedule of public appearances, even in the last months of her life. Poor women who wrote to her to ask for jobs or medical care for their children were helped by her foundation. Ruthless to enemies, arbitrary towards government agencies and officials, she was a symbol of a new life to working people – whatever the real intentions of her and her husband. Juan Perón began to lose his following when she died. He was overthrown by a military junta in 1955, but returned in 1974 with a new wife, Isabel, whom he tried to foist on the public as another Eva. Lacking force or ideas, she merely shored up the patriarchy until Perón died and she was thrust out of office. The military clique that followed ruled Argentina through a system of state terrorism.

Women won the vote in Ecuador in 1929, in Brazil and Uruguay in 1932, in Argentina in 1947, and in Chile in 1949. Bolivia made suffrage universal in 1952, and has even had a woman president. Women in Peru won the vote in 1955, and in Colombia in 1957; once dictator-controlled Paraguay granted it in 1961, all Latin American women could vote. But suffrage is not equal rights: formal political rights don't change entrenched vested interests. In Latin America's family-centred cultures, political behaviour is largely determined by family; and a family's position is largely determined by its class, level of wealth, and traditions.

Still, where women voted and held office, their status improved: more women were accepted in universities, business, and the professions. On occasion, women have decided elections – they kept Perón in office and put in Jorge Alessandri in Chile. Some held high office: Gabriela Mistral, the Nobel Laureate from Chile, was special ambassador to the League of Nations and the United Nations; Mexican writer Rosario Castellanos and Carmen Naranjo of Costa Rica were ambassadors to Israel. But public status does not affect women's subordination in the family. A double standard still infects customs like divorce and domestic responsibility, which change very slowly. Argentinian women were not granted authority over their children until 1985. And, according to one authority, "the Mexican family is founded on two fundamental propositions: the unquestioned and absolute supremacy of the father and the necessary and absolute self-sacrifice of the mother."[24]

The Cuban Revolution of 1959 ushered in a new era, raising hope and intensifying the struggle throughout Latin America. Socialist states made the greatest efforts to abolish sex discrimination in both law and practice. Fidel Castro is a paternalistic ruler, but the government he established in 1959 included important female guerrilla leaders like Haydee Santamaria and Dora Tijerino. The new constitution asserts: "Women have the same rights as men in the economy, political and social fields as well as in the family" (Article 43), and, in 1960, the government set up the Federation of Cuban Women to integrate women into all aspects of the revolutionary process. The Federation of Women developed into an independent, effective organ for mobilizing women and for creating education and health programs, a strong literacy campaign, vocational courses, children's circles, schools for the directors of and workers in these circles, literacy brigades, female militia, a Women's Improvement Plan, and the Ana Betancourt School for Peasant Girls. Fourteen years after its founding, an astonishing 54 percent of Cuban women were members of the federation.

In 1975 Cuba passed the best social legislation for women in Latin America, a Family Code mandating that both sexes share household labour and child care and giving women control of maternity. But too few jobs, boarding schools, and daycare allow men to maintain their old ways, and women still do most of the child care.

In 1979 Nicaraguan socialists overthrew the dictator Anastazio Somoza, who took the entire treasury of the country with him when he fled to exile. From the start, Nicaraguan revolutionaries incorporated women in their movement at every level. Rural and urban women fought Somoza as spies, organized communications networks, provided food and care, fought alongside male soldiers, and filled high-ranking positions in the army. Guerrilla fighter Dora Tijerino joined the Sandinista government after its victory in 1979, and women occupied every level of job.

Although Cuba and Nicaragua have a tradition of machismo, women in both countries made great gains. After the revolution, the FSLN and the women's movement worked together to write and pass the most progressive laws guaranteeing women's rights in the hemisphere.[25] But the unyielding hostility of the United States created severe economic problems for both countries, and outright war in Nicaragua. In addition, there were indications that Sandinista men were shutting women out of high-level government posts even before economic pressure and armed intervention, backed by the United States, toppled the Sandinista government in 1990.

Obsessed with keeping socialism out of the Western hemisphere, the United States forced the overturn of popularly elected socialist governments in Guatemala in 1954, Bolivia in 1971, Chile in 1973, and Nicaragua from 1979 to 1990. It supported military dictators who suppressed dissent in Brazil, Bolivia, Chile, Uruguay, Guatemala, and Argentina – all harsh regimes that unleashed extreme state terrorism. Poor women are vulnerable in every society, but middle-class Latin American women had always been considered outside the public realm, inviolable. The terrorism of this period spared no one, however: men, women, children, even nuns were attacked. Both the state and the rebels who opposed it were imbued with macho ideology, notions of honour and dishonour that allowed no alternative but death or victory. Women in guerrilla movements had to accept this code.

Some women supported rule by the elite. When Chile elected Salvador Allende's socialist government in 1970, 68.3 percent of the women who voted opposed him. Between his election and his inauguration, elite women, dressed in black, surrounded the presidential palace and marched with a coffin bearing the words "Chilean democracy, dead." US corporations cut off shipments and loans to Chile, the CIA fomented upheaval, and the Chilean right wing warned of the erosion of traditional values and the "family." Elite Chilean women believed this propaganda and, frightened by severe rationing, demonstrated against the government. One wealthy woman, fearing expropriation of her estate, rode on horseback to Santiago and stationed herself in front of the presidential palace in a bathing suit – a "decent" Latin American Lady Godiva! She was hailed by the conservative press as an "Amazon of Liberty." Other elite women organized marches in the streets of most Chilean cities every month in the last years of the Allende government. *El Poder Feminino* – Woman Power – is widely perceived as contributing to Allende's fall.

When Augusto Pinochet and his military junta took power in 1973, they stressed women's contribution to "the victory of democracy," but demanded they return to their passive, self-sacrificing roles. Facing widespread opposition, Pinochet and his clique established a terrorist regime that penetrated private life through informants.[26] State terrorism is more extreme than rebel terrorism because the state has more power at its disposal. Argentine and Chilean military oligarchies placed entire segments of the population under suspicion – students, workers, intellectuals. A new word entered the language – *desaparecidos*, the disappeared – people who had been made to disappear, kidnapped, held without due process, tortured, murdered. Yet the majority of the middle and upper classes, especially business people, supported Pinochet until 1981, when a depression or recession injured them. Pinochet consistently held the support of the military and their families, who comprise a separate caste in Chile: well paid, privileged, and living in a world of their own with separate schools and hospitals. When he resigned as head of state, Pinochet continued as head of the country's armed forces and lived in luxury, even splendour.

The government of Argentina also caused people to disappear, leaving their mutilated bodies in remote places. Argentine torturers threw people out of airplanes over the sea, and hundreds of bodies washed up on the beaches of Buenos Aires. Some people had to endure "living death" in hidden camps. Both sexes were tortured, but women were also raped, often in front of children. The Argentine government took away babies born to young women in prison and gave them to military families, then killed the mothers, leaving grandmothers utterly bereft. Political parties and trade unions collapsed or were driven underground; newspapers were closed down and their editors imprisoned. Dissent was banned.

The courage of Latin American women shines forth in their public opposition to these repressive regimes. In the 1970s working- and middle-class women in Chile, Brazil, and Argentina organized protest demonstrations and smuggled information about events out of their countries. Many were killed for their acts. While male Argentines averted their gaze and everyone else was silent, women marched in a circle every Thursday afternoon in the main square of Buenos Aires in front of the Casa Rosada, wearing kerchiefs stitched with names of disappeared children. These Mothers and Grandmothers of the Plaza de Mayo, women of the Families of the Disappeared in Chile and El Salvador, demonstrated carrying photographs of lost children and other kin. In response, Pinochet had sewage shot at them from high-pressure hoses. Over the pope's objections, Catholic clergy, for centuries an obscurantist force holding Latin America in repressive control, helped to organize protest movements run largely by women. Associations of the Relatives of Detained-Missing Persons sprang up in Chile to demand information on over 10,000 *desaparecidos* taken between 1973 and 1983.

Chilean women glued scraps of fabric to a backcloth to form tapestries, or *arpilleras*, to tell the stories of torture, the missing, and other horrors. Smuggled abroad, the *arpilleras* shamed Pinochet before the world. Women's unceasing efforts, despite mounting government terrorism, turned world opinion against Pinochet: even the United States urged him to step down. After he did so in 1990, the Chilean populace defeated his hand-picked candidate. Brazilian and Argentine groups were equally effective. A band of women marching in a public space may not seem much of a weapon against state terrorism, but the women of all the plazas helped to bring down the governments of Argentina, Brazil, and Chile.

Women in Literature

Courage is also needed to write books and articles that expose oppressive regimes. Women who do so often work alone, without the support even of their families, and are easy targets for government wrath. But in Latin America, for a woman merely to write was an act of political rebellion requiring great fortitude.[27]

Latin America's female literary tradition began in the late nineteenth century. One of its first writers, Gertrudis Gómez de Avellaneda (1814–73), a Cuban, achieved some success in Spain as a poet, dramatist, and novelist. Her best-known work was an abolitionist novel, *Sab* (1833), published in a Cuban journal. Her relatives withdrew most copies from publication, and it was omitted from an 1869 edition of her complete works. Her novel, *Two Women* (1842), was the first Latin American fiction to deal with adultery. There is still no complete edition of her work.

After independence (between 1900 and 1960), the consuming interest of Latin American literature was a search for national identity, which was presumed to be male. Indeed, the major concern of most literature is to define humanness, or identity, and it is almost always presumed to be male. In Latin America, men incorporated women into the national identity as symbols of sweetness and emotion, in allegories centred on female figures that represent a territory or a quality. Women had trouble adapting to a tradition in which women function only as poles of male experience. Some poets adopted personae of the oppressed masses, but women were personally in no-win situations: to write freely they had to belong to a bohemian group, but joining such groups alienated their families in a culture in which the family was still the main social institution and refuge. Women who dared to write freely suffered painfully isolated personal lives. Their isolation reinforced the lack of self-esteem so common to Latin American women, and many women writers led anguished lives. Their pain appears in works like *The Diary of Helen Morley*, and Rachel de Queiroz's autobiographical novel, *The Three Marias* (1985).

It is not possible to write against a prevailing current without arguing with that current. Writers who offer a new vision must to some degree be either reactive (which leads to accusations of didacticism) or obscure. Latin American women writers had to challenge men's images of women or abandon the attempt to offer a new vision. Most women simply wrote lachrymose odes to motherhood or tired celebrations of national heroes. Women's sexuality was taboo in literature until the early twentieth century, and, even then, it was easier for a man to write about female sexuality than for a woman. Avant-garde men who emulated Parisian culture created a Modernist movement; they liked sexually free intelligent women and accepted some in their ranks, mostly poets from the Southern Cone (Uruguay, Argentina, Chile). Uruguayan poet Delmira Agustini (1886–1914) adopted the persona of a child to speak boldly about her sexuality.[28]

Most Latin American women writers seem to have lived in anguish, victims of the Latin American belief that *"Mujer que sabe latin, ni tiene marido ni tiene buen fin"* (a woman who knows Latin will find no husband and come to no good). Jean Franco describes some women writers who paid for their achievement with tragic lives: the Chilean Gabriela Mistral (1889–1957, born Lucilla Godoy Alciaga), and the Argentinian Alfonsina Storni, both successful journalists, and Julia de Burgos (1914–53), a Puerto Rican poet.[29]

Three of these women were educated in normal schools and became teachers, *maestras* expected to conform to a nun's standards of celibacy and purity. Mistral felt that women were primarily mothers, that writing was a secondary form of creation for them. She had success as a poet, but considered herself "mutilated" because she had an unhappy early love affair and never married. Her poems, many for children, celebrated the *maestra*. In 1924 she was invited to Mexico to participate in a post-revolutionary literacy campaign and produced a book of readings for women preparing for motherhood that present public life as a male province. Yet she also dealt with public themes: her nationalist poems about Chile did not traditionally glorify war but focused on a journey: an Indian mother and child travel through Chile on foot seeking their roots. This poem was very different from anything her near contemporaries, men like Pablo Neruda, were writing.

Because Mistral celebrated her nation and seemed not to

challenge gender stereotypes, she was acceptable to men and became internationally famous. Representing Chile, she participated in League of Nations meetings and was consul to Italy; she even won the Nobel Prize. But the honours she received may have been based on a stereotyped reading of her work: an edition of her complete poems published after she won the Nobel Prize was arranged by theme – on love, on nature, or for children, for example – and her essays and correspondence have never been published.

Storni, who was born in Switzerland but raised in Argentina, escaped childhood poverty by becoming a *maestra*. A poet and well-known journalist, she wrote on feminism and social issues; to protest female subordination, she tackled the differences between idealized images of Woman and actual women like herself. In one poem she compares herself with Baudelaire: the male poet, filled with contempt and desire, confronts a *femme fatale*, while the female poet toils to squeeze an atom of response or feeling from an emotionally constipated man. In another, addressing a man who imbibes all pleasures greedily yet wants a woman made of foam of mother of pearl, she writes: "You want me white, / You who have held all the wineglasses / In your hand / Your lips stained purple / With fruit and honey."[30] Her love life was tormented; she had a child outside marriage and committed suicide in 1938. The day of her suicide, she wrote a letter to Buenos Aires newspapers that reinforced the myth that women who use their minds or talents outside the domestic realm are damaged beings. Her poetry was never nationally acclaimed like Mistral's, or, posthumously, like de Burgos' works.

The life of de Burgos, another schoolteacher from a poor family, also buttressed the myth of the doomed woman artist: she had an unhappy love affair, began drinking heavily, and died young in penniless exile in New York. Writing from a wide range of experience but against the social and political conventions of her time, she achieved no success in her lifetime and had to publish her work herself. She craved independence and defended the humanity of workers and blacks. After her death, she was nationally (but not internationally) recognized, yet no complete edition of her work has ever been published. A substantial collection, *Obra Poética*, was published in 1961 by the Institute of Puerto Rican Studies. In her most popular poem, "Great River of Loayza," the persona begs to be submerged in the protective embrace of the river: water is a frequent image in her poetry.

Franco calls these women's texts "schizoid" because they alternate between imitating male heroics and drowning in submission to anatomy as destiny. Until recently, however, Latin American women writers had no language but that of religion to describe body or emotion. The great Mexican artist Frida Kahlo (1910–54) painted herself as twins, one adorned, the other naked; she also painted her body (injured in a motor accident) penetrated by surgical instruments, or with her organs hanging outside her carcass, or giving birth to herself. Her paintings are small next to her husband's, the muralist Diego Rivera. That they are equally magnificent has only recently been acknowledged.

Critics called the work of Rosario Castellanos (1925–74), a Mexican poet, novelist, and feminist pioneer, sentimental, bitter, domestic, and, most damning, feminine. Not until Castellanos died did the poet José Emilion Pacheco write: "We were on guard in defense of our privileges; naturally we did not know how to read her." Castellanos had a keen sense of social justice, and she did public work on behalf of Indians and women. After writing a thesis, "On Feminine Culture," for a master's degree from the National University of Mexico in 1950, she returned home, gave the land she had inherited to the Indians, and became a cultural promoter for Chiapas. Her personal experience – disastrous marriage at thirty-two, two miscarriages, one son, a divorce, and the exhilarating discovery of "becoming what one is" late in life – is subsumed in dramatic monologues written in "a public voice brutally frank about private pain":[31]

Beyond my skin, deep in
my bones, I have loved.
Beyond my mouth and its words,
beyond the knot of my tormented sex.
I will not die of sickness
or old age, of anguish or of tiredness.
I will die of love, surrender
to the deepest lap.
I will never be ashamed of these empty hands
or of this hermetic cell they call Rosario.
On the lips of the wind I shall be called
a tree of many birds.

Castellanos may be the most important Latin American woman poet since Sor Juana: she wrote journalism and criticism, directed a university press, taught Latin American literature at university level, and was Mexican ambassador to Israel when she died. She was buried in the national Rotunda of Illustrious Men in Mexico City. Her work, which has had enormous influence, has recently been given an excellent translation into English by Magda Bogin.[32]

The novel was the most problematic literary form for women. Most Latin American males write "national allegories" in which a male protagonist makes a journey of self-discovery that is also the nation's journey, in which women are moral poles in male experience. The only novel about the Mexican Revolution written by a woman, *Cartucho* (Cartridge) by Nelly Campobello, is a tribute to the mother of a supporter of revolutionary Pancho Villa. It does not challenge gender stereotypes. Mexican women's essays often celebrated revolutionary heroes, contributing to machismo and the glorification of the *caudillo*. The Venezuelan Teresa de la Parra's *Memories of Mama Blanca* defends aristocratic values and criticizes men while asserting female superiority. Like later women writers, she saw nationalism and modernization as degradation.

Many current writers use fantasy to suggest values and experience beyond the material surface of life. The Chilean Maria Luisa Bombal uses dream and nightmare to suggest women's imprisonment in stereotypes. Her female characters cannot adapt to the image and confinement required of them and go mad or live in fantasy. Silvina Bullrich depicts Argentina as alienated and apathetic in *Reunión de directorio*. Luisa Valenzuela's novels and brilliant Kafkaesque parables, *Strange Things Happen Here*, use surrealism to describe the former political situation in Argentina. Isabel Allende (a niece of the onetime Chilean president) disclaims political intentions, but *The House of the Spirits* uses surrealism to exalt a "feminine" approach to life and politics. Elena Poniatowska focuses on Mexican history and traditions but tries to depict all Latin America, to speak for those denied a voice who are struggling with poverty, gender roles, physical handicaps, and class or racial discrimination. The Nicaraguan Gioconda Belli, a university student during the Somoza regime, writes revolutionary poems. Rosario Castellanos's novel *Vespers* portrays a woman inciting an indigenous uprising.

Latin American women's low self-image is implicit in the rarity of their autobiographies. The few that exist describe public rather than private struggles. The single exception is Victoria Ocampo, a writer and publisher who was central to the innovative journal *Sur*, which dominated the cultural life of Buenos Aires for several decades. Ocampo broke taboos by having a long relationship with a man she was not married to and by writing about it in her autobiography.

In recent decades, anthropologists used tape to record the life of a subject, leading to a new autobiographical form, the *testimonio*. These recordings give the illiterate – many of them women – a voice.[33] Another sort of *testimonio, I . . . Rigoberta Menchú* (1984), recounts the experience of an indigenous woman who was politically persecuted in Guatemala.[34] Menchú lived in a traditional agricultural community that divided labour sexually. When Efrain Rios Montt's repressive government launched a bloody campaign against dissidents in the northwest highlands, troops occupied Indian communities, killing thousands of indigenous people, and the survivors had no choice but to resist. Menchú's family became prominent in the resistance and, in a brief span, her brother, father, and mother were killed. Priests who consoled her believed in liberation theology and helped her to emancipate herself both as a woman and as a *guerrillista*. Menchú was awarded the Nobel Peace Prize in 1992. Recently, she has come under attack because her memoir is not strictly accurate to her life. She had more education than she admitted, and the events of her book are not always authentic. But the book is a moving and accurate depiction of the experience of Guatamalan Indians in a repressive regime backed by the United States and waging war on its own people.

In 1977 *fem* was founded, the first modern Latin American feminist journal in Mexico to provide a pluralistic non-sectarian approach. Latin American women writers highlight the extreme economic inequality of their societies by focusing on indigenous and working women, especially in biographies and *bildungsromans*. A growing body of female literature deals with the concrete details of women's lives in cultures permeated by Catholic bigotry. Much of it is satirical, like the work of Rosario Ferre, Cristin Peri Rossi, Elena Poniatowska, and Luisa Valenzuela. Women show increasing boldness in writing about politics and sex, especially in poetry, and female sexuality is no longer taboo. Many do not like to be categorized as women and repudiate North American feminism, but several write strongly feminist poetry. Latin American women writers like Allende, Valenzuela, and Poniatowska increasingly earn international recognition.

Women in Latin America Today

Until the nineteenth century, three subcultures coexisted in Latin America: indigenous, traditional, and modern.[35] Indigenous cultures are family-centred and tend to fatalism, a sacred/magical view of the world. Such cultures appear wherever there are large populations of indigenes who were once mainly subsistence farmers. Few indigenous cultures remain in Argentina, Chile, Brazil, Paraguay, Uruguay, or the Caribbean. Only in Paraguay do Amerindians (the Guaraní) play an influential role in shaping society, mainly because Paraguay's Iberian men were killed in wars and rural areas are dominated by Amerindian women.

Traditional cultures follow the old European patterns granting state and church authority over everyday life. Traditional people see life in static terms and expect each generation to follow the same path as the one before. Status is inherited, identity is conferred by family membership, and sex roles are highly differentiated. Sexual inequality, taken for granted, is backed by religion and law. Modern cultures follow the capitalist-industrial model. They allow great social mobility and expect status to be earned, not inherited. They feature nuclear families and extreme individualism; they worship science and rationalism, and progressively challenge sexual inequality. The ambience of each particular society is determined by its particular mix of these subcultures and the number of immigrants it absorbed.

European immigrants with anarchist, socialist, and communist ideas catalyzed Latin American culture with their political ideas and values: they urged education for everyone, regardless of sex. They helped industrialize Latin America and are part of its urban workforce, labour movement, and labour parties. They also helped to create a climate of acceptance of women's intellectual abilities. Today, children are educated without regard to sex to the age of fourteen; even at the university level the difference is small. In 1964–65 the University of Buenos Aires graduated nearly as many women in law and medicine, and over ten times the number of dentists, as United States universities, and the percentage of women graduates in Argentina surpassed those of the United States in almost every category.[36] Because state universities in Latin America charge only nominal fees, women from humble as well as privileged backgrounds are professionally trained in medicine, law, architecture, dentistry, and biochemistry.

All Latin American countries, except Cuba, suffer from extreme social and economic inequality because of the unequal distribution of land: in 1965, 94 percent of the land was owned by 7 percent of the people.[37] Almost all wealth remains in the hands of a few landowning and industrial elites. Because of this economic structure, independence in Latin America did not lead to political or economic independence, and the power elite has always needed help from foreign powers (mainly Britain until the end of the nineteenth century, and the United States since then) to maintain its dominance. The United States, which has claimed hegemonic power since the 1823 Monroe Doctrine, consolidated it in wars against Mexico and Spain, and in repeated military interventions in Central America, Panama, Granada, and elsewhere in the south.

With this huge gap between poor and rich, most Latin American countries are extremely elitist. Men in every kind of society fight fiercely to retain dominance over women, but men are most adamant about it in highly elitist societies. Socialist societies are as unjust, rigid, and obstructional as capitalist societies, but they make some effort to redress the prejudice against women that, under capitalism, is treated as normal. Latin Americans continue to insist that women's place is in the home and that men alone belong in the public sphere. Catholicism remains the dominant religion. North American social scientists describe this situation ideologically, calling Latin American women "marianist." This term means that they base their self-image on the Virgin; they are self-sacrificing, passive, and forgiving; and they are morally and spiritually superior to men. "Marianism" makes them suffer patiently their husbands' infidelities and overbearing machismo. Latin societies entertain a double standard, divide women into categories of good and bad, and maintain a cult of virginity. But within the family, where women's decisions and feelings are respected, women have authority.

Women of the wealthier classes inherit property and manage businesses. When elite women enter politics, they do not challenge class privilege, but support it. Latin American political women dislike American feminism, believing that it focuses on the commonality of women's interests and ignores class differences and conflicts. Female solidarity across class lines is difficult because even socialist women depend on servants. The daughters of the poor become servants, and the fortunate ones among them learn household skills and attend school in the afternoons or evenings. Here, as elsewhere, domestic servants are sexually exploited; if employers refuse to let the girls go to school, they become prostitutes or sink into destitution when they leave service. Males are servants too, but the vast majority are female. Laws make a minimum wage, paid vacations, and retirement plans mandatory for full-time workers, so people hire two or more part-time maids to evade such costs. Servants fear to press employers for compliance because they know they can easily be replaced. In another irony, a high level of professional participation by women is paid for by the exploitation of poor women. Women are caught in such contradictions because they bear the entire burden of raising children.

The overwhelming majority of Latin American women work at home in traditional female occupations: as dressmakers, typists, hand or machine knitters, caterers, translators, accountants, teachers of foreign languages or other subjects, hairdressers, baby sitters, nurses, and repairers of nylons or fine wool clothing. Elite women with "connections" sell luxuries like perfume, imported clothing, electronic equipment, or *haute couture* from their apartments to evade paying taxes. Professional women – lawyers, dentists, doctors – work at home so they can oversee the household at the same time.

Wages are low for everyone, and survival is increasingly precarious for poor people in Latin America. As agriculture was mechanized, women workers were excluded from it. Women migrated to cities, mainly to become domestic servants. However, more are entering industry in runaway shops; modern transport and communications have made possible the phenomenon of the "global factory," in which businesses hire workers, particularly women, anywhere in the world they can pay pittances, often in Asia.

Electrical and electronic assembly enterprises clustered on the United States/Mexico border hire mainly women, who are paid the lowest wages of anyone in the workforce and provided with worse working conditions than men. Most transnational companies hire only women, so men increasingly migrate to the United States. With men absent or unemployed, women cannot form stable families.

A huge influx of people into cities has caused a crisis in housing and every other aspect of life, including schools, sanitation, medical care, air quality, and the availability and quality of water. After the 1970s, working-class women began forming squatters' movements, organizing around issues of housing and work and demanding government attention to their needs, especially in Peru, Argentina, and Mexico. Like working women everywhere, they do two jobs, at work and at home, but lack adequate child care and live in particularly squalid conditions.

Despite hardship in surviving, fertility levels are high in Latin America because of early marriage and strong community pressure, and because male-female power relations in macho societies make it difficult for women to insist on family planning or contraception. Affluent women have big families because servants care for them; poor families have many children out of fear that few will survive to adulthood. Infant mortality is very high, but varies by class and the mother's education: in the 1970s the rates for all classes of mothers compared with those for educated mothers were 96:26 per thousand in Argentina, 126:32 in Colombia, 125:33 in Costa Rica, 176:46 in Ecuador, and 207:70 in Peru. Although infant mortality rates in Latin America have declined since the 1970s, they remain high relative to the industrial world, and rural/urban and class differences persist.

Birth control is a loaded issue. Women's traditional medical lore taught methods of birth control and abortion, but peasant women rarely used them because large families were an asset for farmers. The Catholic Church opposes both with great fervour, but a rapid increase in Latin populations led the United States to promote birth control. Women are now expected to take a political and religious stand as they make personal choices, complicated by the racial and class factors.

Children can provide additional labour or income (child labour is illegal but common in Latin America), but survey after survey shows that Latin American women favour small families. Since they continue to have large ones, the problem lies beyond them. Women who are fully assimilated into the "modern sector," in which children are liabilities, not assets, have controlled their fertility. But Latin governments are pro-natalist, especially in the Southern Cone; fearing the burgeoning power of Brazil, they insist that their countries would be stronger economically and militarily with greater population growth. Government policies on birth control or abortion shape women's lives: most Latin American governments have made abortion illegal except in cases of rape or incest or when bearing a child threatens a woman's life. Argentine women found guilty of abortion are punished by one to four years in prison, and abortionists by up to ten. Adolescent death from self-induced or illegal abortions is commonplace, and illegal abortion accounts for 30–50 percent of all maternal deaths.

In socialist Cuba, education is free. Abortion, legal during the first twelve weeks of pregnancy, is free for minors (who need parental consent) and for women with three children or more. Others must petition the Ministry of Health and pay if the right is granted. Puerto Rico, a "showcase" for population control, bears the questionable distinction of being the only country in the world that has made over a third of its women of childbearing age sterile. The United States assimilated Puerto Rico into its political and economic sphere after the Spanish-American War and transformed the island into a tax heaven for American corporations. Its policies destroyed Puerto Rico's rural economy. While improvements in public health, sanitation, and medical care made Puerto Rico safe for its new rulers, however, Puerto Rican mortality rates actually increased. Americans blamed the population explosion that ensued on Catholicism and male chauvinism, and set up a network of family planning clinics. But abortion only upset the Catholic Church, so the clinics claimed that Puerto Rican women "chose" sterilization. But sterilization was often coerced, and Puerto Rico, claiming genocide, eventually took the case to the United Nations.

North American observers find Latin American women dependent, subject to their parents' authority. They in turn find North American women selfish, individualistic, cavalier in their treatment of the elderly, and lacking in a sense of family responsibility and loyalty. American feminists do not understand that Latin American women see themselves primarily as part of kin-groups, not as individuals. North American social scientists who belittle Latin American feminists for stressing "women's issues" do not understand that such issues are vital everywhere, as quality of life issues.

The most potent cultural influences on Latin American women today are the mass media. The Mexican government censors even government-subsidized films if they offend the military. Mexico banned a Spanish version of Oscar Lewis's *Children of Sanchez* for depicting a family living in marginal poverty in Mexico City, not in revolutionary idealism but jealous rivalry, and sternly dominated by an emotionally remote father with a second family in a *casa chica*. Growing political opposition to government censorship culminated in 1968 in a student uprising, suppressed by a government massacre, at Tlatelolco.

Because the economic reality of Latin America today is international, most Latin American governments are shifting away from the nationalist rhetoric traditionally used by military governments: national debt ties these countries to the International Monetary Fund and economically powerful transnational corporations. Like other Latin governments that are trying to "modernize" their countries, the Mexican government wants to sway people away from reformist ideas towards deregulation, making scarcity the incentive for people to work. Women, often the perpetuators of tradition, are crucial to the modernization of the populace; as low-paid, marginal workers, they are also the target group for employment in new industries. In this scenario, women must be modernized – that is, they must adopt a work ethic. Mass media are the instruments of this modernization.

In both North America and Latin America, women purchase most of the fiction published. In Mexico, each volume in two popular series of comic-strip novels aimed at women sells from 800,000 to a million copies every week, and more than one woman probably reads each copy. These books convey attitudes that are considered proper for their target audience. The bourgeois press, which ensconces women in the domestic world, shapes the consciousness of women of all classes; people always emulate the highest in status. Glossy magazines or soap operas infrequently promote education or emancipation, but, mainly, they encourage consumerism. They target women of the prosperous classes, but reach working-class women with poor, ugly homes. Women immersed in such literature often adopt the values of the dominant class and want bourgeois life as depicted in fiction – sentimentalized, idealized. The demand such fiction creates for material goods causes massive emigration and looting sprees, and provides material for right-wing government propaganda comparing the scarcity in socialist countries with the wealth in the "free world." Much popular culture stresses traditional roles and female subordination. Gender roles are the major theme of popular media. One element missing from all popular culture directed at women is the idea of female solidarity.

*   *   *

Most Latin American countries achieved limited independence in the international sphere. To maintain class supremacy and great economic disparity, their ruling classes bound themselves first to foreign powers, then to transnational corporations with no local loyalties, and eventually to the International Monetary Fund, which is bent on maintaining Western dominance. To keep people poor and quiet, they welcomed dictators. Latin American countries are now ripped by severe poverty, social unrest, and guerrilla movements. In such a climate, whatever men's sympathies, "women's issues" are usually deferred, considered less critical than "men's issues." Women's awareness of this truth, and of their common ground, is growing in Latin America.

Today, Latin American societies place less emphasis on race and ethnicity, but class differences remain huge. Working-class women tend to unite with working-class men to challenge and try to change their societies, which assign privilege by birth to a chosen few. Middle-class women have an investment in maintaining inequality because they are held completely responsible for rearing children, a job assigned to them by men, which they in turn assign to lower-class women. Men have always been able to ignore class lines to achieve male solidarity when they are opposing women. Latin American women, like most women over the ages, are slow to break class ties (which are also family ties) to form solidarity with other women. But without solidarity, women cannot change their lot. Only a few middle-class Latin Americans have seen through the delusions of class, and many of these women are feminists.

CHAPTER 15

ANTI-IMPERIAL
REVOLUTION IN INDIA

I T IS IMPOSSIBLE TO MAKE BROAD GENERALIZATIONS about the huge, sprawling, diverse territory of Southern Asia. To make it comprehensible, writers divide India into an Aryan-Indo-European north and a Dravidian south, into Hindu and Muslim cultures. Social arrangements in northeastern India are similar to those in Southeast Asia; those of northwestern India resemble those of western Asia, yet all these sections speak Indo-European languages and have mainly Muslim populations.[1] In addition, various tribal societies are scattered throughout South Asia from the Himalayas to the Malabar coast. Tribal societies resisted integration into either Aryan or Dravidian social frameworks until the twentieth century. This chapter cannot do justice to India's variety; it will focus on the more cohesive north and Hindu culture, and the past and present of Indian women.

For centuries, India was ruled by invaders. Turkish Muslims defeated the Rajputs in 1192, taking over most of northern India. England began to trade with India on the last day of 1600, when

Queen Elizabeth I signed a charter granting a monopoly over eastern trade to the new East India Company. In 1613 India allowed Britain to found a trading post on the northwest coast: a year later the first cargo of Indian cotton and indigo reached London. After that, England grabbed Indian raw materials – silk, cotton, sugar, indigo – for its factories and shipped manufactured goods back to Indian markets.[2] Some historians claim that England wanted just to trade, that it colonized India almost by accident. But English traders attacked Indian and European trading rivals, and after Emperor Aurungzeb died in 1707 and the Mughal Empire, cleft by internal warfare, gradually collapsed, Britain, perhaps the strongest military and economic power in the world, reached out for control under the aegis of the British East India Company.

This period is often called the Raj (a Hindi word meaning sovereignty). The term denotes both rule by the East India Company in India (which ended in 1858) and rule by the British crown and Parliament (which ended in 1947). By seizing strategic positions in the interior and in areas ringing it, Britain ruled nearly half of India, influencing the native princes who governed the rest. Some Indian leaders were women – Ahilyabi Holkar of Indore; Begum Samra, a widow with an estate east of Delhi; and Mamola Begam of Bhopal. Each, educated by her father or her husband, assumed power and gained her subjects' approval by military leadership, judicial skills, and administrative talents.[3] To serve as an administrator, Englishmen had to know Greek and Latin but nothing about India; they managed their regions incompetently and erratically. The ambitions of the British military precipitated a suicidal mission to Afghanistan (one man survived out of 16,000), the annexation of the Sikh-ruled Punjab (rebellious to this day), and the "Great Mutiny" of 1857. In this revolt, sepoys (Indian soldiers under British command) rebelled, backed by Muslims and Hindus with their own agenda. Britain quashed the mutiny, but, in its wake, the British East India Company was dissolved in 1858.

The Raj

After assuming responsibility for Indian affairs, the British govern-ment conquered by dividing. It disarmed the populace and reor-ganized the army: it assigned men of different ethnic or religious backgrounds and no common cause to each unit, and Europeans commanded most of these units and the heavy artillery. Rulers of small princedoms kept their hereditary rights and possessions if they ceded control over all external affairs. To pay for their regime, the British levied a tax on even the poorest people of half the rental value of their land. When Indians protested, the British argued that the assessments were lower than those of earlier rulers. Those regimes could never collect the taxes they levied, however; the British did. They spent little on health, welfare, or education, devot-ing most of the revenue to courts, police, and, especially, the army. Moreover, the British used the Indian army in their own wars in Burma (now Myanmar), Afghanistan, and China. Indian resources were used not to improve Indian life but to support institutions that repressed the local population or to pay the salaries of English administrators and military men, dividends to East India Company stockholders, or interest on debt held mainly by Englishmen. The English drained India of its wealth.

Perhaps the most injurious part of the Raj was England's eco-nomic policy. As it did with all its colonies, Britain passed laws to prevent India from exporting manufactures, forcing it to absorb British goods. This system undermined India's own handicraft indus-tries. Many villages had long survived on handicrafts, many created by women. Now people had to farm, in a country already too popu-lous for its land. Before the British appropriation, India was poor, regularly swept by famine and epidemic. But under British rule, it suffered the worst famines in its history: 15 million people died in famines between 1877 and 1900. Bengal was a rich cotton-produc-ing area with advanced manufacturing skills – it built warships, for instance. But the British, wanting to raise opium to sell in China, took over its farmland and destroyed its agriculture. Bengal (now Bangladesh and Calcutta) became one of the poorest spots on earth.

Revenues extracted from India made England rich, but British governors of India knew that England's domination could not last. They wanted to create structures to protect English settlers and commerce when it ended.[4] To accomplish this end, Britain suppressed internal warfare, improved sanitary and medical facilities, built railways, roads, and irrigation works, and, in 1833, introduced Western-style education. Many Hindus welcomed Western education, but Muslims did not want their religious-based system displaced by a secular Western system. After the 1880s, when England established civil service examinations and let Indian men compete for positions in administrative bureaucracies, to reject Western education meant foreclosing access to prestigious jobs. Historically, Hindus and Muslims had been rivals; when Muslims, the former ruling class, saw young Hindu clerks surpassing them, animus intensified.

In 1852 a remarkable meeting was held in Bombay of Parsis, Muslims, Hindus, and Jews. The Bombay Association then petitioned the British government for moderate reforms, mainly Indian participation in administrative and judicial affairs. The association tried to use the conqueror's political and philosophical weapons for its own ends, believing this approach more effective than resorting to arms. In this way it foreshadowed the Indian National Congress, which was established in 1885. Feeling nationalist pressure, the British decided to grant a degree of representative government and allowed a few elected Indians to sit on the Viceroy's Legislative Council in 1861. But early in the twentieth century the dictatorial policies of the viceroy, Lord Curzon, provoked a nationalist campaign, a boycott of British goods, and a revival of Indian industries. The Muslim League was founded in 1905, and in 1907 nationalist fervour split the Indian National Congress – weakening Indian unity. But in 1909 the British allowed non-official (and not necessarily elected) majorities to sit on the legislative councils of the Indian provinces.

Like all dominators, the British had to justify their rule – and they sought grounds that would persuade Indians, British citizens, and the English ruling class. Many British officials confused technological and military superiority for moral and racial superiority, and Britons soon saw India and Africa as the "white man's burden."[5] Convinced of the superiority of their moral standards and behaviour, Britons set out to reform India. A major vindication of their rule was to "improve" Indian women's lives.[6] Some scholars think the British focused on women to impugn Indian men's "masculinity" and ability to control their women. But British scrutiny of Indian customs, rituals, and treatment of women produced perhaps the largest ethnographic study ever made of one culture by another.

The first attempt in this analysis was made in 1772, before Britain appropriated India, by Governor General Warren Hastings. He ordered texts governing Hindu society to be chosen, translated, and proclaimed authoritative in all "personal" matters. Brahmin scholars were only too happy to resurrect the law of Manu and have it imposed on all Hindu groups. The same "service" was rendered the Muslims – the *shari'a* was translated and codified as the supreme law of Muslims – although many Muslims continued to follow local custom on marriage, divorce, inheritance, and the rights of women.

Sati, Widow Remarriage, and Women's Rights

One custom the English wanted to eradicate was sati (suttee), the burning of widows on their husbands' funeral pyres. Widows usually remarried until the Mauryan Era (322–200 BC), when Manu decreed that "nowhere is a second husband permitted to respectable women." Upper-caste Hindus soon held that marriage was for life – for women, who could not divorce or remarry if widowed. *Niyoga* (levirate marriage), the forced appropriation of a childless widow by her husband's brother, had been practised, but it faded during the Gupta Era (sixth century), and the emperor Akbar banned it in areas under Mughal control.

By the Middle Ages, higher castes had extended the rule even to children whose marriages were not consummated – which led to many virgin widows twelve or thirteen years old. In such cases, the family – the girl's parents, brothers, or in-laws – had to support her for the rest of her life, and she had to live as a sati (virtuous woman): sleeping on the ground, eating one plain meal a day – without honey, meat, wine, or salt – and avoiding ornaments, coloured garments, and perfumes. She had to spend her life fasting, praying, and performing rites for her husband. Any breach of this discipline brought extreme social opprobrium, rebirth in unhappy circumstances, and danger to the man's soul and next life. A widow's mere existence was inauspicious: considered a bad omen, she was denied the right to attend festive or religious occasions.

It is unclear how and when immolation began: not even Manu urged widows to kill themselves.[7] The first written mention is a recommendation in a third-century text, but sati did not gain legitimacy until after the Muslim invasions. Stories were told about courageous Hindu widows committing *jauhar* (mass suicide) after their husbands were killed in battle by Muslim invaders. But sati was not always a voluntary courageous act: not only were widows forced to live cruel lives but tremendous pressure was placed on them to throw themselves on their husbands' funeral pyres. Many satis were involuntary. By AD 1000, sati was an ideal for Kshatriyas and the practice was spreading to Brahmins.

In late eighteenth-century Bengal, sati took hold with particular ferocity: families drugged widows, tied them to the bodies of their dead husbands, and forced them into the fire with bamboo sticks. They devised an elaborate rite invoking Kali, in which a widow dressed as a bride entered the flames with fanfare acclaiming her for conferring glory on her natal and conjugal families. Of the women burned, 55 percent came from the upper classes, and 45 percent from upwardly mobile lower-caste families. For many families, sati led to social status and a reputation for virtue, but male fear and hatred of women was an important factor in it.[8]

Customs like subjugation, seclusion, and the denial of rights of divorce, remarriage, and property occurred mainly in the higher castes, which could afford to provide for widows. For peasant women, Hindu or Muslim, purdah was an impossible luxury, and remarriage by widows was widely accepted. But why was the suicide of women – who, presumably, were loved – demanded? Why did even feminist Indian commentators try to "explain away . . . defend . . . rationalize" the custom?[9] It is as painful for women as for men to confront a male hatred for women that is as old as patriarchy. Other societies we have examined – Japan and China, for instance – allowed women no escape from oppression but suicide. Other societies also forbade widow remarriage. But sati was unique.

After the British abolished sati in 1829, Indians exalted it even more: widows who expressed even the faintest inclination to commit it, but later wavered, were dragged to the flames kicking and screaming. But many did not have to be dragged: in a society in which a widow's lot was humiliating and miserable, and suicide (even of this painful sort) brought her glory and praise, it was not entirely undesirable. As sati grew more popular, men changed religious myth to justify it, assimilating the protective goddess Chandi with Kali, the unpredictable, punitive mother worshipped mainly by marginal groups like thieves and prostitutes. The bifurcation of Chandi into Durge, the protector, and Kali, the punisher, gave rise to a new theory: men's deaths were their wives' faults. These wives had performed ritual poorly, refusing to make full use of their enormous powers to manipulate natural events and protect men. So widows created their own fate.

Blind to their own practices, the British judged India by Karl Marx's statement that a society's treatment of women was the prime indicator of its level of civilization, and they became obsessed with raising Indian women's status. Early nineteenth-century anthropologists observed that tribal women were not constricted by many regulations on premarital sex, bans on divorce, or marked preference for males. (Current studies, in contrast, do not show tribal peoples to be egalitarian.) Western-educated Indian men in the 1800s wanted to eradicate sati, child marriage, polygyny, and purdah, and they urged the British to pass corrective laws. They promoted female education and widow remarriage and raised awareness of women's lot, but they did not consider women men's equals or want them to be independent, legally, economically, or socially. Having abolished sati, the British tried to advance widow remarriage, raise the marriage age, modify purdah, suppress temple prostitution, and build health and education facilities for women. But most Indians ignored British laws and followed traditional customs.

Their reforms broadened the options for elite women, who were able to benefit from education and dramatically – if slowly – began to enter the professions. Reform movements sprouted in some localities and, by the end of the nineteenth century, spanned the nation, most led by upper-caste men or men of classes allied with Britons. Seeing that reform justified British rule, they were also concerned about Indian social conditions. Some nationalist groups advocated change to prepare people for self-rule. But Britain dragged its feet in acknowledging even the modest demands of the Indian National Congress, and its cautious, corporate approach to independence was discredited at century's end.

During the Raj, the British introduced a multitude of new practices: industry, especially in textile manufacture; cash cropping (raising crops for export rather than subsistence and local markets) and modernized agriculture; modern communications – railways, telegraph, printing presses; government by a bureaucracy chosen partly by educational achievement and supported by systematic taxation, legal codes, and military power; and Western educational systems and ideas – individualism, democracy, progress through science, and equality before the law. All these ideas can raise women's status, but, as we have seen, they are rarely so used. The subject has not been thoroughly studied, but in India these innovations apparently eroded the economic position of lower-caste women. Competition from machine-made textiles and the power loom damaged their traditional work of weaving, spinning by hand on the *charka*, and doing hand embroidery. In the early stages of industrialization, many women and children were hired, but were then dismissed mainly because labour laws passed from 1881 to 1911 limited the hours women could work and banned the employment of children.[10]

Some tribes owned property communally. Women in matrilineal groups in South India, for instance, could ask for maintenance from separated husbands according to joint-family ownership of land; but once British law invested absolute ownership of private property in male heads of household, their rights ended. The British imposed ancient Hindu law on groups not formerly governed by it, annulling the rights women possessed even in patrilineal and patriarchal regions. British administrators overrode Muslim women's inheritance rights, disregarding Muslim law and harming lower-caste women. Restoration of Islamic law later became a nationalist issue for urban Muslims.

Yet British colonial officials made what they saw as Indian women's degradation into a major ideological foundation for British rule in India. They passed laws expected to benefit women, but also set in stone the Brahmanic Laws of Manu, which before the Gentoo Code of 1772 had been applied flexibly. In ignorance of Indian customs and of the complexity of competing legal systems in India, they reduced the flexibility inherent in customary law. Ironically, they created an extensive system to enforce a legal code that further restricted women's independence, right to property, and control over their children.

Women's Education in the Colonial Period, c. 1857–1950

Missionaries and philanthropists built Western-style girls' schools. The first was founded in Calcutta in 1820 by David Hare, a watchmaker who was influenced by European rationalist philosophy. With an explicit evangelical mission, missionaries for a time drew students only from the lower castes. In response, Indian groups suspicious of the missionary agenda opened girls' schools to stop conversion. The first school to attract high-caste women was established in Calcutta in 1849 by Vidyasagar, with the help of J.E.D. Bethune, one of the Governor General's Council, and was called Bethune School (later College). Girls' schools were supported by individuals, reform societies, missionaries, and, after 1854, by modest grants from the Indian government. In 1882 there were 2697 educational institutions for females in India: most were primary schools, but there were also eighty-two secondary schools, fifteen normal schools, and one college, with a total of 127,066 students.[11] The graduates of these schools, a tiny fraction of India's women, became the next generation of leaders of social reform movements.

After the fall of the Mughal Empire, Muslim reformists blamed the collapse on Islam's rigid traditionalism – conservatives considered military defeat divine punishment for moral laxity. An important reformer, Sir Sayyid Ahmad Khan, held British weapons and the British educational and judicial system responsible for the Mughal defeat and British rule. He admired Western technology and ideas, especially science, and tried to inject them into Muslim intellectual life, while defending the Islamic social system from Western criticism. He began reform-oriented exegetical studies of the Qur'an and Hadith, and in 1875 he founded Aligarh University to teach Western science in a Muslim context. But he was less eager to reform laws governing women.

Acknowledging that the Qur'an mandated neither purdah nor denying females education, Khan wanted men to be educated first, especially in Western subjects. He felt female education should emphasize moral and spiritual values, and did what he could to hinder radical reformers who wanted women too to be exposed to Western ideas. Not until the twentieth century were schools founded for Muslim girls, with some Western studies. Since these schools opened over men's opposition, they were especially strict about upholding purdah and stressing family traditions, obedience, and authority. Male students, in contrast, were encouraged to reinterpret tradition.

Rokeya Sakhawat Hossain (1880–1932) has been called the "first and foremost feminist" of Muslim society in Bengal. Born to a conservative father who became wealthy as a landlord, she was taught secretly by her older brother to read and write, then married a supportive man. Hossain gradually liberated herself and went to work in a school for Muslim girls. In 1911 she started the first Muslim girl's school in Calcutta, and introduced adult literacy programs for both Hindu and Muslim women. She also founded the Association of Muslim Women. She wrote a book about the stifling life at one school for girls. Explaining that Muslims did not want girls (who had to travel to reach school) to be seen, the school devised a special bus, without windows but with two blocks of latticework, three inches wide and eighteen inches long, above the front and back doors. The first time the bus was used, the airless heat and darkness in the metal box made the children ill. The Englishwoman who ran the school opened the lattices and hung coloured curtains over the openings. Still it was too hot, and the girls fainted, had headaches all day, and vomited. Parents complained, and many took their daughters out of the school. Muslim men wrote the school letters signed "Brothers-in-Islam," objecting to the curtains because, they said, breezes blew them open and violated purdah rules. They threatened to close the school if this problem was not corrected.

A decade before Charlotte Perkins Gilman's *Herland*, Hossain also wrote a utopian feminist fantasy, *Sultana's Dream* (1905), which reversed the position of Muslim women and men.[12] Women move freely in a garden-city that has been cleaned and made mosquito- and mud-free (mud and mosquitoes were serious problems in Hossain's India) by solar energy and harnessed rain clouds, systems invented by women. After a general war, which women won using concentrated light (lasers), men retreated to their houses. They now live in seclusion, so the streets are crime-free. Society is segregated, but women allow men a wider circle of social intercourse than Muslim men allowed women, letting them see even distant cousins. The men, used to confinement, cook, tend babies, and do domestic work. But women also spend time with their children and cook because they enjoy it and their blooming world. When Hossain's husband read the manuscript of *Sultana's Dream*, he cried, "What a terrible revenge!" This is a staggering statement: he was saying that to impose the same restrictions Muslim women suffered on men would be "terrible revenge." Did that mean that restrictions on women were revenge on them?

At the turn of the century, a mere 725 of India's millions of women worked in the professions.[13] Men who had previously supported reform began to oppose it when a few literate women challenged the authority of men over women. Nevertheless, the percentage of literate women slowly grew – from 0.9 percent in 1901 to 3.4 percent in 1941. By 1936 over 3 million Indian girls and women were studying in 38,262 schools, in contrast to approximately 100,000 in 1882.

Little is known about women's economic activities during the colonial period, but Ramusack writes that some elite women in Bengal were *zamindarins* (landholders), with varying degrees of authority over their estates. Most elite women who worked for pay were in professions that catered to women. Some commoner women became wealthy, mainly as courtesans, especially in Lucknow. They maintained a traditional elite culture and earned enough to buy property and pay taxes. Some women worked in manufacturing, most making jute, matches, and textiles. But then as now, the vast majority of women worked in agriculture. The most visible to the English were the women labouring on tea and coffee plantations. Most women labourers were not included in statistical surveys. Women also worked inside the *zenana* (the women's part of the house) processing food – cleaning or grinding grain.

Western Women in India

Accounts of British colonialism that mention women at all usually place responsibility for the deterioration of the colonial relationship on them. One colonial governor, David Lean, said: "It's a well-known saying that the women lost us the Empire. It's true." The myth is familiar: pure, "vulnerable" European women aroused lust in indigenous men, creating a barrier between them and their white rulers.[14] But this time it had a twist: English wives displaced the local concubines, severing Englishmen's connection to their mentors in indigenous culture. Wives distracted men from their responsibilities; those who isolated themselves from Indian culture were guilty of racism.

At first, the East India Company tried to avoid the expense of shipping Englishwomen to India and encouraged its employees to take Indian wives and concubines. By the turn of the century, more "half-castes" or "Eurasians" than Britons worked for the company, which then tried to limit Eurasians in the civil service. One British woman, Fanny Parkes, the wife of the collector of customs at Allahabad, came in 1822 and "immediately plunged into the rich texture of Indian life: she celebrated Hindu festivals, learned Persian, played the sitar and made vast collections of Indian insects, fossils, religious icons, and animal skulls." Romantic and adventurous, she toured the country without her husband on an Arab horse. She wore Turkish trousers, slept in tents, ordered her servants about in fluent Hindustani, and, with a native crew, sailed for fifty-one days up the Jumna River to Agra to pitch a tent near the Taj Mahal.[15]

After Britain took India from the company in 1857, it sent women to India and created a sizable European community (though men always outnumbered women). As the British approached complete conquest, their moral tone grew sanctimonious and they charged women with maintaining the new morality. The large number of English women permitted the British to create an exclusive society within the alien culture. Wives and hostesses maintained the hierarchy in embattled circumstances, creating social distance from "inferior peoples" by elaborate rituals.[16] Independent-minded women condemned these colonial customs, but most European women patriotically supported the imperial state.

British *memsahibs* brought mid-Victorian piety, prudery, and Christian superiority, sitting "behind silver teapots, corseted, Christian and correct, dressing and behaving exactly as they would have in England, unanimously agreeing that the sooner the natives could be decently clothed and converted the better."[17] A prime example, Charlotte, Lady Canning, believed that Indians should be converted to Christianity by missionaries and often visited mission schools to spur them on.

Not all European women in India were upper class. Women able to find neither work nor husbands, partly because so many men migrated to the colonies, followed them, from prostitutes to doctors. Most found work as domestic servants, though many were missionaries. Female missionaries pioneered *zenana* education, teaching upper-caste Indian women at home, others at schools. *Zenana* education, begun in Bengal in the 1820s, consisted mainly of reading, writing, and enough arithmetic to manage household accounts, but it also included Bible stories and embroidery. Teaching girls in schools was a problem because the trip to the school required abandoning or modifying purdah and relaxing Hindu purity/pollution rules. Parents removed girls from school at about the age of ten to marry. But missionaries were persistent: in 1869 an American Methodist, Isabella Thoburn, took in pupils in Lucknow, laying the foundation for the first Christian college for Indian women.

Since British women were barred from medical schools until 1870 or so, the first woman physicians in India were American. Clara McSwain from Pennsylvania Medical College for Women went to India in 1870; a host of others soon followed, including Ida B. Scudder, who built a major medical complex at Vellore in South India. Confined Indian women were treated through intermediaries, who listed their symptoms for male doctors, sometimes using a doll to describe them. Women giving birth were attended by midwives, "untouchable" because they handled a polluting element, blood, the afterbirth. Two English woman doctors came to India in the 1890s. These pioneers added medical education to curricula, and Indian women began to study medicine, mainly obstetrics and gynecology. Bengali Brahmo women studied new delivery methods emphasizing sanitation to use with relatives and friends.

As Western medicine spread in India, women came to dominate obstetrics and gynecology, reversing the pattern of the West, where male gynecologists gradually eradicated female midwives. Unfortunately, Indian female physicians joined men in denigrating the abilities of midwives, who remained the only medical resource for the vast majority of Indian women. But elite women were increasingly treated by Indian women doctors with Western training. Paradoxically, Indian women were professionally trained because of purdah: they were needed to treat confined women.

European women initiated or catalyzed nineteenth-century Indian reform movements. Margaret Cousins (1878–1954), an Irish feminist theosophist, organized a delegation to petition for the vote and co-founded the Women's Indian Association. Whatever English-speaking women did – collaborated with Indian women, listened to them, or insensitively imposed their own ideas and attitudes – they invariably stirred things up. Missionaries had not been able to convert elite women to Christianity: most converts came from marginal Hindu groups – lower castes and widows. But missionary activities spurred Indian men, who feared women might convert, to establish schools for them. In 1828 a Bengali Brahman reformer, Ram Mohan Roy, founded a rationalist Hindu society, the Brahmo Samaj, in Calcutta. In the 1870s Brahmo Samaj built a Victorian Institution and the Brahmo Girls School; the Hindu Arya Samaj set up Kanya Mahavidyalaya in Jullunder, Punjab; and Muslims opened a girls school within the boys school at Aligarh.

The Gandhi Era

From the first, the Indian National Congress claimed to speak for all India, although its members were graduates of the University of

Calcutta – a narrow class of professional men trained as lawyers, teachers, doctors, and journalists. It included no women and few Muslims. (The Muslims formed their own Muslim League.) After the First World War the Congress tried to include men of other classes, but the Untouchables complained that it represented only caste Hindus and ignored their grievances. The Congress attacked Britain for aggravating Indian poverty by huge spending for military purposes, draining profits from India to London, and ruining Indian industry by means of economic policies. It demanded that Britain employ more Indians in higher administrative ranks and develop representative political institutions in India.

India contributed greatly to the Allied cause during the First World War, hoping, like suffragists, for recognition of its efforts afterwards. Instead, after severe famine and epidemics, including an influenza epidemic that killed 13 million people, the British promulgated the India Act of 1919, which enfranchised a tiny minority of male landowners (about 3 percent of the population) and required them to vote as part of a constituency – as Hindus, Muslims, Sikhs, or landowners. They introduced the principle of "dyarchy," ceding education and health to Indian control, but leaving government firmly in British hands, although Indians now had a majority in the Legislative Assembly. England adopted a harshly repressive governing policy.

Indians erupted in protest campaigns and *hartals* (general strikes) across the country, which the government quashed punitively. The Punjab was a centre of unrest – a number of Europeans had been attacked there, making officials, who remembered the Mutiny of 1857, extremely nervous. In April 1919 the British sent General Dyer to Amritsar with a small force; he banned public meetings, but a huge crowd, including many women and children, gathered on open land called Jallianwala Bagh. Some came intending to defy the ban, but others had come in from the countryside for the annual horse fair and were unaware of it. On April 13 Dyer blocked the exit from Jallianwala Bagh with soldiers and opened fire on the crowd without warning. In this notorious Amritsar Massacre, the troops fired for ten minutes without stopping, killing almost 400 people and wounding over a thousand.

Eighteenth-century India had less ethnic, linguistic, or cultural unity than Europe's nation-states. Only under Asoka in the third century BCE and under the Mughals had a single ruler unified a large segment of India. Nationalism, the belief that the state deserves primary citizen loyalty, is a fairly modern Western concept that did not really exist until the nineteenth century – although most people felt loyalty to a family, clan, city, or religious faith.[18] Nationalism, however, became colonized people's most successful ideological tool against imperialism. Gandhi managed to unify much of India through nationalism.

Mohandas Karamchand Gandhi, deeply influenced by his pious Hindu mother, had studied in England and practised law for twenty years in South Africa. There he campaigned against the country's racist treatment of Indians. He had developed a philosophy of resistance, partly by observing woman suffragists protesting in London. Believing that violence breeds violence and that ends do not justify means, he invented a technique of mass action called *satyagraha* – a loving standing-firm. Often translated as "passive" or "non-violent" resistance, it literally means "soul force" or "the power of truth." Its success depended on the courage of masses of Indians to refuse to obey British orders even when facing their guns, and on Gandhi's belief that the English conscience, sensitized by a long tradition of humane philosophy, would not permit the massacre of thousands of unarmed protesters. The British did kill many resisters, but in the end Gandhi's gamble proved correct – and he always stood in the front lines.

Gandhi returned to India in 1914 and, believing that the Allies were really fighting autocratic militarism, he supported them, against his pacifist principles, in the Great War. But when the British ushered in the repressive regime that unleashed the Amritsar Massacre, he took a stance of non-cooperation and persuaded the

Indian National Congress to follow him. A pacifist who insisted on religious tolerance, he drew support across sectarian lines, even from the Muslim League. He launched his first civil disobedience campaign in 1922, but cancelled it when he discovered that some groups were behaving violently. In the 1920s Motilal and Jawaharlal Nehru – father and son, wealthy, educated, principled Hindus who admired Gandhi – joined the nationalist movement.

The British had no idea how to deal with Gandhi. Britain had levied a salt tax, which brought in considerable revenue. But some independent Indian states had great salt lakes where Indians could get salt free. To keep them from smuggling it into British India, the British built a customs barrier, a thick, high prickly pear hedge 1500 miles long, manned by 12,000 inspectors and tax collectors.[19] To protest the tax and the hedge, Gandhi led a throng on a "march to the sea" to fill pans with sea water and let it evaporate, breaking the law granting the government a monopoly on salt-making. He also led boycotts of state liquor shops. His inclusive, unifying vision healed the split between moral and political principle, showing them to be one. His second mass demonstration, in 1930, led masses of Indians to resign from public office, boycott foreign goods, picket shops and courts, and refuse to pay taxes. The British arrested hundreds of demonstrators, including Gandhi, who was sentenced to six years in jail. Released in less than a year, Gandhi shifted strategy and tried to talk with British leaders. The racist Winston Churchill was disgusted at the mere thought, and the effort proved unproductive.

Gandhi ended his civil disobedience campaign in 1934 and retired from politics to devote himself to helping the poorest of India's poor – the peasants. He built an ashram in central India and worked with the peasants to develop better methods of cultivation, sanitation, and industry – especially spinning and weaving (he spun every day, but he also exploited young girls to wait on and service him). He wanted to approach revolution from a different, positive angle, eschewing money or force to build a decent world from the village level. He especially championed the Untouchables, renaming them Harijan, children of god. (They now call themselves Dalits.)

In 1935 the British took another tack and wrote a new consti-tution allowing princely states and provinces of British India to gov-ern themselves with ministries responsible to elected legislatures. But provincial governors retained great emergency powers, and defence and foreign affairs remained in English hands. In 1937 the Congress party won six of eleven provinces, and it formed ministries in the seven provinces in which it had majorities. The chastened Muslim League (which won only in Bengal, the Punjab, and Sind) made overtures to the Congress, but, unfortunately, the Congress would not compromise. Mohammed Ali Jinnah, president of the Muslim League, gave up all hope of cooperating with the Congress and began to take seriously the idea, first suggested in 1933, of a separate Muslim state.

Women participated hugely in the nationalist movement. They worked for female education, birth control, increasing the age of marriage, dress reform, and nuclear families. Confinement began to be phased out as women entered public life – in politics, the pro-fessions, and social work. And a new companionate marriage emerged. These developments contributed to what journalists called "the new woman." The nationalist leaders – Gandhi and Jawaharlal Nehru of the Indian National Congress, and Jinnah of the Muslim League – were open to enlarging women's sphere. Gandhi is credit-ed with drawing women into nationalist political activities, for he considered female emancipation an essential component of India's regeneration. As he said, "We must be incapable of defending our-selves or healthily competing with other nations, if we allow the better half of ourselves to become paralyzed." Indeed, women were indispensable in the mass movement he created: they maintained the family when men were away fighting colonial rule; and they organized, marched, and picketed. By 1900 women had become deeply involved in the *swadeshi* movement, which exhorted people to use indigenous, not foreign, products. Women contributed extraordinarily to the independence movement and formed their own organizations.

Women in India's Revolution

In 1914 a male reformer and his wife, Sheikh and Begum Abdullah, and Sultan Jahan Begum of Bhopal, the only woman ruler among the princes of India at the time, founded the All-India Muslim Ladies Conference to build a new residence hall for the Aligarh Girls School. New organizations were also founded in this period: the Women's Indian Association (1917), the National Council of Women in India (1925), and the All-India Women's Conference (1927). Elite women took over leadership of the women's social reform movement. For example, Margaret Cousins and Dorothy Jinarajadasa, an English feminist married to a Ceylonese Buddhist, organized the Women's Indian Association. Based in Madras, it advocated woman suffrage and worked for social reforms. Wealthy women founded the National Council of Women in India to sponsor local aid projects – orphanages, working girls' hostels, educational facilities, and prostitutes' homes. It avoided partisan politics.

The largest, most diverse, and most politicized group, the All-India Women's Conference (AIWC), came into being when the governor of Bengal asked women for advice on an educational curriculum appropriate for girls. Cousins did most of the early organizing, but she closely collaborated with Indian women in establishing the Lady Irwin College of Home Sciences in Delhi. In 1932 the AIWC risked public opprobrium by urging public clinics to provide contraceptive information. During the ferment over constitutional reform and civil disobedience in the early 1930s, it joined other women's organizations in demanding the vote for women; in 1934 it began to lobby for a uniform civil code guaranteeing legal rights for women of all religions, especially with regard to marriage, divorce, adoption, and inheritance. In the late 1930s, many of its officers joined the struggle for independence. Its activities diminished in the early 1940s when AIWC officers like Rajkumari Amrit

Kaur and Vijaya Lakshmi Pandit, Jawaharlal Nehru's sister, were jailed for political activity.

Women were central to Gandhi's nationalist agenda, and he attacked dowry, child marriage, and polygamy. He never derided female chastity, but claimed it was an inner quality, not one imposed by external forms like purdah. He supported remarriage for child widows, but admired older widows who withdrew from society. Unlike most revolutionaries, he insisted that political and social agendas must be promoted simultaneously. Gandhi was humane but saw things strictly as a man – he believed in male supremacy and complementary spheres, though he felt that women should be decently treated within them. He urged men to defer to women's greater knowledge of domestic affairs, and women not to devote their lives entirely to domestic work. He claimed that women were men's moral equals, and that Hindu culture excessively subordinated women to men, but he never denounced subordination per se. He disapproved of women earning money outside the home or "undertaking commercial enterprises," and opposed birth control (urging women to use self-control). He created a special role for women in the nationalist movement that did not compete with men's but relied on women's greater moral and spiritual capacity for suffering to serve others. As a result, women thronged to him.

The success of the Non-cooperation Movement required women to boycott foreign goods and to spin *khadi* (homespun, as in the American Revolution). In *An Appeal to the Indian Woman*, Gandhi made spinning women's religious duty (*dharma*): "the economic and . . . moral salvation of India . . . rests mainly with you," he wrote. Basanti Devi (1880–1974) and Urmila Devi (1883–1956), the wife and sister of C.R. Das, the Bengal Congress leader, were among the first women arrested for selling *khadi*. Gandhi ennobled the domestic sphere by giving it political import. Women returned his respect by being in the vanguard of all major independence actions. They faced down police charges during a tax strike in 1928. Gandhi barred women from the Salt March that opened the 1930 civil disobedience campaign because he did not want to be charged with using women as a shield, but Sarojini Naidu led thousands of women in the raid on the Dharsana salt field. Once Gandhi was arrested, women openly challenged British authority, organizing protest marches in Bombay, picketing toddy and foreign cloth shops, promoting hand spinning, and wearing the coarse, itchy *khadi*. Nationalist women endured arrest, detention, verbal abuse, and violence from British authorities for thirty years. Their acts defied the Indian definition of female possibility.

Feminist scholars debate Gandhi's effect on women. Some claim he offered women a way to personal dignity; others say that in the years when women elsewhere were demanding equal rights in law, education, and the vote, Gandhi was encouraging them to be like the goddess Sita, selfless servants of the nation.[20] One wrote that since most of the women in the nationalist movement had grown up in purdah or near it, it is amazing that "they dared as much and . . . accomplished so much."[21] Perhaps most interesting is the claim that the very notion of *satyagraha* exalts "feminine" qualities like the repudiation of violence, the will to fast unto death, and the ability to compromise, thereby revalorizing these qualities.[22]

After the 1930s, women activists began to demand rights. While Gandhi was opposing birth control, the All-India Women's Conference passed a resolution in its favour. Indian women began to demand social reform: they legitimated their entrance into the public sphere by claiming they were upholding ideals of purity; they ended by demanding the extension of male civil rights to women by claiming the right to fulfil their capacities. Some went even further and became revolutionaries.

In the late 1920s, particularly in Bengal, women in their late teens and early twenties joined terrorist groups that targeted British officials and property. British reprisals had fragmented the older revolutionary groups; the new ones accepted women, assigning them the same work as men – smuggling messages and weapons, raiding British armouries, making bombs, and assassinating British officials. Most of these women, like female reformists, were drawn to terrorism by male relatives. Elite, articulate, individualistic, they were marginal in society and marginalized even further by their form of protest – robbery and assassination.

Women's courageous resistance won them powerful allies. The Congress and the Muslim League increasingly accepted the idea of woman suffrage, which was promoted not as a basis for altering sexual-power relations but as an indication of India's readiness for self-government. By 1930 women had won the franchise in all provinces, but national suffrage took decades of struggle mainly by elite women, who fought in many arenas at both the provincial and the national level.

Two Government of India Acts, passed in 1919 and 1935, granted limited male and female suffrage, but in principle and on terms unacceptable to most women's organizations. The franchise was granted to female property owners, but few married Indian women owned property, so the British proposed that the wives of certain classes of male property owners and of military personnel be allowed to vote. Britain gradually enfranchised women in this way, but Indian women demanded universal franchise, not partial steps based on women's relations to men. In the years in which woman suffrage was debated, women argued with men and with each other and campaigned vigorously before committees, conferences, commissions, and legislatures, generally learning political skills.

By the 1930s the National Council of Women in India and the All-India Women's Conference were agitating to reform Hindu laws on marriage and inheritance, which generated more heated controversy than either the franchise or child marriage. These issues fused women and property – an explosive combination – and battles over them continued into the early years of independence. Women's rights activists lobbied for bills to equalize divorce, outlaw polygyny, permit intercaste and interfaith marriage, grant equal rights of guardianship, require both parties' consent to marriage, and grant women equal rights to inheritance. They had little success. The

Hindu Women's Right to Property Act of 1937 gave some widows limited estates during their lifetimes. By the 1940s progressive legal circles and Congress leaders advocated comprehensive reform of the Hindu Code, but, despite the Congress Party's endorsement, the male elite was divided on these issues, especially on divorce. Progress stalled when the Second World War began, along with a Civil Disobedience Campaign.

To eradicate veiling, women used subtle means, trying to draw women who observed purdah into their organizations, stretching the boundaries of the female sphere. Many Indian women did not disapprove of purdah, only its excessive application, and supported segregation in most aspects of life. Although Gandhi, Nehru, and Jinnah denounced the practice, only the All-India Women's Conference of all women's groups sponsored anti-purdah demonstrations. Hindu women deflected Hindu men's antagonism by blaming the practice on Islam, not male oppression, further intensifying the rising tensions between Hindus and Muslims.

Muslim women sought greater freedom while adhering to tradition; they did not challenge but tried to expand the boundaries of purdah, justifying their actions as extensions of their domestic roles. Abadi Banu Begum (1852–1924) offers a striking example of such behaviour. Her sons, the Ali brothers, were active in a campaign to keep the British government from destroying the Ottoman Khalifat, a symbol of Muslim unity. When they were arrested, she toured the country as a mother protecting her children and her religion, and urged Muslims to emulate her sons. Raised in strict purdah, she first spoke in public from behind a veil, a picture of one of her sons standing beside her. But in 1921 she addressed a mass meeting in Punjab (in a joint Hindu-Muslim non-cooperation campaign) and lifted her veil, declaring that all those present were her children in the nationalist cause. Like Victorian women in England and the United States, she accepted her confinement within the domestic sphere, but expanded its purview.

The first Muslim women's organization with a reform agenda

was the All-India Muslim Ladies Conference (Anjuman-e Khawatin-e-Islam), founded in 1914 by literate upper-class wives and relatives of prominent male professionals and educators. In 1918 it passed a resolution condemning polygyny as violating the true spirit of Islam because it was impossible for men to obey the Prophet Muhammad's injunction to treat each wife equally. This resolution caused an uproar in some Muslim journals, but it had no other effect.

In 1940 Mohammad Ali Jinnah, president of the Muslim League, formally declared its intention of forming a separate state. Needing women's support, he claimed that women's "uplift" was essential to the national cause. He encouraged women organized by a female auxiliary of the All-India Muslim League to march and picket. A significant showing in the 1945 elections was crucial to the league's claim to speak for all Muslims: it ran women candidates and let women organize voters, registering and canvassing Muslim women and fundraising. Many of these women were imprisoned when they picketed and protested against the Punjabi government.

When the Second World War erupted, the Congress refused to help England except as an independent state with its own constitution. The British put India off with promises; the Congress had Gandhi begin a new *satyagraha* campaign, a war of words in which Indians informed Britain about each speech in advance. The British arrested every speaker and Indians again filled English jails, but no violence or disruption occurred. In the end, India contributed even more to the British cause than in the First World War, sending 2 million men and many manufactures to fight the Axis.

After Japan invaded Malaya and Burma (Myanmar), the British tried to rally support by making India a dominion with a constitution drafted by Indians – but deferring Indian control until after the war and allowing provinces that opted out of the federation to make separate arrangements with England. Every Indian organization rejected this compromise, suggesting the end was at hand. The war in Europe concluded in May 1945; the war in Asia three months later, when the United States dropped nuclear bombs on Hiroshima and Nagasaki. The British economy was nearly ruined by the war, and Britain depended heavily on American aid. But the United States was not sympathetic to British imperialism in India. In the spring of 1946 a British Cabinet Mission went to India to seek a basis for settlement with Indian leaders and to convince them to reach agreement among themselves because the British really were going to withdraw. Their plan for a federal union safeguarded minorities and left considerable regional autonomy, but several Congress members hinted they would not be bound by any British promises, and Jinnah too rejected the proposal. Deciding the Muslim League must show its strength, he declared August 16, 1946, to be "Direct Action Day." He claimed he had intended only demonstrations, but about 4000 people were killed in riots that day, mainly in Calcutta.

A Labour government succeeded Churchill and, in 1947, Prime Minister Clement Attlee announced that England would leave India in June 1948. He offered the hope that India would remain within the British Commonwealth. With independence imminent, Muslim–Hindu resentment exploded in riots, killing about 12,000 people. The British, who had dragged their feet for almost a century, were now in a hurry to relinquish responsibility and simply accepted partition of the country. The northwest and northeast had the largest concentration of Muslims, but they made up between a fifth and a quarter of the entire population, with communities scattered all over India. In most cases, Indian and Pakistani boundaries could serve as the boundaries of the new states, but Bengal and the Punjab had to be partitioned, and the Punjab's irrigation system had to be severed – to the detriment of both parts. East Bengal became East Pakistan, separated by over a thousand miles from larger West Pakistan. An agricultural region raising cotton, tea, and jute, it was cut off from processing plants and export ports in West Bengal and could barely survive.

Massive mindless violence in the fall of 1947 checked any hope of cooperation between India and Pakistan. It occurred only in Bengal and the Punjab, but reached appalling proportions – about half a million people died. Ten million Indians changed places – Muslims fled to Pakistan; Hindus and Sikhs to India. Over 12 million were left homeless. Frail, in his late seventies, Gandhi exhorted Hindus to end the violence, threatening to fast. He stopped riots in Calcutta; in 1948 he went to Delhi and fasted to force Congress leaders to promise to protect Muslim life and property. When they agreed, he went to pray and was assassinated by a member of a chauvinistic Hindu group. The world mourned him.

Amid the violence and the immense suffering of the partition, Muslim women voluntarily provided medical relief for the wounded and ran blood, food, and clothing drives. In 1949 women veterans of the struggle for freedom founded the All-Pakistan Women's Association to promote the substantive reforms they – and Hindu women – had earned and expected now that their countries were independent. We have seen many examples of women helping in a struggle, only to be excluded once it is over, but what happened to women in India and Pakistan is unique.

Women After Independence

Hindu Women

The period following independence was fulfilling for Hindu women: they won the vote in 1947, when India established universal adult suffrage. Indira Gandhi became prime minister from 1966 to 1977 and again in 1980; Vijaya Lakshmi Pandit was ambassador to Washington and Moscow and high commissioner to the United Kingdom, Padma Naidu was governor of the state of West Bengal, and Sucheta Kripalani was chief minister of Uttar Pradesh. Women were elected to state legislatures and the Lok Sabha (the lower house of the Indian Parliament) in numbers slightly higher than the 3 1/2 percent of women usually elected to such bodies in Western nations. Many of these women were kin of prominent people in the independence movement: Indira Gandhi was Nehru's daughter, Pandit was his sister, and Padma Naidu was Sarojini Naidu's daughter. Almost all the women elected came from the elite class.

Several points need to be made about this phenomenon. First, it was India's traditional feudal structure, not democracy, that enabled elite women to act in the public world. As we have seen, aristocratic societies are made up of families, within which women often have power. This domestic power easily translates into political power in aristocratic states. Second, Indira Gandhi was chosen by an all-male Congress Party leadership because of her relation to Nehru and because they believed they could control a woman. This proved not to be the case; Gandhi was able to hold power for almost twenty years, until she was assassinated in 1984. She and the other women who rose to important positions performed their duties intelligently, proving their ability. But their status was unrelated to ability: they became prominent after independence because of their relation to men. Male systems that allow elite women to hold power do so secure in the knowledge they will not use their position to benefit women at large. No female ruler in history has made substantive improvements in women's lives; few have even tried. This generalization held true in India: Indira Gandhi was no friend to women.

The Preamble of the new Indian Constitution produced in 1950 promises all citizens "equality of status" and guarantees women equal protection under the law and equal opportunity in employment. It also reserves the right to make "rational, reasonable" distinctions by sex to benefit women, a condition women's organizations accepted. But the constitution did not provide a uniform civil code. No single legal code governs marriage and inheritance in India: Hindus, Muslims, Christians, Parsis, Sikhs, and splinter groups – like the residents of former Portuguese Goa and French Pondicherry – each have their own laws. Nehru, who promised women he would reform Hindu personal law, had difficulty doing even that: orthodox male Hindu groups resisted reform. Not until 1954–55 was he able to enact the laws known collectively as the Hindu Marriage Code. His decision to let Muslims follow their personal law – he was trying to reconcile the 10 percent Muslim minority that stayed in India after the creation of Pakistan – disappointed women activists, who felt it was made at the expense of women.

There was resistance to reforms prohibiting child marriage and polygyny, but Nehru encountered the greatest opposition when he tried to guarantee women equal inheritance rights. Not until 1956 was he able to push through the Hindu Succession Act, granting equal and absolute inheritance rights to the widow, mother, sons, daughters (and their immediate heirs) of men who died intestate. Men granted this right with certain conditions: that male heirs could inherit their own *and* part of their father's shares; that men who made formal wills could bar women from inheriting; and that agricultural tenancies were exempt. Thus, powerful conservative male groups in some states prevented widows and daughters from inheriting. Traditionally, women could not inherit land absolutely; in India, their new ability to do so existed only in principle.[23]

The law grants daughters the right to live in their birth family's dwelling, so long as they are unmarried, widowed, or legally separated. Married daughters have no claim at all, not even the right to stay in their fathers' house if they need to flee their in-laws' house because they are being harassed, battered, tortured, or threatened with murder. A father may choose to take in his daughter, but is not bound to do so. It is extremely difficult for women to get out of oppressive marriages because they often have no place to go, and fathers usually get custody of the children. A father is considered the "natural" parent; a mother's claim is secondary. As divorce becomes more common, child custody and support become thorny issues. Some judges have awarded custody of children to mothers, but the law emphasizes the rights of the father's family. In addition, divorced mothers have a hard time supporting their children: laws prohibit discrimination against women in work but place the burden of proof on the individual woman, a demand that daunts even educated women.

The Indian Constitution of 1950 directs that all children up to fourteen shall be given free compulsory education, but this goal is still unattained. Many villages are too poor to finance a school, and schoolchildren need shoes, writing tablets, and pencils. Families with a tiny surplus educate only their sons. The female literacy rate in India has slightly improved – it was 0.69 percent in 1901; 8 percent in 1951, after independence; about 25 percent in 1981; and 38 percent in 1999. Across the board, it is less than half that of males. In the mid-1970s, 99 percent of boys and 68 percent of girls attended primary school. Many villages have no school. Older girls are taken out of school: 33 percent of boys, but only 13 percent of girls attend high school. This attrition is attributed to the need for girls' labour in the household, but is probably connected also to rural communities' demand for female virginity at marriage. Girls are taken from schools at puberty, but even poor families let their sons go to high school. Most middle- and upper-class families educate their daughters, and many attend college. At the college level, then, there is less of a sexual gap in enrolment.

Despite a 1961 law prohibiting dowry, the practice has grown, spreading from upper to lower castes.[24] Historically, dowry is compensation to the groom's family for taking on a dependent non-productive member; bridewealth compensates the bride's family for losing an active productive member. Yet in most societies, all but very rich women work in maintenance or production or both, and most produce children. In India today many wives work, yet dowry continues: families demand higher dowries from educated brides with jobs.

As Western individualism and greed become more visible in India, dowry has become the basis of a hideous new atrocity. Families agree on a dowry, but after the wedding the groom's parents begin to blackmail the bride to squeeze more out of her family – a television set, motorcycle, or wristwatch for the groom, a refrigerator for them. She knows that if their demands are not met, the family may kill her, usually by holding her over the cooking stove so her sari catches fire and she burns to death. Then they can begin the process of getting a new wife – and a new dowry – for their son. Bride burning has become a new form of capital accumulation.[25] Thousands of women have been murdered this way in recent years – 1000 women a year are burned alive in Gujarat state (Gandhi's birthplace) alone.[26] During the last decade, 11,000 to 15,000 women have been killed each year in dowry murders, an increase over the past of 170 percent.[27] Moreover, the murders are often performed by women, by mothers-in-law, although most wife burnings seem to culminate a pattern of battering by husbands.

India's patriarchal socialization has had enormous success in dividing women. The bride's mother-in-law usually decides how dowry items will be distributed (men control all cash) and determines the correct reciprocal relations with the families of women who marry in. Her interests are completely focused on her sons. The same is true of the bride's mother, who may care less about daughters and enjoy creating an appearance of wealth with a large dowry. Some observers believe dowry is inevitable as long as there is overwhelming pressure on girls to marry: 99 percent of Indian women between the ages of twenty-five and forty-four are or have been married.

Moreover, families known to have disposed of daughters-in-law can easily find another family willing to sacrifice its daughter to them. Dowry death is one manifestation of a deeper condition, a belief that pervades Indian culture: that females are worthless. The family of a prominent Rajasthan politician boasts that it has produced no girls in forty years.

Many urban women's groups have mobilized to end this monstrous practice: they do consciousness-raising work, picket households suspected of dowry murder, and set up women's shelters so that brides who sense their conjugal family's intention have some escape. They held a major conference, urged a change in the attitudes of police, and demanded legal reform limiting dowry payments and enforcing inheritance rights. The police rarely do post mortems after suspected dowry deaths and almost never prosecute the murderers.

In general, animist tribal women have more sexual freedom than women of high-god religions.[28] No scripture mandates their inferiority or sanctions male control of female sexuality. Women may have lovers before marriage, choose their husbands, divorce, and remarry. Tribal peoples' greater sexual egalitarianism and ease in daily relations are based less in ideological than economic factors: they do slash-and-burn agriculture and are only loosely part of a money economy, so they are not socially stratified. Subsistence cultures are concerned not with profit and property, but with survival, and they promote women's concerns and individual autonomy. However, as tribal communities are increasingly assimilated into Hindu society, Hindu definitions and expectations of women increasingly restrict their women. Tribal communities are beginning to arrange marriages, demand dowry, and try to control women's movements and their bodies. Because female freedom is equated with low status throughout India, women bear the burden of men's desire to rise socially.

In most Hindu communities, women hold religious festivals celebrating a positive aspect of "femaleness" – fertility, beneficence, or self-sacrifice. Hindus associate women with mother goddesses in the village pantheon; in some places, low-caste women act as priestesses of the goddess, but high-caste Hindus abhor this practice and use only male Brahmin priests. Hindus worship in temples but more at home, where women are the major worshippers. Rites and prayers, however, are imbued with male-dominance. Some women fast each week for their husbands' well-being.

Hindu scriptures (which most women cannot read), sacred legends, and folklore are obsessed with dictating proper female behaviour. Women are enjoined to be meek, self-sacrificing, subordinate to husband and elders, chaste before and after marriage, and totally devoted to husband and children. All women must marry and produce sons because only a son can perform his father's funeral rites. However, a woman's marriage is in the control of her male relatives, who are blamed if she is left unmarried. Upper-caste Hindus believe a woman has only one destined husband in a lifetime and may not divorce or – especially – remarry if widowed or abandoned. These beliefs pervade Hindu culture, influencing even agnostics or atheists.[29]

Worship in Islam is more centred on the mosque, from which women are usually barred. Although Indian Muslims have adopted many Hindu customs, Islam has no major women's festivals. These women are cut off from their religion, bearing its burdens but not its communal pleasures. Even Sikkhism, which mandates spiritual equality between the sexes, allows women no priestly roles or special ceremonies. But it does enjoin women to pray, recite scripture, and work in the communal kitchen attached to every *gudwara*. Men too work there in a rite symbolizing Sikkhism's freedom from the pollution taboos of Hinduism: everyone works together in a caste-free labour force, and everyone together eats what the others have cooked.

Feminism in India

Throughout India, girls are fed less than boys and neglected more, a difference that is visible in the family: girls are pitifully thin and die more often than boys in every decade of early life. Female infanticide exists, although it is illegal, and some towns (especially in Rajasthan) boast they have not had a wedding in over a century (because they produce no girls).[30] Women earn far less than men. Women, who prepare the food, are expected to wait until the men are finished before they can eat. A female construction worker told me, guiltily looking about, that she ate a little something first. She had to, she said: the men never leave anything. Moreover, when the men finish their work, they go out – to town, to the movies, to brothels – or, if they have access to one, they watch television. Women can never relax: they work fifteen or more hours a day.

In the 1970s, after the UN declared 1975 to be the opening year of the Decade for Women, government welfare officials and social reformers were shocked to discover that Indian social programs aimed at "the poor" had benefited mainly men, and that Indian men had not shared their gains with their families but had spent 98 percent of their higher wages on themselves. Decades of "development" (the code for industrialization and modernization of agriculture through mechanization, chemicals, and high-yield crops) had not helped but only harmed women.[31] The government appointed a Committee on the Status of Women to prepare a report on the condition of Indian women for submission to the United Nations.[32]

The committee, nine women and one man, found that, since independence, the ratio of women to men had declined; females were more malnourished and had higher mortality rates than males; and fewer women had paid employment, especially in agriculture and unorganized manufacturing, the two areas where most unskilled women had found work. Only professional women had increased in number. Officials determined to shift their focus from the poor to women.

The 1970s were rocky in India: drought and famine added to problems that arose as a result of the increasing commercialization of agriculture; rising unemployment and rising prices for food and cooking fuel (and its scarcity) triggered violent outbreaks. In the midst of a crisis in December 1974, the committee submitted its report, *Towards Equality*. In June 1975 Indira Gandhi imposed a state of emergency on India, restricting civil rights on grounds of a purported threat to national security. Women activists, galvanized by the suspension of civil rights and new information on women's condition, protested Sanjay Gandhi's (Gandhi's son) forcible imposition of birth control, police rape of women held in local jails, and the new phenomenon of bride burnings. The Indian women's movement revived.

The committee's research was addressed by vital new organizations founded by women. Urban Western-educated groups call themselves feminist, but Madhu Kishwar, the editor of the journal

Manushi (Women), feels that the word "feminism" bears Western connotations, ideas and ideological divisions among women that obscure Indian reality. Some groups prefer the terms *Stree Shakti* (women's power) or *Stree Sangathana* (women's organization).

Groups involved in women's issues can be autonomous, affiliated with institutions, or dedicated to self-help and include consciousness-raising groups, institutions like trade unions and tribal organizations, professional women's associations, women's auxiliaries to political parties, and research networks for academics and activists. They affirm a variety of ideologies – feminist, left-wing political activist, civil libertarian, humanitarian, Gandhian, Marxist, and religious – though most subscribe to a broad agenda.

One of the most important groups is SEWA, the Self-Employed Women's Association, a self-help group founded by Ela Bhatt in Ahmedabad to help women ragpickers and sidewalk vegetable vendors.[33] Bhatt's Gandhian philosophy of self-reliance led her to create an institution for women, especially poor women who cannot get credit in India. They join SEWA, which has a bank to finance their projects, welfare services like legal aid, maternity and widows' benefits, consciousness-raising groups, and a supportive network. SEWA lends money to women to set up small businesses that help them and their children survive; they repay the loans at a rate of about 98 percent.[34] SEWA adds collective strength to women's efforts to found crêches and to end battering and police harassment; it finances woman-owned dairy farms, which are generally clean, efficient enterprises, some of which experiment with cheap forms of solar power. The Working Women's Forum in Madras run by Jaya Arunchalam does similar work.

Women have organized self-help groups – cooperative dairy farms in Gujarat, Madhubani folk painters, housewives marketing a dried snack in Bombay, and women who patrol the streets of Manipur for alcoholics. In Bombay and some rural areas, they demonstrate to embarrass husbands who beat their wives; and in Bombay and elsewhere, they protest rising food prices. Hundreds of groups devise creative projects, asking local women for suggestions for projects. Such groups mobilize on specific issues like bride burning, rape, forced marriage, wife-battering, media sexploitation of women, police violence (including rape) against women, and "Eve-teasing" (harassment of women in public spaces). Most are urban and have sprung up in recent years.

Educated young women founded Saheli (female friend), a Delhi collective, to teach women their legal rights and help them find paid work, especially when they decide to divorce. But they soon had to turn Saheli into a shelter too, as battered wives and girls being forced into unwelcome marriages came to their headquarters for haven. The police broke down their doors, trying to restore the female "property" to its male owners. The Saheli women perform street plays about women's rights. Groups in other states also use this means for reaching illiterate people who rarely or never hear radio or see television: one based in Tamil Nadu put on skits on wife-beating and the enormous burden of women's daily life – fetching wood, fuel, and water, field work, cooking, and child care. Saheli also organizes charivaris, mounting demonstrations in front of the houses of families that murdered their daughters-in-law, and in front of legal courts to pressure judges to take dowry death seriously.

Other young college-educated women go into the countryside, where life is incredibly hard, and live among villagers trying to help women unite, discover a voice, name their needs, and obtain them. What is perhaps most inspiring is that they go to listen, learn, and help, not to impose their own abstract knowledge, and they cross the huge class lines in a spirit of joy, not martyrdom. Other women go to the countryside to unionize agricultural or other unorganized workers in local units.

India remains open to many problem-solving methods. It has not made any system taboo (as the United States did with socialism, and the Soviet Union with capitalism). The split between socialist and mainstream feminists that occurred in the United States and in England did not occur in India. Indian feminists debate different approaches internally; difference does not rupture them. Left-wing women take the initiative on some women's issues, even though left-wing parties in India also insist that "men's issues" (political or economic power) matter more than "women's issues" (survival of women and children and the overall quality of life). Women were highly active politically in Bengal in the 1940s, but the Bengal Communist Party of India (Marxist) has ignored women, and its women's branch degenerated into an auxiliary, mobilizing the vote and sponsoring social and recreational activities. Indeed, all political parties in India have women's wings and they all demonstrate the same failure.

Women founded a feminist press, Kali, and feminist journals like *Manushi* (published alternately in English and in Hindi). *Manushi* defies categorization; it probes every aspect of women's lives, from India's socioeconomic structure, in which 20 percent of the population controls 80 percent of its resources, to poor women's struggles as middle- and upper-class women benefit from new laws, to the daily oppression of women by fathers, brothers, and husbands, who are "virtual prison guards" for "too many women in India." Despite their willingness to acknowledge the behaviour of ordinary men, not just institutions, in oppressing women, Indian feminist journals like *Manushi* do not advocate transforming sex relations, as many Western feminists do. Holding fast to the positive in women's culture, trying to avoid Western individualism, and recognizing that the family can support as well as oppress, they try to find another course.

Muslim Women in India, Pakistan, and Bangladesh

In the past century, Muslim women lost ground in the same ways as Hindu women. Men's life expectancy rose faster than women's, and industrial development, agricultural modernization, and population growth harmed women, especially the poor, who lost jobs in many sectors. About 11 percent of the population of India, over 70 million people, are Muslim. But they are not united; contrary to the male egalitarian principles of Islam, the *Ashraf* (elite) claim Arabic or foreign ancestry and scorn the *Ajlaf* (commoners), who are mainly Indian converts or their descendants.

Ajlaf women have more freedom of movement – they work in the fields and in craft industries with their husbands, or sell petty goods to upper-class women in purdah. Because Ajlaf women have relative freedom, they are less "respectable" than the Ashraf. Like Hindu women, urban, Westernized Ashraf women are entering colleges and the professions, while upwardly mobile Ajlaf become more conservative in gender relations, copying discarded Ashraf norms. Working-class women, Muslim and Hindu, have lost work because of "development," but whether Muslim women work, and what work they do, is also determined by purdah.

Fewer Muslim than Hindu women are educated and participate in paid work or politics – only a handful have sat in parliament since 1952. Muslim women's traditionalism is caused partly by purdah regulations, but also by the uneasy position of Muslims after the traumatic partition in 1947.[35] Most Muslims who went to Pakistan were young, educated, urban professionals; those who stayed behind were a small, rich Muslim class and a mass of frightened, vulnerable poor. A huge gap yawns between them, and to keep the community from fragmenting along class lines, Muslim political leaders play on minority fears of engulfment and rigidly insist on tradition. Pakistan itself, with its Muslim majority, is fundamentalist. Its longtime ruler, General Zia ul Haq, claimed that purdah had an "Islamic" basis, so opposed "promiscuous mingling" of the sexes in education and interpreted family law with great rigidity. After Zia died and Benazir Bhutto became prime minister, she made no improvements in the situation of women. Nor have any governments since.

Every Indian government since independence has shrunk from trying to reform Muslim family law, fearing accusations of "Hindu majority meddling" and a fundamentalist backlash. Although many Muslim nations have reformed their laws, Muslim personal law in

India is static. Despite India's constitutional guarantee of equality for all citizens, Muslim men may marry several wives, divorce by repudiation, and treat women unequally in inheritance. The one advantage Muslim women have over Hindu women is less stigmatization for divorce or widowhood. Polygyny is rare: poor Muslims cannot afford multiple wives. But Islam advocates stricter forms of purdah than Hinduism and tends to discourage female education as corruptive of chastity. Because of purdah, women are less likely to work outside the home, and they endure hopeless poverty without being able to alleviate it.

In Pakistan, women are subject to Qur'anic law as modified by legislation. Islamic authorities dictate the dress and work permissible for Pakistani women. Conservative women wear the burqa, the long cloak covering their heads, faces, and bodies, the cloak Rokeya Sakhawat Hossain loathed. Moderate women conceal themselves with a chaddar, a large shawl, or a duppata, a rectangular scarf. Professional women are slotted into segregated jobs like education and female medicine; women can also work in all-female banks dealing only with women. They are forbidden to take part in international athletic competitions like the Olympics, but can vote, belong to political parties, and run for office. Benazir Bhutto, the daughter of a former prime minister murdered by Zia, became prime minister twice.

Bangladesh (once East Pakistan) became independent in 1971. Its population is mainly Muslim, but its culture resembles Southeast Asian more than Middle Eastern cultures. Physical confinement of women is a cultural ideal, but its poverty means that veiling is rudimentary. Poor women have to work; they bow to the ideal of purdah by trying to avoid contact with unrelated males. Because of poverty and women's subordinate position, in 1981 a woman could expect to live to forty-nine, a man to fifty-three. The maternal mortality rate is one of the highest in world: 27 percent of women between ten and forty-nine years of age die in childbirth. Elite women here, too, are channelled into careers in female education or medicine; here too, women can vote and hold office. The two major political coalitions that opposed the government of former president Ershad were headed by female relatives of former male political leaders, and in 1991 Begum Khaleda Zia was elected prime minister. Yet in both Pakistan and Bangladesh, women are confined in curtained sections in public spaces like buses and railway carriages, offices, banks, and schools, and they must plan expeditions carefully because few women's toilets exist in public places.[36]

Poor rural women cannot be confined because they have to work, but they try to veil themselves. Poor urban women who do not work outside the home are often confined for life to one small room where the family lives. These women call themselves "frogs in a well."[37] A 1960 study of a village near Lahore, Pakistan, listed 97 percent of the women as houseworkers; the other 3 percent did midwifery, spinning, weaving, bread baking, and sweeping. In 1968 only 14.6 percent of Pakistani women over fifteen were paid for their work, and women who worked in their husbands' trades were regarded as subordinates. In the 1960s many Bangladeshi villages kept women completely confined to compounds of between four and ten houses, neither visited from outside nor allowed to meet anyone but residents of their compound.[38] In 1985 I interviewed a woman who lived in such a compound in Delhi. Not yet twenty, she had three children. She was unveiled, illiterate, and very poor, although her literate husband worked for UNICEF and could drive a car. She could do nothing to relieve their poverty because she was not allowed to go out. Her husband did the marketing, errands, and shopping (about which he complained to me: it took up so much of his time, he lamented). So the woman's confinement was intensified by boredom. The young husband, who spoke English, hovered, answering questions for her. He insisted that she could leave the compound, but was murky about just where she could go: it seemed she could visit the compound next door. "She can go to the mosque!" he finally declared, triumphantly. "Ah!" I said. "And where is that? The mosque across the street?" Well, she could not go there, he confessed, but she can go to the woman's mosque. I was surprised. I had never heard of such a thing. Where was it? Embarrassment. There was none.[39]

Purdah forces men to do work done by women in other societies: they buy the food, take children to school, pick them up, take them to doctors and dentists, and do all out-of-house tasks. Muslim or Hindu women from confined backgrounds are often afraid to venture out alone even if their husbands want them to. The husbands must take time off from their jobs to do the chores, lost time that can damage their careers. But here, power over women matters more than money and power in the world. And poor women who cannot read or write, do not own radios or television sets, do little but sit all day, simmering with boredom. They cannot be agreeable to come home to. Yet purdah continues.

Women are organizing. Behbud, a women's welfare organization directed by Nighat Khan, provides vocational training and scholarships for Muslim women, helps them get loans to start small businesses, and offers literacy programs, a library, family planning, and women's health centres. One volunteer tried frantically to get legal help for a woman with cancer who needed a mastectomy, but whose husband had denied permission for the operation even though he knew that, without it, she would die.[40]

India Today

Discussions of women and political power often confuse two very different situations: an extraordinary woman coming to power as an individual in a male governing establishment and political power held by women in general. Since the rise of the state, no state has ever allowed women in general a voice. But rule by family (clan rule, feudalism, monarchies) often brought women to power. Within families, women matter and they hold personal, as opposed to formal, power. Hosts of women have ruled in the past, and even more behind the scenes. But they ruled as men among men: elite women take political power without changing the situation of women as a caste. They do not heed women's voice.

Where women accede to power, they are women only incidentally. They may be seen as extraordinary, able to overcome the "weaknesses" of their sex, but all are subject to special surveillance because of their sex. It may be ironic that a woman, Indira Gandhi, ruled a nation that, more than any other, kills its females, but the two factors are not related. That Indira Gandhi, Golda Meir, or Margaret Thatcher held power does not mean that their countries have less contempt for women than others. Today, women usually come to power in countries with traditions of inherited elite rule: elite men may allow women of their own class to hold power if they have the potential to unify a country, counting on their being malleable to male control – as Indian Congress Party men mistakenly thought Indira Ghandi, and Israeli Labor Party men thought Golda Meir. Whether or not such women defer to male control, men can usually count on them to uphold class interests. Women, not having wives, need servants more than men do. And they know they govern by men's sufferance.

India elects more women to top political posts than other countries because it has a tradition of rule by elite kin-groups: it still has elements of a feudal state. Few monarchies remain, but countries like Pakistan, ruled by elite clans and extended families, within which women can hold influence, run on similar principles. In India, class (caste) distinctions are of huge importance and difficult to overcome. In 1990 the lower house of India's Parliament had a larger percentage of women than the American House of Representatives, and in the upper house, Raya Sabha, 9–10 percent of members were women. Amartya Sen notes that more women were tenured in Delhi University in 1990 than at Harvard.[41] However, as the Indian caste system gradually erodes and becomes less constricting, elite women will no longer be privileged over lower-class men; indeed, fewer women of this generation have important government jobs than in the first generation after independence.

Kerala

Kerala, a southern Indian state, was still matrilineal in the nineteenth century. Matrilineal groups still exist today in southern Tamil Nadu, but such systems were most developed in southern Karnataka and Kerala, which even had a matrilineal Muslim community. The most famous matrilineal group in Kerala was the Nayars, a high-ranking land-owning community that passed property and lineage in the female line.[42] Heads of households (*karanavan*) were men – uncles, not fathers – but women had considerable autonomy, living in *taravad* (matrilineage) houses that men could only visit. Men lived with their grandmothers and mothers. After the evening meal, a man took a lantern or burning branch and went to his wife's house, to spend the night, returning to his maternal house for a bath and breakfast the next day.

Within a *taravad*, older women had authority over younger ones, but no woman was ever abused by a mother-in-law or shunned for being a widow. The *karanavan* arranged a girl's first marriage, usually a useful economic, social, or political alliance. But women could take two or three husbands, serially or simultaneously. If a man visited his wife and found another man's sword and shield outside her door, he was expected to leave quietly. A woman initiated divorce by putting a man's clothes and possessions outside her door. The only limitation on women's marriages was that they had to marry men of their own or a higher caste.

The British outlawed Kerala's matricentric practices; defiant remnants were dampened by the disapproval of Christian missionaries, Tamilians, and other Indians. Nayars were enthralled by Western education and produced many famous intellectuals, including V.K. Krishna Menon, India's first delegate to the United Nations. Nayar women were also educated, and many are professionals. Women in Kerala still have a status they lack elsewhere in India: Kerala is the only state in India with more women than men; many women work for wages; 70 percent are literate (three times the national rate); their average age at marriage is twenty-two (compared with eighteen nationwide); and the birth rate, 33 per 1000 elsewhere, is 23 per 1000 and falling.[43]

Three-quarters of the families in Kerala use sterilization to limit family size, and most of those sterilized are women. But the use of any contraceptive indicates that women have a voice. The director of public health services in Kerala, Vijay Lakshmi, says that, here, women are partners in the family, with "a higher stake in deciding how many children each family has . . . a male cannot just brush his wife aside and make her a child-rearing machine." She disdains northern India, where "women just do the housework and have never learned to read and write." The press advisor to the Indian Ministry of Health and Family Welfare, Rami Chabbra, added: "Our population problem symbolizes the powerlessness of women in our society." A less positive development is that Nayars are beginning to give dowry.

Kerala is one of the few states in India with a strong Communist Party (it won a recent election) and a high proportion of Christians (one-fifth of the population). Both of these facts seem to bear on Kerala's generosity in health and social programs. It has a history of supporting female education and also offers women many job opportunities: they harvest tea and coffee, weave, make textiles from coconut fibres, process fish, and roll cigarettes. Catholic women can choose not to marry but to become nuns: then they teach, nurse, or do social work. Women in Kerala limit the number of their children, to give those they bear a better chance in life as much as to ease their own lot. K. Krishnamurthy, the state health secretary, said: "We have found that women are less selfish than men. They want their wages to be used to improve their families."

*   *   *

Several new trends threaten Indian women — the spread of dowry; the use of amniocentesis to reveal a fetus' sex and abort girls; militant Hindu and Muslim fundamentalism; and a new feature in Indian films — the obligatory rape. Clearly, women in India face a profound, pervasive, and lethal misogyny that infects them as deeply as men. The only cure for this disease is education and solidarity. Indian women make impressive, generous attempts to provide these tools to women in cities and villages, but female solidarity is difficult in so caste-ridden a country. Caste no longer informs every gesture in India, and laws prohibit certain forms of discrimination against low castes. But it remains a potent marker and hinders attempts to organize workers and women. In one large village, organizers had to set up four women's *sangams* (organizations): one for Naickers, two for Harijan colonies at a distance from each other, and one for Mudaliars. In a smaller village, Harijans and Naickers each had a separate *sangam* because higher-ranked women refuse to associate with lower.[44]

Many educated Indian women are strong feminists, working in every possible area to improve women's lot. The first campaigns of the contemporary Indian feminist movement were against dowry and rape, and these campaigns continue still.[45] But now, in an extremely heartening development, the young women who move about the country helping other women are not just the privileged college-educated women of the 1970s and 1980s but the daughters of the overworked, disfranchised, and impoverished women of the countryside.[46] If this group has joined the campaign, victory is assured.

CHAPTER 16

ANTI-IMPERIAL REVOLUTION IN ALGERIA

THE TERRITORY IN NORTH AFRICA NOW CALLED ALGERIA was once inhabited by matrifocal peoples who created one of the most powerful cave-paintings of the Mesolithic period. It shows a naked woman standing behind a naked man, who is holding a bow and arrow. Her hands are raised in a gesture of command, as a force flows from her vulva directly into the penis of the male about to shoot.

Later, Algeria was home to the Berbers. The territory was invaded regularly, and was ruled by Carthage for 700 years, by Rome for 600, and by Vandals, Byzantines, Arabs, Spaniards, and Turks for a total of 300 years. Sunni Muslims arrived in the seventh century; by the twelfth, most Berbers were Muslim. In 1830 its last invaders, the French, imposed Algeria's first strong central government. Of all its conquerors, Muslims most influenced Algeria by introducing Islamic customs – egalitarianism for men; segregation of the sexes in separate spheres; confinement and the veil for women.

Before Islam, Berber clans had an elaborate system of "paths to the fountain," a women's forum where women discussed matters that men could not talk about without "dishonour" and that they learned about only from their wives. In Berber society, a man who was exposed physically or psychologically before men, especially men from other clans and, even more, before women, lost honour. There was a virtual male veil. Berber women did not inherit property, but they could ally with a husband's mother (and thus his father) or with uncles or children; they could withdraw emotionally or sexually and gossip about a man's behaviour or sexual ability. Men could abuse women verbally and physically and repudiate them.[1]

Land was held by the tribe, the communal *'arsh*. Tillers used the land they needed and had usufruct rights. Nomads had free access because all land belonged to God. The Berber concept of private property – *melk* – theoretically allowed land to be sold if the entire tribe consented. In practice, however, it was not sold, but it could be donated to a religion or charity as *Habus* land, worked by the community. The French later confiscated such tracts. Berbers traced ancestry through males and gave fathers absolute authority. The highest ruling body, a tribal council or *djemaa*', controlled *'arsh* lands, adjudicated interclan conflicts, banished men for adultery, and disinherited men who violated tribal norms. Only male heads of clan lineages sat on the *djemaa*', all with equal status. The French nullified them, but they continued underground.

When Spain expelled the Muslims in the sixteenth century, many went to Algeria. Spain then invaded Algeria, forcing the regency of Algiers to ask help from Baba Aroudj (Barbarossa) to defend its coasts. Defence became a corsair activity, and Algiers became a hub for pirates motivated by greed and religious conviction. The French invaded in 1830, writing the final chapter in a long history of conflict between Algerians and the West, when Charles X sent a force to flush out the Barbary pirates who were preying on Mediterranean ships.[2] The French did not at first intend to invade Algeria, but once there they did so. Arab nationalists launched a strenuous opposition to the French, believing they saw conquest as a crusade against Islam, the return of African land to a Latin (Roman) past.

Unlike the British, who adopted a policy of devolution in their empire, granting different parts some degree of autonomy, the French centralized their empire and tried to assimilate their colonies. Insisting that the colonized were French, the administration in each colony not only immersed local people in French culture and language but appointed colonial deputies to Paris to help govern the whole empire. French policy towards Algeria was, in fact, inconsistent, especially in regard to the majority Arab population, but, more than its other colonies, France saw Algeria as a genuine *département* of metropolitan France.[3] Islam proved to be a major obstacle to assimilation, however. Marshall de Bourmont, who led the first French troops to set foot on Algerian territory, had declared that France guaranteed its new subjects their property and religious rights. Nevertheless, religion became the single most important element in French efforts to control Algeria. Like Spaniards in Latin America, the French wanted to eradicate the indigenous religion in Algeria (yet not in Morroco or Tunisia). As the missionary-explorer Charles Foucauld explained: "If we cannot succeed in making Frenchmen of these people, they will drive us out. The only way to make them into Frenchmen is to make them Christians." Foucauld was later killed by desert tribesmen.

The French authorities' obsessive preoccupation with Islam only served to politicize it. Before the French invasion, Algerians had considered themselves Muslim just as Frenchmen considered themselves Catholic: they took their religious identity for granted. They defined themselves primarily by region, tribe, and family. After the arrival of the French, Islam became the most salient element of their identity.[4]

In 1830 Algeria had 6 million inhabitants. Approximately 100,000 French soldiers fought for seventeen years to subdue them;

by 1852, only 2 1/2 million Algerians remained alive. Considering Islam a religion oppressive of women, the French used women to justify their presence (as the British had done in India). They conscripted Algerian men for their armies, seized Algerian lands, and limited the movement of flocks by the many Berbers who were herding nomads. Algerians who survived the wars lost their land and their livelihood and retreated into the family. Women became their emblem too: the veil became far more widespread. After these seventeen years of fierce fighting, despite continued Arab resistance, France decided to colonize the country. By the mid-nineteenth century, Europeans made up about a sixth of the population and were the elite, owning the best land and running the government, industry, finance, and trade. Arabs and Berbers were either peasants or labourers, or they ran shops in the *casbah* (native quarter) of large cities.

In 1873 and 1881 the French began to expropriate Algerian land, dislocating small farmers. As Western economic structures and dominance spread, 84.5 percent of male heads of families in mid-sized cities were unemployed; in Oran, Algiers, and Constantine, the figure was 65.2 percent. Men became monogamous, unable to support several wives, while the wives took work as cleaners or part-time and seasonal servants. By 1900 half a million Europeans (*colons*) lived in Algeria. By 1919 half the peasantry was landless and had moved to Algerian cities or to France. Many of those born in cities or in France (where 76,000 Algerians worked by 1921) became a new class of *petit bourgeoisie* with no firm values. Once homes ceased to be centres of production, rural and urban women lost their chief source of employment and became isolated and dependent on their husbands.

The French tried to make Algeria a French province subject to French law, which meant conforming Algerian law – based on the *shari'a*, the Islamic regulations of marriage, divorce, and property – with French law. Property issues were swiftly brought in line, but Algerian laws governing marriage, divorce, and inheritance could not be changed without extirpating their religious foundation. The naturalization laws passed between the 1800s and 1920s, which initially excluded women, made renunciation of *shari'a* a condition for French citizenship. Few Algerians accepted it. The French granted Algerian men the vote and ended specifically Arab taxes. Workers, mostly males, grew even more macho. French schools opened in Algeria, but even educated Algerians were second class under French rule. Military resistance waned at the turn of the century, as Algerian intellectuals formed reform movements to resist colonial rule or to raise the status of their own people.

Secular and religious reform movements focused on women. Secular reformers, mostly young professionals who had been trained in French schools, chafed under a colonial double standard that encouraged them to believe they were Frenchmen but denied them French political rights. They modelled themselves on the "Young Turks" who reformed Turkey under Kemal Ataturk in the late 1920s, and, indeed, they came to be called the "Young Algerians." They wanted women to participate in public life and, to that end, they advocated female education. They argued that Islam was not necessarily incompatible with "progress," but they conceived of progress in French terms and adopted a French value system. Most Algerians saw them as apologists for colonialism and, therefore, as anti-Muslim.

The religious reform movement, the *ulema* (religious scholars), founded by Shaikh Ibn Badis, dealt with matters that were pressing to most Algerians. Ibn Badis' group also believed that women's status needed improvement and advocated female education, but they wanted girls to attend school only from the age of seven to twelve, educated merely to be believers and mothers. The *ulema* urged segregation after puberty and approved of the veil, but it did not require female seclusion. While the Young Algerians wanted integration into colonial society on secular terms, the religious reformers wanted to improve education, check the spread of alcoholism, drugs, and prostitution, and limit the influence of French culture on young French-educated Algerian men, an influence they perceived as an assault on their cultural integrity.

Above all, these religious reformers wanted to restore Islam to its original form, freed of superstitions and "magical excrescences," and they called their association Al Salafyia (the society of the prophet's companions).⁵ Even as they supported female education, they exhorted women to model their behaviour on the virtuous wives and daughters of Muhammed and his companions. They circulated biographies of legendary women, emphasizing their religious faith, sense of duty, and willingness to sacrifice.

Both sets of Algerian reformers wanted to raise women's status as a means to raise men's, and women's status was one of the main issues they discussed. However, they consulted no female leaders. A feminist manifesto was written by a Tunisian man and condemned by religious reformers. France also offered a poor example – French feminists were co-opted at the end of the First World War, when their husbands took power and silenced them. French men, who were deeply anticlerical and believed that women were more religious than men, denied them the vote. The French Senate tabled motions for woman suffrage in 1929, 1932, and 1933, and, from 1936 to 1938, the socialists, who were indifferent to women, held power. Women's invisibility in both French and Algerian society was emphasized when a man gave the report on the woman question at the International Congress on Mediterranean Women held in March 1932.

During the Second World War, France lost control of its African empire. By 1954 one million French *colons* lived in Algeria: France had poured millions of dollars into Algeria to build French districts and suppress Algerians, and it tried to reassert control when the war ended. Arab and Berber nationalists resented this restoration of a foreign elite to economic and political dominance. A general resurgence of Islam, which had begun in the nineteenth century and now gathered momentum, reinforced Arab nationalism. Nationalist groups coalesced to create the National Liberation Front (FLN) in 1954, and Mostepha Ben Boulaid led 500 insurgents in attacking seventy French installations. The FLN urged Algerians to rise up to demand equal status with Europeans. When cautious Algerians did not rise en masse, the FLN attacked them: "To take no interest in the struggle is a crime; to oppose it is treason."

Nationalists formed the ALN (Armée de Liberation Nationale) to appeal to Muslims. Peasants, not workers, were the staunch Muslims, and by 1956 the ALN had 15,000 to 20,000 men. After January 1955 the ALN accepted women nurses. The following year, the FLN platform enjoined women to lend "moral support to combatants and resisters, gather information, act as liaison agents, take care of military and medical supplies, provide shelter to people sought by the police, and help the families of guerrillas or those who were imprisoned." No provision was made for women combatants, though a few did fight. The majority, however, were nurses, cooks, or laundresses. In any capacity in the FLN, women risked arrest and execution.

The FLN, grounded in the old *djemaa*, valued collective decision-making and, to achieve its goals, political over military means. When the leaders decided that, to attract men to a revolutionary group, they had to overcome the weight of tradition, they decided to include women as bait. Initially they were concerned with protecting girls' virginity, so they approached women who were married to militants, widows, or divorcees. But when these women were killed, their children were left parentless. And single women persisted in volunteering, so the FLN began to use them, keeping cells segregated and allowing no woman to lead. No women were combatants until 1955, when they began to carry messages and bombs and to act as terrorists. A major issue for female revolutionaries was dress. At first, operating inside *casbahs* carrying tracts and doing liaison work, women wore veils. When they began to venture into the European districts of cities, they put on Western dress. But in 1957, when the French authorities realized that women were participating in revolutionary actions, women resumed the veil, strapping bombs, grenades, and machine-gun clips to their bodies beneath the burqa. When the French began to unveil

Algerian women forcibly, women who had repudiated the veil took it up again.[6]

Some nurses demanded and got weapons to protect themselves during French ambushes. Women became militants and many died in combat – 10,949 women's names appear on nationalist lists, 78 percent of them in the countryside. Of these military women (including armed soldiers), two were political commissars and five were terrorists; of those killed, over half were between the ages of fourteen and twenty-four, and 38.8 percent between the ages of twenty-five and forty-nine. Djamila Bouhired, aged twenty-two, the liaison for a terrorist group, was wounded, captured, arrested, tortured (the French used cruel tortures widely in Algeria), and condemned to death. But she was jailed, not killed. Djamila Boupacha, jailed for bomb-throwing, was tortured with electric shocks, cigarette burns, and kicks, and raped with a bottle neck (she was a virgin). She survived and was released at the end of the war. Both women became heroines because they betrayed nothing under torture. Zohra Drif, a law student in a terrorist network, was arrested and sentenced in 1956 to twenty years of forced labour. But the war ended in 1962.

War had given women a chance to change the sexual power structure, unimpeded by religious principles and unopposed by religious leaders. By fighting in the war, women essentially freed themselves from colonial oppression. But the FLN was an underground movement and could not institute reforms. Some leaders tried: in mountainous areas where French troops had trouble getting control and the FLN could act openly, they challenged the prevailing custom of having a bride absent during the signing of her marriage contract, insisting that she witness it along with the groom. Like all revolutionary movements, the FLN needed to rally the widest possible popular support (i.e., male support) and would have preferred not to interfere with male control of women. But the French government had often intervened in Algerian sexual politics, so the FLN did the same, to challenge the French.

In 1958 the war entered a new phase. In September the Provisional Government of the Algerian Republic (GPRA) was founded, its army based in neighbouring Morocco and Tunisia. Colonel Houari Boumédienne rose as a leader in the new government. Born to a middle-class peasant family and educated in Islamic schools, Boumediene wanted agrarian reform and considered the revolution a peasant revolt. Another important figure in the revolution, the socialist Frantz Fanon, was a Haitian physician who came to Algeria in 1956 to work as a psychiatrist at a military hospital. Fanon's lectures, newspaper articles, and books had enormous influence. His books on colonization are still among the most profound and searching on the subject.[7] But Fanon understood neither the lure of Islam nor the fact that women, as much as men, need and deserve independence and self-respect.

As more women joined the struggle, French propaganda targeted them, ostensibly to win them over, but really to turn them against their men. Women are easily used as instruments during conflict because they are always oppressed and open to promises. Like the British appealing to African-Americans during the American Revolution, or companies hiring poor people as scabs during strikes, the powerful always know that society does not value women, and can lure them with offers of rights. French colonial generals, worried that France was losing heart for the war, formed the Secret Army Organization (OAS) to seize power and keep Algeria French. They mounted a coup, ousted the French governor of Algeria, and held a huge rally in May 1958 on the steps of the Governor's Palace in Algiers. The centrepiece of the event was the unveiling of some Algerian women, a symbol for French victory over the last obstacle to the total Frenchification of Algeria.

Women's voluntary participation in the war radically broke the traditional relations between the sexes. It meant that women mingled with men who were not kin, defied parental authority, and left confinement for uncertainty. Many women married fellow combatants, choosing their own husbands. Women whose husbands or sons were arrested travelled alone to detention camps, seeking their loved ones in what must have been terrifying first steps towards freedom. With husbands absent, many women took up the farm work or found jobs to support themselves and their children. But for the family – the realm of male authority – to claim to represent Algerian society, it had to remain intact.[8] Male and female revolutionaries believed that the primary issue was winning the war, not women's rights.

Before the Algerian war was over, France had committed half a million French troops to the conflict, but it never extinguished the FLN. The battle raged in Algeria and in the streets of France, where demonstrations erupted on both sides. Finally, in March 1962, the French president, Charles de Gaulle, agreed with Algerian nationalists that the question of Algerian independence should be put to a referendum in France in April. De Gaulle's prestige and French weariness with the Algerian war prevailed: over 90 percent of the French voted in favour; a referendum in Algeria in July won by almost 100 percent. In July 1962 Algeria became independent.

That is, Algerian men became independent. If, during independence celebrations, an unmarried woman appeared on the streets with a man, male vigilante groups ordered her to marry immediately or go to jail. Algeria's first president, Ahmed Ben Bella, hid patriarchal attitudes under pro-woman rhetoric. The new constitution of September 1962 granted both sexes equality and the franchise, but it also made Islam the state religion and Arabic the official language. Since Islamic law treats women as men's property, contradiction was built into the very founding of the new nation. The authoritarian Ben Bella banned all parties but the FLN and purged it of "radicals" – those who supported workers' right to strike. He also dissolved the French FLN, which favoured a secular state.

The Algerian state deferred to the mullahs, making the Ramadam fast compulsory, banning alcohol, and closing cafés. In 1963 it expropriated all foreign-held agricultural land and, by 1965, over 80 percent of the *colons* had left Algeria. Two million people were out of work. Foreign-educated young male technocrats planned the new state, using a socialist economic model that nationalized large estates owned by the *colons* and created state-owned heavy industry. The model placed a priority on steel works and petrochemical plants, ignoring the well-known social costs of capital-intensive, labour-saving industrialization. Men thrown out of work by this new industry had little choice but to emigrate to France. And the development planners and nationalists did not consider women at all, pretending they were all supported by their husbands or fathers. In 1964 only two women were elected deputies.

While Ben Bella scoured the Qur'an for passages justifying socialism, others tried to defend private property. Ben Bella was too left wing for Muslims, and in June 1965 his opponents rose in a revolt led by Boumédienne. They imprisoned Ben Bella and suspended both the National Assembly and the constitution. Boumédienne, a conservative nationalist authoritarian, wanted to speed up industrial development and transform a mainly agrarian economy into an industrial one. The French bought Algerian oil, iron ore, wine, citrus fruit, and labour, in exchange for exports of French manufactures. Most rural Algerians were subsistence farmers or labourers on French colonists' estates. Women were important in production, and they grew vegetables, fetched water, raised chickens for sale and consumption, wove rugs, and made pottery, blankets, and clothing.

Boumédienne ran the country through a Party Central Committee and included no women in the government. The new state was not concerned specifically with women's participation in industrialization, but industrial societies need literate citizens. Boumédienne extended state power over education and began to educate more females. However, only those girls who had reached school age after 1962 were affected; the overwhelming majority of women remained illiterate. Islam does not explicitly prohibit birth control, but orthodox male Muslims and Algerian nationalists oppose it. In 1967 women bore ten children on average, of whom 6.5 lived to maturity. Algeria's population grew by 50 percent from

1960 to 1970, so in 1966 family "regulation centres" began to give contraceptives to women with four children. Five years later, the Muslims closed them down. Algeria's rulers insisted that women's place was making couscous, a traditional grain dish – in effect, code for confinement in the home.

When Boumediene died in 1978, Colonel Chadli Benjedid headed the government. Less committed to agrarian reform and redistribution of land, Benjedid sharply criticized both agriculture and industry for inefficient bureaucratic management and low productivity. He restructured industry along capitalist lines, aiming at freedom from state control, efficiency, and high profits. Agriculture drew fewer workers of either sex as industrial wages rose, but state-owned industrial plants even today employ few women. The 1988 labour statistics show that only 343,000 women, out of an estimated female population of 11 million, had full-time paid jobs that year. Including housewives who work for wages part time, the number reaches only 523,000. Most employed women today live in urban areas, and they work in the professions and in clerical jobs as often as in domestic service. Hiring women as managers of agricultural enterprises is the most significant change for women since independence, even if few of them have such jobs.[9] The mechanization of agriculture eased farm women's work, but it also lessened their productiveness and their status in rural families. They feel less useful and less content. Increased education has somewhat altered the traditional division of labour: boys who used to herd animals now go to school and their sisters do the herding.

A 1977 survey in Algiers revealed that social class more than religious belief determined people's attitudes towards women working outside the home. Even educated women have difficulty finding jobs, but they are increasingly entering the workforce. Most single women are secretaries, and their brothers control the $200 to $250 a month they earn. They still must do housework in the evenings. An unintended consequence of the state's control of imports was that some women could open shops to manufacture ready-to-wear clothes with relatively little capital. Unable to find jobs, some women set up beautician and hairdressing shops in their homes. Women's opportunities for paid work are likely to continue to be limited, but as women move into the public sphere, men's efforts to suppress them have intensified.

By the time Benjedid took over, Algeria's deteriorating economic situation, urbanization, and disruptions had induced some Algerians to invoke tradition, yearning for a return to an old, "pure" Islam. Male students struck for Arabized education in 1979 and 1980 in Kabylia. The 1978 fundamentalist Muslim revolution in Iran inspired a young graduate in physics from London to form a Muslim brotherhood. The "brothers" focus on women, commanding their segregation from men and forbidding them to work or travel without escorts. "Morals police" spy on women, charging them with *attente de pudeur* if they are alone in a café, at the beach, renting a hotel room, or going out in the company of more than two men. Women seen with foreigners after dark can be questioned or beaten. Women who kiss in public are punished. More women are wearing veils to protect themselves from men or to placate men, and to hide their poverty.

Until 1989 the government tried to undermine the Muslim brothers by allying itself with the orthodox Muslim clergy. It named a committee to reform the Islamic Family Code and to create a new law that mixed *shari'a* with amendments made by the colonial government. No women were named to the revision committee. On International Women's Day, 1979, 200 university women held an open meeting at the industrial workers' headquarters in Algiers and passed a motion to inquire about the membership of the commission. They sent the question to the authorities, but received no reply.

In January 1981 the government forbade women to leave the country. The women's collective met at the University of Algiers to sign petitions and name delegations to visit government officials to denounce such "revolting discrimination." The minister of the interior admitted a delegation of four women and told them that no such law existed. The women procured a draft of the revised Family Code and distributed it clandestinely: it returned women to the legal status of minors. In September 1981 the revision was accepted by the Council of Ministers and, the following month, women launched a campaign of confrontation and embarrassment, holding three major demonstrations in Algiers with a lawyers' collective, labour union representatives, and former freedom fighters. They conducted a national campaign and obtained 10,000 signatures on a petition opposing the code. Tacitly comparing the Algerian government to the French, they paraded independence heroines like Meriem Benmihoub (then a member of the bar), Zohra Drif, and Djamila Bouhired and thereby forced the police to avoid brutality. They made counter demands for monogamy, an unconditional right of women to work, equal inheritance rights, identical ages at marriage, identical divorce conditions, and the best possible protection for abandoned children – and they filmed their protest. It has never been broadcast.

The women who protested were a very small minority, mainly university graduates and professionals, but they forced the government to withdraw the code. However, it was resubmitted in June 1984 and the new version was even worse than the earlier one. Divorce by mutual consent was eliminated, as was the right of a divorced wife to demand housing from her former husband (unless she has custody of the children). Polygyny was permitted in both codes, but the 1981 version had maintained the *shari'a* condition that a man had to provide separate houses for each wife and allowed women to exclude polygyny in marriage contracts. Both conditions were eliminated in the 1984 version. The 1984 Family Code confines women in the family as in a "cell," to protect and preserve them from "social ills." It requires a husband to support his wife; in return, he may marry more than one woman "if he can justify his action." Wives who object may divorce. A man may marry by proxy and divorce at will; a woman may divorce only under specific conditions unless she can pay her husband to grant her a divorce. Women are required to "obey" husbands, "respect" their in-laws, and "breastfeed their children if they can."

There was no uprising of women when the 1984 code was issued – they may have been intimidated by the Muslim brothers. The code satisfied the orthodox clergy, but not the Muslim brothers, who took it as signalling that their persistence would be rewarded by even greater constriction of women. They incited students to attack progressive students with axes and bicycle chains. One was killed and several were wounded. Some Muslims were arrested.

The brotherhood's reading of the political climate was accurate. They were initially suppressed, but the government's new policy of greater democracy gave the brotherhood the status of a political party, the Islamic Front of Salvation (FIS). Since the creation of the FIS, the Muslim brothers have grown even louder in demanding the imposition of an Islamic ethic that bans Western secular customs. It focuses on women: the brotherhood insists that women wear a *hidjab* (ankle-length raincoat-like garment with a scarf completely covering the hair), and some of them also want women to give up their jobs. No birth-control information, contraceptives, or daycare exist in Algeria. The official women's department is a government mouthpiece.

During the revolution, nationalist men talked about and supported a variety of political and social rights to make women adult citizens of the state, but they deferred their implementation until after the revolution. After independence, women's rights were again deferred in favour of development and industrialization. Since 1962 it has become increasingly apparent that political leaders used women cynically: jobs created by the new state have gone to men and, over thirty years later, women still have trouble finding jobs; when they get one, it is usually low-paid and low-prestige work. Most rural women are still illiterate and unemployed. Both the Family Code of 1984 and the state-approved FIS have severely injured women.

In Algeria, Egypt, Tunisia, and other Muslim states, fundamentalism is considered nationalism, and is the only alternative to Westernization. For many Middle Easterners, Westernization means the ills of development: wealth and privileges for a few, high unemployment, strikes, and greater independence for women (although this issue is never publicly acknowledged as a motive to oppose change). No party runs on an anti-woman platform – anywhere. Yet, in Algeria, many men claim women should be more constricted for the cause of nationalism.[10] Muslim men perceive modernization as emasculating, because, for them, "honour" (manhood) is control of women. One historian explains that Islam is based on a belief not in female inferiority, but in female power.[11] Sexual institutions like polygyny, divorce by repudiation, and segregation are strategies for containing female power. Male control over women becomes harder as new forms of production break down female seclusion, as women begin to be educated, and as women work for wages outside the home. But the tacit agenda of fundamentalist groups is apparent – to thrust women forcibly into the veil and out of work. One woman said that "Algeria's 500,000 working women are not going to march to the slaughterhouse silently, even if it means a civil war."[12] A civil war of women against men? But militant Muslims are now killing women simply for appearing on the street bareheaded.[13] In 1995 Algerian militants vowed to kill all women who were married to "atheists" – by which they mean opponents of theocratic government. They also killed twenty or more women who refused to marry Muslim fighters in *zawaj al mutaa* marriage (see volume 1, chapter 11), a non-binding marriage that can last a day or a week.[14]

More recently, bands of armed men, some as large as one hundred, have been massacring Algerians in their homes.[15] Islamic extremists target women in particular. Houria Zedat was training to become a national judo champion when the extremists ordered her to stop practising, put on a veil, and stay home. She ignored them. In the next few years they killed her young brother, slitting his throat before her eyes, shot her mother, and killed her second brother. These men also kidnap attractive young women to serve as sexual slaves in their mountain hideouts. Activists say that thousands of young women have been abducted. One such young woman, kidnapped and raped by a gang of men, was found and liberated. She was treated in a hospital for a year, but at the age of twenty-four she committed suicide.

In the face of this violence, women are standing firm – the first time such a stance has been reported. Some women refuse to wear the veil, and they encourage girls to do the same. Aicha Barki, the head of the Iqra Foundation, which works to end illiteracy, says: "We have crossed the cape of fear."[16]

*   *   *

Every society to some degree holds women responsible for male as well as female sexuality, expecting women, not men, to control male sexual predation. Islam, Orthodox Jewry, and certain Hindus demand segregation of the sexes in schools, institutions, public spaces, and even at home. But only Islamic states demand that women sacrifice all freedom of movement and ease in the world to restrain men. With the growing strength of Islamic fundamentalism, women face a long, difficult struggle.

The illiteracy rate for women in Muslim countries is staggering: in the mid-1970s, 95 percent of Saudi Arabian, 70–95 percent of Iranian, and 98 percent of Afghani women could not read or write. While more girls are being educated in all Muslim countries, many are still removed from school at puberty. In Tunisia in 1975, 63 percent of girls between six and eleven were in school, but only 24 percent of those between twelve and seventeen. In Morocco in the mid-1970s, 30 percent of younger girls and 20 percent of older ones were in school; as of 1982, girls still made up roughly a third of the students in elementary and secondary education and a quarter of university students. In the 1980s women's studies programs proliferated: Beirut College (Lebanon), Cairo University, and Al-Azhar (Egypt), the Centre de Documentation des Sciences Humaines (Wahran, Algeria), the University of Jordan, Kuwait University, and the General Federation of Iraqi Women all sponsored such programs. Still, few women are included in government in Muslim states, and many states have all-male parliaments. In 1999 Kuwaiti women were once again refused the franchise.

Women's groups in most Arab states are composed of upper-class women and are often under government control, especially in one-party states. Women keep trying to participate and be heard: the number of their voluntary associations has doubled in recent decades. They debate ways to integrate women into development as well as the very meaning of development, and discuss the conditions necessary for women to liberate themselves. Rose Ghurayyib, the editor of *Al-Raida*, a journal published by the Institute for Women's Studies in the Arab World at Beirut University in Lebanon, believes that women cannot advance until the Middle East is at peace. She argues that war harmed women's liberation movements in Lebanon, Iraq, Iran, Libya, and other Arab countries, and that "a larger proportion of refugees, illiterates and poor, are women. Violence against them is linked to the violence of war. The participation of Arab women in peace movements and conferences, locally or internationally is . . . imperative."[17]

Still, some Muslim countries have strong feminist groups. Muslim women's rights movements date at least from 1858, when the first girls school was founded in the Ottoman Empire; its first teachers college opened in 1870, and women were first permitted to study in universities in 1914. The Ottoman Empire was dismembered and, in 1923, Kemal Ataturk became head of an independent Turkey; as a nationalist rebel leader, he had enlisted women as soldiers, ammunition carriers, and nurses. In 1926 he abolished Islamic family law and replaced it with a secular civil code that forbade polygamy, set a minimum age for the marriage of girls, and granted the sexes equal rights in divorce, child custody, and inheritance.

By 1934 Turkish women had the right to vote, hold office, and appear in public (in 1920, a woman had been arrested for acting on a Turkish stage). In 1989 Turkish women demonstrated to protest the growth of Muslim fundamentalism. Over 1000 women marched, sang, and carried banners on the anniversary of Turkey's becoming a secular state under Kemal Ataturk. In 1993 a woman, Tansu Ciller, became Turkey's prime minister. Recently, however, a woman elected to the Turkish Senate was denied her seat because she wore a head scarf. She was eventually deprived of her Turkish citizenship.

In the early twentieth century, Muslim women made powerful arguments for reform within Islamic tradition. The Lebanese Nazirah Zein Ed-Din, whose father headed the Lebanese Court of Appeals and encouraged her study of theology, published *Removing the Veil* in 1928.[18] Her arguments were so erudite that critics charged that her book had been written by nine men, including missionaries and lawyers, who wanted to undermine Islam.[19] A feminist, Azizah al-Hibri, wrote that "patriarchy co-opted Islam after the death of the prophet" and cited passages in the Qur'an that were interpreted "loosely and out of context in support of a vicious patriarchal ideology." One passage central to the assertion of male dominance is translated: "Men are in charge of women, because Allah hath made the one of them to excel the other, and because they spend of their property (for the support of women)." Al-Hibri reads this passage differently: "Men are 'qawwamun' over women in matters where God gave of them more than others, and in what they spend of their money"; she points out that the word *qawwamun* can be rendered as "protectors," rather than "maintainers" and believes that the original meaning was "moral guidance and caring."

Feminists have restored the role of women to Islamic history as saints in mystic orders, Muslim scholars, and mothers, influencing the home. But, like black women in the United States and South Africa, Muslim feminists are as concerned about their men as they are about themselves. Western colonization of most of the

Arab world and enduring Western contempt for Islam and for Arabs have fixed the two worlds in opposition. Since feminism arose in the West, and most advances for women – the first schools for girls and pressure to put off the veil – were initiated by Westerners, feminists feel a need to distance themselves from Western ways. Some Arab feminists have resumed the veil to proclaim their distance from Westernization and to affirm their tie to indigenous culture.

Arab women often adopt the veil voluntarily because they dislike elements of Western feminism. They insist that they want liberation with men, not from them. They find American ways particularly repugnant and often blame American women for Western sexual mores. They think American women are oppressed by being objectified as sex objects, and equate "loose" women with feminists. Moreover, many Islamic women do not consider their constriction a subordination. Like many women in the West, they start from an assumption that feminists question: male domination is inherent in nature or in human social structures, and therefore it is inevitable. Many men who deplore the treatment of females by males, having suffered from male predation themselves, share this assumption. Otherwise, though, non-feminists see the same world that feminists see – a species where half of the members prey on the other half – and they seek strategies to deal with this fact and to foster the survival of women and children. So, women in a village in Syria, Toqaan, did not see the veil and laws privileging men as evidence of subordination, but as protecting women and the family from male predation.[20]

In the 1990s world events widened enormously the mutual antagonism of the Muslim and the Western worlds. America's leadership of the Gulf War against Iraq put a strain on all East-West alliances, including that between Israel and the United States. The peace agreement between Israel and the Palestine Liberation Organization begun in the fall of 1993, which seemed to offer grounds for hope for stability in the region, has collapsed in a new, extremely virulent conflict. The terrorist attacks on New York City's

World Trade Center, on the Pentagon, and a nightclub in Bali amount to a renewed declaration of war by Muslims against the West. The United States carried this war – which is continuing to be a live hot war – to Afghanistan and now threatens Iraq, if on rather different grounds. At this writing, the outlook for any harmony between the Muslim world and the West is bleak, and the hope for a restoration of women's rights is faint.

A pitiful footnote is the attempt of elite women in Saudi Arabia to use Western military presence there – including female soldiers – to legitimate their demand to be allowed to drive.[21] On November 6, 1990, seventy veiled Saudi women, having discussed the act with supportive husbands or male kin, had their chauffeurs drive them to a supermarket in Riyadh, then dismissed them and took the wheel themselves. The Saudi police intercepted and arrested the women, releasing them only after they signed a pledge that they would not repeat the action.

These were elite women driving luxury cars. Only wealthy Saudi women would know how to drive; they could learn only in the West, where poor or lower-middle-class women do not go. And they were fighting for a right that must seem an enormous luxury to women of lower classes, but that hardly seems to threaten male supremacy. But, of course, it does: women who drive can escape – like women with whole feet in traditional China or women who lived within running distance of a temple in traditional Japan. The government took a hard line, however. Women with academic jobs were suspended, and fundamentalists defaced their offices. No law bars Saudi women from driving, but the Ministry of the Interior stated that Muslim scholars had determined that driving "degrades and harms the sanctity" of women. Government officials said privately that the women had made a political error: "Now they have made this into a power struggle with the conservatives. They have probably set back driving by women for five more years, maybe a decade." And if they had not? How long would it take these women to get a right they did not claim?

CHAPTER 17

ANTI-IMPERIAL REVOLUTION IN AFRICA

M OST EARLY ARAB AND EUROPEAN INVADERS OF AFRICA settled on the coasts, leaving internal Africa governed by chiefs, monarchs, or consensus communities. After Britain abolished slave trade in 1807 and Africans began exporting palm oil, rubber, and other industrial raw materials to Europe, however, European industrialists clamoured to own the source of these resources. They pressured their governments to appropriate African territory. In the ensuing "scramble" for land, nations vied with each other to grab some of the continent. By the 1880s Britain, France, Spain, Portugal, Holland, and Belgium claimed most of Africa; at the Berlin Conference of 1884–85, they partitioned it.

Despite their sophisticated weapons, Europeans did not conquer Africa easily; they fought for almost a century to subdue it. And almost as soon as the European powers gained African empires, they began to lose them: Spain lost most of its colonies in the Napoleonic wars. The Portuguese, the first Europeans in Africa, were the last out, holding fast to Mozambique, Guinea-Bissau, and

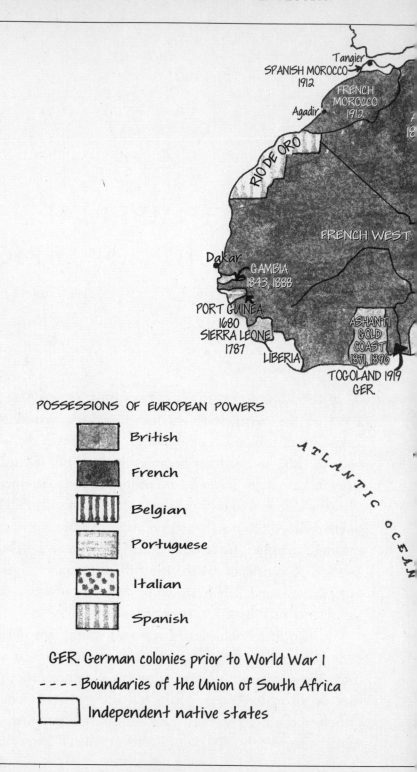

Tangier

SPANISH MOROCCO
1912

FRENCH
MOROCCO
1912

Agadir

RIO DE ORO

FRENCH WEST

Dakar

GAMBIA
1843, 1888

PORT GUINEA
1680
SIERRA LEONE
1787

LIBERIA

ASHANTI
GOLD
COAST
1874, 1896

TOGOLAND 1919
GER.

ATLANTIC OCEAN

POSSESSIONS OF EUROPEAN POWERS

British

French

Belgian

Portuguese

Italian

Spanish

GER. German colonies prior to World War I

- - - - Boundaries of the Union of South Africa

Independent native states

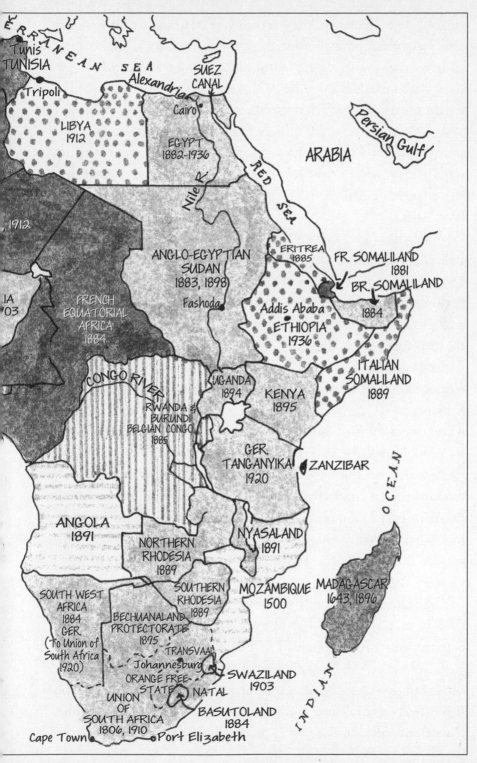

TUNIS
Tunis
Tripoli
LIBYA
1912

1912

1903

SUEZ
CANAL
Alexandria
Cairo
EGYPT
1882-1936
Nile R.

ARABIA

Persian Gulf

FRENCH
EQUATORIAL
AFRICA
1884

ANGLO-EGYPTIAN
SUDAN
1883, 1898
Fashoda

ERITREA
1885
FR. SOMALILAND
1881
BR. SOMALILAND
1884

Addis Ababa
ETHIOPIA
1936

ITALIAN
SOMALILAND
1889

CONGO RIVER
RWANDA &
BURUNDI
BELGIAN CONGO
1885

UGANDA
1894

KENYA
1895

GER.
TANGANYIKA
1920

ZANZIBAR

ANGOLA
1891

NORTHERN
RHODESIA
1889

NYASALAND
1891

SOUTH-WEST
AFRICA
1884
GER.
(To Union of
South Africa
1920)

SOUTHERN
RHODESIA
1889

BECHUANALAND
PROTECTORATE
1895

TRANSVAAL
Johannesburg
ORANGE FREE
STATE
UNION
OF
SOUTH AFRICA
1806, 1910
Cape Town

MOZAMBIQUE
1500

MADAGASCAR
1643, 1896

SWAZILAND
1903

NATAL

BASUTOLAND
1884

Port Elizabeth

RED SEA

INDIAN OCEAN

Angola. They zealously tried to convert Africans to Catholicism. Less racist than other Europeans, they allowed considerable inter-marriage, which made for ambivalence about independence for those with mixed loyalties. In 1951 Antonio Salazar, dictator of Portugal from 1932 to 1968, decreed the colonies "overseas provinces" and sent masses of white settlers mainly to Angola. These people were poor, competing for the same jobs as Africans: cities – and tensions – grew. In 1959 severe economic pressure led Guineans to strike; police killed many. Despite resistance, Portugal refused to leave Africa.

Italy came late to empire-building: it conquered Eritrea and Italian Somaliland and tried to invade Abyssinia (Ethiopia) after 1885. Just before the First World War, it grabbed Libya from the declining Ottoman Empire. In the 1930s Mussolini won Ethiopia and set out to rebuild the Roman Empire, but Italy lost it all after the Second World War. In 1941 Ethiopia became independent under Haile Selassie; in 1972 he was overthrown by a socialist revolution. England made Eritrea a British protectorate, then gave it to Ethiopia in 1952. Somalia became independent in 1960, but there was internal conflict, and in 1968 Major General Mohammed Siad Barre took over the government; he had designs on Ethiopia and made war there until 1988. In 1991 a rebel group overthrew the military regime, and civil war has ripped the country since. The northern part broke off and called itself the Somaliland Republic, but other governments have not recognized it. Eritrea rebelled against Ethiopia in the 1970s, and won independence in 1993. Conflict continues there.

The Dutch, with a very wealthy empire in the South Pacific and Caribbean, stayed aloof from the nineteenth-century "scramble" for colonies, but King Leopold II of Belgium entered the contest and got a colony in the Congo basin. At the 1885 Berlin Conference, European powers recognized this territory as Congo Free State, but it was really a royal fief.[1] Catholic missionaries were sent to indoctrinate and educate the populace, enabling a Belgian journalist to describe the Congo in 1955 as "the most prosperous and tranquil of colonies."[2] But in fact, Congo suffered from an oppression so cruel that shocked writers exposed it, forcing Belgium to put restraints on its citizens' behaviour.[3]

France lost its first colonies in Canada and India to Britain, keeping only some West Indian islands, Algeria, and Senegal. But after France lost the Franco-Prussian war in 1871, its machismo was aroused, and it acquired many African colonies – Mauritania, Ivory Coast, Dahomey, the French Sudan, French Guinea, Upper Volta, and Niger in West Africa; Chad, Gabon, Middle Congo, and Ubangi-Shari in Equatorial Africa; as well as Togoland, Cameroon, and Madagascar. Like Britain, it approached its colonies with an unshakable belief in the superiority of its civilization, even as it acted with cruel savagery. France enlightened its African territories with rationalist philosophy. Following its usual policy of assimilation, it made colonized peoples French citizens with the right to send deputies to the Senate and Chamber of Deputies. Now, to French dismay, Islamic fundamentalists proselytize among the 3.5 million Muslims living in France.[4]

In 1956, weary and unhappy with the Algerian war they were losing and a war in Indochina (Vietnam) they had lost, the French decided to give their colonies more autonomy. A spirit of independence was sweeping all colonies; the French felt they had to choose between granting independence – with the colonies remaining in a loose federation with France – or allowing a host of colonial representatives to vote in French political forums. In 1960 French sub-Saharan African states became independent.

Britain grabbed a huge share of the African pie, but acquired too much territory too quickly to administer all of it efficiently. At first, it made many territories protectorates, turning others (Nigeria, Kenya, Uganda, and the Rhodesias) over to the doubtful mercies of chartered companies. All but Southern Rhodesia eventually became colonies. Gambia, Sierra Leone, the Gold Coast, and Nigeria in the west and Uganda, Tanganyika, Zanzibar, and Nyasaland in the east had few white settlers. But Northern Rhodesia had 73,000 Europeans in 1959, Kenya and Southern Rhodesia even more. Britain also controlled Egypt, the Egyptian Sudan, and the Union (from 1961 the Republic) of South Africa.

Like Belgium, Britain left colonial education mainly to missionaries who shared their culture's assumption of superiority. Such thinking was oppressive to Africans, and led to occasional collisions with local leaders, as it had in India. The Islamic emirates of Northern Nigeria refused to replace Islamic education with European; the Ibos of southern Nigeria, politically fragmented and not tied to a strong belief system, welcomed Western education. They were soon clerks and civil servants for the administration, but bitterly resented in the north. All British colonies produced a new Western-educated middle class at odds with traditional African authorities. The British did not offer practical and vocational education to the extent the Belgians did in the Congo, and college-level training was not available in British colonies until after the Second World War.[5] Universities were started in Nigeria, Uganda, the Gold Coast, and the Sudan only when independence became imminent.

Colonial officials did not educate girls until later in the period and as a subordinate caste. From the first, their education was intended to supply a growing male elite with suitable wives, and schools strongly emphasized domestic science. A vast network of official and voluntary programs "domesticated" women European-style, teaching basic literacy and enough mathematics so women could budget, cook, sew, heal, and know hygiene and child care.[6] Programs designed and promoted by women's clubs in Tanganyika, the Maendeleo wa Wanawake (Women's Progress) movement in Kenya, "improvement associations" in Mombasa, foyers sociaux (housekeeping schools) in Usumbura (Ruanda-Urundi), or mining companies in Northern Rhodesia taught girls that women's primary place was in the home and family, backing this stance with moral precepts.

A major irony of colonization is that Europeans often justified their domination of Africa by promising to improve the lives of African women (as they did in India and Algeria), but instead, their laws, attitudes, and institutions directly or indirectly impoverished them. In this chapter we will discuss women's experience in the colonial period, the independence struggles, and since independence.

Early Colonialism: 1880–1920s

If colonization ended war in a region, Africans at first felt it as a relief; it brought stabilization.[7] The colonists took land, but Africans felt land was to be used, not owned, and had not always used all of theirs: people – followers, not land – signalled status and made a person politically important. Borders had never been clear except in mining country, and became an issue only when profit-motivated elephant-hunting for ivory for export began, because custom entitled the head of the domain where an elephant fell to one tusk. But the colonial powers fixed borders, transformed African economies and social structure, and, in western Africa especially, maintained their rule by force.

Before Europe colonized Africa, Africans lived in self-governing autonomous "tribes."[8] The Europeans partitioned the continent, drawing new borders (allegedly against other "tribes," but really against other Europeans), which disregarded African realities, compacting antagonistic groups and dividing kindred peoples like the Ewe in Ghana and Togo, the Somali in Kenya and Italian and French Somalia, and the Hausa in Nigeria and Niger.[9] Many current African conflicts are rooted in this disregard.

Colonialism had a severe impact on women. It is thought that men took over farming (from women) when the plow was introduced around 1905, and that colonialism destroyed what economic independence and traditional political and social authority women had left.[10] In West Africa, British and French officials ignored women in authority, directing everything through men. For example, the Igbo *omu* (queen mother) managed women's markets and settled their disputes while the male *oba* managed men. The British legitimized the *oba*'s rule by paying him, but not the *omu*, a salary. By the time of independence, the office of the *omu* in many Igbo towns lay vacant.

But some scholars argue that African women in reality had little authority, and that colonialism lessened traditional patriarchal control over women by reducing the likelihood of torture, slavery, or death as punishment for female rebellion, and made divorce possible for women living in intolerable conditions. Throughout Africa, women were subordinate, although in most societies they had some autonomy or control. Women were subordinate in the colonists' home cultures also. Each culture allowed women a few rights or freedoms – but not necessarily the same ones. When Europeans granted African women European women's rights, they violated African custom, and, like the British in India trying to raise the marriage age for girls or eradicate *sati*, they failed. Meanwhile, they had eradicated African women's traditional rights.

From the start of colonization until 1953, European governments tried to keep African women, especially single ones, from migrating. They forbade or restricted women's movement, locking them in villages like hostages to lure their husbands back home. Without women, men were less likely to create African neighbourhoods in European towns, and women would take back male workers who were ill, old, or rejected. To ensure that men from their villages would return, colonial officials pressured African leaders, who already supported this policy. Native courts, a colonial institution, penalized women who migrated even more severely than colonial courts did. In pre-colonial days, divorce was granted by village assemblies made up of men and women, and elder women were heeded.

Colonists introduced taxation, railroads, missionaries, and corvée; they exploited African mines and appropriated African land – and they spread disease. Before colonization, sub-Saharan Africa was protected from foreign epidemics by natural barriers. The period between 1890 and 1930, when many foreigners came to Africa, was the unhealthiest in African history.[11] Ships bearing smallpox had exposed several generations of West Africans to Western diseases before 1800, but smallpox was a serious menace in West Africa into the twentieth century. Africans resisted European diseases somewhat better than Native Americans, Polynesians, Melanesians, or Australian Aborigines. Their slightly greater contact with outsiders may have given them some immunity, African medicine and care may have been better than that of other indigenous populations, and African economic practices were designed in such a way that the economy did not collapse despite widespread death.[12] Also, Africans traditionally valued fertility and childbearing so highly that birth rates were high enough to balance or slightly exceed high death rates until 1945. European practices also spread preventive and curative medicines.

Colonization also introduced a cash economy and wage labour, replaced local goods by imports sold for cash, and imposed taxes, to be paid in cash. At first, colonial governments, pressured by mine and plantation owners, coerced men into wage labour, but as cash became necessary, men migrated seeking wage labour. Colonial governments made property rights individual, "reserving" some land for Africans (land often uninhabitable and miles away from a year-round water source). Decent land was soon overcrowded and grew steadily poorer from over-farming. Europeans blamed primitive African farming methods. Africans had to leave land when tsetse flies invaded, but now had nowhere to go. The Europeans reinforced patriarchism by assigning headmen to oversee production of crops for the European market. But Africans who deferred to Europeans lost their traditional ritual and punitive powers.

Europeans pushed women out of independent or leadership roles, hiring mainly men to work their plantations and construct railways or mines. In central, east, and south Africa, Europeans took men from their villages to build and work large plantations, breaking their resistance by force or the lure of higher wages.[13] When slavery was abolished, household slaves were freed, ending extended households and cooperative farming and fostering nuclear families. Jesuit missionaries brought plows to Africa and lent plows and plowmen to rich men who could set an example.

By gratuitously or accidentally favouring some men above others, imposing corvée on some, and privileging some by giving them decent land, Europeans created classes. African landowners had women and dependent men farm it. Women did not own even the land they had worked for centuries. Landowning men used the earnings from their crops to enlarge their herds, sell cattle, growing richer and more powerful. Marriages were made by bridewealth, and after "buying" a wife, men insisted wives raise their cash crops, not subsistence crops; when markets failed, people starved. In villages that men abandoned to work elsewhere, female control of resources and labour diminished while their workload greatly expanded. The major cause of rural dislocation in Southern and Eastern Africa was colonists' disproportionate reliance on male labour to work their farms and plantations, build roads and railways, and, most significant, to mine the gold, diamonds, and copper that became the economic backbone of South Africa.[14]

Female Strategies for Survival

In East Africa some rural women were able to take advantage of European innovations and the loosened patriarchal control that resulted from economic changes and the removal of men from villages. The rise of cities enabled them to flee unpleasant family restrictions, which often became tighter with the end of slavery. Some were forced to live outside the law, working illegally as prostitutes, but most were petty traders. Whatever their lives were like, they were less controlled by men and their lineages.

In Kenya, Luo women experimented creatively with new crops and farming techniques and increased their trade. The most successful were often Christians: missionaries' stress on agricultural training and hard work led some male converts to help with farm work, easing women's workload. The women used their profits to amass large herds of livestock.

But the experience of Mozambican women in Delagoa Bay was more typical. Men who had left their villages to work in South African mines brought back venereal disease, rapidly infecting women and causing declines in the birth rate and agricultural production. The male chiefs' response was to marry off girls as soon as they began menstruating. Women, already solely responsible for producing food and maintaining the family, were now also mothers at a very young age.

European slave trade increased African slavery – the number of slaves owned by Africans increased, especially after European-run slave markets closed. Slave raids continued after slave trade was abolished, but with no European outlet, the price of slaves fell until even slaves could afford to buy them. Many slaves were female. Much of West Central Africa, populated mainly by matrilineal virilocal Bantu-speakers, escaped the worst depradations of slave raids until the nineteenth century, when raids moved northward.[15] Slave trade came increasingly under the control of African men who lived in all-male coastal commercial centres. Internal traders needed access to these merchants, who dealt only with men, so only men succeeded in business.

Many of these men, who could buy what they needed without wives' help, segregated their wives at home and in public and preferred not to marry free women with obligations to kin. To evade obligations to a matrilineage, the men created endogamous patrilineal trading firms that recruited slave wives. *Yet the wealthy men who formed these companies did not father enough children to reproduce themselves.* Owners and slaves had different economic interests in reproduction: men had to support children for years before they (especially boys) could contribute to the family. They preferred to procreate by cheap slave imports. Women wanted children mainly to share the burden of producing food. But slave women had no rights over their children, who belonged to their owners and might not be able to help aging mothers. Their response to forced marriage and enslavement was to limit the number of children they bore.

In places like the Congo Free State, missionaries and lineage elders joined to attack the growing independence of young women, and disparaged the practice of pawning young girls, which gave elite women access to labour. Elite women lost power and influence. The decline in elite women's status led to the disappearance of an elite female class in this region over the nineteenth century. As a result, European observers saw few differences between slaves and free women: both farmed, and few had time or resources for the leisure activities of earlier elite women. No female leaders emerged in this period: political life was dominated by male traders, and women spent their lives providing food for their families. They took advantage of a few new opportunities, raising food for the wide-scale clandestine slave trade that succeeded abolition and farming the crops that replaced slaves in Afro-European trade. But women's abandonment of subsistence agriculture led to food shortages in some areas – they could not do both cash crop and subsistence farming, and men did not help.

Both colonial and African authorities tried to keep women in the countryside but when the land no longer supported their children, women desperately travelled to cities. But city employers gave them only low-paying, exploitive jobs. (Rural African women were illiterate and untrained in marketable skills, but so were African men: European employers treated literate European women the same way.) Economic options for black women were probably worst in South Africa, where the best job most could find was brewing beer. But this was illegal in many places. Europeans preferred men even as domestic servants; some women found such work but relatively protective families dissuaded others. Domestic service was hard for women with children because they were expected to live in, leaving their own children elsewhere. Many women preferred to do laundry informally. After the First World War began, domestic clothing production increased, and young "coloured" (mixed-race) women in Cape Town entered this industry. Despite abysmal wages and working conditions, it was preferable to working in white people's homes.

Women who wanted to be independent, retain some flexibility, and have a chance to support themselves comfortably had only the usual option: prostitution. Sometimes even this was barred: Johannesburg strictly controlled sexual commerce, allowing poor white women to dominate the field until the early twentieth century (except when severe rural crises impelled large numbers of black women into the cities). But some African women did well as prostitutes. Nairobi (then as now) had far more men than women and prostitutes and brewers working independently could earn enough to amass considerable savings. They invested their money in real estate and by the 1920s made up a significant percentage of African householders in the city. These women often grew estranged from their rural families and sought community elsewhere, joining Islam, or creating fictive kinship bonds based on ethnic notions of blood "brotherhood" and woman-woman marriage.

Women sought employment through marriage: some Central African rural women fleeing poverty and male domination at home migrated to Abercorn in northeastern Rhodesia (now Zimbabwe), a polyethnic commercial town. Clever, sure of their goals, seeing marriage opportunistically (marriage in Africa had always after all been an economic arrangement), many managed to marry up. This appalled colonial authorities; in 1903 they began to support local men in strictly enforcing rules governing bridewealth and marriage, in order to regain control over women.

Once slavery ended, colonial authorities promoted marriage and male dominance as a means of social control. That men should dominate women was the one area of agreement between colonial authorities and male Africans. But sex was the area of greatest collision and most African intractability between Africans and Europeans. Western notions of property and individuality violated

African values, but Europeans simply rode roughshod over Africans; when it came to regulating sex, however (regulating sex anywhere in the world means controlling women), Europeans in Africa encountered obstacles. Although missionaries disapproved of polygyny and female mutilation, they could not end them.

Resistance

Women resisted in both new and traditional ways. Rural African Christian women in a Cape district boycotted local shops and schools in the 1920s. Protesting the terrible burden placed on women by high rates of male migration, limited polygyny, taxation, and land registration, the women succeeded in harming local capitalists. The women's power base lay in rural networks like *manyano* (prayer) groups and later the American Methodist Episcopal Church (AME), which spiritedly took an anti-white, Africanist position. Female coffee-pickers in Kenya organized labour stoppages to demand higher wages and an end to physical and sexual abuse. Organized through work-based networks, they used the form traditional to women of the area to humiliate men: they turned their backs and raised their skirts, mooning them.

Muhumusa in Rwanda

A 1912 uprising in northern Rwanda was led by a woman named Muhumusa.[16] Northern Rwanda was inhabited by the Abahutu (Hutu), farmers in the fertile highlands of Rwanda; Abatuutsi (Tutsi), pastoralists in the hot dry plains, who made up 10 percent of the population; and some Abatwa (Twa), descended from the original gatherer-hunters who still lived in the old way but also by banditry. All three groups shared a common language and culture, and traded with each other, but the Twa were scorned by the two other groups. Most people farmed and raised goats, sheep, and some cattle.

When Rwabugiri, a Tutsi king from the south, conquered the

north, he sent nobles to collect tribute in goods and services from the region. Their arrogance and snobbery aroused resistance, and local leaders formed a ranked bandit society. A new set of leaders emerged – Nyabingi mediums, who took their name from Nyabingi, a powerful woman in the court of Ndorwa before Rwanda defeated it, who was transformed after her death into a spirit. In the nineteenth century, mediums who believed Nyabingi had "chosen" them began to invoke her, begging her to help the sick, poor, or infertile. After mid-century, these mediums, male and female, had strong obedient political followings, most of which opposed Rwabugiri. He blamed the mediums for the defeat of his troops in several battles. When Rwabugiri died in 1895, Kanjogera, his most powerful wife, killed his successor and named her son king, actually taking power herself with her brothers.

But the kingdom never settled into peace under her rule, and when the German military arrived, Kanjogera agreed to a German protectorate over Rwanda in return for help against her rivals. The Germans, however, merely set up two small military outposts on Lake Kivu, supervised by an administrator based in Burundi, who insisted that only missionaries and traders be allowed to work in Rwanda.

After 1900 the north was again invaded by predators. Kanjogera's son Musiinga, imitating his father's expansionist policy, sent agents north with little supervision but with German guns and, sometimes, soldiers. Nobles, aware of northern Rwanda's wealth, bribed lineage leaders or used private armies to seize land; some pretended to represent the ruler, others did not bother. Missionaries cooperated with the nobles, sending their employees along on tax-collecting rounds. Germany, Belgium, and England quarrelled about boundaries and sent expeditions of soldiers and surveyors trooping through, taking food, shelter, and men as porters. When traders seeking ivory and other goods passed through northern Rwanda on their way from East Africa to the Congo, they took what they wanted with little or no recompense, ignoring all protests. Rich, well-armed Roman Catholic White Fathers settled in Rwaza and Nyundu to impose their order, demanding goods and services from the locals.

The horde of newcomers demanded food and service and began to seize land, forcing farmers to work it. To build a town, the Germans forced workers to transport wood and build roads; so did the missionaries. Northern chiefs lost status and wealth. Residents, weakened by epidemics that had swept through in the 1890s and by feeding and servicing the invaders, also faced conflict among local leaders, and fled. The land turned to bush.

Some northerners petitioned Musiinga and tried to ally with the nobles, the Germans, or the missionaries, but nothing helped. Some chose active opposition, robbing the outsiders, burning their houses and disrupting their travel and communications. Others withdrew to new lands in the forest. Basbeya, an Abatwa formerly in Rwaburgiri's personal guard, withdrew to a swamp to hunt and steal from nearby farmers. After a 1905 famine weakened the farmers, Basbeya drove them out. Survivors paid him tribute and many joined his band. His banditry was not politically motivated but was opposed by the government.

Many Nyabingi mediums challenged or defied Rwandan rule, claiming that their power, based in a tie to the spirit, was as legitimate as that of the rulers. One woman medium, Muhumusa, claimed to be an agent of Nyabingi and became prominent, attracting many followers. By 1909 Musiinga and Kanjogera realized that both Basebya and Muhumusa had agents at court – his to inform him of troop movements, hers to overthrow Musiinga. They asked the German soldiers with Maxim guns to chase Basebya back into the swamp and capture Muhumusa. After her capture, she was jailed and exiled outside Rwanda.

In 1911 Muhumusa escaped and returned home. Greatly excited, people thronged to her as she tried to re-establish her old power base by waging war. British soldiers feared her by reputation, and she won several battles easily, which led Basebya to offer her support. Deciding to become a resistance leader, she toured the area with a child said to be the rightful heir to the Rwandan throne. But a British–German force with a cannon and sixty-five rifles attacked Muhumusa's spear-wielding followers and injured her. She was again sent into exile. Her reputation motivated some to rise up and kill Europeans and others to transfer their loyalty to a new medium, Ndungutse, who claimed he had received her power to overcome oppression. His claim transformed the tradition by which mediums passed on their powers to their followers into the idea that "the drive to resist might contain within itself moral force sufficient to legitimate the exercise of power."[17]

After the war, Belgians tried to dominate the north but the spirit that had been solidified and articulated by Muhumusa and Ndungutse continued to spark resistance. Northerners resisted Belgian domination, rebelled against colonialism in 1959, and joined the government of the republic that succeeded it. "Marginal" people and "rootless intellectuals" are often catalysts in peasant revolts.[18] Both Muhumusa and Ndungutse were rootless strangers of unknown parentage. Magnetic, charismatic people who had been exploited, they gave a shape to people's oppressions and were intellectually able to articulate them.[19] Legitimating themselves by claiming both a spiritual and monarchical identity, they drew support from every rank of society, from individuals and blocs. They attacked foreigners and Rwandans, in the process undermining both and creating a spirit that ended colonial rule.

Mekatalili in Tanzania

A woman, Mekatalili, empowered the Giriami of Tanzania to resist British colonization.[20] Over the nineteenth century, the Giriami left the Mombasa area to settle in the Malindi hinterlands, to farm and graze cattle. But Masai raids and disease eradicated the cattle, so they became just farmers. During the migration their political structure changed: the single council of elders in the *kaya* (fortified settlement) was replaced by many local councils. This change de-emphasized rituals and made young men less dependent on their elders, who controlled the medicines used to solve problems needing ultimate arbitration. Severe generational conflicts arose.

Arabs who owned slave-worked maize plantations on the coast began trying after the mid-nineteenth-century to enslave the Giriami. Occasionally, fighting erupted: the Giriami always won on their own terrain, but some were enslavesd, some bought slaves, and some converted to Islam. In time, the British appropriated Arabs' coastal plantations to grow the same crops – cotton, rubber, and sisal. But they needed labour and the London syndicates that owned the plantations pressured the provincial governor to find workers. The Giriami did not need money from contract labour, and fearing enslavement, did not trust the English. The responses of the British reflect their colonial mentality: they dismissed the Giriami fear of enslavement as "irrational," dismissed their form of government, demanding it conform to British standards, and urged the people to defy medicine men, thinking that the reason headmen were not complying was fear of witchcraft. They threatened to take the land by armed force. The Giriami did not know how to resist effectively. An old woman, Mekatalili (Manyazi wa Menza), called the women to a meeting to stop the British from recruiting labour and re-establish the traditional Giriami government.

Mekatalili, a widow without high rank as councillor, had no special position among the Giriami, but she was charismatic and popular. She began a campaign drawing on the tradition of the Giriami prophetess, Mepoho, who probably lived in the nineteenth century. Mepoho had predicted the disruption of Giriami society: she warned that newborns would be smaller, the land would go bad, and youth would disobey and disrespect their elders; boys would take snuff and chew tobacco, girls marry young, and elders lose power. Citing a current drought, Mekatalili recalled these prophecies. She urged the Giriami to end the generational conflict and entreated the women to revive Giriami traditions.

After some rituals and considerable politicking, she called a meeting at the *kaya* in 1913. Women, elders, and young men came, but no headmen. Mekatalili insisted that Europeans were not to blame for the drought, but said that if headmen repaid the wages given them by the British, thereby severing their connection with them, the Giriami would no longer owe them labour service. The people swore oaths – a serious act among the Giriami. Mekatalili did not frame the oaths: she simply laid out the issues, defining the field of discourse. All in all, the gathering reasserted Giriami unity and opposed the British.

The oaths, which involved relations with headmen and the British, were secret: to reveal them meant death. So the British had no idea what was happening when suddenly they could not get anyone to do anything. They blamed the headmen, who in turn became frightened and blamed Mekatalili and the women. Furious, the British pursued Mekatalili, and arrested her along with Wanje (a headman who supported her), and deported them for five years to Kisii, 1000 kilometres away, with a blanket apiece and a little money for food. But in 1914 – almost a year after the oathing – the Giriami went to war against the British.

The war was precipitated by the rape of a Giriami woman by an English policeman and the British dynamiting the *kaya* to punish the Giriami for not building a new one in another location, as ordered. In trying to force the Giriami to evacuate their most fertile land, British troops killed 150 Giriami (one British policeman was killed). Despite their old age, Mekatalili and Wanje escaped and returned but were caught and sent back into exile. The British desperately needed porters during the First World War for their campaign in German East Africa, and used the Giriami; for some years Giriami land was totally disrupted. But in the end, the British lost the war – in 1918, they gave back Giriami land, and pardoned and restored Mekatalili and Wanje. When Mekatalili died, the women's council ended, but she had helped reconstitute Giriami society.

The Women's War in Nigeria

In November 1929 tens of thousands of Igbo women from Calabar and Owerri provinces in Nigeria converged on the Native Administration Centre (which housed the headquarters and residences of district colonial officers, a court, jail, bank, and trader's store). The women chanted, danced, sang mocking songs, and demanded official insignia as Warrant Chiefs (Igbo chosen from each village by the British to sit on the Native Court). They broke into prisons and freed prisoners; they stormed sixteen Native Courts, wrecking or burning most of them. Twice the British summoned troops or police, who killed fifty and wounded fifty. The protest nevertheless went on for a month. The Igbo call it *Ogu Umumwanyi* (the "Women's War"); the British, the "Aba riots." They never understood that the women had rioted out of distress as women.[21]

Most West African societies were patrilineal and patrilocal but women were extremely active politically.[22] The Nigerian Igbo shared language and culture but not political structure: seven and a half million Igbo lived east of the Niger River in democratic villages run semi-autonomously; half a million lived west of the Niger in an area highly influenced by Benin, under a constitutional village monarchy. Both systems were made up of small units in which authority was shared among lineages, kinship, and age groups, among secret and title societies, and oracles, diviners, and other professions. Each sex managed its own affairs through parallel institutions but no distinctions were made between public and private spheres, judicial, executive, and legislative functions, or the political and religious.

The western Igbo had two monarchs, a male *obi*, the acknowledged head of the entire community but actually concerned only with men, and a female *omu*, acknowledged mother of the whole community (*omu* = mother) but actually concerned only with women. The *omu* did not take her position from any relation to a man. Both *obi* and *omu* had parallel councils of twelve advisors; the *omu*'s, the *ilogo*, supervised the community market and could challenge male authority. The *omu* performed rites to prevent calamities like epidemics; she also mediated disputes between women and between spouses, the latter along with the *obi*.

The Igbo preferred consensus, which they thought vital, to judgment. The *omu*, representing all the women of her community, asked their opinion and approval on all major decisions through the *ikporo ani*. This was a body of women from each section or quarter of a village or town, some chosen for lineage but all for achievement: they had to "talk well," enjoy the confidence of their neighbourhood or lineage, and act as liaisons between the *omu* and their constituencies until consensus was reached on every major issue.

Women had other political institutions, notably the *umuada* and the *inyemedi*. The Igbo were exogamous and patrilocal, so women had to leave their homes at marriage. To counter the dislocation and alienation this caused, women invented a lineage system for married women. In their natal villages they were *umuada*, daughters of a village or lineage; in their marital village they were *inyemedi*, co-wives of a village or lineage. They had two homes, with an *otu* (organization) in each. The *otu umuada* included all married, single, widowed, and divorced women of a lineage or village and acted as a political pressure group to stop quarrels and prevent wars. They were very powerful, with higher status than the *inyemedi*, whom they called "our wives," demanding homage or service. The senior woman in the *umuada* could perform rites and sacrifices, purifying new brides from any clandestine sex after becoming betrothed, and absolving adulterous wives.

As in all patrilocal societies, married women were aliens without rights: some villages barred them from burial there until they bore a son; only sons could perpetuate a lineage, or minister to and become ancestral spirits. Not to have a son was the greatest calamity that could befall a couple. But Igbo women were beloved in their natal villages, seen as having left home only temporarily; some villages would not let their daughters be buried in their husbands' villages. To ease wives' lot somewhat was a role of the *otu inyemedi*, headed by the *anasi*, the most senior wife in length of service. They helped members during sickness or stress, gave practical advice, helped discipline lazy, abusive, or adulterous husbands, and punished adultery and other violations of marital law swiftly and drastically. They also planned crops and went on sorties to destroy animals that damaged their crops.

When the British took over Nigeria, they recognized only the *obi*, and gave him a salary, making the *omu* subordinate: she no longer made policy but took orders from the *obi*. Her medicine and rites were replaced by clinics and drugs, the cases she had mediated went to a British-appointed colonial magistrate, and goods were imported, ending her price-fixing in the market. Given the enormous *formal*, institutionalized solidarity among Igbo women, the British were foolish to subvert it. And in 1929, Igbo women rebelled. They had a tradition called "sitting on a man." If a man abused his wife, broke market rules, or let his cows eat women's crops, they gathered at his compound to dance, sing scurrilous songs attacking his manhood, bang on his hut with pestles, wreck it, and tear off the roof. For this war-making, women wore loincloths, smeared their faces with charcoal or ashes, bound their heads with ferns, and carried sticks wreathed with palm fronds.

The women made war on the British to protest a rumoured plan to extend a tax on men to women. Fearing technology, they cut telegraph wires and demanded the removal of the railroad. The men merely put in an appearance. Women thought the British were draining their land and bodies of fertility. Indeed, the British did destroy women's traditional roles. Policy-making became masculinist and elitist, the public sector was split off from the private, and the economic sphere was totally dominated by men. Girls were not educated, and women were increasingly barred from public life. After Nigeria became independent in 1960, the role of the *omu* was revived: an *omu* named in 1972 oversees weaving cooperatives.

But the religion of Nigeria is now Roman Catholic; other institutions are not as important. Female solidarity was broken by stratification and national politics were exclusively male until recently. Women in Nigeria, a cruel dictatorship controlled by Chevron and Shell, recently forced concessions from the oil companies by paralyzing their operations.[23]

South Africa

South Africa was forcibly subdued from the first, although the subjugation was done covertly, hidden from both the British government and people. It has a long history of imperial rule, Western education, and Christianity. Even African resistance leaders grounded their authority not in tradition but in Western reformist protest methods. Most leaders were of the black bourgeoisie, like Charlotte Maxeke, the first black female university graduate in the country, a teacher in the eastern Cape. She became a member of the executive committee of the South African Natives National Congress (later the African National Congress: ANC). African men had long had to carry passes to travel in their own country, but women were not so restricted until 1913. That year, using Gandhi's strategy of passive resistance, and drawing support from African women who feared forced domestic labour in white homes, Maxeke protested about women's passes and the rule was withdrawn.

"Proletarianized" (without land, homes, or work) young black women in Johannesburg sometimes became disruptive, joining male-led Amalaita gangs to burgle houses in the wealthy white suburbs. This method was more threatening but ultimately less effective.[24]

Colonialism: 1920s–1950s

By the end of the First World War, Europeans controlled most of continental Africa, and they expanded cash cropping (still male-dominated). Many men had migrated to jobs in towns and mining areas (which excluded women), but, not wanting black towns springing up in their neighbourhoods, Europeans required African men to live in all-male hostels. Rural women, left alone without male help to clear fields, worked harder but were not able to eke out an existence without trading.

In Kenya and Mozambique the needs of a swelling white population outgrew the availability of black men, and women were hired as *ayahs* (nursemaids). They worked as domestic servants in parts of South Africa, too. Industry also employed women, mainly poor young Afrikaners or, at the Cape, "coloured" (mixed-race) women. A tiny group of black women managed to stay in school long enough to become teachers or nurses, members in their own right of the middle class. The only other African women to rise economically were Nairobi prostitutes, who bought property until Nairobi officials drove them from the streets in the name of health.

Many women migrated to cities to escape the control of husbands, headmen, or fathers. Wanting relationships in freedom, they made short-term informal "marriages": similar to "kept" women in the West, they exchanged domestic and sexual services for support. Such relations, although common in inter-war Nairobi, offended European and African headmen, perhaps because women controlled them: African marriage had always been an exchange among men. Because mine owners had difficulty recruiting labour, they allowed men to have their families live with them in mine areas. This concession drew women to urban centres, thwarting colonial officials and African chiefs who wanted them to stay in the countryside. From 1930 to 1937 South African officials regulated women entering cities (not yet requiring them to carry passes), gradually extending the Natal Code, which defined women as legal minors, to all South African black women. Chiefs and headmen in Northern Rhodesia tried to reclaim their authority over women and young men by gradually recodifying the South African "customary" law.

Even the few powers that women retained in matrilineages vanished eventually. For instance, in Malawi, as nonagricultural female work – iron and salt production, and cloth-making – declined, and household-based cotton production rose in importance, female Mang'anja elders' authority as political leaders beyond their communities dwindled. Earlier conquerors of the Mang'anja, the Kololo, had imposed misogynous rules; the British extended them, replacing the few remaining female heads with men. But Mang'anja women elders retained enough influence to limit the detrimental effects of commercialized farming on women.

In western Kenya Luo women had been experimenting with new crops and tools before the depression, and some had enough success to amass bridewealth for "wives" who enabled them to farm more intensively.[25] But in the 1920s official trading centres superseded local markets; Indians opened permanent shops, and African men took over open-air commerce. Luo women had always depended on trade and commerce, but in the late 1920s and early 1930s, the depression, a plague of locusts, drought, and famine convinced Africans that economic security came not from farming but from formal education and waged work outside the home. Neither was as available to women as to men. In the 1940s Luo men bought shops as investments, local markets were re-established, and women returned to outdoor trade. But agriculture and trade were no longer profitable growing areas of economic activity. Rural Kikuyu women in central Kenya earned wages by picking coffee on European farms – the most menial, lowest paid work. And they were sexually harassed.

Yet in many parts of West and Central Africa, economic changes began to threaten men's control of women, much to colonial rulers' surprise.[26] Successful female traders earned enough to live without husbands and could divorce them. Such independence appalled lineage elders, as well as colonial and local authorities: men who had to grow their own food or cash crops had no free time for other activities. Authorities on every level tried to limit women's mobility and independence by making marriage tighter.

In 1931 it dawned on mining company officials that men's work would improve if their lives were more stable and pleasant, and they let men bring their wives to mining areas. But they did not always provide housing, and if they did, they demanded marriage certificates. In 1933 Native Courts tightened the leash on village women by banning them from working in towns. Such policies created two worlds: adult men working in the "advanced" sector of the economy and women working on farms to support children and elders. Some husbands sent home blankets or gifts; some sent goods to male kin, who passed them to wives they felt behaved well enough to deserve them; some sent nothing. Desperate women went to cities, and colonial government policies plunged them into the "second economy" of informal work and prostitution.

Effects of Colonialism on African Women

Ultimately, expansion of the world economy was disastrous for most women. As women left farming for trade, trade became less important in the overall economy than it had been at the opening of the colonial era. We will examine some effects of colonialism on African women in various parts of Africa.

The Tonga of North Rhodesia

The matrilineal Tonga lived in the Gwembe-Zambezi Valley in Mazabuka, North Rhodesia (later Zambia), but during famines they often moved to the Tonga plateau.[27] There they were welcomed into established communities headed by people with large followings, transient people without strong lineage loyalty. Few could recall ancestors beyond three generations. Men bound themselves to headmen or set up as headmen themselves. Divorced women went to their brothers' houses or made new settlements, taking villagers with them.

But after colonization, European officials decreed that only heads who controlled ten units would be recognized: fewer women than men were acknowledged heads. Missionaries, railway builders, and plantation owners competed for male labour, drawing men away from the community; their departure harmed older women especially. Herds were stricken with Rinderpest in the 1890s, and men – who had an edge of power because of colonial demand for their services – tried to rebuild them by demanding bridewealth. As bridewealth superseded brideservice, the balance between female-controlled resources (male labour) and male resources (cattle: land belonged to neither) tilted in favour of men. In time married women's plot holdings dwindled and their autonomy eroded. Among wealthier commercial farmers, no woman had her own plot; middle-class women had transitory satellite plots, and poor women only scattered fields.

When Seventh-Day Adventist missionaries arrived, they declared Saturday the sabbath, forbidding alcohol, coffee, tea, and tobacco; and they demanded that people live in patriarchal monogamous families. Men were allowed only one wife, but any amount of hired help (which they always used sexually). By 1945 all rich Mazabukan farmers belonged to this church and there was no more available land. Men did little: boys herded cattle; women still worked very hard in the fields and household. Yet if a woman divorced, she owned nothing and had no land to go to.

The Ga of Ghana

The Ga people live in Ussher Town, Central Accra, Ghana, on the coast at the Atlantic terminus of the main slave trade route from the interior.[28] They had lived in the area for over a thousand years and traded with Europeans from the time of their arrival, selling their produce and goods imported from the inland Ashanti. They had longer, closer contact with Europeans than any other Africans. Most Ga commoner men farmed or fished; some traded slaves, gold, or ivory. Ga women also farmed, but they were mainly traders, selling produce or fish and luxury items like linen, knives, pins, cloth, coral beads, bracelets, or mirrors. They sat in the marketplace under shade trees with their wares spread out before them, or hawked them through the streets. They prospered.

Ga society had complex arrangements: people traced clan affiliation patrilineally, inheritance rights cognatically, and maintained bilateral residential rights. That is, they were members of their fathers' clans, inherited from both parents, and lived in the same compound as the parent of the same sex. Women lived with their mothers' female relatives and men lived with their fathers' male relatives, in separate compounds. Women processed food communally in their compounds, supervised by their elders, each night sending dinner to their husbands by a child (preparing dinner seems as hard for men as having babies).

Husbands were expected to give wives money for the family's food and clothing, but women had their own money from trading. Small children lived with their mothers; boys between six and ten years of age could go to their fathers' or live with siblings – brothers and sisters had strong bonds. A husband had to ask his wife to visit him on a given night. No one knows if the marriage pattern arose from economic arrangements or vice versa.

The Ga still live in Accra, but their quality of life has deteriorated. Europeans hire only men as artisans or clerks, jobs which do not require wifely cooperation. Men own property separately: a wife does not necessarily inherit unless a husband gives her a share beforehand. Men conceal the amount of their salaries from wives, doling out allowances to them. Many do not repay wives who (reluctantly) lend them money. Some Ga women still market their husbands' produce outside Accra, but fewer fishers and farmers come to work in the city. Most cooperative couples are self-employed. Women too conceal details of their businesses, especially profits, from their hubands, fearing men will cut back their support of the household (women raise the children). Men tend to demand such information before they give their wives capital, so many wives will not ask husbands for capital. Younger women get less support than older ones but more often get capital from their husbands – as a loan.

Women sell goods for cash: they used to give men a share because they were usually better off than the men. They used to feel an obligation to sell their husbands' produce; now they consider only economic concerns: a woman will say the fish her husband catches aren't her specialty, for instance. Some keep all profits for themselves and are even better off than before. Men are very frustrated: they cannot compel their wives to sleep with them, nor do wives treat them with the old devotion and respect. Most women are illiterate, but they have legal rights.

In central Accra, most women are worse off than they were, but suburban women are worst off. Most city men are artisans, whereas suburban men have succeeded in white-collar work and keep their wives in high-status dependency. Their wives have no money, but need it to run the household, educate the children, give loans to kin and other females, and invest in land and houses. Most women help their mothers – the mother-daughter tie is the strongest cultural bond. Sons help mothers too, but daughters do not help fathers (who do not raise them). Women try to save cash or jewellery. These days most Ga are monogamous because of the high cost of living and the influence of Christianity, but men have rampant extramarital affairs.[29]

The Yoruba in Lagos, Nigeria

Yoruba culture was made up of patrilineal groups ruled by an *ala-afin*. Each lineage had usufruct land and fishing rights, which a lineage head could grant to strangers who offered fealty, labour, or gifts, and who were eventually incorporated into lineages. By the nineteenth century, Lagos was Africa's centre of international trade. Slave trade transformed it from a fairly egalitarian society to a stratified one by concentrating wealth (slaves, arms, ammunition, war canoes, and luxuries) in a few hands. When the Europeans took over, they brought Christianity, which altered the city's economic and political structure. New job opportunities and Western stratification generated an elite, a small group of Christian-educated African men who grew rich and evolved a distinctive culture. But change undermined it almost immediately.[30]

In the 1860s Britain seized Lagos island and a strip of mainland to suppress the slave trade and get a foothold for its own ambitions. When slave trade ended, Lagos exported palm oil. Britain began to rule it directly, importing Christian missionaries whose schools educated an elite. Women, educated short of university, became housewives. Men were educated for top jobs and grew rich, but wealth was not the standard for membership in the elite – rich Muslim merchants were not part of it. This elite class, powerful in Lagos and influential with Europeans and other Africans in the nineteenth century, led the political movements that challenged colonial rule in the next century.

The pivotal element in forming the elite was marriage, either African (Yoruba) or Christian. Yoruba marriage is primarily an economic relation; parents choose their children's mates, often without consulting them, from among their kin. Love is not an issue: emotional needs and intimacy are expected to be satisfied by same-sex relations. Men sexually own their wives, but are themselves polygynous; most have no more than two wives. Divorce is fairly easy – spouses simply stop acting married or return bridewealth. When Christian marriage became possible, women preferred it because colonialism had already undermined traditional economic customs. In Christian marriage, a man's siblings and unofficial children did not inherit unless he specifically provided for them in a written will. It made men owners of wives' bodies but required monogamy, which women preferred and found morally superior. It also made divorce impossible.

The Christianizing of Africans altered their culture in other ways. In Africa Western education was usually provided by missionaries. Missionaries in the Kongo shared colonial rulers' concerns, and until the Second World War tried only to Christianize students, offering little beyond religious instruction. Belgium did not want to create an assertive Westernized elite like that which had emerged in Sierra Leone. But after the war, they began preparing

boys for administration and waged work. They trained a few girls as
Christian wives and mothers (in 1960, on the eve of independence,
under 4 percent of secondary school pupils were girls). When
Kongo became independent, few women had attended anything
but the convent or elementary school and were not hired for wages.
Europeans hired men, who used their wages to buy land (which
they now monopolize). Men rose to run the state.

Missionaries to the Yoruba opened elite girls' boarding schools
to mould women in a Christian image. Obsessed with possible
pregnancy, they implanted shame in their students, training them
in domestic virtues proper for African Christian mothers and wives
for the new male bourgeoisie of teachers, ministers, and evangelists.
The religion of urban South African missionaries was devoted to the
nuclear family as much to Christ.[31] Preoccupied with shielding girls
from premarital sex and pregnancy, they vacillated between training
them for domestic life in their own homes and as servants. African
women embraced the colonial-sponsored cult of domesticity
because it reanimated the traditional but dwindling prestige of
African mothers, and African families were disintegrating from
internal and external pressures.

In an area in which Westernization might improve women's
lives, it failed. Missionaries condemned clitoridectomy and infibulation wherever they remained, for example in the Kikuyu area of
central Kenya. But local people and early nationalist agitators valued these practices and felt the missionaries were attacking ceremonies that lay at the heart of Kikuyu identity. They left mission
churches and set up alternative primary schools for their children.
African women returned to religious traditions to fill women's
needs: women doctors led a new spirit cult in Nyasaland to give
women a voice in their communities; *chisungu* initiation ceremonies remained central to religious life in East-central Africa; in South
Africa, the Lovedu rain queen was still powerful, offering women
religious expression and, they felt, control of weather.

Bemba, Lungu, and Mambwe Women in Abercorn, Rhodesia

Some colonial officials supported women's rights. In Abercorn, Rhodesia, now Mbala in Zambia, during the initial colonial period, no issue was more sensitive than control of women.[32] At the turn of the century, Abercorn was a thriving commercial centre. Because new technology was being installed, more food was needed for workers, and women's value rose because they grew it. As they delivered food to sell to transport and construction workers who made steamboats for Lake Tanganyika, women suddenly saw they could work in workers' camps, administrative centres, and commercial centres. Their new independence aroused a backlash of protective, possessive emotions in men in outlying communities; many accusations of rape and adultery are recorded. But European money vanished once the telegraph lines and steamers were built, the area was deforested, rubber vines were destroyed, and salt from distant Uvinza had become cheaper than the local kind. As central administration grew stronger, the power of district officers weakened and they had to work at keeping good relations with chiefs, whose major complaint was runaway wives who had relations with other men. The court often settled these by payments or the return of children to the chief.

As power was transferred, most matters were referred to Abercorn courts. Records show that women were complainants in civil cases and (usually) victims in criminal cases; they also reveal the conditions under which many women lived. Men who complained about runaway wives could be silenced by receiving goods from their new men. The husband of a woman who ran away from him because he took her wages claimed that she was a slave and he had a right to them. Courts had to discourage slavery, so they denied men's claim to the wages of female dependents. Men also treated children as slaves, sending them to work wherever they chose. Courts sometimes returned children to their mothers, annulling the father's custody. They also tried to prevent male exploitation of pawns who were married off for bridewealth twice the debt they had been pawned for. Women were raped or beaten for refusing sex. Under pressure of economic and social change, men victimized women. British courts often upheld male rights over those of women, but they sometimes considered women as human beings and worked for the welfare of children.

European Women in Colonial Africa

When numbers of European women arrived in Africa, European men blamed them (like Englishmen in India) for ruining their supposedly harmonious former relation with Africans. White women, they said, inhibited men's liaisons with local concubines, which gave them valuable entry to local culture, and they also aroused lust in native men (yet their memoirs show no fear of indigenous men).[33] There *was* a falling-off in harmony between Africans and Europeans after the 1880s – when many evangelical Christian missionaries also arrived, sure of the universal truth of their religion and superiority of their cultures. They attacked local sexual arrangements, especially non-marital liaisons. And European women's presence generated families and European enclaves, both usually xenophobic. Racial prejudice grew with the European population.

According to the "myth of the destructive female," female European colonists were petty, frivolous, racist, unproductive, and dependent, contributing nothing to the imperial project or the indigenous people.[34] European women rarely spoke against their rulers – like men, most supported the imperial venture. However, they all had to work hard, even well-to-do women, in unfamiliar environments running farms and homes and raising children, who (as in India) suffered a very high mortality rate. Many were lower-class women seeking work or marriage. Emigration is frightening: few risk it without need. Male migration to the colonies steadily increased the ratio of women to men in Britain after mid-century: 1042 per 1000 in 1851, it was 1068 per 1000 by 1911. The English called women without husbands or work "redundant" or "surplus," as if women existed only to pair with men and should wither if not plucked. Because they would die if they had no work, they migrated. Most servants in Africa were African, but many British women arriving in South Africa after 1850 became domestic servants. In the 1880s and 1890s, these servants united, forming the British Women's Emigration Association (BWEA). It recruited women by offering them genteel domestic service, potential marriage, and the chance to civilize the world by promoting British values in the colonies – the values of colonial administrators and missionaries.

Women were lured by money: white servants in South Africa could earn as much in two months as their counterparts in England in a year. Between 1902 and 1912, about 1500 white women entered the Transvaal as domestic servants: lower- and middle-class single women competed for the same jobs. But once they arrived, many married or found other work: racial ideology dictated that the most menial work be done by Africans, and many emigrants found work in factories after a year of domestic service. Marriage constituted a loss to an employer but was approved by the colonial state, which wanted to increase the population. For a woman herself, marriage meant entering privileged white society.

Many women came as missionaries. The most famous British female missionary in Africa was Mary Slessor, who lived for forty years in southeastern Nigeria. Her career promoted empire perhaps more than Christianity – she made few real converts but she opposed slavery, human sacrifice at the burial of important people, poison ordeals, and the killing of twins (some Africans thought twins "unnatural" and a threat to the community).[35] She had an enormous influence on the Efik and Ibibio peoples, with whom she lived and built mutual trust and affection. When the British Niger Coast Protectorate was established, Slessor was named Vice Consul and District Magistrate, and she worked against sexual discrimination locally and in England, improving the lives of Efik and Ibibio women (especially those who bore twins), and British women, whom she supported in mission work. She helped extend colonial rule when in 1901 the British used military force to suppress an important local oracle used in the slave trade.

Some female missionaries and colonial administrators' wives, fascinated by the indigenous culture, became ethnographers, studying the mores of a group or its women. Anthropology is supposed to be an "objective" study of cultures in their own terms, but the ideal is not possible; anthropologists in Africa between the wars were closely linked to colonial administrators. Not until the early twentieth century did the study of women seem worthwhile and then male bias kept female anthropologists from prominence. Daisy Bates worked for fifty years among Australian aborgines only to have her material appropriated by A. Radcliffe Brown. Husbands often appropriated their wives' research: classic works of the period by men acknowledge such contribution in a preface, not on the title page.[36] A few – like Audrey Richards in *Chisungu* (1956), a class study of female life cycle rituals – dealt with social problems, but none penetrated the male mystique of colonialism, which would have required a radical assessment of their own culture, not just anthropology itself.

The only European women who tried to undermine imperial rule were reformers. During the 1940s and 1950s reformers interested in African women's concerns helped form African women's organizations on European models. In South Africa, white women made legal and illegal efforts to dismantle racial segregation and white economic exploitation of Africans. Some acted to ease the effects of colonialism and breach the social boundaries that colonialism had placed between ruler and ruled. After the British Colonial Service altered its mission from control to trusteeship and development, women pressured it to hire female officers. In 1938 it dropped its ban on admitting women and after the war began to recruit women educators and social welfare officers.

Female reformers too were ethnocentric, alienating Africans. Their campaign against clitoridectomy split the male Kikuyu community, which denounced them for cultural imperialism. In this case, humane principle, not ethnocentricity or imperialism seems the motive, but they could not halt female genital mutilation.

Two important white women wrote on Africa: Olive Schreiner and Isak Dinesen. Schreiner (1855–1920), born to German missionaries in South Africa, was a reformer who at the turn of the century denounced British treatment of the Boers in South Africa. When the British allied with the Boers, she became a pariah in her homeland by advocating suffrage for Africans and urging white and African workers to unite in class struggle. She went to England and under the pseudonym Ralph Iron published the first sustained imaginative work to reach the West from Africa, *The Story of a South African Farm* (1883). Schreiner, alienated from white South African women, found intellectual kinship in England, where she wrote on women's rights and pacifism. *Woman and Labour* (1911) was one of the most influential feminist works of the period. Schreiner quit the Women's Enfranchisement League in the 1900s when it supported the vote for white women only. Like Isak Dinesen's, her sympathy for Africans was tinged with patronization. Isak Dinesen was the pen name of Karen Blixen (1885–1962), a Danish noblewoman who lived in Kenya. Although her writing was not overtly political, she described the situation in Africa in *Out of Africa* (1938). More popular in Europe and the United States than in Kenya, Dinesen eventually returned to Denmark.

Like most women in strongly authoritarian, repressive societies, white South African women rarely left the home. But a small group of progressive white women opposed white privilege. In the 1930s they organized trade unions, and after the Afrikaner Nationalist Party won the 1948 election and installed apartheid, they joined the massive multiracial nonviolent resistance movement. Massive governmental repression drove activists underground until the 1970s and 1980s, when workers and students again rebelled. Women's issues, however, were a minor part of the agenda of the anti-apartheid movement. Helen Joseph and Ray Alexander Simons, who organized trade unions, were banned and placed under house arrest for working against apartheid; Betty Sacks, Hilda Watts Bernstein, and Ruth First worked through the Communist Party of South Africa. Ruth First, the subject of a film, *A World Apart*, was killed by a South African secret police letter bomb. Other white women too joined black Africans, Asians, and coloured men and women in the ANC.

Local Resistance

The West subjugated Africa but it also educated thinkers to rebel against subjugation: many African nationalists studied in the United States or Europe. African-Americans were very influential, awakened to their heritage by Edward Blyden, a West Indian who in 1850 moved to Liberia and began writing proudly about Africans. Another West Indian, Marcus Garvey, preached "Africa for the Africans," urging African-Americans to return to their motherland (an exhortation with which some white racists agreed). A major influence on Kwame Nkrumah, Garvey was open to using force. But the key figure was W.E.B. Du Bois, who wrote an important history of the slave trade and dreamed of a pan-African movement embracing American and African blacks. In 1919 he organized a Pan-African conference with Senegalese Blaise Diagne, to influence the Peace Conference in Paris.

This was a vain hope, but Pan-African Conferences, held at intervals over the years, were dominated by African-Americans until after the Second World War. By 1945 the fifth Pan-African Conference in Manchester was much more radical. Over 200 delegates attended, among them leading African nationalists like Kwame Nkrumah and Jomo Kenyatta. The delegates unanimously endorsed the "doctrine of African socialism based upon the tactics of positive action without violence." Like the Indian National Congress after the First World War, it turned itself into a non-violent but militant body, ready to confront the colonial powers.

In the 1940s and 1950s, as nationalist movements swept the

continent, women agitated locally. In Lagos, Alimotu Pelewura organized 8,000–10,000 poor illiterate Nigerian marketwomen into the Lagos Market Women's Association. Openly anti-colonial, it protested taxation of women and a price control scheme imposed during the Second World War. In 1945 the association joined a general strike. In the same period, Oyinkan Abayomi, whose husband led the Nigerian Youth Movement, formed the British West African Girls' Club, attracting middle-class Westernized Christian women. The most successful cross-class organization was perhaps the Abeokuta Women's Union, founded by Funmilayo Anikulapo Kuti, who was radicalized while studying in England. Returning to Nigeria as principal of Abeokuta Girls' School, she wore only Yoruba clothing and spoke Yoruba at meetings to identify with fellow union members. Her union agitated against indirect rule and taxation, taking a nationalist approach to women's economic interests.[37]

A Women's Brigade leader, Makatindi Nganga Yeta, a princess, was the granddaughter of a Lozi king who signed the first agreement with the British South Africa Company in 1890; she was the first member of an old aristocratic family to join the Women's Brigade, headed by Betty Kaunda (wife of Kenneth, a resistance leader who later became Zambia's first president) and later the first woman elected to Parliament. At the other end of the social spectrum, Julia Mulenga (Mama Unip), a Bemba woman who sold vegetables at the Lusaka market, joined a political party and went out at night shaking a tin of pebbles to call women to their secret meeting place. She collected money for the party, was always in the front lines during demonstrations, singing slogans and songs, and was known for her courage. The activities of hundreds of such women contributed to the eventual liberation of the country.

In 1950 pass laws were extended to black South African women. The Federation of South African Women, a nonracial group led by the ANC Women's League, was formed in 1954 to fight this change. One day in 1956, 20,000 women, mostly black Africans, delivered petitions to the prime minister, walking to his office in groups of two or three because the government had banned processions that day. But disciplined nonviolent resistance did not work in South Africa, which banned or imprisoned resisters.

East African women who worked for wages (*ayahs* in Mombasa and Nairobi, teachers and nurses in the Sudan) joined newly emerging trade unions. In 1945 northern Tanzanian Pare women marched to district headquarters to protest new taxes they felt would disrupt family and agricultural life. Attacking the local chief, they insisted that the British district officer impregnate them – their metaphoric way of stating that his policies undermined their husbands' position. The government heeded these women to the point of reforming local policies but did not consult them in the decision-making process. South African food and clothing workers also formed unions, making up the core of the Federation of South African Women that agitated against passes for women in the late 1950s. In Usumbura, Muslim women protested a special tax on single women that implied that divorced, widowed, and polygynized women were *malaya* (prostitutes). They protested for several years and finally had the law rescinded.

In the 1950s rural South African women in Natal erupted in rage at forced removals (the government seized people, expropriated their land and houses, and transported them to a wasteland), stock control, and a new system of land allocation that ended female ownership of land. Rising spontaneously, they smashed trucks, burned fields, and attacked any state symbol they came across. The Durban government wanted to foster Municipal Beer Halls, and restricted domestic beer-brewing. This was one of the few trades open to women, who responded violently, invading and burning beer halls, picketing, performing ribald acts, and clashing with police.

In the 1920s Kom women of Cameroon created a tradition of punishing men who offended their community through the *anlu*, a hierarchy with local chapters, dedicated to women's interests. In the 1950s, believing colonial officials were giving their land to the Igbo and angry that local chiefs did not protect their crops from Fulani herders' cattle, Kom women felt their survival threatened. In 1958, about 7000 women gathered at the *anlu* to to mount a year-long protest against British agricultural and market regulations. Colonial officials chose not to use force and none of the protesters was hurt.[38]

A small group of women risked ostracism – if not jail – for activities considered radical by white South Africans, conservative by United States standards, and hopelessly ineffective by African militants. At a tea party in 1955 white housewives, alarmed at African Nationalist Party efforts to erode the already limited franchise of coloured men, founded the Women's Defence of the Constitution League. Keeping vigil for two nights at government offices, despite rocks, garbage, and threats hurled at them by young Afrikaner men, they wore black sashes to mourn the "death" of the Constitution, and later took the name Black Sash.

Some women tried to control their lives and gain a political voice through religion: the Legio Mariae of Kenya, founded by a man, Gaudencia Aoko, was given its character by a Luo prophetess. In Côte d'Ivoire, Marie Lalu founded the Deima religion in 1952, and her work was continued by Princess Geniss. Mai Chaza (Mother Chaza) and Alice Lenshina Mulenga Lubusha founded churches in Zambia. In 1953 Lubusha had a spiritual experience: she died and was taken to God, who entrusted her with two books and told her to return to earth to preach against evil. Her Lumpa Church drew many followers (100,000 members from 1955 to 1957). Its clash with the government in 1964 became a civil war.[39]

In the 1960s Zambian women formed their own brigades, shocking men with their ferocity. Women in the Chilenjie section of Lusaka fought for the right to choose their meat from a butcher shop. Like most shops in the town, butcher shops were owned by whites, who abused Africans. Chilenjie women had to rise very early in the morning, walk miles to the shop, then queue at the window. Those arriving late had to stand in line for hours. Then an African would give money to a butcher through a small window; the butcher randomly chose a cheap cut of meat and threw it unwrapped at the buyer. The Women's League organized a boycott of all butchers, timing it in the wet season when vegetables were plentiful. They waited nine weeks, then marched into the shops and demanded service. The shocked butchers served them.

Nationalist Movements: 1950s–1990s

Transfers of Power

During the 1950s and 1960s, a wave of nationalist movements inundated British and French African colonies in agitation so fierce that it drove colonial rulers to negotiation tables. Finding compromise unacceptable to Africans, most rulers granted independence peaceably, willing to cede political control if they could retain their hold on profitable enterprises.

The Gold Coast, the first British colony in sub-Saharan Africa to win independence, became prosperous through its exports of cocoa after the First World War. When the war ended, as the world's largest producer of cocoa it had a bigger middle class and more money for education and health than most African states. The African party, made up of African professionals and businessmen, asked Kwame Nkrumah to return from London to be its secretary. His views, shaped by British communists, were more radical than theirs, but he returned to the country as an organizer. In 1948 Accra, Kumasi, and other towns exploded in riots that killed 29, and injured 237. These incidents convinced the British that constitutional reform would not mollify the Africans. Suspecting that Nkrumah had incited the riots, British officials had him seized and searched, and felt vindicated when they found a communist party card and a document listing the aims of "The Circle." In 1949 Nkrumah broke with the moderates and formed his own party, aiming for mass support, mainly from trade unions (youth sections and trade unions were the power base of many African nationalist movements). He began a campaign of agitation, strikes, boycotts, and non-cooperation on a Gandhian model.

In 1950 the British sentenced Nkrumah to three years in prison for sedition. He became one of Africa's many "prison graduates," men who moved from prison into power. The British made little effort to keep him from organizing during his imprisonment, and when elections were held in 1951 his was the strongest party. The new British governor, Sir Charles Arden-Clarke, who believed in self-government, released Nkrumah to take over as prime minister (the name given the post in 1952). Unfortunately, on the eve of independence, the cocoa crop was infected with a fungus, severely disrupting the economy. Nkrumah had to win two more elections before Gold Coast became independent Ghana in 1957.

Although reluctant to let go of Gold Coast, the British did not want it enough to commit prolonged armed force. In the face of African discontent, they drew up a new constitution to transfer political power to Africans, and handed over power without violence because the Africans did not demand changes in the economic structure of society, and England would continue to get profits from Ghana. This condition existed in all the African revolutions.

The boundaries drawn for Nigeria by the Nigeria Company between 1885 and 1899 squeezed into one political unit disparate peoples at odds with each other: Yoruba in the Western Region, Ibo in the Eastern, and Muslim emirates in the north. Nigeria was a poor country with almost no middle class, few educational or social services, and no nationalist movement until after the First World War. But in the mid-1950s, with their eyes on Ghana, the Nigerians demanded independence from the British. Three parties reflected the nation's visions. Aware that regional division was the country's most intractable problem, Yoruba chief Awolowo echoed Metternich on Italy: "Nigeria is not a nation. It is a mere geographical expression."[40] Nigeria became independent in 1960, and a republic in 1963. In 1993 military dictator Sani Abacha took over and ruled in league with Western oil interests. Abacha, who in 1995 murdered political dissenters, including Ken Saro-Wiwa, despite worldwide protests, died in June 1998. The new ruler, Olusegun Obasanjo, a

Yoruba Christian, promises democracy, but his strength is not yet clear: in the face of agitation by northern Muslims, he has been silent. Recently, women demonstrating in Warri forced the oil companies to treat workers better.

Sierra Leone became independent in 1961, and a one-party state in 1978. It has been torn by civil war for decades. Uganda, which became independent in 1962, was another artificially created state. Severe internal rivalry divides the peoples who make it up – Buganda, Bunyoro, Toro, and Ankole – who are also caught in local conflicts. The country could not unite enough to form a nationalist movement and Britain simply let it go. The first president, the head (Kabaka) of Buganda, was overthrown in 1966 by his prime minister, Milton Obote, whose troops were led by Idi Amin. When Obote was abroad in 1971, Amin made himself head of state. He systematically murdered all rivals, and his rule, one of the bloodiest ever seen in Africa, ended only when Tanzania sent an army to overthrow him in 1979. Obote became president again in 1980.

Kenya's population contained many Britons and Asians, especially Indians. Imported to build railroads, the Indians opened shops and prospered, to the profound resentment of the Africans. Inspired by Gandhi, Indians agitated for franchise after the First World War. In 1927 the Legislative Council was restructured to include eleven elected Europeans, five elected Indians, one elected Arab and one *nominated* African. At this time, among Kenyan Africans, only the Kikuyu were organized. As they farmed the area near Nairobi, they were most disrupted by European incursions and exposed to European ideas. In 1920 a group of moderate chiefs and elder men formed the Kikuyu Association; the next year, younger men educated in mission schools, with more radical ideas, founded the Young Kikuyu Association. Jomo Kenyatta, educated at a Presbyterian mission school, lived abroad from 1929 to 1946. On his return, he discovered the British had made no progress on producing a new constitution and had condemned the young men's group during the war on grounds of sedition. Africans were not elected to the Legislative Council until 1952, and then only by a complicated method.

Between 1952 and 1955, the disturbance known as the Mau Mau revolt – the only guerrilla struggle for independence in eastern or southern Africa before the 1960s – had white Kenyans shivering in terror. It is not clear who the "Mau Mau" were or if Kenyatta was linked to them: they attacked Africans more than whites. But the rebellion was centred in the Kikuyu, and Kikuyu women, ranked in a clearly defined hierarchy of rural female leaders, held oathing ceremonies that bonded them to the movement. Some women were soldiers but their most crucial role was to maintain supply lines to funnel food, information, medicine, and weapons from towns and reserves to forest retreats. Since no one in the Mau Mau revolt had reflected on the oppressive aspects of gender relationships and the revolutionary strategies required to end them, women's part in the revolt did not lead to change in the actual status of women.

That white settlers had to petition London for troops during the Mau Mau revolt shook their belief that they could rule Kenya. The British drew up a constitution designed to let Africans gain some experience in government, but settlers opposed it, forming a new party to devise a multi-racial state that would safeguard whites' property. Africans had other ideas and formed two main political parties: the Kenya African National Union (KANU), supported mainly by the Kikuyu and Luo, favouring a centralized government; and the Kenya African Democratic Union (KADU), supported by the Masai and smaller groups, which wanted a federation. KANU, led by Kenyatta, won the 1963 election; independence followed later that year. Kenyatta made Kenya virtually a one-party state before he died in 1979. It remained a one-party state ruled until 1994 by the corrupt dictator Daniel Arap Moi. He ruled until 2002, when, under pressure, he retired. The new president, elected by the people on December 27, 2002, is Emilio Mwai Kibaki, an economist who promised free universal education.

Protracted Armed Struggles

Some European nations would not give up their colonies, perhaps because the uprisings were designed to alter the structure of society and would not allow the former imperialist rulers to continue to extract profits from their former vassals.

Portugal would not give up Angola, Mozambique, and Guinea-Bissau; Rhodesian whites vetoed majority rule; and South Africa, technically independent (not a colony), imposed brutal minority rule and apartheid on Africans inside its borders. With roughly 38 million people (about 18 percent white), South Africa reserved 87 percent of the land for whites in 1990 and occupied South West Africa (Namibia) despite UN condemnation and a World Court ruling of illegality. In these countries, there was war, though it went undeclared.

The groups that fought for independence in these nations did not want merely to replace white rulers with black; philosophers of revolution, they wanted to build non-exploitive societies, and they emphasized women's liberation. The Zimbabwe African National Union (ZANU) and the Zimbabwe African People's Union (ZAPU) fought for five years to transform Rhodesia into Zimbabwe in 1980. Namibia's South West African People's Organization (SWAPO) also won independence. The courageous stubborn African National Congress (ANC) under Nelson Mandela forced ruling whites to allow democratic government. Three groups fought Portugal – the Popular Movement for the Liberation of Angola (MPLA), the Front for the Liberation of Mozambique (FRELIMO), and the African Party for the Independence of Guinea and Cape Verde (PAIGC). The Eritrean People's Liberation Front (EPLF) fought for years for independence from Ethiopia, winning it in 1993.

Rhodesia was the virtual fief of one man. Using false pretences, Cecil Rhodes won a Royal Charter to exploit the land between the Transvaal and the Congo Free State, later Northern and Southern

Rhodesia. Rhodes' company ruled both until the 1920s, when they became colonies. Joshua Nkomo, a moderate, founded a nationalist movement in Rhodesia. In 1963 it split into his Zimbabwe African People's Union (ZAPU), and the Reverend Nbabaningi Sithole's more radical Zimbabwe African National Union (ZANU). White settlers used the split to claim that majority rule would cause the internecine strife that had devastated Zaire (once Belgian Congo) since its independence in 1960.

Under Ian Smith, whites declared Rhodesia independent of England in 1965. Deeply embarrassed, the British imposed economic sanctions on the country; these were ineffectual because white-ruled South Africa and Mozambique ignored them. Africans' unremitting struggle against white domination, plus the collapse of the Portuguese empire and the withdrawal of South African aid, brought the white Rhodesian government down. Rhodesia reverted to colony status; the British held elections with universal suffrage in 1980 and Zimbabwe became independent later that year. The election split along tribal lines, foreshadowing future divison: the majority Shona-speaking people voted for ZANU, led by Robert Mugabe; the minority Ndebele (Matabele) people in the south and west of the country continued to support Joshua Nkomo. Disruptions and claims of massacres have sporadically erupted in Zimbabwe since independence. Mugabe made Zimbabwe a one-party state, promising to protect the rights of whites in Zimbabwe, but over the years, most have left, depleting the managerial class. A few years ago, Mugabe began appropriating white-owned land and distributing it to blacks. This has led to further white exodus and a food shortage.

Colonizing East Africa in 1885, England made Zanzibar a protectorate; Germany seized land it called Tanganyika and forced Africans to work on plantations. In 1905 three Matumbi leaders, one of them, Nantabila Naupunda, a female religious leader, led a rebellion in which Africans uprooted cotton on a Kilwa plantation. Slaves and poor free people – indeed, nearly all Africans in southern Tanganyika – followed religious leaders in a full-fledged war, the Maji Maji War. Its most important leader, Kinjikitile Ngwale, taught that all Africans were one and compared the German-forced labour system to slavery in the Zanzibar Empire. The Germans retaliated against the Africans by seizing herds and crops, burning homes and granaries to the ground, and burning crops in the fields. To create a famine, they killed women to keep them from raising food. Against the German Maxim guns, the Maji Maji army used spears, knives, bows and arrows, and shotguns, but it took the Germans two years to defeat the Africans – from 1905 to 1907.

Both Germans *and* Britons plundered the Africans again during the First World War, and German Tanganyika was taken over by the British in 1919. England "requisitioned" crops, herds, and labour during the Second World War. The economy was entirely capitalist. Transnational companies based in Germany and later England owned the plantations; Asians owned smaller companies and most coconut plantations. Slaves were replaced by migrant and day-labourers from nearby villages, mostly women, contracted at very low wages to weed, pluck tea, pick coffee – cash crops, raised main-ly by colonists until independence – and to grade and sort produce.

Cities bloated up: Dar es Salaam had 10,000 people in 1894 but 128,742 in 1957. Most city residents were male until the mid-1950s, when women became 42 percent of residents, most doing small production and trading. In the 1960s women dominated *pombe* (home-brewed beer) production, and the food business, and they fetched and sold firewood, the main fuel for cooking, heating, and agro-processing. They owned 19 percent of the African-owned houses in the city.[41]

Rural women raised export crops, working harder without male help, but men, household heads, received the payments for them. The crops the women raised to feed the family were insufficient, and malnutrition became a permanent feature of African existence for the first time. Colonial appropriation of African land created a dispossessed disruptive populace, tarnishing the colonial image. Yet colonial officials like one secretary of native affairs argued that the state need do nothing for rural people because they had "natural . . . comparatively healthy living conditions."

Men devised a new lifestyle: migrating to cities to work. They kept wives in the villages to support their children and parents, and lovers in town to serve them and contribute their earnings – all women supported themselves. In towns some earned good livings cooking and selling sweetmeats, fish, beans, and cakes, or splitting and selling firewood, yet they were portrayed as immoral. Colonial authorities favoured, regulated, and sometimes imposed bridewealth to "stabilize" marriage by putting wives in bondage. Women mounted major protest actions. In 1945, 500 women in Usangi protested taxation, converging on the headquarters of the colonial chief, mobbing and stoning his car. District authorities were outraged and horrified. One wrote: "Only five hundred women were able to shake the whole security system. What would happen if the thousands of men . . . were to turn violent?"

Women brewers earned so much that Dar es Salaam authorities tried to monopolize beer-brewing – while condemning female brewers for making a profit. Men supported women's resistance. Women's demonstrations seemed spontaneous but were planned by networks strong enough to coordinate sustained protest.[42] The government issued the monopoly, but after three months of effort Tanganyika breweries could not produce *pombe* that was acceptable to Africans. Consumption dropped by half of beer half its usual strength. The municipal breweries wanted to get out of their contract and the government was forced to restore the industry to women.

These women lay the groundwork for the first nationalist political organization in the country: the Tanganyika African National Union (TANU). Created in 1954, it led the fight against British domination. While the small Christian-educated elite stayed home, traditional Muslim women with little or no education joined TANU. Having built solidarity in *ngoma*, dance groups, or women's *lelemama* societies, which integrated Swahili-speaking urban people across ethnic lines, they had hundreds of members organized in a complex hierarchy and saw in TANU a chance both to help the cause of national independence and to end male domination. TANU had strong support in Dar es Salaam, especially among beer brewers, traders and artisans in the "second economy." The majority of card-carrying TANU members in the 1950s were women; all were Muslim, all but one had been active in a *ngoma* group, and all sold *pombe*, fish, and *mandazi* (doughnuts).

Julius Nyerere, a chief's son educated at Makerere and Edinburgh, led TANU when it won independence for Tanzania in 1961, and in 1964 Tanganyika and the Zanzibar islands formed the United Republic of Tanzania. Nyerere, an intelligent dedicated socialist, tried to turn the country into a socialist state. But the unremitting hostility of Western capitalist states, including the United States, caused him difficulties.

In Portuguese colonies, nationalist parties had to fight long cruel guerrilla wars. War lasted eleven years in Mozambique and Guinea-Bissau. Impoverished though Mozambique was during this war, it sent help to the rebels in Zimbabwe, contributing to the victory of Robert Mugabe's ZANU and Joshua Nkomo's ZAPU decades later, in 1980. After Mozambique became independent, though, Southern Rhodesia retaliated by sending the Mozambique National Resistance (RENAMO), a terrorist force, into the country. After whites lost Rhodesia, South Africa backed a greatly expanded RENAMO, claiming that RENAMO wanted Mozambique to expel exiled ANC members, but even after Mozambique agreed to do this, it backed RENAMO terrorism.

Well-financed, armed, and trained RENAMO terrorists utterly disrupted life in rural Mozambique, destroying people, buildings, and vast areas of cultivated land. A third of Mozambican children, half in some regions, died before they reached five. Two hundred thousand children lost one or both parents to death or separation in 1986 alone. RENAMO massacred over 100,000 people in

1987–88. It targeted women, 80 percent of whom lived in rural areas and raised food. Most refugees in camps were women and children. It destroyed farms, so that people starved to death, and it ruined the economy.

Women in the Revolutions

Some nationalist groups put women's rights on their agendas. In the early 1920s the Kenyan East African Association protested the beating and sexual harassment of women on coffee estates. The assocation's leader, Harry Thuku, was arrested in 1922; the association demonstrated, but women members felt the men were too timid. Using their traditional form of bodily display (mooning) to express scorn and resentment, they led a crowd to the police station. But when the group became the Kikuyu Central Association (KCA), it barred women from meetings. Women joined the Mumbi Central Association until 1933, when KCA began accepting women members.

Women took part in armed struggle to the degree that men permitted. Guerrilla movements involve every segment of a population, but not all of them care about freeing women, and to make a commitment to liberate women, leaders first have to recognize their oppression.[43] Revolutionary leaders in Zimbabwe, Mozambique, Angola, and Guinea-Bissau consistently declared their commitment to free women from both colonial and customary domination by what they called degrading practices like polygyny and bridewealth. Women responded eagerly, especially young women educated through primary school. They were eager to end racial, economic, and sexual oppression, and worked as full partners in all phases of struggle. They were vital to the wars of independence in the Portuguese colonies, Tanzania, and Zimbabwe, all of which established socialist governments after liberation.

Robert Mugabe, head of ZANU and now of Zimbabwe, made a commitment to emancipate women. In 1979, he admitted:

Custom and tradition have tended more to favor men than women, to promote men and their status and demote women in status, to erect men as masters of the home, village, clan and nation. Admittedly, women have . . . been allowed sometimes a significant, but at other times a deplorably insignificant role to play. The general principle governing relationships between men and women has, in our traditional society, always been that of superiors and inferiors. Our society has consistently stood on the principle of masculine dominance – the principle that the man is the ruler and the woman his dependent and subject.[44]

A few women incorporated into armed units rose to leadership positions in Zimbabwe. Teurai Ropa, for instance, who finished military training at nineteen, was put on the General Staff of ZANLA, the ZANU army. Twenty-two years old in 1977, she was the youngest member of the ZANU Central Committee and National Executive, but the only woman to hold a ministerial post in Zimbabwe, as secretary for women's affairs. She describes women's activities:

Our women's brigade is involved in every sphere of the armed revolutionary struggle. Their involvement is total. In the frontline they transport war materials to the battlefield and . . . fight their way through enemy territory. . . . They teach the masses how to hide wounded comrades, hide war materials and carry intelligence reports behind enemy lines. . . . At the rear our women comrades' tasks are even more extensive. They are involved in every department of ZANU. They work as commanders, military instructors, political commissars, medical corps, teachers, drivers, mechanics, cooks, in logistics and supplies, information and publicity, as administrative cadres."[45]

After winning the war in Rhodesia early in 1980, ZANU ruled

independent Zimbabwe and soon restored old notions about women's place. In 1983 it launched a campaign to end prostitution, incarcerating several thousand women in prison camps.[46] Using a colonial vagrancy law, police arrested women in streets, hotels, cinemas – even at home – unless they showed proof of marriage or employment. Those without it were sent to a rural "resettlement camp." To arrest prostitutes without their customers is sexist, but it goes beyond anti-prostitution in aiming to impede women's freedom of movement. Prostitution is often the only profession in which women can earn enough to support their children. Anti-prostitution campaigns always aim mainly at women: male prostitutes are rarely arrested. In this case, the police targeted any woman without a male escort, any woman walking around the town.

Zimbabwean women's groups avoid confronting men. Focused on women, they exhort them to end their subservience and deference to men, yet do not exhort men to end their domineering parasitical behaviour. But women politicized during the war respond to reactionary campaigns with creative energy, forming clubs and cooperatives to teach women literacy and domestic science. They build irrigation systems for their fields, arrange revolving credit to buy seed, tools, and fertilizer, and pool resources for money-making projects like handicraft production. Their projects are local immediate responses to a need for income and collective child care, independent of government or party. They are also deeply political. Hundreds with low-level jobs in ZANU attend ZANU leadership-training courses. Even more striking are their spontaneous political protests, most often on economic issues such as rent strikes, food prices, or changes in trade licensing.

When politicians include women in nation-building or development, they usually view them as homemakers, and channel assistance to them through community development and social welfare agencies. Even in socialist states like Tanzania, where ex-President Nyerere supported feminism, men do not see women as economic beings, as producers needing land and jobs. Development schemes for registering and consolidating land gave land and its proceeds to men, totally ignoring women's work. The women so essential to TANU's 1950s success have vanished from public view.

Tanzania has suffered since independence, despite Nyerere's dedication and intelligence. Its mainly agricultural economy is in ruins, partly because development programs focused on men alone.[47] Nyerere resigned as president in 1985 after twenty-three years in office (he was succeeded by President Mwinyi). Before retirement, he pursued *ujamaa* (familyness), resettling peasants in collective villages, nationalizing factories and plantations, and building state-run corporations. He encouraged egalitarianism and discouraged the accumulation of private wealth, but was not deeply committed to sexual equality. One inescapable conclusion is that socialism cannot realize its ideals if it does not support sexual equality. Nyerere did emphasize literacy. Tanzania now enjoys one of the highest rates of primary-school enrolment and literacy in Africa, and has avoided the civil wars and tribal conflicts that plague many other African countries.[48] Tanzania no longer has a socialist economy, however.

In Mozambique, Samora Machel, FRELIMO head who became the country's president, called the emancipation of women "the fundamental necessity for the revolution, a guarantee of its continuity and a precondition for victory." But the government did not push moral change or urge men to alter the division of household labour during the war. And afterward, it did not integrate women in development policy, but stressed cash crops controlled by men. Machel's government did include women in party affairs, as well as village political and economic projects.

But politically active Mozambican women still have to raise both the food and the children; women still produce most household food. At the founding conference of the Organization of Mozambican Women (OMM) in 1973, Machel said, "Generally speaking, women are the most oppressed, humiliated and exploited beings in society."[49] Despite this, OMM was reluctant to question government agricultural policies, and focused on self-help, hygiene, and health. It shies away from disputing the sexual division of labour in and outside the household. Mozambican women are still indoctrinated to "speak with kind words" to husbands. Mozambique's "new women," who are literate, go to cities and work in factories, single by choice or abandoned by their husbands, have the same problems. Most have children and support them even if they have husbands. They are expected to feed the family themselves, even though they lack a *machamba* (family plot), hold jobs, and have husbands with jobs.

In 1986 Machel was killed in a mysterious plane crash over South Africa; the more "pragmatic" Joaquim Chissano became president and turned the country towards capitalism. He ended the pro-woman policy and the few women with high-ranking posts are in the predictable areas of education and social welfare.[50]

In Guinea-Bissau, Luís de Almeida Cabral, seeing the expulsion of the Portuguese as a phase in transition to a socialist society, considered the transformation of internal social relations, including sex relations, integral to his struggle.[51] Envisioning a revolutionary socialist society that would not need unemployment or divide workers and classes like capitalist societies, he stressed women's emancipation. PAIGC (African Party for the Independence of Guinea and Cape Verde) leaders knew women had to take the lead if male domination were to end, and saw that the key to perpetuating oppression lay in ideology, which enables a ruler to convince the oppressed to collude in their own servitude. Ideologies of oppression teach people they are inferior. PAIGC policy was articulated by PAIGC leader Carmen Pereira: "In Guinea-Bissau, we say that women are fighting two colonialisms – one against the Portuguese, the other against men." PAIGC encouraged women to rise up in the 1960s and early 1970s. Once aware of themselves as oppressed, they could envision a freer life. Maria S., an old peasant woman in Guinea-Bissau, explained: "We women really suffer. . . . It is very hard, our life. As for men, the only thing they do is till the land. We are responsible for everything after that. The women alone harvest the rice and we have to transport it without their help, to the village."[52]

When the rebels in Guinea-Bissau won a district, they put their revolutionary theories into practice, trying to raise political awareness, particularly women's. Guinea-Bissau was at war for two years, and its present state is dire.

In 1966, two years after war began in Mozambique, the FREL-IMO Central Committee decided to encourage women to take more active revolutionary roles by widening their range of political and military training. Men opposed this strongly, as a member of the Women's Detachment recalled:

> When we started to work there was strong opposition to our participation. Because that was against our tradition. We then started a big campaign explaining why we also had to fight, that the FRELIMO war was a people's war in which the whole population must participate, that we women were even more oppressed than men and that we therefore had the right as well as the will and the strength to fight. We insisted on our having military training and being given weapons.[53]

The Women's Detachment of the FRELIMO army was formed in 1967. As in Guinea-Bissau, when the rebels took a sector, they instituted revolutionary practices and education. Pauline Mateos, a seventeen-year-old commander in the FRELIMO Women's Detachment, led 200 female guerrillas fifteen and older in these liberated provincial areas. Not everyone embraced revolutionary politics: people had to be convinced, and women were expert at persuasion. Josina Machel, a top woman cadre in FRELIMO, said it was easier for women to approach other women and "men are more easily convinced of the important role of women when confronted with the unusual sight of confident and capable women militants who are themselves the best examples of what they are propounding."[54]

Women responded more eagerly than men to political mobilization because they were more oppressed. And with more to fight for, more to gain, they often surpassed men in political commitment.

Some PAIGC tactics were sexist: cadres urged politicized wives to taunt their husbands: "Go and join the fight. If you don't, I'll wear the pants and I'll go"; "If you don't join the fight, you can stay in the kitchen and do all the cooking and I'll go and join the guerrillas." Josina Machel said: "The presence of emancipated women bearing arms often shames [men] into taking more positive actions." A regional commander of PAIGC's local army reported that at the onset of war, recruiters would take a band of armed women to a village: "*All* the men would join up so as not to be shown up by the women!"[55] Sexist tactics were also effective in Zimbabwe.

Despite all this, and despite the fact that at the start of the war PAIGC trained women as combat guerrillas, when it reorganized the militia into a national army, it took women out of combat, leaving them only in village militias and in some local armed forces. They explained this spuriously: there were more than enough men in the army; working to overcome men's opposition to women slowed the war; women in liberated zones were to lay the groundwork for an egalitarian society *when war ended.* (They might as well have said *in heaven.*)

On the other hand, Cabral always downplayed the importance of military force, stressing more "feminine" activities (yet describing them as male): "Between one man carrying a gun and another carrying a tool, the more important . . . is the man with the tool. We've taken up arms to defeat the Portuguese, but the whole point of driving out the Portuguese is to defend the man with the tool."[56] Still, PAIGC practice sounds much like that of other religious and ideological revolutions.

Stephanie Urdang draws certain conclusions from the situation in Guinea/Cape Verde: no formal political policies of economic and political equality, not even revolutionary socialism, can realize equality unless individual male members of the ruling regime are actually committed to male-female equality; roles do not change, people change them; and while group strategies determine social processes, individual motivations matter.[57] Since relative peace has arrived in these nations only in the 1990s, and Cabral was assassinated, it is too soon to tell if the groundwork laid has diminished men's need for control.

In South Africa, when the ANC drew up a constitution in 1919, it denied women voting rights. It was not changed until 1943. The ANC auxiliary, Bantu Women's League, existed only to provide food and entertainment. The Industrial and Commercial Workers' Union (ICWU) also viewed women mainly as hostesses and wives until it went on strike in East London, South Africa, for six months in 1930. By the second week women were fully engaged.

In later years, however, the Congress Women's League organized huge demonstrations: police arrested over 2000 women demonstrating in Johannesburg in 1958.[58] South African women put the struggle for national liberation before their own. Their demonstrations against passes for women were rooted more in fear for their children than in the idea of women's rights. The government's system of removing men from their villages to work in mines and factories meant most men were absent most of the time. If women had had to carry passes, they would have been forced to work as live-in servants in white houses. In such jobs, they could not take their children, who would be virtually orphaned. They fought fiercely: 20,000 women demonstrated in Pretoria in 1956; protests became angrier as they spread to rural areas. In Bafarutshe Reserve near Botswana, women waged virtual war against those who cooperated in distributing passes.

The South African Black Women's Federation, launched and banned by the white government in the mid-1970s, linked regional women's groups into a new national women's federation in the 1980s, and the ANC finally accepted women in its training camps.

An African specialist writes: "If women's part in nationalist movements were known, Bibi Titi Mohammed, Lilian Ngoyi, Rebecca Njeri Kairi, and Wambui Wagarama would be as famous as Julius Nyerere, Nelson Mandela, and Jomo Kenyatta."[59] But most histories ignore women's activities.

African Women After Independence

Colonialism profoundly and irreversibly altered African society. The cash economy and technology introduced by Europeans and their appropriation of African land (much of which they kept after independence) changed life for both sexes, and both sexes were impoverished. But their situations were different.

African men suffered moral confusion from the collision of African custom and European law. Migrant workers endured sordid loneliness in European-run urban settlements. But men's traditional view of themselves did not change. In a cash economy they could earn money; although paid shamefully, they were still better off than women. They had sexual freedom, perhaps more than before, since prostitutes, concubines, and lovers were available and did not have to be married. Men retained dominance over their wives.

Women as a group were profoundly changed. African women's traditional identity was mainly as mothers. Most African societies endowed motherhood with a near-sacred mystique.[60] African women were happy to be called "mother of [their child]" rather than by their own names. They dreaded barrenness, and some had emotional breakdowns if they did not conceive. Men traditionally sent barren women back to their families, which had to return the brideprice, despite their reluctance to accept a woman whose brideprice might be forfeit forever. Childless women living with a husband's lineage had low status and bore an aura of malignancy. They became scapegoats during troubles, with no place in the community. Many societies refused to bury childless people, but threw their corpses into the bush for wild animals to eat.

Motherhood gave women status; agricultural work gave them

value as commodities, but only *men's* production brought status. Motherhood became even more important after slave trade, wars, and widespread female sterility (resulting from poverty, epidemics, and venereal diseases) depopulated Africa. A global economy and urbanization broke up the traditional family, heightening individualism, but colonial and African governments tried to keep women from becoming "individuals." They forced women to produce food and babies, while forcing or encouraging men to migrate and enter the modern sector. Women alone bore the burden of feeding the community, raising cash crops and rearing children, but they were not rewarded despite their work – harder than before – and their added responsibility. Status now came from money, and women could not even pay for taxes or children's education. When motherhood no longer conferred status, many women developed "dread of motherhood" and resisted having children. Men fought this with harsh controls like divorce for childlessness, but women still hardened towards motherhood.[61]

In Africa, celibacy was traditionally a crime against society, but today's educated young women with good jobs often reject marriage, preferring economic autonomy. In Kenya, where women can inherit and own property, 24 percent of women aged twenty to twenty-four were single in 1984; in 1989, 32 percent.[62] Many feel men are parasites on women. African women do not trust men because they shirk responsibility for supporting their children. In socialist Tanzania, where women are increasingly being pushed into subordination by male appropriation of land, women call marriage "male colonization" and say it is too expensive to maintain a husband.[63]

The keystone of traditional African social organization was control of the labour of women and young men. Production was organized through the family, by male control over access to women – marriage. To control women was to control both production and the reproduction of the production force. All hierarchies – age, status, or power – aimed at this. Colonialism disrupted the traditional family by destabilizing the cornerstone of the economic and social system. Today, economic pressures force most Africans to live in nuclear families, a system alien to other customs, which works under different laws. In many towns, family structures have changed but laws have not. Both matrilineal and patrilineal societies allowed polygyny: marriage, a union of lineages, gave the group stability and continuity. Marriage was fragile, lineage permanent. Such societies see nuclear families as ephemeral.

Pro-natal African governments pressure women to have large families, which many women still consider necessary to their emotional and economic well-being. In most of Africa abortion is illegal and contraception contentious, so unmarried girls leave school to bear children. Propaganda warns that the family is imperilled, not by irresponsible men, but by working women. In 1974 the National Council of Catholic Women in Lusaka declared: "The woman worker ought to know that her income is only a supplement to her husband's income: she ought to be fully aware of her responsibilities as a mother and a wife and never neglect them for the sake of extra-domestic work." A Ghanian woman's magazine lectures: "Women who talk of liberation seem to forget that they were born to be subordinate to men. Many modern families have been wrecked by the attitude of females who have found this hard to accept – educated women. You can see them treat their husbands with a heavy hand, and keep the house and the purse strings under strict control: they actually dominate the man."[64]

Few African women are exposed to ideas that could liberate them. In authoritarian states, political groups are controlled by the government, which forbids independent women's liberation groups and may curb local groups. South Africa backed its coherent national policy of repression with enough force to have widespread effect. The only channels of protest – underground revolutionary parties or movements – were dangerous.[65]

Marriage, Brideprice, and Polygyny

Africa is made up of thousands of small societies: no generalization about any facet of women's lives is true for all. Indeed, all generalizations can be contradicted. Rules governing puberty rites, marriage, brideprice, divorce, and polygyny vary among societies: we do not even know all the variations. What follows is drawn from studies with broad application.

In laws governing marriage, governments consider women's rights but try mainly to avoid offending men, and so do not outlaw traditional customs like bridewealth, polygyny, and clitoridectomy. Laws make more women prefer single motherhood to the constraints of marriage, yet most women marry at some point in their lives. But marriage does not ease most women's lot. Mobility has weakened kinship and marriage bonds, especially in cities. Men, the wage earners, often work far from their homes. Few women can get jobs and farm, sew, or trade. But in a cash economy, they need money and are therefore dependent on men. In some societies, a groom pays a lineage and removes a wife over whom he has virtual rights of *patriapotestas*: young husbands are arrogant in ways they would never have dared to show earlier. Many men beat their wives. Men of different generations lack harmony: men who pay for boys' education demand repayment; fathers or uncles choose a boy's wife, dowry, and marriage rites, invariably choosing a village girl who has been raised to be inferior to her husband. Some boys resent this, wanting congenial educated wives, and may marry the village girl (without her consent) *and* an urban woman (with mutual consent).[66]

Women, caught between Western ideals of love and attraction, and traditional ideals like chastity, find chastity hard to maintain and marriage hard without it. An educated woman who wants to marry well has trouble finding a man and may become the lover ("outside wife") of a married professional. Having two wives and many children gives men status, and few are faithful. Women tolerate infidelity if men are discreet and maintain the family's social and financial status, but outside children cause conflict.

In much of Africa, families marry adolescent girls to much older men, but increasingly women in their twenties marry men their own age. Young people are freer to choose their own partners than in precolonial times; marriage is less an alliance between lineages and more a matter of personal preference as migration and education weaken parents' control of daughters. Some societies have abandoned traditional marriage ceremonies and marriage contracts bridging gendered economic spheres. But without an economic base, marriage suffers from a weak core. Some couples suffer because they cannot talk together. Bemba boys and girls are separated young and never play together; after puberty, male and female siblings live in separate huts. Adults eat and live in segregated units; even community life is segregated. Bemba girls are taught that "a good wife does not talk with her husband. A good wife is expected to go to her man's bed early in the morning and ask him if he has anything to tell her."

Urban couples also live this way. The Ga in Accra maintain their custom of spouses living either in separate houses or separate parts of a house; women or children take food to the men, and women occasionally stay overnight with their husbands. In Tema (an industrial town in Ghana), 82 percent of women live alone; 58 percent of Accra's married women do not live with their husbands. But only 7 percent of married male wage-earners do not live with a wife. (Men are happier about this than women; men like to live with women less for companionship than comfort.[67])

In urban Zambia, educated women tend to avoid marriage yet depend on men's contributions to their lifestyle, but poor market women still raise their daughters traditionally, forcing them to be mutilated and teaching them to subordinate themselves to their husbands. At the same time, they insist that the institution of marriage requires drastic reform. In a study of men of various ethnic groups, all agreed that women who worked in towns were too "big-headed" to accept male control; even those whose wives did not work for wages lamented that women needed not men, but their money.[68] Some, mainly Luo men, wanted wives who were willing to live in villages, and had no "fancy ideas" about urban jobs. But many preferred women who worked: about twenty young men admitted they asked women if they worked before becoming seriously involved with them. They wanted financial assets.

A man starting to date a working woman heaps her with gifts, hoping she will reciprocate. If she does not, he drops her as cheap. Men and women struggle to save money: economic security is more important than romance or sexual attraction. Many urban young men attach themselves to older women, who are more willing than young women to support them. Students, clerks, and unemployed school drop-outs are kept, fed, and clothed by older women but still have sex with younger women (whom they accused of stinginess). The woman lover of one young man bought him land in a village, built him a house, and bought him a wife. Through contacts, she got him a job as a coffee maker at a government office. Many Ganda men in rural areas live this way, and most successful independent female householders have younger lovers whom they pay taxes for, feed, and clothe.

Women bear such heavy economic burdens that they need help from others. But marriage bonds are fragile and kinship ties are attenuated by migration, leaving urban women with no help with children. Africa has no nurturant male model: many African women now view relationships with men instrumentally, using them to get resources and a chance to further their social and economic ambitions.[69] African society condemns women (but not men) who marry for economic gain, yet traditional African marriage was always an economic partnership. But now, women increasingly choose their partners. Many choose to remain independent, especially educated women with good jobs. Many professional women refuse to marry polygynists, refusing to share a husband and his resources with another woman and her children. Yet they rarely find the faithful monogamous marriages they want: most men have outside wives or lovers. Elite women are more likely now than in the past to live with their husbands apart from their matrikin, and are devastated if the men take second wives or abandon them.

The introduction of money sent brideprice soaring. Seen as payment for potential offspring, brideprice recompenses a woman's lineage for the appropriation of her children by a man's lineage. Bridewealth turns women into commodities, and the higher price women fetch, the more jealously men (mainly fathers and brothers) guard them to guarantee their chastity. Thus bridewealth puts women under male surveillance and control throughout their lives.

Divorce is fairly common throughout much of Africa but the rules governing it vary greatly. It is often easy and mutually available, but in patrilineal societies women cannot initiate divorce at all. Divorced women often choose what the Asante call "lover marriage," a long-term informal sexual relationship with a man. After the Second World War, the Ewe of Southern Ghana virtually abandoned traditional and Christian marriage rituals. Even earlier, divorce was common because Ewe women held land rights from their matrikin and could support their children. Many prefer to live alone, and the number of woman-headed households is growing.

In Europe death ends a marriage, and survivors, free of all marital duties, may remarry. This is not always true in Africa. In many societies, widows may not remarry or have a sexual liaison until they have ritual sex with the husband's successor and mourn for a given period. A woman who does not fufil these obligations has essentially committed adultery; the dead husband's kin can demand damages from the next man she has sex with or from her. In colonial times, men abused these rituals: the dead man's kin would demand cash or goods to free a woman, or procrastinate in naming the surrogate husband to keep her bound to the clan, producing food. All women's organizations today, even conservative groups, urge abolition of these customs.

Polygyny is almost universal in Africa. Patrilineal groups favour it because they get the children. It is hard for men in matrilineages to have many wives: wives remain with their natal families and a man would have to visit wives in different villages. Some matrilineages require a wife's consent to a husband's polygyny; patrilineages never do – in principle. In principle, men must treat wives impartially, maintain each in her own house, giving a senior wife certain prerogatives. But sometimes relations between co-wives are bad and lead to accusations of witchcraft. Women use magic to harm each other, or give men drugs to keep them from having erections with another wife. Emotional insecurity and rivalry can arouse a wife's hatred for a man and her children by him. Some women go mad repressing emotions considered unacceptable in their society. Women's emotional state worsens during pregnancy, when husbands cohabit only with other wives.

Rural Women

The effects of colonialism pervade Africa even after independence. African men still raise cash crops on women's land, and women still do the work, and work to feed the family. Men do not share the money they earn from cash crops with women or their children. In most places, men took the best land, expecting women to feed the community on the land that was left. Corrupt governments often do not pay men either, but men spend what money they get on capital investment like trucks or fertilizer. Generally, women and children eat more poorly than men and have high mortality rates. Colonists and postcolonial development experts gave men tools and advice on raising cash crops or encouraged their migration to plantations, mines, or towns to work, leaving women at home trying to feed all of society.[70]

During colonialism, Europeans introduced cocoa as a cash crop in southern Ghana. Women worked their husbands' cocoa farms and produced their families' food. Women own only 5 percent of cocoa farms, and those are small. Cocoa prices fell in the 1960s, and men used to cash migrated to towns for work, leaving the women to feed themselves, the children, the elders, the sick and impaired. The trend begun during the colonial era of giving women sole responsibility for subsistence has continued, but cocoa farms monopolize the best land despite the fall in price and women must feed the community on increasingly infertile land. To supplement their poor yields, many combine farming with trade, food processing, and waged labour – when they can get it.

Luo, Luyia, and Gusii men in western Kenya control women by controlling access to land: women have no rights to land or child custody in their fathers' lineage. Most men migrate, leaving women to work the land. But for access to land and livestock, a woman must be married. By making it nearly impossible for women to survive outside marriage, these groups put the responsibility for maintaining marriages on women. Marriage is extraordinarily stable: landless women are reluctant to leave their children. But husbands cannot divorce women who have had their children and farmed their land. If a husband dies, the lineage gives the wife to another man, so she retains access to land. The growing influence of Christianity, which disapproves of such levirate marriage, has led some women to refuse new husbands. But those who do lose access to land, animals, and their children.[71] The only alternatives to marriage are prostitution or woman-woman marriage, but it is hard for a woman to amass enough wealth to buy a woman.[72] Moreover, employers expect the wives of migrant male labourers to feed them, so they pay scanty wages and men send little money home. Western Kenya's soil has lost its fertility and most plots are small: women own only 5 percent of individually held land titles. They are in a desperate condition.

Among the worst hit women are South Africans, who live in deep poverty with almost no way to earn money. Women and children suffer extreme malnutrition, and infant mortality rates are staggering. In South Africa, 95 percent of wage-earners work in Lesotho and 70 percent of rural households are run by women whose farming brings in almost no cash and too little food to sustain them. To supplement occasional remittances and bridewealth payments from husbands, they farm cooperatively, brew beer, trade, and sell sex.

Increased trade throughout Africa has helped some women grow more economically and personally independent, weakening the control of husbands and kin groups. But husbands and lineages give women less economic support and help in child care (this preceded female independence, is not a consequence of it), and women cannot get capital, so cannot enlarge petty local trade operations in low-margin items into more profitable long-distance trade in commodities and manufacture. Yet, according to the World Bank, women produce 70 percent of Africa's food, without tractors, oxen, or even plows. Beyond survival – and many do not survive – few are rewarded for this productiveness. In ten African countries where women and children make up 77 percent of the population, women have the legal right to own property in only 16 percent of households.[73]

Urban Women

Dire conditions in the countryside impel women to go to cities. It is hard for women to find work in towns but enterprising women increasingly do so, some with their husbands. In most cities, employers did not hire women for wages until after the Second World War. In South Africa, Kenya, and Mozambique, local industries hired a few women to process food or tobacco and manufacture clothing. Industry hired large numbers of women during the Mau Mau revolt of 1952–56 in Kenya, but fired them when men again became available. Many women now work in factories and service industries in South Africa, the most industrialized African country. They do low-paid, semi-skilled work, most in clothing or food processing or preparation, at least until machines are introduced, when men usually replace them. More women are clamouring for work but many employers will not hire women.

One job that opened to African women was domestic service, in cities like Lourenco Marques (Maputo) and Johannesburg, and in

Kenya to Kikuyu women. The lowest-paid, most exploited of all urban workers (especially in South Africa), servants are often required to live in an employer's house, where they cannot raise their own children. The system has made it impossible for them to support and care for their children at the same time. Female domestic servants have little bargaining power and employers make extraordinary demands on their time. Young women with urban kin often work as servants for them in exchange for their school fees.

Even in cities, men expect women to take exclusive responsibility for feeding the children. Many urban women now are single heads of household, juggling to survive by various independent casual jobs and through relationships with men, which they manipulate to their own advantage with extreme skill. Women must be resourceful and motivated enough to create a job. Their usual resorts – petty trading and preparing food – are saturated. Many become prostitutes. A study in Kinshasa (Zaire) showed prostitutes earned a higher income than any other women and many men. But they must earn it every day to feed their children. Those with husbands who contribute to their support work only when they need money.

Some African societies were stratified before colonialism, but class distinctions were neither universal nor commonplace. Now most people are ranked by class, age, and status. Stratification is paradoxical for women, for whom higher status often means less freedom. In some regions, some women found jobs in industry or large-scale agricultural projects, gaining enterprise and autonomy.

Birth Control

In Africa fewer than 5 percent of couples use modern contraceptives. People in many non-industrialized societies tend to resist contraception: many children die, and couples produce prolifically hoping a few will survive. Many African men fear contraception will free women sexually from their control. Some Zambian family planning clinics require women to bring letters of permission from their husbands before they help them.

Yet many African men shirk responsibility for the children they father, thinking of children as a kind of free good: once they have secured a wife, blessings will flow to them. While men monopolize the benefits of a wage economy, women, often malnourished to start with are further depleted by long, often uninterrupted breast-feeding, feeding, clothing, sheltering, and educating their children. They pay for babies in hard labour and bodily wear and tear. Women in industrialized nations bear children over a three- to five-year period; African women bear them over eighteen to twenty years; between two and six of every 1000 African women die in childbirth, 100–500 times the Western European rate.

Men oppose contraceptives even though AIDS, transmitted heterosexually in Africa, has spread like rumour through Zambia, Zaire, Burundi, Rwanda, Uganda, and Tanzania, and more slowly in Kenya, Congo, Zimbabwe, and Malawi. Half the adults in Uganda, the worst-hit country, may have AIDS. In Botswana and Zimbabwe, a quarter of all adults are infected, according to UNAIDS.[74] Thirty to forty percent of military and civilian leaders in some states are believed infected. Men also refuse to be tested or allow their wives to be tested for AIDS. African women gladly use contraceptives if they can get them, but they are legal in few states, and men oppose their use. Legality makes contraceptives morally acceptable and more available, bolstering the resolve of women willing to break with tradition and defy their husbands. Contraceptive use has more than doubled in Zimbabwe in the last five years to about 27 percent.

Family planning and health programs tend to fail with illiterate women, but some planners offer basic literacy. There is a close correlation between women's education and children's health – in Kenya, for instance, women's education seems responsible for over an 80 percent drop in infant mortality in the last twenty years. It is understandable that people whose traditional religion centred on fertility find contraception immoral. Historians are unsure how widespread traditional beliefs are today, but more than any other people in the world, Africans want many children.

Education, Religion, and Political Participation

Although male sexism is the major impediment to waged work for African women, they are also hampered by lack of education. Formal education in Africa discriminated against females from the start, in accord with both Western and African mores. Families wanted girls locked into field- and homework, and feared education might free them to abandon these. Most West Africans are illiterate; only a small elite is literate, fewer girls than boys. Girls who go to school rarely go beyond the primary level.

Most African governments dismiss female education. In Ghana, which supported it more than other African states, in 1960, at the end of the colonial period, 33 percent of girls and 54 percent of boys of fifteen had any schooling. In 1970, after a decade of independence, 62.6 percent of boys and 53.4 percent of girls 6–14 were in school. But older students were mainly male – 36.5 percent of males and 16.6 percent of females 15–24, 0.3 percent of males and 0 females 25 and older. In 1971 Zaire (now Congo), women were 5 percent of university students; in 1974, one in thirteen; in 1975, one in ten.

In new African states, Africans were hired in high-ranked jobs in government and industry. As they expanded female education, they began to hire educated professional women – but most in stereotypic low-paid female fields. Educated women, denied the high pay they deserve, often use men (the deniers) to support them in luxurious lifestyles. A very few Western-educated women work in acceptably female professions like teaching, nursing, and social welfare. In sex-segregated Mombasa, Muslim men require women in such jobs to deal only with women. Swahili women were encouraged to educate themselves for professional work, but the small Christian elite encourages domestic dependency for women.

The increasing stratification of women creates great tension as more girls go on to university to become teachers, nurses, and secretaries and others rise in the social hierarchy by careful marriages.

Women's groups claim to speak for all women yet may define lower-class women in ways that suit elite interests. In the 1970s Maendeleo, Kenya's major national women's organization, was a militant group fighting for all women's rights, but under a dictatorial regime, it became the organ of an exclusive, politically connected urban elite alienated from rural members.

Women's changing role touches the profoundest level of people's feelings. What the West calls subconscious behaviour, Africans may see as witchcraft. As women's power and independence erode, some resort to witchcraft, often a source of female cohesion and strength.[75] For Luo women of Kenya and Tanzania, relations with a husband's family are primary: a woman spends her life with them, yet they treat her with suspicion until she has a child. Even then, her mother-in-law or other female kin may compete with her to keep her from getting enough land and cattle to maintain her husband and children. Living in perpetual insecurity and struggle, she may flare up in "possession" when tension becomes unbearable. Women use accusations of witchcraft to eject or socially demote weaker females, especially old women. Older women, who used to have high status, may be blamed for all the ills affecting other women in the family. This is partly because of education: educated young women have higher status than their female elders and feel guilty about it, while the older women resent it. Mutual bad feelings generate accusations of witchcraft.

Women, the mainstay of most independent Christian communities, outnumber male members two-to-one, and support the priests with their labour. They conduct choirs and organize mutual aid, social activities, and prayer meetings for the sick. But the few male members aged twenty-five to forty-five monopolize all the responsible positions in the congregations, and young men who attend sect schools look down on elders. Women are drawn to these churches by a need for a social and emotional centre; most are marginal in their society.

Many African churches are independent – that is, they are controlled by Africans and reject some tenets of their father churches.

Most independent churches broke away over women's issues – genital mutilation and polygyny. All independent African Christian churches tolerate polygyny but try to limit it by demoting polygynous men from prestigous positions. African Christian churches stress respect for wives. The Congolese Jamaa movement stresses the creation of a vital bond between mates through mutual respect and comradeship. Jamaa women, less inhibited than other women, are freer to speak out and manage social functions; some Jamaa husbands even help in the house. Thus, many men suspect the movement. They resent losing their prerogative as "*bwana*, the household head, who reigns over his woman and his children."[76] Men often demand that their wives give up their membership or be divorced. Many new religions are extremely reactionary.

In urban areas of northern Sudan, Muslim men keep women secluded and segregated, but women meet each other at *zaar*, spirit-possession ceremonies, multi-ethnic events with regular meetings for dance, and healing rituals. They do not challenge their confinement or infibulation, which in this century marks middle-class status for women. In some regions religion is blatantly used to enforce patriarchy.[77] Women in the matrilineal Malawi village of Magomero who have lost economic power adopt their husbands' religion, although it supports patrilineal inheritance to their detriment: dependency generates self-destruction.

Men associate women's religions with reactionary politics, claiming that women are conservative by nature. In truth, "modernization" is masculinization; new methods narrow experience into linear progress towards a goal and ends into means or instruments. From the beginning of Western "modernization," in the fourteenth century, it belittled "feminine" activities like procreation and maintenance as marginal non-work requiring no skill and deserving no reward. But far more than Western women, African women have been denied a chance to become modern at even the lowest level, as factory and office workers. Bound to the land, expected to procreate and support the community by agricultural labour even as this became impossible, African women often support conservative positions. For example, in Nigeria, Ibo women futilely protested the introduction of oil-mills, which improved the quality and quantity of palm oil and raised the average wage. They did so because only men could run the oil-mills. Formerly, women prepared the oil and their husbands sold it, and women kept part of it to sell and keep the profits. Now, they get nothing.

After almost three decades of independence, only five states have multi-party systems (Senegal, Gambia, Botswana, Madagascar, and Mauritius). Thirty-eight of the forty-five African states have single-party systems or no parties at all: over half are ruled by military governments that exclude women from authority. But few African states grant women many rights. Many, such as the Pare district of Tanzania or Lesotho, limit women's participation in political process to the local level and allow even that only where there are few men. In twenty-nine states, women vote, are elected to legislatures, fill professional or high-ranking government jobs, yet remain minors, needing a father's consent to their marriage whatever their age or experience, even if they are widows. The Ibo and Yoruba dual-sex systems, which gave women political power through parallel institutions, have changed to a Western unisex model favouring men. Nigerian women no longer have much political voice: few are elected to office: those in office are appointed by men and are indebted to them.[78] In the north, a Muslim government has installed *shari'a* law. Some African states passed laws that improve women's situation but don't enforce them.

African men insist on a double standard. For example, Tanzanian men are extremely promiscuous, but try to keep their wives from working outside the home where they might meet other men, and from using contraceptives, which would free them to choose their own sexual life. Africans also tend to scapegoat women. Throughout Africa, all problems – high divorce rates, illegitimacy, or the vanishing of African customs – are blamed on women. Young urban women especially are verbally and physically abused for wearing make-up, mini-skirts, or foreign hairstyles. Irresponsible promiscuous men condemn professional women who marry late or never, for immorality. Such scapegoating, hardly unique to Africa, is especially strong in societies with strong Western influence. In Africa, as in other post-colonial societies, men justify imposing constrictions on women by invoking "authenticity," claiming that as the bearers of African (or Islamic, or Hindu) culture, women must be protected from Western influences like cosmetics, wigs, or short skirts. Men who are unable to withstand neocolonial forces that subordinate Africa demand women do so.

They demand mainly symbolic "authenticity" – clothes, hairstyles, or sexual habits minimally affect economic or political systems. But men's surveillance of women's dress and morality keeps women from being effective in the political arena. A sex that is constantly being corrected is unlikely to be taken seriously in the political realm. The few brave women who do enter politics are continually reminded by hecklers *and friends* that their proper place is "beside the three cooking stones with the children." Single or persistent women are discredited by charges of sexual immorality. But women fight back.

Women's Protests since Independence

Market women and beer-brewers in Nairobi and Kampala created formal support organizations, sometimes investing their funds in collective enterprises. Women traders in Lusaka formed groups to protest their economic grievances. In Nakuru, a small town in Kenya, women formed associations to buy farmland collectively, with some success. Urban Zambian women use "love medicines" to get control of their marital and economic lives. Kenyan Masai women unite to protect women charged with adultery. The sustained pressure of Sudanese women's groups forced legal reform of women's economic and family position. But the Women's Union has been careful not to attack strongly held "traditions" like infibulation. The Somali government supported a campaign against infibulation by the Women's Democratic Organization in 1977.

Most significant are female industrial workers in South Africa, who were deeply involved in labour protest in the 1970s and 1980s. In the 1990s, a few active women trade unionists forcefully protested the division of time and labour in the household. Women organized squatters groups, struck over rents, and protested as members of women's organizations, parents of young children were arrested by the government, and were taken political prisoner in the liberation movement of the 1980s. South Africa has vigorous articulate political women across the board, but the younger generation of African men has been making very strong anti-woman statements that the older generation symbolized by Nelson Mandela does not counter.

Still, more and more women are speaking out politically. In Birnin Kudu in 1988, Nigeria's former first lady, Maryam Babangida, held a women's conference, "Better Life for Rural Women," inspiring Ladi Adamu, a Fulani, to run in the first Nigerian election since 1983. As an appointed councillor, she built support among rural women by teaching villagers about immunization, digging wells, installing modern water pumps, and building roads to remote villages in the countryside. She was elected to the new thirteen-member local government council, but its chairman, Falalu Mohammed Rukur Gantsa, a *mallam* (Islamic teacher), denied her an office, secretary, car, or portfolio.[79] When the council goes on official inspections, Gantsa puts the men in air-conditioned cars and sends Adamu in a pickup truck. In a 1980s debate on women, all speakers were men. When government councillor Adamu stood to speak, the chairman cut the power off. She held a dead microphone. Adamu says, "In this part of the country, people always think that a woman who speaks out must not follow tradition and must be a prostitute." The chairman's hatred wins her the people's sympathy.

Ugandan president Yower Museveni's government is working to rebuild the country after two decades of devastating violence caused by male rivalry and a murderous ruler, Idi Amin. Museveni's regime is one of the most progressive in Africa on the subject of women.[80] He has appointed women to his cabinet, even to the vital post of Minister of Agriculture. Every parliamentary district reserves an at-large seat for a woman. But over 80 percent of the mostly illiterate population live in the country. As educated people returned from exile after the civil war following Idi Amin's brutal rule, women attorneys started the Uganda Association of Women Lawyers and a Women's Legal Aid Clinic to help uneducated poor women, which teach rural women their legal rights and visit rural villages to talk to them.[81] Women do not know wife-beating is illegal or that unless the state recognizes a marriage, a woman is not legally married and lacks protection if her husband dies. In Buwunga, Sarah Bahalaal-iwo, chairwoman of the Association, sat on the grass with local women, telling them about their right to own property: "If you inherit land from your father or earn enough to buy some yourself, register it in your own name, not your husband's. A husband may try to take all the household possessions during a divorce or separa-tion. He might beat you up, but don't give in. Fight back."

Even politically prominent women are abused. The Kenyan government planned to build a $200-million sixty-storey tower, the tallest commercial structure in Africa, to hold a larger-than-life statue of President Daniel Arap Moi.[82] It was to be erected in Uhuru Park, a popular downtown park, but Kenya cannot afford it – already $400 million in debt, Kenya is seeking loans for an oil pipeline, a sugar project, and equipment for Kenya Airways. But Kenyans know they have to keep their mouths shut. The only per-son daring enough to protest was Professor Wangari Maathai, head of the Green Belt Movement, an environmental group.

Maathai studied on scholarship in the United States in the 1960s, and became a professor of veterinary medicine at the Uni-versity of Nairobi. Her husband, a member of Parliament, sued for divorce, charging her with adultery with another Parliament mem-ber. She lost. When she accused the judge of incompetence, he jailed her, releasing her only after she promised to apologize.

Deciding to run for Parliament, she resigned her university chair only to discover that a technicality disqualified her. She then devoted herself to the Green Belt Movement, run by the National Women's Council of which she was chair. The movement plants trees to beautify the land, stop soil erosion, provide fuel (which helps women), and earn women income: for each tree surviving over three months outside the nursery, the woman who planted it earns 50 Kenya cents (2.3 cents US), often the only cash she earns. Maathai won a United Nations Environmental Program Global 500 award for protecting the environment.

When the tower was announced, Maathai filed a lawsuit contending that Uhuru Park was the wrong place for it: the suit was dismissed. When she urged that the tower be built elsewhere, prominent politicans and the president attacked her. Kenyan police evicted her group from its building. The president said his opponents "had insects in their heads" – a woman ought to know that Kenyan tradition forbade a woman from criticizing a man. Chances are that the tower will not be built or will not be so tall – but not because of Maathai. To date, it is not built, and Moi is no longer in power.

Other educated women take risks to help poor women. Female doctors and health workers organize locally against clitoridectomy and infibulation. African women work with the global women's movement and write world literature. Among the female writers best known outside Africa are Buchi Emecheta and Flora Nwapa of Nigeria, Grace Ogot of Kenya, and South African Bessie Head, who now lives in Botswana, Miriam Tlali of South Africa (the first South African woman to have her work published outside the country), and Mariama Ba of Senegal.[83]

Women's Experience in Socialist States

In 1952, overriding the desire of a majority of Eritreans for independence, the United Nations federated it with Ethiopia, but guaranteed it democratic rights. Over a decade, Ethiopian emperor Haile Sellassie abolished those rights. Demonstrations and appeals to the UN in protest won Eritreans only more repressive controls. In 1961 a desperate populace formed the Eritrean Liberation Front (ELF) and rose up in arms. The leaders of the ELF were mostly chiefs from the north, traditional Muslims. Women involved in 1950s protests and an underground independence movement joined the ELF to fight for independence, but it did not want them participating, and sent women who came to fight in the 1960s to work in offices in neighbouring Sudan. (A maxim in Eritrean society is "women and donkeys are made to be beaten.")

In 1970 a group of intellectual, left-leaning, socially conscious Eritreans founded the Eritrean People's Liberation Front (EPLF), and in 1972 a virtual civil war exploded between the two groups, which reconciled in 1974. The EPLF was committed to democracy and wanted to eliminate discrimination against women and other Eritrean minorities. EPLF encouraged women's participation, and many women joined. At first, men aspersed women in EPLF military forces as weak and treated them as dangerously divisive temptations. But as the EPLF got control of more territory, women were highly successful in promoting egalitarian land reform (the EPLF distributes land to women *and* men), education for Muslim females, and more egalitarian marriage. By 1978 women made up 13 percent of EPLF soldiers and those in local militias in villages and towns under EPLF control. A year later, they were 13 percent of front-line fighters and 30 percent of the EPLF as a whole; by 1989, they were 23 percent of front-line fighters and 40 percent of the front as whole. They were still excluded from the upper ranks of the organization; at the first EPLF congress in 1977, women were 10 percent of delegates but not one was elected to the Central Committee. At the second, in 1988, about 25 percent of delegates were women and 8 percent (six) were elected to the Central Committee.[84]

The ELF became defunct in 1981, and the EPLF controls Eritrea. The government claims to remain committed to women's equality, and the new constitution, passed in 1997, guarantees equality on the basis of sex and other qualities. However, war broke out between Eritrea and Ethiopia in 2000, and after an agreement between the opponents, a UN peacekeeping force occupied the country. Education is a priority in the country: most Eritreans are illiterate, women more than men: in 1980, 95 percent of women were illiterate; in 1988, 90 percent, as of 2000, 85 percent.[85] Women were 53 percent of students before a terrible drought; over 27,000 women registered for literacy courses in 1983, but only 9390 attended, because people fled their villages during a famine that year. At the largest EPLF child's school (Revolution School), girls comprised nearly half of the students in the late 1980s and over a third of the teachers were female. In 1988, women were over half the first graduating class of the EPLF Institute of Technology.

As a *de facto* government, the EPLF redistributed land extensively, assigning it not to households, but to individuals, including women, who now have legal rights to land. About 80 percent of the population live by agriculture and/or herding; families raise subsistence crops but it is taboo for women to plow. Men are forcibly conscripted, or go to Arab countries or the Sudan for waged work, or graze herds wherever they can; women must support the children. Many female-headed households are in precarious condition. The EPLF urges village cooperatives to work land for the disabled and plow for women without men but some women defy the century-old taboo and plow. They are beginning to enter agricultural training programs; eighty women were graduated in 1985. Women participate in the government: 30 percent of the seats in Parliament are reserved for them, and as of 2000 there were two female ministers in the cabinet and two female ambassadors.

Rural women train to be health workers and tailors, facing obstacles in the latter, traditionally considered men's work. Many women went to Asmara to work in the 1950s; they now make up about 40 percent of permanent workers and 72.9 percent of permanent employees in textile factories. Most are unskilled and poorly paid.

Progressive laws governing marriage, divorce, child custody, property ownership, and equal pay have abolished child marriages and arranged marriages, and granted women custody of children and economic support after divorce. But the most significant change may be EPLF pressure on men to take responsibility for maintaining the community: "All fighters, men and women, commanders and rankers, share cooking, fetching wood and water, and cleaning."[86] "You see men looking after children everywhere in Eritrea," writes a scholar.[87] But men not under military discipline do not share in household work or child care, although the peasant association tries to teach them about equality. Two scholars report widespread male resistance to change, and the government has a habit of taking over female projects.[88]

The defeat of Portugal by FRELIMO and the MPLA in Mozambique and Angola reverberated through European-dominated colonies, and sent a wave of hope through the black townships of South Africa.[89] Hope revived the dormant tradition of resistance, drew an angry young generation into the ANC, and fuelled 1976 student uprisings. Mozambique sacrificed to help Africans win Zimbabwe; when Angola won independence in 1975, it sacrificed to support SWAPO, the military wing of the Namibian liberation movement, which provided bases and refuge for civilians fleeing South Africa's *apartheid* army. Without Angolan support, Namibia would still be a South African colony; without Cuban support, Angola could not have helped Namibia.[90] When South African troops invaded Angola at Cuito Cuanavale, 50,000 Cuban soldiers helped the Angolans stop them in perhaps the most crucial military confrontation in the region since the Boer War.

But victory costs as much as defeat and one cost is the ideals that fuelled the fight. In Mozambique and Angola, revolutionary socialist ideals have almost been extinguished by sorrow, hunger, and destruction. Africa's capitalist autocracies suffer too: children in Malawi, closely allied with the United States and South Africa, die faster than perhaps any others on earth. Most of the problem arose from South Africa's relentless determination to destabilize these countries. With rich natural resources extracted by cheap African labour kept subordinate by apartheid, white South Africa made itself a power machine. The measurable costs of destabilization surpass $60 billion, or two-fifths of the gross domestic products of all these countries, by UN estimates. The immeasurable costs are refugees irremediably scarred by grief and rage, millions of deaths, and the ideals that inspire revolutions – which would, if realized, improve everyone's life.

Political ideals die in socialist *and* capitalist states: the multiparty governments of Zimbabwe and Botswana used the South African threat to justify repressive legislation restricting the right to dissent; Mugabe made Zimbabwe a single-party system. Fifteen years of war against the United States and South Africa have strengthened the MPLA, Angola's ruling party, but have also made it more politically rigid, and despite a treaty, the civil war continues intermittently. In Zimbabwe, whites still own most of the best farmland, although Mugabe is now pursuing a policy of land appropriation. White power structures quietly work to secure control of South Africa's economy despite the ANC victory. The government sold off the state iron and steel company; the De Beers company, subsidiary of a huge Anglo-American transnational conglomerate that dominates South African mining, moved half its assets to a new holding company in Switzerland.

That no socialist state created in this century has been humane, just, or egalitarian, is partly a result of our almost universal faith in domination, government from above. One cannot deplore the decline of Soviet hegemony over eastern Europe or of single-party governments in Africa. The governing party of the Congo officially abandoned Marxist ideology in 1990, adopting a social democratic platform. In 1991, after over two decades of one-party politics, it legalized opposition parties. Huge protests in Benin forced the president, Mathieu Kerekou, to grant multi-party elections and disavow Marxism-Leninism. Nyerere supported competing parties in

Tanzania. Autocratic capitalist states too fall in this domino game: Félix Houphouët-Boigny, the only ruler of Côte d'Ivoire since independence in 1960, agreed to legalize opposition parties and to resign as head of the ruling party – but he died first. Zambia too was dominated by one man, President Kenneth Kaunda, from independence in 1964. In 1991, in a referendum, Zambians chose multi-party elections and Kaunda lost the presidency to Frederick Chiluba. Zaire's president for the last twenty-five years, Mobutu Sese Seko, promised to allow two parties tocompete with his own for power, but never did so and was overthrown by Laurent Kabila, who came to power at the head of a rebel force, promising democracy, but delivered nothing before he died. His son, Major General Joseph Kabila, presently rules newly renamed Kongo.

Colonialism did not really end. It left a legacy in law, in ownership (Europeans still hold much of Africa's richest land), and above all in borders. Not only the best land, but virtually all government aid went to whites. Africans in colonies were generally not allowed to compete with Europeans in growing cash crops, but had to work *for* them to pay the new taxes imposed on them. European mapmakers ignored political arrangements like the linked Ibo villages of eastern Nigeria or sprawling Yoruba towns scattered across western Nigeria, or indigenous political systems like democratic village councils dedicated to consensus. As a result, in the sixty to eighty years that colonial governments ruled, they never acquired moral legitimacy in the eyes of the people.

It is a cruel irony that exploitive and brutal as colonialism was, what has followed has sometimes been worse. Some governments – Britain in India and Belgium in the Congo – intervened to restrain private companies. Few European colonial governments were totally irresponsible. If they were not checked by their own consciences, or the forces of public opinion, they were restrained by the expectation that they would still be governing the colony for the foreseeable future. They had every interest in making sure that it remained reasonably prosperous and was not stripped of all its assets.

Multinational companies have no such automatic check upon their operations. In some areas, neocolonialism has proved worse than colonialism.[91] In addition, AIDS is gradually wiping out entire populations across the continent.

There is some cheering news. For example, a 1993 editorial observed that South Africa, once "one of the world's most sexist governments . . . has emerged as one of the . . . most progressive." With 106 women in parliament, it "moved from 141st place on the list of countries with women in Parliament, to 7th." This leap from 2.7 percent to 26.5 percent, means that "South African women are now better represented than their British counterparts."[92] In addition, women have joined across geographical, racial, class, religious, and political lines to create a forum for discussion of issues like economics, housing, and education. Women from groups formerly at war, like the ANC and the Inkatha Freedom Party, have joined together with women from other political parties (the Azanian People's Organization and the Democratic Party, for instance) and groups like the Rural Women's Movement, the Executive Women's Club, the Methodist Women's Manyanos, the Union of Jewish Women, the South African Domestic Workers Union, the South African Association of University Women.[93]

On the other hand, women are not well represented in the provincial parliaments, and are absent from regional executive committees. Activists are uncertain that female ministers are able or willing to use gendered analyses and approaches to the matters they deal with.

Namibian women were mobilized in the liberation struggle, and although the liberation movements remained male-dominated, women for the first time came together in discussion of gender issues and began to act in their own interests in local organizations. With independence, they took part in political life, and constituted almost a third of local government representatives in 1990 – partly because a law required political parties to include a specific number of women among their candidates. The Namibian constitution, written in gender-inclusive language, explicitly forbids discrimination on the grounds of sex, and authorizes affirmative action. Women still make up only a tiny fraction of representatives at national and regional levels, but got a boost by the ratification of the Convention on the Elimination of All Forms of Discrimination against Women in 1992.[94]

The government of Kenya has been outright hostile to female empowerment, but Kenyan women are tremendously active, and have formed self-help groups to build water cisterns, schools, bridges, dispensaries, and roads. They have created groups to help rural women earn money, something long denied them. In Central Province, women learned to build permanent roofs for their houses and were so successful and famed that they came to be known as *mabati* (iron-roofing) women groups.[95] In an even more revolutionary development, women's groups are buying land and businesses.[96]

Green Zones, an agricultural project in Mozambique, reserves land around Maputo for women only. Most of the women who participate in it are single – unmarried, widowed, or divorced – and raise crops alone. They have been very successful.[97]

The most heartening fact about these examples is that they abound. With so many women are working for themselves with other women, having seen through the cultural blinders of patriarchal customs, they cannot be stopped. They, and their children, and their men, will all benefit.

CHAPTER 18

WOMEN AND DEVELOPMENT

T HE VAST MAJORITY OF WOMEN ALIVE TODAY are poor and live
in non-industrial countries. Most of them strain to raise children with little or no help from men, much less their governments
or global agencies. For some decades now, non-industrial countries
have been the object of charitable attention from institutions like
the United Nations, churches, and foundations. This attention is
called "development." Examples of development projects include
increasing cash-crop production, building wells in a village, or
establishing industries to exploit a country's oil or gas.

Transnational corporations also invest in projects to exploit natural resources and a large, unskilled labour force. Unjust and cruel
as colonialism was, the conditions that have followed it are often
worse. Western companies abuse Third World workers and pollute
their environment without check, returning little of the profit to
the subject nation. Yet national governments cooperate in these projects because they hope the "development" will benefit the country
economically.

The term "development" sounds neutral, like something grow-ing by itself, in the way children or plants do. But development pro-grams are rooted in political ideologies and created by policy-makers with their own agendas. They are large- or small-scale efforts to force and direct growth in goal-directed, linear ways. "Masculine" process-es are useful, but sometimes narrow; planners see only one goal and one road towards it and they often shape goals to serve men's need for status, which is attained by rank, wealth, and "boy toys." Development projects, however altruistic at root, often benefit mainly a neocolonial elite, along with the European and American capitalist investors behind them. As technological advances in the Green Revolution increased farms' yields and efficiency, huge agribusinesses swallowed more land and used more machines. In many Third World countries, small farmers have been dispossessed, like English peasants centuries earlier; they now work as migrants or day labourers "surviving precariously in the outskirts of overpopu-lated cities."[1]

The Planners: Theories, Attitudes, and Policies

Global charitable organizations, transnational corporations, and most national governments are headed by men. Their schemes ignore women, not so much from malice as from a variety of un-conscious motives. The one issue that can unite men as a caste, their one point of agreement, is the definition of manhood as control. Some men control other men, but all men are supposed to control "their" women. Theoretically, the price men pay for dominance is bearing the burden of dependent inferiors. And many men do. Because they support their families, the men who determine policy ignore the overwhelming number who do not; consequently, all governments, institutions, corporations, and moralists assume that men, in general, use all or most of their income to feed, shelter, and clothe women and children, and that helping men is therefore help-ing whole families.

This assumption is false, as are its corollaries: that to develop national economies is inherently good and benefits everyone; that women's needs and interests are basically the same as men's; and that women's participation in technological, economic, and organizational innovations is irrelevant to national development.[2] Policymakers assume that the male sex is friendly to the female sex. Much as one wishes that this assumption were true, experience shows that, with many exceptions, in homo sapiens the male is a predator on the female.

Government policies reflect masculine values even on the local level. Governments consider assistance to cash-crop farmers, who are always male, an investment. To guarantee that cash cropping will show increasing returns, governments offer men incentives like seeds, machines, fertilizers, and improvement loans. As long as women's work continues to be the feeding of men and children (however poorly) without such help, governments gladly leave that responsibility to them. Projects focused on women funded by donor agencies other than the United Nations receive dramatically less money and attention than larger (male) development projects.[3] A study of planners, to determine the extent to which they contribute to the "domestication of women" ("housewifization") – treating women as if they were dependants of men who actually supported them – found blatant bias in project after project.[4] Even planners who considered themselves "liberated" showed a total lack of information about women and a widespread unconscious bias. Development planners act "as if women didn't exist at all."[5]

Development planners did not recognize that their schemes harmed women until Ester Boserup's pioneering work of 1970, *Women's Role in Economic Development*, challenged the accepted belief that modernization and industrialization raised women's status.[6] Boserup alerted scholars to the fact that colonial rule, urbanization, and a world market economy disrupted women's position, especially in Asia, Latin America, and Africa, changing patterns in the sexual division of labour and marginalizing women formerly equal to men in political decision-making, access to and control over resources, and legal rights and privileges. Urbanization made women economically dependent on men, while a world market system excluded women from land tenure and ownership. Yet neither urbanization nor a world market system needed to injure women: the changes are sex-neutral. They harmed women because they were made by men who ignored women, who assumed that men supported women.

Generally, development has not benefited women. It can foster sexual equality by making women more central in the economy and in political life, as it did to some degree in the West. Similarly, it can exclude women from paid production, relegating them to household or informal work, as has occurred in much of the Third World. But everywhere it creates a female proletariat that works for low wages, allowing employers to accumulate capital at minimal cost.[7] Even when planners try to include women, they subordinate them to their own narrow vision of "progress," blind to women's lives or needs.[8] They encourage women to produce for a market, to earn income, while, like state planners in socialist Europe, completely ignoring the fact that someone has to raise the children and that women usually take that responsibility. Planners of irrigation projects ignore women's use of water, although everywhere in the world it is women who must fetch it. A Tanzanian man complained: "Water is a big problem for women. We can sit here all day waiting for food because there is no woman at home. Always they are going to fetch water."[9]

Planners are not interested in helping women get control over land, increase subsistence production, or produce the clothing or other goods they and their children need. Development planners are interested only in income – cash – which can be earned only by producing something that can be sold at market. Poor Third World women with no money to buy anything can get money only by producing something for people with money – urbanites in their own countries or Westerners.[10] Integrating women into development as presently defined means getting these women to produce not what they need, but what others will buy.

Development has three major forms: mechanizing agriculture; investing capital to transform traditional manufacturing and handicrafts into large-scale enterprises; and expanding markets to include more small communities. Development officials urge training, especially in new technologies, but exclusively for men. If they consider women at all, it is as housewives whose support men need to be productive and stable at work. The only form of development for women is training them in domesticity. Women who are allowed to continue productive (non-domestic) activities are relegated to two lines of work: to subsistence, traditional handicrafts or to domestic service and clerical and low-paid professional duties in teaching, nursing, and social work.

In industrial societies, wealth flows from parents to children. In traditional agricultural societies, children start to help in the household by the time they are five, and by adolescence they contribute as adults. In Africa, parts of Asia, and other areas that live mainly by farming, parents value children for providing income or labour. In the past, in Africa especially, fathers' authority over children could last throughout their lives; many had total control over adult sons' labour and surplus, and children were responsible for maintaining their parents in old age. The introduction of wage labour shattered this ancient tradition. The shift from a mainly agricultural economy, in which children were assets, to a predominantly industrial economy, in which children are burdens, is reflected in changes in custody law: where children have no value as property, courts begin to award women custody after divorce. Worldwide, in societies where children do not support aging parents, many men do not support children.

Studies of projects in which men were given new technologies for cash cropping show that, while income may increase, nutritional levels fall. The reason is that the income belongs to the men, who use it to throw "prestige feasts" or buy transistor radios; in

Cameroon, men use their income to pay their children's school fees, but in Kenya, men buy liquor, gamble, and pay prostitutes while their families starve. The women can no longer feed the family because their work and land is used for the men's cash crops.[11] In India, researchers found that men spend about 80 percent of their earnings on "toys": motorcycles, wristwatches, radios, television sets, and entertainment like movies, alcohol, and prostitutes. Migrant workers in Africa send home an average 10 percent of their earnings: women residents in the hostels in Cape Town roll their eyes at the cars in various states of disrepair that clutter up the space around them. In the United States, too, a huge number of men desert wives and the children they have fathered so they can spend more on themselves and force the family onto welfare.

Studies also show that, when women have resources or earn income, children's nutritional levels and well-being improve. Indian women consistently spend 95 percent of their wages on their children. As the saying goes: "A penny to a woman is a penny for the family; a penny to a man is a penny for the man." Yet when a Zambian tax code was amended in 1986 to give women half of a child allowance that men had formerly received, men sneered that women would waste it on "perming their hair, buying make-up and expensive dresses." In places where women are excluded from wage labour or earn little, or where men take their wives' wages as their own, women are forced into dependence by a lopsided system that enforces male dominance. These women have difficulty negotiating what they need. Since women take responsibility for children, the world's children are at risk.

Agricultural Development

In areas where women traditionally did subsistence agriculture, cash cropping created competition between the sexes. Some cash-cropping schemes require women's labour yet do not acknowledge it. If a crop needs heavy watering, for instance, women must find the water; fetching water is woman's work, for which women are not paid. Cash cropping can undermine systems of mutual responsibility: in many polygynous societies, most people live in monogamous relationships with mutual cooperation. A man who raises cash crops may earn enough to buy a second wife, who provides extra labour. But he then gives less support to his first wife and children. Cash crops lead men into debt for seed, fertilizers, and mechanical devices. If crops fail from drought, pests, or other natural causes, or if markets fall disastrously, the farmer earns little or nothing. He has no food, but has a debt. Some projects fail because planners ignore women's expertise.[12]

In a project called "Operation Flood," Indian women were lent money to buy buffalo to produce milk for sale. Tending buffalo is women's work because it is arduous, dirty, and menial: doing the milking, cleaning the pen every morning and night, walking miles to find grass and fodder at a field's edge or on uncultivated land considered common property, and lugging it back. Once the dairy scheme was launched, landlords claimed that all grass growing on or around their fields was private property. They accused the poor women who collected grass in the traditional way of stealing it and they beat and harassed them.[13] The women had to pay back their loans every month, even when the buffalo calved or were ill. Many could not pay because, when the milk was sold, men took the milk money. But the women were saddled with the burden of keeping the animal. Before Operation Flood, the villagers drank the milk they produced. Now they export it to cities. Since most poor city people cannot afford to buy milk at market prices, dairies use it for luxury products – ice cream, sweets, or baby food. Operation Flood benefited the middle class who could afford to buy such products, while health levels declined in the villages that participated in the project.

Many scholars of development direct their animus mainly at capitalism, blaming capitalist greed, policies, and attitudes for the annihilation of peoples who have lived for millennia by subsistence farming. Their outrage is understandable, but capitalists do not have a monopoly on attitudes that are destroying ways of life that kept the human race alive over the millennia. The problem is a value system that is spreading across the globe and is now nearly universal. In socialist countries too, large-scale plans dispossess peasants from the land their ancestors farmed, direct production at the market, and ignore the fact that women are generally responsible for raising the next generation of humans.

In a socialist state committed to equality, women spread manure to fertilize their crops and carry their produce on their heads as they trudge the many miles to market. Nearby, men quickly spread chemical fertilizers and, when the crops grow, transport them on bicycles and trucks.[14] Such scenes recur regularly in India, Greece, and Turkey. In the former Soviet Union, men almost exclusively use large machines, while women lift and carry heavy loads by hand and do the most menial work.

Development programs ignored women's role in agriculture until the late 1970s, after the United Nations decreed the Decade for Women and after food crises had occurred in many parts of the world. At that point, groups in several countries devised ways to benefit women – and thus children and men. Everyone gained when women were given a voice.

In the Gambian villages of Jahally and Pacharr, women used primitive tools to grow rice in a swamp with poor water distribution. Women did most of the cultivation but got only 16 percent of the government credits for land improvement – the rest went to men. Since every development program for improvement and irrigation shifted more land and rice from women's to men's control, women warily resisted the UN International Fund for Agricultural Development (IFAD) and a donor consortium's offer of $16 million for a project to increase production. IFAD drew up regulations protecting women's rights, but village men demanded that women be ousted from the land allocation committee. The women, who were losing valuable planting time, formed a committee and asked to launch the project on their own. The government's and the donor's tact, combined with the women's energy, finally persuaded the men: 2500 swamp acres were drained and an irrigation system installed. Women got credit for seeds, fertilizers, threshers, and levelling and irrigation machines. Yields rose from one ton or less an acre to three tons, so less rice had to be imported for cash. The Agency for International Development (AID) found that agricultural projects that gave women themselves the resources appropriate to their particular kind of farming were much more likely to succeed than those that did not.

Since 1980, Oxfam America's projects in India have focused exclusively on poor women.[15] Sakuti, group leader of the Khond tribal people in southern Orissa, says that women spend their 10 rupees on food for the family, but men spend half their earnings on drink. Women walk ten kilometres or more for firewood to sell, work far harder than men, and hide their money from them. This is true too of Malayalee tribal women in the Kalrayan Hills of Tamil Nadu, who do field work, housework, and raise children. Unlike Hindu women, tribal women can remarry after divorce or widowhood, but only men inherit land and sit on the *panchayats*, traditional village councils that settle disputes and grant divorces. Women field workers are paid 5 rupees a day, men 8. Men divorce sick or injured wives who can no longer do field work: without husbands they are destitute even if they do work. KALWODS, an agency for women in the area, helped Poochie buy a dairy cow. A divorcee living with an eleven-member extended family in a tiny one-room house, Poochie repaid her loan and now earns 10 rupees a day selling milk. Literacy classes and women's meetings enabled her to write her name and gave her the confidence to confront government officials and lead women's group meetings.

CODES, a local development society supported by Oxfam in Sathumadurai, a farm village in northern Tamil Nadu, funded palm-leaf weaving cooperatives and other projects. The women wanted a crafts centre and a dairy cooperative. The village had a seldom-used temple where men sometimes gambled, but the men would not let the women use it. When they received Oxfam funding, the women bought a small building in the village, but, because they were all illiterate, they made men both president and secretary of the cooperative. They worked hard, yet after two years they were still operating at a loss. They persuaded the men to resign, elected a woman president, and hired Sivagami, an educated woman from a neighbouring village, to keep the books and handle the money. They began to earn a substantial profit. Sixty women, most of whom did not own animals before, purchased milk cows and buffaloes. Siv, a Harijan who used to be harassed by everyone from village boys to government officials, now walks proudly, a respectable businesswoman. Men who opposed the women's cooperative are happy – the women let them help decide how to use the money they earn.

Industrial Development

Colonial governments outlawed local manufacturing to make room for their own products. In many regions, industrialization destroyed the home manufacture of textiles and pottery by flooding local markets with cheap imported manufactured goods. Family industries (in which women were important) could not compete. In recent decades, transnational corporations have backed much of the industry introduced in Third World countries. Wherever they operate, these companies are concerned only with profit and they ignore the effects of their activities on the people and the environment. The people most victimized by such enterprises are women.

Because transnational corporations can muster labour pools across continents, they profoundly affect people in any area. Transnational disregard of local needs undermines the traditional social structures in any region. Such enterprises "internationalize" workers: they inure them in Western values and assumptions that are foreign to their cultures and that do not exist outside work.[16] Women who work in factories or offices especially may find themselves violating prevailing cultural norms. Transnational corporations often hire women because they think women are more docile and obedient than men, will work for almost nothing, lack experience in labour organizing, and are more likely to tolerate frequent job turnover. Consequently, women constitute the majority of the labour force in industries like electronics, garment manufacture, and assembly. Transnational companies are not the only exploiters: repressive national governments with an investment in keeping workers tractable and silent punish those who protest low wages and poor working conditions. Women everywhere are so used to oppression they often do not recognize it.

Third World women who made traditional goods for home use or sale (like African women who made cloth, bread, clothing, and bricks) were easily incorporated into the first stage of industrialization, producing foodstuffs and clothing for growing urban populations. Before 1970, for example, small Latin American businesses hired many female seamstresses and embroiderers. But when demand increases, companies with low-level technology cannot fill the orders and industries with the capital for machines move in. They replace large female workforces with a small male workforce to run the new machines, sending women back to traditional jobs in handicrafts, petty trade, or domestic work – cooks, maids, washerwomen, and nannies. Women do not become part of the later stages of industrialization. Most industries developed to substitute for imports were highly capitalized and used a male labour force; they hired women only in domestic or supportive jobs, as cleaners, clerks, and secretaries. Capitalism boasts about people's "freedom" to sell their labour: the epitome of this freedom is the working-class woman prostitute, who is "free" to sell her labour and her body, but in reality must do either or both to survive.[17]

Employers justify not hiring women on the ground that they are unskilled and illiterate, but so are most men. However, when it suits their purposes, industries hire mainly women. Since the 1960s, burgeoning export industries in India have created new jobs for women – because of their "nimble little fingers" – in plants making clothes for export and in a small pharmaceutical industry. Those who fit this stereotype, which appears also in Latin America and elsewhere in Asia, are paid very low wages.

Transnational corporations hire females for intensive labour in the processing stage of production at a low minimum wage. They prefer single girls willing to work for next to nothing, believing they are better educated, work harder, complain less, and are less likely to unionize or be tired or absent than adult women with family responsibilities. Businessmen admit these reasons openly: Texas Instruments in Curazao prefers women because their sex dictates low wages.[18] Foreign corporate managers in Singapore claim that women have special qualities – docility, diligence, a tolerance for repetitive tasks, and "swift fingers." The personnel officer of INTEL Corp., a US semi-conductor firm in Malaysia, said: "We hire girls because they have less energy, are more disciplined and are easier to control."[19]

In Mexico, companies find it advantageous to assume that women's wages are "extra," a mere supplement to the income of a father, husband, or son. Men paid such wages or given such unstable jobs would either move to other jobs or organize and strike for higher pay.[20] In Morocco, a female machinist earns about 70 percent of a male machinist's pay. Male workers and factory managers shrug off the inequity by saying that women "work for lipstick" and other small personal luxuries.[21] This attitude allows employers to continue to pay women shameful wages, and men to demand that all household work be done as efficiently as if women did not work outside the home. Hot meals on the table at the right time, marketing, laundry, child care – all these tasks remain the responsibility of those who are working only to buy frivolous items fit for a vain sex!

Women's wage levels reflect the segregation of the industrial workforce. In much of the developing world, male workers are trained and typically earn three to four times more than women, who are untrained. The wage disparity seems to increase with industrialization.[22] We have focused on factory work, but men dominate office work, too, in the Third World. Most women still live in the countryside, far from any source of waged work.

By removing men from rural areas, industrialization breaks down once supportive kinship ties. It can make formerly self-sufficient women dependent on wages by taking over the markets for which they produced. But paid work can also give women status by giving them income. In some cases, it gives them mobility too, enabling them to free themselves from oppressive patriarchal bonds.

Medical Aid and Education

Some efforts to improve the health of women and children in Third World countries have been very effective. UNICEF, for instance, devised a simple program of vaccinating infants and teaching mothers a basic diarrhea remedy that has saved the lives of countless African children, 40 percent of whom die before the age of five. But corporations obsessed with profit are indifferent to human well-being, and Third World governments have few controls over them. Pharmaceutical companies dump birth-control devices like IUDs and high-estrogen birth-control pills on unsuspecting populations, often with the support of US aid programs. They charge many times more than they do in industrialized countries for such products. Companies exhort mothers to use powdered milk, although in countries with unsafe water it produces milk that makes babies sick or kills them. Such policies have been challenged by feminist networks like the International Contraception, Abortion and Sterilization Campaign based in London.

Educational aid is one of the most successful programs in parts of the Third World, especially Africa, where, right after independence, foundations were laid for university education to train African professionals. Within twenty years, universities in Nigeria, Zambia, Senegal, Ghana, and Congo were filled with students studying for degrees in engineering, computer science, and agronomy. But most programs aid male students. World Bank support in Tanzania, however, helped to improve primary and adult education, including that for females, and brought the literacy rate up to 80 percent.

The percentage of rural African girls in school remains very low, and girls still have a different curriculum from boys, one male authorities consider fitting for them. Of the few African women who attend university, most are urban-born or raised and they gravitate towards or are channelled into professions that are considered appropriate for respectable young ladies: nursing and teaching. Still, women do not have a monopoly even on these professions: in most of Africa, half the nurses are male.

Men against Women

Most students of development agree that policies detrimental to women arise from a pervasive male belief that men support women and that governmental and institutional support for women is therefore not necessary. They attribute such policies to men's failure to notice women's plight, rather than from malice towards them. But this claim is hard to swallow: most Third World policy-makers grew up in communities where women led hard lives; they may even have watched their own mothers struggle to keep them from starving. When even visitors notice women's hard lot, how can a native not be aware of it?

Blaming women for male failures is a traditional patriarchal tactic. World governments scapegoat women to an extraordinary degree for failures in their own policies and in capitalist development. In Nigeria, where national policies emphasized "masculine" values – profit, self-aggrandizement, and power – oil became the main source of government revenue in the early 1970s. The Nigerian government (like the colonial English) ignored or dismissed food farming, small commodity production, and small-scale trading – all activities in women's domain. It was not just unsupportive but somewhat hostile to the women who fed the nation.

When the price of oil fell and the massive investment in aggrandizing public works and industrialization that had begun when oil revenues were high brought little return, an extreme economic crisis occurred. The Federal Military Government mounted a coup and took control in 1984–85. The FMG swiftly blamed the crisis on "indiscipline" – the "failure of particular social groups to perform adequately their prescribed social role, preventing society from functioning as it should."[23] The "indisciplined" groups included almost all Nigeria's women. Wives and working mothers were said to neglect their children; single women were said to be prostitutes leading men into undisciplined behaviour; and petty traders were said to hoard goods and create a crisis in consumer items. Women, the most marginal and vulnerable members of the population, were at fault for the failure of wide-scale policies, just as the Vestal Virgins were to blame whenever Rome lost a war.

In truth, if one looks to blame a person or a group, one can always find grounds. Petty traders made an easy target because high inflation and shortages angered citizens, who easily blamed traders for these problems. But traders are the most powerless link in the retail food chain. The FMG sent soldiers to the markets to beat the traders and force them to lower prices. All this action could possibly accomplish was to drive traders' families into destitution, but blaming small traders fit into the FMG development ideology. This ideology in turn derived from colonial ideology, which divided Nigeria into traditional (backward) and modern sectors and urged modernization through industrialization and urbanization, as in the West. Women, whether traders or subsistence farmers, who inhabited this traditional sector in need of modernization, were suddenly responsible for its existence, as if, without them, Nigeria would suddenly be modern.

Men try to repress women when women's economic power begins to rise.[24] Male passersby who assaulted Egyptian women workers as they walked to work claimed that the women were "loose" because they were walking alone in the streets at an odd hour and it was the responsibility of any male to "teach them a lesson."[25] In many countries, men invoke religion to repress women. When militant Pakistani Muslims complained about women's growing independence, Zia ul Haq limited female legal and civil status.[26] The Ayatollah Khomeini had done so earlier in Iran, and insurgent Muslim militants try to enforce strict compliance in most Muslim countries today. Individual men too, threatened by women with independent incomes, use religion to restore them to their "proper" subordinate position in the family – in the West as well as in the East. As soon as a family in Harbassi, India, attains some prosperity (partly from women's work), men force their wives to withdraw from agricultural labour and live in confinement.

If men are hostile enough, planners may cancel a women's project. A large project aimed at women in Burkina Faso was opened to both sexes for fear of male sabotage.[27] Men can also push women out of a project. A state-owned steel mill in Ciudad Guayana, Venezuela, tried to integrate women into previously all-male production jobs.[28] Women had worked at the mill for years, but only in the office. Low-ranking men, mainly day labourers who felt the factory was an all-male domain, were extremely hostile to the women. Foremen harmed labouring women even more by sexual harassment. Female engineers encountered discrimination mainly from paternalism and dead-ending: men treated them in a patronizing way and did not promote them.

But the most blatantly exploitive form of development is what is called sexploitation or sex-tourism: tours for men to Third World countries to visit brothels created especially for them and "womaned" by virtual slaves – girls, often just children, who have been sold into servitude by poor peasant fathers. Sex-tourism was proposed as a development strategy by international aid agencies. The sex industry was first planned and supported by the World Bank, the International Monetary Fund, and USAID.[29] Thailand, the Philippines, and South Korea are the present centres of Southeast Asian sex-tourism. Parties of Japanese businessmen are flown to one of these places by their companies as a reward. American workers at a construction site in Saudi Arabia, totally fenced off from the culture around them, were flown to Bangkok every two weeks to be serviced by Thai women working in massage parlours. Another part of the sex industry is marriage brokerage: private companies, most of them in West Germany, sell Asian or Latin American women as wives, openly advertising them as "submissive, non-emancipated, [and] docile." Both industries are maintained by a support network of multinational tourist enterprises, hotel chains, airlines, and related industries and services.

A New York-based international women's rights organization, Equality Now, estimates that twenty-five sex-tour companies operate in the United States alone.[30] These groups take American and foreign male tourists to brothels throughout Southeast Asia, where millions of women and girls are forced into prostitution.

Women's Responses to Development

Since poor men usually earn small or irregular incomes, it has always been risky for women to rely on them for support and they often turned to other women for material help.[31] They do so in the Third World today. Poor rural women in the Dominican Republic in the 1960s lived with men but preferred not to marry. They supported themselves by their own efforts and those of close female kin.[32] The survival strategies of urban African-American women often bypass support from men, depending on their own work, welfare payments, and female support networks. Women in Nairobi shantytowns generously help each other get established producing bootleg beer and give each other extensive financial and emotional support, especially during the regular police raids.

Women hostile to a male development project may resist or subtly subvert it. Third World women farmers resist coercion by developers – forced crop cultivation, forced labour in government projects, and forced marketing of crops. Women workers resist government efforts to outlaw off-the-books businesses like beer brewing, food processing, and prostitution. Female entrepreneurs evade tax laws and zone regulations. This resistance contributed to a drop in crop sales to official marketing agencies, a decline that affected food supplies and foreign-exchange earnings. Women's insistence on their right to move where they choose, to settle in towns, and to support themselves, threatened the ruling classes in several African countries. Officials in Kenya, Tanzania, and Zimbabwe ordered periodic round-ups of "unattached" townswomen to expel them from cities.

In the mid-1970s, growing political unrest in the Third World and women's increasing inability to feed their families – especially in Africa, where children were dying of starvation – led governments to fear that their labour force was shrinking. Western development agencies came up with the idea of Women in Development (WID). But WID programs do not empower women but control them; they co-opt female protest. WID officials infiltrate autonomous women's groups and networks to spy on women's activities in off-the-books work and self-organized groups.[33] Nearly all international agencies now have a WID policy in addition to a development policy and post special WID staff in Third World "recipient" countries to liaise with local women's groups. Women's projects are almost always low in funding and prestige and are separated from overall development programs. Agencies favour "income-earning" projects that pay women little or nothing but require a great amount of labour. The heads of these projects use the earnings for private ends and sometimes embezzle them. WID projects are widely considered Band-Aid programs applied to situations of extreme deprivation. Nevertheless, WID policy has been adopted by government and non-governmental organizations in the Third World.

Like Western industrialization, development in the Third World grows in soil already poisoned by sexism. Yet it can give an enterprising woman a chance for freedom from male domination. Development changes a society and shifts it from one kind of economy to another. How we work affects all other aspects of our lives, including the make-up of the family and its power arrangements. Change enables people at the bottom of society to manoeuvre for advantage. Development projects have added to women's physical burden and decreased their economic security by destabilizing households and communities. But they have brought education to some areas, and education and jobs raise women's self-esteem.

Any ability to move is a step forward for many Third World women; for some, just taking that step brings joy. Some women intend to gain freedom from male control. In Tanzania, many rural women migrate to cities, extricating themselves from the intricate web of male control over their work in peasant households. Some avoid marriage. While they face sexual subordination in the wider society, working for minimum wages at jobs riddled with sexual discrimination and rarely being promoted, no repression is as painful as that by family: "Paid work away from home releases [women] from the grip of the patriarchal family system, and gives them a measure of economic independence and status in the family which they may never have had before. Despite the exploitative nature of the work, social disapproval of independent working women and the multitude of other problems these women confront, many . . . see their work as liberating."[34]

Feminists are perplexed about how they should view work that combines exploitation with liberation. Factory work may improve women's well-being but exploit them miserably at the same time. Companies and governments in international markets profit from women's disadvantages in all labour markets. But if disadvantaged women organize and win even minimal improvements in wages and working conditions, they lose their jobs because transnational companies move elsewhere. Development and industrialization both neglect women and target, liberate, and exploit them – as they do men. Women suffer more because of sexism at every level, from the bosom of the family to the community to corporate and government decisions. Male insistence on retaining prerogatives over women – and their solidarity on this point – is now accompanied by a degree of selfishness that threatens human survival, as men increasingly refuse to take responsibility for children.

Third World women need a two-pronged approach: practical help and strategic help.[35] Projects that address women at all almost always offer the first – wells, grain mills, health facilities, and help in reproduction. Such male-directed projects almost never try to help women strategically, empowering them to end male violence and obtain abortions, equal pay, and access to waged work. The ramifications of the masculine value system are endless: many Third World countries actively seek huge populations, imagining that people make them strong in the same way that "big men" of the past had huge followings. The long-term consequences of this value system may be to destroy the very society or culture it claims to strengthen.

Welfare Systems

Welfare systems are not usually discussed in the same breath with development projects, but development is to the Third World what industrialization was to the West, and welfare is the institution the West uses to ameliorate industrialization. Women's philanthropic work in the nineteenth and twentieth centuries provided the impetus to welfare systems. As this work was "professionalized," men took it over, retaining women as unpaid volunteers or low-level staff. Women and children are the main recipients of welfare assistance because they are the most vulnerable, poorest members of society. Welfare is an intermeshing set of social programs intended to alleviate the consequences of economic and personal life cycles like inflation/unemployment and impoverished motherhood, illness, and old age.[36] The term "welfare" also usually describes programs for giving the poor more access to education or medical care, or requiring those who benefit most from amenities like garbage collection, police protection, or schools to pay for their larger share through graduated taxes.

People have argued about the nature of poverty for centuries. Indeed, arguments about human nature are often really about inequity. To posit Man as an aggressive, predatory, selfish creature who, ever since his emergence on earth, has fought to possess resources – women, land, and goods – is to hold that economic inequity is programmed by nature and is therefore ineradicable. In this case, to the victor belong the spoils (women, money, status, goods), and those without them are inferior beings, natural losers in the Great Game. People who hold this position claim that everyone starts from the same gate and runs the same track; winners are literally the best, a superior breed.

But to posit that humans began as one species among many, sharing and cooperating with each other to survive, and that this structure most benefits humans, is to find economic inequity unjust, a consequence of millennia of predation and indoctrination. People who hold this position believe that humans retain little of their natural programming and that our special talent for symbolic thought is also a special burden, since we believe our own propaganda. They believe that people start out in life in very different positions, and that centuries of acquisitiveness have put some people so far behind that they cannot "win" without severely deforming themselves. "Winners," deformed by convincing themselves they have won by desert, think that welfare is an attempt to allay the most visibly heartbreaking miseries of losing. In this way, welfare alleviates their guilt of having been born a winner.

We no longer live in small lineage groups in which everyone is entitled to land and animals, helps everyone else (even if in a ritualized, rule-bound way), and cares for the sick, the old, and the children. Nor is it likely that we will ever again live in communal kin-groups. Socialism, in its various forms, was an experiment in enabling humans to maintain their present economic level, yet give all citizens such security. Initiated in a hostile environment in which self-defence was necessary, all socialist states became oppressive and most have failed. Welfare, less radical an effort, has encountered somewhat less antagonism. It is a bandage on a gaping wound, but it eases life for some people.

After the eighteenth century, revolutionary agitation spread in the West for the abolition of slavery, the right to a living wage, and universal manhood suffrage. Women had to fight harder, longer, and virtually alone for the right to education, work, and equality in law, but their struggles changed the social discourse, introducing the idea that humanness, not sex and class, endows people with rights. Before the Second World War, many countries offered relief for the poorest, maternity benefits and leaves for woman workers, allowances for families with many children, some old age pensions or health care for the indigent or for members of state insurance programs, and other forms of relief of economic distress. After 1945 these programs were coordinated and made comprehensive; most important, they were based on a new rationale: that every citizen had a right to a minimum standard of life. By the later twentieth century, the idea was legitimate that the state provides what is necessary for survival when people cannot provide for themselves.

At the core of the idea of social welfare is a belief in universality: policy-makers wanted all citizens to have access to help, financed by deductions from their wages. But many citizens – middle-class married women – worked without pay. Planners argued whether to treat such women as individuals, eligible for benefits because they were citizens or merely as part of a unit, minors controlled by a male wage-earner. Britain and France decided this question differently.

During the interwar years, British feminist pressure led to the establishment by 1945 of many state programs to aid poor women and their families. Eleanor Rathbone wanted family allowances based on the number of children to be paid to mothers; trade unions demanded that men receive a "family wage." Rathbone argued that the needs of single men and men with large families were different, implying that men spent most of their wage on themselves: paying mothers allowances was the best way for the state to acknowledge the importance of mothers' contribution. But male-dominated labour unions and political parties baulked at empowering women, under the guise of economic concerns, and during the war Lord Beveridge, the major architect of the British welfare state, chose a scheme different from Rathbone's. He defined a family as a wage-earning male citizen supporting a wife and several children. Beveridge's program gave women access to money only through husbands, assuming that most married women did not work outside the home and that the few who did would work intermittently, so would neither pay contributions nor acquire a claim to benefits. Most women would be exempt from the program, unable to be economically independent. Married women who did contribute and qualify earned lower benefits than men or single women.

After the Second World War, the French set up a Conseil National de la Résistance (CNR) to create a system like Britain's to help citizens survive in case of unemployment, accident, or sickness. The CNR, made up of representatives of all major political parties (including the Communists) that had resisted the German occupation, created the Securité sociale, which entitled all working people to social security whatever their marital status. French legislators tied the system to a general overhaul of existing labour law, decreeing better working conditions along with social security, and making payments, responsibilities, and benefits as equal as possible. Women became eligible for social security when they began to work for wages, but the plan did not recognize the special contribution of mothers and did not pay child allowances. It did provide maternity leaves and pre- and post-natal protections.

The difference in the two systems was rooted in different male thinking in the two countries. Neither British nor French men were concerned with women's well-being; both were extremely misogynous. As we have seen, British trade unions spent more energy excluding women from the workforce than fighting employers, and the left supported government groups in keeping women dependent. Frenchmen believed that a dynamic economy depended on women working outside the home. A higher percentage of women worked for wages in France than in most industrialized countries, and the French left believed that women would support socialism only if they worked for wages. Throughout the interwar period, the Communist Party especially tried to organize women in trade unions and political groups. Many French feminists believed that female emancipation depended on economic independence. They demanded better training and jobs, and tried to organize women in unions.

The outcome in both countries helped and harmed women. Laws decreeing equal access to work and family allowances helped more women enter the workforce. As states took over philanthropic work, they hired women as clerks to maintain the system, as managers of charity organizations and as social workers to liaise with families needing help. Welfare law mandated more schools, and the schools hired women teachers disproportionately to men. National health plans hired women nurses, paramedical workers, and clerical staff. Extended education kept youngsters in school longer. At the same time, older people and mothers of young children got benefits small enough to keep them in poverty but close enough to their potential take-home pay to deter them from seeking jobs. Without waged work, they did not identify with organizations beyond their community. Welfare indirectly gave people a basis for political organization that was not based on personal networks and the traditional political parties. This was a major shift: politics in the early twentieth century had been characterized by class conflict – and class was determined mainly by work and social relations within the workplace.

Governments throughout the West instituted welfare systems after the Second World War. For the first time in history, governments of large nations moved to improve their people's well-being. But their programs varied in their degree of fidelity to reality, not stereotypes: the best were created in the Scandinavian states; the worst in the United States. Many commentators felt that welfare had eradicated old conflicts, that class and sex warfare were over. Having announced the "end of ideology," they were shocked at the eruptions of the late 1960s as workers went on strike, students occupied schools, both workers and students took to the streets, and feminism arose – partly from the new trend of forming political alliances on grounds other than work. Feminists intensified this new networking scope by advocating democratic pluralism and opposing broad state control over citizens' lives. They appealed to women across lines of nation, class, colour, and social position based solely on the experience of subordinate status all women share. Urging women to add to or to replace class with sex-based affiliations, women's movements changed the make-up of traditional political parties. Insisting on women's difference from men and on decentralization, they challenged welfare systems – universalist programs imposed on people by the state.

Global markets have changed work relations both in the Third World and in the West. Transnational corporations with no necessary home base feel no need to abide by the laws of any state or care about the welfare of any citizens. Devoted to profit, they control resources greater than those of many nations. They spread across the world, enormously mobile, superseding national economies with a global economy, building factories, buying raw materials, and hiring workers to assemble and sell their products wherever it is cheapest to do so. They shut factories in places that offer high wages and expensive social programs, and open them in Third World countries with low wages and no social programs. They fire full-time workers for whom they have to contribute to costly social programs and hire part-time workers at minimum wage with no benefits in what has been called "McJobs." Capitalism has responded to the massive efforts of labour unions by cancelling their gains.

Many European nations provide universal health care, free education, child allowances, and free or subsidized child care that make women's lives more bearable. Of the industrial countries, only the United States does not offer its citizens such care. It is hard to oppose welfare programs that keep a family from starving, even if they reinforce women's dependence on men and their subordinate image (as men realize when they design them). But debate about whether welfare programs harm or help women is becoming irrelevant as governments, especially in the United States, eradicate it. In 1997, responding to men's clamorous protests against welfare mothers, the United States passed a law requiring localities to offer welfare recipients jobs, which they cannot refuse and still retain welfare. It is too soon to know the long-term consequences of this new system, in terms of malnutrition, infant and female mortality, and general well-being.

As multinational corporations devise more strategies to evade laws requiring decent working conditions, a wage people can live on, fair employment and promotion policies, and environmental concerns, the efforts of working women and men over the last century and a half fall into oblivion. What they are faced with now is the necessity of worldwide organizing – a huge task. Perhaps in time women and men will be able to find global human solidarity, which will enable them to turn what multinationals offer to their advantage.[37]

PART EIGHT

THE TWENTY-FIRST
CENTURY:
DAWN

THE FEMINIST MOVEMENT IS THE MOST IMPORTANT revolution that has ever occurred on earth. Its nature is so radical that many people, even women themselves, do not perceive it; moreover, it is rooted in qualities so natural they go unspoken. Many women seem, basically, to be spiritually anarchic: they do not easily bow to authority, rarely revere authority, and are loath to act against their own values in the name of authority. The feminist movement challenges the very root of patriarchy, the idea that one person can be humanly superior to others and entitled to have authority over them.

But to create a non-patriarchal world in the face of 5000 years of patriarchal culture is a massive and overwhelming task. It cannot be compassed in a century and a half. Feminism might gain power if it created a violent revolution, but violent revolutions fail, not in seizing power but in establishing their values. The means destroy the ends. It will require years of gradual change, as humane values rise to the surface of life after five millennia of suppression.

The feminist revolution was well under way as the twentieth

century ended. Despite periods of quiet struggle, feminists have worked steadily since 1848. After the Nineteenth Amendment to the US Constitution was passed, women worked in areas of personal concern, on committees, in women's organizations, and in government. Women's social reform network grew during the Depression into "America's most vital institutions of resistance to despair."

In settlement houses and community centres, women nourished the hungry. While "the United States retreated from its commitment to the League of Nations . . . the women of the peace movement" agitated for mutual security politics and the World Court.[1] Ida B. Wells' anti-lynching movement continued to agitate through the 1920s; in 1930, southern white women, led by Jessie Daniel Ames, repudiated men's claim that lynching was intended to protect the "honour" of southern womanhood. Thousands of southern women joined the group she founded, the Association of Southern Women for the Prevention of Lynching.[2] Women, most notably Eleanor Roosevelt, worked on issues of environment, health care, housing, and civil and human rights. "Fifty years after ER worked to place human rights on the international agenda, the Universal Declaration of Human Rights [was] adopted by the United Nations on 10 December 1948."[3]

Set back by the Second World War and the tyrannical social movement for conformity that followed it, women rose again in the 1960s, during the Vietnamese war, with protest on their lips. This phase of the movement, which still continues, has heaped success upon success, provoking a severe global backlash. Undeterred, women continue, now campaigning globally and leaving no area of life untouched. Through these years, the women's movement has remained true to itself: it remains a horizontal movement, with ad hoc leaders but no final authority; active in many fields and causes, but with no dogma and no heresy. The women's revolution asks people to live for it, not die for it; women believe, with Emma Goldman, that revolutions are to dance at.

CHAPTER 19

THE HISTORY OF FEMINISM

FEMINISM IS A GLOBAL REVOLUTION, the most important revolution in philosophical and political thought since patriarchy emerged. Because it is anti-patriarchal, feminism does not conform to patriarchal structures. Patriarchal organizations have heads, dogmas, fixed agendas, and hierarchical organization: their principles, structure, and even the rivalries among their leaders can be analyzed in terms of power, without much reference to actual life. Although their reality is always complex and messily human, they aim at a near-mathematical perfection of form – which requires that they be in some sense cut off from actual life. In addition, because patriarchy is rooted in a falsehood – the belief that one human can be superior to others – its laws and "facts" are matters of language, not concrete reality. A man is *declared* divine in an utterance, much as the son is declared god by the *word* of god in the biblical book of John.

Feminist acts are immersed in real life: campaigns arise when they are needed, then they fade. Leaders are ad hoc: women who lead local movements may abandon leadership roles after winning their goals or switch to different movements. Their authority is personal, not linguistically pronounced. Moreover, no woman has authority over others in the feminist movement itself (outside the employer/employee relationship): each woman is her own rabbi. This is something the media have never understood: no woman can speak for other women. Each woman speaks for herself. No one can say what "the feminist movement" believes or extract obedience from her cohorts.

Over time, women have been oppressed by different forces and have devised different strategies to resist. All those strategies are in some sense feminist, even if the word and the concept were unknown at the time. Movements or groups may be unconsciously feminist or may repudiate the name *feminist*: a person or thought is feminist if it regards women as being as important as men, overtly or tacitly.

Feminism has many forms, so scholars refer to it in the plural: feminisms. Most historians define feminism as an attempt to change women's position in society – one that often takes the form of a political movement or organization. I define *feminism* as a set of values that encompasses all attempts based on a female perspective, by either women or men, to improve the lot of any group of women.[1] Because helping one group of women may, in fact, harm another, feminist groups are sometimes at odds with each other. But in all forms, feminism is a movement to help women as a group against the oppression of men as a group.

Since women's only universal experience is growing up as girls in a world owned and ruled by men, feminism is not monolithic. All feminists are influenced by their society and by class, colour, religion, region, history, and politics. For a woman, simply standing up for oneself is a feminist act, so demanding equal rights with men makes one a feminist. But the ultimate goal of feminism is to change society. Feminists work to educate both sexes, to show the suicidal nature of domination. They try to empower women to fight for themselves individually and in groups. Women's criticism of men is noticed, singled out, and commented upon, but men's unremitting war on women is so normal and everyday that many people see it not as a political act but as a fact of nature.

Elite classes are not permanent, fixed minorities; they change over time. Elitehood is not given by nature: the elite always rises from lower classes and always falls back into them. But elites continue to exist, testifying to the power of the idea of superiority. People may hate or scorn elites, yet be awed by them and strive to be part of them. As long as we feel this way, elites will continue to exist. They are exclusive: to claim superiority, a group must exclude most people. No psychology degree is necessary to understand that this need to claim superiority arises from feelings of inferiority too strong to allow equality – and this claim is relevant to the relationship between males and females.

Feminism is the only philosophical and political movement to challenge the legitimacy not of a particular elite but of elitehood itself – the *idea* of superiority. Male rebellions always challenge the supremacy of a particular class or group. The rebels insist they are equal or morally superior to an elite (of state or church) and therefore deserve rights and privileges. Many men think feminism is another movement of this kind – that it asserts that women are equal (or superior) to men and deserve the same rights. When men accept women in colleges, well-paid jobs, or professions, they feel they have responded to feminist demands: they are assimilating women, just as earlier elites assimilated earlier waves of the disenfranchised. Bewildered that feminists still protest, they ask: What *do* women want?

Most people, especially most men, do not give much thought to feminism; they think they know what it is and don't bother to read its documents. They do what Rokeya Hossain did in her utopia: reverse the present situation, put women in men's seats, and imagine – with horror – women treating men as men treat women. This scenario provokes considerable hostility. But feminism does not aim to reverse the present situation. It is not just a campaign for equality. The assertion of equality is a first step in gaining women a voice in the male world, a necessary prerequisite for the real goal – changing that world. The male landscape is one of unremitting war for power and control that defines people only as winners or losers. The goal of feminism is to create a cooperative world in which no one wins (which isolates) or loses (which undermines).

This goal is clearly a major undertaking, not to be achieved in a few generations. It is a task we cannot accomplish as we are presently constituted, for all of us – women and men, feminists and patriarchists – are infected with patriarchal values and modes of thought. It is a task we can only work towards. But unlike male revolutions, feminism does not ask its adherents to sacrifice, to kill or die for it, but to live and enjoy it. It is a revolution one can dance at. Its ends *and* means stress cooperation, felicity, and the fostering of life. Every success improves life for some women; we do not need to eradicate patriarchy completely to savour joy.

Historical Feminism

In Western Europe and the United States

Richard Evans theorizes that nineteenth-century feminism was rooted in liberalism, in the eighteenth-century Enlightenment.[2] Liberalism, an intellectual revolution that arose from economic change, challenged the medieval belief that the classes – nobles, clergy, and a "third estate" of commoners, serfs, and villeins – were immutable. Liberals defined humans as free, reasonable, and equal before god. They impugned the legitimacy of hereditary aristocracies, which were based in an old assumption of divine pedigree. The rulers of society, they argued, should be those whose superiority was based in industry and ability. But liberalism was one more male movement that preached equality but meant a new elitism. Liberals demanded the removal of legal restrictions barring men of their class from competing with upper-class men, but they never thought that industrious able peasants, slaves, and workers were also their equals.

Since nineteenth-century women had no voice in society, feminism could not succeed without male support, and liberals were the main backers of feminism in almost every country. National feminist groups "took on the colouring of the liberals around them, whether they were anti-clerical, as in France or Italy, nationalist, as in Finland or Bohemia, or moderate and rather timid, as in Germany and Russia."[3] Those most opposed to middle-class liberalism, mainly conservative agrarian or aristocratic groups, also most strongly opposed feminism. Socialism, however, challenged liberal political and economic power with the liberals' own argument, forcing liberals to face their hypocrisy. Acknowledging the accuracy of the socialist diagnosis but disliking the left's revolutionary solution to social problems, liberals chose an approach they could control — state intervention.

In Evans' view, liberalism collapsed as socialism rose; propertied people abandoned liberalism for more conservative politics after communism triumphed in 1917. Simultaneously, he claims, feminism declined: the female suffrage movement was a highly successful movement for status, not sex equality, and, after the 1920s, feminist movements died or were suppressed in nations where women won the vote. No other countries granted women suffrage until after the Second World War.

This hypothesis does not account for the continual politicking of women in the United States and elsewhere for more humane government policies towards the poor, as well as justice for women. Nor does it account for the revitalization of the 1960s, feminism's "second wave." Feminism is unquestionably rooted in the notion of rights first articulated in eighteenth-century France. Feminists began their assault on male privilege by championing others — middle-class men in the salon world of the Enlightenment; poor men and women in the French Revolution; African-Americans in the nineteenth-century United States. This is not to say that all feminists are democratic egalitarians: many nineteenth-century feminists were biased and blind, like most people who live in biased cultures. Some middle-class women assumed that poor women should live like white middle-class women and tried to "lift" others out of their group, not empower them. Some white women felt superior to people of colour; presumably some women of colour felt the reverse. This diversity is true today as well. But despite prejudice and personal limitations, the nineteenth-century feminist movement laid the foundation for a full-fledged assault on patriarchal thought.

The notion that all human beings have inherent rights is a revolutionary one. Carried to its logical conclusion, it subverts the idea of superiority. We speak here not of small superiorities – one person's talent for playing the piano or catching a baseball or giving speeches. Class is posited on a transcendent superiority that, as we have seen in this history, began as an assertion of divine ancestry. Divine forebears produced kings and nobles. While the nature of elite classes has changed greatly over the millennia, the sense that they have a superior pedigree remains, hovering over them like haloes. If no person born lacks human rights, however, no one is inferior. And if no one is inferior, no one can be superior.

In a totally male-dominated world, to challenge belief in superiority was to challenge the existence of god. Early feminists had to tread lightly. In the fourteenth century, Christine de Pisan could only hope that heaven would provide the justice women were denied on earth. Early feminists had to "prove" that women were human, capable of rational thought. To disarm blanket disdain for their sex, they sought "exceptions" (female leaders or moral exemplars). But by the mid-nineteenth-century they, if not their opponents, could take women's moral judgment and intellectual and physical capacities as givens and begin to demand human rights.

All women's defences of their sex and arguments for enlarged scope challenge patriarchal thinking, the thrust of which is to place greater and greater constraints on women. That women's arguments were couched in terms familiar to an era, posited on a basic agreement with those terms, is not surprising. People, no matter how radical, tend to reflect the values of their own time and to accept them, to some degree. Nineteenth-century middle-class feminism exploited liberal discourse, a language current in the period. Christine de Pisan expressed feminist ideas in the religious, monarchial terms her period understood. During the French Revolution, women were foreclosed from feminist consciousness and female solidarity by the lack of a language to express such ideas. They had to use revolutionary or religious discourses, both of which ignored or constricted them. African-Americans, labour unionists, anarchists, and socialists also used male discourses current in their time. The feminist project is so huge, so radical, that women have had to think their way through it step by step, tearing the veils of masculist culture.

What women never had was a feminist discourse. And before they could create one, they had to penetrate their own patriarchal biases. Most nineteenth-century women believed that, by natural endowment, environment, or training, human females were moral, nutritive, peaceloving, and philosophically disinterested (unselfish), while males were competitive, self-aggrandizing, belligerent, and self-interested.[4] Others saw humans as a single species with equal intellectual and spiritual endowments, deserving of equal or similar opportunities. In the United States, women of both persuasions achieved a solidarity that lasted only until they won the ballot. Then the women's movement splintered. It did not decline, as Evans holds, along with liberalism: it fragmented because the great victory had been won, and now smaller ambitions had to be pursued.

The division was precipitated by the Equal Rights Amendment. In 1923 militant suffrage activists renewed the National Woman's Party and tried to exploit their momentum by lobbying for a constitutional amendment for full legal equality. The NWP was highly effective: focusing solely on the United States Constitution, it created women's voting blocs, lobbied national political leaders, and used direct action techniques – picketing, demonstrating, accepting imprisonment.[5] But an equal rights amendment would annul protective legislation for women, which many groups felt was needed by women who, unlike men, carry, bear, and raise babies. So groups that allied with the NWP to win the ballot – major women's voluntary organizations and the Women's Bureau of the United States Department of Labor – opposed the ERA. This split, between those who see women as in need of special protections because they raise children (unpaid labour in our world) and those who see women as capable beings deserving of the same rights as men, continues to this day as a conflict between conservative and liberal women.

During the second wave of feminism in the late 1960s, women started consciousness-raising groups to pool their experience. From them came a language of shared experience: the feminist discourse. Never before were there words to describe concepts like prejudice against women (sexism), men's belief in their transcendence and superiority (machismo), the double standard as a cohesive in society (the personal is political), the construction of masculinity and femininity (gender), or the political ramifications of gender (sexual politics). This language was forged by a host of women – poets, theorists, activists – struggling with themselves, each other, and social forces. By creating this discouse, they created a feminism profoundly different from any earlier form. No longer dependent on male categories of thought, intent on demystifying patriarchal attitudes, it did not so much resuscitate nineteenth-century feminism as use it as a springboard into revolutionary philosophy and politics. It could name the enemy – patriarchy; name the kind of world it wanted – feminist; and list the ways men denied rights to women. For the first time, women could move from a defensive position – vindicating their sex from diminishment and attack, insisting women were human beings and so entitled to rights – to an aggressive demonstration of how sexism brings men political, social, and economic gain and emotional and biological loss.

This revolutionary feminism emerged in the mid-1960s in the United States and England. In the United States, the events usually credited with precipitating it were the publication of *The Second Sex* by Simone de Beauvoir (1953) and *The Feminine Mystique* by Betty Friedan (1963) and women's experience in the anti-war campaign. Although de Beauvoir was an essentialist who believed women were limited by their biology, she compiled a mass of information demonstrating their subjection by law and custom, in the process re-opening the argument about women's nature and place. Friedan's book galvanized middle-class housewives who were smothering in invented lives. Female protesters of American participation in the Vietnam War, relegated to serving and sex by anti-war men who publicly attacked domination as immoral, left to form women's groups. Later, women members of human rights groups followed suit, tired of male leaders' denial of humanness to women.

To these milestones I would add the invention of the birth-control pill in 1955 and the "sexual revolution" of the late 1950s and 1960s, in the wake of revelations about female sexuality by Kinsey (1953) and Masters and Johnson (1966).[6] Not all feminists consider the change in sexual mores called the sexual revolution a benefit to women, since it increased male objectification of women and male irresponsibility about marriage and fatherhood. However, Barbara Ehrenreich, Elizabeth Hess, and Gloria Jacobs show that the sexual revolution did not really change male sexual behaviour, only permitting men to be more open, but changed women's sexual behaviour dramatically.[7]

Masters and Johnson legitimated clitoral orgasm, which Freud had called "immature." Legitimation of the clitoral orgasm legitimated female sexuality: it is hard to argue that god made asexual the only sex with an organ devoted entirely to providing sexual pleasure. Sexual freedom is essential to feminism. People afraid to enter the public world lest they lose their all-important virginity, or lest they be spoken about disparagingly, cannot act independently. But people who had internalized traditional mores could not simply drop them. Nor could women trained to defer to men change their behaviour overnight. Many were thrust into painful conflict, their sense of justice and rights warring with ingrained behaviour.

Internal war made them angry, and their shared anger gave women's groups cohesion and a centre.

Differences about the nature of femaleness continue to divide feminists. Unable to assume a common biological female identity, socialists and Marxists insisted women were defined by their social identities.[8] Radical feminists, essentialists for whom anatomy was destiny, believed all women were united by nature – biology – and could be freed only by technology. Shulamith Firestone suggested hatching babies in bottles.[9] They formed the "women's liberation movement" in an implicit alliance with nineteenth-century middle-class feminism. They marginalized black or lesbian groups. While narrowing their movement, they stretched the idea of Woman (and social history in general) by searching for women's history. Since examining women in history subverts the idea of a single entity, Woman, the radical feminists deconstructed the very idea they were founded on.

At the same time, women's liberationists of the 1960s appealed to women and articulated goals in general terms, assuming a unity grounded in their shared experience as a second sex, victims of oppression, and in their common response. They had low hopes for themselves, a sense of inadequacy, and narrow horizons. The movement tried to create solidarity among women, a sense of sisterhood arising from shared perceptions. It was not then called feminism (a term reserved for the fiercely attacked "radical feminists"). Most women's liberationists remained aloof from campaigns for sexual equality, but women everywhere demanded just that – legal and economic equality, equal opportunity at work and in education, an end to the double standard and the laws that bolster it.

There are other feminisms: socialist, Marxist, lesbian separatist, feminists of colour, mainstream feminism. Some French feminists focus on women's bodies, trying to render sensuous experience in "female" syntax.[10] Mainstream feminists work for greater political representation and equal rights in every area for women. In the Third World, feminists live in rural villages, earn local women's trust to discover what they need, and work through feminist, government, or development agencies to help them get it. Feminist scholars research history, biology, psychology, social life, science, literature, music, art, and other disciplines free of the distortions created by exalting maleness. Feminist artists express a female perspective in their work. Ordinary women who may not call themselves feminists work in their communities to improve life for themselves, other women, and their children – across the globe.

Feminism has certain defining characteristics. It uses collective, not individualist, language: feminists speak of "we," not "I."[11] Feminists invented a political form called the consciousness-raising group. Few exist today, but feminist political organizations are structured like consciousness-raising groups: they are usually self-organized, and leaders cannot command others. Even highly intense campaigns like Women Strike for Peace were based on grassroots organization. Women's groups stress participation, not representation. Feminists invented a new concept, "sexual politics" (a term made famous by Kate Millett), the perception that sex differences are political differences, that men's sex alone gives them power over women, that to learn your gender role is to learn your place in society. Feminists invented the discipline of gender studies and recognized that gender (the qualities assigned to the sexes by society) is constructed and symbolic, not biological.

Feminists, both female and male, have succeeded amazingly in a little over thirty years in undoing double-standard laws and practices, rethinking social structures, politics, and gender, and overturning some of the unwritten laws of male supremacy. Feminist ideas and language have become public discourse in the West, valid currency in the world of thought. But sexism cannot be eliminated without eliminating the foundations of Western society, and we do not have a blueprint for what to put in its place. We have ideals, principles, but no structures. To create feminist structures will take time: it can happen only slowly, as patriarchy gradually erodes and young people grow up with brains less cluttered by an invidious ideology. Until then, we must foster cooperative egalitarian ideas and structures wherever possible. The great worries are co-option and obliteration. Our female descendants may be blinded by the bit of carrot they are offered, as some of us are – or men may obliterate feminists from history as they have in the past. Robin Morgan notes that the latest wave of feminism is not the second, but more like the ten thousandth.[12] Women rebel and often win a victory. But tendencies towards widescale female autonomy have been quickly suppressed in history.

Feminism in Asia and the Middle East

Women's rights movements emerged in Asia and the Middle East in the late nineteenth and early twentieth centuries.[13] In Asia and Africa the force driving emergent feminism was often a nationalism aimed at ending colonial domination. When intellectuals and professionals who had studied abroad or in modern schools at home joined local capitalists thwarted by imperialist economic policies to fight colonial and economic domination, they either expelled the colonists or negotiated themselves into power.[14] Yet most new states established authoritarian, hierarchical social structures. Third World revolutions or reforms and feminism were rooted in local material circumstances and thinking: no ideology was simply imported from the West. But Western feminism, thought, and examples (especially the Irish struggle against Britain, with its martyred freedom fighters and hunger strikers) influenced events in these nations.

The competition between economic systems that characterized the West for fifty years had an impact on women and feminism in other places as well. While not at all feminist in intention, capitalism can work to women's advantage. Industry prefers cheap, docile workers – qualities associated with women – and as industry grew, especially textile-related businesses, so did the demand for women workers. China manufactured silk and allied products; Iran, carpets; Japan, textiles and other goods; India, textiles; Egypt, cotton; and

Turkey, rugs and textiles. Women's labour was crucial in plantation-raised cash crops like tea, rubber, coconut, sugar, and other agriculture. Confined women were of no use to industry: when Shah Reza Khan passed laws to bring women out of seclusion, he argued, "One half of the country's working force has been idle."[15] Thus, when fundamentalist Muslims take power, they immediately force women out of jobs. Jobs allow women some money of their own and provide them with a place where they can meet each other and speak together – a necessity for slave rebellions everywhere.

Socialists, who always promised much to women, felt they had to deliver something when they had won their struggles. For a time, women were part of a contest between socialist and capitalist systems competing to see which system delivered more to the female half of the population. On the whole, socialists gave women fairer laws and social services; capitalists gave them stuff – some of it necessary, like tampons. Western women missionaries, socialists, theosophists, and freethinkers, who were often dissidents at home, visited Asia and introduced its women to the discourse and activities of women elsewhere in the world.[16] The wife of a Dutch colonial official influenced Indonesia's pioneer feminist, and Dutch socialist feminists helped inspire Indonesian feminism.[17] An American spread feminist revolution in the Chinese revolutionary army, Japan, and India.[18]

What has made the huge difference for women in Third World countries are the United Nations conferences devoted to women's issues that have been held over the last decades (see chapter 21). Feminist pressure on national delegations to the United Nations has changed the surface of the discourse about women. The importance of the conferences to ordinary women cannot be overstated.

Turkey

One of the earliest feminist reformers was Mustapha Kemal in Turkey. His reforms inspired discussion and change in many other societies and became an example that stood for decades. Kemal (later called Ataturk, "the father of the Turks") acted from true respect for women. Deeply impressed by the courage and militancy of Turkish women during the Balkan wars and the First World War when they did everything from farming to working in banks, from nursing to fighting in battle, he accepted Anatolian women in his army. He married (and divorced) an educated woman who appeared with him in public unveiled. He expanded educational opportunities for women and introduced a new civil code that barred polygamy and marriage by proxy and gave women equal rights to divorce, child custody, and inheritance. The code raised the minimum age of marriage to seventeen for women and eighteen for men and, shockingly, allowed Muslim women to marry non-Muslim men (the reverse had always been permitted). It separated marital property and gave women the right to control their own. These reforms caused a sensation: Turkey was the first Muslim state to replace the *shari'a* with a civil code. The government urged, but did not compel, Turkish women to abandon the veil, and Kemal campaigned for Western dress.

But these reforms rarely affected the majority of Turkish women, bound to the land and to men's control. Although a woman was prime minister of Turkey a few years ago, a woman who recently ran for Parliament and was elected was denied her seat because she wore a headscarf. Later, the state revoked her citizenship. One wonders what rights women do possess in Turkey today.

Egypt

In Egypt after the First World War, professional and business men led by Saad Zaghlul formed the Wafd party to spur Egyptian self-determination; it drew intellectuals, peasants, and women. Wafd men, secular Muslims who favoured female education, created a climate in which women could write on feminist issues. Malak Higni Nassif (1886–1918) wrote as Bahissat El Badia (Searcher in the Desert); she was a forceful journalist concerned with veiling, seclusion, education, marriage, and divorce. One of the first Egyptian women to qualify as a teacher, in 1900, she left Cairo for a desert area when she married her polygynist husband. Her experience of patriarchal subjection among secluded rural women made her a keen critic of the system and, in 1911, she addressed the Egyptian Legislative Assembly and proposed a program to improve women's situation. She endorsed universal elementary education, urging that women be trained to heal and teach other women, but also said that girls should be taught religion, hygiene, first aid, and child rearing. She was the most famous of the many women who wrote for Arabic women's journals after the turn of the century.

Newly confident, women joined the nationalist anti-British movement. When the British suppressed the Wafd in 1919, violent demonstrations erupted: militant nationalists, including women, engaged in Wafd-led strikes and assassinations.[19] Socialist and Communist Party members organized factory workers, tram drivers, waiters, and lamplighters to strike over wages and work hours. Their demonstrations in Cairo and Alexandria drew enough support to mount a general strike in 1924. The government suppressed both parties and arrested Charlotte Rosenthal, among others, as a Communist leader. Women are rarely specifically mentioned in discussions of labour movements, but are always affected by them. Elites often repress workers by targeting women: for example, the militant Muslims trying to force women back into confinement in Egypt today also focus on women in their efforts to repress workers' movements and deflect working-class men from the labour struggle.[20]

In 1922 England granted Egypt nominal independence. The drafters of the new constitution supported female education, yet ignored women's political rights. Their main reward to women was to raise girls' minimum age of marriage to sixteen. A major militant, Huda Sharawi (1882–1974), a wealthy, educated woman who had founded a girls' school, formed the Egyptian Feminist Union with other middle-class women in 1923. In March 1924, when the Egyptian Parliament opened, Egyptian women held a demonstration demanding suffrage. The union was the main women's group concerned with social welfare, education, and legal equality of the sexes. Sharawi became famous when she cast her veil into the sea after returning from an International Conference of Women in Rome in 1924. This act was scandalous because her husband was an eminent pasha, and many prominent women imitated her. In 1925 she started a French-language journal (*L'Égyptienne*) for French-speaking women in Egypt's elite, to discuss issues like Turkish reforms of laws regulating women and Islam's treatment of women.

Egyptian men kept women on so tight a leash that, when the University of Cairo admitted women in 1928, orthodox men revolted, causing a crisis in the government. Not until 1962 did Al-Azhar University admit women students. Some Egyptian women were educated nevertheless, even earning professional degrees, but most remain illiterate. Muslim leaders and laymen firmly opposed woman suffrage until 1956. In 1979 women's pressure forced Parliament to reserve 30 of its 392 seats for women and to liberalize marriage and divorce laws in their favour. But in 1985 the Supreme Court struck down the provision allowing women to divorce husbands who had taken second wives. Egypt remains a major site of female genital mutilation.

Japan

The Orient tried to preserve its integrity by intense xenophobia, but the West pushed in anyway. Japan repelled all efforts to colonize it, outdoing the West at its own game by rapidly industrializing. In the late nineteenth century several male reformers urged that women's status be raised. One wrote, "Combining Western women's rights with [the] traditional virtues of our women . . . will produce models of perfection." In 1870 the government gave concubines the same rights as wives. In 1872 an enslaved prostitute escaped, causing a scandal: the government declared itself averse to prostitution, voided prostitutes' debts to the houses that imprisoned them, and freed them. But it did not ban prostitution. Some men suggested that the traditional Japanese family should be replaced with nuclear families. Tokutomi Soho, an influential liberal who later switched to conservatism, called the traditional family a "breeding ground of every abuse, servility, double-dealing, jealousy, alienation and treachery," where women were treated as the "natural slaves" of men, with no independent life or identity: "Women are not recognized as human beings," he said.[21]

Much of the non-Western world in the late nineteenth century abandoned traditional dress. In Japan the emperor led the way, cutting his hair in a Western style; the government urged long-haired samurai to imitate him. But when a group advocated short hair for women, the government decreed this style illegal and required women not only to claim health reasons for wearing short hair but also to get government permission. Female appearance seems always to be symbolic: Japanese feminists cut their hair to protest women's lack of rights and adopted Western dress. When the bourgeoisie took up Western dress, it became a sign of status.

Influenced by liberal ideas, the government decreed that all Japanese should be literate, even girls. Girls' secondary schools taught mainly morality and "womanly virtues" until Christian missionaries opened girls' schools after 1870 with a richer curriculum. By 1927 women made up a third of the teachers in coeducational primary schools; by 1910, 99 percent of boys and 97 percent of girls attended elementary school, but women were still barred from the universities in Tokyo and Kyoto. In 1941 40 women and 30,000 men attended the imperial universities.

Educated women entered the workforce as teachers, nurses, physicians, and clerical workers. They had already entered industry, making up 60 percent of factory workers by 1876, most in textiles. These women were treated worse in Japan than elsewhere. Young single women from poor rural families who went to factories to work were put in prison-like dormitories and worked fifteen hours a day for a contracted period. Working conditions were harsh, and half of them left after a year, drained to exhaustion. Most ran away, but some committed suicide. In 1886 one hundred women struck at a silk mill in Kofu when the owner proposed to increase working hours and reduce wages. Their partial success encouraged other female mill workers to strike in subsequent years. Scorned as ignorant farm girls, they were the "pioneers of Japan's modern labor movement."[22] They had almost no contact with Liberal Party feminist activists, nor did male trade unionists organize them.

Male reformers founded Merokusha (Meiji Six Society) to spread liberal ideas, support female education, and attack concubinage, the double standard, and traditional marriage. Japanese journalists were inspired to enter the new discourse, and they translated Western feminist works by John Stuart Mill and others. This climate encouraged women to speak out and join the rights movement, which became the Liberal Party. Many women joined, and the best known of them all, Kishida Toshiko, who was intelligent, beautiful, and from a rich family, was made lady-in-waiting to the Meiji empress. After two years, stifled by court life, she left and began speaking publicly: after an appearance on a Liberal Party platform in 1882, she spoke publicly across Japan. One of her speeches was titled "The Government Lords It over the People; Men Lord It over Women." She demanded equal educational opportunities for women, training for work that provides economic independence, and a single standard in sexual codes, law, and civil and property rights. She had great impact on women and inspired the founding of women's groups like the Kyoto Women's Lecture Society. She also motivated Japanese women to agitate politically.

The government intensified its repression of the Liberals and, in 1890, barred women from political parties, political groups, or political meetings. This law radicalized women, many of whom became socialists or anarchists. Fukuda Hideko, who joined the socialists, began publishing a journal, *Sekai Fujin* (Women of the World), as a forum for socialist debate on women's issues. It, too, was shut down by the state.

The main opposition to the Japanese government at this time

came from leftist groups – socialists, communists, and anarchists – in all of which women were prominent. The most famous of these women, Kanno Suga (1881–1910), with only an elementary school education, left her merchant husband to become a reporter. As a member of the Osaka Women's Reform Society, she edited a newspaper while caring for a consumptive younger sister. Conflict with socialist men radicalized her; she joined the radical socialist faction and was among those arrested in 1908 for raising banners declaring "Anarchism" and "Anarcho-Communism." Released from jail in 1909, she and some colleagues started a new journal, which she edited. It was suppressed after two issues. In despair, Suga planned to assassinate the emperor. With twenty-five others, she was arrested for treason in 1910 and condemned to death. People from all over the world protested and won reduced sentences for many, but not Suga. At her trial, she eloquently attacked the authoritarian government and faced execution bravely.

Other left-wing women and trade union activists also fought a despotic government. In 1918 women stevedores refused to load rice onto ships at Ootsu because the price of rice in Japan was soaring. This insubordination triggered the Rice Riots – widespread demonstrations, strikes, and uprisings by miners, peasants, and workers in other ports which lasted several months. Repressive tactics backfired and the government fell.

At the same time, feminism was flowering in literature. In 1911 Hiratsuka Raicho (1886–1971) founded the group Seitosha (Bluestockings) and a journal, *Seito*, to disseminate women's philosophy, literature, and culture, avoiding economics and politics.[23] In 1915 Ito Noe became editor of *Seito*. A bolder feminist, she discussed issues like abortion and prostitution, which frightened many moderate women into dropping out of Bluestockings, causing it economic problems. The last issue of *Seito* was published in early 1916 and Bluestockings gradually dissolved. Noe married the anarchist Osugi Sakae. They were very poor and, constantly harassed by the police, lived as virtual political prisoners for the next six years. In September 1923 Ito, Osugi, and his five-year-old nephew were murdered by military police as "enemies of the state." Ito was only twenty-nine, but she and her colleagues left a legacy: Bluestockings raised feminist consciousness in Japan, and *Seito* deeply influenced the generation who created the Japanese women's movement.

Seito published Yosano Akiko (1878–1942), one of the Shin-shisha group who revolutionized Japanese poetry in the early twentieth century. Akiko analyzed patriarchy and the family, urged female economic independence, and wrote anti-militarist revolutionary work. Her poetry dealt with erotic love from a female perspective: her theme and her unconventional lifestyle made her notorious. She dared to deflate the war hysteria the government promoted during the 1904–5 Russo-Japanese War, opening one poem, "Do not die a purposeless death on the battlefield."[24] People wanted her prosecuted for treason. In 1911 *Seito* published "Sozo-rogoto" (famous in the anglophone world as "Mountain-moving Day"), which compared women's power to a long-dormant volcano. It ends:

> The mountain-moving day is coming
> I say so, yet others doubt.
> Only a while the mountain sleeps
> In the past
> All mountains moved in fire,
> Yet you may not believe it.
> Oh man, this alone believe,
> All sleeping women now awake and move.[25]

Persecution of leftist groups in the 1920s suppressed female militants and silenced most feminists, but a few courageous women kept debate alive. Ishimoto Shizue studied Margaret Sanger's work and tried to launch a birth-control campaign in Japan. Sanger visited Japan in 1922, but the police kept her from speaking. The ban aroused interest and her writings were translated into Japanese, setting off a debate on birth control.

In 1919 Hiratsuka, Ichikawa Fusae, and others formed the Association of New Women to campaign for equal rights, suffrage, unionization of women, and repeal of the 1890 law barring women from political activity. In 1928 a leading political party urged woman suffrage, and the Japanese press began to support it. But a government minister told women, "Go back to your homes and wash your baby's clothes! This is the job given to you and there is the place in which you arc entitled to sit!" Women's hope rose when he was replaced by a minister more sympathetic to women's issues, but in 1931 a women's suffrage bill that passed the lower house of the Diet was rejected by the upper.

In the 1920s conservative businessmen and the army held Japanese economic and political life in a stranglehold that precluded the growth of democratic institutions. Their power boosted by the 1930s Depression, they adopted militaristic expansionist policies to gain total control. Inflamed by the racist immigration policies of the United States and Australia and the Naval Agreements of 1931 (fixing a ratio of 10:10:7 ships for the United States, Britain, and Japan), Japan occupied Manchuria and northern China. In 1937 it launched a full-scale invasion of China, Vietnam, Indonesia, Singapore, and Malaysia and, in 1941, bombed Pearl Harbor, an American base in Hawaii. Japan entered the Second World War as a German ally.

The men who had furiously demanded that women stay home now urged them to work in factories. Easing laws restricting women's work, they exhorted them to produce more "subjects of the Emperor" and passed a Motherhood Protection Law (1937), giving benefits to poor mothers. "Women were told that their children were not their own property but the Emperor's"; they were to send their sons away "joyfully, as the Emperor's soldiers," producing the means for aggression.[26] Although Japanese women's suffrage organizations denounced government policies, most women supported the war effort. The war ended in 1945 with Japan's defeat, after the United States dropped atomic bombs on Hiroshima and Nagasaki.

Japanese women could not vote until the American occupation in 1945. In 1946 they elected thirty-nine women deputies. Japanese men, forced by treaty to abandon militarism, turned their energy to economic aggression, but the tone of Japanese society remains much the same. Social pressure on women to be a "good-wife, wise-mother" remains intense. Continued suppression still hurtles some Japanese women into the terrorist groups.

Feminist Strategies

It is remarkable that people with no rights, no money, and often no education, denied the right to speak in public or even to occupy the public sphere, were able to overthrow the laws and customs constricting them. To do so, they adopted strategies based on their diagnosis of the causes of women's oppression. It is questionable whether anti-feminist and conservative women believe that women matter as much as men, but because they link women's secondary status to their biology, they make it inalterable. Yet some conservative thinkers urge change in the distribution of power between the sexes. Liberal feminists consider women's oppression unfair discrimination and work to change laws and attitudes to end the bias.

Most activists believe feminism can reach its goals without radically changing society, but others do not. Traditional Marxist feminists locate women's oppression in the class system. Socialist feminists are rooted in traditional Marxism, but find gender and class oppression inseparable. Radical feminists see the oppression of women as the most fundamental oppression and the cornerstone of patriarchy; they believe that social, political, and economic structures must be profoundly changed to create a just and benign world. Feminists of all persuasions believe that colour, class, and caste raise the toxicity of sexual oppression significantly and exponentially.[27]

The overwhelming majority of feminists espouse no particular philosophy, but simply move in the world as feminists, joining group protests when an issue has importance to them personally. They spread feminist ideas by the way they carry themselves, speak, and build personal relationships. Some feminists have fixed channels of expression – lobbying, networking, activism, or writing and teaching theory. For some, the overriding task is rethinking patriarchal attitudes and structures, concentrating on philosophy, political theory, psychology, sociology, history, literary criticism, or science; others want to feminize their religion. Some want to revalorize the female body, sexuality, and emotional texture; or spread feminist attitudes through the popular media; or create and foster feminist art. A band of dedicated feminist activists works mainly with grassroots women's groups.

All feminists are in some sense activists, seeking the most effective means to change harmful institutions and practices. But patriarchal laws and customs limit women's courses of action and render them powerless, voiceless. When women cannot vote, own property, or hold political office, how do they persuade men to support them? How have women managed to change the laws and customs that perpetuated their subordination? How have they gained a voice on issues considered strictly male – war, militarism, tyranny, injustice?

Before people can act for themselves, they must think for themselves. All societies conceal – mystify – the facts of subjugation, largely through language and religion. Most cultures profess that the sexes are equal, that women's lot has improved over the ages, or that women enjoy – or need – subordination. To think otherwise, women have to defy their culture, a terrifying prospect. Women who do so, if they are not validated from outside, suspect they are mad. Their first strategy is to talk to each other; their second is to read – writing is essential to feminism. The third is acting in solidarity with other women on an issue of passionate concern.

Feminist action ranges from guerrilla warfare or terrorism to direct action to conventional political action. Direct action differs from conventional political action in being militant. Militant action means confrontation and risk. In some nations, rallies are an accepted part of political discourse, but in others they are illegal and risky. In the 1960s and 1970s in the United States, supposedly a liberal democracy, soldiers killed students rallying at Jacksonville State and Kent State universities and, in 1979, five members of the Communist Workers Party at an anti-KKK rally. People may be beaten at rallies and at marches supporting labour, civil rights, anti-war, feminist, or gay rights movements. In South Africa, police killed children rallying for education in their own language. Participants in the Lesbian Strength March in London in June 1984 did not intend civil disobedience, but when the police arrested two lesbian photographers, demonstrators sat down spontaneously and blocked roads until the two were released.

Most feminist acts are nonviolent. Nonviolent direct action may involve destruction of property, but it never plans injury to living creatures – though demonstrators may erupt in violence if attacked violently. Women have always performed nonviolent collective actions. In classical Athens, women rose up to defend a female right to practise medicine when Agnodice, who treated Athenian women and dressed as a man, was denounced and exiled. Their action freed her. Women in the Iroquois Confederation established a centuries-long peace by boycotting sex and childbearing until men conceded them the power to decide on war and peace.

The nonviolent direct action tactics of militant British woman suffragists influenced Gandhi's ideas on nonviolent resistance and *satyagraha*. Gandhi wrote about the women's movement "more than a year before he discovered Thoreau's 'Civil Disobedience.'"[28] He followed British news closely and knew about the first arrests of English suffragists in Manchester and London in 1905 and 1906, when he was formulating South African Indians' demands for legal, political, and human rights. In 1906 he went to London to plead his cause; three days after he arrived, eleven women were arrested for demonstrating at the House of Commons. A few days later

Gandhi published an article commending the suffragists' courage and choice of prison over fines, taking his title from their slogan "Deeds Better than Words." Again in London in 1909, he attended a mass meeting celebrating the release from prison of the first group of suffrage hunger strikers and held them up as an example to Indians: "When we consider the suffering and courage of these women, how can the Indian satyagrahi stand comparison with them?"[29]

Direct Action Strategies[30]

Women held mass demonstrations everywhere in the first half of the twentieth century. Egyptian women demonstrated against the British and French occupation of Cairo and Damascus in 1919, and in 1923, against the veil and for women's rights. Chinese women rallied in the streets for women's suffrage in 1924. Some women demonstrate with prayer. In 1957 forty women in Santiago, Cuba, walked in a procession mourning sons killed by Batista's police. Others followed "praying in unison and fingering their rosaries," carrying a banner reading "Stop the murder of our sons." More women joined the procession, swelling it to a thousand or more, in the first public display of broad, effective, organized civic resistance in Cuba "under the aegis of the *fidelista* movement."[31] When African women rallying in Ixopo, South Africa, in 1959 were ordered by the police to disperse, they "fell down on their knees and began to pray! The police hung around helplessly."[32]

Circles, symbolic of equality, sharing, and strength, are a favoured female form. In 1904 Iranian women ringed a group of mullahs with their bodies to protect them from government forces. Thousands of women encircled the Pentagon in November 1980, linking hands or scarves or anything that enabled them to surround the building. On December 12, 1982, 30,000 women encircled the missile base at Greenham Common in England. Some penetrated the base on January 1, 1983, to dance in circles on the missile silos. On International Women's Day, March 8, 1983, women surrounded a military base at Comiso, Italy. That December, American women circled 10 Downing Street to protest Britain's harbouring of American Cruise and Pershing missiles.

Because women have historically been silenced, they often use the technique of "truth-saying" – speaking, writing, or otherwise publishing censored truths – to empower women and protest male domination. Since 1982 Israeli socialist feminists have demonstrated to protest their militaristic society and Israel's invasion of Lebanon, and they have distributed pamphlets and led workshops on the link between militarism and male supremacy. In 1987 and 1988 Palestinian women mounted mass truth-saying demonstrations to protest Israeli policies in the occupied territories. They marched, held sit-ins, interfered with arrests, harassed Israeli soldiers arresting Palestinians, and protected children with their bodies.

Women use singing, dancing, and keening (wailing) as tools. During a miners' strike around 1910, women hooted at scabs for "taking the bread from their children's mouths," as Mother Jones charged. The sheriff arrested them for disturbing the peace and they were sentenced to thirty days in jail. Mother Jones advised them to take their babies to jail and sing all night, spelling each other, sleeping by day. Five nights of "howling" was enough for the sheriff: he freed them. Australian women mounted a series of demonstrations against rape in 1981: sixty-one were arrested and sang to those outside the jail, who sang back, all afternoon and evening as they were processed. "Back and forth the voices rang, the women inside and the women outside singing to each other."[33] In 1982 British women protesting its military build-up stood outside Parliament keening, touching the members emotionally. With sound, "we could actually penetrate the building."[34]

In the 1830s sixty women's Anti-Slavery Societies in the United States imitated Englishwomen who had helped win the abolition of the slave trade and slavery in Britain "by their needles, paint brushes, and pens, by speaking the truth." They kept the issue of slavery constantly in the public eye by stitching the words "May the points of our needles prick the slaveholder's conscience" on bags, pen-wipers, needle-books, pin-cushions, and other items.

The Congressional Union disrupted President Wilson's speech to Congress on December 4, 1916, by unfurling an embroidered banner in the gallery. In the 1970s and 1980s, women in Chile dec-orated *arpilleras* with pictures of torture and starvation and smug-gled them abroad to expose the Pinochet government's policies. Women in the "Chipko" (hug the trees) movement in India assert the harmony between humankind and nature.[35] In 1973, tribal women in the Garhwal Himalayas tried to stop commercial devas-tation of their forests by tying a *rakhi* (a sacred thread symbolic of the brother-sister relationship) around trees, pledging their lives to save them. When axemen brought contractors and armed police, the women hugged the trees, chanting slogans. The Chipko move-ment became a widespread, well-organized ecological movement.

Women in Chile, Argentina, El Salvador, Lebanon, and other countries embroidered the names of the disappeared on their ker-chiefs or pinned their pictures on their clothes when they demon-strated, demanding information about political prisoners or their release. The women who keened at the British Parliament in 1982 carried "trees of life," twigs beautifully adorned with ribbons or sequins in suffragist colours (green, purple, white) and doves of peace. In August 1985, 15,000 people enclosed the Pentagon with a fifteen-mile "ribbon" of over 25,500 panels, each a yard long, dec-orated or embroidered mainly by women over nearly three years.

Women's graffiti caused a male outcry at Brown University in 1990 when they wrote on toilet walls the names of men who had raped them.[36] In 1916 women's suffrage militants chalked "Votes for Women" on sidewalks and walls. In Brazil, men commonly use a "defence of honour" to justify killing wives or lovers supposedly for infidelity. Feminists launched a campaign against this custom in 1980. Demonstrations and public denunciations had little effect, but the whole country was shaken by the news that Belo Horizonte (capital of Minas Gerais, the most traditional state in Brazil) had awakened to a blanket of graffiti saying: "He who loves does not kill – Down with the farce of honour – How many more corpses until women's oppression is acknowledged?" After that, women demonstrated at each trial. By 1981 feminist pressure had forced the government to reconsider legal assumptions in such crimes.[37]

Weaving webs is a symbol of the women's peace movement because it resembles women's actions: each link in a web is fragile, but a spider's web can halt a lion, an African proverb reminds us. Since 1981 women at peace encampments at Greenham Common, Seneca Falls, Hasselback, and elsewhere have decorated barbed wire fences around missile sites with woven webs, yarn, drawings, banners, and items like baby clothes to express their values and feelings. The Women's Pentagon Action encircled the entire Pentagon with a woven braid in 1981 and blocked entrances with webs of brightly coloured yarn.

When women take power into their own hands, they assert female autonomy. Women were excluded from the dedication of the Statue of Liberty in 1886, so in 1986 a group called Women Rising in Resistance sailed a boat around the island to reclaim it under the rubric "Take Liberty." Taking liberty may involve escape from slavery, prison, or domestic abuse. Harriet Tubman, a major taker of liberty, led hundreds of black slaves to freedom (see volume 2). In many countries, Japan and England, for instance, the law often treated "free" women as slaves. Puerto Rico passed a law in 1824 penalizing those "who hid runaway slaves, minors, or married women who left their legal owners, parents or husbands to live by themselves, take refuge in the interior of the island, or abandon it altogether."[38] Slaves who wrote passes for blacks or taught others their secretly acquired knowledge of reading and writing were taking liberty. African-American Susie King Taylor recalled, "I often wrote passes for my grandmother, for all colored persons, free or slave were compelled to have a pass."[39] In twentieth-century South Africa, blacks took the liberty of publicly burning passes. Sojourner Truth took the liberty of boarding segregated trolley cars and staring down angry conductors. After years of such actions she was sued, and won, announcing that "before the trial was ended, the inside of cars looked like pepper and salt."

In nineteenth-century China, single women formed sisterhoods to avoid marrying. In 1920s China, women followed Nationalist armies in the Northern Expedition. In each region they reached, they formed independent women's unions to encourage women to ban footbinding, harbour runaway slaves and prostitutes, intimidate wife beaters, and grant divorces on their own authority. They set up a women's political school in Hankou in 1926.[40]

Polls show that women everywhere are anti-war, but they do more than favour peace – they take liberties for it. Women built peace encampments at over a hundred sites in the 1980s, at Greenham Common and Molesworth in England, Comiso in Italy, Hunsrück in West Germany, Nanoose in Canada, Seneca Falls and Puget Sound in the United States, Soesterburg in Holland, and Pine Gap in Australia. Shibokusa women have protested Japan's occupation by American troops since the 1950s, to save their land and their way of life. They sit in, disrupt military exercises, and build cottages on or around the military base, "small bastions of ordinary life amid the soldiers' incessant preparations for death."[41] Peace camps assert women's right, authority, and power to take the environment and the future in their own hands and to create an alternative society – the webs, baby clothes, plants, and other symbols they use to decorate their encampments signify life, harmony with nature, and simple equality.

Igbo women's tradition of "sitting on a man" discomfited British officials in 1929. The New York Female Moral Reform Society embarrassed many in 1834 when it printed the names of local men who entered brothels. In 1938 the entire membership of the Women's Association in China followed Mother Tsai to a local official to complain about an opium and gambling den, then "stalked" into the den itself and "peremptorily" ordered the men home.[42] In the 1980s rural Indian women held "people's courts," blackened the face of a rapist landlord, and paraded him on a donkey. Feminist activists in Delhi demonstrate in front of middle-class homes where women have been killed in dowry deaths, trying to confront the perpetrators physically. These acts are a kind of *charivari*, a medieval shaming exposure that used noisy mockery, parading on animals, and singing. So too are street theatre (a form of instruction), burnings (like that of President Wilson's effigy by the National Woman's Party in 1918–19), demonstrations at Miss America contests, nude sit-ins, mock trials of public officials by women in witch costumes, *gheraos* in India, "die-ins" (pageants mourning the nuclear arms race), picketing, silent vigils, and chaining oneself to a fixed object to target political persecution.

Direct actions always strive to get attention, and some involve making trouble. One tactic is to interrupt speakers or disrupt meetings of parliamentary or political bodies, as women disrupted a 1969 New York State legislative hearing on abortion, shouting "*We are the real experts!*" An elderly Navajo woman disrupted a 1985 White House honours ceremony to denounce Reagan's economic policies. Trespass, sit-ins, blockades, and occupations serve the same purpose. In 1962, at a rally to protest nuclear testing, a member of Women Strike for Peace climbed the fence at Camp Mercury, Nevada. Women climbed the White House fence, invaded missile bases, and demonstrated on the steps of the Supreme Court.

One form of trespass, the sit-in, first occurred in the United States in 1838, when the Anti-Slavery Convention of American Women adopted a policy of sit-ins and ride-ins. American civil rights, labour, feminist, anti-war, and anti-nuclear movements, like protest movements elsewhere, often organize sit-ins. They become blockades, if people use their bodies to bar entrances, as at the Women's Pentagon Actions and at women's peace camps. Sit-ins lasting over a few days are occupations. In Iran in 1979, during a series of massive demonstrations after International Women's Day, 15,000 women seized the Palace of Justice in Teheran and occupied it for several days. In 1982 black women students occupied the office of the president of Medgar Evers College in Brooklyn, New York, remaining there for more than a hundred days. The Grassroots Group of Second-Class Citizens occupied the Illinois State Capitol building for four days. In 1983 welfare protesters occupied the Pennsylvania State Capitol for over two weeks.

In the Middle Ages, women mounted small-scale strikes. They struck in late eighteenth-century England, with men in Pawtucket, Rhode Island, in 1824, and alone in Dover, New Hampshire, in 1828 and in Lowell, Massachusetts, in 1834. In 1888 women match workers in London mounted a successful strike. In 1909–10 approximately 25,000 women shirtwaist makers struck in Philadelphia and New York. The largest strike of women workers in history, it was crucial to the development of the International Ladies' Garment Workers Union, one of the most important unions in America.

Most American unions excluded blacks, but in 1933, when 900 black female pecan workers in St. Louis went on strike, white women workers struck with them. To divide them, the factory owner offered whites higher wages. They responded by marching on City Hall, 1500 strong, black and white. The owner gave in.[43] In the 1880s Mexican women were so important in organizing workers and strikes that Carmen Huerta was named to preside at the Second Congress of Workers in 1880. Women dominated the many strikes in the French tobacco industry between 1870 and 1900. In Vienna in 1893, women workers' first strike won them a ten-hour day, a minimum wage, and other demands from textile manufacturers. In 1904 women textile workers in Crimmitschau, Germany, struck for over twenty-two weeks. Women still strike – metalworkers in Brazil in 1980, textile workers in Poland in 1981, bakers in India, and Asian textile workers in Birmingham, England, in 1984. In October 1984 tens of thousands of Icelandic women struck for twenty-four hours to protest discrimination against women. Mothers, bus drivers, secretaries, teachers, and others closed down the city of Reykjavik.

To stop lynchings, Ida B. Wells used her paper, the *Memphis*

Free Speech, to lead a boycott of white businesses in Memphis in 1892. When whites threatened to burn her newspaper down, she got a job as an independent journalist and urged blacks to boycott Atlanta streetcars. In the 1940s and 1950s, African-American women boycotted with the slogan "Don't Buy Where You Can't Work."[44] When Rosa Parks refused to sit in the back of a bus in 1956, she triggered a black boycott of buses in Montgomery, Alabama. Black women were vital in this boycott, setting off the great thrust of direct actions for black civil rights in the 1950s and 1960s.

As colonial women boycotted tea in the pre-revolutionary period in America, colonized Indian women boycotted commercial salt, British cloth, and liquor during the Indian independence struggle. In the 1980s women organized networks internationally to boycott Nestlé products, protesting its irresponsible promotion of infant formula in the Third World. Men worked in the boycott, but women conducted the campaign.

Women deface images of women's bodies as objects for sale, as commodities, or those that show sexual violence against women. At the Women's Pentagon Action in 1981, three women were charged with defacing federal property for spilling blood at the entrance to the building. In June and July 1982, after the United States Congress defeated the Equal Rights Amendment, women wrote in blood on copies of the US Constitution and on the marble floors of the Illinois State Capitol building; they spray-painted female statues at the National Archives building in Washington, DC.

Hand spinsters in Leicester, England, protested the introduction of spinning machines in 1788 by wrecking them. Militant American temperance crusaders like Carrie Nation smashed liquor bottles, bars, glasses, and mirrors, trying to close down saloons in the 1870s. In 1972 tribal women in India protested male alcoholism and wife-beating, and rural rich men's exploitation and sexual harassment. They joined the Maharashtra Workers Union, but acted on their own. In rage, they broke bootleggers' alcohol-storage pots, attacked alcoholic men with brooms, and beat their wives too.

They paraded men who molested women through the village on a donkey, festooned with a garland of footwear.[45]

After 1908, militant British suffragists used the tactic of damaging or destroying property: they broke windows in posh London shops, tore up turf in polo fields, and burned down empty buildings to "attack the secret idol of property." Annie Kenney acknowledged the risk to human life in burning houses, but the protesters made sure the buildings were empty. "Providence protected us," they said: no one was killed in suffragist militant actions.[46] In 1977 Rochester Women Against Violence Against Women chained and glued the doors of a cinema showing "snuff" films. To protest thousands of kidnappings and disappearances in the unending war, Lebanese women blocked Beirut roads with burning tires in 1984. Hundreds of women built and burned barricades near London in 1985 to obstruct a nuclear Cruise missile convoy.

Sabotage is usually a covert terrorist act, but after 1912, British suffragists performed acts of sabotage like cutting telegraph wires. In 1985 women from the peace encampment at Hunsrück, West Germany, sabotaged concrete used for construction at the Hasselbach base. In 1987 Katya Komisaruk destroyed the computer console for a missile guidance system at Vandenburg Air Force Base. None of these acts injured anyone.

Women in China and Japan committed suicide to protest their suffocating lives – the only form they were allowed. Such acts are personal, but personal despair can arise from political powerlessness. Self-injury as a political act is tied to a cause outside the self and expresses hope. Political suicides perform an act epitomizing powerlessness in hope of forcing change. The most famous feminist suicide is that of Emily Wilding Davison, who in 1913 threw herself in front of the British king's horse, crying "Votes for women!" Nhat Chi Mai, a Buddhist nun, protested the Vietnam War by writing to the United States government, "I offer my body as a torch / to dissipate the dark," then immolating herself.

Less final self-injuries, like fasts and hunger strikes, are also rooted in hope. Hunger strikers like imprisoned suffrage militants in England and the United States, Ilwa women in Mauritius in 1978 and 1981, and eight Illinois women who fasted for thirty-six days in 1982 for the Equal Rights Amendment wanted to force people to see that women's lack of social, economic, legal, and political equality was a matter of life and death. Another risky act is putting one's body on the line by lying down in front of vehicles or on roads or tracks. In the 1929 Ecuadorian railroad strikes, Tomasa Garcés lay on railroad tracks to stop trains from leaving the station; in the 1940s Korean Louise Yim barred the doorway of her school to keep Japanese soldiers from taking over the school: "You will have to run a bayonet through me if you want to enter," she said. Ordered to fix bayonets, the soldiers eventually withdrew. The Indian women of the "Chipko" movement risked violence from commercial lumbermen when they hugged trees.

Such acts do not always achieve their goal, and gains can be retracted in the next generation, the next decade, or the next year. But women's actions often led to significant changes and to permanent improvements in their lives – suffrage, removal of discriminatory laws and customs, recognition that women are human. Women's protests significantly contributed to India's achieving independence, to the overthrow of the Marcos regime in the Philippines, and to the ouster of military dictatorships in Argentina and Chile. Women's actions are a legacy that women and other disenfranchised groups can draw on for courage and inspiration, a tradition of the socially powerless exerting power.

Women are sometimes violent. They revolted in twelfth-century Arab harems, in third- and eighteenth-century China; female terrorists worked in China and Russia in the nineteenth century.[47] In the 1980s women made up half the terrorists on Interpol's Wanted list and dominated some terrorist organizations. The Baader-Meinhof gang that terrorized Germany in the 1970s was 80 percent female; the women were known to have better ideas, to be calmer under pressure, and to be more intellectual than their male "leader,"

Andreas Baader. Ulrike Meinhof, its noted journalist leader, criticized Baader for keeping them constantly on the run without planning their next move. He spent his energy trying to control women who could have organized the group without him. Yet the press, unable to treat the women seriously, called one of them, Astrid Proll, "The Gun Girl."[48]

Dr. Margherita Cagol and her husband founded the Italian Red Brigades; the Japanese Red Army is led by Fusako Shigenobu, whom the press calls "The Red Queen of Terror." Of thirty-five Red Army Faction members in Hamburg, 80 percent are women; its last leader, Inge Viett, is a former nursery-school teacher. Viett, on the run since the 1970s, was twice imprisoned and escaped, once by sawing through her cell bars. When two policemen approached her in Paris, she shot them, killing one. In 1989 RAF blew up the director of the Deutsche Bank. Nathalie Menigon (press name "The Wild Beast of Terror") and Joelle Aubron (who once wanted to be a nun) were members of Action Directe, a French anti-NATO group that was captured after killing Georges Besse, the head of Renault. Susanne Albrecht, a lawyer's daughter, was arrested in East Germany in June 1990 for participating in the 1977 killing of her godfather, Jurgen Ponto, head of the Dresdener Bank. And sweet-faced Palestinian Leila Khaled, now a mother of two children, hijacked two airplanes decades ago.

Anti-terrorist police now consider women as likely as men to plan and realize terrorist attacks, yet they still draw stereotypical gender distinctions. Christian Lochte, an ex-judge who runs a surveillance unit in a Hamburg federal internal security agency, says: "Women shoot without hesitation, whereas men tend to think about escape routes. In a terrorist group, it is the women who organize things, who hold everything together. Men are good at arranging the fine details of an operation, but women will figure out safehouses, who to trust and how to run the daily life of the group." They are taken aback, however, by what they perceive as women's greater penchant for violence, their willingness to shoot and kill even people they know well, and they hypothesize that women have to prove themselves in a way men do not. Perhaps. But I suspect these men have no inkling of the rage inflaming the hearts of a sex that is belittled even as it expresses that anger in an ultimate way.

Feminist Accomplishments in Law and Politics

Law, a seemingly impersonal arbiter of human affairs, is in fact not impersonal at all. Supposedly a tool to achieve justice, it is not concerned with justice (as many jurists have pointed out); rather, it delineates the rights or privileges of the elite. This bias is true everywhere. Even in small-scale societies, social control fields are almost always sexually differentiated.[49] Men in gathering-hunting societies rarely use physical force on women, but they have other "legal" means to control them. For example, Luo members of an independent African Church in Kampala intimidate women, force them to confess before the group, and limit their access to property.[50] Women may be prevented from obtaining legal redress: rules pinpointing situations particular to women combine with lack of access to the courts to control them.

Thus, to obtain a hearing at law is a major accomplishment for women. Law alone cannot transform a patriarchal into an egalitarian society; feminists must continually struggle to educate and compel compliance. But without laws asserting equality, women can only plead, persuade, and pressure. Law, vital in feminist struggle, was the first area feminists sought to change.

The ultimate arbiter of law in the United States, the Supreme Court, generally reflects mainstream opinion. Illuminated by feminist ideas and moved by feminist pressure, the court made some landmark decisions after 1964. To fathom the groundbreaking nature of the new decisions, one should recall that, as recently as 1961, the United States Supreme Court justified the categorical exemption of women from jury service by invoking woman's place at the "center of home and family life."[51]

An inspiring feature of egalitarian movements is that the achievements of one oppressed group benefit others. Nineteenth-century American white women, still tacking their cause onto others' pursuits, first walked out of the house and onto the platform from an urgent wish to abolish slavery. Fighting for abolition gave them confidence; men's hostility to women on platforms gave women the impetus to fight for themselves. Demanding the right to be treated as human beings, they contributed significantly to the liberation of slaves in the United States. In the twentieth century, African-Americans fighting for the right to be treated as human beings returned the favour, contributing significantly to the liberation of women in the United States. African-American activism prompted passage of the Civil Rights Act of 1964, which provided the foundation for many challenges of laws upholding the double sexual standard.

The struggle began when the Civil War ended and whites in the south (and later, the north) formed vigilante groups to keep black Americans subordinate. Of many such groups, the largest and oldest, the Ku Klux Klan, held a special animus for teachers in black or integrated schools, intimidating, beating, or even killing them. Women teachers (black, white, north and south) heroically faced the KKK. Mrs. Baldwin, a teacher who came to a southern town in 1868, could not find a place to live because the KKK had threatened local families. It mailed her "vile books and pictures," threatening to kill her if she did not leave town. It did murder Julia Hayden, a seventeen-year-old black teacher in charge of a freedmen's school in Tennessee.[52] Teachers still went south.

In 1909 black militants like Ida B. Wells and Mary Church Terrell, along with white progressives like Jane Addams, Mary White Ovington, and Lillian Wald, formed the National Association for the Advancement of Colored People (NAACP) to end lynching. They worked courageously and untiringly, using nonviolent direct action techniques: educating people by publicizing lynching stories, mounting demonstrations, investigating riots, bringing legal suits on behalf of victims, and indefatigably pressing for anti-lynching laws. The NAACP worked with the National Association of Colored Women led by Mary Talbert, who also formed the Anti-lynching Crusaders, bringing together Zona Gale, Florence Kelly, Grace Nail Johnson, and Alice Dunbar Nelson to wage a publicity campaign in national newspapers and periodicals "until not a single person who reads the daily press shall be ignorant of the fact that we are the only country that burns human beings at the stake."

Whites hurt by the Great Depression of 1929 scapegoated blacks: the lynching rate doubled in 1930. In response, Jessie Daniel Ames founded the Association of Southern Women for the Prevention of Lynching, which became expert in pressuring the press as well as sheriffs, state senators, and governors dependent on local votes, including those of women. On several occasions this group thwarted lynchings by mustering the press and law officers when they received early warning of mobs forming. One woman alone changed the thinking of many whites about blacks: from 1925 to 1966 Lillian Smith wrote essays, speeches, and articles in the Chicago *Defender* and a popular novel, *Strange Fruit,* about a black-white relationship (Billie Holiday recorded the song of the same name). Smith taught whites that racism, not Negroes, was the problem and that it profoundly injured both blacks and whites.

The Fifteenth Amendment guaranteed black men the right to vote; the Nineteenth enfranchised all women. But the Klan or other groups denied African-Americans the vote in the south. In the 1940s Moranda Smith, the first woman regional director for an international union in the south, fought this curb by "teaching workers how to negotiate the registration process" and leading groups "to the courthouse to demand the right to vote." Her colleagues called her "a striking spark of the union spirit that set thousands of workers into militant motion for labor's cause."[53] Smith was fair game for Klan persecution. The risk of challenging white structures was immeasurably greater for blacks than whites, even in the 1960s, after law and public opinion had succeeded in reducing the number of lynchings.

Fannie Lou Hamer expected to be killed. Born in 1917, she worked on a plantation in Ruleville, Mississippi, for over eighteen years but was fired after she began working as field secretary for the Student Nonviolent Coordinating Committee (SNCC). In 1964 she lost a race for Congress but became vice-chair of the Mississippi Freedom Democratic Party (MFDP) delegation to the Democratic National Convention in Atlantic City. It became her route to unexpected fame. Mississippi's Democratic Party completely ignored its black citizens. Hamer and Aaron Henry, vice-chairs of a black Mississipian delegation, were determined to publicize the fact that the delegation sent to the Democratic National Convention represented less than half Mississippi's residents. Hamer, Annie Devine, and Victoria Gray Adams challenged the seating of the Mississippi delegation at the 1964 Democratic National Convention. Testifying before the credentials committee, Hamer told of trying to register to vote and being beaten for it in Winona, Mississippi, in 1963. Speaking simply and movingly, she educated the entire nation. The MFDP rejected Hubert Humphrey's insulting proposal of two votes in the regular delegation and was not seated at the convention. Neither this failure nor knowing that, returning home, they would face the Klan crushed Hamer, who ruminated, "You can kill a man, but you can't kill ideas. Cause that idea's going to be transferred from one generation till, after awhile, if it's not too late for all of us, we'll be free."

The next year the MFDP challenged the state's all-white congressional delegation. The campaign, known as Mississippi Challenge, led to passage of the Voting Rights Act of 1965. Morton Stavis, a white civil rights lawyer, compiled and presented to Congress evidence of civil rights abuse in Mississippi; in 1966, with three other lawyers, he founded the Center for Constitutional Rights. The Mississippi action totally changed the make-up of Democratic Party conventions, which now feature a brilliant rainbow.

Hamer courageously faced continual threats from the Klan and its sympathizers until she died of natural causes in 1977, having helped transform a failure into a freedom.

By participating in southern civil rights activism in the 1960s, some whites shared the suffering inflicted by the Klan on thousands of blacks. White Andrew Goodman and Michael Schwerner were murdered along with black James Chaney in Philadelphia, Mississippi, in 1964; Viola Liuzzo, mother of five children, marched in Montgomery to protest the Alabama state policy of denying voter rights. She was shot and killed by Klansmen on March 25, 1965, as she shuttled marchers in her car between Montgomery and Selma. But whites and blacks often conflicted within the civil rights struggle. White men tended to take over, without necessarily understanding the pressures on southern blacks, and to take credit for the accomplishments of the campaign. Black men responded by forming new organizations and excluding whites.

Black and white men both impeded female solidarity. Men derided women who challenged the sexual division of work and excluded them from leadership roles and a voice in the intellectual side of movement work – in both the civil rights and the anti-war campaigns. White women in the civil rights movement inspired feminism in some white men, but their presence created a deep rift with black women and caused tensions between black men and black women.[54] Most white women in the movement were middle class, privileged compared with blacks. Organizing gave them confidence and a sense of political efficacy. Southern black women were far more likely than white women to be brutalized by the police and jailed. Inspired by their tough, hardworking, activist mothers, they resented white women's racial insulation from the more dangerous and dehumanizing aspects of the movement.

This tension was exacerbated by black men's behaviour. They made sexual advances to white women, accusing them of racism if they refused. If they accepted, black women accused them of betraying their sisters. Black women's anger became a powerful force within SNCC, creating a barrier that sisterhood could not transcend. Black women already felt cruelly torn between the male-dominated civil rights movement and white-dominated feminism, while white women felt belittled by all – mainly by white northern New Leftists. In time, each group created a separate movement.

Civil rights agitation initiated in the 1950s intensified in the 1960s and led to passage of the Civil Rights Act of 1964. This significant comprehensive law is divided into eleven main titles.[55] Two titles deal with voting rights and desegregation in public facilities: Title V set up a Commission on Civil Rights; Title VII listed practices prohibited to employers and labour unions, obliged the federal government to set up an "affirmative" program of equal employment opportunity for all workers and job applicants, and created an Equal Employment Opportunity Commission (EEOC) to monitor compliance with the law. The act had outlawed discrimination by race, colour, religion, and national origin until Representative Howard Smith of Virginia added sex, hoping to defeat it (joking that the addition would guarantee every woman's right to a husband). Martha Griffiths of Michigan and other congresswomen rose in support of the bill, and conservatives, counting on the inclusion of sexual equality to cause the whole bill to fail, also supported it. It passed.

When the EEOC began operating in the summer of 1965, it expected virtually all complaints to come from blacks, but in the first year, 25 percent came from women. To handle them, the commission and the courts had to analyze female job categories and work patterns closely. A section of Title VII, women's greatest tool in achieving equality, required employers who wanted to define job categories by sex to show that sex was a "bona fide occupational qualification," not just a traditional one.

By 1968 American feminism was fully in the public eye. In 1971 the Supreme Court held that laws treating women and men differently might violate the constitution. In a landmark case, *Reed v. Reed,* the court used the Equal Protection Clause of the Fourteenth Amendment to assert that state legislatures cannot penalize people for their sex without a reasonable explanation for different treatment.[56] Sally Reed sued her estranged husband for the right to manage her dead son's estate. They were Idaho residents, and Idaho law preferred male relatives to manage a deceased person's estate – men were named administrators automatically. Reed held that this practice violated her rights under the Equal Protection clause of the Fourteenth Amendment. The court asked a question it never asked before feminism arose: What is the rational relationship between sex and the law's purpose? The state had not compared the Reeds' relative abilities to manage the property; it privileged men as a convenient way to end disputes. The court found this custom to be an arbitrary distinction based on sex and a violation of the Fourteenth Amendment's Equal Protection clause. It was the first application of the Fourteenth Amendment to women, the first major constitutional bar to discrimination by sex by legislatures, and the first legal treatment of women held accountable to constitutional principles.

In 1972 and 1978 the Civil Rights Act was amended to give the EEOC substantial new powers and responsibilities. In 1978 Congress passed the Pregnancy Discrimination Act, enlarging the definition of sex to include pregnancy, childbirth, or related medical conditions. The EEOC was willing to acknowledge that sexual harassment is a form of sex discrimination, but the term was not defined. For example, posting pictures of naked or semi-naked women in a workplace did not qualify as harassment until 1991, when Judge Howell Melton of the Federal District Court in Jacksonville, Florida, held that maintaining "a boy's club atmosphere" – an unrelenting "visual assault on the sensibilities of female workers" – constituted harassment.[57] But this case was brought by the feminist NOW Legal Defense and Education Fund, not by the EEOC, which as a government agency reflects government attitudes and policies. The EEOC never endorsed the concept of comparable worth. Republican administrations do not fight sexism; under Reagan and Bush I the executive branch systematically undermined the EEOC by failing to appoint personnel and by cutting funding.

In the classical republican tradition, political identity was not a right but a purchase. Men bought citizenship through property ownership and military duty. In the United States, male, but not female, citizens owe the state military service. Men need not actually perform that service: the existence of the obligation confers status. Women served as nurses in the armed forces, but did not make up substantial numbers of the military until the Second World War, when the services set up women's sections. Accepting volunteers who fit narrow guidelines and exempting them from combat, the armed forces limited women's numbers and their rank (until 1967 no woman could hold a command position), and granted them fewer benefits than men of the same rank. During the Vietnam War, these restrictions were modified slightly, and in 1976 West Point, Annapolis, and the Air Force Academy admitted women.

In 1980 President Jimmy Carter recommended resuming selective service registration in peacetime, requiring women as well as men to register. The ensuing debate, occurring simultaneously with debate over the Equal Rights Amendment, exposed male legislators' urgent need for a double standard. They did not object to women in the military, but feared that treating the sexes equally in draft registration would force equal treatment elsewhere.[58] They finally passed the Military Selective Service Act of 1980, ordering peacetime draft registration for men but not women. Men challenged this law, claiming it denied them the equal protection by law guaranteed by the Fifth Amendment. In 1981 the Supreme Court upheld the law in *Rostker v. Goldberg*, almost entirely because women were excluded from combat, without questioning the reasons for or the wisdom of the bar. Legal historian Leo Kanowitz pointed out that excluding women from combat (which is the usual practice) implies that men are less precious than women. As a point of comparison, in Israel, women are drafted but limited to noncombat assignments and are sometimes not given weapons; in the former Soviet Union, most servicewomen were nurses or administrators.

In 1989 Roberta Achtenberg and Clare Migden, self-declared lesbians, were elected to the San Francisco Board of Supervisors (city council), and Dale McCormick became the first declared lesbian elected to the State Senate of Maine. Lesbians are being elected to head mixed gay groups as well – some claim because the AIDS epidemic has killed off gay male leaders and women are filling a void. Perhaps lesbians' support of men in the AIDS struggle has won them gay male loyalty,[59] or perhaps the AIDS crisis has moved gay men closer to women's values. The two groups (insofar as they are coherent) have in the past been divided by different agendas: men were more concerned with sexual liberation and creating power bases; women focused more on social issues like child custody and care or women's health. Now both groups are urgently concerned with social issues and health care.

On the issue of peace, a gender gap has appeared in the political realm: in 1964–65, as the United States started to build a significant force in Vietnam, polls showed a gap of 12 points between the sexes on the use of military force. As Bush took the country into the Gulf War, the gap was 25 points. To the question "Shall the United States attack Iraqi forces in Kuwait?" men answered 48 percent against and 48 percent for; women were opposed by 73 percent to 22 percent.[60] But the gender gap has yet to suffice to win an election for a liberal administration, make women 50 percent of governing bodies, or keep the United States out of war or "police actions." In New Zealand, self-declared lesbian legislator Marilyn Waring brought down the government and her own party in June 1984 by persuading her country to refuse to permit nuclear submarines to refuel there. She prepared the ground for 1999, when Prime Minister Helen Clarke, the head of the Labour Party, led a coalition of centre-left parties, including the Green Party.

Women dared to express their commitment to peace in

"Women Strike for Peace" (WSP) in 1961. The 1930s American "Red Scare" went on until the fall of communism: capitalist interests dictated suppression of all dissent. In the 1950s (as in 1990–91 and in 2002–3), peace movements were seen as dissent, and people who deplored aggression as suspect. Government bodies like the House Committee on Un-American Activities (HUAC) and the Senate Internal Security Subcommittee interrogated members of peace organizations, trying to smell out communists. Women's non-hierarchical methods generated a hugely successful action, yet protected women from political persecution. For HUAC, opposing war or nuclear testing was radical; it commandeered membership lists of "radical" groups in order to intimidate the populace.

Five Washington, DC, women, appalled at the arms race in both the capitalist United States and the socialist Soviet Union, joined SANE, the Committee for a Sane Nuclear Policy, a highly structured male-dominated group opposed to the arms race.[61] In 1960 the Senate Internal Security Subcommittee ordered Nobel Laureate physicist Linus Pauling, who opposed nuclear testing, to reveal the names of the scientists who collected signatures on an anti-nuclear petition. Nervous SANE leaders began their own internal Red hunt, expelling communists and communist sympathizers. The women – Dagmar Wilson, Jeanne Bagby, Folly Fodor, Eleanor Garst, and Margaret Russell – were already frustrated by SANE's slow reactions to international crises and the men's reluctance to deal with "mother's issues" like milk contamination from radioactive fallout in nuclear tests. Upset by SANE's "Red Hunt" and convinced that no political body on earth cared about human life, they sought a way to call attention to the moral dimensions of the nuclear arms race. Remembering British women's marches at Aldermarston and civil rights sit-ins, they decided on a strike.

Their approach was to call friends and acquaintances across the country, spreading their idea in "female" style networking. The women they called contacted others, directly or by telephone. Women dug out Christmas card lists and sent chain letters. Within a year, the idea of a one-day strike for peace had become a national women's movement, with local chapters in sixty communities and offices in ten cities. From the first, the WSP was a non-hierarchical participatory network of activists whose greatest strength was the Washington founders' willingness to let each group act in ways that best suited its constituency. The women returned this confidence with trust and admiration. Knowing the dangers of keeping lists, they kept none. As an unforeseen benefit, the WSP could never accurately gauge its numbers, so its legend grew even when its membership did not. But on November 1, 1961, about 50,000 women in over sixty cities across the country left their kitchens and offices for a day to strike for peace. The demonstration and their demand – "End the Arms Race, Not the Human Race" – created a sensation across the country.

The WSP celebrated its first anniversary the following November, a month after the 1962 Cuban Missile Crisis. Confident and with a sense of urgency, it planned new protests. But in early December HUAC subpoenaed Dagmar Wilson, the national WSP spokeswoman, and thirteen women peace activists from the New York metropolitan area, three of whom had not even been part of the WSP. The surveillance establishment and right-wing press had from the beginning recognized what the Rand Corporation called the WSP's potential "to impact on military policies." The FBI had put the WSP under surveillance from its first public planning meeting in Washington in October 1961.

Days after HUAC summonses began to arrive, about fifty New York area "key women" held an emergency meeting and decided to support any woman summoned before HUAC, whatever her past or present affiliations, if she supported the WSP's position opposing both Russian and American nuclear policies. It would support the three women not in the WSP, if they wished, along with the WSP women. In sharp contrast to SANE in 1960, the WSP refused to isolate or criticize any woman for her affiliations or conduct at the hearing. This decision "not to cower" before the committee or to conduct internal purges, but to respect each woman's right to act for peace and to conduct herself according to the dictates of her conscience, was courageous in that period.

The politically unknown but savvy WSP leaders understood that, if HUAC was to succeed, it needed press support for its tactics of intimidation and persecution. They saw the hearing as a war between the sexes in which female common sense, openness, humour, hope, and naiveté fought male rigidity, solemnity, suspicion, and dark theories of conspiracy and subversion. In December 1962, in the Old House Office Building of the United States Congress, a hearing was held to determine the extent of Communist Party infiltration into "the so-called 'peace movement' in a manner and to a degree affecting the national security." It lasted three days, during which, for the first time, HUAC was belittled with humour and treated to a dose of its own moral superiority. Instead of refusing to testify, like radicals and civil libertarians of the 1950s, large numbers of the WSP participants volunteered to "talk." About one hundred women telegraphed Representative Francis Walter, the HUAC chair, offering to come to Washington to tell all about their movement. (The offers were refused.) This original WSP tactic exposed the committee's real intent – to smear those it chose to investigate, not to get information. At the hearings, the women captured the sympathy and support of much of the national media and strengthened the movement instead of destroying it. A typical newspaper account read:

> The dreaded House Un-American Activities Committee met its Waterloo this week. It tangled with 500 irate women. They laughed at it. Kleig lights glared, television cameras whirred, and 50 reporters scribbled notes while babies cried and cooed during the fantastic inquisition.

> When the first woman headed to the witness table, the crowd rose silently to its feet. The irritated Chairman Clyde

Doyle of California outlawed standing. They applauded the next witness and Doyle outlawed clapping. Then they took to running out to kiss the witness . . . Finally, each woman as she was called was met and handed a huge bouquet. By then Doyle was a beaten man. By the third day the crowd was giving standing ovations to the heroines with impunity.[62]

In *Thirty Years of Treason*, Eric Bentley wrote: "In the 1960s a new generation came to life. As far as HUAC is concerned, it began with Women Strike for Peace." And in 1970, *Science* reported that "Wiesner [Jerome Wiesner, Kennedy's science advisor] gave the major credit for moving President Kennedy toward the limited Test Ban Treaty of 1963, not to arms controllers inside the government but to the Women Strike for Peace and to SANE and Linus Pauling."

The WSP used Friedan's "feminine mystique" to legitimate women's right to a voice on foreign and military policy, just as eighteenth-century women used the concept of Republican motherhood to justify their demand for female education, and nineteenth-century women used the cult of true womanhood to legitimate their work in ante-bellum reform movements. Accepting the confines of a traditional female role, facing HUAC with courage, candour, and wit, WSP raised women's sense of political power and self-esteem. The WSP-HUAC hearing is a monument to courageous, principled women unafraid to take a stand against Cold War paranoia. But despite (or because of) women's success in making HUAC and what it stood for look foolish, men have consigned the event to oblivion.

Accomplishments in Conditions of Work

The number of women in medicine, law, and management has grown by 300 to 400 percent since the early 1970s. But the fact that women now make up more than half of the American workforce has not changed the stereotype of working husband and home-bound wife. Since women almost always also rear children and maintain the home, their contribution to society is greater than men's. Moreover, men's participation in the workforce is gradually dropping as women's rises sharply.

One group of women is leaving the workforce: in the United States, because more women are in universities and colleges, 73 percent of women between the ages of twenty and twenty-four worked in 1985, compared with 71.8 percent in October 1990. Many find the pay offered in expanding areas of work (often under $8 an hour) insufficient to cover child care. Of the 58 million married women living with a husband, 51.7 percent work outside the home – almost 60 percent of those with children under six, and 75 percent of those with older children. Counting those both with and without male support, 52 percent of women with children under one year old work outside the home. In Sweden, which has government-financed child care, over 80 percent of women aged twenty-five to fifty-four work outside the home; the figure is 74 percent in the United States.[63]

Feminism has made it more difficult for male employers to claim that women are unreliable workers because of pregnancy and child-rearing. Indeed, studies of women in military service show that female soldiers, despite menstruation or pregnancy, miss fewer days on duty than males, are less often absent without leave, and get into less trouble with drinking or drugs. Yet many male officers resent them, fearing men will lose their solidarity. They cite an old army saying: "Soldiers don't fight for their country, they fight for their friends." (They seem to believe men and women cannot be friends.) Men spend less time together because married soldiers live with their spouses. One general has acknowledged that women's presence has transformed the military.

Since the mid-1970s, working-class women have become more radicalized, profoundly altering the organizational and ideological balance of the feminist movement. Some commentators find this assertiveness a mixed blessing because, when any group dominates, the focus narrows.[64] Many American feminists opposed directing women's energies to passing the Equal Rights Amendment, since campaigns for equality help middle-class women, often to the detriment of working-class women. When working-class women take over, the agenda tilts towards economic projects.

In the 1970s Canadian working-class women fought for limited practical goals – equal pay and training, getting women hired in non-traditional jobs – which meant tackling the issue of sexual harassment. Mothers over twenty-five began entering the workforce and unions in dramatically greater numbers. To cut costs, the government downgraded working conditions for professional women like nurses and teachers, who increasingly turned to unions and professional associations for support. Hoping "affirmative action" would be cheaper and easier than writing, passing, and enforcing rigorous equal value laws, the government and organized labour made propaganda stars of the few women who worked in heavy industry (rail, steel, mining, manufacturing, and forest products) and were members of male-dominated heavy industrial unions, ignoring the fact that unions, socialist feminists, and women job-hunters had had to campaign to overcome employers' opposition to hiring women in such jobs.

Sexual harassment, an explosive issue for working-class people, is unlike other "women's issues" – daycare, equal pay, and maternity leave. It exposes men's deep unacknowledged hatred of women. Women are harassed not just by supervisors but by fellow workers. When a supervisor harasses a woman, the act has a class dimension: the man is telling her that she holds her job at his pleasure, emphasizing her inferiority to him in both class (or position) and sex. Male workers' running comments on women's sexuality, appearance, and incompetence express hate, tacitly threaten rape or battery, and appropriate a woman's sexuality. Supervisors tell a woman she is there at his will; fellow workers tell women they do not belong there at all.

Sexual harassment reinforces male solidarity across class lines, even if all the men in a workplace do not participate or witness in silence. It splinters working-class solidarity by dividing men and women, and strengthens elite or upper-class domination. This factor is important in understanding why governments foster sexual sadism towards women. Ruling classes are always small; working classes, large. To control the majority, the minority must divide it by sex, colour, or any other trait. Men who challenge women for acquiescing in male domination should ponder their long submission to this divisive technique.

Advanced capitalist economies – Canadian, American, and European – are being transformed, seemingly permanently. New technology and "deindustrialization" (moving industry to other parts of the globe) take work from growing numbers of Westerners of all ages, sectors, and levels of skill and education. The move of industry leaves behind ghostly cities, unemployed masses, and economic and emotional depression. Employers who remain are often highhanded and treat their workers poorly.[65]

Women office-workers must trade off their wages, lower than factory wages, for "clean" jobs that let them wear nice clothes and claim status. Secretaries may have as much education as their male bosses, yet are slotted into a female occupation that allows their male bosses to treat them like servants. An important development for working women was the formation of Local 925 of the Service Employees' International Union. Women in banking and insurance companies in cities like Cleveland, Boston, and Washington, DC, have organized to deal with sex discrimination and poor treatment in offices.[66] At first, organizers formed groups to negotiate solutions piecemeal. This process proved unsatisfactory and they eventually affiliated with the Service Employees International Union as Nine to Five: The National Association of Working Women, District 925 of the Service Employees International Union. Nine to Five has 12,000 members and the union, 50,000, almost all women. The movie *Nine to Five* inspired women across the country to form similar but independent groups like Women Employed and Working Women.[67]

Few clerical workers are unionized, but women form vital networks at work, which some believe do not challenge managerial authority but perpetuate and ease women's "adjustment to a stuck situation."[68] Others think these networks can potentially create solidarity in opposition to management. Using "feminine" modes like gossip about family life, secretaries create a "world which male bosses . . . cannot penetrate, thus allowing women to get away with doing . . . things that cannot be controlled."[69]

Unions like Nine to Five and the Coalition of Labor Union Women help women discover their own feminism. Eighteen months after the Textile Workers Union of America won bargaining rights in a National Labor Relations Board election, workers at the Oneita Knitting Mills in South Carolina struck. The strike lasted from January to June 1973, though the national boycott that accompanied it was never widely known.[70] But the strike succeeded because of black solidarity, white cooperation, and male support – a rare occurrence in labour union history. The character of the thousand-strong Oneita workers had changed: new workers were mostly black, younger, and more militant than earlier generations (85 percent were female, 75 percent were black, and the strike committee was 50 percent black and about 75 percent female). Strikes in small southern towns can challenge the entire power structure of the community, where factory owners, political leaders, and church leaders are all extraordinarily influential. In Oneita, black women challenged the power structure of their community, got help, and won. They were strongly supported by the black community, especially political leaders and clergy, and by unionized workers – Steelworkers, Rubber Workers, Retail Workers, and Furniture Workers from nearby communities. Some of these unions were mostly black; others were racially mixed. Some of Oneita's black union activists had worked in the southern civil rights movement, where they had gained political experience and ties to sympathetic blacks and whites, both local and statewide.

The 1976 boycott of J.P. Stevens, a textile manufacturer, drew more attention and support than any other except the United Farm Workers in 1989–90.[71] For forty years, the Textile Workers Union and its forerunner, the Textile Workers Organizing Committee, tried to organize the workforce (about half female and 25–30 percent black) at Stevens mills in North and South Carolina. It agitated at the Roanoke Rapids, North Carolina, plant in the 1940s, 1950s, 1960s, and 1970s, and finally won an election in 1974. Workers felt that Stevens violated labour laws, discriminated against women and blacks, maintained poor health and safety conditions, and paid women poorly. Because Stevens owned plants all over the south and simply transferred work from a struck plant, striking was useless unless all the plants cooperated. And Stevens was extremely tough in negotiations. One rank-and-file woman, Crystal Lee Jordan (later Sutton), took the lead at the Roanoke Rapids plant and urged an unusual route – a consumer boycott. It was hugely successful: workers at ten Stevens plants won collective bargaining agreements.

When an inexperienced man was hired as loan officer at $700 a month at the Citizen's Bank of Willmar, Minnesota, the women in the bank were outraged.[72] Female tellers started at $400–$500 a month, with no overtime pay, and were rarely promoted. The women filed charges of sex discrimination with the EEOC.[73] In December 1977 eight women went on strike. The Willmar Eight action was the first strike against a bank in Minnesota history and it so upset the owners that they sold the bank. The strike went on for a long time and permanently altered the women's lives: townspeople felt threatened by it; husbands, relatives, and friends grew angry with the women, who were not hired by the new bank owners. But by arousing fears of similar action in other banks (especially after a documentary made about the strike was shown across the country), these women influenced banking policy. The action transformed them into committed feminists/unionists, supported by women's and union groups across the nation.

The city of San José, California, paid jobs dominated by women 18 percent less than jobs dominated by men, even though both categories had the same number of evaluation points (equal skill or training).[74] After this discrepancy was verified by an outside consultant, the American Federation of State, County and Municipal Employees (AFSCME) tried to negotiate the inequity. San José's female mayor and the mainly female city council resisted the union, which, after six months, filed charges with the EEOC, charging that the city used segregated job classifications to underpay workers. In July 1981 Local 101 of the AFSCME went on strike. Nine days later, over 800 workers, 70 percent of them women, won $1.5 million in restitution, plus regular pay increases of 15.5 percent. This strike is notable for two reasons: the men in a mixed local strongly supported the women, even though only 30 percent of the bargaining unit was female; and the union dealt successfully with a technical legal issue – comparable worth.

African-American Women

African-American and African-British women often feel excluded or slighted by white feminists, but black and white feminists in America have also worked together for their mutual benefit. However, African-American women emerge from a different historical and social context from Euro-American women and they face a more excruciating problem. Euro-American women are tied to men who are unambiguously either part of the problem or part of the solution. But black men in America are so severely subjugated and exploited that they live virtually as a colonized population and, some believe, are being exterminated. This dire situation significantly influences the attitudes of black women.

Many African-Americans are mired in a poverty that is impossible to overcome because of discrimination: they cannot get decent jobs or move to certain neighbourhoods. Poor schools offer poor education, which leads to low-paid jobs or unemployment, and a cycle of hopelessness sets in. After the Supreme Court decreed segregated schools illegal in 1954 (the *Brown* decision), the south integrated its schools fairly successfully. But in almost all northern cities, more black students attended de facto segregated schools (with 90–100 percent black enrolment) after the decision than before it.[75] Moreover, educated black inner-city men do not get better-paying jobs as educated white inner-city men do. A study of ten urban ghettos showed educated black men no more likely to get jobs than uneducated; in some, they were more likely to be unemployed.[76]

African-American women have struggled to maintain their families and their community despite these obstacles, both raising and supporting their children. During the 1930s they organized neighbourhood "Housewives Leagues" in Chicago, Baltimore, Washington, Detroit, Harlem, and Cleveland to boycott white shops that excluded blacks from clerical and sales positions. "Don't Buy Where You Can't Work" boycotts gained an estimated 75,000 jobs for blacks and had "an economic impact comparable to that of the CIO's organizing efforts, and second only to government jobs as a new source of openings."[77] During the Second World War, black people were given limited opportunities in defence work – the percentage of black women employed in industry grew from 6.5 to 18 percent – but in low-paying, low-skill jobs. Blacks were barred from clerical and sales jobs until the 1960s.[78]

Because white America sees many African-Americans in poverty, it fails to realize the size of the black middle and elite classes that arose in the late nineteenth century. Nineteenth-century black female philanthropists used a rhetoric of "racial uplift," based on the notion that oppressed groups are responsible for their oppression and must "improve" themselves (a message today of Louis Farrakhan). In this climate, many blacks were educated and achieved prosperity and confidence. These were the African-Americans who launched the Civil Rights Movement, using strategies of non-violent direct confrontation – sitting-in at lunch counters, staging mass demonstrations, boycotting public transportation, taking "freedom rides," and registering to vote. Malcolm X revolutionized African-American thinking in the early 1960s by revalorizing black identity.[79] He created a new discourse, bringing terms like Black, Afro-American, and African-American into widespread use. "Black" became a new political-class identity when black nationalism grew strong enough to inspire mass resistance. Such organizations were not sex-segregated, but their official leaders were all male.

In disproportionately large numbers, women became the backbone of local organizations. A woman, Ella Baker, ran Martin Luther King Jr.'s campaign of peaceful protest and helped found the Southern Christian Leadership Conference (SCLC) and the Student Nonviolent Coordinating Committee.[80] Older working-class women, "mamas," inspired and supported younger workers, black, white, male, and female; they fed and housed civil rights workers, risking their jobs and sometimes their lives. Fannie Lou Hamer, Angela Davis, Assata Shakur, and hosts of other black women stood on the front lines of the Black Power movement. Black men formed the SNCC and the Black Panther Party (BPP). The Panthers, an international revolutionary organization focused on self-help and pride in race and heritage ("Black is Beautiful"), taught that Africans in the United States were colonized people. If some members planned terrorist actions against oppression, they never carried them out. Mainly they initiated self-help programs like feeding black children. The government immediately acted to suppress the new movement.

J. Edgar Hoover's FBI infiltrated King's inner circle and persecuted him with threats and intimidations. But he did not stop and he was murdered. Although there is no proof the FBI killed him, by 1967 Hoover considered the Panthers, not organized crime or the Communist Party, the greatest threat to "national security." A 1970 top-secret Special Report for President Nixon called the Panthers "the most active and dangerous black extremist group in the United States." The government worried less about its "hard-core members" (estimated at about 800) than the respect in which blacks held it: "A recent poll indicates that approximately 25 per cent of the black population has a great respect for the BPP, including 43 per cent of blacks under 21 years of age."[81] It set up Cointelpro, a counter-intelligence program, "to expose, disrupt, misdirect, discredit or otherwise neutralize the activities of black nationalist hate-type organizations and groupings, their leadership, spokesmen, membership and supporters."[82] It spread false rumours about Panther leaders and forged letters implicating them in robbing the party treasury, informing for pay, holding secret Swiss bank accounts, and having affairs with white women.

Cointelpro tapped phones, monitored shipments of *The Black Panther*, and infiltrated meetings, rallies, and headquarters. It assassinated twenty-eight Panthers in eighteen months in the late 1960s. Before dawn on December 4, 1969, the FBI induced the Illinois State Attorney's office to send police to a Chicago apartment where some Panther leaders were staying. They fired multiple rounds into the apartment, killing two leaders, Fred Hampton and Mark Clark, in their sleep and wounding four others. John Kifner, of the *New York Times* Chicago bureau, the first reporter at the scene, verified that what was described as a fierce exchange of gunfire was a unilateral police barrage – only one shot was fired from Hampton's apartment.[83] Most shots were aimed at the inside corners of the room holding the beds. Hampton's bodyguard, William O'Neal, an FBI infiltrator, had given the FBI a floor plan of the apartment; an autopsy revealed he had also given Hampton a sleeping drug the night before the raid. Government agencies mobilized to destroy the Black Panthers simply because of their potential to muster substantial social or political force.[84] Julia Cade of the American Civil Liberties Union (ACLU) National Prison Project counts at least fifteen former Black Panthers still in jail. The rest are dead. The party was wiped out within a decade.

Legal codes adopted during and after slavery were aimed primarily at black men, as the main threat to the existing "system" of white domination. Unemployment among black men is twice or more the national average; black men fill American prisons. The United States imprisons a larger percentage of its citizens than any other country in the world, having surpassed South Africa and the former Soviet Union. The USSR used to imprison 268 people per 100,000; Afrikaners, 333 per 100,000. The United States jails 426 per 100,000. The figures are even more shocking if we look at the racial breakdown: apartheid South Africa imprisoned 729 black males per 100,000; the United States imprisons 3109 per 100,000.[85]

This is the context of African-American life today. The United States government has systematically crushed all attempts by blacks to forge solidarity in the face of oppression: lynch mobs may be gone, but black males can be killed simply for walking in a white neighbourhood; police regularly harass, beat, or kill blacks on suspicion of a crime or without it, and selectively persecute black drivers. Demoralized, intimidated black men may express their rage in criminal acts; crime may bring prosecution, but it will not bring down on their heads the entire apparatus of government suppression. Political organizing, even when aimed at building peaceful black solidarity, does.

A black mother knows her son has one chance in three of avoiding prison before he is twenty-one. In such a climate, black women naturally cleave to and support their men, and devote huge energies to enabling their children to survive. As they were under slavery, African-American women remain the backbone of the family. All poor families have strategies to deal with poverty, strategies middle-class thinkers like Daniel Moynihan deprecate, yet which enable people to survive. But class, not race, is the main influence on family forms and behaviour, which vary little with colour. The more affluent a family grows, the more it acts like others on its economic level. Yet social critics adopt Moynihan's dictum that black families are maladaptive because they are headed by women and they focus mainly on the matrifocal family. Research shows, however, that the most common family structure among blacks is a married couple living together in a relatively egalitarian relationship.[86]

Some black women understand and forgive black men for vic-timizing women as white men do. Some don't. Women continue in the forefront of civil rights actions in government offices and insti-tutions, but are reluctant to insist on their own needs if these needs might pit them against men's. Black men as a group are extremely hostile to feminism in black women and often refuse to share gains in rights and freedoms with women. Stokely Carmichael and Charles Hamilton mention not one woman, not even Angela Davis, in *Black Power: The Politics of Liberation in America*. Black working-class women suffer oppression on three levels – sex, colour, and class. But a dramatic upsurge of organizational activity has occurred among African-American women since 1970, a date that also marks an African-American female literary renaissance.

American black women have created literature since Phillis Wheatley paved the way in the eighteenth century, yet only men are included in the African-American literary tradition. This canon omits Harriet Jacobs' vivid story of her escape from slavery, Harriet Wilson's *Our Nig* (1859), the first African-American novel, and Harlem Renaissance figures Zora Neale Hurston and Alice Dunbar-Nelson.[87] *Black Writers of America*, an ambitious anthology, includes no women.[88] Except for Gwendolyn Brooks and Margaret Walker, no woman had status in the black literary establishment before the 1970s. Alec Haley simply stole parts of Margaret Walker's *Jubilee*, the first modern slave narrative novel, for *Roots*. But in 1988 Oxford University Press began issuing the Schomburg Library of Nineteenth-Century Black Women Writers in thirty volumes.[89]

Dismissed by male-dominated literary establishments, whether black or white, black women announced their own literary tradition in 1970 with the publication of extraordinary first novels by Toni Morrison (*The Bluest Eye*), Alice Walker (*The Third Life of Grange Copeland*), and Toni Cade's anthology *The Black Women*, a collec-tion of poems, stories, and essays that "reflect the preoccupations of the contemporary Black woman in this country." Ignoring the def-initions of male experts and white feminists, they defined themselves.[90] In 1977 Barbara Smith published a landmark essay, "Toward a Black Feminist Criticism." Responding to strong pressure on black women to support black men, she showed that black men omit or denounce black women writers and that white feminists exclude them, while everyone ignores black lesbian writing. She urged black women to speak for themselves and to deal with sexual as well as racial and class politics.

The most egregious example of black male writers' animosity for women writers is their attitude to Toni Morrison. For years a senior editor at Random House, winner of many awards and the respect of mainstream American literary organizations, Morrison won the Nobel Prize in 1994. And she is a great writer – in my opinion the greatest living American author. Her highly acclaimed novels – *The Bluest Eye, Sula, Song of Solomon, Tar Baby, Beloved, Jazz, Paradise,* and others – deal with the pain of African-American men and women, describing their lives honestly and sympathetically. Yet black men accuse her of "selling out," being a tool of white feminism, a black man hater who engenders "sexual immorality among black women."[91]

Black women's experience is unique – they do not experience racism as black men do, nor sexism as white women do. The two prejudices, compounded, interact dynamically to create something devastating. Black women writers courageously break taboos to talk not just about the racism that splits black and white feminists but about the issues that divide women of colour from each other.[92]

Today, African-American women writers enjoy a wide audience, black and white, female and male, and are reaching out to women of colour across the world. The global black women's literary renaissance is informed by Black consciousness or nationalist thinking as well as the women's movement. But women of colour suffer "triple jeopardy" worldwide.[93] As Burakumin women in Japan are discriminated against by sex, class, and caste, women of internally colonized groups – South African, Palestinian, Amerindian, Northern Irish, Japanese Ainu, and some Pacific women – are oppressed sexually, racially, and nationally. Women disinherited economically or politically because of sex at home are locked out because of race when they emigrate to industrialized societies. In 1987 a collective of unemployed black women founded Black-womantalk, the first black female publishing house in England, to deal with such women's problems. And in 1994, American writer Meredith Tax founded Women's WORLD: World Organization for Rights, Literature, and Development, an organization intended to help women writers of the Third World find and deal with pub-lishers in the First World and to become better known.

The new scholarship on Afro-American women builds largely on Angela Davis' perception that black women's domestic work was "the only labor of the slave community which could not be directly and immediately claimed by the oppressor."[94] Many black women describe mother-centred worlds the heroine must leave to become herself or from which she continues to draw consolation and strength. "The memories of the mothers handed down through the daughters" keep communities together, Temma Kaplan notes.[95] Mothers in oppressed societies use language, symbol, and song to open the future for their children, just as Harriet Tubman used spir-ituals as signals when she led people to freedom. Similarly, Gertrude "Ma" Rainey, the "Mother of the Blues," and Bessie Smith sang to affirm ties among women and to urge them not to depend on men, a tradition that directly influenced Billie Holiday.[96]

Lesbians

When Gore Vidal wrote that there are heterosexual and homosexual acts, but no heterosexual and homosexual people, he suggested the ambiguity of sexuality, the fact that most people are capable of a range of behaviours wider than they may choose to live out. Women and men may perform both hetero- and homosexual acts over a lifetime, yet consider themselves strictly homo- or heterosexual. An estimated 6 to 13 million lesbians live in the United States, and 1.5 million of them are mothers – most were married, but some adopted children or used artificial insemination.[97] Lesbians may be feminists or not, activists or not, white, black, Latina, Asian, Native American, or European. They have taken part in all the direct actions discussed here; their contribution to feminist work is not discussed separately. But it is necessary to discuss lesbianism as a source of contention within feminism, and the particular contribution lesbians have made to feminist thinking.

Lesbians demanded a distinct voice in all early feminist groups, believing that patriarchal censure of lesbianism illuminates its attitudes towards all women. Lesbians, the most totally woman-identified women, asked women's organizations to support them. Some organizations drew back from associating with lesbians, mirroring patriarchal prejudice; others wanted to avoid identification with them, fearing male hostility. Men call women who speak up *bitches* or *dykes*, names women feared.

Dissension over lesbianism as a feminist position split early mainstream feminist organizations (only the issue of legal abortion was more divisive). It was partly healed at the women's conference in Houston in 1977 when Betty Friedan, the most famous opponent of public support for lesbianism, stood first in a line of women who spoke publicly in favour of including women's right to their own sexuality as a plank in the conference proposal. Her statement brought down the huge hall: purple and white balloons went soaring and the crowd roared, as if all those thousands of women were lesbians. Indeed, the public stance of many mainstream feminists today is that "we are all gay and black."

Among the most influential forces that changed women's attitudes were penetrating writings by lesbians on patriarchal attitudes towards women.[98] Lesbians by and large have written the most insightful analyses of women's issues because, of all women, they are least afraid of male censure. Lesbians love sons, fathers, brothers, and male kin – and even ex-husbands or male lovers – but, less likely than heterosexual women to be emotionally or economically dependent on men, they are often more honest and direct. They have produced a brilliant body of work that analyzes men's use of women in bolstering patriarchy and in the ideology of heterosexuality. Patriarchy has forced women into heterosexuality through early marriage (justified by men's insistence on virgin wives), wifely subordination to husbands, outlawing institutions that let women live alone without male domination, opposing wages sufficient to support a woman and her children, and sanctions against contraceptives and abortion.

These analyses moved directly into the centre of feminist thinking, enlarging both radical and mainstream feminist theory. With the courage to think what many straight women repress and to say what many straight women only think, lesbians have contributed hugely to feminist actions and theory.[99]

CHAPTER 20

THE POLITICAL
IS PERSONAL,
THE PERSONAL
IS POLITICAL

BECAUSE ALL GOVERNMENTS PRIVILEGE MEN and discriminate against or ignore women, women often feel like pariahs, people without a country. They can be torn between loyalty to their country and family, which may dismiss them, and loyalty to self, to the integrity of their existence. For millennia, women have been emotionally tortured by this conflict, but feminism offers an insight that points a way out of the dilemma. Feminism teaches that the personal is political, and the political, personal: the way one is treated in one's family reflects the power relations between the sexes in the country at large; and the way a state views females in terms of power will be reflected in one's domestic situation. Both are reflected in the situation in the world at large. Seeing this correlation, women can pinpoint what needs to be changed.

Now, at the dawn of the twenty-first century, women of every colour, culture, and class can connect with global feminism. "Global feminism" refers to a network of indigenous feminist groups and the emergence of a feminist culture – women hearing and teaching each other, using participatory democracy as means and end, and, in the process, developing a global perspective. They try to avoid nationalism as a prevailing determinant, calling their movement "global" rather than "international." The motto of global feminism is "Think Globally, Act Locally." And just as local problems are part of global situations, so personal problems are part of political and economic situations. Everything coheres.

The Political Is Personal

Conferences have been the major instrument for connecting women globally. But to work effectively, they must be run by women, not governments, their content dictated by women, from grassroots organizers to women who manage institutions. Conferences managed by governments or agencies are always shams. Charlotte Bunch, who has dedicated her life to global feminism, writes that the 1975 UN International Women's Year Conference in Mexico City was treated as a joke by the media and most governments, who used it as a perk for wives, lovers, and female creditors.[1] When the United Nations declared the Decade for Women (1975–85), it did not intend to foster feminism; rather, it intended to find a way to control the direction the "woman issue" took in the face of emerging global feminism. But nothing seemed to emerge from it: the representatives carped at each other, arguing about Israel versus the Arab states, while representatives from African countries bristled at Western women's criticism of genital mutilation. This, they insisted, was an internal matter, a cultural difference, and no business of Westerners. Westerners begged to differ: the torture and mutilation (and sometimes, death) of children and girls as a result of clitoridectomy or infibulation was a crime against women and a concern to all women. Male power entities totally ignored the Plan of Action the conference drew up to improve women's status.

Inadvertently, however, the UN had empowered women, as thousands of female private citizens descended on Mexico City for the meeting. They came in great numbers, women from all parts of the globe, lacking governmental status. As non-governmentals (NGOs), they could not speak in public or offer resolutions. No doubt the official delegates mocked them. But these women could do something else: they could and did talk together. They found areas of agreement; they exchanged telephone numbers. With no government assistance, they were becoming a lobby.

Many were leaders of non-governmental women's groups, eager to meet each other and discuss issues they were passionate about. Among these non-governmental groups were the Center for Women and Global Leadership, led by Charlotte Bunch; the International Reproductive Research Action Group (IRRAG), led by Rosalind Petschetsky; the Women's Environmental and Development Organization (WEDO), run by Bella Abzug; and several different organizations that operate within the United States, for which Gloria Steinem agitates. Originally founded to monitor the language of male development and population projects, to insure that women were remembered, WEDO became something far more potent. When the NGO women met, sparks flew, and talks went on late into the night. They stayed in contact, grateful for each other's support and advice. Much of what was accomplished at later meetings was a result of the interaction of these non-governmental groups.

The year 1975 was named the beginning of the Decade of Women, and some steps were taken to improve the lot of women. India, for instance, launched development projects like the Self-Employed Women's Association (SEWA) (see chapter 15) to raise women's income. Another microcapitalist project was initiated in Bangladesh in 1976, by Professor Muhammed Yunus, whose Grameen Bank made small loans of $50 to $100 to women for investment in entrepreneurial projects. In a few years, the bank made $900 million from these loans, which the women repaid at a rate of about 98 percent. Third World women don't seem to default. And since women who make money spend it on their children, the long-term consequence of improving women's lot was that their children received some education. This outcome would have important consequences.

At the Asian and Pacific Centre for Women and Development conference in Bangkok in 1979, feminists listed their goals: they wanted to assure the right of every woman to equity, dignity, and freedom of choice through the power to control her own life and body within and outside of the home and to remove all forms of inequality and oppression in society. For them, feminism is a world view affecting all aspects of life, all intimately interconnected: "The personal is political." They decided that the most important step was building women's movements independent of governments and male political parties. They did not argue that women should not work within these channels but that they must have their own power base. Grassroots organizing and autonomous organizations give women control of the direction of their movement.

By the Mid-Decade UN Conference on Women in Copenhagen (1980), the mood had changed, not because governments had adopted feminism but because they no longer found it amusing. Threatened by women in groups discussing politics, governments wanted to control the second conference tightly. When word got out that the preamble committee was discussing sexism across traditional political lines, for example, governments hastily sent their most loyal delegates to seize control of the committee and re-establish traditional divisions (between North and South, Israel and the Arab states, for instance). A prime law of patriarchy is divide and conquer, and the governments succeeded to the degree that the word *sexism* appeared in the final report only in a footnote describing what some countries saw as one cause of women's oppression, as if women's subordination was always local and due to local circumstances, and not a matter of male complicity.[2] Government and UN officials often feel that their political, economic, and social power, their jobs and lifestyles, depend on perpetuating existing political divisions. They were not about to let a few idealistic women in Copenhagen get out of hand and upset their rule. They knew that if women ever united globally against sexism, men would lose their prerogatives. And, indeed, they successfully kept control of the Mid-Decade Conference at the official level.[3]

Copenhagen was perhaps even more rancorous than Mexico City, but women triumphed on the unofficial level, holding their own autonomous NGO forums, which permitted real conversation and networking across political lines, especially among feminists. Intended to transcend divisive nationalistic agendas, they did not affect the official surface of the UN conferences. The media were hardly aware of them, and the various squabbling governments continued in their arrogant ways. But the discussions changed the participants, introducing them to new friends and new ideas.[4]

Only at a global conference can women place the family, whose structure and power relations vary with culture, in a larger context. Kenyans talked of female exploitation in the family. Working women earn too little to pay for scarce expensive child care and must leave their children with uneducated pre-adolescent girls, often relatives. Ignorant of rudimentary cleanliness and hygiene, the girls exchange their work for board, lodging, and a little pay if they are lucky. Many try to attend school if they get time off. They tend children and do housework and other tasks for very little reward: in short, they are exploited. Exploited working women can work only by exploiting poorer female relatives who cannot find even a low-wage manual job. At maturity, these girls marry men of their own class or move into casual work – trading, hawking, prostitution. Their poverty makes them eminently exploitable by both their families and the outside world. Their family teaches them social skills, ignoring the time when they have to find marginal work, but family exploitation also reinforces their poverty and dependence.[5]

Marriage, divorce, widowhood, and aging present very different problems for Western and for Third World women. In the Third World, divorced women are ostracized and destitute, owning nothing and lacking welfare. Not to marry at all (many do not) is socially demeaning and impoverishing, but in places like South Africa, poverty and the work structure make marriage difficult. Only 28.2 percent of black South African women marry.[6] But married or not, countless women worldwide live alone much of their adult lives.

A major project that emerged during the decade was Development Alternatives with Women for a New Era (DAWN), an India-based international organization that brings together Third World women activists, researchers, and policy-makers developing a global perspective on women's economic and political situation.[7] DAWN sponsored workshops on feminism and socialism. Panellists who had fought in socialist-feminist wars in Cuba, Nicaragua, Tanzania, Zimbabwe, and China stated that socialists try harder than capitalist states to better women's condition, yet they openly admitted socialism's limits for women.

A follow-up conference held by the Organisation for Economic Co-operation and Development (OECD) committed itself to targets for 2015: to reduce poverty by half, mainly through education and the extension of human rights to poor people. The World Bank announced that its main reason for existing was to eradicate poverty, and it became the largest contributor in the world to the social sector.

By the time of the UN Third World Conference on Women in Nairobi in 1985, at the end of the Decade of Women, the NGO women had broken through the barrier and were able to influence events. Third World women broke the precedent of 1975 and 1980 and criticized their countries' oppressive social and political practices. African women criticized African customs harmful to women, including clitoridectomy and infibulation, and reported on their many efforts to end it. Just as important, Third World women got together to critique the kind of development that was being imposed on their countries. For the first time, they suggested a feminist analysis of structural adjustment programs at the UN – an economic critique. We saw in chapter 18 how development programs focused on men and how some of them destroyed a traditional women's economy. The women in Nairobi insisted that the macro-economic framework of development projects had to be changed. In addition, the Asian Women's Research and Action Network (AWRAN) produced a detailed report on government repression of Philippinas. Domestic violence, not on the agenda in 1975, was a major subject in 1980 and 1985, when delegates passed proposals urging governments to try harder to help victims.

The UN Decade for Women saw some improvements: the State of the World's Women Report, issued at its end, disclosed that, in 1985, 90 percent of nations had official agencies dedicated to women's advancement, half of which had been created during the decade. Only twenty-eight states had required equal pay for equal work before 1975; in 1985, ninety did so. Most participating countries granted women constitutional and legal equality; sixty-five signed the Convention on the Elimination of All Forms of Discrimination against Women.[8] Changes can be tokens or can even disguise a worsening of women's situation, but legal changes give women the tools to forge real change. And incorporating women's new status in official documents gives it a legitimacy it had not formerly possessed.

Nevertheless, at the end as at the beginning of the UN decade, women performed two-thirds of the world's work, raised 45 percent of its food, earned one-tenth of its income, and owned one-hundredth of its property. Moreover, woman-hating religious groups and authoritarian governments throughout the world are undermining recently won rights to property, constitutional equality, and reproductive choice. Aware of this reaction, DAWN, in the vanguard of a movement to forge a global feminism that privileges no group of women, suggested that "feminism cannot be monolithic" in issues, goals, or strategies but should "reflect the concerns of women from different regions, classes, nationalities and ethnic backgrounds." It supports diverse approaches based on a shared opposition to oppression by sex and hierarchy as "the first step in articulating and acting upon a political agenda."

Success bred more UN conferences. A 1990 World Summit on Children, held in New York, was largely ignored at the time, but it had important reverberations. It set goals for the year 2000, made up of measurable targets in improving the health and education of children, and set an agenda for the twenty-first century. The United Nations Children's Fund (UNICEF) became the direction-maker for children's projects in the developing world.

In 1992 the Earth Summit, the UN Conference on Environment and Development, was held in Rio de Janeiro. It was a blockbuster. Stephen Lewis of UNICEF, who was present, described Bella Abzug "bludgeoning" Maurice Strong (the Canadian director-general of the UN Environmental Program and secretary-general of the conference) into submission, forcing him to allow the NGOs to be heard publicly! This was, Lewis says, the moment when governments began to listen to civil society. Here, women questioned who had the authority to shape Agenda 21, the agenda for sustainable development that was the object of this environmental meeting. The United Nations Development Fund for Women (UNIFEM), led by Noelene Heyser, played a strong role here, bringing peasant women from many countries to the UN to explain their work and claim the right to shape the agenda: it is, after all, they who have to live out the consequences of such agendas. No such people had ever been brought before that august body before, yet the women had a great impact. In the end, governments accepted that international covenants were necessary to protect the environment, and follow-ups were planned for Kyoto and Montreal.[9]

But the most thrilling conference, says Lewis, was the 1993 World Conference on Human Rights, held in Vienna. Women took over, especially Charlotte Bunch and Bella Abzug, and "governments ran for cover." The Asian and Latin American women's caucuses were brilliant, and Bunch and Roxanna Carillo of UNIFEM mounted an extraordinary "Day of Testimonies," in which twenty-five women from all over the world described personal violations they had experienced – physical, sexual, legal, and other kinds – before an audience of a thousand – which offered them utter silence and muffled tears. All the judges declared that things had to change.

This conference was extraordinarily important: it destroyed the line between public and private that, for centuries, had been sacrosanct in liberal theory. Liberal men insisted that to guarantee freedom in the private realm, it was necessary to distinguish between it and the public realm. But doing so guaranteed only men's freedom. The private realm is, after all, the first and most profound site of female victimization. So, a human rights organization would criticize states that tortured or imprisoned journalists, writers, or political figures, but not raise a murmur of protest against states that made legal the physical battering and torture, or even murder, of women. The division between public and private meant that women's human rights were violated. But this abuse did not seem a serious problem to men who, consciously or not, do not think of women as fully human.

The decision to abandon the distinction between public and private was, essentially, a recognition that the political is personal, the personal political. In 1993, after years of splintering argument, the human rights women succeeded in getting the human rights men to admit that women had human rights. This admission means that women were declared to be human beings – a matter that had been in contention for millennia. The very idea was world shaking.

The admission that women have human rights did not change the lives of women immediately, but it will. It represents a shift in thinking that makes women matter in a way they had not previously. It brings women to a level equal with men in global awareness and lays the groundwork for future thought, legislation, and institutions. Ever since Aristotle, the world at large has seen women as "defective men," not as human beings with rights not to be assaulted, maimed, tortured, or killed, as people needing, as men do, food, clothing, medical care, and education. Of course there are still people who don't believe women are fully human – the Human Rights declaration can't change that. But it fixed new assumptions for future behaviour.

In addition, the 1993 conference appointed a female rapporteur to handle women's rights issues. Without a rapporteur, items cannot be placed on the human rights agenda. One of the subjects the rapporteur will investigate is the report that, in some countries, women who are about to be executed are routinely raped first. One of the items demanded by the NGO women was the ability to monitor all resolutions in a realistic way. They are determined to avoid a set of paper resolutions that everyone signs at the meeting and then goes home and forgets. And they planned follow-up conferences for reports from the various monitors.

In 1994 the International Conference on Population and Development in Cairo changed the basic assumptions about population control, a subject of great concern because of fears that huge population growth in Africa and Asia will cause unrest and insurgence in the world. For generations, institutions have tried to cut back the birth rate. The formulaic cure for large families has been to raise men's income, based on the assumption that, when men consider themselves middle class, they sire fewer children so they can spend more on the nutrition, education, and medical care of each child. But when development projects in Asia and Africa did raise men's income levels, women's and children's nutritional levels went down and the birth rate stayed up.

Birth control is a ticklish subject. Development agencies believe that in countries where many children die young, men want large families to guarantee that a few will survive; that in Africa in particular, a large brood of children testifies to a man's virility and power; and that men dislike birth control because it gives women a sexual freedom men do not want them to have. In addition, the opposition of certain religious groups, especially the Catholic Church, has made it a dicey matter. And large official conferences do not tackle dicey things. But experiments conducted in several places, including Bangladesh, one of the world's poorest countries with one of the world's highest birth rates, concentrated on women; instead of money, they gave them education on birth control and access to it. In a few years, the Bangladeshi birth rate dropped significantly.

The heroine of the Cairo conference was Nafis Sadik, the Pakistani head of the United Nations Fund for Population Activities (UNFPA), who dared to face down Pope John Paul II. During a private meeting with him, held before the conference, Sadik did not dissemble, apologize, or make nice, but told the Pope that the Vatican would not dictate to the world's women. Reporting on their unfriendly meeting, she gave an inspirational speech to the entire conference. She, along with Bella Abzug of WEDO and Noeleen Heyser of UNIFEM, helped set the entire development movement on a new course. Women had never been the centre of birth-control discussion. It was apparently assumed by developers that women's wombs were owned and controlled by men. Abzug insisted that reproduction was not women's sacred duty but their right – the right to be in control of their own bodies, their own lives.

The impact of Vienna has been enormous, says Lewis. Inspired by the human rights principles enunciated the year before, the conference placed women firmly at the centre of any discussion of population, just as they had been positioned in the poverty discussion. Knowledge about children's poverty gained through work for the 1990 conference enriched this discussion. Henceforth, family planning would be seen as part of women's education and women's rights. Where women had greater equality with men, the population dropped. After this conference, there would be no development without the massive education and empowerment of women: this is the new mainstream thinking and, because it is written in a document signed by most of the world's governments and because it sets standards for the world, it has become part of the thinking of those governments.

A Pledge to Gender Justice, written by members of the Third Preparatory Committee for the Fourth World Conference, was endorsed by over 100 organizations worldwide. Heyser writes: "At Nairobi, women outlined a comprehensive plan of Forward Looking Strategies for the Advancement of Women. At Rio, women were recognized as managers of natural resources and the moving force for sustainable development. At Cairo, women's health, empowerment and reproductive rights were placed at the centre of population-related development policies. At Copenhagen, the political, economic, and social empowerment of women was recognized as key to eradicating poverty, unemployment and social disintegration."[10]

Early in 1995, a conference was held that did not focus on women: the Summit on Social Development, held in Copenhagen, was intended to address poverty, social disintegration, and employment. Again, there were battles between North and South, and complaints about a decline in assistance to the South by the World Bank and the International Monetary Fund (IMF). Although women were not on the agenda, Abzug created a women's caucus and joined the press briefings held by the men. Her group insisted that you cannot understand poverty without looking at the feminization of poverty; you cannot look at social disintegration without looking at women's role in the family; and you cannot look at employment without paying attention to women's supposedly "casual" work. The world over, women's work is unvalued, often unpaid, and often part time; it is unrecognized, secondary work, "working for lipstick." Yet this casual work feeds most of the world's children and must be recognized and valued whether it is paid or not. Gro Brundtland of Norway gave a powerful speech pointing out that poverty was largely female, and the phrase, "feminization of poverty," entered the language. The final plan to deal with poverty mentioned this feminization of poverty and urged universal education and universal health care. For the first time in history, many of the world's states committed themselves to these two goals.

In 1995 the UN Fourth World Conference on Women was held in Beijing. It was the largest women's conference in history: 50,000 people participated, women and men, governmental representatives and NGOs. Hillary Clinton, the wife of the president of the United States, appeared. Despite the hostile atmosphere generated by the Chinese government, everything came together. Heyser describes it as "not a UN conference on women, but a women's conference on the world."[11] The conference succeeded in placing women's issues at the centre of concern. Every part of the agenda created in earlier sessions became part of the official international agenda: violence against women, health and education, inheritance rights, and women's rights to own their own bodies. It set women's agenda for empowerment and emphasized the need to look at economic and political power in all countries. The conference gathered a million signatures on a petition to end violence against women and made a commitment to declare rape a war crime. Through a General Assembly resolution, a trust fund was set up to support campaigns to end violence against women, focusing on four areas: family violence, traditional practices, violence in war and crisis situations, and economic violence. It also established a monitoring system.

In just twenty-five years, these conferences have forged an entirely new conception of women on a global level. For the first time in history, governments recognize that women are human beings with human rights; that they are central to development projects attempting to eradicate poverty; and that their education and health care is doubly important, since women are the ones who care for, and often support, the children. Violence against women has been declared not a male right but a crime, whatever religious legal codes may hold. Human rights organizations are now committed to taking a stand against violence towards women. In a world in which the political and the personal are identical, taking a global perspective means using our knowledge of sexual politics, feminist theory, and experience to expose the connections between "women's issues" and world problems.

It is not possible to overestimate the importance of these conferences. Governments are not, of course, suddenly converted to feminism; they are as misogynist as ever. But the agreements they signed give the women of every country a tool, a weapon, for forcing changes in law or in enforcement of existing law. Perhaps the most important accomplishment of Beijing was to provide funding for women activists in each country to monitor compliance. We have seen how the daughters of peasant women in India, helped by groups like SEWA, are now the college-educated missionaries to other peasant villages, succeeding the philanthropic privileged college-educated women of the earlier generation (see chapter 15). When change is being impelled from the bottom, from the grassroots, it is inevitable. The revolution Rosa Luxemburg and Emma Goldman wanted, the revolution from below, is happening now. It is called feminism, and it owns the twenty-first century.

The Personal Is Political

Physical Abuse of Women

Date rape and sexual harassment were, Gloria Steinem says, just life – until women turned them into crimes.[12] Nowadays, everywhere in the world, women are organizing against the most pervasive oppression they suffer – personal abuse in the home. Patriarchists often claim that men dominate the public realm, but women dominate men and the home. Yet the home – the sanctuary from the harsh outside world, sacred to religionists of all persuasions, and the place even liberal men believe women should be if they have children – is the primary site of female persecution, where girls are taught from infancy the true status of their sex: to be owned and controlled by men.

Many – perhaps most – human beings emerge from childhood bruised, scarred, or deformed from emotional or physical punishment and deprivation. We lug our pain into adulthood, buried under layers of defences, to inflict it, intentionally or willy-nilly, on others. A more just and humane world demands a more just and humane upbringing and an end to physical punishment.

The patriarchal law that men "own" women and children also gave men the right to abuse them physically, like their animals. It bears pondering that people may treat animals better than women and children. Children of both sexes are beaten, even tortured. In general, boys are punished more often and more severely than girls, to teach them that they must be obedient to the Father. But in adolescence, boys are given far greater freedom than girls and forced to do less domestic maintenance or none at all. The overall message boys get is that they must obey the Man, but can exercise power and enjoy freedom once they are men. Girls are taught submission and are confined in the home from infancy to marriage.

Both sexes are sexually abused as infants or children, but here the balance tilts the other way: more girls than boys are abused and for longer periods. Sexual abuse has only recently entered public discourse, but experts suggest that girls subjected to repeated molestation and rape feel voided (as do adult women who have been raped), feel that their will, their existence as human beings, has been obliterated. (I do not know of studies of boys in this regard, but their feelings are probably similar.) Women rarely sexually abuse children, but they batter them more often than men. What is remarkable is not that women beat their children but that men, who spend little time with children (most statistics claim children spend 90 percent of their time with their mothers and 10 percent with their fathers), are responsible for nearly half the battering and most of the sexual abuse.[13]

Nineteenth-century women instigated reform of child welfare laws, and women's movements organized the reform. Women in the West finally got exclusive responsibility for rearing children after children became financial liabilities rather than assets; they found paternal discipline too strict. To try to protect children was to challenge patriarchy, yet women softened child-rearing norms, "senti-mentalizing" the Calvinist tradition. Feminists campaigned against corporal punishment and, by the mid-nineteenth century, the pros-perous classes frowned on it. But child-beating was not considered a social problem in the United States until the 1870s. Reformers focused mainly on poor families, blaming drunkenness, ignorance, or poverty for the ill-treatment of children. By the early twentieth century, child-welfare advocates had found that most children suf-fered not from assault but from neglect. Parents were absent or inattentive. Children were sometimes sent to reform schools on stubborn-child charges. Society wanted to protect children, but reformist thinking was stuck in a patriarchal rut: children were still property to be controlled by all-powerful fathers. If biological or marital fathers were not up to the mark, the state would step into the breach.

Nineteenth-century feminists redefined family and, particular-ly, mothering norms, but for most women, especially poor urban women, motherhood was hard or impossible. Many mothers were isolated from support networks of kin; caretakers are isolated by small children, who are accepted in few public places or workplaces. Cities grew dangerous for children, and the new norms of mother-ing, which involved "psychological parenting," increased the grounds on which a mother could "fail" (the very idea of failing at motherhood was inconceivable before the nineteenth century). Social workers asked to intervene in family conflicts were invited by the weaker members of the family power structure, women and children – yet they were the people who suffered most from that intervention. Fathers might be outraged at losing face, but agency action usually led not to prosecution and jail, but removal of child-ren from the family. Mothers (and children) dreaded this outcome far more than fathers.[14]

In every country, family relations have always been socially reg-ulated, although community standards and methods for achieving conformity vary. The idea of failing at motherhood or of an autonomous family is foreign to most people in the world. The idea of family autonomy arose in the nineteenth-century West to offer a personal, caring haven from the public realm of instrumental relations. In the 1950s Talcott Parsons asserted that professionals had taken over family functions like child care, education, therapy, and medical care and that this was progress – it left families more time and energy to devote to emotional interaction. But the Frankfurt school of German Marxists condemned the decline of family autonomy, blaming it in part for the horrors of totalitarianism. Such thinking now dominates left-wing criticism of social control, which continues to identify the "private" sphere as somehow natural, producing strong egos and inner direction, in contrast to the invasive public sphere, which produces passive conformist populations.[15] The right wing, too, has attacked social welfare programs over the last decade in its campaign to keep women dependent. The unacknowledged agenda of the left may not be different.

"Family autonomy" is a foolish idea, especially since the power of the male household head it is intended to protect has eroded. The United States Census Bureau defines a family as a household of two or more people related by blood or law. In 1960, 94 percent of the American population lived this way; in 1977, 90 percent. The other 10 percent lived alone, with unrelated people, or in institutions (hospitals, prisons, orphanages, old-age homes). But the Census Bureau definition masks different kinds of "families" made up of parent-child, childless couples, or those with grown children not at home (recently called "broken families" or "remnants").[16] In 1989 only one in four families was made up of two parents and children. In 1991 there were 9.7 million single-parent families – 8.4 million of them headed by women.[17]

"Family" is not identical to household: people share households without considering themselves family, and people who do not live together feel like family.[18] The 1975 *Journal of Home Economics* suggests that *family* denotes interdependency, interconnection, intimacy, and commitment over time.[19] But many people are not intimate or interdependent with kin, sharing only a common past. Permanence is not a mark of kinship: early death used to rearrange family relationships regularly. Today, one of two marriages in the United States ends in divorce.

Social agencies have helped poor women who need protection from physical attack at home or in shielding their children from abuse. Social control is desirable to some reformers so long as policies give mothers both legal custody and the power to support their children while tending them according to their own standards of care. A beneficent social policy could help battered women by enabling them to leave abusive situations and live in comfort and dignity without men, while teaching them to expect decent treatment from others. It would be hard to empower children similarly. It is also hard to know when a child is better off apart from its mother. One of the cruellest elements in child abuse is that the abuser may also be the main source of affection – that the one who loves also hates – while the other parent is indifferent.

Millions of women raise children and support them in a society that undervalues their sex and pays them little more than half the standard (male) wage for their work. In the United States in the early 1990s, 60 percent of working women did not have job-protected maternity leave; 75 percent of working women were single or married to men earning under $15,000 a year; 50 percent of babies under a year had working mothers, yet federal funds for day-care (already insufficient) had been cut by 25 percent since 1980. European women, on average, have maternity leave of five months at full pay; in France, 90 percent of three-year-olds attend government-sponsored pre-schools; in Sweden, parents can work six-hour days until their child reaches eight; and in Italy, working women get two years' credit towards seniority with each new child. Women in Europe earn 70–80 percent of the male wage. Women in the United States earn less than that.

Social policy on child abuse cannot be discussed out of this context. Like every other issue involving women, it is inextricable from a web of culture. What we are talking about when we talk about "women's issues" is life itself, issues disdained by those pursuing power. Patriarchy defines women as mothers, and mothers as nurturant, provident creatures who live entirely for others. This ideology of mothering is so widespread, ancient, and powerful that it remains, even if one's lived experience does not validate or even correspond to it. A woman may see her experience as an aberration, or may intensify her efforts to achieve this ideal, or may blame herself or her own mother in a destructive cycle.[20] But whatever women do, no such being can possibly exist.

Blame of the mother, pervasive in American culture, is most striking in cases of incest. Most important studies of incest show that the mother is the main focus of the daughter's anger, hatred, and sense of betrayal, even though the father was the abuser.[21] Women molested or raped in childhood almost always direct their rage mainly at women, not men. Incest victims tend to regard all women, including themselves, with contempt. The mother in an incestuous family is likely to be a defeated woman, defeated by the same force that is eradicating her daughter – male power in the family, backed by political and economic power in the outside world. Incest victims also tend to blame and despise themselves for the incest. Since girls often identify with their mothers, contempt for the mother drains them of all faith in female power. Boys who are severely physically abused by their fathers also often bow, later, to their fathers' "rightness," despising their mothers' helplessness.

One accomplishment of feminism has been to expose and bring into common knowledge the facts of female abuse. The National Organization for Women has calculated that, in the United States, a husband or lover beats a woman every fifteen minutes. Every year, 500–750 women of the beaten millions strike back. At least 40 percent of women who kill do so in self-defence. Men have beaten, molested, imprisoned, raped, tortured, and murdered children, wives, and lovers for millennia. In past societies, indeed until the feminist movement of the nineteenth century, men's right to perform such acts was given by law (and still is in Muslim law). Even after such rights were rescinded, women could not get help from police or social agencies and could not escape unless their families were sympathetic – and not all of them were. Even so, men can pursue the women who leave, and they often kill the entire family. Men sexually assaulted their children with impunity, and few were prosecuted for it. Not until nineteenth-century women joined in solidarity to end these horrors and agitate for laws forbidding assaults of women and children, whatever their relation to men, did people in general believe that such acts could be opposed effectively.

Women continue to further this humane agenda, with significant effects.[22] In the United States a few years ago, feminist activists urged lawyers for the first time to use a plea of self-defence for such women. Some women won new trials or reviews on this ground and were released from jail. The efforts of these reformers have led just and humane men to act. In December 1990 Richard F. Celeste, the outgoing governor of Ohio, granted clemency to twenty-six of over one hundred such women in Ohio prisons; in January 1991 Governor William D. Schaefer of Maryland commuted sentences for eight women similarly convicted. Women's and criminal justice groups lobby other governors and are working across the country for laws explicitly allowing battered women charged with violence against their abusers to introduce evidence of their abuse and its psychological effects in their defence. Missouri, Ohio, and Louisiana now have such laws; Schaefer lobbied for one in Maryland in 1991. Similar legislation is being considered in other states.[23]

Women across the world have created shelters for battered women, rape crisis centres, and centres for displaced homemakers. They have to beg every year for government funds (which are cut whenever money is tight), but they try to provide a safe home, food, and clothing for battered women and their children, a haven for rape victims, and counselling and retraining for displaced homemakers. Until such shelters were founded in the late twentieth century, women were allowed no escape from male abuse.[24] If this were all feminism had accomplished, it would be remarkable.

The Body: Reproduction, Sexuality, Health, and Violence

Women in Brazilian shantytowns told DAWN workers that their main problem was reproduction. The Brazilian left, campaigning against population control, had distributed a flyer showing a man giving women birth-control pills and the women demanding resources instead. The Sao Paulo women said this was a false representation: they wanted both. Forming "Proyecto Esse Sexo que e Nosso" (Project for This Sex That Is Ours), DAWN produced illustrated booklets about women's health, reproduction, and sexual pleasure. The most effective educational material for poor women in Brazil, these pamphlets are now distributed by the government.[25]

After women in the slums of Lima, Peru, asked their Women's Centre for information on sex, health, and birth control, the Manuela Ramos Movement centre held workshops on women's lives on personal, informational, and organizational levels. They offered discussion of women's bodies, sexuality, and roles as human beings, mothers, and citizens, along with information on health, primary education, and neighbourhood organization.

Women of Southeast Asia organized projects to assist victims of battery and rape, but also to change rape laws and community attitudes. In Indian towns, women banged pots and pans outside the houses of men particularly abusive to their wives and agitated against rampant "dowry deaths." They forced passage of a law requiring any "accidental death" or "suicide" of a woman in the first seven years of marriage to be investigated for foul play.

Before global feminism, Africans refused to discuss female genital mutilation. But in 1984, women from twenty-four African countries held a conference in the Sudan, African Women Speak on Female Circumcision. They advocated its total eradication, declaring that the Qur'an in no way supported it. In Nigeria, Africa's most populous nation, girls are married very young (from eleven to thirteen) and most are genitally mutilated. As a result, many have agonizing childbirths. Obstructed birth can tear a hole between the birth canal and the bladder. Without corrective surgery, this damage renders a twelve-year-old incontinent for life. About 20,000 women, mainly northern Nigerian Muslims, suffer this disability (vesicovaginal fistula, or VVF). Their husbands divorce them; their families shun them. Nigerian women's groups have recently mounted a campaign against early marriage.[26]

In Latin America, the Catholic Church demands that contraceptive and abortion information be suppressed, but complications from illegal abortions are the major cause of death of Latin American women between the ages of fifteen and thirty-nine. In Colombia, feminists have set up illegal clinics to perform sanitary abortions, with a sliding payment scale. Movements for legal abortion are increasing across the continent: several Latin American women (including a Peruvian nun, Rosa Dominga) signed the *New York Times* ad placed by Catholics demanding choice.

While the governments of China, Singapore, Malaysia, and India have forcibly sterilized women or penalized them economically, the Kampuchean government coerces women to "recover" the population massacred by a previous government. Population policies almost always focus on women, as if men had nothing to do with conception. Many states use coercion, which often backfires. A Bangladeshi program bribing women with wheat for using contraception heightened local opposition to birth control. In China, India, and Korea, government pressure leads to murdered female babies. Feminists advocate programs like the Bangladeshi "Seven Village Women's Self-Reliance Movement," which integrates family planning with a range of services to improve family income, education, and health.[27]

Female sexual slavery may be the most serious human rights violation in Asia. Poor Indian families sell daughters as servant/concubines to Arabs or as Devadasis; they are impressed for life as prostitutes in temples or brothels run by priests. As we have seen, "tourism to Third World countries, particularly in Asia, became a growth industry in the 1970s and continues to be propagated as a development strategy by international aid agencies. In fact, this industry was first planned and supported by the World Bank, the IMF and USAID."[28] Sex-tourism helped make up for the economic loss when the American military left Southeast Asia. Companies in Thailand, the Philippines, and South Korea lure women by promising good jobs, then enslave them in brothels where male customers treat them sadistically. They also sell Asian women as "compliant" mail-order brides to Western men. Organized multi-million-dollar transnational businesses offer sex-tour packages to men from wealthy regions – Japan, Europe, North America, and the Middle East – systematically selling women's bodies as part of packaged tours, feeding various middlemen, and bringing foreign capital into the country.

When a national economy relies on prostitution – as in Vietnam and the Philippines when American troops were stationed there, or in Thailand, with brothels patronized mainly by Japanese businessmen – only a global feminism can fight back. Women are mere commodities in brothels: most of the money they bring in ends in men's hands. Feminists try to end such practices in their own countries, but since the traffic is international, steps must be taken on that level. Philippinas protest sex-tourism and militarism simultaneously, giving shelter to women who escape and teaching them skills that allow more control over their lives. Japanese feminists, who first opposed this traffic, worked with Southeast Asian feminists to expose local travel agencies and companies that ran such businesses and to expose the men's practices to their wives.

Feminist groups like GABRIELA in the Philippines and the Women's Information Centre in Thailand help victims of forced prostitution and try to spread suspicion of deceitful ads and jobs abroad. They also denounce their governments for complicity in sex-tourism, which brings in much-needed foreign capital and is sometimes even included in the budget for national development plans. Women from Japan, Thailand, Korea, and the Philippines worked the crowd at the International Tourism Conference in Manila in 1982, demonstrating there and at national airports, embarrassing everyone involved. Feminists in Holland and West Germany, where Southeast Asian women are brought as prostitute-slaves and mail-order wives, set up centres for foreign women try-ing to escape, demonstrate at airports when sex-tours leave for Asia, and confront traffickers in their own countries.

Female sexual pleasure and lesbianism are not on the agendas of any government, and feminists raise these issues over opposition. Brazilian feminists incorporate them in women's health projects, and a workshop on these subjects took place at the first Feminist Encuentro for Latin America and the Caribbean held in Colombia in 1981. At the second Encuentro in Peru in 1983, the lesbian ses-sion drew half the 600 participants and had to move to a bigger room. Since then, lesbian feminist groups have formed in Peru, Brazil, Mexico, Chile, Argentina, and the Dominican Republic. In Chile, feminists invented a board game called "knowing our sexual-ity," which they still play with women in the barrios. The women get so heated about the issues that they manage to make only a few moves a week. Lesbianism was discussed in workshops at a Costa Rica health conference and in Nairobi in 1985, and a regional les-bian-feminist conference was held in 1987 in Mexico.[29]

Years ago, the Boston Women's Health Collective produced *Our Bodies, Ourselves*. Widely translated, it revolutionized women's health care. The Black Women's Health Network in Atlanta devel-oped a holistic approach to health, self-affirmation, and race/sex oppression that Kenyan women have adopted. For several years, the Geneva Women's Health Clinic (Dispensaire des Femmes) has offered non-medical collective feminist health care, using Western and herbal treatments, and has trained women to establish clinics in Costa Rica, Brazil, Nicaragua, and India.

PART EIGHT: THE TWENTY-FIRST CENTURY: DAWN

Work

Of all countries, India has created the most projects to help women economically, perhaps because of a highly developed moral sense among many Indians or because elite women have considerable influence in the country and many dedicate themselves to the plight of the poor. One of them, Ela Bhatt, founded the Self-Employed Women's Association (SEWA), which organizes women in informal vocations. SEWA helps women earn more by forcing banks to give them credit – it creates a credit system within the cooperative and trains women in various skills. It also eases their isolation: many Indian women are confined at home; they work alone and need middlemen to sell their work. SEWA eliminated these men, who generally exploit the women. It also created a women's political base. The Working Women's Forum, Annapurna Mahila Mandal, Bhagavatula Charitable Trust, Bangladeshi Chanchte Shekha, Bangladesh Rural Advancement Committee, and many other organizations help working women form dairy cooperatives, economic and social planning groups, savings groups that invest in small businesses and lease land, local credit organizations, and a global project, Women's World Banking, that has been very valuable.

In Nigeria, the Street Foods Project organized the (primarily) women who sell food on the streets and pushed for laws regulating selling zones, making them safer and cleaner and protecting women from male harassment. It also trains women in marketing and other skills. In Ghana, Flight Lieutenant Jerry J. Rawlings seized control and, in 1979, tried to force market women to accept his price controls by whipping violators and bulldozing their stalls. The women persisted in their practices. He razed the Accra market; next morning the market women were in place in the ruins. By 1986 he conceded the battle, unveiling a new central market with a cement floor, steel roof, and no price controls.[30]

Togo market women have kept its president in power for the last twenty years. Gnassingbé Eyadéma knows he must defer to the

· 766 ·

market women's lobby, the Professional Association of Retailers. Other women in the region share the market women's pride and power – the music of a favourite local song, "If My Husband Goes Out, I Go Out Too," is illustrated with a bird flying out of a cage.[31]

Feminist projects aim mainly to help women, but women want to improve their families and communities, not just themselves. To improve their families' lives, Latin American women came up with the idea of Comedores Populares (People's Food Places), communal kitchen-dining rooms for slum families. They created them (sometimes with help from a local church or development organization) and run them, usually rotating responsibility for buying and preparing food. Communal cooking enables them to feed their families more cheaply but also gives them more free time and company – each woman no longer works alone in her house. Together, the women discuss their problems – from male abuse to water sanitation – and find communal solutions. They even mount demonstrations to call attention to grievances like rising food prices.

On the whole, development agencies have ignored women's needs as they introduce technology to a region, yet women are often expected to maintain tools that may be impractical for their region. The 1985 Nairobi conference held Tech and Tools sessions to discuss the technology women felt was appropriate for them. Its slogan, "If it's not appropriate for women, it's not appropriate," tacitly contested development experts' belief that women require less-sophisticated machines than men and suggested that women were experts in practical needs. African women took the lead, demonstrating useful tools like indirect solar dryers to preserve food for storage, community stoves, and hand-held or cast-iron maize shellers.

Mind and Heart

Women have initiated many projects to discover, express, and foster female culture. Historians probe archives to discover an obliterated women's history; women approach their disciplines from a woman's perspective, producing original criticism of literature, art, and film and studies in psychology, sociology, science, medical research, political analysis, and just about every other field. Their work has provided a foundation of knowledge for succeeding generations; their ideas offer fertile soil for new ways of thinking. This enterprise, too, is global. Feminists encourage women to record their life stories. Feminist groups across the world – the Centro de Documentacion Sobre La Mujer in Peru, for example – seek the history of their country's women.

Women make audiovisuals – film, video, and slides – documenting every aspect of women's lives in their culture. Film festivals are a regular feature at women's conferences in India and Latin America; and in Africa and Asia, groups use video to raise the consciousness of illiterate rural women. In some Latin American countries, television helps raise women's consciousness: in Mexico, soap operas offer information on birth control to make it more socially acceptable. On Argentinian television, spot features present famous actors of both sexes conversing about equality at work and domestic violence. A spot feature in Costa Rica concerns a family preparing to go out for a walk. It first shows the men reclining, waiting while the women rush about cooking, cleaning, and dressing; then it segues into a scene of the whole family working together around the house, finishing the chores before their outing. It is titled, "Democracy Begins at Home" – a slogan also used by Chilean women to raise consciousness.

SISTERN, a women's theatre collective in Jamaica, uses drama to educate urban poor and rural women. It publishes a newsletter and scripts, mounts photograph exhibits, and made a video, *Sweet Sugar Rage*, documenting its use of theatre with female sugar workers. Throughout the Third World, feminist groups use March 8, International Women's Day, as an occasion for marches, demonstrations, and cultural festivals. Every year since 1983, Lima women have marked the day with a massive festival, drawing 7000–8000 people, which displays women's art and publications

– a boon for women who would never see such things elsewhere.

To raise the consciousness of United States Hispana, women initiated Proyecto La Mujer, one-day conferences in three Illinois cities. Many Latinas are confined to home and church, where they encounter nothing new or stimulating.[32] The conferences introduced Latina community women and scholars, poets, and artists to each other. In the spring of 1983, creative women from Hispanic barrios held sessions in Aurora, Joliet, and Elgin to explore Latina image and identity through the perspective of Midwest Hispanic women artists and poets. It was not an academic intellectual exercise but a dialogue among women. The artists read poetry and showed photographs, sculptures, and other art offering new images of Hispana. Over three hundred women attended, proud that a conference was held just for them, eager to discuss their feelings as a scorned minority in Anglo culture. They themselves planned conferences for the following years.

Feminists in many countries work to encourage parents to send their daughters to school and to establish non-sexist curricula and sophisticated research centres. A woman in a rural area near Calcutta opened a school for children who work part of the day. When she found that families were sending only sons, she began to accept boys only from families that sent their daughters.

In Saudi Arabia, a bastion of male privilege and female constriction, women fought for education. A million Saudi girls now go to school, and 100,000 females study for advanced degrees. As a result, more educated women are entering the workforce. The 50,000 female teachers and clerks employed by the government in the General Administration for the Education of Girls make up 80 percent of the country's female workforce. The Ministry of Health employs 5000 female nurses and doctors; a few thousand women work as tellers, bank loan officers, merchants, and manufacturers. Naila al-Mosly, a petroleum engineer, manages a reservoir engineering department at Aramco with 186 employees, 50 of them Saudi men.[33]

Women's studies is now an accepted discipline in colleges and universities in both First World and Third World countries, and women's research centres dot the globe, from Senegal to Lima, Santiago, and Mexico, from the Dominican Republic, to India, and the United States.

A Voice: The Political Is Personal

Women who demand human rights challenge traditional patriarchal families. This demand is always painful, particularly for Third World women living in tight-knit kin-groups. The experience is illuminating, however, because it reveals the woman-hatred underlying traditional structures. The families of poor women, especially in rural India, may attack women just for attending a women's meeting or conference. Most of these women have had no association with outsiders and they rarely leave the domestic environs unaccompanied by kin. For them to attend a women's conference is to take independent action that is the first step towards a radical break.

In one Hawaiian community, women who were upset mainly by male violence eased their problem by addressing both the political and the economic situation – and so related the personal to the political. The thousand-year history of the Hawaiian community of Wai'anae, five valleys on the leeward side of Oahu, Hawaii, is told in ancient chants and "talking story." Then, people lived cooperatively, using land from the mountains to the sea in a reciprocal communal economy.[34] Hawaii's annexation to the United States in 1898 terminated Hawaiians' rights in the islands, however, and the horticulture and fishing that gave them their identity.

In the 1980s Ho'oipo De Cambra and Sister Anna of the local Health and Community Council found more local women coming for help than they could deal with. They started the Wai'anae Women's Support Group, in which women met to talk about their lives, their desire for community and freedom, and ways to escape from victimization. Many of them were battered; many children were abused. Wai'anae has one of the highest unemployment rates in Hawaii – almost 30 percent. Many people lack houses, jobs, and food, and the men frequently erupt in violence. Accepting anger as a signal of something wrong, the group tried to identify the wrong and change it. They initiated a program called Peace Education. Eight of the nine public schools in Wai'anae now offer this two-week program, which teaches students to examine their anger and aggressiveness and to learn to create harmony in the family. The women hold health seminars for women and girls, and they drew up and submitted a grant proposal for a Women's Handicraft Cooperative to create a cottage industry. Working in groups, the women came to see that all their concerns were interrelated and basically political. In 1985 they helped homeless Hawaiian beach people who had been evicted from beach parks by the Honolulu City officials. They made a film to promote nuclear disarmament: many of them protested the US Navy's control and test-bombing of the island of Kaho'olawe and joined with a Native Hawaiian move-ment, the Protect Kaho'olawe 'Ohana (family).

In India, where technology and industrialization have not ben-efited women, the "feminization of poverty" is a major problem.[35] Women were excluded from new jobs by social considerations and lack of training. As industrial wages and working conditions improved, men took traditionally female jobs in jute, mining, and textiles. But in the 1970s, as feminist consciousness emerged, Indian women began to change their lives. During a famine in Ma-harashtra, leftist women organized lower-middle-class and poor women to protest price rises, adulteration of products, and cheating at ration shops. Thousands demonstrated with rolling pins, thalis, and brooms. Tribal women protested prosperous men's economic exploitation and sexual harassment, along with alcoholism and wife-beating in their own families. One of most brilliant campaigns women initiated in this period was the "Chipko" (hug the trees) movement, which grew into a widespread and well-organized eco-logical movement.

In 1979 a fourteen-year-old girl was raped by two constables at a police station. The High Court convicted the rapists, but the Supreme Court reversed the judgment, ruling that the girl had consented because there were no wounds on her body. Middle- and upper-class women and the women's fronts of leftist political parties erupted together to protest this decision. That year, needing a base and forum of their own, women founded Vimochana to help battered women. It drew battered wives and their kin, whose suffering became a window on woman-hatred in general. Vimochana uses consciousness-raising to empower women to deal with personal and structural violence. It helps women who are harassed about their dowries, those with bigamous husbands who abandon them without support, and sexually harassed or exploited women. It deals with structural violence by organizing women in slums, in industries, or in working women's hostels around issues of oppression and discrimination. Seeing struggles for justice as interrelated, many Vimochana women join groups that are committed to changing consciousness – peasant and workers' associations, for instance – and sometimes lead them in actions.[36]

Women are in the vanguard of peace movements and groups opposing nuclear energy and militarism. In Europe, North America, and Australia, women's groups focus mainly on nuclear energy, on weapons, and, during wars, on anti-war demonstrations. South Pacific women in the Nuclear Free Pacific Movement try to stop nuclear testing. Everywhere, women work locally.

Nowhere have women campaigned as indefatigably against war and the nuclear arms race as in England. Women were important in the 1980s Campaign for Nuclear Disarmament, but their most famous peace action was the Greenham Common. In 1979 NATO announced plans to place hundreds of American nuclear missiles in Western Europe in a broad intensification of the nuclear arms race. The first installation, planned for 1983, was of ninety-six ground-launched Cruise missiles at a US air base at Greenham Common, near Newbury, about sixty miles west of London. In September

1981, forty British women walked 120 miles from Wales to Greenham Common to protest and publicize this use of British soil.[37]

The media ignored the march, just as they ignored anti-war marches in the United States during the Gulf War – an omission that is really censorship. Their plans thwarted by lack of media attention, the women decided to stay at the base until the British public became aware of the American scheme to use England and Europe as a shield against the Eastern bloc, keeping war from American soil. The Greenham Common women's peace camp developed from this vigil outside the gates of the base. They put up tents and settled in, many with children. The small, stubborn peace camp grew, and on December 11, 1982, 20,000 women formed a nine-mile human chain around the base.[38] They "redecorated" the site, adorning the barbed-wire fence with thousands of bits of fabric, poems, personal treasures, children's pictures, toys, and clothes. Originally, the protesters wanted to start a public debate on the new nuclear weapons, but as more and more women joined them and they received international attention, they decided to try to block the deployment of missiles at Greenham.

Both the British and the US governments ignored them, and missiles began to arrive at the base in November 1983. But the women remained, maintaining permanent vigil in protest. They put up comfortable tents and shelters, until the government evicted them from the land outside the base. They remained until the base closed in 1992. The number of women actually camping out at Greenham varied over time, but they continued, day and night, in all seasons, in sun or rain (mostly rain in that part of England!).[39] Moreover, their protest inspired large numbers of British women to agitate for peace and to build peace camps in Europe and the United States. Every year after Greenham began, 50,000 women at a time demonstrated at the base, infusing the peace movement with new life.

Some might not consider Greenham a feminist action. It was

not intended to gain any right for women or to raise women's status, and it drew non-feminist women who were passionate about peace. But it was in the profoundest sense feminist because it was an attempt to force men to heed a female voice, to inform political leaders that much of the population ardently opposed war and wanted leaders to adopt a different stance. War and weapons are a "women's issue," although men deny it.

From 1975 to 1991, war raged in the once beautiful Lebanese city of Beirut. A factionalist war among Christians, Muslims, and Druzes, surrogates for outside forces (Israel and Syria), it defied solution. Evelyne Accad urged the Lebanese to adopt both nationalism and feminism – the first to overcome factionalism and unite the country; the second to alter its value system of "ownership and possession."[40] Lebanon has a tradition of freedom of expression non-existent in other Arab countries; it has long welcomed political refugees, including many women writers. When Egypt banned Nawal el-Saadawi's *Al-Mar'ah Wa Al-Jins* (Women and Sex) in 1972 and expelled her from her job in the Ministry of Health, she fled to Lebanon. Republished there, her book became a bestseller in the Arab world, a "stepping stone" in Arab feminism. Similarly, the Syrian writer Ghada Al Samman ignored the war to settle there, and she founded a publishing house in a place without censorship.

Lebanese women's lives are regulated by the laws of their religious communities, not national laws. But these communities are insular and prevent people from talking together. In communities where women are confined or kept under surveillance, isolation equals ignorance. To help end the suicidal war, some women joined political parties – Kataëb (Christian Maronite), PPS (Popular Pro-Syrian), Amal (Muslim Shiite), PSP (Progressive Socialist Druze), PLO (Palestinian Liberation Organization), Murabitun (Muslim Sunni), Phalangist, Ba'ath, National Block, and Communist – but these groups only increased the general paranoia and rivalry. At the UN World Conference for Women in Copenhagen in 1980, women did converse. They agreed that the solution was negotiation to achieve peace, harmony, and nurturance, not dominance, and decided only feminism could unify people across parochial differences.

Since then, Lebanese women have formed interdenominational groups aimed at achieving peace. They organized peace marches, sit-ins, and hunger strikes. Standing defiantly between the guns of the divided city, they appealed to fighters by visiting refugee camps and military headquarters and sticking flowers in gun nozzles. To eliminate militia checkpoints where people were kidnapped, they went from East to West Beirut, from Phalangist to Progressive checkpoint, begging men in the name of their wives, mothers, and sisters to stop the butchery. They blocked passageways dividing the two sides of the capital, organized all-night sit-ins, and stormed local TV stations, interrupting the news to broadcast their demands. In May 1984 Imam Khalifeh, a kindergarten teacher and member of the Institute for Women's Studies in the Arab World in West Beirut, organized a peace march by women from both sides of the city who were to meet at the only crosspoint, the Museum passage. They were halted by a "blind" shelling – a randomly aimed shelling – that killed and wounded many from both sides.

In 1997 Rachel Ben Dor, whose son was a soldier in the Israeli army, formed Four Mothers – Leave Lebanon in Peace. This group generated a large anti-war movement and was initially treated with scorn and derision. But in June 2000 it was honoured as the force responsible for Israel's unilateral withdrawal from Lebanon.[41]

Women pioneer environmental movements too. In 1975 Cathy Hinds moved her family to Gray, a small town near Portland, Maine, to benefit from the fresh air and quiet of the country.[42] The water smelled bad, but country water often does, she thought. When she bathed her two- and five-year-old daughters, they cried, complaining that the water burned them: but it was not too hot. The children developed skin rashes; Hinds had a miscarriage; and her older daughter began to have dizzy spells. Cheryl Washburn, a neighbour with similar problems, asked her doctor if her problems could be connected with their water; he scoffed and prescribed tranquillizers. But other neighbours too spoke of dizziness, headaches, and respiratory problems; and they could all see they had similar rashes.

The neighbourhood women met in their houses to discuss the problem. Washburn contacted the city health officer, who sent water samples to be tested. But the technology did not yet exist to test water for a range of chemicals, and it was months before a Massachusetts lab identified three contaminants: trichloroethylene, trichloroethane – both toxic and potentially carcinogenic – and dimethyl sulfide, perceptible through its smell. Eventually dozens of contaminants were found in the local water.

The group stopped drinking the water, and gradually learned that it was not safe either for cooking or even bathing: even fumes from the water were hazardous. In January 1978 dozens of wells in the neighbourhood were capped. Trying to track down the source of the contamination, the health officer homed in on a waste recycler, the McKin Company, which had grown to handle wastes for 300 companies. McKin was closed, but the chemicals remained.

America discovered the consequences of decades of unregulated dumping of toxic chemicals in 1978, when Love Canal hit the news. An abandoned waterway in Niagara Falls, New York, Love Canal held over 20,000 tons of toxic chemical wastes dumped by the Hooker Chemical Company. In the early 1950s Hooker filled the canal, covered it with soil, and donated it to the local Board of Education, which built houses on it and a school. Early residents complained of health problems, but government officials ignored them until the late 1970s, when they began to study birth defects, miscarriages, and stillbirths in the area. The rates were abnormally high, as was the rate of chromosome damage (which can cause cancer). A local woman, Lois Gibbs, organized residents and led the fight for compensation and fair treatment. After years of struggle, the government moved several thousand families and shut the houses up. They were recently resold, despite questions about their safety.

But officials conducted no health studies on the residents of Gray. The Gray health officer proposed one, but the state of Maine would not fund it. Hinds and Washburn formed the Environmental Public Interest Coalition (EPIC). When McKin ignored an order to excavate and remove contaminants, the women grew sceptical of government assurances of a clean-up and called a press conference. A state official was at Hinds' door next morning. Hinds took him and some reporters to the site and demanded that it be cleaned up in two weeks. When the official demurred, she threatened that EPIC would do it themselves, with the press documenting their work. Pressured by fear of publicity and by EPIC, the state, believing that EPIC was a big organization, did the job. But the contamination problem was not over. After reading studies suggesting that McKin had polluted the river, spreading toxins further, Hinds lobbied until the McKin site was placed on the Superfund list for clean-up by the government. After warning the people who bought her house of possible residues, Hinds moved away, but still works on pollution. She co-founded the Maine Citizens Coalition on Toxics, which joined a state citizens group, the Maine People's Alliance.

Latin American women focus on militarism and the machismo tradition that is a major source of the coups that plague the continent. Asian and African women try to build bridges between opposing factions. As civil war wracks Sri Lanka, Women for Peace organize northern Tamil and southern Sinhalese women, circulate peace petitions, hold public meetings, and publish newsletters criticizing government policy. In one pamphlet, a Tamil and a Sinhalese mother talk about their sons, who have been killed in the conflict, and urge its end. Feminists in the New Delhi Ankur project help widows of Sikh men who were killed by Hindus in the riots that followed Indira Gandhi's assassination. They try to forge ties between them and the Dalit (untouchable) women who live in the same housing project and whose caste was set against the Sikhs during the riots. Similarly, some Israeli women reach out to Palestinian women.

Knowing their sons were murdered, in July 1987 mothers dared to protest in authoritarian South Korea. Mothers, wives, and female kin of political prisoners held a huge rally at the headquarters of the ruling Democratic Justice Party in Seoul. They threw eggs as they shouted "Down with dictatorship!" They hurled bottles at a bus carrying policemen convicted of torturing student prisoners to death, demanding the release of all political prisoners. Fifteen of them were arrested.

Women's groups fight local governments too. In 1985, wanting to stop the erection of a state prison in a residential area with dozens of schools in East Los Angeles, a predominantly Mexican-American neighbourhood, women asked their parish priest to organize them. Every week 400 women marched, wrote letters, and lobbied in Sacramento – and they stalled the project. Next, they derailed a plan for an above-ground pipeline to carry oil from offshore rigs in Santa Barbara through East Los Angeles to Long Beach, bypassing affluent white coastal communities. They also incorporated as a nonprofit organization and allied with a mainly black group in south-central Los Angeles to keep a toxic waste incinerator from being built in their area.[43]

Hands

Women reach out hands to other nations, classes, or neigh-bourhoods with rigid, exclusive, or threatening boundaries. African-American Mildred Tudy and Mexican-American Maria Fava worked separately to improve living conditions and bridge racial enmity in the Williamsburg-Greenpoint neighbourhood of Brooklyn. Their agitation forced the city to take some necessary steps and, in the process, they introduced other low-income women to feminism and improved their own lives. White women join black women to fight the Ku Klux Klan in many localities.[44] Women lead citizens' groups opposed to the use of nuclear power; they were "the most committed and energetic opponents of the city and General Motors" during problems in Poletown; and they make up the majority of community leaders dealing with toxic waste or those involved in community groups in Chicago and other cities.[45]

Women in regional and global networks and grassroots groups reach out, forming bonds that strengthen both sides and allow them to learn from each other. Global feminism has influenced existing international women's organizations like the World YWCA, which is now concerned with non-Western women. Most important, in a profound shift from patriarchal thinking, women's networks give priority to the voices of women on the local level and try to avoid making decisions from the top down. Feminists approach the world differently from other "underdog" groups: they don't want a bigger slice of the patriarchal pie, as men do, and they don't want to inject a few women into the highest echelons of power while the rest remain marginal or in abject poverty.

Rather, women want to expose the fraudulence of the highest value of the male world – power as domination, a recipe for contention and isolation. They want to transform social and economic relations by stressing cooperation and nutritiveness – a recipe for felicity. They hope that, through global networking, they can discover an alternative structuring principle to male hierarchy, which today seems the only possible structure. If women can realize an alternative structure, they can literally change the world.

Antifeminism and Conservative Feminism

Both right- and left-wing parties historically used women to support and maintain men; both have traditionally been sexist. Today, however, some leftist men reject explicitly masculinist ideologies, sympathizing with or supporting a degree of female liberation: some are even feminists. Right-wing movements tend to be nationalistic and/or religious and macho, exalting militarism and a cult of manliness and male supremacy. It is difficult for feminists to understand how women can support an ideology that openly subordinates them and supports militarism, which may kill their sons and daughters. Yet many do. This section will focus on conservative women in the United States.

Most North American antifeminists are part of a New Right that is a coalition of three main groups: businessmen threatened by changes in capitalism, religious fundamentalists, and groups dedicated to specific issues like abortion.[46] They ally with each other on the grounds on which they agree with each other – their opposition to feminism, social welfare programs, and what they consider state invasion into the private sphere of the family. All three are male-dominated, but mobilize women as local and national fronts and to serve men and the male cause.

Antifeminist women seem to operate out of a feeling of weakness. They fear a feminist agenda, which they believe devalues the work and security of mothers and wives. Some oppose divorce because it threatens women's financial security, or daycare because it offers an alternative to the established form of the family, or legal abortion for a variety of reasons, but mainly for allowing men to copulate with impunity instead of having to "pay" for it with marriage. Some antifeminist women have attained power in their worlds and do not want the rules of the game to change; they know that belittling other women and the feminist movement pleases the men they deal with. Antifeminists accede to male dominance: having achieved some measure of security or success by deferring to it, they fear change.

Antifeminist women are not fools. They see the same world feminists see and diagnose it similarly. Many men consider feminists man-haters, but conservative antifeminist women generally hold men in much lower esteem than feminists do. They think men are what they are by nature and are profoundly sceptical of their potential for change. They believe sex differences pervade all aspects of existence – body, mind, emotion, morality – and are extreme and unbridgable, rooted in nature. Many consider men untrustworthy, less worthy and moral than women, "slightly inferior" exploiters who are a threat unless they are under women's moral guidance and control. Seeing the sexes as virtually different species, these women cast men in the role of protectors whose manliness depends on their fulfilling this role. They exploit male rivalry and fear of other men to persuade their men to protect them from those men, who are presumed to be predatory or irresponsible.

Most of the conservative women interviewed by Robyn Rowland loathe violent, aggressive male values and consider life-affirming, caring, conservationist female values superior to men's and in need of cultivation.[47] Others identify with violent aggressive male values in an aggressive violent world. Both are pro-family, pro-children, and pro-woman and continually bargain with men not to use their power over them. Yet they see women as responsible for their own lives: women's good management produces "good" husbands who reflect the women's worth. Thus, antifeminist women see men as overgrown children in need of control, and life as a sexual power struggle they are determined to win.

Andrea Dworkin believes that right-wing women see women's position realistically, responding not with feminists' assertions of sisterhood but a "self-protective sense of repulsion."[48] The powerless do not easily put faith in the powerless: they "need the powerful" – and the powerful are male. Without sisterhood, antifeminist groups discriminate by race and class. They try to fight for themselves while maintaining the appearance of acting within the parameters laid down by males.

Without hope of changing the status quo, antifeminists fight for themselves within it. They want to be "equal but different," and they see feminism as a movement aimed at sameness with men. They are convinced that feminism devalues motherhood and family life. The issue most dividing them from feminists is abortion. A conservative woman says: "I believe that feminists have fallen into a male trap. They are attempting to adapt women to a wombless male society, instead of adapting society to meet the needs of women." Unable to believe that sexual politics can change, they try to exploit them for their own and their children's benefit.

Feminists and antifeminists differ not in their appraisal of the world but in their degree of hope or, perhaps, idealism. Essentially, the difference rests on whether we believe gender differences are biologically or culturally determined, whether our roles in life are inevitably tied to our genitals. If gender is inextricable from sex and given by birth, all men are violent, aggressive, appropriational, and dominant, despite their emotional, moral, and spiritual inferiority to women. This attitude is a council of despair for both sexes, and especially for mothers of sons.

Second-wave American feminists' demand for equality with men both at law and in access to education, work, credit, and status was emphasized in the media presentation of American feminism. But most American feminists also support the values held by the antifeminists. Feminists also want a world that values nutritiveness, compassion, and harmony. The strategy of groups that seek equality was to enter the public realm to change it (although that has not happened) and to enlarge women's possibilities. Women as a caste have never wanted to end their association with motherhood and children, but only to make it less absolute, insisting that women are human beings capable of the full range of human behaviour. Indeed, most feminists, including lesbians, are mothers who take profound satisfaction in their children.

The emphasis on equality generated a conservative "pro-family" movement within feminism, according to Judith Stacey, a kind of backlash that repudiated sexual politics, "the distinctively radical core of the women's liberation movement of the 1960s and 1970s."[49] She believes that conservative feminists do not want to interpret personal or social relationships in terms of sexual power because, to do so, threatens "the family"; for them, the fight against male domination deflects attention from more important agendas. The germinal insight of feminist thought, Stacey asserts, was that "woman" is a social category historically and socially constructed on a base of subordination: feminist sexual politics attempted to transform gender and sexuality using the New Left insight that "the

personal is political." Politicizing intimate relationships, particularly female-male ones, was the "most explosive and threatening aspect
of feminist sexual politics" and the form new conservative feminists
particularly reject.

Conservative feminists feel that 1970s feminists' rage against
men and their assertion that the traditional family oppressed
women gave women an either/or choice between family and car-
eer/equality. Thinkers like Betty Friedan, Jean Bethke Elshtain, and
Carol McMillan support "the family," but disagree on what it is. For
Friedan, "the family is who you come home to"; Elshtain defines a
family as connected by marriage or kinship. Both want women to
ignore men's war on women. Believing that the "tired welfare state"
alienates and antagonizes conservatives, Friedan urges feminists to
avoid "incendiary sexual issues" like lesbianism and abortion on
demand. Elshtain fears that politicizing personal life will end privacy and politics and lead to totalitarian control over both. In a bureaucratic capitalist and totalitarian socialist world, she finds family
life the only nursery of the values needed to resist corporate power
and antidemocratic tendencies.

Elshtain criticizes feminists for assimilating to the "masculine"
world – accepting market imperatives and instrumental rationality,
and seeking technocratic solutions to moral and political problems.
She urges a "politics of limits" that eschews utopian dreams and
does not try to change what, she believes, cannot be changed without dire human consequences – biology, gender, family, and sexual
morality. Above all, Elshtain urges resisting state intervention in private life and calls for "social feminism," which places children at the
centre of feminist concern, preserves traditional families and communities, maintains clear boundaries between public and private
life, and preserves those aspects of gender differentiation "necessary"
to social life.

Friedan, Elshtain, and McMillan believe that Western feminists
have bought into a male division of experience that sees public life,
career, and male rationality as more significant and demanding than

motherhood and the qualities associated with it. McMillan criticizes Western rationalist logic and values on serious grounds: as presenting a false dichotomy and hierarchy between reason and emotion, culture and nature; and using it to privilege technology, manipulative skills, and control of the natural environment, as well as to denigrate women, mothering, and domesticity.[50] Accepting this distorted version of experience, feminists and sexists alike, according to McMillan, seek worldly power, while feminists – misguidedly – seek equality and androgyny.

McMillan urges that these values be rearranged in a society that better prepares women for their "natural" relationship to children. She urges opposition to all interference with "natural" female reproduction and mothering – most forms of birth control, abortion, unisex education, daycare, and even co-parenting. Friedan and Elshtain also seek to maintain gender roles, instead of trying to achieve androgyny – an early feminist goal.

One can interpret part of the conservative feminist agenda as one based in fear and despair at the overwhelming difficulty of altering the most deeply rooted human attitudes – towards sex, gender, and family. But part of its analysis seems to me to be on target: a feminist society should be centred on children. Moreover, we cannot overestimate the importance of the philosophical foundations of patriarchy, its division of experience into two distinct realms: mind, ruled by men; body, in which women are immersed. One is volitional, the other necessary; one is granted the right to dominate, the other the requirement to obey. And there is no question that in struggling to change patriarchal values, women are stumped by the so-far-immovable male refusal to take responsibility for children. All efforts at equality founder on the fact that women give birth and take the responsibility for raising children. If feminists have not yet succeeded in integrating human activities and values, the fault lies less with them than with the men who impede them and the difficulty of a task that cannot be compassed in a generation.

Only after we recognize that women's subordination to men is systemic and structural can we begin to build a base for a humane, felicitous world. One of feminism's most important achievements is its deconstruction of the family as a natural unit and its reconstruction as a social unit.[51] This breakdown made possible the recognition that the private realm idealized as the nursery of humane values is, in fact, the primary site of women's subjection.

Stacey argues that the conventional nuclear family generates effective and economic self-sufficiency; inward-turning, it gets its strength from a strong bond between husband and wife, often based in domination. Other family forms, like black urban ghetto matrifocal domestic networks or white urban networks in nineteenth-century Britain and America, survive only if women reach out and forge relations with kin, neighbours, and friends.[52]

The difficulty in maintaining long-term commitment, which is one basis of conservative feminists' fears, results not from feminism, but from the sexual revolution, efficient contraception, and the fact that marriage no longer creates an economic unit necessary to a society. Few people live on the land, and most people live longer. Monogamy may not be a typical human trait. Marriage for life meant something very different when most people died young. Societies that desire marriage for life must enforce it by forbidding divorce, and even then, men (and sometimes women) often take lovers or leave. Women do commit themselves – but less to marriage than to children. It may be harder to maintain an egalitarian than a power relationship enforced by law and custom: subordinate partners must accept whatever dominant partners do, so one gets his way and the other is silent. But the problems resulting from the end of marriage would be less severe if men took more responsibility for children.

Women who fear male power and lack faith in change reject feminism, but still continue to struggle for some autonomy, for structures to protect their children, and for decent lives. Underneath the serious disagreements among antifeminists, conservative feminists, and feminists, most women – indeed, probably most people – would like a safer, more felicitous world in which everyone has a voice and children are protected. Regardless of their conflicts, feminists of all persuasions are allied, as are antifeminists. In a few hundred years, historians will see that, in the late twentieth and early twenty-first centuries, almost the entire female sex was moving in the same direction along different paths.[53]

CHAPTER 21

THE FUTURE OF FEMINISM

FEMINISM IS AN ALIVE AND HEALTHY SPIRIT in the hearts of millions of women and some men, a burgeoning movement across the globe. It is not a "masculine" movement – a party with a dogma, central headquarters, fixed leaders, and levels of command. Ironically, feminism has been accused of having exactly that – of imposing "politically correct" ideas on poor, bewildered men. There are issues on which the majority of feminists are agreed, most of them centring on their insistence that women own their own bodies, but it is because churches, governments, and the male sex have laid claim to those bodies for millennia that these items cause contention.

Some basic feminist assumptions are fixed and inflexible: that women matter as much as men and share the same human rights to food and nourishment, health care, education, paid work on every level, security to walk about unmolested, sexual partners of their choice, and freedom to create their own lives. Many women lack some or all of these rights, but some men do too. The goal of the UN conferences is to create a world in which no one lacks these rights.

Beyond that, women choose their own paths. Non-Western women often complain of the Western obsession with individualism and prefer a more community-oriented vision. Some women worry more about protecting women; others worry about attaining real equality with men in the business world, for instance. Feminists' stubborn refusal to be co-opted by the media during the puritanical impeachment hearings of Bill Clinton indicates the more complex reality. Journalists expected (and hoped for) an across-the-board feminist condemnation of a man who fornicated outside his marriage and did not hesitate to involve a much younger subordinate – an abuse of power no matter who provoked whom. But once feminists saw that the relationship was volitional on Monica Lewinsky's side and not sexual harassment, they shrugged. Most men seem to believe that feminists are puritanical about sex, but that is far from the case. They do not agree even about sexual requirements like monogamy, for instance.

Feminism is a loose set of beliefs based on the single belief that women matter as much as men. The leaders do not inherit their mantles from a foremother, and they do not get chosen by an elite. Rather, they arise from the mass of women because they are in some way extraordinary – more intelligent, hardworking, perceptive, or savvy. They bear more responsibility than others, not more power. The movement does not endow its officeholders with power, as men's movements do. Those feminist leaders who have any power earned it through work. The power feminism wants is the power to change life, not power to hold in one's hand and gloat over. The women who are leaders in women's groups reside in thousands of villages, towns, and cities across the globe; they spread feminism daily by living it and talking about it. Feminism brings joy to people's hearts – it is truly a gospel, a good news. Some people think feminists must adhere to a code of appearance – no make-up, no nail polish, no high heels, uncomplicated short hair – but lots of feminists wear make-up and dye their hair. Feminists are single heterosexuals, married women, women in heterosexual love affairs, single lesbians,

lesbians in committed relationships, lesbians in homosexual love affairs, celibate women, and women who move from one type of sexual relationship to another. They are of every colour and religion – there are even Mormon, Muslim, and orthodox Jewish feminists, despite their sects' strong disapproval of feminism.

Most feminist campaigns are particular, aimed at changing a certain law or custom, or improving life for a certain group of women. Actions with larger goals like peace require widespread support. Many feminist actions have been successful: change may be slow and gradual, but much change has occurred in the past thirty years, particularly in cultural and educational areas. Most people today are aware of the existence of feminism, even if many have a distorted idea of its nature. Feminist concepts have entered ordinary discourse in most societies, and the philosophy they incorporate has lightened the hearts and burdens of uncounted women and men. Feminist theoretical work is building a vital new epistemology, a foundation for the future.

Because feminism is a living entity in the lives of millions of women, it is growing and becomes more widespread with every decade. In the present century, it will reach most women throughout the world. The twenty-first century will be the century for feminism. At the same time, however, feminism has been silenced. The swallowing of businesses by global corporations means that a smaller and smaller number of men have greater and greater power in the world. The number of men who control the media worldwide is tiny – perhaps fewer than the fingers on two hands. This near monopoly has resulted in serious censorship, one different from any before known.

Censorship is as old as the state. John Milton railed elegantly at censorship by the Catholic Church, "sometimes five Imprimatures are seen together dialogue-wise in the piazza of one title page, complimenting and ducking each to other with their shaven reverences, whether the author, who stands by in perplexity at the foot of his epistle, shall to the press or to the sponge"; but the year after he wrote the great *Areopagitica*, he himself became chief censor of England.

Censorship is not always overt: even before the rise of multinational corporations, literature was censored, not just by theocrats in Iran or Rome but by invisible forces. Censorship has always existed in the United States. Certain things could not be said publicly or printed; the taboo depended on the era, but usually included explicit sex. Although publishers have always claimed that market forces alone dictated their decisions, tacit agreement today would prevent a publisher from printing a book that is explicitly anti-Semitic, say, or racist. Yet there has never been a bar to misogyny: explicitly woman-hating books (and films and songs) have always been common. Until the 1970s, in contrast, a feminist view of life was not permitted because men felt it was man-hating. It required men who were unaware to stretch their sympathies too far, and they found feminist work incomprehensible.

Since the rise of the feminist movement in the late 1960s, however, men of all levels have been exposed to feminist ideas, feminist theory, and feminist terms. Feminist work is not incomprehensible now, except to those whose minds are wilfully shuttered. Yet, since the 1980s, less and less work by feminists has appeared. Newspapers, magazines, and television almost never feature a feminist writer, although feminism is one of several important intellectual movements in our current world. There is no discussion of feminist ideas; even feminist magazines rarely feature dialogue. Only on public radio (and there, rarely) is there any mention of this worldwide revolution. There is a blackout on feminism, as if it did not exist.

Even intellectual men write about history and literature as if feminism had never occurred. They are somehow able to ignore the huge changes it has generated in customs, laws, and every discipline – history, psychology, and literature especially. Feminism is the most transforming revolution to occur since the industrial revolution: it has changed the discourse. Men's censorship seems to be based on the hope that ignoring it will make it go away. This is not the sort of censorship that can be attacked in the old ways: we cannot protest that a certain kind of book is not being published or picket a newspaper that omits a certain kind of news from its pages. It is questionable how many people even notice: Did you notice that television reportage almost totally ignored the many huge protests mounted against the Gulf War in New York, London, and San Francisco? I saw two half-minute reports on CNN during the entire war, and only from friends did I have knowledge of the huge marches that actually occurred.

This censorship does not appear to be political, but we know now that everything is political. Twenty-first-century censorship is the silence of controllers who do not want any changes in the status quo. Since the collapse of European socialism and the seeming triumph of capitalism, global businesses censor discussion of any political, economic, or moral system that might lead to change: it avoids serious discussion of leftist politics and of feminism, though mockery of feminism is of course permitted. But it is essential that feminism be discussed. As a truly revolutionary point of view, any realization of the feminist vision will require huge changes in every human endeavour. How this should be done requires thought and planning. To censor feminist discussion is, therefore, profoundly destructive to the movement, and we must find ways around it.

The world we inhabit has been constructed almost entirely from a male perspective. For women to matter in this universe, they must now be written in to the structures that were originally set up to exclude them. This inclusion cannot be done by adding a paragraph to a chapter in a traditional male history. Women's presence completely alters a context. It is not the physical fact of a woman's body on a panel that changes it, but her perspective on its deliberations, since this point of view has never before been considered. As two scholars have described the addition of women's studies programs to college curricula: "The fact that our understanding of homo sapiens has incorporated the perspective of only half of the human race makes it clear that women's studies is not an additional knowledge merely to be tacked on to the curriculum. It is, instead, a body of knowledge that is perspective transforming and should therefore transform the existing curriculum from within and revise the common notion of what constitutes an 'objective' or 'normative' perspective."[1] To assert that women matter is to demur from traditional morality and to change the value system we live by.

A feminist world would be arranged differently from the existing world in every aspect and on every level. Starting with basic morals, feminists would alter the structure and relations of families and of economic, cultural, and political institutions. To reform society is indeed an overwhelming task: people resist even small changes, and those with the most power, who have most to lose, resist most powerfully. This obstacle paralyzes feminists, and we have not yet taken the necessary next step: devising a rough blueprint for a better system. Feminism has a clear value system, but no structural plan for reordering economic, political, and social life. Indeed, feminists are wary of large-scale plans: they tend to be applied rigidly and from the top down (like socialist systems), and so lead to tyranny, not democracy. Present feminist policy – supporting local groups in self-created projects – works well on the small scale, the structure all new burgeoning belief systems have used. Christianity, Islam, and socialism, for example, all began with small "cells" of believers building a new church in joy.

The dominant metaphor for hierarchy has always been the family. Of course, it is the family already structured by patriarchy that is referred to – triangular, a group with one dominant male, subordinate female or females, and subordinates beneath them (children, servants, hangers-on). The dominant male has absolute power in this structure and is presumed to have the well-being of his subordinates at heart. There is no safety valve in the design if he proves not so inclined; only escape or revolution can save the group from wretchedness. But for women, escape is almost never possible, since there is nowhere else to go.

So the family is an imperfect analogy for hierarchy. First, it's true that small children do need authority and to be protected and

THE FUTURE OF FEMINISM

directed by adults. But children affect their parents as much as the reverse – only a cruel parent would hand out orders to children while ignoring their desires and needs. Most governments, in contrast, pay little heed to their citizens unless the citizens organize. Second, children grow up: much of the parenting one does is aimed at helping the child grow up, teaching it to be independent. Governments do not want independent thought from their citizens, only economic independence. Third, most people, except those brutalized into a zombie-like submissiveness, do not like authority and do not feel that others have the right to authority over them. Because authority is always an imposition, it needs to be backed by might. The family is a far more flexible and two-way structure than hierarchy. Even severely unhappy families with a dictatorial parent are less rigid than hierarchies.

The dominant metaphor for feminism is anarchy. The anarchy I refer to is that of the planets, which move in more or less fixed patterns, each realizing its own orbit in harmony, but not collusion, with the others. No planet dominates; indeed, so far as we know, no element dominates space. Each part follows its own truth. A young female entomologist found this same kind of anarchy in anthills, contradicting the belief of generations of scientists that anthills are dominated by the queen.[2] (It's interesting that the most famous entomologist of our period is Edward Wilson, the leading exponent of sociobiology – a defence of hierarchical power relations on the ground that they are true to nature because exemplified by such entities.)

Feminists do not have the power to build large-scale alternative structures. At present, we cannot even conceive of them. What political arrangement, for instance, would enable people to have great autonomy in their lives and make each person her own boss, her own rabbi? Women have created small-scale alternative worlds in their families or their communities. These alternatives are so far experimental, but from these experiments grow a body of knowledge of what works and what doesn't, in family, political, and economic structures and in ideas for future trial.

Alternative Family Structures

In 1975 Cuba became the first country, capitalist or socialist, to mandate a Family Code requiring men to "cooperate" in housework and child care, even if they are the only family members who work outside the home. Clause 26 of the Family Code reads: "If one of the spouses contributes only through his or her work in the home and child care, the other spouse must provide full economic support, without this meaning that he or she be relieved of the obligation of cooperation with housework and child care."[3] Clause 28 carries the principle of sexual parity even further: "Both spouses have the right to exercise their professions or crafts and must lend each other reciprocal cooperation and aid to this effect." The law requires parents to organize their home life so children get proper care.

This code generated a debate on the division of labour: it legitimated men who, despite mockery, helped maintain their homes; it enlarged the views of adolescents, who now see adult responsibilities as including work both outside and within the home. The Family Code is only one tool in Cuba's effort to integrate women into the workforce without disrupting the family. The government placed particular emphasis on building daycare centres, especially in areas with the most working mothers. These centres accept babies when they are forty-five days old, the point at which paid maternity leave ends. The economy cannot support enough infant centres (*circulos*) to accommodate all children, so those whose mothers work outside the home are given priority.

Almost all Cuban workshops have dining rooms or allow workers to use one at a nearby factory. Grade-school children enjoy hot-lunch programs, and many junior-high students board at school. Teenagers spend the school week in boarding schools across the country and return home to their families on weekends – a boon to many parents and children of that age. Neither child support nor custody is automatic in Cuba's Family Code: a wife who works for

wages with a husband who studies may be responsible for supporting the children; and, on marriage break-up, some men get child
custody. Cuba's family policy seems increasingly successful. But the
government still considers the heterosexual nuclear family the basic
cell of society and harshly punishes homosexuality as "counter-rev-
olutionary." Recently, however, official hostility towards same-sex
love has been muted.[4]

Sweden based its family policy on the principle that an economy that requires two incomes to support a family must give parents
a reasonable chance to combine work with family life. Swedish
family policy emphasizes shared parenting; the Prime Minister's Advisory Council on Equality between Men and Women reported in
1975 that "fathers are now accorded the same degree of responsibility and importance in the children's lives as has always been
accorded to mothers." To realize this balance, the government set up
a three-part program to expand public child-care facilities, give parents of small children more time off from work, and, to combat
stereotypes, educate people about gender roles and parenting.

A national program of sex-role education was launched in
1969. Children of both sexes in elementary and secondary schools
were taught about gender stereotypes, career options, and techniques and responsibilities of child care. Today, all official curricula presume that both sexes will fill the same adult roles, be concerned about careers, and need to learn about parenting. A parental
insurance system introduced in 1974, financed by an 85 percent
contribution from employers and a 15 percent contribution from
the central government, entitles one parent at a time to stay home
with a newborn baby for nine months while receiving 90 percent
of full pay. One parent may use all the paid leave, parents may
divide it, or, if their employers are willing, both may work half-
time for 90 percent pay. A recent addition lets parents use the last
three months of paid leave gradually until a child reaches the age
of eight. In 1979 parents were granted the legal right to a six-hour
workday for a child's first eight years, or a full leave of absence for

eighteen months (but without compensation after the nine-month period).

National boards of health and welfare polled Swedish children to discover what they talk about to one another and their questions about life problems. They were surprised by the children's concern about sharing responsibility and looking out for one another. Often lonely and forlorn, they wonder why their elders live as they do, why adults work so hard. They wonder why they were brought into the world and what will become of them. Feelings of isolation are common in industrial societies in which production is separated from the household. Swedish child psychologists and welfare workers are now proposing that children be integrated young into the adult job world – visiting parents' workplaces, attending daycare centres connected to workplaces, and being allowed to work in their teens. It is a testimony to the values of the Swedish people that, despite their highly industrialized society, children's physical and mental environment and the quality of their relationships with parents and other adults are important enough to be contentious issues in national elections.

But the sexual division of labour at work or at home has remained unaffected. Even if both spouses work for wages, the husband expects the wife to do most of the child care and the housework. Men complain that work takes so much out of them they have nothing left to give their families; they insist that home is a place for recovery and rest. But for women, who also work hard outside the household, home is a place of work. Men get away with irresponsibility because they earn far more than women, who remain concentrated in unskilled and low-paid jobs. The Advisory Council on Equality between Men and Women noted in 1975: "In spite of pay equalization between the sexes, great differences remain, above all because women and men work in different occupations."[5]

The United States has no policy and few social programs to assist families with two working parents or single heads of household. Shared parenting is a luxury reserved for willing professionals and the self-employed; unsupported by government, daycare is expensive and scarce. But thousands of resourceful young adults with children have tried communal living.

People committed to sexual monogamy and private parenting, but who found living in a nuclear family burdensome and emotionally unfulfilling, formed the Circle of Families. Residential collectives made up of nuclear units, circles of families sometimes accept single childless adults, but require everyone to participate in communal child-rearing. In 1973 a Philadelphia circle, the Philadelphia Life Center, consisted of thirteen houses and one hundred children and adults – singles, childless couples, and parents ranging from their twenties to their sixties. In a circle of families in Brooklyn, New York, four adults split a twelve-hour day into four three-hour housework duties. Each adult has nine hours free and works three hours in the household, sharing laundry, cooking, shopping, and child care equally.[6]

Tensions arise in communes as they do in families. In the symbology of television or glossy magazines, family conflict signals failure or lack of love. But people in intentional communities expect conflict and consider the process of resolving it an essential element of growth. They work on building equal, non-oppressive relations, giving special attention to pressures arising from lack of privacy. They hold regular meetings to let off steam and offer each other care, concern, and criticism. Many communards consider these the most rewarding aspect of communal life. The men in the Philadelphia Life Center formed a discussion group to deal with the discomfort some felt about domestic work and nurturing, asking what it means to be a man and how they have been brought up to view the male role.

An early 1970s study of thirty-eight counter-culture communes (also called hippie and anarchist communes) showed that most communards had joined in search of traditional values – support, acceptance, love, a sense of place, and a model for child-rearing.[7]

Seeing themselves as an extended family of peers, some groups adopted the same surname. One called itself "The Family." Such communities can assimilate varied living arrangements – monogamous couples, unmarried couples, heterosexual and homosexual acts, and individuals moving in and out of relationships in what the authors call "serial monogamy." They stress that while celibacy is rare and couples' relations may be fragile, sex is not promiscuous or disordered. Communities practising group marriage are rare and are usually torn by so many personal conflicts that few survive even a year.

Lesbian women have experimented with both small and large communes. For years the "Community" in Portland, Oregon, functioned as a network, offering members residence in one of several dwellings scattered throughout the city as well as paid work in commune-run enterprises like a gas station, child-care centre, health clinic, bookstore, and house-painting business. It required members to place a primary value on being a lesbian; to identify with the counter-culture youth movement and advocate its ideals; and to devote most of their time and energy to Community recreational, cultural, and political activities.

Members of the Community spent virtually all their time together – at work, play, friendship, or love. The Community expected ex-lovers to remain friends; if they could not, they were asked to leave. Portland State University anthropologists who studied personal and group relationships in the Community asserted that members found the commune's support, acceptance, and companionship more stable and enduring than any love relationship, and eventually made sexual relationships secondary. The Womanshare Collective in Grants Pass, Oregon, also offered collective living – providing a home and a connection with people and with the land, although the particular members and land might vary over time.

Alternative Economic Structures

Socialism

Feminism, emphatically egalitarian and therefore democratic, is inherently socialist, but twentieth-century socialist states were not feminist. They used feminist rhetoric and made greater efforts than other kinds of government to treat the female of the species as part of society, but gave feminism mostly lip service. A real feminist society was too radical for them. As a result, they failed women, but failed men too. They failed humanity by structuring society from the top down – an absurd way to realize a democratic philosophy. Today, no existing government in the world is sympathetic to feminism. Efforts to create equal rights and a single standard, even by governments that claim they want to reward women for their contribution to revolution, came to grief on the loud and unwavering opposition of men at every level of education and power, in and out of government.

For decades, socialist feminists believed that socialist revolution would emancipate women. More pessimistic views have emerged recently. The priorities of socialist states foster male domination and worsen women's situation in some ways. Industrial socialist states like the Soviet Union assimilated women into paid work, including the professions, without redefining sexual power relations. In all socialist states, industrialized or not, women's workload increased: maintaining the family and raising children under conditions made difficult by national priorities (placing arms and heavy industry above food, child-care facilities, and other necessities), women also had to work full-time for wages and work politically if they wished to get ahead. Nor did socialist states establish anything near sexual parity in political bodies. Government apologists justified such failures, citing scarce resources, international pressure, and underdevelopment, but one woman best summed up the situation: "If a country can eliminate the tsetse fly, it can get an equal number of men and women on its politburo."[8]

What most determines a nation's treatment of women is not its economic or political structures but its values. Militant states, even without huge armies and extensive arsenals (like some Muslim states), are more emphatically anti-woman than pacific states. Whatever their economic/political form, cultures that see men as killers consider women mere breeders and servants. Some feminists think war can benefit women by expanding their sphere: "the longer women assume the . . . roles once held by men, the more likely they are to retain them."[9] They argue that women, when they participate in armed combat for an extended period, have a better chance of retaining the right to take fully human roles in society once the combat has ended.[10]

But I feel this is wishful thinking. Women have worked and fought courageously in every socialist revolution in this century, but in no socialist state are they equal to men. In Algeria, Vietnam, as well as the old USSR and China, women were sent back to the couscous or its equivalent. Eritrea has had a mass organization for women longer than any country but Vietnam. The victorious Eritrean revolutionary forces were strongly feminist, but as their new society is built, women are dwindling into unimportance there.

The 1960s wave of feminism inspired women in Peru, Mexico, and Brazil to mobilize for feminist demands. Socialist revolution-aries formed the Nicaraguan Sandinista Front (FSLN) to overthrow dictator Antonio Somoza in 1962; women joined in 1963. When the revolution began, some Sandinista leaders seemed aware of the importance of women's liberation and Nicaragua's need for it. The first FSLN platform treated sex equality as part of social equality, and in 1969 promised to abolish "the odious discrimination that women have been subjected to" and "establish economic, political, and cultural equality between women and men." It marshalled thousands of women to overthrow the Somoza regime and achieve equality through the Association of Women Confronting the National Problem (AMPRONAC), founded in 1977.

By the time the FSLN ousted Somoza in July 1979, women

made up 30 percent of combatants. When the Sandinistas took power, they were determined to create a true socialist state, not a one-party state that suppressed dissent. Committed to a socialism strong enough to allow a mixed economy, nonalignment, and political pluralism, they allowed political dissent (within certain limits) and left 60 percent of the country's economic assets in private hands, nationalizing only Somocista assets. "Sandinismo" meant a socialism more democratic, independent, and moderate than Third World socialisms. Nicaragua became a symbol of hope to socialists throughout Latin America and beyond. But the appeal of this humane approach made the Reagan administration ferocious in its determination to destroy the Sandinistas.

Within weeks of taking power, the Sandinistas banned media sexploitation of women and named female FSLN cadres to senior positions (ministers, vice-ministers, regional party coordinators). Female combat soldiers became administrators and police. The government reaffirmed its commitment to women's liberation by proclaiming in the Estatuto Fundamental (a draft of their constitution) "the unconditional equality of all Nicaraguans without distinction of race, nationality, creed, or sex" and pledging to "remove by all means available" obstacles to achieving it.

In five years, the Sandinistas reduced illiteracy from over 50 percent to 13 percent, doubled the number of schools, increased school enrolment, eradicated several mortal diseases, provided basic healthcare services, and built more housing than Somoza in decades of rule. The land reform program cancelled peasants' debts and gave thousands of people land or secure jobs on state farms or cooperatives. Reform of family law confronted the unequal power relations between the sexes, along with men's right to evade responsibility for children while holding exclusive legal right to them. Women acquired custody rights, and men were required to contribute to the household and to child maintenance (when paternity was acknowledged). The land reform program gave women title to land and wages for their work, and encouraged them to participate and lead in cooperatives.

These actions had some negative results. Elite women who dealt in imports and luxury goods were more highly taxed. They gained legal rights, but lost business. Often bearing sole responsibility for children and family health care, women are especially concerned with housing and food. Many government campaigns helped women with practical problems, but reinforced their exclusive responsibility for those problems. The government did little or nothing to remove other mechanisms that subordinate women, and many male privileges over women remain in place.

After a few years, the FSLN's image abroad began to tarnish. Economic scarcity and constant war against US-backed forces were grinding down the Sandinista experiment; they stopped trying to improve women's position. In October 1984 Minister of Defence Tomás Borge acknowledged that certain important advances had been made, but "all of us have to honestly admit that we haven't confronted the struggle for women's liberation with . . . courage and decisiveness. From the point of view of daily exertion, women remain fundamentally in the same conditions as in the past."

Sandinista efforts to build popular support for feminist campaigns to raise women's consciousness were thwarted by the Catholic Church. Afraid of losing popular support as war tensions mounted, the FSLN realized only those parts of liberation programs that fit in with other goals and enjoyed popular support without arousing strong opposition – mostly in social welfare, development, social equality, and political mobilization to defend the revolution. Today, most Nicaraguan women remain at the bottom of the economic structure, eking out a living as domestic servants or producing or trading petty commodities. Few of them benefited from the socialization of child care and domestic labour: in mid-1984, forty-three child-care centres tended about 4000 children, and further expansion was not envisaged because of financial hardship caused by the contra war.

In time, of course, under unremitting American pressure, the Sandinistas were voted out of office and Nicaragua returned to its capitalist economy (which like many Latin American economies, privileges a tiny elite). The Nicaraguan revolution is an extreme example of the difficulty of constructing a socialist society in face of poverty, underdevelopment, and external intervention – and most socialist revolutions encountered such interference. Post-revolutionary Mozambique suffered South African attacks; South Yemen and China, dire scarcity; Cuba, a US blockade; and Vietnam, a devastated landscape. In any case, most socialist states supported women's emancipation only half-heartedly.[11] It should be clear by now that women's emancipation requires a feminist revolution.

Hilkka Pietilä

At the 1985 UN Conference in Nairobi, Finn Hilkka Pietilä proposed an alternative system for thinking about economic matters.[12] Since then, she has developed her theory. Pietilä argues that all of life is based on two primary sectors: the household economy, in which labour is unpaid and voluntary, and which is necessary (in the sense I have been using this term throughout these volumes) for the survival of most humans; and the economics of living nature – production based on cultivating the living potential of nature, rather than on extracting products from it. She calls this sector the "free economy."

Beyond these sectors are two others: the "protected sector" and the "fettered economy." The first involves elements most governments protect and regulate so prices and terms can be determined independently, without too much pressure from the global economy: production and labour for domestic markets and public services – food production, house and infrastructure construction, administration, education, health, transport, and communication. The fettered economy – large-scale production for export (usually called the open economy) – is tied to world markets. The international market determines its terms – prices, competition, and demand. At present, Pietilä writes, the entire life of society is geared to support this sector, yet it accounts for only a modest proportion of total production in any one nation and in the world. Money payment is not the only criterion for assessing work, she says; it can be gauged by volume of labour power (number of workers) or work time (number of hours) needed for a process. Volumes of input or output can be expressed in physical units or in number of people cared for.[13]

This way of depicting economies is more useful and more reflective of reality than current methods of analysis. It allows free resources to be used in free and protected sectors and, if the market wants GDP figures, the market can pay for them. Pietilä's model includes women's (and men's) unpaid work (at present invisible in economic models) as a factor in an economy. Some Finnish women determined to put this principle into practice by using their reproductive work for political ends. *Ms. Magazine* reported that in June 1986, over four thousand Finnish women went on strike, proclaiming "No natal for no nukes."[14] A delegation of women presented the minister of trade and commerce with a statement declaring their resolve not to bear children until Finland changed its pro-nuclear energy policy. On October 24, 1985, women in twenty-two countries organized "time off for women" activities or full-scale strikes to inform governments that they wanted all women's work, including unwaged work, made visible in the Gross Domestic Product.

An Alternative Political Structure: Anarchy

We have referred to anarchy several times in the course of this work, yet the reader may have only a vague sense of what it is, partly because definitions of anarchy are heavy on negatives but vague about positives. Anarchists oppose domination, hierarchies, and all forms of coercion. The communes discussed earlier do not call themselves anarchistic, yet they live in anarchy – without a head. The anarchist communities that thrived in Barcelona before the Spanish Civil War and present-day grassroots feminist groups in

Europe and North America follow in the communalist-anarchist tradition of Bakunin, Kropotkin, and Goldman. It is, in fact, easy to live without a head in a small group. But a large-scale society combining freedom and community is difficult to envision.

An anarchist society would be, first of all, egalitarian: society (including work structures) would foster reciprocity and cooperation (which anarchists traditionally call "mutualism"), ending the need for economic inequality or differential work incentives.[15] The institutions in and through which people interact would encourage them to cooperate, not compete, with one another. Society would not be managed by a centralized hierarchy; people would organize groups to meet their own needs. Leaders would arise on an ad hoc basis, leading in certain ways in given situations. No chairs of authority would give some people the right or authority to "command" in all situations. Instead of trying to dominate nature, people would find ways to live in harmony with the physical environment, as simple societies did. Anarchists insist that means be consistent with ends, that the process of change is the change, that we accomplish revolution by living in revolutionary ways. An illustration of these principles is the 1973 Vancouver Women's Health Collective.[16]

In early 1973, women from local feminist health services (including abortion referral and self-help groups) joined to form the Vancouver Women's Health Collective to offer advice on health, contraception, and abortion. It fitted diaphragms and had a drop-in service. Through collective women's study groups, it tried to inform the public as well as medical and nursing students; it ran a self-help clinic aimed at empowering women to take responsibility for their own health. The members were determined to use feminist principles in their collective workplace as well.

Accepting the same premise as most corporations and bureaucracies – that withholding information keeps people powerless and that the more information people have in a given situation, the more power they have and the more responsibility they take – they structured the collective to distribute information, power, and responsibility as equally and widely as possible. Refusing to vest authority in individual managers who controlled information, they rotated coordinating and administrative positions among all members and held weekly meetings to decide all matters of policy, large or small, by consensus. Each member took a turn at every job, teaching her successor what was necessary to perform it.

The collective engaged in self-criticism at their weekly meetings, reversing the usual arrangement in which a boss alone has the authority to criticize workers or systems. In theory, all members of the collective participated equally in running the organization and in making and carrying out decisions. In practice, however, inevitably some members had more time to contribute, some had been around longer and knew more, and newcomers needed to learn more before they could fully take part. But the structure guaranteed that no one felt oppressed by the work.[17]

Linda Light and Nancy Klieber distinguish "social power" – power to dominate or control others – from "personal power" or autonomy (these terms roughly correspond with my "power over" and "power to").[18] Hierarchical organizations force individuals to compete for both, but collectively organized workplaces increase personal power for everyone. Sharing social power generates personal power, which makes people independent, self-reliant, self-actualizing, and confident. They feel better about themselves, and they act more creatively and responsibly in cooperating with others towards a common end. Workers in collectives have more freedom and autonomy than those in hierarchical organizations, and evidence suggests these benefits carry over to personal life, raising self-confidence and political efficacy outside workplaces.

Marcia Freedman describes anarchy in practice in an international women's conference, the International Tribunal for Crimes against Women, in Brussels in March 1976. She ruefully confesses that she was invited because she was the only feminist legislator in the world at the time.[19] Radical feminists took over the imposing

Palais de Congress for five days. She felt "like a country bumpkin in the big city, not because of the building . . . but . . . the women who occupied it." The Palais was filled with woman advocates – for prostitutes, battered women, incest victims, female prisoners, and against coerced sterilization and pregnancy, genital mutilation, and pornography. They had set up hundreds of exhibit tables and papered the walls with disturbing political posters. A long queue of women waited patiently to enter a curtained-off corner of the vast foyer labelled "Self-Help." Admitted ten at a time, they were shown a speculum and taught how to examine their vaginas, recognize signs of vaginal infections, and treat them with yogurt and vinegar.

The delegates had voted to bar men, and they exploded at the presence of male journalists. The organizers apologized for sitting on a platform above the audience, for creating an agenda for others, and for placing time limits on speakers. Feminist insistence on democratic decision-making can seem impracticable, but in the long run it saves time because it reaches consent, unifying a group before an action. Issuing orders and demanding obedience seems more efficient, but it leads to conflict, defection, and revolt later on. Female style does not preclude defection, but reduces it by giving members a personal stake in the action.

The ideal feminist organization is the leaderless group. Freedman writes: "We are anarchists not by ideology but by need. We are moved by an underclass appreciation of power – by our certainty that the kind of power that oppresses us can never be ours – to envision a utopia in which there is no governance other than self-governance," in which bonding, caring, and sharing replace authority. The Brussels conference showed anarchy in effective action. Anarchic structure lets people exercise and relinquish power; everyone is heard when there is a flexible centre of attention.

Anarchist organizations may spend more time in decision-making than hierarchical organizations, but they have two major benefits: everyone derives power from their work, and this empowerment improves morale. The draining power struggles that characterize large organizations are far less prevalent in collectives. In strongly hierarchical organizations, most of people's energy is spent jostling for advancement or just maintaining their position or their institutional power. Energy is diverted from the actual work of the organization. And, as already explained, since collectives reach decisions by consensus, people do not subvert and undermine them later. Anarchist structures not only improve lives but are more efficient in the long term. Unfortunately, no matter how committed they are to cooperative, noncompetitive modes of work, collectives must compete in a competitive outside world.

An Alternative Politics: Citizenship

Societies often deny women citizenship by granting it only to those who will defend their country in armed struggle, an activity for which women's bodies were deemed unfit (or too precious). As Kathleen B. Jones reads Western political theory, it bifurcates experience and marginalizes women as familial incarnations of love, who nurture only their own families.[20] The particularity of women's passion made them unfit (by nature) for a seemingly more universal passion for political virtue and public duty. By locking women in the realm of the necessary, philosophers implicitly denied them the mark of humanness, volition, and the power and right to choose actions and life. Indeed, they granted volition only to propertied males. But as revolutions swept formerly commoner males into elite seats, that distinction was blurred among men. Only women are still seen as beasts of burden, created by nature to serve and maintain the human race.

There is no evidence that women are by nature more loving than men. The capacity for nurturing and cooperation that many females exhibit may result from a socialization that prepares them to take responsibility for children. Women's affections are perforce particular – they have been imprisoned in the domestic realm. Concern for the particular does not disqualify a person from con-

cern for the whole: indeed, compassion for others grows from compassion for one's own. Without feeling for the particular, one is not
likely to feel for the universal. The entire philosophical edifice is a
justification of elite male scorn for labour that does not lead to
power.

The liberal understanding of citizenship, Jones notes, implies
that for women to become full citizens, they must become like men
– that is, not produce babies from their bodies. So Shulamith Firestone urged artificial reproduction.[21] If women no longer became
pregnant, gave birth, and nourished babies from their bodies, they
would no longer be second-class citizens, sex would be freed of
taboos, the workforce could be fully age- and sex-integrated, and
people would contract to live together. A less extreme and simpler
solution, so far apparently impossible, is for men to take equal responsibility for child-rearing and domestic maintenance.

Western philosophers have long held autonomy to be the great
goal of life. Yet total autonomy isolates totally, engendering madness, and studies show that personality is defined by relationships.
Feminists believe that people become selves through their personal,
sexual, and productive relationships. The ideal, fully democratic,
feminist society can be sustained only by organizing society at all
levels – family, workplace, community, and state – in more open
and ambiguous organizational structures and behavioural codes
than characterize the partial democracies now existing in most
Western nations. In feminist political theory, the nation-state is an
outmoded political form.

An important accomplishment of feminist theory has been to
reintroduce the body into political discourse. Thinking about the
political significance of women's bodies has generated extraordinarily
vital thinking about pornography and reproductive rights.
One feminism, "difference feminism," stresses the political significance of female culture, embracing the concrete, particular, and
bodily, revalorizing them, but without challenging the context of
domination that transforms "every alternative voice into a new song

of self-sacrifice." Jones urges us to embrace the "cherished ideals and precious human values" that grow in the female social world and to discard domination and subordination.[22]

For early feminists, aware of the need to invent an egalitarian, personal form of political organization, feminist political community was a family (sisters) or friendship group. They proposed substituting intimate forms of interaction modelled on family and friendship structures for the alienated hierarchical interactions of citizens in bureaucratic systems, and exchanging ties of affection for power links (domination/subordination) as the way to bind the social order. Feminists disliked pursuing instrumental goals: they preferred a sense of community to competitive hierarchies, just as they preferred trust to suspicion as the motivating political impulse. Feminist political scientists suggest empowerment as the criterion for citizenship.[23]

Jones argues that defining "citizen" as a sister or friend in a feminist polity is transforming. Belonging to a polity as to a family of equals intensifies the experience of membership. When men use the family as a political model, they stress dominance/subordination – the leader as "father" of the state-family. Care-taking is an implied, not a primary, concern. A feminist family, in contrast, is a community of absolute equals. Families tend to demand total commitment from members, but also to nurture and accept them partially or wholly as persons, not functions. Families and friends grow stronger, more intense solidarity than citizens in a modern state, and their relationships have many dimensions, not just the formal self-presentation. Families and friends are bound by complex psychological bonds of body, heart, and will.

Of course, psychological bonds and their messy, often unconscious underpinnings are precisely what male hierarchies try to avoid. And the degree of commitment expected from a sister can undermine autonomy and self-development – which are also feminist ideals. Sisterly rivalry is just as intense and debilitating as the sibling rivalry men display in competitions. When feminists feel tension and contradiction, Jones notes, they turn rigidly "political-ly correct." Dissent is harder in a polity ruled by a family's "general will" than in a community based in friendship.

Traditional citizenship precludes all other loyalties – to a family, sex, class, race, or place. The French revolutionaries' ideal citizen was Brutus, who executed his own sons for "treason." Elshtain calls the female version of such citizenship "Spartan motherhood" (mothers' civic duty is to sacrifice their sons to the state's wars).[24] Such citizen-ship also requires a combative, oppositional stance on political action, which cannot be fused with a feminist citizenship based on intimate particular bonds like maternity. Feminists value full equality, multiple interests and loyalties, and experiencing body and emotion – not blotting them out. Above all, they do not advocate sacrificing life to the pursuit of power. Concluding that feminist values cannot be adapted to the patriarchal conception of citizenship, Jones urges feminists to transform the practice and concept of citizenship to fit their values, and, in the process, to create a new polity.

But the difficulty of realizing feminist ideals remains. We can-not even imagine a feminist political structure without considering the unresolved problem of balancing bondage with autonomy. The male thinking that makes autonomy an ideal (for men) has made it an absolute, if rhetorical, requirement for "manhood." Men pretend to autonomy, pretend to be the cowboy on a high horse, alone in the mesa, dwarfing even the bluffs. The ideal forces men – or they force themselves – to live deceitful lives that make them sick, men-tally or physically. Men who live as though they were independent often collapse when their wives or women friends die, overwhelmed by unmet needs. But Western women also try to act or be autonomous. Their stress on individualism often alienates Third World women, many of whom are bound to extended families that organize production. When a family's survival depends on each member chipping in labour or income, no one feels independent.

Our need for bonds and our need for autonomy are hard to bal-ance, and they seem to contradict each other. No political structure

I know of has focused on balancing these basic human needs. Anarchy still remains a vision: it has been realized only in relatively small communities and only for brief periods. But it is essential that the political thinkers who devise a new structure be feminist, to guarantee that women – the easiest group to bind because they take responsibility for children – are not bound more than they wish to be. And also to ensure that the proposed bonds exist to ease the isolation and to increase the felicity for the entire community, and not to enable someone to dominate.

An Alternative Society: Motherhood and Children

Men appropriate children as they appropriate women, by legislating them into possessions. Men's control over children varies among societies, but in most present-day societies, children are named for their fathers, the less certain parent. In past societies that permitted abortion and infanticide, fathers controlled whether children lived or died. In most societies before the twentieth century, fathers had exclusive rights to determine a child's residence, diet, medical care, education, and marriage (often without their consent), and always got custody of children after divorce. This is still the case in many countries. Men's ownership of children is/was a lever in their control of women, who, emotionally bound to their children, were effectively bound to the fathers who owned them. But no law now or ever required men to do the work of raising children. Laws in some states required men to support them, but women have little or no recourse if they fail to do so, and none if they do so more poorly than they can afford. Yet both law and social sanction require women to care for children; the state removes children from mothers who fail to do so according to its standards. Parenting is divided: men get the power, and women get the work.

Children are an asset in agricultural economies because they start to work at an early age, and social pressure requires them to support or care for elderly parents. But in advanced industrial societies, children must be fed, sheltered, clothed, and educated for many years and do not contribute to the household until they are mature – if then. They are expensive, time-consuming drains, assets only in terms of love. So, in industrial society, the law often grants mothers custody of children. In modern semi-egalitarian marriage, fathers do not have an exclusive right to determine all elements of a child's life, but they still try to control childbirth and the child care they rarely perform.

The belief that women are responsible for children, and men are not, derives from prehistory, when fatherhood was unknown and children were named for and belonged to their mothers. Women did the work of reproducing and most of the work of maintaining the human race, but they controlled their work and reaped any rewards. This is the way things are because, literally, this is the way they have always been. But does that necessarily mean this is the way they must be? Is it impossible for men to enrich themselves by caring for children? Clearly, men's genes do not preclude it – judging from how many men increasingly tend children now – and with pleasure.

But Heidi Hartmann and other feminists feel this division of labour makes the struggle for equality futile. Since men's work (the production of things) is fundamentally different from women's work (the production and reproduction of human beings), the two can never be equal.[25] Feminist analysis has rooted women's oppression in sexuality, marriage, and the family. It has discovered some basic strategic principles: the need for autonomous women's movements; the need to refuse to postpone women's struggles or subordinate them to any male-dominated state, party, class, colour, or national movement; and the need to defend lesbian choice. Some feminists believe these analytic and strategic illuminations, more than classic demands for equal pay, equal work, reproductive freedom, and child care, are the legacy of 1960s feminism.

But not everyone does the kind of work assigned their sex, and many people do both kinds of work. The decision to stop fighting for equality arises from despair at male intransigence in taking responsibility for children. Thwarted, feminists feel they must seek another direction – and the feminism of the future must have a broader agenda. The tendency to care for others (which humans probably learn) is a vital necessity in a species whose young are born helpless and remain relatively so for years. At the core of that care-taking is motherhood – the rock on which all feminist efforts come to grief – for equality cannot be achieved as long as women alone are responsible for raising the human race, nor can we single-hand-edly create a feminist world. To persuade men to join with us will require a complete change in most men's experience of life; they will finally have to grow up by taking daily, ordinary responsibility for the children of the world.

Reproducing the human race is the essential human act; we do not need to invoke a specious "natural law" to know that nature programs species to stay alive long enough to reproduce themselves. But unlike flies or fish, human young, born altricial, require years of nurturing to survive. Rearing children is as essential as giving birth to them. Society's primary task is to foster both phases of this essential process: childbirth and child-rearing. Child welfare must lie at the centre of any feminist polity. Yet, increasingly, the values and tendencies both of the West and the Third World endanger children and mothers.

Biological motherhood will probably not be done away with in the near future, and perhaps never. Many women would fight to the death to retain this most profound of all human experiences and bonds. But biological motherhood is not identical to rearing a child. Millions of children have been raised by people other than biological mothers. Biological motherhood is the profoundest and most enduring human bond, but all human bonds are breakable. Biological motherhood is necessary, but it is not a prerequisite for mothering. Adoptive parents can mother as well as a biological mother. The fact that only women give birth does not mean that only women should mother.

The major task facing future feminists is to devise an economic and social structure that fosters procreation and child-rearing without locking women into forced procreation or motherhood. Not all women want to or can give birth: but those who do are making an essential contribution to society that deserves – and requires – support. Similarly, not all women and men want to rear children: but those who do deserve and require support. All humans should contribute to well-being. The only purpose of human life beyond continuation is to foster and enrich the life that exists – one's own, by fostering one's own talents, and the lives of others – by taking care and by creating and maintaining society, culture, technology, or a polity. For such a structure to be realized, men must recognize that immortality lies in future generations and that manhood lies in taking responsibility for living future humans. To contribute to creating felicity for everyone's children is one of the most satisfying tasks on earth.

The difficulty of discussing any single problem women face demonstrates the integrity of women's lives, which are of a piece and cannot be compartmentalized. A feminist world would recognize this integrity as human, not female, and would start where feminism always starts, with the most basic, the most profound – our own bodies, emotions, thoughts, and sexuality. The only political structure that permits such recognition is participatory democracy, a polity based in small local units in which every person has a voice. The only way to guarantee that all children born will be raised in decent circumstances is to distribute wealth in a more egalitarian way to allow every child the same right to air and water, food, protection, medical care, education, and work.

Given that we emerge from roughly five millennia of patriarchy, feminists have accomplished enormous things in a little over a century. As women across the globe gradually overcome economic discrimination, enforced economic dependence, and political and social disenfranchisement, we exchange male-identification – an alien definition of our being – for woman-identification, a positive self-definition that reveals female excellence.[26] Feminists are testing new kinds of lives and community. Women want more jobs with more responsibility and more recompense. We have a right to power on the same terms as men, even if relatively few pursue it: culture, biology, or some combination of the two, teaches us that pursuit of power is the pursuit of misery. But women must have a voice in political decision-making.

All feminist goals are ultimately connected to the quality of life, autonomy, pride, dignity, freedom, joy, meaningfulness, and sense of self that Sheila Ruth calls "spiritual matters."[27] Feminism also addresses the divisiveness of gender and class stratification. It enhances bonds among same-class women who, in the process, forge the solidarity to counter male divisions and redefine "politics" – "men's issues" and "women's issues" – from a women's perspective, creating a new way of looking at the world. Moreover, divisions among women can heal when we recognize a kinship based on our position in a men's world and our almost universal concern for the young and for human well-being. This healing is part of the feminist project.[28]

NOTES

CHAPTER 1

1 George Dorsey, *Man's Own Show: Civilization* (New York: Harper and Bros., 1931).

2 For the political difference between wife- and sister-status, see Karen Sachs, *Sisters and Wives: The Past and Future of Sexual Equality* (Westport, Conn.: *Contributions in Women's Studies*, 10, 1979). For an analysis of Kongo in these terms, see Susan Herlin Broadhead, "Slave Wives, Free Sisters: Bakongo Women and Slavery c. 1700–1850," in *Women and Slavery in Africa*, eds. Claire Robertson and Martin Klein (Madison, Wisc.: University of Wisconsin Press, 1983).

3 For more information on women in this empire, see Margaret Strobel, *Muslim Women in Mombasa, 1890–1975* (New Haven: Yale University Press, 1979).

4 Basil Davidson, *The Story of Africa* (London: Mitchell Beazley, 1984).

5 Howard Zinn, *A People's History of the United States* (New York: Harper & Row, 1980).

6 Frederick Cooper, "Islam and Cultural Hegemony: The Ideology of Slaveowners on the East African Coast," in *The Ideology of Slavery in Africa*, ed. P. Lovejoy (Beverly Hills: Sage Publications, 1981).

7 Mtoro bin Mwinyi Bakari, *Desturi za Waswahili*, ed. and trans. by J.W.J. Allen as *The Customs of the Swahili People* (Berkeley: University of California Press, c. 1981).

8 Cooper, *Ideology of Slavery in Africa*.

9 Marcia Wright, "Women in Peril," *African Social Research* 20 (1975): 800–19.

10 Julian Cobbing, "The Mfecane as Alibi: Thoughts on Dithakong and Mbolompo," *Journal of African History* 29 (1988): 487–519.

11 George E. Brooks, Jr. "The Signares of Saint-Louis and Gore: Women Entrepreneurs in Eighteenth-Century Senegal," *Women in Africa: Studies in Social and Economic Change*, ed. Nancy J. Hafkin and Edna G. Bay (Stanford, Calif.: Stanford University Press, 1976).

12 E. Frances White, "Creole Women Traders in the Nineteenth Century," Working Papers No. 27, African Studies Centre, Boston University; and *Sierra Leone's Settler Women Traders: Women on the Afro-European Frontier* (Ann Arbor: University of Michigan Press, 1987).

13 Babatunde Agiri, "Slavery in Yoruba Society in the 19th Century," in *The Ideology of Slavery in Africa.* ed. P. Lovejoy (Berkeley: Sage Publications, 1981).

14 Anna Hinderer, *Seventeen Years in the Yoruba Country: Memorials of Anna Hinderer*, edited by her friends (London: Seeley, Jackson & Holliday, 1852).

15 Citations in this sections come from Christine Qunta, who is herself quoting Tendai Mutunhu, "Nehanda of Zimbabwe," *Ufahamu*; and from Terence O. Ranger, *Revolt in Southern Rhodesia 1867–70* (London: Heinemann, 1967).

16 David Sweetman, *Women Leaders in African History* (London: Heinemann, 1984).

17 R.S. Baden-Powell (founder of the Boy Scouts), a guest at the ceremony at which Prempeh was forced to bow to the British governor, wrote about her: "the only man among them was the Queen."

18 Iris Berger, "Rebels or Status-Seekers? Women as Spirit Mediums in East Africa," Hafkin and Bay, *Women in Africa.*

19 For some examples, see M.J. Bessell, "Nyabingi," *Uganda Journal* 6, 2 (1938), cited by Berger in "Rebels or Status-Seekers?"

20 The section on Africa could not have been written without the help of Marcia Wright and Susan Hall, who worked tirelessly to help protect me from mistakes. Marjorie Mbilinyi also consulted on this section, and Christine Gailey was a consultant on Dahomey. Sources not noted in the text are M. Kwamena-Poh, *African History in Maps; African Women South of the Sahara,* ed. Margaret Jean Hay and Sharon Stichter (New York: Longman, 1984); Marjorie Mbilinyi, "'Women in Development': Ideology and the Marketplace," in *Competition: A Feminist Taboo?,* ed. Valerie Miner and Helen E. Longino (New York: Feminist Press, 1987), and "Wife, Slave and Subject of the King: The Oppression of Women in the Shambala Kingdom," *Tanzania Notes and Records* 88–89 (1982): 1–13; Claire Robertson, "Ga Women and Socioeconomic Change in Accra, Ghana," in Hafkin and Bay; *Slavery in Africa; Historical and Anthropological Perspectives,* ed. Suzanne Miers and Igor Kopytoff (Madison: University of Wisconsin Press, 1977); Rosalyn Terborg-Penn, "Women and Slavery in the African Diaspora: A Cross-Cultural

Approach to Historical Analysis," *Sage* 3, 2 (fall, 1986): 11–15; Marcia Wright, "Justice, Women, and the Social Order in Abercorn, Northeastern Rhodesia, 1897–1903," in *African Women and the Law: Historical Perspectives*, ed. Margaret Jean Hay and Marcia Wright; and Marcia Wright, "Technology, Marriage and Women's Work in the History of Maize-Growers in Mazabuka, Zambia: a Reconnaissance," *Journal of African Studies* 10, 1 (October 1983): 71–85.

CHAPTER 2

1 Alice Kessler-Harris, *Women Have Always Worked: A Historical Overview* (New York: The Feminist Press, 1981).

2 Carroll Smith-Rosenberg, "The Female World of Love and Ritual: Relations Between Women in Nineteenth-Century America," *Signs* 1, 1 (autumn 1975): 1–29.

3 Françoise Basch, *Relative Creatures: Victorian Women in Society and the Novel*, 1837–67 (London: Allan Lane, 1974); and *Rebelles Américaines au XIXième Siècle: mariage, amour libre, et politique* (Paris: Meridiens Klincksieck, 1990).

4 For concrete examples of women's experience, see Diane Balser, *Sisterhood and Solidarity: Feminism and Labor in Modern Times* (Boston: South End Press, 1987). For direct quotations from women factory workers of the period, see *Victorian Women*, ed. Erna Olafson Hellerstein, Leslie Parker Hume, and Karen M. Offen (Stanford, Calif.: Stanford University Press, 1981).

5 Joan W. Scott and Louise A. Tilly, *Comparative Studies in Society and History*, Vol. 17 (Cambridge: Cambridge University Press, 1975); and Louise A. Tilly and Joan W. Scott, *Women, Work and Family* (New York: Holt, Rinehart and Winston, 1978).

6 For a moving account of women in the Lowell mills, see Harriet Robinson, *Loom and Spindle or Life Among the Early Mill Girls* (1898: reprint. Kailua Hawaii: Press Pacifica, 1976).

7 Jacqueline Dowd Hall, Robert Korstad, James Leloudis, "Cotton Mill People," *American Historical Review* 91, 2 (April 1986): 245–85.

8 Christine Stansell, *City of Women: Sex and Class in New York, 1789–1860* (New York: Alfred A. Knopf, 1986) and "Women, Children, and the Uses of the Streets: Class and Gender Conflict in New York City, 1850–1860," *Feminist Studies* 8, 2 (summer 1982): 309–32.

9 Cited in Diane Balser, *Sisterhood and Solidarity*, 34.

10 Joan W. Scott and Louise A. Tilly, *Comparative Studies in Society and History*, Vol. 17 (Cambridge: Cambridge University Press, 1975).

11 Dolores Janiewski, "Making Common Cause: The Needlewomen of New York, 1831–69," *Signs* 3, 1 (1976).

12 Rosalyn Baxandall, Linda Gordon, Susan Reverby, "Boston Working Women Protest, 1869," *Signs* 3, 1 (1976).

13 Ibid.

14 Munby's portraits can be found in Michael Hiley, *Victorian Working Women: Portraits from Life* (Boston: David R. Godine, 1979).

15 Visiting the Wigan pits, intrigued by the dress and demeanour of the Pit Brow girls, Munby called Wigan "the picturesque headquarters of rough female labour." George Orwell visited Wigan fifty years later, and noticed only men; Beatrix Campbell corrected his oversight, on a visit to Wigan fifty years later, when the pits were closed and the town was dying. Beatrix Campbell, *Wigan Pier Revisited: Poverty and Politics in the Eighties* (London: Virago, 1984).

16 Cited by Tilly and Scott in *Women, Work and Family.*

17 Leonore Davidoff, "Mastered for Life: Servant and Wife in Victorian and Edwardian England," *Journal of Social History* VII, 3 (spring 1974).

18 Theresa McBride, "The Long Road Home: Women's Work and Industrialization," *Becoming Visible: Women in European History*, ed. Renate Bridenthal, Claudia Koonz and Susan Stuard (Boston: Houghton Mifflin, 1987).

19 Christine Stansell, *City of Women: Sex and Class in New York, 1789–1860* (New York: Alfred A. Knopf, 1986).

20 William Blackstone, *Commentaries,* 1893, cited in Davidoff, "Mastered for Life."

21 Katherine Schlegel, "Mistress and Servant in Nineteenth-Century Hamburg: Employer/Employee Relationships in Domestic Service, 1880–1914," *History Workshop Journal* 15 (spring 1983): 60–77.

22 Lee Holcombe, *Victorian Ladies at Work*, ed. Lee Holcombe (Hamden, Conn.: Anchor Books, 1973).

23 Ruth Rosen and Sue Davidson, "Introduction," *The Maimie Papers*, ed. Ruth Rosen and Sue Davidson (Old Westbury, NY: Feminist Press, 1977).

24 Mary Gibson, *Prostitution and the State in Italy*, 1860–1915 (New Brunswick, NJ: Rutgers University Press, 1986).

25 For a description of the living conditions of a group of British prostitutes, see Frances Finnegan, *Poverty and Prostitution: A Study of Victorian Prostitutes in York* (Cambridge: Cambridge University Press, 1979).

26 W.R. Greg, "Prostitution," *Westminster Review* (1850).

27 This information comes from Rosen and Davidson, *The Maimie Papers.*

28 Judy Walkowitz, *Prostitution and Victorian Society: Women, Class, and the State* (Cambridge: Cambridge University Press, 1980).

29 For a description of the life of an early twentieth-century prostitute in her own words and from her own perspective, see Rosen and Davidson, *The Maimie Papers.*

30 Friedrich Engels, *The Condition of the Working Class*, (1844: Harmondsworth: Penguin, 1987).

31 Basch, *Relative Creatures.*

32 Tilly and Scott, *Women, Work and Family.*

33 Ibid.

34 Louis Reybaud, cited by Tilly and Scott, *Women, Work and Family.*

35 Stansell, *City of Women.*

36 Cited by Ellen Ross, in "Survival Networks: Women's Neighbourhood Sharing in London Before World War I," *History Workshop Journal* 15 (Spring 1983): 4–27.

37 In the 1980s, the women in Wigan lived on beans on toast and tea, giving any real food they could afford, like a steak and kidney pie, to their men. The men, who eat better, spend much of their wages at the pub. Campbell, *Wigan Pier Revisited.*

38 Ellen Ross, "'Fierce questions and taunts': Married life in working-class London, 1870–1914," *Feminist Studies* 8, no. 3 (Fall 1982).

39 Robinson, *Loom and Spindle.*

40 Ann Whitehead, "Sexual Antagonism in Herefordshire," *Dependence and Exploitation in Work and Marriage*, ed. D. L. Barker and S. Allen (London: Longman, 1976).

41 Ross, "Fierce Questions and Taunts."

42 Ross, "Survival Networks."

43 Stansell, "Women, Children, and the Uses of the Streets."

44 Ross, "Survival Networks."

45 Stansell, *City of Women.*

46 Stansell, "Women, Children, and the Uses of the Streets."

47 Stansell, *City of Women.*

48 Ibid.

CHAPTER 3

1 Spain (1820), Naples (1820), and Greece (1821). The Greek uprising succeeded; revolutions in Naples and Spain were crushed, but the latter quickened a liberation movement in Latin America.

2 Popular uprisings in Modena, Bologna, and Parma gained neither reform nor national unification. With heavy military force and difficulty, Russia put down a Polish uprising (1830–31). Uprisings erupted in Switzerland and parts of Germany and Italy, civil war in Portugal and Spain.

3 Less serious disruptions troubled Spain, Denmark, Rumania, Ireland, Greece, and Britain.

4 Barbara Taylor, *Eve and the New Jerusalem: Socialism and Feminism in the Nineteenth Century* (New York: Pantheon Books, 1983).

5 Its name changed several times, ending as *La tribune des femmes.*

6 Charles Fourier, "Théorie des Quatre Mouvements," in *The Utopian Vision of Charles Fourier*, ed. Jonathan Beecher and Richard Bienvenue, (Boston: Beacon Press, 1971), 194–96.

7 *The Need to Welcome Female Strangers Kindly; Travels of a Pariah; Walks through London; A Worker's Union.*

8 *The Liverpool Standard*, 1839: Barbara Taylor, "The Men Are as Bad as Their Masters . . .": "Socialism, Feminism and Sexual Antagonism in the London Tailoring Trade in the 1830s," in *Sex And Class in Women's History*, ed. Judith L. Newton, Mary P. Ryan, and Judith R. Walkowitz (London: Routledge and Kegan Paul, 1983).

9 Françoise Basch, *Relative Creatures: Victorian Women in Society and the Novel, 1837–67* (London: Allan Lane, 1974).

10 Fredericka Bremer, a Swedish visitor, was highly impressed by a knitting machine. She described it in *The House of the New World: Impressions of America* (1853).

11 *The New Harmony Gazette*, October 1, 1825.

12 Gerda Lerner, *The Majority Finds Its Past* (New York: Oxford University Press, 1979).

13 Catherine Clinton, *The Other Civil War* (New York: Hill and Wang, 1984).

14 E.J. Hobsbawm, *The Age of Revolution: Europe 1789–1848* (London: Cardinal l988).

15 Ibid.

16 Karl Marx and Frederich Engels, *The Communist Manifesto* (1848: reprint, London: Penguin, 1985), trans. Samuel Moore (1888), ed. A.J.P. Taylor (1967).

17 In our own time we have seen rulers rob their countries of their wealth and flee, or murder large numbers of citizens. Elected officials start wars that kill their own citizens to benefit an elite. In the mid-nineteenth century, Austrian, Prussian, and Russian rulers cooperated in brutally suppressing their people.

18 Ferdinand VII, the authoritarian king of Spain, quashed democratic agitation with help from France, which sent him 200,000 soldiers in 1823. When Ferdinand died, his widow Maria Christina allied with middle-class liberals to get the throne for her daughter Isabella. In return for their help in defeating Ferdinand's reactionary brother Don Carlos, she granted them a constitution that gave them – but not the lower and working classes – a voice in the legislature. Eventually, their fear of this silent majority led the middle class to welcome an authoritarian dictator.

After Napoleon's defeat, Louis XVIII, Louis XVI's brother, was given the French throne. He also mollified the middle class with a constitutional charter establishing legal equality and a bicameral parliament, but limiting the vote by age and property ownership to about 100,000 men. He died in 1824, succeeded by his brother, the reactionary Charles X, who immediately indemnified nobles whose property had been seized during the revolution, and restored exclusive control of education to the Church. Wealthy middle-class deputies rebelled, passing a vote of no confidence in the government. Charles dissolved the chamber and called for new elections, which defeated his candidates. He dissolved the chamber again, issuing laws repressing the press and suffrage.

The 1848 revolution in France sparked uprisings across Europe. In Vienna as in Paris, students massed the barricades; the Austrian government took the same action as the French, but its soldiers would not fire. The Austrian Emperor abdicated in favour of his nephew, and Metternich's government fell, replaced by one that promised a liberal constitution. The collapse of Austria's government heartened leaders in its subject states – Hungary, Bohemia, Czechoslovakia, and the Italian city-states. People everywhere clamoured not just for bread and work but for a new society. As French rebels were demanding universal (male) suffrage and a republic, central Europeans were calling for constitutional systems. Rebels in Germany and Italy, still divided into petty states ruled by absolute princes, demanded some form of national unity. Even the Slavs, forgotten by history, rose up demanding nationhood: to Marx's dismayed disapproval, nationalism proved stronger than class in most of the 1848 revolutions.

In Milan, Naples and Sicily, Venice, Lombardy, and Tuscany, working-class armies successfully fought Austria for national unity and reform. Three hundred and fifty people were killed in the Milan insurrection: a few were students, clerks, or from landowning families; the rest were workers, 74 of them women. But ruling aristocrats in these principalities feared and detested workers (a "mortal menace") more than they feared Austria. Their fears of the lower classes and quarrels with each other precluded Italian unity; the cities were soon reconquered by Austria. The Czechs also squabbled once they had power: being anti-German, they refused to ally with German-speaking Austrians who wanted a united Germany. Their quarrels weakened them enough for Austria to reassert its control.

In Prussia, uprisings forced King Friedrich Wilhelm to concede a popular elected assembly. But the assembly proved hostile to Russia and granted self-government to Poles in the section of partitioned Poland under Prussian rule. Then the Germans in Prussian Poland rebelled against the Polish government and the Prussian army crushed the Poles. Other German states and principalities tried to quiet unrest by expanding relief programs or encouraging emigration. Hungary presented the Austrian emperor with a set of laws decreeing equality before the law, abolishing peasant corvée, tithes, and tax exemptions for aristocrats, and demanding a liberal constitution with a property-based franchise giving the vote to about a quarter of all adult males. Austria was at war in Italy and accepted these reforms, but as it gradually subdued the Italians and improved its military situation, it sent troops into Hungary and defeated it. Thus ended the revolutions of 1848.

19 Roger Price, *The Revolutions of 1848* (London: Macmillan, 1988).

20 Hobsbawm, *Age of Revolution.*

21 Kathleen B. Jones, "Citizenship in a Woman-Friendly Polity," *Signs*, 15, 4 (summer 1990): 781–812.

22 Ibid.

23 Françoise Basch was consultant for this section. Also consulted was Dolores Hayden, *Seven American Utopias: The Architecture of Communitarian Socialism* (Cambridge, Mass.: MIT Press, 1975).

NOTES

Chapter 4

1 Lee Virginia Chambers, *Schiller, Liberty, a Better Husband: Single Women in America: The Generations of 1780–1840* (New Haven: Yale University Press, 1984.)

2 Greg is quoted in Françoise Basch, *Relative Creatures* (London: Allan Lane, 1974).

3 Cited in Basch, *Relative Creatures.*

4 Leonore Davidoff, "Mastered For Life: Servant and Wife in Victorian and Edwardian England," *Journal of Social History* VII, 3 (spring 1974).

5 Ann Douglas Wood, "The Fashionable Diseases," in *Clio's Consciousness Raised*, ed. Mary S. Hartman and Lois Banner (New York: Harper & Row, 1974).

6 Carroll Smith-Rosenberg, "Puberty," in Hartman and Banner, *Clio's Consciousness Raised*, quoting a nineteenth-century physician describing puberty in women and men.

7 Smith-Rosenberg, "Puberty."

8 Michel Foucault, *Power/Knowledge*, ed. Colin Gordon (New York: Pantheon, 1980), 217.

9 The propaganda was produced by Francis Place and Richard Carlile.

10 Maryanne Cline Horowitz, "The 'Science' of Embryology Before the Discovery of the Ovum," in *Connecting Spheres: Women in the Western World, 1500 to the Present,* ed. Marilyn J. Boxer and Jean H. Quataert (New York: Oxford University Press, 1987).

11 Basch, *Relative Creatures,* 23.

12 Bonnie S. Anderson and Judith P. Zinsser, *A History of Their Own* (vol. II) (New York: Harper and Row, 1988).

13 Parkes, cited by Basch, *Relative Creatures,* 11; and Marion Reid, *A Plea for Woman Being a Vindication of the Importance and Extent of Her Natural Sphere of Action* (London and Edinburgh: 1843).

14 Later called *The Englishwoman's Review.*

15 Linda K. Kerber, "Separate Spheres, Female Worlds, Woman's Place: The Rhetoric of Women's History," *Journal of American History* 75, 1 (1988): 9–39.

16 Marilyn Ferris Motz, *True Sisterhood: Michigan Women and Their Kin, 1820–1920* (Albany, NY: State University of New York Press, 1983).

17 Sarah Lewis, *Woman's Mission* (1839).

18 Martha Vicinus, *Independent Women: Work and Community for Single Women, 1850–1920* (Chicago: University of Chicago Press, 1985). The discussion of single women throughout is indebted to this work.

19 American readers may be unaware that in Britain, "college" can mean a secondary school as well as one of university level.

20 Vicinus, *Independent Women.*

21 Information about Elizabeth Fry comes from Anderson and Zinsser.

22 It is still expected of women that when they marry they will adapt to their husbands' economic and social level, live his life rather than their own. This is the problem of Isabel Archer in Henry James' *A Portrait of a Lady.* She rejects suitors whose lives are fixed in order to marry, disastrously, a man who seems to promise that she can create her own.

23 Cited by Anderson and Zinsser.

24 Florence Nightingale, "Method of Improving the Nursing Service of Hospitals," (1869).

25 Maria Ramas, "Freud's Dora, Dora's Hysteria," in *Sex and Class in Women's History,* ed. Judith L. Newton, Mary P. Ryan, and Judith R. Walkowitz (London: Routledge and Kegan Paul, 1983).

CHAPTER 5

1 Ellen Moers, *Literary Women* (New York: Doubleday, 1977); Joseph Kestner, *Protest and Reform, 1827–1867* (Madison: University of Wisconsin Press, 1985).

2 The quotation from Thomas Carlyle is from his *Chartism* (1840).

3 Moers, *Literary Women.*

4 Elaine Showalter, *A Literature of Their Own* (Princeton: Princeton University Press, 1977). In addition to the writers listed above, Elizabeth Stone, Eliza Meteyard, Geraldine Jewsbury, Camilla Toulmin, Julia Kavanagh, Fanny Mayne, and Dinah Craik were part of the earlier generation mentioned by Showalter.

5 Tillie Olsen, "Introduction," Rebecca Harding Davis, *Life in the Iron Mills,* ed. Tillie Olsen (1861: reprint, New York: Feminist Press, 1972).

6 Gaye Tuchman and Nina E. Fortin, *Edging Women Out: Victorian Novelists, Publishers, and Social Change* (New Haven: Yale University Press, 1989).

7   Nancy A. Hewitt. "Friends: Agrarian Quakers and the Emergence of Women's Rights in America," *Feminist Studies* 12, no. 1 (spring 1986): 28–49.

8   Blanche Glassman Hersh, *The Slavery of Sex: Feminist-Abolitionists in America* (Chicago: University of Illinois Press, 1978).

9   Ibid.

10 Catherine Clinton, *The Other Civil War* (New York: Hill and Wang, 1984).

11 Ibid.

12 The discussion of Graceanna Lewis comes from Lee Virginia Chambers-Schiller, *Liberty, a Better Husband: Single Women in America: The Generations of 1780–1840* (New Haven: Yale University Press, 1984).

13 See Sidney Bremer, "Lost Continuities: Alternative Urban Visions in Chicago Novels, 1890–1915," *Soundings* 64, 1 (spring 1981): 29–51.

14 Ann Douglas, *The Feminization of American Culture* (New York: Alfred A. Knopf, 1977).

15 Clinton, *The Other Civil War*.

16 Carr managed to study abroad, but suffered from exclusion from life classes, the stigma of seriousness in a woman painter, and from constrictions on middle-class women's conduct – obstacles that despite her early assertiveness kept this stubborn forceful woman from painting for fifteen years.

17 Darlene Clark Hine, *Black Women in White: Racial Conflict and Cooperation in the Nursing Profession, 1890–1950* (Bloomington: Indiana University Press, 1989).

18 Christine Stansell, *City of Women: Sex and Class in New York, 1789–1860* (New York: Alfred A. Knopf, 1986). The discussion of charity organizations in New York is drawn from Stansell's book.

19 On November 2, 1989, a Texas judge was cleared of charges of bias for granting a light sentence to a man found guilty of murdering two gay men. Judge Jack Hampton explained: "These homosexuals, by running around on weekends picking up teen-age boys, they're asking for trouble. . . . I put prostitutes and gays at about the same level. And I'd be hard put to give somebody life for killing a prostitute." (*The New York Times*, November 2, 1989), 25.

20 Clinton, *The Other Civil War*.

21 Angela Y. Davis, *Women, Race, and Class* (New York: Random House, 1981).

22 Raya Dunayevskaya, "The Black Dimension in Women's Liberation," in *Women's Liberation and the Dialectics of Revolution* (Atlantic Highlands, NJ: Humanities Press International, 1985).

23 Eleanor Flexner, *Century of Struggle: The Woman's Rights Movement in the United States* (Cambridge, Mass.: Harvard University Press, 1959; reprint, 1996).

24 Gloria I. Joseph, "Sojourner Truth: Archetypal Black Feminist," in *Wild Women in the Whirlwind: Afra-American Culture and the Contemporary Literary Renaissance* (New Brunswick, NJ: Rutgers University Press, 1990).

25 Hewitt, "Friends."

26 Clinton, *The Other Civil War.*

27 Chambers-Schiller, *Liberty, a Better Husband.*

28 Carroll Smith-Rosenberg, "The Female World of Love and Ritual: Relations Between Women in Nineteenth-Century America," *Signs* 1,1 (autumn 1975). See also her *Disorderly Conduct* (New York: Alfred A. Knopf, 1985).

29 Material on black women's clubs has been drawn mainly from Paula Giddings, *When and Where I Enter* (New York: William Morrow, 1984).

30 Giddings, *When and Where.*

CHAPTER 6

1 Herbert Gutman, *The Black Family in Slavery and Freedom, 1750–1925* (New York: Pantheon, 1976).

2 Over 180,000 African-Americans fought for the Union; several thousand spied for it, although they were at greater risk than whites. Almost half a million deserted southern plantations, helping to cripple the economy of the south.

3 Catherine Clinton, *The Other Civil War* (New York: Hill and Wang, 1984).

4 Ibid.

5 Ibid.

6 Tracey Weis did research for this segment.

7 Paula Giddings, *When and Where I Enter: The Impact of Black Women on Race and Sex in America* (New York: William Morrow, 1984). The emphasis is Giddings'.

8 Ibid.

9 The historian was Leslie Howard Owens, *This Species of Property: Slave Life and Culture in the Old South* (New York: Oxford University Press, 1976), 195.

10 Jacqueline Jones, "'My Mother Was Much of a Woman'": Black Women, Work, and the Family Under Slavery," *Feminist Studies* 8, 2 (summer 1982): 235–269.

11 Ibid.; and Jacqueline Jones, *Labor of Love, Labor of Sorrow: Black Women, Work, and the Family from Slavery to the Present* (New York: Basic Books, 1985).

12 Eugene Genovese, *Roll, Jordan, Roll: The World the Slaves Made* (New York: Random House, 1974).

13 Jones, *Labor of Love, Labor of Sorrow.*

14 Dorothy Sterling, *We Are Your Sisters: Black Women in the Nineteenth Century* (New York: Norton, 1984).

15 Quoted by Giddings, *When and Where.*

16 Ibid.

17 Jones, *Labor of Love, Labor of Sorrow.*

18 Ibid.

19 David Katzman, *Seven Days a Week: Women and Domestic Service in Industrializing America* (Chicago: University of Illinois Press, 1981).

20 Jacqueline Grant, "Black Women and the Church," *Some of Us Are Brave*, ed. Gloria T. Hull, Patricia Bell Scott, Barbara Smith (Old Westbury, NY: The Feminist Press, 1982).

21 Linda Perkins, "Heed Life's Demands: The Educational Philosophy of Fanny Jackson Coppin," *Journal of Negro Education* (summer 1982).

22 E. Franklin Frazier, *Black Bourgeoisie* (New York: The Free Press, 1957).

23 East African Islamic slaveholders in Africa were not at first racist, but justified slavery by asserting the superiority of Islam to other religions. Only after huge numbers of African slaves adopted Islam, which forbids the enslavement of Muslims, did owners resort to racism to vindicate their practice. Ancient slaveholding states – Mesopotamia, Greece, Rome, Islamic states or the later Ottoman Empire – were not racist. Slaves and owners often shared colour and even ethnic background. Aristotle justified Athenian slavery by arguing that anyone so craven as to accept slavery was humanly inferior, deserving of enslavement.

24 Jacquelyn Down Hall, *Revolt Against Chivalry: Jessie Daniel Ames and the Women's Campaign Against Lynching* (New York: Columbia University Press, 1979).

25 Clinton, *The Other Civil War.*

26 Philip Bruce, *The Plantation Negro as a Freeman: Observations on His Character, Condition, and Prospects in Virginia* (New York: G.P. Putnam's Sons, 1889).

27 This atmosphere is illustrated by a case cited by Giddings. Henry Smith, a black man in Paris, Texas, accused in 1893 of raping a five-year-old white girl, was tortured with red-hot irons and condemned to be burned alive. The town made the day of his burning a holiday so schoolchildren could attend it, and the railroads ran excursion cars for rural people. After Smith was ashes, the mob attacked each other in greed for souvenirs – the man's bones, teeth, and buttons.

28 Giddings, *When and Where.*

29 Some other early black artists were Robert M. Douglass Jr. (1809–1887), the brother of abolitionist Sarah Douglass, an abolitionist painter who became an expatriate; and May Howard Jackson (1877–1931), one of the first black sculptors to reject European conventions and use racial problems as a theme. She studied at the Pennsylvania Academy of Fine Arts, and despite the high quality of her work, remained unsuccessful.

30 Wilson's authorship was established only a few years ago by Henry Louis Gates. See David Ames Curtis and Henry Louis Gates, "Establishing the Identity of the Author of *Our Nig,*" in *Wild Women in the Whirlwind: Afra-American Culture and the Contemporary Literary Renaissance,* ed. Joanne M. Braxton and Andrée Nicola McLaughlin (New Brunswick, NJ: Rutgers University Press, 1990).

31 Giddings, *When and Where,* mentions Emma Dunham Kelly, *Megda* (1891); Frances Ellen Watkins Harper, *Iola Leroy* (1892); and Victoria Earl Matthews "Aunt Lindy" (1893). Alice Dunbar Nelson, who was part of the Harlem Renaissance, had been publishing poetry and short stories long before it began: *Violets and Other Tales* (1895) and *The Goodness of St. Rocque* (1898). In 1965 Pauline Hopkins' *Contending Forces* (1900) was called "the most powerful protest novel authored by a Black woman with the exception of Anne Perry's *The Street.*"

32 Samella Lewis, *Art: African-American* (New York: Harcourt Brace Jovanovich, Inc., 1978).

33 Mary Schmidt Campbell, *Harlem Renaissance: Art of Black America,* Introduction (New York: Harry N. Abrams, 1987).

34 Giddings, *When and Where.*

35 Ibid.

36 Frazier, *Black Bourgeoisie.*

37 Ruth Bordin, *Woman and Temperance: The Quest for Power and Liberty, 1873–1900* (Philadelphia: Temple University Press, 1981).

38 Blanche Wiesen Cook, "Female Support Networks and Political Activism: Lillian Wald, Crystal Eastman, Jane Addams, and Emma Goldman," *Chrysalis* 3 (autumn 1977); and "Feminism, Socialism, and Sexual Freedom: The Work and Legacy of Crystal Eastman and Alexandra Kollontai," *Stratégies Féminines/ Stratégies Féministes*, eds. Françoise Basch et al. (Paris); English edition, ed. Judith Friedlander et al. (Bloomington: Indiana University Press, 1986).

39 Jane Addams, *Twenty Years at Hull House* (New York: 1910; reprint, Princeton: 1981), 65.

40 Cited by Clinton, *The Other Civil War.*

41 Ibid.

42 Ibid.

CHAPTER 7

1 Kathi Kern, *Mrs. Stanton's Bible* (Ithaca: Cornell University Press, 2001), 34.

2 "Twentieth-Century Foxes," *Ms. Magazine*, X, 1 (December 1999– January 2000).

3 Cited in Catherine Clinton, *The Other Civil War* (New York: Hill and Wang, 1984).

4 Nancy Cott, *The Grounding of Modern Feminism* (New Haven: Yale University Press, 1987). The discussion of the split in the women's movement after suffrage was won is indebted to Cott's book and to a review of it by Ruth Rosen, "A Serious Case of Déjà-vu," *The Women's Review of Books* V, 3 (December, 1987).

5 Ruth Rosen and Sue Davidson, Introduction, *The Maimie Papers*, ed. Ruth Rosen and Sue Davidson (Old Westbury, NY: Feminist Press, 1977).

6 Nancy Cott, "Eighteenth-Century Family and Social Life Revealed in Massachusetts Divorce Records," *The Journal of Social History* 10 (fall 1976): 20–43.

7 Françoise Basch, *Relative Creatures: Victorian Women in Society and the Novel, 1837–67* (London: Allan Lane, 1974).

8 Barbara Taylor, *Eve and the New Jerusalem: Socialism and Feminism in the Nineteenth Century* (New York: Pantheon Books, 1983).

9 All quotations in this paragraph come from Jill Liddington and Jill Norris, *One Hand Tied Behind Us: The Rise of the Women's Suffrage Movement* (London: Virago, 1978).

10 Joni Seager and Ann Olson, *Women in the World: An International Atlas* (Simon and Schuster: New York, 1986).

CHAPTER 8

1 Heidi Hartmann, "Capitalism, Patriarchy, and Job Segregation by Sex," *Signs*, I (spring 1976), 137–69; "The Unhappy Marriage of Marxism and Feminism: Toward a More Progressive Union," *Capital and Class*, 8 (summer 1979) 1–33.

2 Ava Baron, "Women and the Making of the American Working Class: A Study of the Proletarianization of Printers," *Review of Radical Political Economics* 14, 3 (fall 1982): 23–42.

3 But fear of Asians peaked during the Second World War, when thousands of Japanese-Americans, some of whose forebears had been in America longer than those of many European immigrants, had their property confiscated, were placed in concentration camps, and were deprived of all civil rights.

4 Meredith Tax, *The Rising of the Women* (New York: Monthly Review Press, 1989).

5 Ibid.

6 Ibid.

7 Ibid.

8 Ibid.

9 Ruth Milkman, "Organizing the Sexual Division of Labor: Historical Perspectives on 'Women's Work' and the American Labor Movement," *Socialist Review* 49: 95–150.

10 The discussion of Rose Pastor Stokes derives from Catherine Clinton, *The Other Civil War* (New York: Hill and Wang, 1984) and from Arthur and Pearl Zipser, *Fire and Grace: The Life of Rose Pastor Stokes* (Athens, Ga.: University of Georgia Press, 1990).

11 Alma Herbst, *The Negro in the Slaughtering and Meatpacking Industry in Chicago* (Boston: Houghton Mifflin, 1932).

12 Rosalyn Terborg-Penn, "Survival Strategies among Afro-American Women Workers: A Continuing Process," *Women, Work, and Protest: A Century of U.S. Women's Labor History*, ed. Ruth Milkman (Boston: Routledge & Kegan Paul, 1985).

13 Blanche Wiesen Cook, "Female Support Networks and Political Activism: Lillian Wald, Crystal Eastman, Jane Addams, and Emma Goldman," *Chrysalis* 3 (autumn 1977); and "Feminism, Socialism, and Sexual Freedom: The Work and Legacy of Crystal Eastman and Alexandra Kollontai," *Stratégies Féminines/ Stratégies Féministes*, ed. Françoise Basch et al. (Paris); English edition, ed. Judith Friedlander et al. (Bloomington: Indiana University Press, 1986).

14 Tax, *The Rising of the Women.*

15 Candace Falk, *Love, Anarchy, and Emma Goldman* (New York: Holt, Rinehart and Winston, 1984).

16 Ibid.

17 Milkman, "Organizing The Sexual Division of Labor."

18 Ibid.

19 Ibid.

20 Sarah Boston, *Women Workers and the Trade Union Movement* (London: Davis-Poynter, 1980).

21 Ibid.

22 Barbara Taylor, "'The Men Are as Bad as Their Masters . . .': Socialism, Feminism and Sexual Antagonism in the London Tailoring Trade in the 1830s," in *Sex and Class in Women's History*, ed. Judith L. Newton, Mary P. Ryan, and Judith R. Walkowitz (London: Routledge & Kegan Paul, 1983).

23 Ibid.

24 Cynthia Cockburn, *Brothers: Male Dominance and Technological Change* (London: Pluto Press, 1983).

25 Ibid.

26 Engineer Thomas Wright, in 1868. Cited in Cockburn, *Brothers.*

27 Eleanor Rathbone, *The Disinherited Family*, republished as *Family Allowance* (London: Allen and Unwin, 1949).

28 Cockburn, *Brothers.*

29 Other sources used in this chapter are Mary Stevenson, "Women's Wages and Job Segregation," *Labor Market Segmentation*, ed. Richard C. Edwards, Michael Reich, and David M. Gordon (Lexington, Mass.: D. C. Heath, 1975); and Sidney and Beatrice Webb, *History of Trade Unionism* (London: Longmans, Green Christian Co., 1920).

CHAPTER 9

1 In 1871 Tennie Claflin (Victoria Woodhull's sister) published *Constitutional Equality* (New York: Woodhull, Claflin & Co.). and pointed out that "where five years ago one paper in a hundred only, contained something about the progress of the Woman Question, now only one in a hundred can be found that has not a very considerable space devoted to it." She linked this to the Civil War and women's "bold advance . . . into the heat and strife of active business life."

2 Bram Dijkstra, *Idols of Perversity: Fantasies of Feminine Evil in Fin-de-Siècle Culture* (New York, Oxford: Oxford University Press, 1986); Klaus Theweleit, *Male Fantasies* vol I. Minneapolis: University of Minnesota Press, 1987). I have also drawn from Reinhold Heller, the catalogue for an exhibit of fin-de-siècle paintings of this sort shown at the David and Alfred Smart Gallery of the University of Chicago in 1981, *The Earthly Chimera and the Femme Fatale: Fear of Woman in Nineteenth-Century Art.*

3 Anthony Ludovici, *Enemies of Women: The Origins in Outline of Anglo-Saxon Feminism* (London: Carroll and Nicholson, 1948). Ludovici cites this characteristic as specific to late nineteenth-century men, and "almost endemic in England" during this time.

4 Dykstra, *Idols of Perversity.*

5 Horace Bushnell, "Women's Suffrage: The Reform Against Nature," *The New Englander,* 28, 109 (October 1869).

6 Nicholas Francis Cooke, *Satan in Society* (1870; New York: Edward F. Hovey, 1881).

7 Ibid.

8 Pierre-Joseph Proudhon, *On Pornocracy, or Women in Modern Times* (1875).

9 Franz Wedekind, *Earth Spirit* and *Pandora's Box.*

10 See Mark Twain's *Eve's Diary* (1906) and Oscar Wilde's *The Picture of Dorian Gray* (1891) and *Salome* (1893).

11 For a scholarly study of theories of impregnation, see Thomas Lacquer, *Making Sex: Body and Gender from the Greeks to Freud* (Cambridge, Mass.: Harvard University Press, 1990). Norman Mailer resuscitated the old-husband's-tale that orgasm is necessary to conception in *Prisoner of Sex*.

12 Harry Campbell, *Differences in the Nervous Organization of Man and Woman* (1891).

13 Dykstra, *Idols of Perversity*; Charles Darwin, *The Descent of Man*. "It is generally admitted that with woman the powers of intuition, of rapid perception, and perhaps of imitation, are more strongly marked than in man."

14 *The Atlantic Monthly* (1866).

15 Herbert Spencer, *Social Statics* (1850); *First Principles* (1862).

16 Carl C. Vogt, *Lectures on Man*.

17 Herbert Spencer, *The Study of Sociology* (1873).

18 Maurice Hamel, *Salon de 1890* (Paris, 1890); Albert Aurier, *Mercure de France* (August 1891).

19 See Emile Zola, *The Sin of Father Mouret*.

20 For instance, Paul Adam, "On Children," *La Revue Blanche* (1895), wrote that girls between eight and thirteen "found a perverse pleasure in watching sedentary middle-aged men expose themselves to them for a few pennies," and concludes "virtually all vices fester in the mind of the child. . . . Evil in adults is a sign of their not having grown up." Lombroso and Ferrero agreed, writing in *The Female Offender*: "What terrific criminals would children be if they had strong passions, muscular strength, and sufficient intelligence; and if, moreover, their evil tendencies were exasperated by a morbid psychical activity! And women are big children; their evil tendencies are more numerous and more varied than men's, but generally remain latent. When they are awakened and excited they produce results proportionately greater." (New York: D. Appleton, 1986).

21 This figure is exalted also by Camille Paglia, *Sexual Personae* (New Haven: Yale University Press, 1990).

22 Dykstra, *Idols of Perversity*.

23 Ibid.

24 Walter Pater, *Marius the Epicurean* (New York: Macmillan, 1907).

25 Charles Baudelaire, "Metamorphoses of the Vampire" (1852). This poem

was deleted from the first edition of *Flowers of Evil* (1857).

26 Charles Darwin, *The Descent of Man*. The animal is the Asiatic Antilope saiga.

27 Dykstra, *Idols of Perversity*.

28 Emile Tardieu, in *La Revue Blanche* (1895).

29 Dykstra, *Idols of Perversity*.

30 William Graham Sumner, "Sociology," in *War and Other Essays* (1881).

31 Barbara Ehrenreich, Foreword to Theweleit, *Male Fantasies*.

32 Theweleit, *Male Fantasies*.

33 Ibid.

34 Heinrich Teuber, *Bergmannsfrauen* (1927).

35 Theweleit, *Male Fantasies*.

36 Michael Rohrwasser, *Saubere Mädel, Starke Genossen* [*Spotless Maidens, Sturdy Comrades*] (Frankfurt, 1975).

37 Theweleit, *Male Fantasies*.

38 Ibid.

39 Edward Fuchs, *The Gallant Age, History of Manners* [*Sittengeschichte*], 6 vols. (Munich, 1909–12).

40 Thomas Stephen Szasz, *The Manufacture of Madness* (New York: Harper & Row, 1977).

41 Theweleit, *Male Fantasies*, 358.

PART SEVEN: THE TWENTIETH CENTURY

1 Barbara Ehrenreich writes that the First World War abolished the threat of internal class warfare within most of the belligerents and tamed socialism, at least temporarily. See Barbara Ehrenreich, *Blood Rites* (New York: Henry Holt & Co., 1997), 30.

CHAPTER 10

1 Some of the material in this section is drawn from my *Beyond Power* (New York: Summit Books, 1985). I am also indebted to Beatrix Campbell, personal communication.

2 Charles Sowerwine, "The Socialist Women's Movement from 1850 to 1940," in *Becoming Visible: Women in European History*, ed. Renate Bridenthal, Claudia Koonz, and Susan Stuard (Boston: Houghton Mifflin Company, 1987).

3 My account of Luxemburg's life is indebted to Elzbieta Ettinger, *Rosa Luxemburg: A Life* (Boston: Beacon Press, 1986).

4 Ibid.

5 The topography of Lithuania gave birth to its political myths, writes Simon Schama, *Landscape and Memory* (New York: Vintage Books, 1996).

6 Mikhail Bakunin and Sergej Nechaev, *The Catechism of a Revolutionary* (Geneva: Georg & Co., 1896).

7 Until 1903, male students of law and political science were registered as "jurists," and female students as "women students in political science." Verena Stadler-Labhart, *Rosa Luxemburg an der Universität Zurich* (Zurich: Hans Rohr Verlag, 1978).

8 She had considerable company. Isaiah Berlin wrote in 1972: "No influential thinker . . . foresaw its future – at any rate, no one clearly foretold it . . . Nationalism was, by and large, regarded in Europe as a passing phase." Berlin, *Against the Current* (New York: Viking Press, 1980), 337.

9 Ettinger, *Rosa Luxemburg*.

10 Richard J. Evans, *The Feminists* (London: Croom Helm, 1977).

11 Sowerwine, "The Socialist Women's Movement from 1850 to 1940."

12 Temma Kaplan, "Women and Communal Strikes in the Crisis of 1917–1922," in Bridenthal, Koonz, and Stuard, eds., *Becoming Visible*.

13 Women scholars stress that working-class women felt legitimate invading public spaces because they lived near administrative centres, not in a separate part of the city. Ibid.

14 Ibid.

15 A detailed account of the anarchist movement in Malaga, Cadiz, and Seville provinces can be found in Temma Kaplan, *Anarchists of Andalusia, 1868–1903* (Princeton: Princeton University Press, 1977).

16 Ibid.

17 Ibid.

18 Candace Falk, *Love, Anarchy, and Emma Goldman* (New York: Holt, Rinehart and Winston, 1984).

19 Their morality and repressiveness is the subject of Federico Garcia Lorca's great novel, *The House of Bernarda Alba* (1945).

20 See Ann Snitow, "The Church Wins, Women Lose," *The Nation*, April 26, 1993; "Poland Takes Steps to Ease Abortion Law," *New York Times*, August 30, 1996; "Polish Court Voids Liberal Abortion Law," *New York Times*, May 29, 1997; "Pope Urges Poland to Ban Abortion," *International Herald Tribune*, June 10, 1997; "Anti-Abortion Law Reimposed in Poland," *New York Times*, December 18, 1997.

21 Nanette Funk, "Introduction: Women and Post-Communism," in *Europe and the Former Soviet Union*, ed. Nanette Funk and Magda Mueller (New York: Routledge, 1993).

22 Renata Siemienska, "Wybierane i Glosujace," in *Kobiety: Dawne i Nowe Role*, cited by Elzbieta Matynia, "Finding a Voice: Women in Postcommunist Central Europe," in *The Challenge of Local Feminisms: Women's Movements in Global Perspective*, ed. Amrita Basu (Boulder, Col.: Westview Press, 1995).

23 Ibid.

24 Ann Snitow, "Feminist Features in the Former Eastern Bloc," *Peace and Democracy News* 7, 1 (1993).

25 Matynia, "Finding a Voice."

CHAPTER 11

1 Shashkov, *History of Russian Women* (1898), cited by Fanina W. Halle, *Women in Soviet Russia* (New York: Viking, 1935).

2 Richard Stites, *The Women's Liberation Movement in Russia: Feminism, Nihilism, and Bolshevism, 1860–1930* (Princeton: Princeton University Press, 1978).

3 The Byzantine word for "home," "house," or "building" was *terremnon*; *terem* was a lord's keep or tower. By calling women's quarters *terem*, the Tatars made husbands into lords. The Russian word for "prison," *tyurma*, derives from the same term, showing women's reality.

4 Peter Kolchin, *Unfree Labor: American Slavery and Russian Serfdom* (Cambridge, Mass.: Harvard University Press, 1987).

5 Richard Stites, "Women and the Revolutionary Process in Russia," in *Becoming Visible: Women in European History,* ed. Renate Bridenthal, Claudia Koonz, and Susan Stuard (Boston: Houghton Mifflin, 1987).

6 Stites, *Women's Liberation Movement.*

7 Barbara Engel, "Women as Revolutionaries: The Case of the Russian Populists," in Bridenthal, Koonz, and Stuard, eds., *Becoming Visible.*

8 Stites, *Women's Liberation Movement,* 141–42.

9 International Women's Day was inaugurated in the United States in 1909 and in Europe in 1911 to celebrate the work, goals, and community of working-class women. It is celebrated on March 8 in the West, and on February 23 in Russia. It is rarely even noticed in the United States.

10 Walter Karp, *The Politics of War: The Story of Two Wars Which Altered Forever the Political Life of the American Republic, 1890–1920* (New York: Harper & Row, 1979).

11 Bernice Glatzer Rosenthal, "Love on the Tractor: Women in the Russian Revolution and After," in Bridenthal, Koonz, and Stuard, eds., *Becoming Visible.*

12 Y. Bochkaryova and S. Lyubimova, *Women of a New World* (Moscow, 1969).

13 Temma Kaplan, "Women and Communal Strikes in the Crisis of 1917–1922," in Bridenthal, Koonz, and Stuard, eds., *Becoming Visible.*

14 Aleksei Tarasov-Rodionov, *February 1917* (New York: Covici-Friede, 1931).

15 Kaplan, "Women and Communal Strikes."

16 Louise Bryant, *Six Months in Russia* (New York: George H. Doran Co., 1918).

17 V.I. Lenin, *On the Emancipation of Women* (Moscow, nd), cited by Stites, "Women and the Revolutionary Process in Russia."

18 Stites, "Women and the Revolutionary Process in Russia."

19 Anonymous, "Interview with a Career Woman," in *Women and Russia: Feminist Writings from the Soviet Union,* ed. Tatyana Mamonova (Boston: Beacon Press, 1984).

20 Ekaterina Alexandrova, "Why Soviet Women Want to Get Married," ibid.

21 Tatyana Mamonova, *Russian Women's Studies: Essays on Sexism in the Soviet Union* (New York: Pergamon Press, 1989).

22 Katrina vanden Heuvel, "Glasnost for Women?" *The Nation*, June 4, 1990.

23 Yekaterina Nikolayeva, "I Don't Want to Be Sorry I'm a Woman," *Moscow News*, 1989.

24 Heuvel, "Glasnost for Women?"

25 Mamonova, ed., *Women and Russia*.

26 Lynn Mally, personal communication, December 1999.

27 Elizabeth Waters and Anastasia Posadskaya, "Democracy Without Women Is No Democracy: Women's Struggles in Postcommunist Russia," in *The Challenge of Local Feminisms: Women's Movements in Global Perspective*, ed. Amrita Basu (Boulder, Col.: Westview Press, 1995).

28 Ibid.

29 Mary Buckley, personal communication.

Chapter 12

1 Sharon L. Sievers, "Women in China, Japan, and Korea," in *Restoring Women to History*, ed. Renate Bridenthal, Claudia Koonz, and Susan Stuard (Bloomington, Ind.: Organization of American Historians, 1987).

2 Elisabeth Croll and Delia Davin, consultants for this section, personal communication.

3 Sievers, "Women in China."

4 Muriel Evelyn Chamberlain, *Decolonization: The Fall of the European Empires* (Oxford: Basil Blackwell, 1985).

5 One of her poems, "Women's Rights," articulated her desire to be a Chinese Joan of Arc:

We want our emancipation!
For our liberty we'll drink a cup.
Men and women are born equal,
Why should we let men hold sway?
We will rise and save ourselves,
Ridding the nation of all her shame.
In the steps of Joan of Arc,
With our own hands will we regain our land.

6 Croll and Davin, personal communication.

7 Cited by Sievers, "Women in China."

8   Margery Wolf, *Revolution Postponed: Women in Contemporary China* (Stanford: Stanford University Press, 1985).

9   Kay Ann Johnson, *Women, the Family and Peasant Revolution in China* (Chicago: University of Chicago Press, 1983).

10 Sievers, "Women in China."

11 Ibid.

12 Helen Snow, *Women of Modern China* (The Hague, 1967).

13 An important source throughout the following sections was Elisabeth J. Croll, *Feminism and Socialism in China* (New York: Schocken Books, 1980).

14 Croll and Davin, personal communication.

15 Janet Salaff and Judith Merkle, "Women and Revolution: The Lessons of the Soviet Union and China," in *Women in China: Studies in Social Change and Feminism*, ed. Marilyn B. Young (Ann Arbor, Mich.: Center for Chinese Studies, University of Michigan, 1973).

16 Elisabeth Croll, *The Politics of Marriage in Contemporary China* (Cambridge: Cambridge University Press, 1981).

17 Sheryl WuDunn, *New York Times*, December 3, 1989.

18 Sheryl WuDunn, "The Prisoners of Tiananmen Square," *New York Times Magazine*, April 8, 1990. See also Dai Qing, *The River Dragon Has Come* (1998).

19 Naihua Zhang with Wu Xu, "Discovering the Positive within the Negative: The Women's Movement in a Changing China," in *The Challenge of Local Feminisms: Women's Movements in Global Perspective*, ed. Amrita Basu (Boulder, Col.: Westview Press, 1995).

CHAPTER 13

1   Renate Bridenthal, "Something Old, Something New: Women between the Two Wars," in *Becoming Visible: Women in European History*, ed. Renate Bridenthal, Claudia Koonz, and Susan Stuard (Boston: Houghton Mifflin, 1987).

2   Renate Bridenthal, "Two: The Family Tree: Contemporary Patterns in the United States," in *Household and Kin: Families in Flux*, ed. Amy Swerdlow, Renate Bridenthal, Joan Kelly, and Phyllis Vine (New York: The Feminist Press, 1981).

3   In the United States, Henry Ford wrote a book called *The International Jew: The World's Foremost Problem*, purporting to be the minutes of a cabal

of Russian Jews plotting to destroy Christianity and the white race and to take over the world. The Rev. Charles Coughlin broadcast a weekly radio program of virulent anti-Semitism. In Arkansas, Gerald L.K. Smith founded the Christian Nationalist Crusade, which became a national movement to persecute Jews. Gerald Winrod, an apocalyptic fundamentalist preacher in Kansas, also gained a huge following in a movement called the Jayhawk Nazis.

4   Yet some Nazi writers projected a prehistoric matriarchy and exalted Brunhilde as the Ideal Woman. See Claudia Koonz, "The Fascist Solution to the Woman Question in Italy and Germany," in Bridenthal, Koonz, and Stuard, eds., *Becoming Visible*. This section is indebted to this article and to Koonz' *Mothers in the Fatherland: Women, the Family and Nazi Politics* (New York: St. Martin's Press, 1987).

5   Koonz, *Mothers in the Fatherland*.

6   Ibid.

7   Ibid.

8   Ibid.

9   Sybil Milton, "Women and the Holocaust: The Case of German and German-Jewish Women," in Renate Bridenthal, Altina Grossmann, and Marion Kaplan, eds., *When Biology Became Destiny: Women in Weimar and Nazi Germany* (New York: Monthly Review Press, 1984).

10 Koonz, *Mothers in the Fatherland*.

11 The first Italian feminist novel, *A Woman*, by Sibella Aleramo, implied that fascism had liberated women from an ugly male world by denying them entry to higher education, the professions, and political power and allowing them to look inward, build female solidarity, and cultivate self-esteem based on their domestic responsibilities, thereby enriching "their race."

12 Koonz, *Mothers in the Fatherland*.

13 For a vivid depiction of Italy during this period, read Elsa Morante's classic *History: A Novel*, trans. William Weaver (New York: Random House, 1977), about a Jewish Italian woman.

14 For a portrayal of such women's lives, see Paola Drigo's *Maria Zef*, trans. Blossom S. Kirchenbaum (Lincoln: University of Nebraska Press, 1989), published in Italy in 1939; and Maria Messina, *A House in the Shadows*, trans. John Shepley (Marlboro, Vt.: The Marlboro Press, 1990). These short, brilliant novels picture female lives more oppressed and benighted than any in literature – even Islamic works. Yet they are set in Italy, the nursery of art, music, and literature.

CHAPTER 14

1 Muriel Evelyn Chamberlain, *Decolonization: The Fall of the European Empires* (Oxford: Basil Blackwell, 1985).

2 Ann M. Pescatello, "Latina Liberation: Tradition, Ideology, and Social Changes in Iberian and Latin American Culture," in *Liberating Women's History*, ed. Berenice A. Carroll (Urbana: University of Illinois Press, 1976).

3 Ann Pescatello, *Power and Pawn: The Female in Iberian Families, Societies, and Cultures* (Westport, Conn.: Greenwood Press, 1976).

4 Marysa Navarro, "Women in Pre-Columbian and Colonial Latin America," in *Restoring Women to History: Women in Latin America and the Caribbean*, ed. Marysa Navarro and Virginia Sánchez Korrol (Bloomington: Indiana University Press, 1999).

5 *Women in Latin American History: Their Lives and Views*, ed. June Hahner (Los Angeles: UCLA Latin American Center Publications, 1976).

6 Navarro, "Women in Pre-Columbian and Colonial Latin America." Navarro was a consultant to this project.

7 Jean Franco, personal communication. Franco was a consultant to this project.

8 Virginia Sánchez Korrol, "Women in Nineteenth- and Twentieth-Century Latin America and the Caribbean," in Navarro and Korrol, eds., *Restoring Women to History*.

9 Quoted in Evelyn Cherpak, "The Participation of Women in the Independence Movement in Gran Colombia, 1780–1930," in *Latin American Women: Historical Perspectives*, ed. Asunción Lavrin (Westport, Conn.: Greenwood Press, 1978).

10 *Women in Latin America*, ed. Susan Hill Gross and Marjorie Wall Bingham (St. Louis Park, Minn.: Glenhurst Publications, 1969).

11 Maria Dundas Graham, *Journal of a Voyage to Brazil and Residence There during Part of Three Years, 1821, 1822, 1823* (New York: Praeger, 1969).

12 Chamberlain, *Decolonization*.

13 Ibid.

14 Franco, personal communication.

15 Mary K. Vaughan, "Primary Schooling in the City of Puebla, 1821–1860" (unpublished paper, University of Illinois at Chicago, 1986). Quoted by Korrol, "Women."

16 Korrol, "Women."

17 Margaret Randall, *Mujeres en la Revolution* (Mexico: Siglo xxi, 1972).

18 Gross and Bingham, eds., *Women in Latin America*.

19 Temma Kaplan, "Women and Communal Strikes," in *Becoming Visible: Women in European History*, ed. Renate Bridenthal, Claudia Koonz, and Susan Stuard (Boston: Houghton Mifflin, 1987).

20 See, for instance, the memoirs of Magda Portales of Apra and Benita Galeana of the Mexican Communist Party.

21 *The Children of Sanchez*, by Oscar Lewis, describes the impoverished Jesús Sánchez with a *casa chica* and a second family.

22 Maria Giminez was a consultant to this project.

23 For further reading on Eva Perón, see Nancy Caro Hollander, "Si Evita Viviera," in *Women in Latin America: An Anthology from Latin American Perspectives*, ed. Eleanor B. Leacock (Riverside, Cal.: Latin American Perspectives, 1979), and Marysa Navarro, "The Case of Eva Perón," *Signs* 3, 1 (1977).

24 Benjamin Keen and M. Wasserman, *A Short History of Latin America* (Boston: Houghton Mifflin, 1984).

25 Daisy Garth, "The Present Situation of Nicaraguan Women," in *Genes and Gender VI: On Peace, War, and Gender*, ed. Anne E. Hunter (New York: The Feminist Press, 1991), 133.

26 Aryeh Neier and Cynthia Brown, "Pinochet's Way," *New York Review of Books*, June 25, 1987.

27 Franco provided much of the information in this section.

28 Many Latin American women are nicknamed "La Nena" (baby) and called that name into old age.

29 Franco, personal communication.

30 This poem can be read in its entirety in *Contemporary Women Authors of Latin America*, ed. Doris Meyer and Margariet Fernández Olmos (Brooklyn, NY: Brooklyn College Press, 1983). Poems by other Latin American woman writers appear in *The Defiant Muse: Hispanic Feminist Poems from the Middle Ages to the Present*, ed. Angel and Kate Flores (New York: The Feminist Press, 1986).

31 Dan Bellm, "A Woman Who Knew Latin," *The Nation*, June 26, 1989.

32 *The Selected Poems of Rosario Castellanos*, ed. Cecilia Vicuña and Magda Bogin; trans. Magda Bogin (St. Paul, Miss.: Graywolf Press, 1989).

33 Carolina María de Jesús' *Child of the Dark* (1962) describes her struggle to survive as a single mother of three children living in near starvation in squatter settlements in Sao Paulo. June Nash made a film, *I Left My Life in the Mine*, the *testimonio* of a woman abused by sexist male miners who insisted that women in mines brought bad luck. *Let Me Speak!* (1978), by Domitila Barrios de Chungara with Moema Viezzer, is also an account of Bolivian miners: Barrios de Chungara organized women to visit their jailed miner husbands, present their demands to management, and provide mutual assistance during strikes. In 1975 she was a delegate to the Women's International Congress held in Mexico. Franco comments that while Barrios de Chungara had no sympathy for the problems of lesbians or prostitutes, middle-class feminists were uninterested in her account of male miners' plight.

34 Her book is available in English. See *I . . . Rigoberta Menchú, An Indian Woman in Guatemala*, ed. Elizabeth Burgos-Debray (London: Verso, 1984).

35 Elu de Lenero, "Women's Work and Fertility," in *Sex and Class in Latin America*, ed. June Nash and Helen I. Safa (New York: Praeger, 1976).

36 Maria Giminez, personal communication.

37 This is not to say there is no inequality in Cuba, only that there is less there than in other Latin American states. William W. Murdoch, *The Poverty of Nations* (Baltimore: The Johns Hopkins University Press, 1980).

CHAPTER 15

1 Barbara N. Ramusack, "Women in South and Southeast Asia," in *Restoring Women to History* (Bloomington, Ind.: Organization of American Historians, 1988).

2 Marian Fowler, *Below the Peacock Fan: First Ladies of the Raj* (Toronto: Penguin Books, 1987).

3 Stewart Gordon, "Legitimacy and Loyalty in Some Successor States of the Eighteenth Century," in *Kingship and Authority in South Asia*, ed. J.F.Richards (Madison: University of Wisconsin Publication Services: South Asian Studies 3, 1978).

4 Mountstuart Elphinstone, governor of Bombay in the 1820s, wrote that it was preferable "to have an early separation from a civilized people,

rather than a violent rupture with a barbarous nation, in which it is probable that all our settlers and even our commerce would perish along with all the institutions we had introduced into the country," cited by Muriel Evelyn Chamberlain, *Decolonization: The Fall of the European Empires* (Oxford: Basil Blackwell, 1985).

5 Veena Oldenburg, personal communication. Veena Oldenburg was a consultant to this project.

6 Ramusack, "Women."

7 Ashis Nandy, *At the Edge of Psychology* (Delhi: Oxford University Press, 1980).

8 Ibid.

9 Vina Mazumdar, "Comment on Suttee," *Signs* 4, 2 (1978): 268–73.

10 *Cross-Cultural Study of Women*, ed. Margot I. Duley and Mary I. Edwards (New York: The Feminist Press, 1986).

11 Maria Mies, "Historical, Cultural, and Social Determinants of Female Roles," in her *Indian Women and Patriarchy* (New Delhi: Concept Publishing, 1980).

12 Rokeya Sakhawat Hossain, *Sultana's Dream* and selections from *The Secluded Ones*, ed. and trans. Roushan Jahan (New York: The Feminist Press, 1988).

13 Ironically, as elite women cast off purdah, lower-caste women adopted it in what is called Sanskritization – the emulation of elite styles, customs, and language by lower classes, a practice that leads in time to a rise in their ritual status.

14 The claim that outsiders find one's own women irresistible justified white oppression of blacks in America, and the confinement of Hindu and Muslim women.

15 Fowler, *Below the Peacock Fan.*

16 Margaret Strobel, "Gender and Race in the Nineteenth- and Twentieth-Century British Empire," in *Becoming Visible: Women in European History*, ed. Ranate Bridenthal, Claudia Koonz, and Susan Stuard (Boston: Houghton Mifflin, 1987).

17 Fowler, *Below the Peacock Fan.*

18 Chamberlain, *Decolonization.*

19 Fowler, *Below the Peacock Fan.*

20 See, for instance, Radha Krishna Sharma, *Nationalism, Social Reform and Indian Women* (Patna and New Delhi: Janaki Prakashan, 1981); Pratima Asthana, *Women's Movement in India* (New Delhi: Vikas Publishing, 1974); Jana Matson Everett, *Women and Social Change in India* (New York: St. Martin's Press, 1979); and Maria Mies, *Indian Women and Patriarchy* (New Delhi: Concept Publishing, 1980).

21 Geraldine H. Forbes, "Caged Tigers: 'First Wave' Feminists in India," *Women's Studies International Forum* 5, 6 (1982): 525–36.

22 Oldenburg, personal communication.

23 Duley and Edwards, eds., *Cross-Cultural Study.*

24 Ursula Sharma, *Women, Work and Property in North-West India* (London: Tavistock, 1980).

25 Oldenburg, personal communication.

26 Barbara Crosette, "India Studying 'Accidental' Deaths of Hindu Wives," *New York Times*, January 15, 1989.

27 Mary Anne Weaver, "Gandhi's Daughters," *New Yorker*, January 10, 2000.

28 J. Mencher and J. Lessinger, "Women in India," notes written for this study.

29 Ibid.

30 Weaver, "Gandhi's Daughters."

31 Personal communication, Vina Mazumdar, Delhi, 1984. See also her "Social Reform Movement in India – From Renade to Nehru," in *Indian Women from Purdah to Modernity*, ed. B.R. Nanda (New Delhi: Vikas Publishing, 1976).

32 The committee's findings and recommendations are cited throughout these sections.

33 See Ela R. Bhatt, "Organising Self-Employed Women Workers," in *Women and Development: Perspectives from South and Southeast Asia*, ed. Rounaq Jahan and Hanna Papanck (Dacca: Bangladesh Institute of Law and International Affairs, 1979).

34 Personal communication, Ela Bhatt, Ahmadabad, 1974.

35 Shahida Lateef, "Modernization in India and the Status of Muslim Women," in *Modernization and Social Change among Muslims*, ed. Imtiaz Ahmad (New Delhi: Manohar Publications, 1983).

36 Oldenburg, personal communication.

37 Ibid.

38 Florence McCarthy studied these villages. Reported in Hannah Papanek and Gail Minault, *Separate Worlds* (Delhi: Chanakya Publications, 1982).

39 Marilyn French, "Women and Work in India," in *Women: A World Report,* ed. Debbie Taylor (London: Methuen, 1985).

40 Barbara Crossette, "Pakistani Women Seek Basic Rights," *New York Times,* March 26, 1990; "In a Pakistan Village, Democracy of a Feudal Kind," ibid., May 2, 1990; "Village Women Earn Respect (and Rupees, Too)" ibid., July 9, 1990.

41 Amartya Sen, "More Than 100 Million Women Are Missing," *New York Review of Books,* December 20, 1990.

42 Mencher and Lessinger, "Women in India."

43 Steven R. Weisman, "Births Are Kept Down but the Women Aren't," *New York Times,* January 29, 1988.

44 Mencher and Lessinger, "Women in India."

45 Radha Kumar, "From Chipko to Sati: The Contemporary Women's Movement," in *The Challenge of Local Feminisms: Women's Movements in Global Perspective,* ed. Amrita Basu (Boulder, Col.: Westview Press, 1995).

46 Temma Kaplan, personal communication.

CHAPTER 16

1 Peter R. Knauss, *The Persistence of Patriarchy* (New York: Praeger, 1984).

2 Marnia Lazreg, "Gender and Politics in Algeria: Unraveling the Religious Paradigm," *Signs* 15, 4 (1990): 755–80.

3 Muriel Evelyn Chamberlain, *Decolonization: The Fall of the European Empires* (Oxford: Basil Blackwell, 1985).

4 Lazreg, "Gender and Politics."

5 Ibid.

6 Knauss, *The Persistence of Patriarchy.*

7 See Frantz Fanon, *The Wretched of the Earth,* trans. Constance Farrington (New York: Grove Press, 1963), and *A Dying Colonialism,* trans. Haakon Chevalier (New York: Grove Press, 1967).

8 Lazreg, "Gender and Politics."

9 Ibid.

10 Kay Boals, "The Politics of Cultural Liberation: Male-Female Relations in Algeria," in *Liberating Women's History*, ed. Berenice A. Carroll (Urbana: University of Illinois Press, 1976).

11 Fatima Mernissi, *Beyond the Veil: Male-Female Dynamics in a Modern Muslim Society* (New York: Wiley, 1975).

12 Youssef M. Ibrahim, "Algerians Choose the Protest Vote," *International Herald Tribune*, June 27, 1990.

13 About thirty women were killed for this act between 1992 and 1994, and in February 1994 militant Muslim men publicly vowed to kill women who appear bareheaded in public. See Youssef M. Ibrahim, "Bareheaded Women Slain in Algiers," *New York Times*, March 31, 1994.

14 Youssef M. Ibrahim, "Algeria Militants Vow to Kill Women Linked to Government," ibid., April 5, 1995.

15 Youssef M. Ibrahim, "As Civil War Drags On, Atrocities Grow," ibid., December 28, 1997.

16 Ibid.

17 Cited in *Cross-Cultural Study of Women*, ed. Margot I. Duley and Mary I. Edwards (New York: The Feminist Press, 1986), 437.

18 Nazirah Zein Ed-Din, "Removing the Veil and Veiling: Lectures and Reflections towards Women's Liberation and Social Reform in the Islamic World," trans. Salah-Dine Hammoud. Reprinted in *Women's Studies International Forum* 5, 2 (1982): 221–26.

19 Duley and Edwards, eds., *Cross-Cultural Study*.

20 Louise E. Sweet, "In Reality: Some Middle Eastern Women," in *Many Sisters: Women in Cross-Cultural Perspective*, ed. Carolyn J. Matthiason (New York: The Free Press, 1974).

21 Youssef M. Ibrahim, "Saudi Women Take Driver's Seat in a Rare Protest for the Right to Travel," *New York Times*, November 7, 1990; "Saudi Women Disciplined," ibid., November 13, 1990; James LeMoyne, "Ban on Driving by Women Reaffirmed by Saudis," ibid., November 15, 1990.

CHAPTER 17

1 Muriel Evelyn Chamberlain, *Decolonization: The Fall of the European Empires* (Oxford: Basil Blackwell Inc., 1985), 68.

2 Chamberlain cites *The Transfer of Power in Africa: Decolonization*, ed. P. Gifford and W.R. Louis (New Haven: Yale University Press, 1982), 305.

3   For example, Mark Twain described a pile of human hands higher than his head; Joseph Conrad described slaves chained at the neck and linked together, in "Heart of Darkness."

4   Alan Riding, "France Fears Fallout from Algerian Turmoil," *The New York Times*, October 12, 1993.

5   Except for Fourah Bay Teachers' Training College in Sierra Leone, Achimota in the Gold Coast, and Makerere in Uganda.

6   Iris Berger, "Women of Eastern and Southern Africa," in *Restoring Women to History*, ed., Cheryl Johnson-Odim and Margaret Strobel (Bloomington, Ind.: Organization of American Historians, 1988).

7   Marcia Wright, personal communication. Wright was a consultant for all the African sections of this book.

8   According to Meredith Turshen, it is an anachronism to call these groups tribes, peoples, societies, or nations, but it is unclear what one should call them. Meredith Turshen, "Victims of Development," *The Women's Review of Books* IV, 8 (May 1987): 11–12.

9   Jennifer Seymour Whitaker, *How Can Africa Survive?* (New York: Harper & Row, 1988).

10 Esther Boserup, *Women's Role in Economic Development* (London: Allen and Unwin, 1970).

11 K. David Patterson and Gerald W. Hartwig, "The Disease Factor: An Introductory Overview," *Disease in African History, An Introductory Survey and Case Studies*, ed., Hartwig and Patterson (North Carolina: Duke University Press, 1978), 3–24.

12 Patterson and Hartwig, "The Disease Factor."

13 Jeanne K. Henn, "Women in the Rural Economy: Past, Present, and Future," in *African Women South of the Sahara*, ed. Margaret Jean Hay and Sharon Stichter (New York: Longmans, 1984).

14 Berger, "Women of Eastern and Southern Africa."

15 E. Frances White, "Women of Western and Western Central Africa," in Berger, *Restoring Women to History* states that women carried their agricultural knowledge across the continent as they moved to their husbands' homes.

16 Alison L. Des Forges, "'The Drum Is Greater than the Shout': The 1912 Rebellion in Northern Rwanda," in *Banditry, Rebellion and Social Protest in Africa*, ed. Donald Crummey (London and Portsmouth, New Hampshire: James Currey/Heinemann, 1986).

17 Ibid.

18 Eric R. Wolf, *Peasant Wars of the Twentieth Century* (New York: Harper and Row, 1969).

19 Des Forges, "'The Drum Is Greater than the Shout.'"

20 Cynthia Brantley, "Makatalili and the Role of Women in Giriama Resistance," in Crummey, ed., *Banditry, Rebellion and Social Protest in Africa.*

21 Judith Van Allen, "'Aba Riots' or Igbo 'Women's War'? Ideology, Stratification, and the Invisibility of Women," in *Women in Africa: Studies in Social and Economic Change*, ed. Nancy J. Hafkin and Edna G. Bay (Stanford, Calif.: Stanford University Press, 1976).

22 Kamene Okonjo, "The Dual-Sex Political System in Operation: Igbo Women and Community Politics in Midwestern Nigeria," in Hafkin and Bay, *Women in Africa.*

23 See *The New York Times*, August 9, 2002.

24 Berger, "Women of Eastern and Southern Africa."

25 Berger, "Women of Eastern and Southern Africa."

26 E. Frances White, "Creole Women Traders in the Nineteenth Century," (African Studies Center, Boston University), Working Papers No. 27.

27 Marcia Wright, "Technology, Marriage and Women's Work in the History of Maize-Growers in Mazabuka, Zambia: A Reconnaissance," *Journal of African Studies*, 10, 1 (October 1983): 71–85.

28 Claire Robertson, "Ga Women and Socioeconomic Change in Accra, Ghana," Hafkin and Bay, eds., *Women in Africa.*

29 Diana Gladys Azu, "The Ga Family and Social Change," *African Social Research Documents*, 5 (Leiden: Africa-Studiecentrum, 1974).

30 Kristin Mann, *Marrying Well: Marriage, Status and Social Change among the Educated Elite in Colonial Lagos* (Cambridge: Cambridge University Press, 1985).

31 Deborah Gaitskell, Judy Kimble, Moira Maconachie, and Elaine Unterhalter, "Class, Race and Gender: Domestic Workers in South Africa," *Review of African Political Economy*, 27–28 (1983): 86–108.

32 Marcia Wright, "Justice, Women, and the Social Order in Abercorn, Northeastern Rhodesia, 1897–1903," *African Women and the Law: Historical Perspectives*, ed. Margaret Jean Hay and Marcia Wright (Boston: Boston University Papers on Africa VII, 1982).

33 Margaret Strobel, "From Lelemama to Lobbying: Women's Associations in Mombasa, Kenya," in Hafkin and Bay, eds., *Women in Africa.*

34 Ibid.

35 Ibid.

36 Ibid.

37 Cheryl Johnson, "Class and Gender: A Consideration of Yoruba Women during the Colonial Period," in *Women and Class,* ed. Claire C. Robertson and Iris Berger (New York: Africana Publishing Co., 1986).

38 Shirley Ardener, "Sexual Insult and Female Militancy," in *Perceiving Women,* ed. Shirley Ardener (London: J.M. Dent and Sons, 1975).

39 Maria Rosa Cutrufelli, *Women of Africa: Roots of Oppression* (London: Zed Press, 1983).

40 Obafemi Awolowo, *Path to Nigerian Freedom* (London: Faber & Faber, 1947).

41 Margery Mbilinyi, "'City' and 'Countryside' in Colonial Tanganyika," *Economic and Political Weekly: Review of Women Studies* XX, 43 (October 26, 1985).

42 Ibid.

43 Stephanie Urdang, *And Still They Dance: Women, War and the Struggle for Change in Mozambique* (New York: Monthly Review Press, 1989); and "Women in National Liberation Movements," in *African Women South of the Sahara,* ed., Margaret Jean Hay and Sharon Stichter (New York: Longman, 1995).

44 Urdang, "Liberation," quoting Robert Mugabe, "Opening Speech to the First Zimbabwe Women's Seminar, May 1979," *Zimbabwe News,* Maputo.

45 Ibid.

46 Gay W. Seidman, "Women in Zimbabwe: Postindependence Struggles," *Feminist Studies* 10, 3 (fall 1984): 432–440.

47 For an example, see James L. Brain, "Less than Second-Class: Women in Rural Settlement Schemes in Tanzania," in Hafkin and Bay, *Women in Africa.*

48 Paul Lewis, "Nyerere and Tanzania: No Regrets at Socialism," *The New York Times* (December 24, 1990).

49 Samora Machel, "The Liberation of Women Is a Fundamental Necessity for the Revolution" (1973), in Samora Machel, "Mozambique: Sowing the Seeds of Revolution," in *Speeches by Samora Machel* (London, undated).

50 Urdang, *And Still They Dance.*

51 Stephanie Urdang, *Fighting Two Colonialisms: Women in Guinea-Bissau* (New York: Monthly Review Press, 1979).

52 Urdang, "Liberation."

53 Ibid.

54 Ibid.

55 Ibid.

56 Cited in Urdang, "Liberation."

57 Urdang,"Liberation."

58 Cutrufelli, *Women of Africa: Roots of Oppression.*

59 Iris Berger, *Women of Eastern and Southern Africa.*

60 Whitaker, *How Can Africa Survive?*

61 Cutrufelli, *Women of Africa: Roots of Oppression.*

62 Jane Perlez, "Elite Kenyan Women Avoid a Rite: Marriage," *The New York Times* (March 3, 1991).

63 Marja-Liisa Swantz, *A Creative Role Denied? The Case of Tanzania* (New York: St. Martin's Press, 1985).

64 All quotations from Cutrufelli, *Women of Africa: Roots of Oppression.*

65 For example, Deodolinda Rodriguez, who founded OMA, a women's organization in Angola, died in a Zaïre concentration camp.

66 Cutrufelli, *Women of Africa: Roots of Oppression.*

67 Ibid.

68 Christine Obbo, *African Women* (London: Zed Press, 1980).

69 Mann, *Marrying Well.*

70 For a comparison of past and present agricultural practices, see Lucy E. Creevy, "The Role of Women in Malian Agriculture," *Women Farmers in Africa: Rural Devlopment in Mali and the Sahel* (Syracuse, NY: Syracuse University Press, 1986).

71 Margaret Jean Hay, "Women as Owners, Occupants, and Managers of Property in Colonial Western Kenya," in Hayand Wright, *African Women and the Law.*

72 For a discussion of this problem in Kenya, see Regina Smith Oboler, *Women, Power, and Economic Change: The Nandi of Kenya* (Stanford, Calif.: Stanford University Press, 1985).

73 Jane Perlez, "Uganda's Women: Children, Drudgery and Pain," *The New York Times* (February 24, 1991).

74 Salim Muwakkil, "Outlook," *Houston Chronicle* (March 11, 1999).

75 Cutrufelli, *Women of Africa: Roots of Oppression.*

76 E. Van Loock, "La Jamaa, Vue dans le Concret," *Le Mariage, La Vie Familiale, l'Éducation Coutumière* (Bandundu, 1966) cited by Cutrufelli, *Women of Africa: Roots of Oppression.*

77 Landeg White, *Magomero: Portrait of an African Village* (Cambridge: Cambridge University Press, 1987).

78 Kamene Okonjo, "Sex Roles in Nigerian Politics," in *Female and Male in West Africa*, ed. Christine Oppong (London: George Allen and Unwin, 1983).

79 James Brooke, "For Women in Politics, the Microphone Is Dead," *The New York Times* (August 22, 1988).

80 Jane Perlez, "For the Oppressed Sex, Brave Words to Live By," *The New York Times* (June 6, 1990).

81 Jane Perlez, "When the Trouble Is Men, Women Help Women," *The New York Times* (June 5, 1989).

82 Jane Perlez, "Skyscraper's Enemy Draws a Daily Dose of Scorn," *The New York Times* (December 6, 1989); "Kenya Decides to Reduce Planned 60-Story Tower," *The New York Times* (February 12, 1990).

83 Some other important African women writers are Barbara Kimenyi (Uganda), Noemia de Sousa (Mozambique), Martha Mvungi (Tanzania), Rebeka Njau and Charity Waciuma (Kenya), and Amelia House of South Africa.

84 Veronica Rentmeesters, "Eritrea: Will Women's Liberation Survive the Liberation Struggle?" presented at the Thirty-Second Annual Meeting of the African Studies Association. Atlanta, Georgia (Nov. 1–4, 1989), No. 89:82.

85 Cheryl Hatch, "Women of War," *Christian Science Monitor* (March 8, 2000).

86 Trish Silkin, "Eritrea: Women at War," *Spare Rib* (April, 1979: 20–23).

87 Jenny Rossiter, "The Quality of Life," in *Eritrean Journey,* ed., Doris Burgess et al. (London: War on Want, 1985).

88 Atsuko Matsuoka and John Sorenson, "After Independence: Prospects for Women in Eritrea," in *Proceedings of Women's Worlds* (Norway: University of Tromsø, 1999).

89 Steve Askin and Colin Darch, "Southern Africa – Hope Deferred," *The Nation* (May 28, 1990).

90 Ibid.

91 Chamberlain, *Decolonization,* 77.

92 J. Wilhelm and D. Streak, "South African Parliament a World Leader in the Fight for Sexual Equality," *Sunday Times* (May 29, 1994).

93 Amanda Kemp et al., "The Dawn of a New Day: Redefining South African Feminism," in *The Challenge of Local Feminisms: Women's Movements in Global Perspective,* ed., Amrita Basu (Boulder, Col.: Westview Press, 1995).

94 Dianne Hubbard and Colette Solomon, "The Many Faces of Feminism in Namibia," in Basu, *The Challenge of Local Feminisms.*

95 M. Monsted, *Women's Groups in Rural Kenya and Their Role in Development* (Copenhagen: Center for Development Research, 1978). Cited in Wilhemina Odoul and Wanjiku Mukabi Kabira, "The Mother of Warriors and Her Daughters: The Women's Movement in Kenya," in Basu, *The Challenge of Local Feminisms.*
    Mazingira Institute also provides examples of women's groups that have transformed mutual welfare activities into revolving loan societies, investor groups, highly structured labour collectives, and so on. Mazingira Institute, *Women and Development: A Kenya Guide* (Nairobi, 1992), 8. Even more revolutionary, women's groups have bought land, business premises, and other properties.

96 Odoul and Kabira, "The Mother of Warriors and Her Daughters."

97 Stephanie Urdang, personal communication. Special thanks are due to Susan Hall, who tried hard to keep me from making errors in all the African sections.

CHAPTER 18

1 Lourdes Arizpe and Josefina Aranda, "Women Workers in the Strawberry Agribusiness in Mexico," in *Development and the Division of Labor by Gender*, ed. Eleanor Leacock and Helen I. Safa (Boston: Bergin and Garvey, 1986).

2 *Cross-Cultural Study of Women*, ed. Margot I. Duley and Mary I. Edwards (New York: The Feminist Press, 1986).

3 Gita Sen and Caren Grown, *Development, Crises, and Alternative Visions: Third World Women's Perspectives* (New York: Monthly Review Press, 1987).

4 Barbara Rogers, *The Domestication of Women: Discrimination in Developing Societies* (London: Tavistock, 1980); the term "housewifization" comes from Maria Mies, *Patriarchy and Accumulation on a World Scale: Women in the International Division of Labour* (London: Zed Books, 1986).

5 Hanna Papanek, "The Differential Impact of Programs and Policies on Women in Development," in *Women and Technological Change in Developing Countries*, ed. Roslyn Dauber and Melina Cain (Boulder, Col.: Westview, 1981).

6 Ester Boserup, *Women's Role in Economic Development* (New York: St. Martins, 1970).

7 Susan Tiano, "Women and Industrial Development in Latin America," *Latin American Rsearch Review* 21, 3 (1986): 157–70.

8 Cathy A. Rakowski, personal communication. Rakowski was a consultant on this book.

9 Statistics and quotation from Jennifer Seymour Whitaker, *How Can Africa Survive?* (New York: Harper & Row, 1988), 152.

10 Maria Mies, "Historical, Cultural, and Social Determinants of Female Roles," in her *Indian Women and Patriarchy* (New Delhi: Concept Publishing, 1980), and *Patriarchy and Accumulation on a World Scale*.

11 Irene Tinker, "New Technologies for Food-Related Activities: An Equity Strategy," in Dauber and Cain, eds., *Women and Technological Change in Developing Countries*.

12 See, for example, Jennie Dey, "Gambian Women: Unequal Partners in Gambian Rice Development Projects?" in *African Women in the Development Process*, ed. Nici Nelson (London: Frank Cass and Company, 1981).

13 Mies, "Historical, Cultural, and Social Determinants."

14 Stephanie Urdang, personal communication.

15 Viji Srinivasan, Oxfam-America's program director for India and Bangladesh, lists many development projects for women there. Oxfam-America Special Report, *Women's Projects in India* (winter 1986/87).

16 Sue Ellen M. Charlton, *Women in Third World Development* (Boulder, Col.: Westview, 1984).

17 Deborah Fahy Bryceson, "Women's Proletarianization and the Family Wage in Tanzania," in *Women, State, and Ideology*, ed. Haleh Afshar (Albany: State University of New York Press, 1987).

18 Rakowski, personal communication.

19 Quoted in F. Frobel, J. Kreye, and O. Heinrichs, *The New International Division of Labour* (Cambridge: Cambridge University Press, 1980).

20 Arizpe and Aranda, "Women Workers."

21 Susan Joekes, "Working for Lipstick? Male and Female Labor in the Clothing Industry in Morocco," in *Women, Work, and Industry in the Third World*, ed. Haleh Afshar (London: Tavistock, 1985).

22 Susan Tiano, "Gender, Work, and World Capitalism: Third World Women's Role in Development," in *Analyzing Gender*, ed. Beth Hess and Myra Marx Ferree (Beverly Hills, Cal.: Sage, 1987).

23 Carolyne Dennis, "Women and the State in Nigeria: The Case of the Federal Military Government, 1984–5," in Afshar, ed., *Women, State, and Ideology*.

24 Rae Lesser Blumberg, "A General Theory of Gender Stratification," in *Sociological Theory* (San Francisco: Jossey-Bass, 1984).

25 Sue Ellen Charlton, *Women in Third World Development* (Boulder, Col.: Westview, 1984). Charlton is citing a study by Mona Hammam.

26 Sen and Grown, *Development, Crises, and Alternative Visions*.

27 Rogers, *The Domestication of Women*.

28 Rakowski, notes for this study.

29 Mies, *Patriarchy and Accumulation on a World Scale*, 137–42.

30 Marina Budhos, "Putting the Heat on Sex Tourism," *MS.*, March/April 1997.

31 Ellen Ross, "Fierce Questions and Taunts: Married Life in Working-Class London, 1870–1914," *Feminist Studies* 8, 3 (1982): 575–602. Ross is discussing poverty in another time and place, of course.

32 Ibid.

33 Marjorie Mbilinyi, "'Women in Development' Ideology and the Marketplace," in *Competition: A Feminist Taboo?* ed. Valerie Miner and Helen E. Longino (New York: The Feminist Press, 1987).

34 Asoka Bandarage, "Victims of Development," *Women's Review of Books* 5, 1 (1987): 1–4.

35 Maxine Molyneux, "Mobilization without Emancipation? Women's Interests, State, and Revolution," in *Transition and Development: Problems of Third World Socialism*, ed. Richard R. Fagan, Carmen Diana Deere, and José' Luis Coraggio (New York: Monthly Review Press, 1986).

36 Jane Jenson, "Both Friend and Foe: Women and State Welfare," in Renate Bridenthal, Claudia Koonz, and Susan Stuard, eds., *Becoming Visible: Women in European History* (Boston: Houghton Mifflin, 1987). Jenson refers to an interconnected set of social programs designed to alleviate the consequences of economic and individual life cycles: poverty, illness, unemployment, and old age.

37 In addition to the sources cited in the notes, the following were of help in researching this chapter: Eve E. Abraham-Van der Mark, "The Impact of Industrialization of Women: A Caribbean Case," in *Women, Men, and the International Division of Labor*, ed. June Nash and Maria Patricia Fernandez-Kelly (Albany: State University of New York State Press, 1983); Pamela M. D'Onofrio-Flores, "Technology, Economic Development, and the Division of Labour by Sex," in *Scientific-Technological Change and the Role of Women in Development*, ed. Pamela M. D'Onofrio-Flores and Sheila M. Pfafflin (Boulder, Col.: Westview, 1982); Linda Y.C. Lim, "Capitalism, Imperialism, and Patriarchy: The Dilemma of Third-World Women Workers in Multinational Factories," in Nash and Fernandez-Kelly, eds., *Women, Men, and the International Division of Labor*; Nancy M. Lutz, "Image of Docility: Asian Women and the World Economy," in *Racism, Sexism, and the World System*, ed. Joan Smith et al. (New York: Greenwood Press, 1988); Heleieth I.B. Saffioti, "Female Labor and Capitalism in the United States and Brazil," in *Women Cross-Culturally: Change and Challenge*, ed. Ruby Roholich-Leavitt (The Hague: Mouton, 1975); Janet W. Salaff, *Working Daughters of Hong Kong: Filial Piety or Power in the Family?* (Cambridge: Cambridge University Press, 1981); Marianne Schmink, Judith Bruce, and Marilyn Kohn, eds., *Learning about Women and Urban Services in Latin America and the*

Caribbean (New York: The Population Council, 1986); Zenebeworke Tadesse, "Women and Technology in Peripheral Countries: An Overview," in D'Onofrio-Flores and Pfafflin, eds., *Scientific-Technological Change*; M. Vaughan, "Women, Class, and Education in Mexico, 1880–1928," in *Women in Latin America: An Anthology from Latin American Perspectives* (Riverside, Cal.: LAP, 1979).

PART EIGHT: THE TWENTY-FIRST CENTURY

1 See Blanche Wiesen Cook, *Eleanor Roosevelt*, Vol. 2 (New York: Viking, 1999), 63.

2 Ibid., 190.

3 Ibid., 7.

CHAPTER 19

1 Juliet Mitchell and Ann Oakley argue that without a fixed definition for woman beyond biological femaleness, feminism cannot have a single definition. *What Is Feminism? A Re-examination*, ed. Juliet Mitchell and Ann Oakley (New York: Pantheon Books, 1986). Theorists discuss feminisms because various groups hold different basic assumptions and favour different approaches. In *The Cause*, Ray Strachey defined a *feminist* as a person whose central concern and preoccupation was the position of women and the struggle for their emancipation, and *feminism* as a conscious political choice by people who shared not a theory but an ideal. Roy Strachey, *The Cause: A Short History of the Women's Movement in Great Britain* (London: G. Belland and Sons, 1928). Rosalind Delmar, in "What Is Feminism?" in Mitchell and Oakley's volume of the same name, defines feminist as a person who believes "women suffer discrimination because of their sex . . . have specific needs which remain negated and unsatisfied, and that the satisfaction of these needs would require a radical change (some would say a revolution even) in the social, economic and political order."

2 Richard J. Evans, *The Feminists* (London: Croom Helm, 1977).

3 Ibid.

4 Nancy F. Cott, "Feminist Theory and Feminist Movements: The Past Before Us," in Mitchell and Oakley, eds., *What Is Feminism?*

5 Ibid.

6 Alfred Kinsey, *Sexual Behavior in the Human Male* (1948) and *Sexual Behavior in the Human Female* (1953); William H. Masters and Virginia E. Johnson, *Human Sexual Response* (1966).

7 Barbara Ehrenreich, Elizabeth Hess, and Gloria Jacobs, *Re-Making Love* (New York: Anchor Press, 1987).

8 Mitchell and Oakley, *What Is Feminism?* Introduction.

9 Shulamith Firestone, *The Dialectic of Sex: The Case for Feminist Revolution* (New York: Bantam Books, 1971).

10 Americans Mary Daly and Susan Griffin also write in a "female" language; Daly creates brilliant neologistic puns that contain a critique of patriarchy.

11 During a 1989 conference in Paris of Soviet, French, and American women writers, a Soviet writer lamented that all the writers, even the communists, continually used the word "I." Only the Americans, she said, spoke of themselves in the plural, supported each other, and sought consensus – she used the image of a bird flying with two wings. Unlike the French or the Soviet representatives, the American delegation had a large component of feminists.

12 Robin Morgan, *The Demon Lover* (New York: W.W. Norton, 1989).

13 Many are described in Kumari Jayawardena, *Feminism and Nationalism in the Third World* (London: Zed Books, 1986).

14 Ibid.

15 L.P. Elwell-Sutton, *Persian Oil: A Study in Power Politics* (London, 1955), 34.

16 For example, Annie Besant, Margaret Cousins, Sister Nivedita (Margaret Noble), and feminists and reformers like Carrie Chapman Catt and Margaret Sanger (USA), Ellen Key (Sweden), Mary Carpenter (Britain), and Dr. Aletta Jacobs (Holland).

17 Ms Ovink-Soer influenced Kartini.

18 Agnes Smedley (1892–1950). In Japan and India she worked with Vir Chattopadhyaya.

19 Afaf Lutfi al-Sayyid Marsot, "The Revolutionary Gentlewomen in Egypt," in *Women in the Muslim World*, ed. Lois Beck and Nikki Keddie (Cambridge, Mass.: Harvard University Press, 1978), 269.

20 Nawal El-Saadawi, private communication, New York, 1990.

21 Jayawardena, *Feminism and Nationalism*, 230.

22 Sharon L. Sievers, *Flowers in Salt: The Beginnings of Feminist Consciousness in Modern Japan* (Stanford, Cal.: Stanford University Press, 1983).

23 Pauline C. Reich, "Japan's Literary Feminists: The Seito Group," headnote to excerpts from the work of Hiratsuka Raicho, translated by Pauline C. Reich and Atsuko Fukuda, *Signs* 2, 1 (1976): 280–91.

24 "Ode to My Younger Brother Who Was Drafted by the Army."

25 Her work is collected in *Tangled Hair* (1901).

26 Noriko Sano, "Japanese Women's Movements during World War II," *Feminist International* 2 (Tokyo, 1980).

27 These categories are based on those drawn by Alison Jaggar and Paula Rothenberg, *Feminist Frameworks: Alternative Theoretical Accounts of the Relations between Women and Men* (New York: McGraw Hill, 1984).

28 James D. Hunt, *Gandhi in London* (New Delhi: Promilla, 1978).

29 Ibid., 137–38.

30 This section is drawn from Berenice A. Carroll, "'Women Take Action!': Women's Direct Action and Social Change," *Women's Studies International Forum* 12, 1, ed. Berenice A. Carroll and Jane E. Mohraz (New York: Pergamon Press, 1989).

31 Gene Sharp, *The Politics of Nonviolent Action* (Boston: Porter Sargent, 1973).

32 Described by Albert Luthuli; see ibid., 138.

33 Robin Morgan, *Sisterhood Is Global* (Garden City, NY: Doubleday, 1984).

34 Alice Cook and Gwyn Kirk, *Greenham Women Everywhere* (Boston: South End Press, 1983), 65.

35 Madhu Bhushan, "Vimochana: Women's Struggles, Nonviolent Militancy and Direct Action in the Indian Context," in Carroll and Mohraz, eds., *Women's Studies International Forum*.

36 William Celis 3rd, "Date Rape and a List at Brown," *New York Times*, November 18, 1990.

37 Morgan, *Sisterhood Is Global*, 84.

38 Federico Ribes Tovar, *The Puerto Rican Woman: Her Life and Evolution Throughout History* (New York: Plus Ultra Books, 1972).

39 *Black Women in White America*, ed. Gerda Lerner (New York: Random House, 1973).

40 Morgan, *Sisterhood Is Global*, 149.

41 Leonie Caldecott, "At the Foot of the Mountain: The Shibokusa Women of Japan," in *Keeping the Peace*, ed. Lynn Jones (London: The Women's Press, 1983), 104.

42 Agnes Smedley, *Portraits of Chinese Women in Revolution* (Old Westbury, NY: The Feminist Press, 1976), 123–26.

43 Paula Giddings, *When and Where I Enter* (New York: William Morrow, 1984), 232–33.

44 Ibid., 257.

45 Bhushan, "Vimochana."

46 Midge Mackenzie, *Shoulder to Shoulder* (New York: Alfred A. Knopf, 1975).

47 Morgan, *The Demon Lover*.

48 Eileen MacDonald, "Face to Face with the Girls Behind the Gun," *The European*, June 15–17, 1990.

49 Daisy Dwyer, "Outside the Courts: Extra-Legal Strategies for the Subordination of Women," in *African Women and the Law: Historical Perspectives*, ed. Margaret Jean Hay and Marcia Wright (Boston: Boston University Papers on Africa VII, 1982).

50 Ibid.

51 Deborah L. Rhode, "Feminist Perspectives on Legal Ideology," in Mitchell and Oakley, eds., *What Is Feminism?*

52 Patricia A. Gozemba and Marilyn L. Humphries, "Women in the Anti-Ku Klux Klan Movement, 1865–1984," in Carroll and Mohraz, eds., *Women's Studies International Forum*.

53 "Tobacco Workers Honor Fighting Union Leader," *The Union Voice* (Winston-Salem, June 3, 1951), cited by Lerner, *Black Women in White America*, 272–74.

54 Kathleen B. Jones, "Citizenship in a Woman-Friendly Polity," *Signs* 15, 4 (1990): 781–812.

55 *Women's America: Refocusing the Past*, ed. Linda K. Kerber and Jane De Hart-Mathews (New York: Oxford University Press, 1987).

56 Susan Cary Nicholas, Alice M. Price, and Rachel Rubin, *Rights and Wrongs: Women's Struggle for Legal Equality* (New York: Feminist Press, 1986).

57 Tamar Lewin, "Nude Pictures Are Ruled Sexual Harassment," *New York Times*, January 23, 1991.

58 Kerber and De Hart-Mathews, eds., *Women's America*.

59 Katherine Bishop, "Lesbians Clear Hurdles to Gain Posts of Power," *New York Times*, December 30, 1990.

60 Louis Harris, "The Gender Gulf," ibid., December 7, 1990.

61 Amy Swerdlow, "'Ladies' Day at the Capitol: Women Strike for Peace Versus HUAC," *Feminist Studies* 8, 3 (1982): 493–520, and *Women Strike for Peace: Traditional Motherhood and Radical Politics in the 1960's* (Chicago: University of Chicago Press, 1993).

62 Bill Galt, *Vancouver Sun*, December 14, 1962.

63 Louis Uchitelle, "Women's Push into Work Force Seems to Have Peaked, for Now," *New York Times*, November 24, 1990.

64 See, for instance, Heather Jon Maroney, "Feminism at Work," in Mitchell and Oakley, eds., *What Is Feminism?*

65 Ibid.

66 Michele Hoyman, "Working Women: The Potential of Unionization and Collective Action in the United States," in Carroll and Mohraz, eds., *Women's Studies International Forum*.

67 Karen Nussbaum, personal communication.

68 Rosabeth Moss Kanter, *Men and Women of the Corporation* (New York: Basic Books, 1977).

69 Jane Barker and Hazel Downing, "Word Processing and the Transformation of the Patriarchal Relations of Control in the Office," *Capital and Class* 10 (spring 1980): 64–97.

70 Hoyman, "Working Women."

71 Ibid.

72 Ibid.

73 The National Labor Relations Board could not help them because of a technicality.

74 Hoyman, "Working Women."

75 David B. Tyack, *One Best System: A History of American Urban Education* (Cambridge, Mass.: Harvard University Press, 1974).

76 Bennett Harrison, *Education, Training, and the Urban Ghetto* (Baltimore: Johns Hopkins University Press, 1972).

77 Karen Anderson, "Last Hired, First Fired: Black Women Workers during World War II," *Journal of American History* 69, 1 (1982): 82–97.

78 Tracy Weis, notes provided for this study. Tracy Weis was a consultant in this project.

79 Andrée Nicola McLaughlin, "Black Women, Identity, and the Quest for Humanhood and Wholeness," in *Wild Women in the Whirlwind: Afro-American Culture and the Contemporary Literary Renaissance*, ed. Joanne M. Braxton and Andrée Nicola McLaughlin (New Brunswick, NJ: Rutgers University Press, 1990).

80 Temma Kaplan, personal communication.

81 Noam Chomsky, Introduction to *Cointelpro: The FBI's Secret War on Political Freedom*, ed. Cathy Perkus (New York: Monad Press, 1975).

82 Quotation from a memo cited by Alexander Cockburn, "Beat the Devil," *The Nation*, July 2, 1990.

83 Cockburn, "Beat the Devil."

84 Chomsky, Introduction to Perkus, ed., *Cointelpro*.

85 Statistics from the Sentencing Project using Justice Department figures. See Tom Wicker, "The Iron Medal," *New York Times*, January 9, 1991.

86 On the egalitarianism of black families, see Lewis Hylan, *Blackways of Kent* (New Haven, 1964); Peter Kunkel and Sara Sue Kennard, *Spout Spring: A Black Community* (New York, 1971); Virginia Heyer Young, "Family and Childhood in a Southern Negro Community," *American Anthropologist* 72 (April 1970): 269–88, all cited by Diane K. Lewis, "The Black Family: Socialization and Sex Roles," *Phylon: The Atlanta University Review of Race and Culture* 36, 3 (1975): 221–37.

87 Other important literary ancestors are Nella Larson, Marita Bonner, Alice Childress, Ann Petry, and Carlene Hatcher Polite.

88 Calvin Hernton, "The Sexual Mountain and Black Women Writers," in Braxton and McLaughlin, eds., *Wild Women in the Whirlwind. Black Writers of America* was edited by Richard Barksdale and Keneth Kinnamon.

89 Joanne M. Braxton, "Afra-American Culture and the Contemporary Literary Renaissance," in Braxton and McLaughlin, eds., *Wild Women in the Whirlwind*.

90 Cheryl A. Wall, "Taking Positions and Changing Words," in *Changing Our Own Words: Essays on Criticism, Theory, and Writing by Black Women*, ed. Cheryl A. Wall (New Brunswick, NJ: Rutgers University Press, 1989).

91 Hernton, "The Sexual Mountain."

92 The first problem is addressed in *Common Differences: Conflicts in Black and White Feminist Perspectives*, ed. Gloria I. Joseph and Jill Lewis (Garden City, NY: Anchor Press/Doubleday, 1981); the second in *But Some of Us Are Brave*, ed. Gloria T. Hull, Patricia Bell Scott, and Barbara Smith (Westbury, NY: The Feminist Press, 1982).

93 McLaughlin, "Black Women."

94 Angela Davis, "The Role of Black Women in the Community of Slaves," *The Black Scholar* 3, 4 (1971). Her place in the new scholarship is described in Elizabeth Higginbotham and Sara Watts, "The New Scholarship on Afro-American Women," *Women's Studies Quarterly* 16, 1–2 (1988): 12–21.

95 Temma Kaplan, Introduction to *The Barnard Occasional Papers on Women's Issues* 3, 2 (1988): 2–3.

96 Angela Y. Davis, "Black Women and Music: A Historical Legacy of Struggle," in Braxton and McLaughlin, eds., *Wild Women in the Whirlwind.*

97 William A. Henry III, "The Lesbians Next Door," *Time*, November 8, 1990.

98 See, especially, Gayle Rubin, "The Traffic in Women," in *Toward an Anthropology of Women*, ed. Rayne Rapp Reiter (New York: Monthly Review Press, 1975); and Adrienne Rich, *Of Woman Born* (New York: Bantam Books, 1976), and "Compulsory Heterosexuality and Lesbian Existence," *Signs* 5, 4 (1980): 631–60.

99 See, for instance, Betsy Ettorre, "Compulsory Heterosexuality and Psych/atrophy: Some Thoughts on Lesbian Feminist Theory," in *Radical Voices: A Decade of Feminist Resistance from Women's Studies International Forum*, ed. Renate D. Klein and Deborah Lynn Steinberg (Elmsford, NY: Pergamon Press 1989).

In addition to the sources cited in the notes, the following works enriched my understanding of the material: Susan Porter Benson, "The Clerking Sisterhood: Rationalization and the Work Culture of Saleswomen in American Department Stores, 1890–1960," *Radical America* 12 (March–April 1978): 41–55; Renate Bridenthal, "Two: The Family Tree: Contemporary Patterns in the United States," *Household and*

Kin: Families in Flux, ed. Amy Swerdlow, Renate Bridenthal, Joan Kelly, and Phyllis Vine (New York: The Feminist Press, 1981); Nadine Brozen, "Despite Women's Gains in States, Studies Find Few in the Top Posts," *New York Times*, October 24, 1986; Cynthia B. Costello, "'WEA're worth it!' Work Culture and Conflict at the Wisconsin Education Association Insurance Trust," *Feminist Studies* 11, 3 (1985): 497–518; E. Franklin Frazier, *Black Bourgeoisie* (New York: The Free Press, 1957); William R. Greer, "Women Now the Majority in Professions," *New York Times*, March 19, 1986; Janheinz Jahn, *Muntu* (New York, 1961), trans. Marjorie Grene (New York: Grove Press, 1961); Barbara Melosh, *"The Physicians Hand": Work Culture and Conflict in American Nursing* (Philadelphia: Temple University Press, 1982); United States Department of Education, National Center for Education Statistics, *Digest of Education Statistics*, 1994.

CHAPTER 20

1 Charlotte Bunch, *Bringing the Global Home: Feminism in the '80s* (Denver, Col.: Antelope Publications, 1985). Charlotte Bunch was a consultant for this book.

2 Ibid.

3 Azar Tabari, "The Women's Movement in Iran: A Hopeful Prognosis," *Feminist Studies* 12, 2 (1986): 343–60.

4 Jean O'Barr, "Reflections on Forum '85 in Nairobi, Kenya: Voices from the International Women's Studies Community," *Signs* (spring 1986): 584–608.

5 Rudo Gaidzanwa, "Reflections on Forum '85 in Nairobi, Kenya: Voices from the International Women's Studies Community," ibid.

6 Angela Davis, *Women, Race and Class* (London: Women's Press, 1982).

7 Amrita Basu, "Reflections on Forum '85 in Nairobi, Kenya: Voices from the International Women's Studies Community," *Signs* (spring 1986): 584–608.

8 Elaine Sciolino, "U.N. Finds Widespread Inequality for Women," *New York Times*, June 23, 1985. The United States is not one of them.

9 Stephen Lewis, special representative for UNICEF and advisor to the executive director, personal communication.

10 *A Commitment to the World's Women*, ed. Noeleen Heyser (New York: UNIFEM, 1995).

11 Noeleen Heyser, personal communication.

12 Andrea Dworkin, *Life and Death* (New York: The Free Press, 1996), 215–16.

13 Linda Gordon, "Feminism and Social Control: The Case of Child Abuse and Neglect," in *What Is Feminism? A Re-examination*, ed. Juliet Mitchell and Ann Oakey (New York: Pantheon Books, 1986); and Linda Gordon, "Family Violence, Feminism, and Social Control," *Feminist Studies* 12, 3 (1986): 453–78.

14 Gordon, "Feminism and Social Control."

15 Ibid.

16 Renate Bridenthal, "Two: The Family Tree: Contemporary Patterns in the United States," in *Household and Kin: Families in Flux*, ed. Amy Swerdlow, Renate Bridenthal, Joan Kelly, and Phyllis Vine (New York: The Feminist Press, 1981).

17 "Only One U.S. Family in Four Is 'Traditional,'" *New York Times*, January 30, 1991.

18 Bridenthal, "Two."

19 *Journal of Home Economics* (1975): "Family is defined as a unit of intimate, transacting, and interdependent persons who share some values and goals, resources, responsibility for decisions, and have commitment to one another over time."

20 Deborah Pope, Naomi Quinn, and Mary Wyer, "The Ideology of Mothering: Disruption and Reproduction of Patriarchy," *Signs* 15, 3 (1990).

21 Janet Liebman Jacobs, "Reassessing Mother Blame in Incest," ibid.

22 Ann Jones has written about battered women in *Women Who Kill* (New York: Holt, Rinehart, and Winston, 1980), *Everyday Death: The Case of Bernadette Powell* (New York: Holt, Rinehart, and Winston, 1985), and *Next Time She'll Be Dead: Battering and How to Stop It* (Boston: Beacon Press, 1994); and with Susan Schecter, *When Love Goes Wrong* (New York: HarperCollins, 1992). Linda Gordon writes about child abuse: two of her articles are cited above; Beatrix Campbell has written about child sexual abuse in *Unofficial Secrets* (London: Virago Press, 1988), and has made a television documentary about ritual child sexual abuse.

23 Tamar Lewin, "More States Study Clemency for Women Who Killed Abusers," *New York Times*, February 21, 1991.

24 Except for the Aboriginal women's community in Australia and in Japanese temples, where women could live celibate for years to earn a divorce, but lose their children.

25 Charlotte Bunch, personal communication.

26 James Brooke, "A Nigerian Shame: The Agony of the Child Bride," *New York Times*, July 17, 1987.

27 Bunch, *Bringing the Global Home.*

28 Maria Mies, *Patriarchy and Accumulation on a World Scale: Women in the International Division of Labour* (London: Zed Books, 1986), 137–42.

29 Bunch, *Bringing the Global Home.*

30 James Brooke, "West African Women: Political Inroads," *New York Times*, August 10, 1987.

31 Ibid.

32 Irene Campos Carr, "Proyecto La Mujer: Latina Women Shaping Consciousness," in *Women's Studies International Forum* 12, 1, ed. Beatrice A. Carroll and Jane E. Mohraz (New York: Pergamon Press, 1989).

33 Youssef M. Ibrahim, "Saudi Women Quietly Win Some Battles," *New York Times*, April 26, 1989.

34 Alice Yun Chai and Ho'oipo De Cambra, "Evolution of Global Feminism through Hawaiian Feminist Politics," in Carroll and Mohraz, eds., *Women's Studies International Forum.*

35 Madhu Bhushan, "Vimochana: Women's Struggles, Nonviolent Militancy and Direct Action in the Indian Context," ibid.

36 Ibid.

37 Anne Witte Garland, *Women Activists: Challenging the Abuse of Power* (New York: The Feminist Press, 1988).

38 Amanda Sebestyen, "Britain: The Politics of Survival," in *Sisterhood Is Global*, ed. Robin Morgan (Garden City, NY: Doubleday, 1984).

39 Garland, *Women Activists.*

40 Evelyne Accad, "Feminist Perspective on the War in Lebanon," in Carroll and Mohraz, eds., *Women's Studies International Forum.*

41 Deborah Sontag, "Israel Honors Mothers of Lebanon Withdrawal," *New York Times*, June 3, 2000.

42 Material on Hinds from Garland, *Women Activists.*

43 "Mothers Group Fights Back in Los Angeles," *New York Times*, December 5, 1989.

44 Patricia A. Gozemba and Marilyn L. Humphries, "Women in the Anti-Ku Klux Klan Movement, 1865–1984," in Carroll and Mohraz, eds., *Women's Studies International Forum.*

45 Garland, *Women Activists.*

46 Robyn Rowland, "Women Who Do and Women Who Don't Join the Women's Movement," in *Radical Voices*, ed. Renate D. Klein and Deborah Lynn Steinberg (Elmsford, NY: Pergamon Press, 1989).

47 Ibid.

48 Andrea Dworkin, *Right-Wing Women: The Politics of Domesticated Females* (London: The Women's Press, 1983).

49 Judith Stacey, "The New Conservative Feminism," *Feminist Studies* 9, 3 (1983): 559–83, and "Are Feminists Afraid to Leave Home? The Challenge of Conservative Pro-family Feminism," in Mitchell and Oakley, eds., *What Is Feminism?*

50 Carol McMillan, *Women, Reason, and Nature* (Princeton: NJ: Princeton University Press, 1982).

51 Rayna Rapp, "Household and Family," in Rapp, Ellen Ross, and Renate Bridenthal, "Examining Family History," *Feminist Studies* 5 (spring 1979): 181.

52 See, for instance, Carol Stack, *All Our Kin: Strategies for Survival in a Black Community* (New York: Harper & Row, 1974); and Nancie Gonzalez, "The Anthropologist as Female Head of Household," *Feminist Studies* 10, 1 (1984).

53 Allison Brown, "Women's Resistance Camp: Hunsrück, West Germany," in Carroll and Mohraz, eds., *Women's Studies International Forum*; Garland, *Women Activists*; Tami Hultman, "Reflections on Forum '85 in Nairobi, Kenya: Voices from the International Women's Studies Community," *Signs* (spring 1986): 584–608.

CHAPTER 21

1 Elizabeth Langland and Walter Gove, *A Feminist Perspective in the Academy* (Chicago: University of Chicago Press, 1981), 3.

2 Douglas Foster, "Bugged," *New York Times Magazine*, October 31, 1999. The entomologist is Deborah Gordon. Her analysis appears in *Ants at Work* (New York: W.W. Norton, 1999).

3 Amy Swerdlow and Phyllis Vine, "The Search for Alternatives: Past, Present, and Future," in *Household and Kin*, ed. Amy Swerdlow, Renate Bridenthal, Joan Kelly, and Phyllis Vine (New York: The Feminist Press, 1981).

4 Ibid.

5 All material on Sweden is from ibid.

6 Ibid.

7 Bennet M. Berger, Bruce M. Hacket, and R. Mervyn Miller, "Child-Rearing Practices of the Communal Family," in *Family in Transition*, ed. Arlene S. Skolnick and Jerome H. Skolnick (Boston: Little, Brown, 1970); and Bennet M. Berger et al., "Supporting the Communal Family," in *Commitment and Community: Communes and Utopias in Sociological Perspective*, ed. Rosabeth Moss Kanter (Cambridge, Mass.: Harvard University Press, 1972).

8 Maxine Molyneux, "Mobilization without Emancipation? Women's Interests, State, and Revolution," in *Transition and Development: Problems of Third World Socialism*, ed. Richard R. Fagan, Carmen Diana Deere, and José Luis Coraggio (New York: Monthly Review Press, 1986).

9 Arlene Eisen, *Women and Revolution in Vietnam* (London: Zed Books, 1984).

10 Veronica Rentmeesters, "Eritrea: Will Women's Liberation Survive the Liberation Struggle?" Paper presented at the Thirty-Second Annual Meeting of the African Studies Association, Atlanta, Georgia, November 1–4, 1989.

11 Molyneux, "Mobilization without Emancipation?"

12 See discussion and diagram in Marilyn Waring, *If Women Counted* (San Francisco: Harper & Row, 1988), 300–4.

13 Hilkka Pietilä, "A New Picture of Human Economy: A Woman's Perspective," paper presented at the International Interdisciplinary Congress on Women, San José, Costa Rica, February 1993.

14 *MS.*, November 1986.

15 Martha A. Ackelsberg and Kathryn Pyne Addelson, "Anarchist Alternatives to Competition," in *Competition: A Feminist Taboo?* ed. Valerie Miner and Helen E. Longino (New York: The Feminist Press, 1987).

16 Ibid.

17 Information on the Vancouver Women's Health Collective cited by Acklesberg and Addelson from Nancy Klieber and Linda Light, *Caring for Ourselves: An Alternative Structure for Health Care* (Vancouver, BC: School of Nursing, University of British Columbia, 1978).

18 Ibid.

19 Marcia Freedman, *Exile in the Promised Land* (New York: Firebrand Books, 1990).

20 Kathleen B. Jones, "Citizenship in a Woman-Friendly Polity," *Signs* 15, 4 (1990): 781–812.

21 Shulamith Firestone, *The Dialectic of Sex: The Case for Feminist Revolution* (New York: Bantam Books, 1971).

22 Jones, "Citizenship."

23 Ibid.

24 Jean Bethke Elshtain, *Women and War* (New York: Basic Books, 1987).

25 Heidi Hartmann, "Capitalism, Patriarchy and Job Segregation by Sex," *Signs* 1 (spring 1976): 137–69.

26 Sheila Ruth, "A Feminist World View," in *Radical Voices*, ed. Renate D. Klein and Deborah Lynn Steinberg (Oxford: Pergamon, 1983).

27 Ibid.

28 In addition to the sources cited in the text, the following have enriched my understanding: R.D. Boyer and Herbert M. Morais, *Labor's Untold Story* (New York: Radio and Machine Workers, 1972); Birgit Brock-Utne, *Feminist Perspectives on Peace and Peace Education* (New York: Pergamon Press, 1989); Susan Brownmiller, *Against Our Will: Men, Women, and Rape* (New York: Simon and Schuster, 1975); Laurie Cashdan, "Anti-war Feminism: New Directions, New Dualities: A Marxist-Humanist Perspective," *Women's Studies International Forum* 12, 1, ed. Berenice A. Carroll and Jane E. Mohraz; Melvyn Dubofsky, *We Shall Be All: A History of the Industrial Workers of the World* (Chicago: Quadrangle Books, 1969); Nancy Hewitt, "Sisterhood in International Perspective: Thoughts on Teaching Comparative Women's History," *Women's Studies Quarterly* 16, 1/2 (1988): 22–32; Judy Kimble and Elaine Unterhalter, "'We Opened the Road for You, You Must Go Forward': ANC Women's Struggles, 1912–1982," *Feminist Review* 12 (October 1982): 11–35; Eva Nordland, "What Does Security Mean to Women?" paper delivered at Women Negotiating for Peace conference, Halifax, June 5, 1985; Betty Reardon,

"Sex and the War System," paper for the Institute for World Order (1982) and the basis for her *Sexism and the War System* (Syracuse, NY: Syracuse University Press, 1996); Deborah L. Rhode, "Feminist Perspectives on Legal Ideology," in Juliet Mitchell and Ann Oakley, eds., *What Is Feminism? A Re-examination* (New York: Pantheon Books, 1986); Barbara Roberts, "No Safe Place: The War against Women," *Our Generation* 15, 4 (1983): 7–26; Azar Tabari, "The Women's Movement in Iran: A Hopeful Prognosis," *Feminist Studies* 12, 2 (1986): 343–60.

SELECTED
BIBLIOGRAPHY

Abdalla, Raqiya Haji Dualeh. *Sisters in Affliction: Circumcision and Infibulation of Women in Africa*. London: Zed Books, 1982.

Abraham-Van der Mark, Eve E. "The Impact of Industrialization of Women: A Caribbean Case." In *Women, Men, and the International Division of Labor*, ed. June Nash and Maria Patricia Fernandez-Kelly. Albany: State University of New York Press, 1983.

Accad, Evelyne. "Feminist Perspectives on the War in Lebanon." In *Women's Studies International Forum*, 12, 1, ed. Berenice A. Carroll and Jane E. Mohraz. New York: Pergamon Press, 1989.

Ackelsberg, Martha A., and Kathryn Pyne Addelson. "Anarchist Alternatives to Competition." In *Competition: A Feminist Taboo?* ed. Valerie Miner and Helen E. Longino. New York: The Feminist Press, 1987.

Addams, Jane. *Twenty Years at Hull House*. First published 1910. New York: Macmillan, 1981.

Afshar, Haleh, ed. *Women, State, and Ideology*. Albany: State University of New York Press, 1987.

Allen, Paula Gunn. *The Sacred Hoop: Recovering the Feminine in American Indian Traditions*. Boston: Beacon Press, 1986.

Altekar, A.S. *The Position of Women in Hindu Civilization*. Banaras, India: Motilal Barnarsidass, 1956.

Ammerman, Nancy. *Bible Believers: Fundamentalists in the Modern World*. New Brunswick, NJ: Rutgers University Press, 1987.

Anderson, Bonnie S., and Judith P. Zinsser. *A History of Their Own*. New York: Harper & Row, 1988.

Anderson, Karen. "Last Hired, First Fired: Black Women Workers during World War II." *Journal of American History* 69, 1 (1982): 82–97.

Ardener, Shirley. "A Comparative Study of Rotating Credit Associations." *Journal of the Royal Anthropological Institute* 94, 2 (1964).

— "Sexual Insult and Female Militancy." In *Perceiving Women*, ed. Shirley Ardener. London: J.M. Dent & Sons, 1975.

Arizpe, Lourdes, and Josephina Aranda. "Women Workers in the Strawberry Agribusiness in Mexico." In *Development and the Division of Labor by Gender*, ed. Eleanor Leacock and Helen I. Safa. Boston: Bergin and Garvey, 1986.

As, Berit. "The Feminist University." In *Radical Voices: A Decade of Feminist Resistance*, Women's Studies International Forum, ed. Renate D. Klein and Deborah Lynn Steinberg. Elmsford, NY: Pergamon Press, 1989.

Asthana, Pratima. *Women's Movement in India*. New Delhi: Vikas Publishing, 1974.

Avery, T.L., and E.F. Graham. "Investigations Associated with the Transplanting of Bovine Ova." *Journal of Reproductive Fertility* (1962): 212–17.

Azu, Diana Gladys. *The Ga Family and Social Change*. African Social Research Documents, vol. 5. Leiden: Africa-Studiecentrum, 1974.

Babatunde Agiri. "Slavery in Yoruba Society in the 19th Century." *The Ideology of Slavery in Africa*, ed. P. Lovejoy. Berkeley, Cal.: Sage Publications, 1981.

Bakan, David. *And They Took Themselves Wives*. San Francisco: Harper & Row, 1979.

Bakari, Mtoro bin Mwinyi. *The Customs of the Swahili People*, ed. and trans. J.W.T. Allen. Berkeley: University of California Press, c.1981.

Bakunin, Mikhail, and Sergej Nechaev. *The Catechism of a Revolutionary*. Geneva: Georg & Co. 1896.

Balser, Diane. *Sisterhood and Solidarity: Feminism and Labor in Modern Times*. Boston: South End Press, l987.

Bandarage, Asoka. "Victims of Development." *Women's Review of Books* 5, 1 (1987).

Barker, Jane, and Hazel Downing. "Word Processing and the Transformation of the Patriarchal Relations of Control in the Office." *Capital and Class* 10 (spring 1980).

Baron, Ava. "Women and the Making of the American Working Class: A Study of the Proletarianization of Printers." *Review of Radical Political Economics* (1982): 23–42.

"Barring Women from Jobs." *New York Times*, October 3, 1989.

Barringer, Felicity. "Sentence for Killing Newborn: Jail Term, Then Birth Control." *New York Times*, November 18, 1990.

Barry, Kathleen. *Female Sexual Slavery*. New York: New York University Press, 1979.

Basch, Françoise. *Rebelles Americaines au XIXeme Siecle: Mariage, Amour Libre, et Politique*. Paris: Meridiens Klincksieck, 1990.

— *Relative Creatures: Victorian Women in Society and the Novel, 1837–67*. New York: Schocken, 1974.

Basch, Françoise, et al., eds. *Stratégies Féminines/ Stratégies Féministes.* First published in Paris. English edition, ed. Judith Friedlander et al. Bloomington: Indiana University Press, 1986.

Basu, Amrita. "Reflections on Forum '85 in Nairobi, Kenya: Voices from the International Women's Studies Community." *Signs* (spring 1986): 584–608.

— ed. *The Challenge of Local Feminisms: Women's Movements in Global Perspective.* Boulder, Col.: Westview Press, 1995.

Baxandall, Rosalyn, Linda Gordon, and Susan Reverby. Archives: "Boston Working Women Protest, 1869." *Signs* 3, 1 (1976).

Bayat-Philipp, Mangol. "Women and Revolution in Iran." *Women in the Muslim World* (1978).

Belkin, Lisa. "Report Clears Judge of Bias in Remarks about Homosexuals." *New York Times*, November 2, 1989.

Bellm, Dan. "A Woman Who Knew Latin." *The Nation*, June 26, 1989.

Benson, Susan Porter. "The Clerking Sisterhood: Rationalization and the Work Culture of Saleswomen in American Department Stores, 1890–1960." *Radical America* 12 (March–April 1978).

Berger, Bennet M., Bruce M. Hacket, and R. Mervyn Miller. "Child-Rearing Practices of the Communal Family." *Commitment and Community: Communes and Utopias in Sociological Perspective*, ed. Rosabeth Moss Kanter. Cambridge, Mass.: Harvard University Press, 1972.

Berger, Iris. "Women of Eastern and Southern Africa." In *Restoring Women to History*, ed. Renata Bridenthal, Claudia Koonz, and Susan Stuard. Bloomington, Ind.: Organization of American Historians, 1988.

Berger, John. *Ways of Seeing.* London: Penguin Books, 1972.

Bessell, M.J. "Nyabingi." *Uganda Journal* 6, 2 (1938).

Beyer, Lisa. "Life Behind the Veil." *Time*, November 8, 1990.

Bhatt, Ela R. "Organising Self-Employed Women Workers." In *Women and Development: Perspectives from South and Southeast Asia*, ed. Rounaq Jahan and Hanna Papanek. Dacca: Bangladesh Institute of Law and International Affairs, 1979.

Bhushan, Madhu. "Vimochana: Women's Struggles, Nonviolent Militancy and Direct Action in the Indian Context." In *Women's Studies International Forum*, 12, 1, ed. Berenice A. Carroll and Jane E. Mohraz. New York: Pergamon Press, 1989.

Bishop, Katherine. "Lesbians Clear Hurdles to Gain Posts of Power." *New York Times*, December 30, 1990.

— "Scant Success for California Efforts to Put Women in Construction Jobs." *New York Times*, February 15, 1991.

Blumberg, Rae Lesser. "A General Theory of Gender Stratification." In *Sociological Theory*, ed. Randall Collins. San Francisco: Jossey-Bass, 1984.

Boals, Kay. "The Politics of Cultural Liberation: Male-Female Relations in Algeria." In *Liberating Women's History*, ed. Berenice A. Carroll. Urbana: University of Illinois Press, 1976.

Bochkaryova, S., and Y. Lyubimova. *Women of a New World*. Moscow, 1969.

Bohlen, Celestine. "East Europe's Women Struggle with New Rules, and Old Ones." *New York Times*, November 25, 1990.

Bordin, Ruth. *Woman and Temperance*. Philadelphia: Temple University Press, 1981.

Boserup, Ester. *Women's Role in Economic Development*. New York: St. Martin's Press, 1970.

Boston, Sarah. *Women Workers and the Trade Union Movement*. London: Davis-Poynter, 1980.

Bottigheimer, Ruth B. *The Bible for Children: From the Age of Gutenberg to the Present*. New Haven: Yale University Press, 1996.

Boulting, William. *Women in Italy*. London: Methuen, 1910.

Boxer, Marilyn J., and Jean H. Quataert. *Connecting Spheres: Women in the Western World, 1500 to Present*. New York: Oxford University Press, 1987.

Boyer, R.D., and Herbert M. Morais. *Labor's Untold Story*. New York: Radio and Machine Workers, 1972.

Brantley, Cynthia. "Makatalili and the Role of Women in Giriama Resistance." In *Banditry, Rebellion, and Social Protest in Africa*, ed. Donald Crummey. Portsmouth, NH: Heinemann, 1986.

Braxton, Joanne M. "Afra-American Culture and the Contemporary Literary Renaissance." In *Wild Women in the Whirlwind: Afro-American Culture and the Contemporary Literary Renaissance*, ed. Joanne M. Braxton and Andrée Nicola McLaughlin. New Bunswick, NJ: Rutgers University Press, 1990.

Bremer, Sidney. "Lost Continuities: Alternative Urban Visions in Chicago Novels, 1890-1915." *Soundings* 64, 1 (1981): 29-51.

Bridenthal, Renate, Claudia Koonz, and Susan Stuard. *Becoming Visible: Women in European History*. Boston: Houghton Mifflin, 1987.

Bridenthal, Renate. "Two: The Family Tree: Contemporary Patterns in the United States." In *Household and Kin: Families in Flux*, ed. Amy Swerdlow et al. New York: The Feminist Press, 1981.

"British Study Finds Leukemia Risk in Children of A-Plant Workers." *New York Times*, February 18, 1990.

Broadhead, Susan Herlin. "Slave Wives, Free Sisters: Bakongo Women and Slavery c. 1700–1850." In *Women and Slavery in Africa*, ed. Claire Robertson and Martin Klein. Madison, Wis.: University of Wisconsin Press, 1983.

Brock-Utne, Birgit. *Feminist Perspectives on Peace and Peace Education*. New York: Pergamon Press, 1989.

Brooke, James. "Ex-Rebel in a Muumuu Becomes a Potent Force." *New York Times*, September 24, 1990.

— "For Women in Politics, the Microphone Is Dead." *New York Times*, August 22, 1988.

— "'Honor' Killing of Wives Is Outlawed in Brazil." *New York Times*, March 29, 1991.

— "A Nigerian Shame: The Agony of the Child Bride." *New York Times*, July 17, 1981.

— "Paraguay Trailblazer: The Would-Be Mayor." *New York Times*, March 7, 1991.

— "West African Women: Political Inroads." *New York Times*, August 10, 1987.

Brooks, George E., Jr. "African 'Landlords' and European 'Strangers': African-European Relations to 1870." In *Africa*, ed. Phyllis M. Martin and Patrick O'Meara. Bloomington: Indiana University Press, 1986.

Brophy, Julia. "Custody Law, Childcare, and Inequality in Britain." In *Child Custody and the Politics of Gender*, ed. Carol Smart and Selma Sevenhuijzen. New York: Routledge, 1989.

Brotman, Harris. "Engineering the Birth of Cattle." *New York Times Magazine*, May 15, 1983.

Brown, Allison. "Women's Resistance Camp: Hansruck, West Germany." *Women's Studies International Forum*, 12, 1, ed. Berenice A. Carroll and Jane E. Mohraz. New York: Pergamon Press, 1989.

Brown, Cynthia, and Aryeh Neier. "Pinochet's Way." *New York Review of Books*, June 25, 1987.

Brownmiller, Susan. *Against Our Will: Men, Women, and Rape*. New York: Simon & Schuster, 1975.

Brozen, Nadine. "Despite Women's Gains in States, Studies Find Few in the Top Posts." *New York Times*, October 24, 1986.

Brun-Gulbrandsen, Sverre. "Sex Roles and the Socialization Process." In *The Changing Roles of Men and Women*, ed. Edmund Dahlstrom. London: Duckworth, 1967.

Bryant, Louise. *Six Months in Russia*. New York: George H. Doran, 1918.

Bryceson, Deborah Fahy. "Women's Proletarianization and the Family Wage in Tanzania." In *Women, State, and Ideology*, ed. Haleh Afshar. Albany: State University of New York Press, 1987.

Bryk, Felix. *Circumcision in Man and Woman*, trans. David Berger. New York: American Ethnological Press, 1934.

Budhos, Marina. "Putting the Heat on Sex-Tourism." *MS.*, March–April 1997.

Bunch, Charlotte. *Bringing the Global Home: Feminism in the '80s*. Denver, Col.: Antelope Publications, 1985.

Burke, B. Meredith. "Ceausescu's Main Victims: Women and Children." *New York Times*, January 10, 1989.

Burns, John F. "Afghan-Relief Agencies Report Intimidation." *New York Times*, May 24, 1990.

— "After a 20-Year Truce, Abortion Debate Is Revived in Canada as Court Strikes Down Restrictive Law." *New York Times*, February 20, 1985.

— "Moscow Gone, Najibullah Boasts and Kabul Stands." *New York Times*, March 12, 1989.

Burrows, Mrs. "A Childhood in the Fens about 1850–69." In *Life as We Have Known It*, by Cooperative Working Women, ed. Margaret Llewelyn Davies. London: Virago, 1977.

Caldecott, Leonie. "At the Foot of the Mountain: The Shibokusa Women of Japan." In *Keeping the Peace*, ed. Lynn Jones. London: The Women's Press, 1983.

Campbell, Beatrix. *The Iron Ladies: Why Do Women Vote Tory?* London: Virago, 1987.

— *Unofficial Secrets*. London: Virago Press, 1988.

Campbell, Helen Stuart. "One of the Fur Sewers." In *Prisoners of Poverty: Women Wage-Workers, Their Trades and Their Lives*. Boston, 1889.

Campbell, Mary Schmidt. Introduction, *Harlem Renaissance: Art of Black America*. New York: Harry N. Abrams, 1987.

Carr, Irene Campos. "Proyecto La Majer. Latina Women Shaping Consciousness." In *Women's Studies International Forum*, 12, 1, ed. Berenice A. Carroll and Jane E. Mohraz. New York: Pergamon Press, 1989.

Carroll, Berenice A. "'Women Take Action!' Women's Direct Action and Social Change." In *Women's Studies International Forum* 12, 1, ed. Berenice A. Carroll and Jane E. Mohraz. New York: Pergamon Press, 1989.

Cashdan, Laurie. "Anti-war Feminism: New Directions, New Dualities: A Marxist-Humanist Perspective." In *Women's Studies International Forum* 12, 1, ed. Berenice A. Carroll and Jane E. Mohraz. New York: Pergamon Press, 1989.

Castro, Janice, and G. Bolte. "Get Set: Here They Come!" *Time* 136, 19 (1990).

Celis, William 3rd. "Date Rape and a List at Brown." *New York Times*, November 18, 1990.

Chai, Alice Yun, and Ho'oipo De Cambra. "Evolution of Global Feminisms through Hawaiian Feminist Politics." In *Women's Studies International Forum*, ed. Berenice A. Carroll and Jane E. Mohraz. New York: Pergamon Press, 1989.

Chamberlain, Basil Hall. *Things Japanese*. London: John Murray, 1905.

Chamberlain, Muriel Evelyn. *Decolonization: The Fall of the European Empires*. Oxford: Basil Blackwell, 1985.

Chambers-Schiller, Lee Virginia. *Liberty, a Better Husband – Single Women in America: The Generations of 1780–1840*. New Haven: Yale University Press, 1984.

Chaney, Elsa M. *Supermadre: Women in Politics in Latin America*. Austin: University of Texas Press, 1979.

Charlton, Sue Ellen. *Women in Third World Development*. Boulder, Col.: Westview Press, 1984.

Cherpak, Evelyn. "The Participation of Women in the Independence Movement in Gran Colombia, 1780–1930." In *Latin American Women: Historical Perspectives*, ed. Asunción Lavrin. Westport, Conn.: Greenwood Press, 1978.

Chomsky, Noam. Introduction, *Cointelpro: The FBI's Secret War on Political Freedom*, ed. Cathy Perkus. New York: Monad Press, 1975.

— *World Orders Old and New*. New York: Columbia University Press, 1996.

Church, George J. "The View from Behind Bars." *Time* 136, 19 (1990).

Clinton, Catherine. *The Other Civil War*. New York: Hill and Wang, 1984.

Cobbing, Julian. "The Mfecane as Alibi: Thoughts on Dithakong and Mbolompo." *Journal of African History* 29 (1988): 487–519.

Cockburn, Alexander. "Beat the Devil." *The Nation*, July 2, 1990.

Cockburn, Cynthia. *Brothers: Male Dominance and Technological Change*. London: Pluto Press, 1983.

Cohn, Carol. "In the Rational World of Defense Intellectuals." *Signs* 12, 4 (1987).

Cook, Alice, and Gwyn Kirk. *Greenham Women Everywhere*. Boston: South End Press, 1983.

Cook, Blanche. *Eleanor Roosevelt*, 2 vols. New York: Viking, 1992, 1999.

Cook, Blanche Wiesen. "Female Support Networks and Political Activism: Lillian Wald, Crystal Eastman, Jane Addams, and Emma Goldman." *Chrysalis* 3 (autumn 1977).

— "Feminism, Socialism, and Sexual Freedom: The Work and Legacy of Crystal Eastman and Alexandra Kollontai." In *Stratégies Féminines/Stratégies Féministes*, ed. Francois Basch et al. English edition, ed. Judith Friedlander et al. Bloomington: Indiana University Press, 1986.

Cooper, Frederick. "Islam and Cultural Hegemony: The Ideology of Slaveowners on the East African Coast." In *The Ideology of Slavery in Africa*, ed. P. Lovejoy. Beverly Hills: Sage Publications, 1981.

Costello, Cynthia B. "WEA're worth it!" Work Culture and Conflict at the Wisconsin Education Association Insurance Trust." *Feminist Studies* 11, 3 (1985): 497–518.

Cott, Nancy. "Feminist Theory and Feminist Movements: The Past before Us." In *What Is Feminism: A Re-examination*, ed. Juliet Mitchell and Ann Oakley. New York: Pantheon Books, 1986.

Cowell, Alan. "Egypt's Pain: Wives Killing Husbands." *New York Times*, September 23, 1989.

Crean, Susan. *In the Name of the Fathers: The Story Behind Male Custody*. Vancouver: Amanita Publications, 1988.

Creevy, Lucy E. "The Role of Women in Malian Agriculture." In *Women Farmers in Africa: Rural Devlopment in Mali and the Sahel*, ed. Lucy E. Creevy. Syracuse, NY: Syracuse University Press, 1986.

Croll, Elisabeth J. *Feminism and Socialism in China*. New York: Schocken Books, 1980.

— *The Politics of Marriage in Contemporary China*. Cambridge: Cambridge University Press, 1981.

Crosette, Barbara. "India Studying 'Accidental' Deaths of Hindu Wives." *New York Times*, January 15, 1989.

— "India's Population Put at 844 Million." *New York Times*, March 26, 1991.

— "Pakistani Women Seek Basic Rights." *New York Times*, March 26, 1990.

Curtis, David Ames, and Henry Louis Gates. "Establishing the Identity of the Author of *Our Nig*." In *Wild Women in the Whirlwind: Afra-American Culture and the Contemporary Literary Renaissance*, ed. Joanne M. Braxton and Andrée Nicola McLaughlin. New Brunswick, NJ: Rutgers University Press, 1990.

Cutrufelli, Maria Rosa. *Women of Africa: Roots of Oppression*. London: Zed Press, 1983.

D'Onofrio-Flores, Pamela M. "Technology, Economic Development, and the Division of Labour by Sex." In *Scientific-Technological Change and the Role of Women in Development*, ed. Pamela M. D'Onofrio-Flores and Sheila M. Pfafflin. Boulder, Col.: Westview Press, 1982.

Dauber, Roslyn, and Melinda L. Cain, eds. *Women and Technological Change in Developing Countries.* Boulder, Col.: Westview Press, 1981.

Davidoff, Leonore. "Mastered for Life: Servant and Wife in Victorian and Edwardian England." *Journal of Social History* 7, 3 (1974).

Davidson, Basil. *The Story of Africa.* London: Mitchell Beazley, 1984.

Davis, Angela. "Black Women and Music: A Historical Legacy of Struggle." In *Wild Women in the Whirlwind: Afra-American Culture and the Contemporary Literary Renaissance,* ed. Joanne M. Braxton and Andrée Nicola McLaughlin. New Bunswick, NJ: Rutgers University Press, 1990.

Davis, Angela Y. *Women, Race, and Class.* New York: Random House, 1981.

— "The Role of Black Women in the Community of Slaves." *The Black Scholar* 3, 4 (1971).

Davis, Devra Lee. "Fathers and Fetuses." *New York Times,* March 1, 1991.

DeBerg, Betty A. *Ungodly Women: Gender and the First Wave of American Fundamentalism.* Minneapolis: Fortress Press, 1990.

Degler, Carl N. "The Changing Place of Women in America." In *The Woman Question in American History,* ed. Barbara Welter. Hinsdale, Ill.: The Dryden Press, 1973.

Dennis, Carolyne. "Women and the State in Nigeria: The Case of the Federal Military Government, 1984–5." In *Women, State, and Ideology,* ed. Haleh Afshar. Albany: State University of New York Press, 1987.

DeParle, Jason. "Child Poverty Twice as Likely after Family Split, Study Says." *New York Times,* March 1, 1991.

Dey, Jennie. "Gambian Women: Unequal Partners in Gambian Rice Development Projects?" In *African Women in the Development Process,* ed. Nici Nelson. London: Frank Cass and Company, 1981.

Dijkstra, Bram. *Idols of Perversity: Fantasies of Feminine Evil in Fin-de-Siècle Culture.* New York: Oxford University Press, 1986.

Dobrokhotova, Valentina. "Woman Worker." In *Women and Russia: Feminist Writings from the Soviet Union,* ed. Tatynana Mamonova. Boston: Beacon Press, 1984.

Dorsey, George. *Man's Own Show: Civilization.* New York: Harper & Brothers, 1931.

Douglas, Ann. *The Feminization of American Culture.* New York: Alfred A. Knopf, 1977.

Downing, Jane, and Hazel Barker. "Word Processing and the Transformation of the Patriarchal Relations of Control in the Office." *Capital and Class* 10 (spring 1980).

Drigo, Paolo. *Maria Zef,* trans. Blossom S. Kirchenbaum. Lincoln: University of Nebraska Press, 1989.

Dubofsky, Melvyn. *We Shall Be All: A History of the Industrial Workers of the World.* Chicago: Quadrangle, 1969.

Duggan, Lynn, and Nancy Folbre. "Women and Children Last." *New York Times,* January 8, 1994.

Duley, Margot I., and Mary I. Edwards, eds. *Cross-Cultural Study of Women.* New York: The Feminist Press, 1986.

Dullea, Georgia. "In Male-Dominated Korea, an Island of Sexual Equality." *New York Times,* July 9, 1987.

Dunayevskaya, Raya. "The Black Dimension in Women's Liberation." In her *Women's Liberation and the Dialectics of Revolution.* Atlantic Highlands, NJ: Humanities Press International, 1985.

Dworkin, Andrea. *Right-Wing Women: The Politics of Domesticated Females.* London: The Women's Press, 1983.

— *Life and Death.* New York: The Free Press, 1996.

Dwyer, Daisy. "Outside the Courts: Extra-Legal Strategies for the Subordination of Women." In *African Women and the Law: Historical Perspectives,* ed. Margaret Jean Hay and Marcia Wright. Boston: Boston University Papers on Africa VII, 1982.

Ed-Din, Nazirah Zein. "Removing the Veil and Veiling: Lectures and Reflections Towards Women's Liberation and Social Reform in the Islamic World," trans. Salah-Dine Hammoud. Reprinted in *Women's Studies International Forum* 5, 2 (1982): 221–26.

Ehrenreich, Barbara. *Blood Rites.* New York: Henry Holt, 1997.

— "Sorry, Sisters, This Is Not the Revolution." *Time* 136, 19 (1990).

Ehrenreich, Barbara, and Deirdre English. *For Her Own Good.* Garden City, NY: Doubleday, 1979.

Ehrenreich, Barbara, Elizabeth Hess, and Gloria Jacobs. *Re-Making Love.* New York: Anchor Press, 1987.

Eisen, Arlene. *Women and Revolution in Vietnam.* London: Zed Books, 1984.

El Dareer, Asma. *Woman, Why Do You Weep? Circumcision and Its Consequences.* London: Zed Books, 1987.

Elshtain, Jean Bethke. *Women and War.* New York: Basic Books, 1987.

Elwell-Sutton, L.P. *Persian Oil: A Study in Power Politics.* London: Lawrence & Wishart, 1955.

Engelberg, Stephen. "Abortion Ban, Sought by Church, Is Rejected by Polish Parliament." *New York Times*, May 18, 1991.

Engels, Frederich, and Karl Marx. *The Communist Manifesto*. 1848.

Ettinger, Elzbieta. *Rosa Luxemburg: A Life*. Boston: Beacon Press, 1986.

Ettorre, Betsy. "Compulsory Heterosexuality and Psych/atrophy: Some Thoughts on Lesbian Feminist Theory." In *Radical Voices: A Decade of Feminist Resistance from Women's Studies International Forum,* ed. Renate D. Klein and Deborah Lynn Steinberg. Elmsford, NY: Pergamon Press, 1989.

Evans, Kathy. "Afghan Edict Tells Women How to Dress." *The Guardian*, June 23, 1990.

Evans, Richard J. *The Feminists*. London: Croom Helm, 1977.

Everett, Jana Matson. *Women and Social Change in India*. New York: St. Martin's Press, 1979.

Fabbro, David. "Peaceful Societies: An Introduction." *Journal of Peace Research* 15 (1978).

Falk, Candace. *Love, Anarchy, and Emma Goldman*. New York: Holt, Rinehart and Winston, 1984.

Fanon, Frantz. *The Wretched of the Earth*, trans. Constance Farrington. New York: Grove Press, 1963.

— *A Dying Colonialism*, trans. Haakon Chevalier. New York: Grove Press, 1967.

Faure, Christine. "Absent from History," trans. Lillian S. Robinson. *Signs* 7, 1 (1981): 71–86.

Fein, Esther B. "Soviet Military's High Death Rate Draws Scrutiny." *New York Times*, February 10, 1991.

Finnegan, Frances. *Poverty and Prostitution: A Study of Victorian Prostitutes in York*. Cambridge: Cambridge University Press, 1979.

Firestone, Shulamith. *The Dialectic of Sex: The Case for Feminist Revolution*. New York: Bantam Books, 1971.

Flexner, Eleanor. *Century of Struggle*. Cambridge, Mass.: Harvard University Press, 1980.

Forbes, Geraldine H. "Caged Tigers: 'First Wave' Feminists in India." *Women's Studies International Forum* 5, 6 (1982): 525–36.

Forges, Alison L. Des. "'The Drum Is Greater than the Shout': The 1912 Rebellion in Northern Rwanda." In *Banditry, Rebellion, and Social Protest in Africa*, ed. Donald Crummey. Portsmouth, NH: Heinemann, 1986.

Foster, Douglas. "Bugged." *New York Times Magazine*, October 31, 1999.

Foucault, Michel. *Power/Knowledge*, ed. Colin Gordon. New York: Pantheon, 1980.

— *Discipline and Punish: The Birth of the Prison*, trans. Alan Sheridan. New York: Pantheon Books, 1977.

Fowler, Marian. *Below the Peacock Fan: First Ladies of the Raj*. Toronto: Penguin Books, 1987.

Franco, Jean. "The Incorporation of Women: A Comparison of North American and Mexican Popular Narrative." *Studies in Entertainment*, ed. Tania Modleski. Bloomington: Indiana University Press, 1985.

Frank, Douglas W. *Less than Conquerors: How Evangelicals Entered the Twentieth Century*. Grand Rapids, Mich.: W.B. Eerdmans, 1986.

Franklin, Frazier, E. *Black Bourgeoisie*. New York: The Free Press, 1957.

Freedman, Marcia. *Exile in the Promised Land*. New York: Firebrand Books, 1990.

French, Marilyn. *Beyond Power*. New York: Summit Books, 1985.

— "Women and Work in India." In *Women: A World Report*, ed. Debbie Taylor. London: Methuen, 1985.

Friedan, Betty. *The Second Stage*. New York: Summit Books, 1981.

Frobel, F., J. Kreye, and O. Heinrichs. *The New International Division of Labour*. Cambridge: Cambridge University Press, 1980.

Fromm, Erich. *Love, Sexuality, and Matriarchy: About Gender*. New York: Fromm International Publishing, 1997.

Funderburk, A.R. "The Word of God on Women's Dress." *Moody Bible Institute Monthly* 22 (January 1922): 759.

Gaidzanwa, Rudo. "Reflections on Forum '85 in Nairobi, Kenya: Voices from the International Women's Studies Community." *Signs* (spring 1986): 584–608.

Gaitskell, Deborah, et al. "Class, Race and Gender: Domestic Workers in South Africa." *Review of African Political Economy* 27–28 (1983): 86–108.

Garland, Anne Witte. *Women Activists: Challenging the Abuse of Power*. New York: The Feminist Press, 1988.

Garth, Daisy. "The Present Situation of Nicaraguan Women." *Genes and Gender VI: On Peace, War, and Gender*, ed. Anne E. Hunter. New York: The Feminist Press, 1993.

Gibson, Mary. *Prostitution and the State in Italy, 1860–1915*. New Brunswick, NJ: Rutgers University Press, 1986.

Giddings, Paula. *When and Where I Enter*. New York: William Morrow, 1984.

Gold, Allan R. "Sex Bias Is Found Pervading Courts." *New York Times*, July 2, 1989.

— "Study Finds Sex Bias in Connecticut Legal System." *New York Times*, September 8, 1991.

Gonzalez, Nancie. "The Anthropologist as Head of Household." *Feminist Studies* 10, 1 (1984).

Gordon, Ann D., and Mari Jo Buhle. "Sex and Class in Colonial and Nineteenth-Century America." In *Liberating Women's History*, ed. Berenice A. Carroll. Urbana: University of Illinois Press, 1976.

Gordon, Deborah. *Ants at Work*. New York: W.W. Norton, 1999.

Gordon, Linda. "Family Violence, Feminism, and Social Control." *Feminist Studies* 12, 3 (1986): 453–78.

— "Feminism and Social Control: The Case of Child Abuse and Neglect." In *What Is Feminism? A Re-examination*, ed. Juliet Mitchell and Ann Oakey. New York: Pantheon Books, 1986.

— "Voluntary Motherhood: The Beginnings of Feminist Birth Control Ideas in the United States." In *Cleo's Consciousness Raised*, ed. Mary S. Hartmann and Lois Banner. New York: Harper & Row, 1974.

Gozemba, Patricia A., and Marilyn L. Humphries. "Women in the Anti-Ku Klux Klan Movement, 1865–1984." In *Women's Studies International Forum*, 12, 1, ed. Berenice A. Carroll and Jane E. Mohraz. New York: Pergamon Press, 1989.

Graham, Maria Dundas. *Journal of a Voyage to Brazil and Residence There During Part of Three Years, 1821, 1822, 1823*. New York: Praeger, 1969.

Granet, Marcel. *Chinese Civilization*. London: K. Paul, Trench, Trubner & Co., 1930.

Grant, Jacqueline. "Black Women and the Church." In *Some of Us Are Brave*, ed. Gloria T. Hull, Patricia Bell Scott, and Barbara Smith. Old Westbury, NY: The Feminist Press, 1982.

Gray, Francine du Plessix. "Reflections: Soviet Women." *The New Yorker*, February 19, 1990.

— *Soviet Women: Walking the Tightrope*. New York: Doubleday, 1990.

Greer, William R. "Women Now the Majority in Professions." *New York Times*, March 19, 1986.

Gross, Susan Hill, and Marjorie Wall Bingham, eds. *Women in Latin America*. St. Louis Park, Minn.: Glenhurst Publications, 1969.

Grossman, R. "Women's Place in the Integrated Circuit." *Southeast Asia Chronicle* 66 (1979): 1–17.

Gutman, Herbert. *The Black Family in Slavery and Freedom, 1750–1925*. New York: Pantheon, 1976.

Hafkin, Nancy J., and Edna G. Bay, eds. *Women in Africa: Studies in Social and Economic Change*. Stanford, Cal.: Stanford University Press, 1976.

Hahner, June, ed. *Women in Latin American History: Their Lives and Views*. Los Angeles: UCLA Latin American Center Publications, 1976.

Hall, Basil. *Travels in North America in the Years 1827 and 1828*. Philadelphia: Carey, Lea & Carey, 1829.

Hall, Jacqueline Dowd. *Revolt against Chivalry: Jessie Daniel Ames and the Women's Campaign against Lynching*. New York: Columbia University Press, 1979.

Hall, Jacqueline Dowd, Robert Korstad, and James Leloudis. "Cotton Mill People." *American Historical Review* 91, 2 (1986): 245–285.

Halle, Fanina W. *Women in Soviet Russia*. New York: Viking, 1935.

Hansen, H. H. "Clitoridectomy, Female Circumcision in Egypt." *Folk* 14/15 (1972/1973).

Harrell-Bond, Barbara E. *Modern Marriage in Sierra Leone*. The Hague: Mouton, 1975.

Harris, Louis. "The Gender Gulf." *New York Times*, December 7, 1990.

Harrison, Bennett. *Education, Training, and the Urban Ghetto*. Baltimore: Johns Hopkins University Press, 1972.

Hartman, Mary S., and Lois Banner, eds. *Clio's Consciousness Raised*. New York: Harper & Row, 1974.

Hartmann, Heidi. "Capitalism, Patriarchy, and Job Segregation by Sex." *Signs* 1 (spring 1976): 137–69.

— "The Unhappy Marriage of Marxism and Feminism: Toward a More Progressive Union." *Capital and Class* 8 (summer 1979): 1–33.

— "The Family as the Locus of Gender, Class, and Political Struggle." *Signs* 6, 3 (1981).

Hatem, Mervat. "The Politics of Sexuality and Gender in Segregated Patriarchal Systems: The Case of Eighteenth- and Nineteenth-Century Egypt." *Feminist Studies* 12, 2 (1986): 250–74.

Hay, Margaret Jean, and Marcia Wright, eds. *African Women and the Law: Historical Perspectives*. Boston: Boston University Papers on Africa VII, 1982.

Hay, Margaret Jean, Marcia Wright, and Sharon Stichter, eds. *African Women South of the Sahara*. New York: Longman, 1984.

Hayden, Dolores. *Seven American Utopias: The Architecture of Communitarian Socialism.* Cambridge, Mass.: MIT Press, 1975.

Heise, Lori. "The Global War against Women." *World Watch.* Reprinted in *Washington Post*, April 9, 1989.

Henn, Jeanne K. "Women in the Rural Economy: Past, Present, and Future." In *African Women South of the Sahara*, ed. Margaret Jean Hay and Sharon Stichter. New York: Longman, 1984.

Henry, William A. III. "The Lesbians Next Door." *Time*, November 8, 1990.

Herbst, Alma. *The Negro in the Slaughtering and Meatpacking Industry in Chicago.* Boston: Houghton Mifflin, 1932.

Herman, J., and L. Hirschman. "Father-Daughter Incest." *Signs* 2, 4 (1977): 735–57.

Hernton, Calvin. "The Sexual Mountain and Black Women Writers." In *Wild Women in the Whirlwind: Afra-American Culture and the Contemporary Literary Renaissance*, ed. Joanne M. Braxton and Andrée Nicola McLaughlin. New Bunswick, NJ: Rutgers University Press, 1990.

Hersh, Blanche Glassman. *The Slavery of Sex: Feminist-Abolitionists in America.* Chicago: University of Illinois Press, 1978.

Hess, Beth, and Myra Marx Ferree, eds. *Analyzing Gender.* Beverly Hills, Cal.: Sage, 1987.

Heuvel, Katrina vanden. "Glasnost for Women?" *The Nation*, June 4, 1990.

Hewitt, Nancy A. "Friends: Agrarian Quakers and the Emergence of Woman's Rights in America." *Feminist Studies* 12, 1 (1986): 28–49.

— "Sisterhood in International Perspective: Thoughts on Teaching Comparative Women's History." *Women's Studies Quarterly* 16, 1/2 (1988): 22–32.

Hewlett, Sylvia Ann. "Feminism's Next Challenge: Support for Motherhood." *New York Times*, June 17, 1986.

Heyser, Noeleen, ed. *Commitment to the World's Women.* New York: UNIFEM, 1995.

Hiley, Michael. *Victorian Working Women: Portraits from Life.* London: Gordon Fraser, 1979.

Hilton, Anne. *The Kingdom of Kongo.* Oxford: Clarendon Press, 1985.

Hinds, Michael deCourcy. "Better Traps Being Built for Delinquent Parents." *New York Times*, December 9, 1989.

Hine, Darlene Clark. *Black Women in White: Racial Conflict and Cooperation in the Nursing Profession, 1890–1950.* Bloomington: Indiana University Press, 1989.

Hirschman, Albert O. *The Passions and the Interests: Political Arguments for Capitalism before Its Triumph*. Princeton, NJ: Princeton University Press, 1977.

Hitchens, Christopher. "Minority Report." *The Nation*, February 13, 1989.

Hoagland, Sarah Lucia. "Androcentric Rhetoric in Sociobiology." In *Radical Voices: A Decade of Feminist Resistance*, Women's Studies International Forum, ed. Renate D. Klein and Deborah Lynn Steinberg. Elmsford, NY: Pergamon Press, 1989.

Hobsbawm, E.J. *The Age of Revolution: Europe 1789–1848*. London: Cardinal, 1988.

Hochstedler, Carol. *The Tale of Nazame*. Ithaca: Cornell University East Asian Papers, 1979.

Hofstadter, Richard. *Anti-intellectualism in American Life*. New York: Random House-Vintage, 1962.

Hollander, Nancy Caro. "Si Evita Viviera . . ." *Women in Latin America: An Anthology from Latin American Perspectives*, ed. Eleanor B. Leacock et al. Riverside, Cal.: Latin American Perspectives, 1979.

Hollander, Nancy Caro, and Marysa Navarro. "The Case of Eva Perón." *Signs* 3, 1 (1977).

Horowitz, Maryanne Cline. "The 'Science' of Embryology before the Discovery of the Ovum." In *Connecting Spheres: Women in the Western World, 1500 to the Present*, ed. Marilyn J. Boxer and Jean H. Quataert. New York: Oxford University Press, 1987.

Horton, Robin. "African Traditional Thought and Western Science." *Africa* 37 (January 1967).

Hosken, Fran. *The Hosken Report: Genital and Sexual Mutilation of Females*. Lexington, Mass.: Women's International Network News, 1979.

Hossain, Rokeya Sakhawat. *Sultana's Dream* and selections from *The Secluded Ones*, ed. and trans. Roushan Jahan. New York: The Feminist Press, 1988.

Hubbell, Stephen. "Jordan Votes the Islamic Ticket." *The Nation*, December 25, 1989.

Hubbs, Joanna. *Mother Russia: The Feminine Myth in Russian Culture*. Bloomington: Indiana University Press, 1989.

Hultman, Tami. "Reflections on Forum '85 in Nairobi, Kenya: Voices from the International Women's Studies Community." *Signs* (spring 1986): 584–608.

Hunt, James D. *Gandhi in London*. New Delhi: Promilla, 1978.

Hunter, Anne E. *Genes and Gender VI: On Peace, War, and Gender*. New York: The Feminist Press, 1993.

Hurst, Jane. *The History of Abortion in the Catholic Church: The Untold Story.* Washington, DC: Catholics for a Free Choice, 1989.

Huston, Nancy. "The Matrix of War: Mothers and Heroes." In *The Female Body in Western Culture: Contemporary Perspectives,* ed. Susan Suleiman. Cambridge, Mass.: Harvard University Press, 1986.

Ibrahim, Youssef M. "Algeria Militants Vow to Kill Women Linked to Government." *New York Times,* May 4, 1995.

— "Algerians Choose the Protest Vote." *International Herald Tribune,* June 27, 1990.

— "Bareheaded Women Slain in Algiers." *New York Times,* March 31, 1994.

— "Saudi Women Quietly Win Some Battles." *New York Times,* April 26, 1989.

Jacobs, Janet Liebman. "Reassessing Mother Blame in Incest." *Signs* 15, 3 (1990).

Jagger, Alison, and Paula Rothenberg. *Feminist Frameworks: Alternative Theoretical Accounts of the Relations between Women and Men.* New York: McGraw Hill, 1984.

Jahn, Janheinz. *Muntu: An Outline of the New African Culture,* trans. Marjorie Grene. New York: Grove Press, 1961.

Jain, Devaki. *Women's Quest for Power: Five Indian Case Studies.* Sahidabad, Uttar Pradesh: Vikas Publishing, 1980.

Janiewski, Dolores. "Making Common Cause: The Needlewomen of New York, 1831–69." *Signs* 1, 3 (1976).

Jayawardena, Kumari. *Feminism and Nationalism in the Third World.* London: Zed Books, 1986.

Jensen, Jane. "Both Friend and Foe: Women and State Welfare." In *Becoming Visible: Women in European History,* ed. Renate Bridenthal, Claudia Koonz, and Susan Stuard. Boston: Houghton Mifflin, 1987.

Joekes, Susan. "Working for Lipstick? Male and Female Labor in the Clothing Industry in Morocco." In *Women, Work, and Industry in the Third World,* ed. Haleh Afshar. London: Tavistock, 1985.

Johnson, Cheryl. "Class and Gender: A Consideration of Yoruba Women during the Colonial Period." In *Women and Class,* ed. Claire C. Robertson and Iris Berger. New York: Africana Publishing Co., 1986.

Johnson, Kay Ann. *Women, the Family and Peasant Revolution in China.* Chicago: University of Chicago Press, 1983.

Johnston, David. "Hoover: Still a Shadow Not to Be Stepped on," *New York Times,* September 9, 1991.

Jones, Ann. *Everyday Death: The Case of Bernadette Powell.* New York: Holt, Rinehart, and Winston, 1985.

—— *Next Time She'll Be Dead: Battering and How to Stop It.* Boston: Beacon Press, 1994.

—— *Women Who Kill.* New York: Holt, Rinehart, and Winston, 1980.

Jones, Ann, and Susan Schecter. *When Love Goes Wrong.* New York: Harper Collins, 1992.

Jones, Jacqueline. *Labor of Love, Labor of Sorrow: Black Women, Work, and the Family from Slavery to the Present.* New York: Basic Books, 1985.

—— "'My Mother Was Much of a Woman': Black Women, Work, and the Family under Slavery." *Feminist Studies* 8, 2 (1982): 235–69.

Jones, Kathleen B. "Citizenship in a Woman-Friendly Polity." *Signs* 15, 4 (1990): 781–812.

Jordan, Winthrop D. *White Over Black.* Chapel Hill: University of North Carolina Press, 1968.

Joseph, Gloria I. "Sojourner Truth: Achetypal Black Feminists." In *Wild Women in the Whirlwind: Afra-American Culture and the Contemporary Literary Renaissance*, ed. Joanne M. Braxton and Andrée Nicola McLaughlin. New Bunswick, NJ: Rutgers University Press, 1990.

Kamm, Henry. "Afghan Peace Could Herald War of Sexes." *New York Times*, December 12, 1990.

Kandell, Jonathan. *La Capital: The Biography of Mexico City.* New York: Random House, 1986.

Kanter, Rosabeth Moss. *Men and Women of the Corporation.* New York: Basic Books, 1977.

Kaplan, Temma. *Anarchists of Andalusia, 1868–1903.* Princeton, NJ: Princeton University Press, 1977.

—— *Crazy for Democracy: Women in Grassroots Movements.* New York: Routledge, 1997.

—— *Red City, Blue Period: Social Movements in Picasso's Barcelona.* Berkeley: University of California Press, 1992.

—— "Women and Communal Strikes in the Crisis of 1917–1922." In *Restoring Women to History*, ed. Renata Bridenthal, Claudia Koonz, and Susan Stuard. Boston: Houghton Mifflin, 1987.

Karp, Walter. *The Politics of War: The Story of Two Wars Which Altered Forever the Political Life of the American Republic, 1890–1920.* New York: Harper & Row, 1979.

Katzman, David. *Seven Days a Week: Women and Domestic Service in Industrializing America.* Chicago: University of Illinois Press, 1981.

Keen, Benjamin, and M. Wasserman. *A Short History of Latin America*. Boston: Houghton Mifflin, 1984.

Keller, Bill. "Raisa Gorbachev Hits Back: The Women Are All for Me." *New York Times*, May 27, 1989.

Kerber, Linda K. "Separate Spheres, Female Worlds, Woman's Place: The Rhetoric of Women's History." *Journal of American History* 75, 1 (1988): 9–39.

Kerber, Linda K., and Jane De Hart-Mathews, eds. *Women's America: Refocusing the Past*. New York: Oxford University Press, 1987.

Kessler-Harris, Alice. *Women Have Always Worked: A Historical Overview*. New York: The Feminist Press, 1981.

Kestner, Joseph. *Protest and Reform, 1827–1867*. Madison: University of Wisconsin Press, 1985.

Kieffer, George H. *Bioethics: A Textbook of Issues*. Reading, Mass.: Addison-Wesley, 1979.

Kimble, Judy, and Elaine Unterhalter. "'We Opened the Road for You, You Must Go Forward': ANC Women's Struggles, 1912–1982." *Feminist Review* 12 (October 1982): 11–35.

Klein, Viola. "The Historical Background." *Women: A Feminist Perspective*, ed. Jo Freeman. Palo Alto, Cal.: Mayfield, 1979.

Klieber, Nancy, and Linda Light. *Caring for Ourselves: An Alternative Structure for Health Care*. Vancouver: School of Nursing, University of British Columbia, 1978.

Knauss, Peter R. *The Persistence of Patriarchy*. New York: Praeger, 1984.

Knowlton, Robin Willis. "Rape in the United States Continues at One of the Highest Rates in the World." *In These Times*, September 23, 1987.

Kochman, Thomas. "Cross-cultural Communication: Contrasting Perspectives, Conflicting Sensibilities," *The Florida FL Reporter* 9 (spring/fall 1971): 3–16, 53–54.

Kolchin, Peter. *Unfree Labor: American Slavery and Russian Serfdom*. Cambridge, Mass.: Harvard University Press, 1987.

Koso-Thomas, Olayinka. *Circumcision of Women: A Strategy for Eradication*. Atlantic Highlands, NJ: Zed Books, 1987.

Kurtz, Howard. "Correspondents Chafe Over Curbs on News." *Washington Post*, January 16, 1991.

Lab, Louise. *Sonnets*, trans. Graham Dunstan Martin. Austin: Edinburgh Bilingual Library 7, University of Texas Press, 1972.

Lacroix, Paul. *History of Prostitution,* trans. Samuel Putnam. New York: P. Covici, 1926.

Ladner, Joyce A. "Racism and Tradition: Black Womanhood in Historical Perspective." In *Liberating Women's History,* ed. Berenice A. Carroll. Urbana: University of Illinois Press, 1976.

Lamb, Sharon. "Acts without Agents: An Analysis of Linguistic Avoidance in Journal Articles on Men Who Batter Women." *American Journal of Orthopsychiatry* 61, 2 (1991).

Langland, Elizabeth, and Walter Gove. *A Feminist Perspective in the Academy.* Chicago: University of Chicago Press, 1981.

Laquer, Thomas. *Making Sex: Body and Gender from the Greeks to Freud.* Cambridge, Mass.: Harvard University Press, 1990.

Lateef, Shahida. "Modernization in India and the Status of Muslim Women." In *Modernization and Social Change among Muslims,* ed. Imtiaz Ahmad. New Delhi: Manohar Publications, 1983.

Laurence, William L. *Dawn Over Zero: The Study of the Atomic Bomb.* London: Museum Press, 1974.

Lazreg, Marnia. "Gender and Politics in Algeria: Unraveling the Religious Paradigm." *Signs* 15, 4 (1990): 755–80.

Leacock, Eleanor B., ed. *Women in Latin America: An Anthology from Latin American Perspectives.* Riverside, Cal.: Latin American Perspectives, 1979.

Leacock, Eleanor B., and Mona Etienne, eds. *Women and Colonization.* Boston: Bergin and Garvey, 1980.

Leacock, Eleanor B., and Helen I. Safa, eds. *Development and the Division of Labor by Gender.* Boston: Bergin and Garvey, 1986.

Lenero, Elu de. "Women's Work and Fertility." *Sex and Class in Latin America,* ed. June Nash and Helen I. Safa. New York: Praeger, 1976.

Lerner, Gerda. *The Creation of Patriarchy.* New York: Oxford University Press, 1986.

— *The Majority Finds Its Past: Placing Women in History.* Oxford: Oxford University Press, 1979.

Levathes, Louise. "A Geneticist Maps Ancient Migrations." *New York Times,* July 27, 1993.

Lewin, Tamar. "Child Care in Conflict with a Job." *New York Times,* March 2, 1991.

— "Implanted Birth Control Device Renews Debate over Forced Contraception." *New York Times,* January 10, 1991.

— "Jobless Pay for Mother." *New York Times,* March 13, 1991.

— "More States Study Clemency for Women Who Killed Abusers." *New York Times*, February 21, 1991.

— "Nude Pictures Are Ruled Sexual Harassment." *New York Times*, January 23, 1991.

— "Older Women Face Bias in Workplace." *New York Times*, May 11, 1991.

— "Women Found to Be Frequent Victims of Assaults by Intimates." *New York Times*, January 17, 1991.

Lewis, Barbara. "The Limitations of Group Action among Entrepreneurs: The Market Women of Abidjan, Ivory Coast." In *Women in Africa: Studies in Social and Economic Change*, ed. Nancy J. Hafkin and Edna G. Bay. Stanford, Cal.: Stanford University Press, 1976.

Lewis, Diane K. "The Black Family: Socialization and Sex Roles." *Phylon: The Atlanta University Review of Race and Culture* 36, 3 (1975): 221–37.

Lewis, Michael. "Parents and Children: Sex-Role Development." *School Review* 80 (February 1972): 229–40.

Lewis, Paul. "UNICEF Sees Death of Infants Ebbing." *New York Times*, December 19, 1990.

Lewis, Samella. *Art: African American*. New York: Harcourt Brace Jovanovich, 1978.

Lightfoot-Klein, Hanny. *Prisoners of Ritual: An Odyssey into Female Genital Circumcision in Africa*. New York: Harrington Park Press, 1989.

Lindqvist, Sven. *Exterminate All the Brutes*. New York: The New Press, 1996.

Lockhart, James. *Spanish Peru, 1532–1556*. Madison: University of Wisconsin Press, 1968.

Loock, E. Van. "La Jamaa, Vue dans le Concret." In *Le Mariage, La Vie Familiale, l'Education Coutumière*. Bandundu, 1966.

MacDonald, Eileen. "Face to Face with the Girls behind the Gun." *The European*, June 15–17, 1990.

Macfarlane, Alan J. *Love and Marriage*. Cambridge: Cambridge University Press, 1986.

Mackenzie, Midge. *Shoulder to Shoulder*. New York: Alfred A. Knopf, 1975.

MacKinnon, Catherine A. "Pornography: Not a Moral Issue." In *Radical Voices: A Decade of Feminist Resistance*, Women's Studies International Forum, ed. Renate D. Klein and Deborah Lynn Steinberg. Elmsford, NY: Pergamon Press, 1989.

Mamonova, Tatyana. *Russian Women's Studies: Essays on Sexism in the Soviet Union*. New York: Pergamon Press, 1989.

Mann, Kristin. *Marrying Well: Marriage, Status and Social Change among the Educated Elite in Colonial Lagos*. Cambridge: Cambridge University Press, 1985.

Margolick, David. "Can Bankruptcy Reduce the Price of a Divorce?" *New York Times*, March 2, 1991.

Marsden, George M. "Defining American Fundamentalism." In *The Fundamentalist Phenomenon*, ed. Norman J. Cohen. Grand Rapids, Mich.: William B. Eerdmans, 1990.

Marsot, Afaf Lutfi al-Sayyid. "The Revolutionary Gentlewomen in Egypt." In *Women in the Muslim World*, ed. Lois Baeck and Nikki Keddie. Cambridge, Mass.: Harvard University Press, 1978.

Maslin, Janet. "Bimbos Embody Retro Rage." *New York Times*, June 17, 1990.

Matsubara, Hisako. *Cranes at Dusk*. Garden City, NY: Dial Press, 1985.

Mazumdar, Shudha. *Memoirs of an Indian Woman*. Armonk: M.E. Sharpe Inc., 1989.

Mazumdar, Vina. "Comment on Suttee." *Signs* 4, 2 (1978): 268–73.

— "The Social Reform Movement in India: From Renade to Nehru." In *Indian Women from Purdah to Modernity*, ed. B.R. Nanda. New Delhi: Vikas Publishing, 1976.

Mbilinyi, Marjorie. "'City' and 'Countryside' in Colonial Tanganyika." *Economic and Political Weekly: Review of Women Studies* 20, 43, October 26, 1985.

— "Wife, Slave and Subject of the King: The Oppression of Women in the Shambala Kingdom." *Tanzania Notes and Records* 88–89 (1982).

McBride, Theresa. "The Long Road Home: Women's Work and Industrialization." In *Becoming Visible: Women in European History*, ed. Renate Bridenthal and Claudia Koonz. Boston: Houghton Mifflin, 1977.

McLaughlin, Andreé Nicola. "Black Women, Identity, and the Quest for Humanhood and Wholeness: Wild Women in the Whirlwind." In *Wild Women in the Whirlwind: Afra-American Culture and the Contemporary Literary Renaissance*, ed. Joanne M. Braxton and Andrée Nicola McLaughlin. New Brunswick, NJ: Rutgers University Press, 1990.

Melosh, Barbara. *The Physician's Hand: Work Culture and Conflict in American Nursing*. Philadelphia: Temple University Press, 1982.

Merchant, Carolyn. *The Death of Nature: Women, Ecology and the Scientific Revolution*. New York: Harper and Row, 1979.

Mernissi, Fatima. *Beyond the Veil: Male-Female Dynamics in a Modern Muslim Society*. New York: Wiley, 1975.

Messina, Maria. *A House in the Shadows*, trans. John Shepley. Marlboro, Vt.: The Marlboro Press, 1990.

Mies, Maria. *Indian Women and Patriarchy*. New Delhi: Concept Publishing, 1980.

— *Patriarchy and Accumulation on a World Scale: Women in the International Division of Labour*. London: Zed Books, 1986.

Milkman, Ruth. "Organizing the Sexual Division of Labor: Historical Perspectives on 'Women's Work' and the American Labor Movement." *The Socialist Review* 10 (January/February 1980): 95–150.

Mill, J.S. *On The Subjection of Women*. London: Everyman, 1965.

Millet, Kate. *Going to Iran*. New York: Putnam, 1982.

Milton, Sybil. "Women and the Holocaust: The Case of German and German-Jewish Women." *When Biology Became Destiny: Women in Weimar and Nazi Germany*, ed. Renate Bridenthal, Altina Grossmann, and Marion Kaplan. New York: Monthly Review Press, 1984.

Mitchell, Juliet, and Ann Oakley, eds. *What Is Feminism? A Re-examination*. New York: Pantheon Books, 1986.

Moers, Ellen. *Literary Women*. New York: Doubleday, 1977.

Molyneux, Maxine. "Mobilization without Emancipation? Women's Interests, State, and Revolution." In *Transition and Development: Problems of Third World Socialism*, ed. Richard R. Fagan, Carmen Diana Deere, and José Luis Coraggio. New York: Monthly Review Press, 1986.

Money, John. "Delusion, Belief, and Fact." *Psychiatry* 11 (1948).

— *The Destroying Angel*. Buffalo: Prometheus Books, 1985.

— "Sex, Hormones, and Other Variables in Human Eroticism." In *Sex and Internal Secretions*, vol. 2, ed. W.C. Young. Baltimore: Johns Hopkins University Press, 1961.

Morante, Elsa. *History: A Novel*, trans. William Weaver. New York: Random House, 1977.

Morgan, Robin. *The Demon Lover*. New York: W.W. Norton, 1989.

— *Sisterhood Is Global*. Garden City, NY: Doubleday, 1984.

Motz, Marilyn Ferris. *True Sisterhood: Michigan Women and Their Kin, 1820–1920*. Albany: State University of New York Press, 1983.

Murdock, William W. *The Poverty of Nations*. Baltimore: The Johns Hopkins University Press, 1980.

Mutunhu, Tendai. "Nehanda of Zimbabwe," *Ufahamu*.

Nandy, Ashis. *At the Edge of Psychology*. Delhi: Oxford University Press, 1980.

Nelson, Nici, ed. *African Women in the Development Process*. London: Frank Cass, 1981.

Nicholas, Susan Cary, Alice M. Price, and Rachel Rubin. *Rights and Wrongs: Women's Struggle for Legal Equality*. New York: Oxford University Press, 1976.

Nightingale, Florence. *Method of Improving the Nursing Service of Hospitals*. London, 1869.

Noble, Kenneth B. "Liberian Warfare Has Roots in 1985: Revolt Now against Doe Was Ignited by Coup Reprisals, Specialists Believe." *New York Times*, June 5, 1990.

— "Low-Paying Jobs Foreseen for Most Working Women." *New York Times*, December 12, 1985.

Nordland, Eva. "What Does Security Mean to Women?" Unpublished paper, Women Negotiating for Peace conference, Halifax, June 5, 1985.

O'Barr, Jean. "Reflections on Forum '85 in Nairobi, Kenya: Voices from the International Women's Studies Community." *Signs* (spring 1986): 584–608.

O'Faolain, Julia, and Lauro Marinte. *Not in God's Image*. London: Temple Smith, 1973.

O'Flaherty, Wendy Doniger. *Women, Androgynes, and Other Mythical Beasts*. Chicago: University of Chicago Press, 1980.

Obbo, Christine. *African Women*. London: Zed Press, 1980.

Oboler, Regina Smith. *Women, Power, and Economic Change: The Nandi of Kenya*. Stanford Cal.: Stanford University Press, 1985.

Okonjo, Kamene. "Sex Roles in Nigerian Politics." In *Female and Male in West Africa*, ed. Christine Oppong. London: George Allen & Unwin, 1983.

Olsen, Tillie. "Introduction," to Rebecca Harding Davis, *Life in the Iron Mills*, ed. Tillie Olsen. First published 1861. New York: The Feminist Press, 1972.

O'Reilly, Jane. "Naming the Sacred." *MS.*, January/February 1991.

Orenstein, Peggy. "*MS.* Fights for Its Life." *Mother Jones* 15, 7 (1990).

Ostow, Mortimer. "The Fundamentalist Phenomenon: A Psychological Perspective." In *The Fundamentalist Phenomenon*, ed. Norman J. Cohen. Michigan: William B. Eerdmans Publishing Co., 1990.

Ostrogarski, Mosei. *The Rights of Women*. New York: Scribner's, 1893.

Owens, Leslie Howard. *This Species of Property: Slave Life and Culture in the Old South*. New York: Oxford University Press, 1976.

Ozment, Steven. *When Fathers Ruled*. Cambridge, Mass.: Harvard University Press, 1983.

Packard, Vance. *The People Shapers*. New York: Bantam, 1979.

Paglia, Camille. *Sexual Personae*. New Haven: Yale University Press, 1990.

Papanek, Hanna. "The Differential Impact of Programs and Policies on Women in Development." In *Women and Technological Change in Developing Countries*, ed. Roslyn Dauber and Melina Cain. Boulder, Col.: Westview Press, 1981.

Papanek, Hannah, and Gail Minault. *Separate Worlds*. Delhi: Chanakya Publications, 1982.

Pardoe, Julia. *The City of the Sultans and Domestic Manners of the Turks in 1836*. Philadelphia: Carey, Lea & Blanchard, 1837.

Patterson, K. David, and Gerald W. Hartwig. "The Disease Factor: An Introductory Overview." In *Disease in African History: An Introductory Survey and Case History*, ed. David Patterson and Gerald W. Hartwig. Durham, NC: Duke University Press, 1978.

Peires, J.B. "'Soft' Believers and 'Hard' Unbelievers in the Xhosa Cattle-Killing." *Journal of African History* 27 (1986): 443–61.

Perkins, Linda. "'Heed Life's Demands': The Educational Philosophy of Fanny Jackson." *Journal of Negro Education* (summer 1982).

Perkus, Cathy, ed. *Cointelpro: The FBI's Secret War on Political Freedom*. Introduction by Noam Chomsky. New York: Monad Press, 1975.

Perlez, Jane. "Elite Kenyan Women Avoid a Rite: Marriage," *The New York Times*, March 3, 1991.

— "For the Oppressed Sex, Brave Words to Live By." *New York Times*, June 6, 1990.

— "Kenya Decides to Reduce Planned 60-Story Tower." *New York Times*, February 12, 1990.

— "Skyscraper's Enemy Draws a Daily Dose of Scorn." *New York Times*, December 6, 1989.

— "Uganda's Women: Children, Drudgery and Pain." *New York Times*, February 24, 1991.

— "When the Trouble Is Men, Women Help Women." *New York Times*, June 5, 1989.

Pescatello, Ann M. "Latina Liberation: Tradition, Ideology, and Social Changes in Iberian and Latin American Culture." In *Liberating Women's History*, ed. Berenice A. Carroll. Urbana: University of Illinois Press, 1976.

— *Power and Pawn: The Female in Iberian Families, Societies, and Cultures*. Westport, Conn.: Greenwood Press, 1976.

Peterson, Betsy. *Dancing with Daddy*. New York: Bantam, 1991.

Polikoff, Nancy D. "Fathers' Rights, Mothers' Wrongs." *The Women's Review of Books* 7, 9 (1990).

Pollitt, Katha. "A New Assault on Feminism." *The Nation*, March 26, 1990.

Pollock, Scarlet, and Jo Sutton. "Father's Rights, Women's Losses." In *Radical Voices: A Decade of Feminist Resistance*, Women's Studies International Forum, ed. Renate D. Klein and Deborah Lynn Steinberg. Elmsford, NY: Pergamon Press, 1989.

Pope, Deborah, Naomi Quinn, and Mary Wyer. "The Ideology of Mothering: Disruption and Reproduction of Patriarchy." *Signs* 15, 3 (1990).

Porter, Gina. "A Note on Slavery, Seclusion and Agrarian Change in Northern Nigeria." *Journal of African History* 30 (1989): 487–91.

Power, Marilyn. "Falling Through the 'Safety Net': Women, Economic Crisis, and Reaganomics." *Feminist Studies* 10, 1 (1984): 31–58.

Pratap, Anita. "Romance and a Little Rape." *Time*, August 13, 1990.

Price, Roger. *The Revolutions of 1848*. London: Macmillan, 1988.

Purvis, Andrew, and T. Johnson. "A Perilous Gap." *Time*, November 8, 1990.

Qunta, Christine N. "Outstanding African Women, 1500 BC–1900 AD." In *Women in Southern Africa*, ed. Christine Qunta. London: Allison & Busby, 1987.

Ramas, Maria. "Freud's Dora, Dora's Hysteria." In *Sex and Class in Women's History*, ed. Judith L. Newton, Mary P. Ryan, and Judith R. Walkowitz. London: Routledge and Kegan Paul, 1983.

Ramusack, Barbara N. "Women in South and Southeast Asia." In *Restoring Women to History*, ed. Renate Bridenthal, Claudia Koonz, and Susan Stuard. Bloomington, Ind.: Organization of American Historians, 1988.

Randall, Margaret. *Mujeres en la Revolución*. Mexico: Siglo xxi, 1972.

Ranger, Terence O. *Revolt in Southern Rhodesia, 1867–70*. London: Heinemann, 1967.

Rapp, Rayna. "Household and Family." In *Examining Family History*, ed. Rayna Rapp, Ellen Ross, and Renate Bridenthal. *Feminist Studies* 5 (spring 1979): 181.

Rathbone, Eleanor. *The Disinherited Family*, republished as *Family Allowance*. London: Allen and Unwin, 1949.

Reardon, Betty. *Sexism and the War System*. New York: Syracuse University Press, 1986.

Reddock, Rhoda E. "Women and Slavery in the Caribbean: A Feminist Perspective." *Latin American Perspectives* 12, 1 (1985): 63–80.

Redford, Donald B. *History and Chronology of the Eighteenth Dynasty*. Toronto: University of Toronto Press, 1967.

Reed, Evelyn. *Women's Evolution: From Matriarchal Clan to Patriarchal Family*. New York: Pathfinder Press, 1975.

Reich, Pauline C. "Japan's Literary Feminists: The Seito Group." Headnote to excerpts from the work of Hiratsuka Raicho, trans. Pauline C. Reich and Atsuko Fukuda. *Signs* 2, 1 (1976): 280–91.

Remondino, P.C. *History of Circumcision from the Earliest Times to the Present.* Philadelphia: F.A. Davis Co., 1891.

Rentmeesters, Veronica. "Eritrea: Will Women's Liberation Survive the Liberation Struggle?" Unpublished paper, Thirty-Second Annual Meeting of the African Studies Association. Atlanta, Georgia, 1989.

Rhode, Deborah L. "Feminist Perspectives on Elgal Ideology." In *What Is Feminism? A Re-examination,* ed. Juliet Mitchell and Ann Oakey. New York: Pantheon Books, 1986.

Rice, John R. *I Am a Fundamentalist.* Murfreesboro: Sword of the Lord Publishers, 1975.

Rich, Adrienne. "Compulsory Heterosexuality and Lesbian Existence." *Signs* 5, 4 (1980): 631–60.

— *Of Woman Born.* New York: Bantam Books, 1976.

Riding, Alan. "France Fears Fallout from Algerian Turmoil." *New York Times,* October 12, 1993.

— "Women to the Fore! What Would Franco Say?" *New York Times,* May 30, 1989.

Roberts, Barbara. "No Safe Place: The War against Women." *Our Generation* 15, 4 (1983): 7–26.

Robertson, Claire. "Ga Women and Socioeconomic Change in Accra, Ghana." In *Women in Africa: Studies in Social and Economic Change,* ed. Nancy J. Hafkin and Edna G. Bay. Stanford, Cal.: Stanford University Press, 1976.

Robinson, Harriet. *Loom and Spindle or Life among the Early Mill Girls.* First published 1898. Kailua: Press Pacifica, 1976.

Robinson, William J. *Married Life and Happiness.* New York: Eugenics Publishing Company, 1922.

Rogers, Barbara. *The Domestication of Women: Discrimination in Developing Societies.* London: Tavistock, 1980.

Rohrlich-Leavitt, Ruby, ed. *Women Cross-Culturally: Change and Challenge.* The Hague: Mouton, 1976.

Rohter, Larry. "Rape Case in Mexico Fuels Outrage at Police." *New York Times,* January 31, 1990.

Rose, Steven. *Against Biological Determinism.* New York, Shocken Books, 1982.

— *Towards a Liberatory Biology.* New York, Schocken Books, 1982.

Rose, Steven, et al. *Not in Our Genes.* New York: Pantheon, 1984.

Rosen, Ruth, and Sue Davidson. Introduction, to *The Maimie Papers*, ed. Ruth Rosen and Sue Davidson. Old Westbury, NY: Feminist Press, 1977.

Rosenberg, General Robert. "The Influence of Policymaking on C3I." Incidental paper, Seminar on C3I. Cambridge, Mass.: Harvard University, Center for Information Policy Research, 1980.

Ross, Ellen. "Fierce Questions and Taunts: Married Life in Working-Class London, 1870–1914." *Feminist Studies* 8, 3 (1982): 575–602.

— "Survival Networks: Women's Neighbourhood Sharing in London before World War I." *History Workshop Journal* 15 (spring 1983): 4–27.

Rossi, Alice. "A Biosocial Perspective on Parenting." *Daedalus* 106 (spring 1977).

Rowland, Robyn. "Women Who Do and Women Who Don't Join the Women's Movement." In *Radical Voices: A Decade of Feminist Resistance*, Women's Studies International Forum, ed. Renate D. Klein and Deborah Lynn Steinberg. Elmsford, NY: Pergamon Press, 1989.

Rubin, Gayle. "The Traffic in Women." In *Toward an Anthropology of Women*, ed. Rayne Rapp Reiter. New York: Monthly Review Press, 1975.

Ruth, Sheila. "A Feminist Analysis of the New Right." In *Radical Voices: A Decade of Feminist Resistance*, Women's Studies International Forum, ed. Renate D. Klein and Deborah Lynn Steinberg. Elmsford, NY: Pergamon Press, 1989.

Saadawi, Nawal el. *The Hidden Face of Eve: Women in the Arab World.* Boston: Beacon Press, 1982.

Sachs, Karen. *Sisters and Wives: The Past and Future of Sexual Equality.* Westport, Conn.: Contributions in Women's Studies 10, 1979.

Sahrma, Radha Krishna. *Nationalism, Social Reform and Indian Women.* Patna and New Delhi: Janaki Prakashan, 1981.

Salaff, Janet, and Judith Merkle. "Women and Revolution: The Lessons of the Soviet Union and China." In *Women in China: Studies in Social Change and Feminism*, ed. Marilyn B. Young. Ann Arbor: Center for Chinese Studies, University of Michigan, 1973.

Sánchez Korrol, Virginia. "Women in Nineteenth- and Twentieth-Century Latin America and the Caribbean." In *Restoring Women to History*, ed. Renata Bridenthal, Claudia Koonz, and Susan Stuard. Bloomington, Ind.: Organization of American Historians, 1988.

Sanday, Peggy Reeves. *Female Power and Male Dominance: On the Origin of Sexual Inequality.* New York: Cambridge University Press, 1981.

— *Fraternity Gang Rape: Sex, Brotherhood, and Privilege on Campus.* New York: New York University Press, 1990.

Sandelowski, Margarete J. "Failures of Volition: Female Agency and Infertility in Historical Perspective." *Signs* 15, 3 (1990).

Sanderson, Lilian Passmore. *Against the Mutilation of Women*. London: Ithaca Press, 1981.

Sano, Norkio. "Japanese Women's Movements during World War II." *Feminist International* 2. Tokyo, 1980.

Schama, Simon. *Landscape and Memory*. New York: Vintage Books, 1996.

Schechter, Susan. *Women and Male Violence: The Visions and Struggles of the Battered Women's Movement*. Boston: South End Press, 1982.

Schlegel, Katherine. "Mistress and Servant in Nineteenth-Century Hamburg: Employer/Employee Relationships in Domestic Service, 1880–1914." *History Workshop Journal* 15 (spring 1983): 60–77.

Schmidt, William E. "British Study Finds Leukemia Risk in Children of A-Plant Workers." *New York Times*, February 18, 1990.

— "Who's in Charge Here? Chances Are It's a Woman." *New York Times*, May 21, 1991.

Schrieber, Le Anne. "Where Are the Doctors Who Will Do Abortions?" *Glamour*, September 1991.

Sciolino, Elaine. "UN Finds Widespread Inequality for Women." *New York Times*, June 23, 1985.

Scott, Joan Wallach. "The Modern Period." *Past and Present* 101 (November 1983): 141–57.

Scott, Joan W., and Louise A. Tilly. *Women, Work and Family*. New York: Holt, Rinehart and Winston, 1978.

Scott, Russell. *The Body as Property*. New York: Viking Press, 1981.

Scully, Diana. *Understanding Sexual Violence: A Study of Convicted Rapists*. Boston: Unwin Hayman, 1990.

Seager, Joni, and Ann Olson. *Women in the World: International Atlas*. New York: Simon & Schuster, 1986.

Sebestyen, Amanda. "Britain: The Politics of Survival." In *Sisterhood Is Global*, ed. Robin Morgan. Garden City, NY: Doubleday, 1984.

Seidman, Gay W. "Women in Zimbabwe: Postindependence Struggles." *Feminist Studies* 10, 3 (1984): 432–40.

Sen, Amartya. "More Than 100 Million Women Are Missing." *New York Review*, December 20, 1990.

Sen, Gita, and Caren Grown. *Development, Crises, and Alternative Visions: Third World Women's Perspectives*. New York: Monthly Review Press, 1987.

Shaarawi, Huda. *Harem Years: The Memoirs of an Egyptian Feminist*, trans. Margot Badran. New York: The Feminist Press, 1987.

Shalvi, Alice. "The War of All Mothers." *Networking for Women* 4, 3 (1991).

Sharma, Ursula. *Women, Work and Property in North-West India*. London: Tavistock, 1980.

Sharp, Gene. *The Politics of Nonviolent Action*. Boston: Porter Sargent, 1973.

Showalter, Elaine. *A Literature of Their Own*. Princeton, NJ: Princeton University Press, 1977.

Sievers, Sharon L. *Flowers in Salt: The Beginnings of Feminist Consciousness in Modern Japan*. Stanford, Cal.: Stanford University Press, 1983.

— "Women in China, Japan, and Korea." In *Restoring Women to History*, ed. Renata Bridenthal, Claudia Koonz, and Susan Stuard. Bloomington, Ind.: Organization of American Historians, 1988.

Smart, Carol. "Power and the Politics of Child Custody." In *Child Custody and the Politics of Gender*, ed. Carol Smart and Selma Sevenhuijsen. New York: Routledge, 1989.

Smedley, Agnes. *Portraits of Chinese Women in Revolution*. Old Westbury, NY: The Feminist Press, 1976.

Smith, Daniel Scott. "Family Limitation, Sexual Control, and Domestic Feminism in Victorian America." In *A Heritage of Her Own: Toward a New Social History of American Women*, ed. Nancy F. Cott and Elizabeth H. Pleck. New York: Simon & Schuster, 1979.

Smith, J.C. *The Neurotic Foundations of Social Order*. New York: New York University Press, 1990.

Smith-Rosenberg, Carroll. "The Female World of Love and Ritual: Relations between Women in Nineteenth-Century America." *Signs* 1, 1 (1975): 1–29.

Smole, W.J. *The Yanomama Indians: A Cultural Geography*. Austin: University of Texas Press, 1976.

Snitow, Ann. "The Church Wins, Women Lose." *The Nation*, April 26, 1993.

— "Feminist Features in the Former Eastern Bloc." *Peace and Democracy News* 7, 1 (1993).

Snow, Helen. *Women of Modern China*. The Hague, 1967.

Solomon, Joan. "Menopause: A Rite of Passage." *MS.*, December 1972.

Sontag, Deborah. "Israel Honors Mothers of Lebanon Withdrawal." *New York Times*, June 3, 2000.

Sowerwine, Charles. "The Socialist Women's Movement from 1850 to 1940." In *Restoring Women to History*, ed. Renata Bridenthal, Claudia Koonz, and Susan Stuard. Bloomington, Ind.: Organization of American Historians, 1988.

Spender, Dale. *Invisible Woman: The Schooling Scandal.* London: Wirters & Readers, 1982.

Staccy, Judith. "Are Feminists Afraid to Leave Home? The Challenge of Conservative Profamily Feminism." In *What Is Feminism? A Re-examination,* ed. Juliet Mitchell and Ann Oakey. New York: Pantheon Books, 1986.

— "The New Conservative Feminism." *Feminist Studies* 9, 3 (1983): 559–83.

Stack, Carol. *All Our Kin: Strategies for Survival in a Black Community.* New York: Harper & Row, 1974.

Stadler-Labhart, Verena. *Rosa Luxemburg an der Universit at Zurich.* Zurich: Hans Rohr Verlag, 1978.

Stampp, Kenneth M. *The Peculiar Institution.* New York: Random House/ Vintage Books, 1956.

Stansell, Christine. *City of Women: Sex and Class in New York, 1789–1860.* New York: Alfred A. Knopf, 1986.

Steinem, Gloria. *Outrageous Acts and Everyday Rebellions.* New York: Signet Books, 1986.

— "Sex, Lies, & Advertising." *MS.,* July/August 1990.

Steinfels, Peter. "6,000 Form Rival Baptist Organization." *New York Times,* May 12, 1991.

— "Idyllic Theory of Goddesses Creates Storm." *New York Times,* February 13, 1990.

Stellman, Jeanne Mager, and Joan E. Bertin. "Science's Anti-Female Bias." *New York Times,* June 4, 1990.

— eds., Introduction, *The Barnard Occasional Papers on Women's Issues* 3, 2 (1988).

Sterling, Dorothy. *We Are Your Sisters: Black Women in the Nineteenth Century.* New York: Norton, 1984.

Stetson, Erlene. "Studying Slavery." *But Some of Us Are Brave,* ed. Gloria T. Hull, Patricia Bell Scott, and Barbara Smith. Old Westbury, NY: The Feminist Press, 1982.

Stites, Richard. "Women and the Revolutionary Process in Russia." In *Restoring Women to History,* ed. Renata Bridenthal, Claudia Koonz, and Susan Stuard. Boston: Houghton Mifflin, 1987.

— *The Women's Liberation Movement in Russia: Feminism, Nihilism, and Bolshevism, 1860–1930.* Princeton: Princeton University Press, 1978.

Strachey, Ray. *The Cause: A Short History of the Women's Movement in Great Britain.* London: Virago, 1978.

Straus, M. R. Gelles, and S. Steinmetz. *Behind Closed Doors.* New York: Doubleday, 1980.

Strobel, Margaret. *Muslim Women in Mombasa, 1890–1975.* New Haven: Yale University Press, 1979.

— "From *Lelemama* to Lobbying: Women's Associations in Mombasa, Kenya." In *Women in Africa: Studies in Social and Economic Change,* ed. Nancy J. Hafkin and Edna G. Bay. Stanford, Cal.: Stanford University Press, 1976.

Sudarkasa, Niara. "The Status of Women in Indigenous African Societies." *Feminist Studies* 12, 1 (1986): 91–103.

Sudetic, Chuck. "Romania Seeks to Reduce Abortions." *New York Times,* January 17, 1991.

Sung, Marina H. "The Chinese Lieh-nü Tradition." In *Women in China: Current Directions in Historical Scholarship,* Historical Reflections Directions Series 3, ed. Richard W. Guisso and Stanley Johannesen. Waterloo, Ont.: University of Waterloo Press, 1981.

Swantz, Marja-Liisa. *A Creative Role Denied? The Case of Tanzania.* New York: St. Martin's Press, 1985.

Sweet, Leonard I. *The Minister's Wife: Her Role in Nineteenth-Century American Evangelism.* Philadelphia: Temple University Press, 1983.

Sweet, Louise E. "In Reality: Some Middle Eastern Women." In *Many Sisters: Women in Cross-Cultural Perspective,* ed. Carolyn J. Matthiason. New York: The Free Press, 1974.

Sweetman, David. *Women Leaders in African History.* London: Heinemann, 1984.

Swerdlow, Amy. "Ladies' Day at the Capitol: Women Strike for Peace versus Huac." *Feminist Studies* 8, 3 (1982): 493–520.

— *Women Strike for Peace: Traditional Motherhood and Radical Politics in the 1960's.* Chicago: University of Chicago Press, 1993.

Swerdlow, Amy, and Phyllis Vine. "The Search for Alternatives: Past, Present, and Future." In *Household and Kin,* ed. Amy Swerdlow et al. New York: The Feminist Press, 1981.

Tabari, Azar. "The Women's Movement in Iran: A Hopeful Prognosis." *Feminist Studies* 12, 2 (1986): 343–60.

Tarasov-Rodionov, Aleksei. *February 1917.* New York: Covici-Friede, 1931.

Tax, Meredith. *The Rising of the Women.* New York: Monthly Review Press, 1989.

Taylor, Barbara. *Eve and the New Jerusalem: Socialism and Feminism in the Nineteenth Century.* New York: Pantheon Books, 1983.

— "'The Men Are as Bad as Their Masters...': Socialism, Feminism and Sexual Antagonism in the London Tailoring Trade in the 1830s." In *Sex and Class in Women's History*, ed. Judith L. Newton, Mary P. Ryan, and Judith R. Walkowitz. London: Routledge & Kegan Paul, 1983.

Terborg-Penn, Rosalyn. "Survival Strategies among Afro-American Women Workers: A Continuing Process." In *Women, Work, and Protest: A Century of U.S. Women's Labor History*, ed. Ruth Milkman. Boston: Routledge, Kegan & Paul, 1985.

— "Women and Slavery in the African Diaspora: A Cross-Cultural Approach to Historical Analysis." *Sage* 3, 2 (1986): 11–15.

Terry, Don. "Ex-Officer Held in Girls' Sex Assault." *New York Times*, June 14, 1989.

Theweleit, Klaus. *Male Fantasies*, vol. 1: *Women, Floods, Bodies, History*. Minneapolis: University of Minnesota Press, 1987.

Tiano, Susan. "Gender, Work, and World Capitalism: Third World Women's Role in Development." In *Analyzing Gender*, ed. Beth Hess and Myra Marx Ferree. Beverly Hills, Cal.: Sage, 1987.

— "Women and Industrial Development in Latin America." *Latin American Research Review* 21, 3 (1986): 157–70.

Tilly, Louise A., and Joan W. Scott. *Comparative Studies in Society and History*, vol. 17. Cambridge: Cambridge University Press, 1975.

— *Women, Work & Family*. New York: Holt, Rinehart and Winston, 1978.

Tinker, Irene. "New Technologies for Food-Related Activities: An Equity Strategy." In *Women and Technological Change in Developing Countries*, ed. Roslyn Dauber and Melinda L. Cain. Boulder, Col.: Westview Press, 1981.

— "Reflections on Forum '85 in Nairobi, Kenya: Voices from the International Women's Studies Community." *Signs* (spring 1986): 584–608.

Tovar, Federico Ribes. *The Puerto Rican Woman: Her Life and Evolution throughout History*. New York: Plus Ultra Books, 1972.

Tucker, Patricia. *Love and Lovesickness*. Baltimore: John Hopkins University Press, 1980.

— *Sexual Signatures*. Boston: Little Brown, 1975.

Turshen, Meredith. "Victims of Development." *The Women's Review of Books* 4, 8 (1987): 11–12.

Tyack, David B. *One Best System: A History of American Urban Education*. Cambridge, Mass.: Harvard University Press, 1974.

Uchitelle, Louis. "Women's Push into Work Force Seems to Have Peaked, for Now." *New York Times*, November 24, 1990.

U. S. Department of Education, National Center for Education Statistics. *Digest of Education Statistics,* 1994.

Urdang, Stephanie. *And Still They Dance: Women, War and the Struggle for Change in Mozambique.* New York: Monthly Review Press, 1989.

— *Fighting Two Colonialisms: Women in Guinea-Bissau.* New York: Monthly Review Press, 1979.

— "Women in National Liberation Movements." In *African Women South of the Sahara,* ed. Margaret Jean Hay and Sharon Stichter. New York: Longman, 1984.

Vaughan, M. "Women, Class, and Education in Mexico, 1880–1918." In *Women in Latin America: An Anthology from Latin American Perspectives,* ed. Eleanor Leacock et al. Riverside, Cal.: Latin American Perspectives, 1979.

Vicinus, Martha. *Independent Women: Work and Community for Single Women, 1850–1920.* Chicago: University of Chicago Press, 1985.

Walkowitz, Judy. *Prostitution and Victorian Society: Women, Class, and the State.* Cambridge: Cambridge University Press, 1980.

Wall, Cheryl A. "Taking Positions and Changing Words." In *Changing Our Own Words: Essays on Criticism, Theory, and Writing by Black Women,* ed. Cheryl A. Wall. New Brunswick, NJ: Rutgers University Press, 1989.

Waring, Marilyn. *If Women Counted.* San Francisco: Harper & Row, 1988.

Wasserman, M., and Benjamin Keen. *A Short History of Latin America.* Boston: Houghton Mifflin, 1984.

Webb, Sidney and Beatrice. *History of Trade Unionism.* London: Longmans, Green Christian Co., 1920.

Weisman, Steven R. "Births Are Kept Down but the Women Aren't." *New York Times.* January 29, 1988.

— "Broken Marriage and Family Brawl Pose Hard Test for a Cohesive Caste." *New York Times,* February 21, 1988.

— "In Crowded Japan, a Bonus for Babies Angers Women." *The New York Times,* February 17, 1991.

Whitaker, Jennifer Seymour. *How Can Africa Survive?* New York, Harper & Row, 1988.

White, E. Frances. "Creole Women Traders in the Nineteenth Century." Working Papers No. 27, African Studies Center, Boston University.

— *Sierra Leone's Settler Women Traders: Women on the Afro-European Frontier.* Ann Arbor: University of Michigan Press, 1987.

— "Women of Western and Western Central Africa." In *Restoring Women to History,* ed. Renata Bridenthal, Claudia Koonz, and Susan Stuard. Boston: Houghton Mifflin, 1987.

White, Landeg. *Magomero: Portrait of an African Village.* Cambridge: Cambridge University Press, 1987.

Wicker, Tom. "The Iron Medal." *New York Times,* January 9, 1991.

Wieseltier, Leon. "The Jewish Face of Fundamentalism," *The Fundamentalist Phenomenon,* ed. Norman J. Cohen. Michigan: William B. Eerdmans Publishing Co., 1990.

Wilkerson, Isabel. "Jury in Illinois Refuses to Charge Mother in Drug Death of Newborn." *New York Times,* May 27, 1989.

Willasden, S.M., et al. "The Production of Monozygotic Twins of Preselected Parentage by Micromanipulation of Non-surgically Collected Cow Embryos." *Theriogenology* 15, 1 (1981): 23–27.

Wilson, E.O. *Sociobiology: The New Synthesis.* Cambridge, Mass.: Harvard University Press, 1975.

Wolf, Eric R. *Peasant Wars of the Twentieth Century.* New York: Harper & Row, 1969.

Wolf, Margery. *Revolution Postponed: Women in Contemporary China.* Stanford: Stanford University Press, 1985.

Wood, Ann Douglas. "The Fashionable Diseases." In *Clio's Consciousness Raised,* ed. Mary S. Hartman and Lois Banner. New York: Harper & Row, 1974.

Wright, Marcia. "Justice, Women, and the Social Order in Abercorn, Northeastern Rhodesia, 1897–1903." In *African Women and the Law: Historical Perspectives,* ed. Margaret Jean Hay and Marcia Wright. Boston: Boston University Papers on Africa VII, 1982.

— "Technology, Marriage and Women's Work in the History of Maize-Growers in Mazabuka, Zambia: A Reconnaissance." *Journal of African Studies* 10, 1 (1983): 71–85.

— "Women in Peril." *African Social Research* 20 (1975): 800-19.

WuDunn, Sheryl. "The Prisoners of Tiananmen Square." *New York Times Magazine,* April 8, 1990.

Zhang, Naihua, with Wu Xu. "Discovering the Positive within the Negative: The Women's Movement in a Changing China." In *The Challenge of Local Feminisms: Women's Movements in Global Perspective,* ed. Amrita Basu. Boulder, Col.: Westview Press, 1995.

Zinn, Howard. *A People's History of the United States.* New York: Harper & Row, 1980.

Zipser, Arthur and Pearl. *Fire and Grace: The Life of Rose Pastor Stokes.* Athens: University of Georgia Press, 1990.

INDEX

A

Abacha, Sani, 608
Abayomi, Oyinkan, 604
Abdullah, Sheikh and Begum, 520
Abella y Ramirez, María, 470
Abeokuta Women's Union (Nigeria),
604
abolitionists, 100, 150–51, 167–73,
704–5
as racists, 170–71
and women's rights, 170, 177,
220–21, 225, 231, 683, 715
abortion, 224, 805, 812
Catholic Church and, 354–55
in Europe, 121, 354–55, 424, 433,
446
opposition to, 780, 781, 784
in Russia, 370, 384, 385, 389,
392–93
in Third World, 496–98, 545,
626, 663, 763
Abyssinia. *See* Ethiopia
Abzug, Bella, 744, 749–50, 752, 753
Accad, Evelyne, 774
Achtenberg, Roberta, 722
Acorn, George, 65
Action Directe (France), 713
Acton, William, 119–20
Adams, John Quincy, 168
Adams, Lucretia, 197
Adams, Victoria Gray, 717
Adamu, Ladi, 641
Addams, Jane, 214, 237, 260, 265,
266, 297, 715–16
adultery, 123, 125, 409, 445
among Native Americans, 192–93
in Third World, 14, 477, 595, 598
The Advocate, 167

affirmative action programs, 649–50,
728
Afghanistan, 502, 503, 562, 566
AFL-CIO, 275
Africa, 8, 9, 570–72, 627. *See also*
specific countries; East Africa; West
Africa
Arabs in, 14, 572, 584
colonialism in, 573–80, 589–92
Europeans and, 7–8, 17–21, 321,
567–72, 574
malnutrition in, 613, 632, 668
medical aid in, 663–64
nationalism in, 320, 607–16
political structures in, 583–84,
586–89
revolts in, 603–7
slavery in, 7, 8–30
women in, 576–80, 618–19,
624–50
rural, 624–33
urban, 633–34
white, 599–603
and World Wars, 585, 613
African-Americans, 184, 188,
193–211, 262–65, 603, 730–37.
See also African-American women
and civil rights, 716–19, 733–34,
737
in cultural life, 207–10
discrimination against, 197,
200–1, 263, 265, 715–19, 732,
735–36
and labour movements, 245, 262,
265, 716, 730–31
and religion, 198, 200, 210
African-American women, 184–85,
667, 732–39, 765

Carillo Puerto, Felipe, 474
Carlo, Adelia de, 470
Carlyle, Jane, 130
Carlyle, Thomas, 102, 147
Carmichael, Stokely, 737
Carnegie, Andrew, 249
Carpenter, Mary, 142, 143
Carr, Emily, 158
Carranza, Venustiano, 474
Carroll, Lewis, 303
Carter, Jimmy, 721
Cary, Mary Ann Shadd, 225
castas, 457, 464, 469
caste. *See* class
Castellanos, Rosario, 481, 489–90,
    491
Castro, Fidel, 482
Cather, Willa, 156
Catherine de Medici, 320
Catherine (the Great) of Russia,
    360–61
Catholic Church, 437
    and abortion, 354–55, 496, 763
    in Africa, 570–71, 589
    and birth control, 496, 752, 763
    in Europe, 111, 354–55, 422
    and fascism, 352, 432, 434–35,
        442–45
    in Latin America, 453, 461–62,
        470, 485, 494, 496, 802
    and leftist movements, 422,
        444–45
    and women, 444–45, 466, 802
Catt, Carrie Chapman, 225, 229
Celeste, Richard F., 761
celibacy, 97, 625
censorship, 222, 270–71, 498, 704–5,
    773, 789–91
Center for Constitutional Rights
    (U.S.), 717
Center for Women and Global
    Leadership, 744
Chabas, Paul, 303
Chabbra, Rami, 544

Chad, 571
Chaney, James, 718
Chang, Sophia, 400
Chao Wu-chieh, 403–4, 413
Chapman, Maria Weston, 169
charitable organizations. *See*
    philanthropy; social work
Charity Organisation Society (Britain),
    143
Charles X of France, 108, 547
chastity, 396, 404, 424, 627, 630
Chaza, Mai (Mother Chaza), 606
Cheng, Soumay, 400–401
Ch'en Tu-hsiu, 404
Chernyshevsky, Nikolai, 268, 363–64
Chertkoff, Genia, 471
Chester, Susan, 214
Chiang Kai-shek, 407–10. *See also*
    Soong Mei-ling
Chicago Women's Alliance, 250
Chicago Women's Club, 178–79, 183
Child, Lydia Maria, 72, 169, 173
child abuse, 67–68, 70, 303, 756–57,
    759–60
    by fathers, 166, 268, 360, 380,
        756
    by mothers, 756
    social policy on, 759–61, 770–71
child care, 88, 273, 415, 727, 813
    in Africa, 560, 634, 746
    in Europe, 63–64, 69, 424, 427,
        446, 727, 795–96
    in Latin America, 482, 496, 794,
        802
    in Russia, 370, 381–82, 386, 389
child custody, 692, 759, 812
    in Africa, 559, 598, 632, 646
    in Asia, 409, 529
    in Britain, 123, 125, 126
    industrialization and, 655, 813
    in Latin America, 463, 794–95,
        801
child labour, 50–52, 196, 279, 497,
    746

in Europe, 37–38, 40, 41, 43,
49–52, 424
child marriage, 521, 529, 762–63
children, 14–15, 141, 142, 303–4,
635, 656. *See also* child abuse;
child care; child custody; child
labour; family allowances;
illegitimacy; motherhood
in Africa, 594, 598
in China, 417–19
as criminals, 70–71, 72
diet of, 65, 257, 631, 656, 751
education of, 51–52, 67, 72, 250,
795
in Europe, 436, 795–96
in families
fathers and, 66, 67, 598, 655,
756–57, 813
as widows, 506, 521
as women's responsibility,
381–82, 464–65, 654,
812–15
with working mothers, 63–65
industrialization and, 655, 812–13
in Latin America, 462–63, 497,
794–95, 801
and slavery, 16, 25, 195–97,
577–78, 598
value of, 624–25, 655
Children of Sanchez, 498
Children's Aid Society, 72
child support
from fathers, 529, 625, 635, 801
from governments, 385, 446, 759
Chile, 455, 483–85, 493, 712
literature in, 487–88, 491
women in, 467, 470, 481, 705,
765
Chiluba, Frederick, 648
China, 409
and conflict, 399, 403, 699, 712,
803
civil war (1945–49), 406–12

Cultural Revolution (1966),
415–16
Republican Revolution (1911),
399–403
Europeans in, 394–95, 503
immigrants from, 246–48, 252
People's Republic of, 413–16
protests in, 405, 419–20, 707
Western influence in, 397–99,
403, 407
women in, 395–97, 402–3,
416–21, 690, 763, 800
The Chinese Women's Journal, 401
Chipko movement (India), 705, 712,
771
Chissano, Joaquim, 620
Chopin, Kate, 156
Chou En-lai, 406
Christianity, 26, 423. *See also* Catholic
Church; Protestants
in Africa, 26, 580, 593, 595–97,
599, 632, 636–38
in Asia, 399, 514, 515, 544
and repression of women, 128,
198, 357–58, 636
Christine de Pisan, 684, 685
Churchill, Winston, 518, 526
Church Missionary Society, 26
Ciller, Tansu, 564
Circle of Families (U.S.), 797
circumcision, female. *See* genital
mutilation
cities, 70–72. *See also* slums
families in, 628–29, 757
migration to, 422–23, 496
in Africa, 576, 578–79, 589,
590, 592, 613–15
women in, 59, 414, 417
in Africa, 576, 578–79, 590,
592, 613, 633–34
citizenship, 808–12
civil disobedience, 524, 589, 602–7
Gandhi and, 517–18, 521–22

civil service. *See* white-collar workers
civil war. *See also specific wars*
  in Africa, 570, 609, 611, 642–45, 647
  in China, 406–12
  in Russia, 378, 379
  in Spain, 349, 350–52
  in United States, 48, 159–62, 185–88, 199–200
Claflin, Tennessee, 222–23
Clark, Amy, 186
Clark, Mark, 735
Clarke, Edward, 154–55
Clarke, Helen, 722
Clarke, Mary, 130
class, 60, 352–53, 682, 684, 736. *See also* class-consciousness; class struggle; elites; middle class; working class
  in Africa, 9, 604, 634, 636–37
  among African-Americans, 181–82, 210
  in Asia, 396, 507, 542, 545
  discrimination by, 545, 777, 781
  industrial revolution and, 35–38, 39
  in Latin America, 466, 500
  and sexuality, 59–60, 425, 463, 464
  socialism and, 345, 353
  and women, 117, 177, 224, 728–29
class-consciousness, 39, 105, 351, 423
  among women, 42, 47–48, 99, 181–82, 250
class struggle, 105–7, 323–24, 333, 345, 346
Cleveland, Emmeline, 162
Cleyre, Voltairine de, 271
Clinton, Bill, 788
Clinton, Hillary, 754
clitoridectomy, 120. *See also* genital mutilation

opposition to, 316, 743, 747–48
  in Africa, 597, 601–2, 643
clitoris, 120–21, 687. *See also* clitoridectomy
clothing, 118, 284–85, 695. *See also* garment industry; tailors
  of Muslim women, 539, 560, 692
  and veil, 524, 550, 552–53, 564–65, 692–94, 703
  nineteenth-century, 55–56, 118
  reformed, 100, 118, 176, 364, 692, 695
clubs
  political, 77, 111, 459–60
  women's, 60, 77, 178, 572, 618
  and African-Americans, 179–82, 205, 263
Coalition of Labor Union Women (U.S.), 730
Cobbe, Frances Power, 231
Cobbing, Julian, 17–18
CODES (India), 659–60
Cointelpro, 734
Coit, Stanton, 213
Colden, Cadwallader, 164
Coles, Elizabeth, 23
collectives, 765, 805–8
  for health care, 765, 805–6
  in Soviet Union, 379, 383–84, 387
  in Third World, 414, 619
colleges. *See* universities
Colombia, 454, 456, 457, 466, 481, 763
colonialism. *See also* colonies
  in Africa, 613–14, 624–26, 631, 640, 665
  and capitalism, 34–35, 575
  and religion, 548, 564–65
  resistance to, 289, 320–21, 550, 585, 586
  successors to, 648–49
  and women, 573–76, 592–603
colonies. *See also* colonialism

F

Himmler, Heinrich, 435
Hindemith, Paul, 305
Hindenburg, Paul von, 431, 438
Hinderer, Anna, 25
Hinds, Cathy, 775, 777
Hindus, 526–33
    attitudes toward women of,
        532–33, 562
    and education, 504, 515
    laws of, 505, 523–24
    and Muslims, 504, 524, 526–27
Hippocrates, 122
Hip-Yee Tong, 247
Hiratsuka Raicho, 697, 699
history, 17–20, 688
Hitler, Adolf, 308, 340, 351, 425–27
    racial aims of, 433–34, 436–37
    rise of, 310, 339, 342, 430–31
    and women, 428–32, 436, 441
Hobsbawm, Eric, 103, 113
Hofmannsthal, Hugo von, 305
Holiday, Billie, 716, 739
Holkar, Ahilyabi, 502
home life, 63–64, 71, 464–65. *See also*
    domesticity as ideal; family;
    housework
homesteaders, 188–91
homosexual men, 133–34, 306–8,
    384, 722, 739, 795. *See also*
    lesbianism; lesbians
Hong Kong, 395
Hooker Chemical Company, 776
Hoover, J. Edgar, 202, 206–7, 264,
    734
Hosmer, Harriet, 158
hospitals, 135–38, 163
Hossain, Freda, 75
Hossain, Rokeya Sakhawat, 511–12,
    539, 681
Hostos, Eugenio Maria de, 467
Houphouët-Boigny, Félix, 648
House Committee on Un-American
    Affairs (HUAC), 723, 724–26

housewives, 251, 606, 655. *See also*
    domesticity as ideal; housework;
    wives
Housewives Leagues (U.S.), 733
housework, 99, 189, 388–89, 557, 804
    in communes, 796–98
    done by men, 62, 638, 794, 797
    in utopian communities, 88, 99
    working women and, 662, 794,
        796
housing, 189, 416, 475–76, 496, 559.
    See also communalism
Hovey, Marion, 162
Howe, Elias, 48
Howe, Julia Ward, 221
Hsiang Ching-yu, 405, 406
Huerta, Carmen, 709
Hughes, Langston, 208, 209, 210
Hugo, Victor, 305
Humphrey, Hubert, 717
Hungary, 355, 422, 439
Hunt, Harriot K., 162
Hunt, Jane, 174
Hurston, Zora Neale, 209, 737
husbands, 68, 141, 594–95, 598, 633
Hutu people, 580

I

Ibibio people, 600
Ibn Badis, Shaikh, 550
Ibo people, 572, 608, 639
Iceland, 709
Ichikawa Fusae, 699
Igbo people, 573–74, 586, 605, 707
illegitimacy, 59–61, 379, 385
immigrants, 166, 248, 465, 493,
    599–600. *See also* immigration
    discrimination against, 202–3,
        246–48
    in United States, 149–50, 190–91,
        245–48
        as workers, 42–43, 48, 62–63,
            183, 241, 243, 248, 249

Louis Philippe of France, 108, 109,
  112
L'Ouverture, Toussaint, 458–59
Lovett, William, 94
Lowell, James Russell, 169
Lowell Manufacturing Company,
  40–43, 66–67, 242, 709
Lübeck, Gustav, 332
Lubusha, Alice Lenshina Mulenga, 606
Luddites, 92
Ludovici, Anthony, 298
Lungu people, 598–99
Luo people, 576–77, 591, 606, 610,
  629, 632, 637, 714
Lutz, Bertha, 470
Luxemburg, Rosa, 314, 327–41
  in Germany, 332, 336–41
  on war, 336–37, 374
Luyia people, 632
lynching, 201, 204–5, 264, 271
  opposition to, 678, 709–10,
  715–16
Lyons, Mary, 151–52
Lytton, Constance, 234–35
Lytton, 2nd Earl of, 235

M

Maathai, Wangari, 642–43
Macarthur, Mary, 283
Macauley, Eliza, 86
Macéo, Antonio, 460
Machado, Gerardo, 477
Machel, Josina, 621–22
Machel, Samora, 619–20
machismo, 317, 477, 550, 686,
  779–80
  in Latin America, 482–83, 494,
  496, 777
MacKenzie, Midge, 234
Maclure, William, 98
Madagascar, 571, 639
Maendeleo wa Wanawake
  (Tanganyika), 572, 637

magazines, 115, 155. *See also* feminists,
  publications of
Maharashtra Workers Union (India),
  710
Maji Maji War (1905), 612–13
Malawi, 590–91, 635, 638, 646. *See
  also* Nyasaland
Malaysia, 699, 763
Malcolm X, 734
male domination, 149, 295–96, 315,
  353, 656, 779–80
  in Africa, 20, 30–33, 579, 591,
  617, 620, 624–26
  among African-Americans,
  193–94, 198–99
  in Asia, 415, 532
  development and, 652, 668–69
  in Europe, 315, 317, 360
  feminism and, 680–81, 779, 780,
  782–83
  and political movements, 220,
  269, 718–19, 799, 810
  and religion, 532, 565
  resistance to, 30–33, 580–89,
  667–68
  and sexuality, 298–99
  and working women, 53–55,
  57–58, 244, 285–86
malnutrition, 613, 632, 668
Malthusian League, 425
Maltzan, Maria von, 440
Mambwe people, 598–99
Mamola, Begam, 502
Mamonova, Tatyana, 388, 390, 391
Manchu dynasty, 394, 398–99, 402
Mandela, Nelson, 611, 641
Mang'anja people, 591
Mantatisi (Mmanthatisi), 19
manufacturing. *See* factories;
  industrialization
Manushi, 534–35, 537
Manyazi wa Menza (Mekatalili), 583,
  584–85
Mao Tse-min, 404

Service Employees International Union
(U.S.), 729
settlement houses, 72, 143–44,
213–15
Seventh-Day Adventists, 593
Seward, William H., 168
sewing machines, 43, 48, 248
Sewingwomen's Protective and
Benevolent Union (U.S.), 46
sex, 100, 192, 215, 222, 507, 798. *See
also* free love; morality; sexual
freedom; sexuality
in Africa, 579–80, 590
in Europe, 166–67, 221–22,
298–99
men's attitudes toward, 66, 590
in Soviet Union, 381–82
sexism, 379, 411, 686, 745–46
in Africa, 622, 649
of transnational companies,
669–70
in United States, 721
sex-tourism, 666–67, 763–64
sexual abuse. *See also* rape; sexual
harassment
of children, 70, 756
and prostitution, 56–57
of servants, 53–56, 472, 495, 593
sex-tourism as, 666–67, 763–64
of workers, 37–38, 268
sexual freedom, 49, 59, 687. *See also*
free love
in Africa, 554–55, 624, 751–52
and class, 59–60, 425, 464
in Latin America, 464, 469–70
socialism and, 265–73
in Soviet Union, 387–88
sexual harassment, 720, 728–29, 755
protests against, 771–72
sexuality, 316, 739, 765
of children, 303–4
images of, 299–301, 304–5, 487
in India, 507, 532–33
in literature, 487, 492

male, 306–7
and male dominance, 298–99,
300–301
patriarchy and, 741
theories of, 306–8, 316
in nineteenth century, 119–21,
133–34, 214, 222, 230,
298–303, 317
women as transcending, 115–17,
119–20, 298–99, 310–11, 463,
477
sexual politics, 74–76, 686, 689,
754–55, 781–83
sexual revolution, 687, 785
Shaftesbury, Lord Ashley, 8th Earl of,
50, 58, 60
Shaka, 17–18
Shakers, 81, 96–98
Shakur, Assata, 734
Shambala people, 15–16
Sharawi, Huda, 693–94
sharecropping, 12, 197–98, 245
shari'a, 505, 692
in Africa, 549–50, 558, 559, 639
Shelley, Percy Bysshe, 82, 86
shelters, 531, 536, 761–62
Shirt Sewers' Cooperative Union
(U.S.), 46
Shona people, 27–28, 612
Shoulder to Shoulder, 234
Showalter, Elaine, 147
La Siempreviva, 473
Sierra, Justo, 466
Sierra Leone, 609
Sigourney, Lydia, 156
Sikhs, 502, 527, 533, 777
Simons, Ray Alexander, 602–3
Singapore, 420, 699, 763
single women, 69, 166, 177, 248, 472
in Algeria, 557
in Asia, 417, 695–96
in Europe, 44, 91, 129–31,
362–63
in Latin America, 453, 463

V

benefits for, 672–74, 699
in China, 396, 406, 413, 415, 416
in Cuba, 794–95
in Europe, 329, 431, 673–74
fascism and, 433, 445–46
in India, 512, 521, 534, 540, 543–44
in Islamic countries, 636, 769
in Japan, 695–96
in Latin America, 452, 463, 465, 469–71, 479, 495–96, 498–99
in Mexico, 466, 472, 496
in Russia, 363, 368–70, 373, 377, 384, 386–87
unskilled, 48, 104, 245, 279, 281, 534, 645
in wartime, 187–88, 238
workhouses, 92
working class, 94. *See also specific occupations and countries;* proletarians
charitable organizations and, 143, 180–83
and domestic ideal, 114, 128–29
and fascism, 310, 311–12
and feminism, 87, 95, 177
industrialization and, 37, 39–70
and marriage, 124, 125
women in, 297, 538, 728
African-American, 734, 737
assistance for, 672–74
in Europe, 325–26, 349–50
in Latin America, 452, 479–80, 496, 500
in nineteenth century, 37, 39–70, 91, 165–66
poverty of, 165–66, 495–96, 672
radicalization of, 727–28
and socialism, 325–26, 344–45

and suffrage movement, 237, 292
violence toward, 67–68
waged work for, 129, 288–92
and womanly ideals, 203, 463
Working Women's Association (U.S.), 46, 47
Working Women's Protective Union (U.S.), 175, 182
Working Women's Union (U.S.), 249
Working Women (U.S.), 729–30
World Anti-Slavery Convention (1840), 173
World Bank, 663–64, 666, 747, 753, 764
World Court, 611
World War I. *See* First World War
World War II. *See* Second World War
Wright, Frances (Fanny), 85, 89, 99–101, 168, 173, 176
Wright, Marcia, 15, 20
Wright, Martha, 174

X

xenophobia, 202–3, 246–48, 264–65

Y

Yaa Asantewa of Edweso, 29–30
Yakunin, Gleb, 392
Yemen, 803
Yeta, Makatindi Nganga, 604
Yim, Louise, 712
YMCA (Young Men's Christian Association), 264
Yoko, Mme, 23
Yoruba people, 22, 24–27, 595–97, 604, 608–9
Yosano Akiko, 698
Young, Brigham, 191
Yüan Shi-k'ai, 401, 403

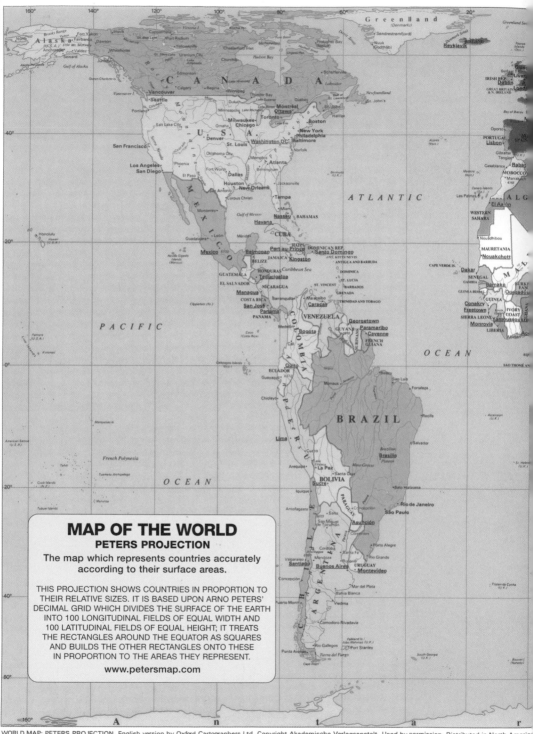

MAP OF THE WORLD
PETERS PROJECTION
The map which represents countries accurately
according to their surface areas.

THIS PROJECTION SHOWS COUNTRIES IN PROPORTION TO
THEIR RELATIVE SIZES. IT IS BASED UPON ARNO PETERS'
DECIMAL GRID WHICH DIVIDES THE SURFACE OF THE EARTH
INTO 100 LONGITUDINAL FIELDS OF EQUAL WIDTH AND
100 LATITUDINAL FIELDS OF EQUAL HEIGHT; IT TREATS
THE RECTANGLES AROUND THE EQUATOR AS SQUARES
AND BUILDS THE OTHER RECTANGLES ONTO THESE
IN PROPORTION TO THE AREAS THEY REPRESENT.

www.petersmap.com

WORLD MAP: PETERS PROJECTION. English version by Oxford Cartographers Ltd. Copyright Akademische Verlagsanstalt. Used by permission. Distributed in North America